The
Classic 1000
Cake and Bake
Recipes

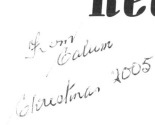

D0522621

Wendy Hobson

foulsham
LONDON • NEW YORK • TORONTO • SYDNEY

foulsham

The Publishing House, Bennetts Close,
Cippenham, Slough, Berkshire, SL1 5AP, England

ISBN 0-572-02803-2

Typeset in Great Britain by Grafica, Bournemouth.
Printed in Great Britain by St Edmundsbury Press, Bury St Edmunds, Suffolk

Contents

Introduction

This collection of recipes covers everything from crisp biscuits and small cakes to rich fruit cakes, gâteaux and granary and herb breads. It could be the only cookery book you will need to keep all your favourite cake and bake recipes to hand. The range is vast and you will find every taste catered for.

The chapters are arranged so that you will find a suitable cake for the occasion simple to locate. If you need a quick cake to make for the children, turn to No-bake Cakes; if you are looking for a family favourite, try Teatime Favourites – or everybody's favourite, Chocolate Cakes! And never be afraid to use your imagination, and whatever you have in the cupboard, if you fancy substituting ingredients to make your own unique recipes. So use the collection, find out your favourites – and I hope you will enjoy them all!

Making Cakes

Equipment
You do not need vast quantities of cake-making equipment, but it is worth buying the best quality you can afford as it will last longer and give better results. The following list gives you the basics that you will need.

- Scales, measuring jug and spoons.
- Mixing bowls.
- Wooden and metal spoons and spatula.
- Whisk.
- Sieve (strainer).
- Food processor and mixer (if possible).
- Rolling pin.
- Greaseproof (waxed) paper or non-stick baking parchment.
- Cake tins (pans). The best are sturdy, black to conduct the heat, and those with loose bases make it easier to remove the cake. Remember to use a deep cake tin for sponge cakes otherwise the mixture will rise above the top of the tin and the cake will spoil.
- Bun tin (patty pan), muffin tin, loaf tins.
- Baking sheet.
- Microwave containers
- Wire cooling rack.
- Sharp serrated knife and palette knife.
- Airtight tins.

Ingredients

- Use your discretion in substituting ingredients and personalising the recipes. Make notes of particular successes as you go along.
- Eggs are medium unless otherwise specified.
- Always wash fresh produce before preparing it. Peel and scrub ingredients as appropriate to the recipe. For example, carrots can be washed, scrubbed or peeled, depending on whether they are young or old.
- The use of spices, such as cinnamon and nutmeg, is a matter of personal taste. Taste the food, where appropriate, as you cook and adjust the seasoning to suit your taste.
- You can use fresh or dried herbs in most recipes, but where fresh herbs are specified only use half the amount of dried. Do not use dried herbs for garnishing or adding at the end of a recipe.
- Two leaves of gelatine are equivalent to 5 ml/1 tsp of powdered gelatine.
- Use whichever type of butter or margarine you prefer. Some margarines state on the packet the uses for which they are most suitable. If the recipe indicates that the butter or margarine should be softened, make sure you have butter at room temperature; soft margarines can be used straight from the fridge.
- You can use fresh, dried or easy-blend dried yeast for bread and yeast-cake recipes. 15 g/½ oz of fresh yeast is equivalent to 20 ml/4 tsp of dried yeast. Dried yeast will take slightly longer to dissolve than fresh yeast. If you are using fresh yeast, you can mix it into the flour once dissolved without waiting for the recommended 20 or so minutes. If you are using easy-blend yeast, simply mix it with the dry ingredients, then add the warm liquid and knead to a dough. The ideal temperature for water to be added to yeast or dough is hand-hot or 38°C/100°F.

Preparation and Cooking

- Use either metric, imperial or American measures; never swap from one to another.
- Spoon measurements are level: 1 tsp = 5 ml; 1 tbsp = 15 ml.
- Use whatever kitchen gadgets you like to speed up the preparation times: mixers for whisking, food processors for grating, slicing, mixing or kneading, blenders for liquidising.
- Approximate sizes are given for baking tins (pans) but use your discretion in selecting the right one for a particular recipe. For example, if a 23 cm/9 in square tin is recommended, you can successfully use a 30 × 18 cm/12 × 7 in tin instead. In general, a square measurement has been given in most recipes as it is much easier to assess a suitable size.

- Cake and bread weights are approximate.
- Cake tins (pans) are round unless otherwise specified.
- Lining cake tins makes it easier to remove the cake from the tin without it breaking. You can use re-usable silicon sheets or greaseproof (waxed) paper. To line a circular tin, draw round the base of the tin on to the paper and cut out to fit the base. Cut a strip long enough to fit round the inside of the tin and about 2.5 cm/1 in taller than the tin. Fold up 1 cm/½ in along the bottom edge of the strip and snip up to the fold at regular intervals. Press into the greased tin so that the fold is on the base of the tin and the snipped strip is on the base. Place the base circle on top. To line a loaf tin (pan), or a square or rectangular tin, cut a rectangle of paper large enough to fit the tin and stand the tin on top. Fold up the edges so that it fits the tin. Cut away four rectangles from the corners of the paper, then shape the cross-shaped piece of paper into the greased tin.
- All ovens vary so cooking times have to be approximate. If you are using a fan oven, refer to the manufacturers' instructions on recommended cooking times and temperatures as both are likely to be reduced.
- There are several ways to test whether a cake is done, depending on the type of cake: the top will be golden brown; the cake will start shrinking from the sides of the tin; a sponge-type cake should spring back if pressed gently with a fingertip; a thin skewer inserted in the centre of a fruit cake will come out clean.
- Cakes and biscuits should generally be removed from the baking tin once cooked. Gently peel off any lining paper and cool on a wire rack. This has not been listed in every recipe. Where it is better to leave cakes in a tin to cool before removing them, this has been included.
- Leave dough to rise in a warm, but not hot, place for best results. If you want the dough to rise more slowly, leave it in a cooler place.
- When bread is cooked, it should be firm and golden brown. Using oven gloves, take it carefully out of the tin and tap it on the base. It will sound hollow if it is cooked. If not, return it to the tin and the oven for a further 5 minutes, then test again.

Storing Cakes and Breads
- Sponges, light cakes and breads are all best eaten soon after baking. Only heavier fruit cakes or rich cakes improve if they are stored, carefully wrapped in foil, in an airtight container.
- Biscuits will keep for a couple of days if stored separately in an airtight container.
- Most cakes can be successfully frozen if as soon as they are cold they are wrapped in clingfilm (plastic wrap) and a freezer bag and frozen. They will keep for up to three months.

Sponges, Plain Cakes and Roulades

*P*lain cakes are delicious served with drinks or tea, or you can add icings (frostings) and fillings (pages 228–37) to make them more of a special treat. Don't be put off by thinking that a roulade is difficult to make. The cake will often break a little when you roll it up, but it will still taste delicious and have that authentic home-made touch!

All-in-one Sandwich Cake

Makes one 20 cm/8 in cake

100 g/4 oz/½ cup butter or margarine, softened
100 g/4 oz/½ cup caster (superfine) sugar
2 eggs
100 g/4 oz/1 cup self-raising (self-rising) flour
5 ml/1 tsp baking powder
150 ml/¼ pt/⅔ cup double (heavy) cream
Icing (confectioners') sugar, sifted, for dusting

*P*lace all the ingredients except the cream in a bowl and beat together until smooth. Spoon the mixture into two greased and lined 20 cm/8 in sandwich tins (pans) and bake in a preheated oven at 160°C/325°F/gas mark 3 for 35 minutes until springy to the touch. Leave to cool on a wire rack.

Whip the cream until stiff. Sandwich together the cakes with the cream and dust with icing sugar.

Almond Cake

Makes one 20 cm/8 in cake

100 g/4 oz/½ cup butter or margarine, softened
225 g/8 oz/1 cup soft brown sugar
2 eggs, lightly beaten
175 g/6 oz/1½ cups plain (all-purpose) flour
2.5 ml/½ tsp bicarbonate of soda (baking soda)
1.5 ml/¼ tsp baking powder
A pinch of salt
120 ml/4 fl oz/½ cup plain yoghurt
5 ml/1 tsp almond essence (extract)

*B*eat together the butter and sugar until light and fluffy. Gradually beat in the eggs, then fold in the flour, bicarbonate of soda, baking powder and salt. Stir in the yoghurt and almond essence. Spoon the mixture into a greased and lined 20 cm/8 in cake tin (pan) and bake in a preheated oven at 180°C/350°F/gas mark 4 for 1 hour until golden brown and springy to the touch. Leave to cool in the tin for 10 minutes before turning out on to a wire rack to finish cooling.

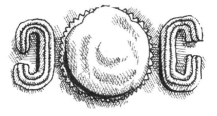

Angel Food Cake

Makes one 23 cm/9 in cake

*75 g/3 oz/¾ cup plain
(all-purpose) flour
25 g/1 oz/2 tbsp cornflour
(cornstarch)
A pinch of salt
225 g/8 oz/1 cup caster (superfine)
sugar
10 egg whites
1 tbsp lemon juice
1 tsp cream of tartar
1 tsp vanilla essence (extract)*

Mix the flours and salt with a quarter of the sugar and sift well. Whisk half the egg whites with half the lemon juice until foamy. Add half the cream of tartar and a teaspoonful of sugar and whisk until they form stiff peaks. Repeat with the remaining egg whites, then fold them together and gradually whisk in the remaining sugar and the vanilla essence. Very gradually fold the flour mixture into the egg whites. Spoon into a greased 23 cm/9 in springform ring mould (tube pan) and bake in a preheated oven at 180°C/350°F/gas mark 4 for 45 minutes until firm to the touch. Invert the tin on to a wire rack and leave to cool in the tin before turning out.

Blackberry Sandwich

Makes one 18 cm/7 in cake

*175 g/6 oz/¾ cup butter or margarine,
softened
175 g/6 oz/¾ cup caster (superfine)
sugar
3 eggs, beaten
175 g/6 oz/1½ cups self-raising
(self-rising) flour
5 ml/1 tsp vanilla essence (extract)
300 ml/½ pt/1¼ cups double (heavy)
cream
225 g/8 oz blackberries*

Cream together the butter or margarine and sugar until pale and fluffy. Gradually beat in the eggs, then fold in the flour and vanilla essence. Spoon into two greased and lined 18 cm/7 in cake tins (pans) and bake in a preheated oven at 190°C/375°F/gas mark 5 for 25 minutes until springy to the touch. Leave to cool.

Whip the cream until stiff. Spread half over one of the cakes, arrange the blackberries on top and spoon over the remaining cream. Cover with the second cake and serve.

Golden Butter Cake

Makes one 23 cm/9 in cake

*225 g/8 oz/1 cup butter or margarine,
softened
450 g/1 lb/2 cups caster (superfine)
sugar
5 eggs, separated
250 ml/8 fl oz/1 cup plain yoghurt
400 g/14 oz/3½ cups plain
(all-purpose) flour
10 ml/2 tsp baking powder
A pinch of salt*

Cream together the butter or margarine and sugar until light and fluffy. Gradually beat in the egg yolks and yoghurt, then fold in the flour, baking powder and salt. Whisk the egg whites until stiff, then carefully fold into the mixture with a metal spoon. Spoon into a greased 23 cm/9 in cake tin (pan) and bake in a preheated oven at 180°C/350°F/gas mark 4 for 45 minutes until golden brown and springy to the touch. Leave to cool in the tin for 10 minutes, then turn out on to a wire rack to finish cooling.

All-in-one Coffee Sponge

Makes one 20 cm/8 in cake

100 g/4 oz/¹⁄₂ cup butter or margarine,
softened
100 g/4 oz/¹⁄₂ cup caster (superfine)
sugar
100 g/4 oz/1 cup self-raising
(self-rising) flour
2.5 ml/¹⁄₂ tsp baking powder
15 ml/1 tbsp instant coffee powder,
dissolved in 10 ml/2 tsp hot water
2 eggs

Blend together all the ingredients until well mixed. Spoon into a greased and lined 20 cm/8 in cake tin (pan) and bake in a preheated oven at 180°C/350°F/gas mark 4 for 30 minutes until well risen and springy to the touch.

Czech Sponge Cake

Makes one 15 × 25 cm/ 10 × 6 in cake

350 g/12 oz/3 cups plain
(all-purpose) flour
100 g/4 oz/²⁄₃ cup icing (confectioners')
sugar, sifted
100 g/4 oz/1 cup ground hazelnuts or
almonds
15 ml/1 tbsp baking powder
150 ml/¹⁄₄ pt/²⁄₃ cup milk
2 eggs, lightly beaten
250 ml/8 fl oz/1 cup sunflower oil
225 g/8 oz fresh fruit
For the glaze:
400 ml/14 fl oz/1³⁄₄ cups fruit juice
20 ml/4 tsp arrowroot

Mix together the dry ingredients. Stir together the milk, eggs and oil and add to the mixture. Pour into a greased 15 × 25 cm/6 × 10 in shallow cake tin (pan) and bake in a preheated oven at 180°C/350°F/gas mark 4 for about 35 minutes until firm. Leave to cool. Arrange the fruit over the sponge base.

Boil together the fruit juice and arrowroot, stirring until thickened, then spoon the glaze over the top of the cake.

Simple Honey Cake

Makes one 20 cm/8 in cake

100 g/4 oz/¹⁄₂ cup butter or margarine,
softened
25 g/1 oz/2 tbsp caster (superfine)
sugar
60 ml/4 tbsp clear honey
2 eggs, lightly beaten
175 g/6 oz/1¹⁄₂ cups self-raising
(self-rising) flour
2.5 ml/¹⁄₂ tsp baking powder
5 ml/1 tsp ground cinnamon
15 ml/1 tbsp water

Beat together all the ingredients until you have a soft dropping consistency. Spoon into a greased and lined 20 cm/8 in cake tin (pan) and bake in a preheated oven at 190°C/375°F/gas mark 5 for 30 minutes until well risen and springy to the touch.

All-in-one Lemon Sponge

Makes one 20 cm/8 in cake

100 g/4 oz/¹⁄₂ cup butter or margarine,
softened
100 g/4 oz/¹⁄₂ cup caster (superfine)
sugar
100 g/4 oz/1 cup self-raising
(self-rising) flour
2.5 ml/¹⁄₂ tsp baking powder
Grated rind of 1 lemon
15 ml/1 tbsp lemon juice
2 eggs

Blend together all the ingredients until well mixed. Spoon into a greased and lined 20 cm/8 in cake tin (pan) and bake in a preheated oven at 180°C/350°F/gas mark 4 for 30 minutes until well risen and springy to the touch.

Lemon Chiffon Cake

Makes one 25 cm/10 in cake

225 g/8 oz/2 cups self-raising
(self-rising) flour
15 ml/1 tbsp baking powder
5 ml/1 tsp salt
350 g/12 oz/1½ cups caster (superfine)
sugar
7 eggs, separated
120 ml/4 fl oz/½ cup oil
175 ml/6 fl oz/¾ cup water
10 ml/2 tsp grated lemon rind
5 ml/1 tsp vanilla essence (extract)
2.5 ml/½ tsp cream of tartar

Mix together the flour, baking powder, salt and sugar and make a well in the centre. Mix the egg yolks, oil, water, lemon rind and vanilla essence and blend into the dry ingredients. Beat together the egg whites and cream of tartar until stiff. Fold into the cake mixture. Spoon into an ungreased 25 cm/10 in cake tin (pan) and bake in a preheated oven at 160°C/325°F/gas mark 3 for 1 hour. Turn off the oven but leave the cake for a further 8 minutes. Remove from the oven and invert on to a cooling rack to finish cooling.

Lemon Drizzle Cake

Makes one 900 g/2 lb cake

100 g/4 oz/½ cup butter or margarine,
softened
175 g/6 oz/¾ cup caster (superfine)
sugar
2 eggs, lightly beaten
175 g/6 oz/1½ cups self-raising
(self-rising) flour
60 ml/4 tbsp milk
Grated rind of 1 lemon
For the syrup:
60 ml/4 tbsp icing (confectioners')
sugar, sifted
45 ml/3 tbsp lemon juice

Cream together the butter or margarine and sugar until light and fluffy. Gradually add the eggs, then the flour, milk and lemon rind and mix to a soft dropping consistency. Spoon into a greased and lined 900 g/2 lb loaf tin (pan) and bake in a preheated oven at 180°C/350°F/gas mark 4 for 45 minutes until springy to the touch.

Mix together the icing sugar and lemon juice and spoon over the cake as soon as it comes out of the oven. Leave in the tin to cool.

Lemon and Vanilla Cake

Makes one 900 g/2 lb cake

225 g/8 oz/1 cup butter or margarine,
softened
450 g/1 lb/2 cups caster (superfine)
sugar
4 eggs, separated
350 g/12 oz/3 cups plain
(all-purpose) flour
10 ml/2 tsp baking powder
200 ml/7 fl oz/scant 1 cup milk
2.5 ml/½ tsp lemon essence (extract)
2.5 ml/½ tsp vanilla essence (extract)

Cream together the butter and sugar, then mix in the egg yolks. Stir in the flour and baking powder alternately with the milk. Stir in the lemon and vanilla essences. Whisk the egg whites until they form soft peaks, then gently fold into the mixture. Turn into a greased 900 g/2 lb loaf tin (pan) and bake in a preheated oven at 150°C/300°F/gas mark 2 for 1¼ hours until golden brown and springy to the touch.

Madeira Cake

Makes one 18 cm/7 in cake

175 g/6 oz/¾ cup butter or margarine,
softened
175 g/6 oz/¾ cup caster (superfine)
sugar
3 large eggs
150 g/5 oz/1¼ cups self-raising
(self-rising) flour
100 g/4 oz/1 cup plain (all-purpose)
flour
A pinch of salt
Grated rind and juice of ½ lemon

Cream together the butter or margarine and sugar until pale and soft. Add the eggs one at a time, beating well between each addition. Fold in the remaining ingredients. Spoon into a greased and lined 18 cm/7 in cake tin (pan) and level the surface. Bake in a preheated oven at 160°C/325°F/gas mark 3 for 1–1¼ hours until golden brown and springy to the touch. Leave to cool in the tin for 5 minutes before turning out on to a wire rack to finish cooling.

Marguerita Cake

Makes one 20 cm/8 in cake

4 eggs, separated
15 ml/1 tbsp caster (superfine) sugar
175 g/6 oz/1½ cups plain
(all-purpose) flour
100 g/4 oz/1 cup potato flour
2.5 ml/½ tsp vanilla essence (extract)
25 g/1 oz/3 tbsp icing (confectioners')
sugar, sifted

Beat together the egg yolks and sugar until pale and creamy. Gradually beat in the flour, potato flour and vanilla essence. Whisk the egg whites until stiff and fold into the mixture. Spoon the mixture into a greased and lined 20 cm/8 in cake tin (pan) and bake in a preheated oven at 200°C/400°F/gas mark 6 for 5 minutes only. Remove the cake from the oven and make a cross on the top with a sharp knife, then return to the oven as quickly as possible and bake for a further 5 minutes. Reduce the oven temperature to 180°C/350°F/gas mark 4 and bake for a further 25 minutes until well risen and golden brown. Leave to cool, then serve dusted with icing sugar.

Hot Milk Cake

Makes one 23 cm/9 in cake

4 eggs, lightly beaten
5 ml/1 tsp vanilla essence (extract)
450 g/1 lb/2 cups granulated sugar
225 g/8 oz/2 cups self-raising
(self-rising) flour
10 ml/2 tsp baking powder
2.5 ml/½ tsp salt
250 ml/8 fl oz/1 cup milk
25 g/1 oz/2 tbsp butter or margarine

Whisk together the eggs, vanilla essence and sugar until light and fluffy. Gradually beat in the flour, baking powder and salt. Bring the milk and butter or margarine to the boil in a small pan, then stir into the mixture and blend well. Spoon into a greased and floured 23 cm/9 in cake tin (pan) and bake in a preheated oven at 180°C/350°F/gas mark 4 for 40 minutes until golden brown and springy to the touch.

11

Milk Sponge Cake

Makes one 20 cm/8 in cake

150 ml/¼ pt/⅔ cup milk
3 eggs
175 g/6 oz/¾ cup caster (superfine)
   sugar
5 ml/1 tsp lemon juice
350g /12 oz/3 cups plain
   (all-purpose) flour
5 ml/1 tsp baking powder

Heat the milk in a pan. Beat the eggs in a bowl until thick and creamy, then add the sugar and lemon juice. Pour in the flour and baking powder, then gradually beat in the hot milk until smooth. Spoon into a greased 20 cm/8 in cake tin (pan) and bake in a preheated oven at 180°C/350°F/gas mark 4 for 20 minutes until well risen and springy to the touch.

All-in-one Mocha Sponge

Makes one 20 cm/8 in cake

100 g/4 oz/½ cup butter or margarine,
   softened
100 g/4 oz/½ cup caster (superfine)
   sugar
100 g/4 oz/1 cup self-raising
   (self-rising) flour
2.5 ml/½ tsp baking powder
15 ml/1 tbsp instant coffee powder,
   dissolved in 10 ml/2 tsp hot water
15 ml/1 tbsp cocoa (unsweetened
   chocolate) powder
2 eggs

Blend together all the ingredients until well mixed. Spoon into a greased and lined 20 cm/8 in cake tin (pan) and bake in a preheated oven at 180°C/350°F/gas mark 4 for 30 minutes until well risen and springy to the touch.

Moscatel Cake

Makes one 18 cm/7 in cake

175 g/6 oz/¾ cup butter or margarine,
   softened
175 g/6 oz/¾ cup caster (superfine)
   sugar
3 eggs
30 ml/2 tbsp Moscatel sweet wine
225 g/8 oz/2 cups plain
   (all-purpose) flour
10 ml/2 tsp baking powder

Cream together the butter or margarine and sugar until light and fluffy, then gradually beat in the eggs and wine. Fold in the flour and baking powder and mix until smooth. Spoon into a greased and lined 18 cm/7 in cake tin (pan) and bake in a preheated oven at 180°C/350°F/gas mark 4 for 1¼ hours until golden brown and springy to the touch. Leave to cool in the tin for 5 minutes, then turn out on to a wire rack to finish cooling.

All-in-one Orange Sponge

Makes one 20 cm/8 in cake

100 g/4 oz/½ cup butter or margarine,
   softened
100 g/4 oz/½ cup caster (superfine)
   sugar
100 g/4 oz/1 cup self-raising
   (self-rising) flour
2.5 ml/½ tsp baking powder
Grated rind of 1 orange
15 ml/1 tbsp orange juice
2 eggs

Blend together all the ingredients until well mixed. Spoon into a greased and lined 20 cm/8 in cake tin (pan) and bake in a preheated oven at 180°C/350°F/gas mark 4 for 30 minutes until well risen and springy to the touch.

Plain Cake

Makes one 23 cm/9 in cake

50 g/2 oz/¼ cup butter or margarine
225 g/8 oz/2 cups plain
  (all-purpose) flour
2.5 ml/½ tsp salt
15 ml/1 tbsp baking powder
30 ml/2 tbsp caster (superfine) sugar
250 ml/8 fl oz/1 cup milk

Rub the butter or margarine into the flour, salt and baking powder until the mixture resembles breadcrumbs. Stir in the sugar. Gradually add the milk and mix to a smooth dough. Press gently into a greased 23 cm/9 in cake tin (pan) and bake in a preheated oven at 160°C/325°F/gas mark 3 for about 30 minutes until light golden brown.

Spanish Sponge Cake

Makes one 23 cm/9 in cake

4 eggs, separated
100 g/4 oz/½ cup granulated sugar
Grated rind of ½ lemon
25 g/1 oz/¼ cup cornmeal
25 g/1 oz/¼ cup plain (all-purpose)
  flour
30 ml/2 tbsp icing (confectioners')
  sugar, sifted

Beat the egg yolks, sugar and lemon rind until pale and foamy. Gradually whisk in the cornmeal and flour. Beat the egg whites until stiff, then fold into the batter. Spoon the mixture into a greased 23 cm/9 in square cake tin (pan) and bake in a preheated oven at 220°C/425°F/gas mark 7 for 6 minutes. Remove from the tin immediately and allow to cool. Serve sprinkled with the icing sugar.

Victoria Sandwich

Makes one 23 cm/7 in cake

175 g/6 oz/¾ cup butter or margarine,
  softened
175 g/6 oz/¾ cup caster (superfine)
  sugar, plus extra for sprinkling
3 eggs, beaten
175 g/6 oz/1½ cups self-raising
  (self-rising) flour
60 ml/4 tbsp strawberry jam
  (conserve)

Beat the butter or margarine until soft, then cream with the sugar until pale and fluffy. Gradually beat in the eggs, then fold in the flour. Divide the mixture evenly between two greased and lined 18 cm/7 in sandwich tins. Bake in a preheated oven at 190°C/375°F/gas mark 5 for about 20 minutes until well risen and springy to the touch. Turn out on to a wire rack to cool, then sandwich together with jam and sprinkle with sugar.

Whisked Sponge Cake

Makes one 20 cm/8 in cake

2 eggs
75 g/3 oz/⅓ cup caster (superfine)
  sugar
50 g/2 oz/½ cup plain
  (all-purpose) flour
120 ml/4 fl oz/½ cup double (heavy)
  cream, whipped
45 ml/3 tbsp raspberry jam (conserve)
Icing (confectioners') sugar, sifted

Whisk together the eggs and sugar for at least 5 minutes until pale. Fold in the flour. Spoon into a greased and lined 20 cm/8 in sandwich tin and bake in a preheated oven at 190°C/375°F/gas mark 5 for 20 minutes until springy to the touch. Leave to cool on a wire rack.

Cut the cake in half horizontally, then sandwich the two halves together with cream and jam. Sprinkle icing sugar over the top.

Windmill Sponge Cake

Makes one 20 cm/8 in cake

For the cake:
*175 g/6 oz/1½ cups self-raising
(self-rising) flour*
5 ml/1 tsp baking powder
*175 g/6 oz/¾ cup butter or margarine,
softened*
*175 g/6 oz/¾ cup caster (superfine)
sugar*
3 eggs
5 ml/1 tsp vanilla essence (extract)
For the icing (frosting):
*100 g/4 oz/½ cup butter or margarine,
softened*
*175 g/6 oz/1 cup icing (confectioners')
sugar, sifted*
*75 ml/5 tbsp strawberry jam
(conserve)*
*Sugar strands and a few crystallised
(candied) orange and lemon slices
to decorate*

Cream together all the cake ingredients until you have a soft cake mixture. Spoon into two greased and lined 20 cm/ 8 in cake tins (pans) and bake in a preheated oven at 160°C/325°F/gas mark 3 for 20 minutes until golden brown and springy to the touch. Leave to cool in the tins for 5 minutes, then turn out on to a wire rack to finish cooling.

To make the icing, cream the butter or margarine with the icing sugar until you have a spreadable consistency. Spread the jam over the top of one cake, then spread with half the icing and place the second cake on top. Spread the remaining icing over the top of the cake and smooth out with a palette knife. Cut a 20 cm/8 in circle of greaseproof (waxed) paper and fold into 8 segments. Leaving a small circle in the centre to hold the paper in one piece, cut out alternate segments and place the paper on top of the cake as a stencil. Sprinkle the uncovered sections with sugar strands, then remove the paper and arrange the orange and lemon slices in an attractive pattern on the undecorated sections.

Swiss Roll

Makes one 20 cm/8 in roll

3 eggs
*75 g/3 oz/⅓ cup caster (superfine)
sugar*
*75 g/3 oz/¾ cup self-raising
(self-rising) flour*
Caster (superfine) sugar for dusting
75 ml/5 tbsp raspberry jam (conserve)

Whisk together the eggs and sugar for about 10 minutes until very pale and thick and the mixture trails off the whisk in ribbons. Fold in the flour and spoon into a greased and lined 30 × 20 cm/12 × 8 in Swiss roll tin (jelly roll pan). Bake in a preheated oven at 200°C/400°F/gas mark 4 for 10 minutes until well risen and firm to the touch. Sprinkle a clean tea towel (dish cloth) with caster sugar and invert the cake on to the towel. Remove the lining paper, trim the edges and run a knife about 2.5 cm/1 in in from the short edge, cutting half-way through the cake. Roll up the cake from the cut edge. Leave to cool.

Unwrap the cake and spread with jam, then roll up again and serve sprinkled with icing sugar.

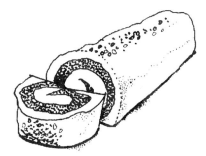

Apple Swiss Roll

Makes one 20 cm/8 in roll

100 g/4 oz/1 cup plain (all-purpose)
*   flour*
5 ml/1 tsp baking powder
A pinch of salt
225 g/8 oz/1 cup caster (superfine)
*   sugar*
3 eggs
5 ml/1 tsp vanilla essence (extract)
45 ml/3 tbsp cold water
Icing (confectioners') sugar, sifted, for
*   dusting*
100 g/4 oz/1 cup apple jam
*   (clear conserve)*

Mix the flour, baking powder, salt and sugar, then beat in the eggs and vanilla essence until smooth. Stir in the water. Spoon the mixture into a greased and floured 30 × 20 cm/12 × 8 in Swiss roll tin (jelly roll pan) and bake in a preheated oven at 190°C/375°F/gas mark 5 for 20 minutes until springy to the touch. Sprinkle a clean tea towel (dish cloth) with icing sugar and invert the cake on to the towel. Remove the lining paper, trim the edges and run a knife about 2.5 cm/1 in from the short edge, cutting half-way through the cake. Roll up the cake from the cut edge. Leave to cool.

Unroll the cake and spread with apple jam almost to the edges. Roll up again and dust with icing sugar to serve.

Brandy Chestnut Roll

Makes one 20 cm/8 in roll

3 eggs
100 g/4 oz/½ cup caster (superfine)
*   sugar*
100 g/4 oz/1 cup plain (all-purpose)
*   flour*
30 ml/2 tbsp brandy
Caster (superfine) sugar for
*   sprinkling*
For the filling and decoration:
300 ml/½ pt/1¼ cups double (heavy)
*   cream*
15 ml/1 tbsp caster (superfine) sugar
250 g/9 oz/1 large can chestnut purée
175 g/6 oz/1½ cups plain
*   (semi-sweet) chocolate*
15 g/½ oz/1 tbsp butter or margarine
30 ml/2 tbsp brandy

Whisk together the eggs and sugar until until pale and thick. Gently fold in the flour and brandy with a metal spoon. Spoon into a greased and lined 30 × 20 cm/12 × 8 in Swiss roll tin (jelly roll pan) and bake in a preheated oven at 220°C/425°F/gas mark 7 for 12 minutes. Place a clean tea towel (dish cloth) on the work surface, cover with a sheet of grease-proof (waxed) paper and sprinkle with caster sugar. Invert the cake on to the paper. Remove the lining paper, trim the edges and run a knife about 2.5 cm/1 in from the short edge, cutting half-way through the cake. Roll up the cake from the cut edge. Leave to cool.

To make the filling, whip the cream and sugar until stiff. Sieve (strain) the chestnut purée, then beat until smooth. Fold half the cream into the chestnut purée. Unroll the cake and spread the chestnut purée over the surface, then roll up the cake again. Melt the chocolate with the butter or margarine and brandy in a heatproof bowl set over a pan of gently simmering water. Spread over the cake and mark into patterns with a fork.

Chocolate Swiss Roll

Makes one 20 cm/8 in roll

3 eggs
75 g/3 oz/⅓ cup caster (superfine)
sugar
50 g/2 oz/½ cup self-raising
(self-rising) flour
25 g/1 oz/¼ cup cocoa (unsweetened
chocolate) powder
Caster (superfine) sugar for dusting
120 ml/4 fl oz/½ cup double (heavy)
cream
Icing (confectioners') sugar for
sprinkling

Whisk together the eggs and sugar for about 10 minutes until very pale and thick, and the mixture trails off the whisk in ribbons. Fold in the flour and cocoa and spoon into a greased and lined 30 × 20 cm/12 × 8 in Swiss roll tin (jelly roll pan). Bake in a preheated oven at 200°C/400°F/gas mark 4 for 10 minutes until well risen and firm to the touch. Sprinkle a clean tea towel (dish cloth) with caster sugar and invert the cake on to the towel. Remove the lining paper, trim the edges and run a knife about 2.5 cm/1 in from the short edge, cutting half-way through the cake. Roll up the cake from the cut edge. Leave to cool.

Whip the cream until stiff. Unwrap the cake and spread with cream, then roll up again and serve sprinkled with icing sugar.

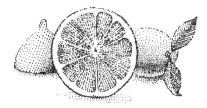

Lemon Roll

Makes one 20 cm/8 in roll

75 g/3 oz /¼ cup self-raising
(self-rising) flour
5 ml/1 tsp baking powder
A pinch of salt
1 egg
175 g/6 oz/¾ cup caster (superfine)
sugar
15 ml/1 tbsp oil
5 ml/1 tsp lemon essence (extract)
6 egg whites
50 g/2 oz/⅓ cup icing (confectioners')
sugar, sifted
75 ml/5 tbsp lemon curd
300 ml/½ pt/1¼ cups double (heavy)
cream
10 ml/2 tsp grated lemon rind

Mix the flour, baking powder and salt. Beat the egg until thick and lemon-coloured, then slowly beat in 50 g/2 oz/¼ cup of the caster sugar until pale and creamy. Beat in the oil and lemon essence. In a clean bowl, beat the egg whites until they form soft peaks, then gradually beat in the remaining caster sugar until the mixture holds stiff peaks. Fold the egg whites into the oil, then fold in the flour. Spoon into a greased and lined 30 × 20 cm/12 × 8 in Swiss roll tin (jelly roll pan) and bake in a preheated oven at 190°C/375°F/gas mark 5 for 10 minutes until springy to the touch. Cover a clean tea towel (dish cloth) with a sheet of greaseproof (waxed) paper and dust with the icing sugar, then invert the cake on to the towel. Remove the lining paper, trim the edges and run a knife about 2.5 cm/1 in in from the short edge, cutting half-way through the cake. Roll up the cake from the cut edge. Leave to cool.

Unroll the cake and spread with lemon curd. Whisk the cream until stiff, and stir in the lemon rind. Spread over the lemon curd, then roll up the cake again. Chill before serving.

Lemon and Honey-cheese Roll

Makes one 20 cm/8 in roll

3 eggs
75 g/3 oz/⅓ cup caster (superfine)
  sugar
Grated rind of 1 lemon
75 g/3 oz/¾ cup plain (all-purpose)
  flour
A pinch of salt
Caster (superfine) sugar for dusting
For the filling:
175 g/6 oz/¾ cup cream cheese
30 ml/2 tbsp clear honey
Icing (confectioners') sugar, sifted,
  for dusting

Whisk together the eggs, sugar and lemon rind in a heatproof bowl set over a pan of gently simmering water until thick and foamy and the mixture trails off the whisk in ribbons. Remove from the heat and whisk for 3 minutes, then fold in the flour and salt. Spoon into a greased and lined 30 × 20 cm/ 12 × 8 in Swiss roll tin (jelly roll pan) and bake in a preheated oven at 200°C/ 400°F/gas mark 6 until golden brown and springy to the touch. Cover a clean tea towel (dish cloth) with a sheet of greaseproof (waxed) paper and sprinkle with caster sugar, then invert the cake on to the towel. Remove the lining paper, trim the edges and run a knife about 2.5 cm/1 in from the short edge, cutting half-way through the cake. Roll up the cake from the cut edge. Leave to cool.

Mix the cream cheese with the honey. Unroll the cake, spread with the filling, then roll up the cake again and dust with icing sugar.

Lime Marmalade Roll

Makes one 20 cm/8 in roll

3 eggs
175 g/6 oz/¾ cup caster (superfine)
  sugar
45 ml/3 tbsp water
5 ml/1 tsp vanilla essence (extract)
75 g/3 oz/¾ cup plain (all-purpose)
  flour
5 ml/1 tsp baking powder
A pinch of salt
25 g/1 oz/¼ cup ground almonds
Caster (superfine) sugar for
  sprinkling
60 ml/4 tbsp lime marmalade
150 ml/¼ pt/⅔ cup double (heavy)
  cream, whipped

Beat the eggs until pale and thick, then gradually beat in the sugar, water and vanilla essence. Mix in the flour, baking powder, salt and ground almonds and beat to a smooth batter. Spoon into a greased and lined 30 × 20 cm/12 × 8 in Swiss roll tin (jelly roll pan) and bake in a preheated oven at 180°C/350°F/gas mark 4 for 12 minutes until springy to the touch. Sprinkle a clean tea towel (dish cloth) with sugar and invert the warm cake on to the cloth. Remove the lining paper, trim the edges and run a knife about 2.5 cm/1 in from the short edge, cutting half-way through the cake. Roll up the cake from the cut edge. Leave to cool.

Unroll the cake and spread with marmalade and cream. Roll up again and sprinkle with a little more caster sugar.

Lemon and Strawberry Roulade

Makes one 20 cm/8 in roll

For the filling:
30 ml/2 tbsp cornflour (cornstarch)
75 g/3 oz/⅓ cup caster (superfine) sugar
120 ml/4 fl oz/½ cup apple juice
120 ml/4 fl oz/½ cup lemon juice
2 egg yolks, lightly beaten
10 ml/2 tsp grated lemon rind
15 ml/1 tbsp butter
For the cake:
3 eggs, separated
3 egg whites
A pinch of salt
75 g/3 oz/⅓ cup caster (superfine) sugar
15 ml/1 tbsp oil
5 ml/1 tsp vanilla essence (extract)
5 ml/1 tsp grated lemon rind
50 g/2 oz/½ cup plain (all-purpose) flour
25 g/1 oz/¼ cup cornflour (cornstarch)
225 g/8 oz strawberries, sliced
Icing (confectioners') sugar, sifted, for dusting

To make the filling, mix together the cornflour and sugar in a pan, then gradually add the apple and lemon juices. Stir in the egg yolks and lemon rind. Cook over a low heat, stirring continuously, until very thick. Remove from the heat and stir in the butter. Spoon into a bowl, place a circle of greaseproof (waxed) paper on the surface, cool, then chill.

To make the cake, beat all the egg whites with the salt until they form soft peaks. Gradually beat in the sugar until stiff and shiny. Whisk together the egg yolks, oil, vanilla essence and lemon rind. Stir in a spoonful of the whites, then stir the yolk mixture into the egg whites. Fold in the flour and cornflour; do not overmix. Spread the mixture into a greased, lined and floured 30 × 20 cm/

12 × 8 in Swiss roll tin (jelly roll pan) and bake in a preheated oven at 200°C/400°F/ gas mark 4 for 10 minutes until golden. Invert the cake on to a sheet of greaseproof (waxed) paper on a wire rack. Remove the lining paper, trim the edges and run a knife about 2.5 cm/1 in in from the short edge, cutting half-way through the cake. Roll up the cake from the cut edge. Leave to cool.

Unroll and spread the cool cake with the lemon filling and arrange the strawberries on top. Using the paper to help you, roll up the roulade again and dust with icing sugar to serve.

Orange and Almond Swiss Roll

Makes one 20 cm/8 in roll

4 eggs, separated
225 g/8 oz/1 cup caster (superfine) sugar
60 ml/4 tbsp orange juice
150 g/5 oz/1¼ cups plain (all-purpose) flour
5 ml/1 tsp baking powder
A pinch of salt
5 ml/1 tsp vanilla essence (extract)
Grated rind of ½ orange
Caster (superfine) sugar for sprinkling
For the filling:
2 oranges
30 ml/2 tbsp powdered gelatine
120 ml/4 fl oz/½ cup water
250 ml/8 fl oz/1 cup orange juice
100 g/4 oz/½ cup caster (superfine) sugar
4 egg yolks
250 ml/8 fl oz/1 cup double (heavy) cream
100 g/4 oz/⅓ cup apricot jam (conserve), sieved (strained)
15 ml/1 tbsp water
100 g/4 oz/1 cup flaked (slivered) almonds, toasted

Beat together the egg yolks, caster sugar and orange juice until pale and fluffy. Gradually fold in the flour and baking powder using a metal spoon. Whisk the egg whites and salt until stiff, then fold into the mixture with the vanilla essence and grated orange rind using a metal spoon. Spoon into a greased and lined 30 × 20 cm/12 × 8 in Swiss roll tin (jelly roll pan) and bake in a preheated oven at 200°C/400°F/gas mark 6 for 10 minutes until springy to the touch. Turn out on to a clean tea towel (dish cloth), sprinkled with caster sugar. Remove the lining paper, trim the edges and run a knife about 2.5 cm/1 in in from the short edge, cutting half-way through the cake. Roll up the cake from the cut edge. Leave to cool.

To make the filling, grate the rind of one orange. Peel both oranges and remove the pith and membranes. Halve the segments and leave to drain. Sprinkle the gelatine over the water in a bowl and leave until spongy. Stand the bowl in a pan of hot water until dissolved. Leave to cool slightly. Beat the orange juice and rind with the sugar and egg yolks in a heatproof bowl, set over a pan of gently simmering water, until thick and creamy. Remove from the heat and stir in the gelatine. Stir occasionally until cool. Whip the cream until stiff, then fold into the mixture and chill.

Unroll the cake, spread with the orange cream and sprinkle with the orange segments. Roll up again. Heat the jam with the water until well blended. Brush over the cake and sprinkle with the toasted almonds, pressing down gently.

Back-to-back Strawberry Swiss Roll

Makes one 20 cm/8 in roll

3 eggs
75 g/3 oz/⅓ cup caster (superfine) sugar
75 g/3 oz/¾ cup self-raising (self-rising) flour
Caster (superfine) sugar for dusting
75 ml/5 tbsp raspberry jam (conserve)
150 ml/¼ pt/⅔ cup whipping or double (heavy) cream
100 g/4 oz strawberries

Whisk together the eggs and sugar for about 10 minutes until very pale and thick, and the mixture trails off the whisk in ribbons. Fold in the flour and spoon into a greased and lined 30 × 20 cm/12 × 8 in Swiss roll tin (jelly roll pan). Bake in a preheated oven at 200°C/400°F/gas mark 4 for 10 minutes until well risen and firm to the touch. Sprinkle a clean tea towel (dish cloth) with caster sugar and invert the cake on to the towel. Remove the lining paper, trim the edges and run a knife about 2.5 cm/1 in in from the short edge, cutting half-way through the cake. Roll up the cake from the cut edge. Leave to cool.

Unwrap the cake and spread with jam, then roll up again. Cut the cake in half lengthways and place the rounded sides together on a serving plate with the cut sides facing outwards. Whip the cream until stiff, then pipe over the top and sides of the cake. Slice or quarter the strawberries if they are large, and arrange decoratively over the top of the cake.

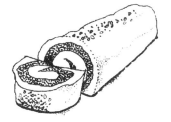

Chocolate Cakes

*C*hocolate is a favourite with most people, so there is a lot of choice here for both quick and easy and more complicated chocolate cake recipes. There are also a couple of carob recipes included for variety. You will find the world-famous chocolate Sachertorte in International Cakes on page 159.

All-in-one Chocolate Cake

Makes one 20 cm/8 in cake

100 g/4 oz/½ cup butter or margarine,
  softened
100 g/4 oz/½ cup caster (superfine)
  sugar
100 g/4 oz/1 cup self-raising
  (self-rising) flour
15 ml/1 tbsp cocoa (unsweetened
  chocolate) powder
2.5 ml/½ tsp baking powder
2 eggs

*B*lend all the ingredients together until well mixed. Spoon into a greased and lined 20 cm/8 in cake tin (pan) and bake in a preheated oven at 180°C/350°F/gas mark 4 for 30 minutes until well risen and springy to the touch.

Chocolate Banana Loaf

Makes one 900 g/2 lb loaf

150 g/5 oz/⅔ cup butter or margarine
150 g/5 oz/⅔ cup soft brown sugar
150 g/5 oz/1¼ cups plain
  (semi-sweet) chocolate
2 bananas, mashed
3 eggs, beaten
200 g/7 oz/1¾ cups plain
  (all-purpose) flour
10 ml/2 tsp baking powder

*M*elt the butter or margarine with the sugar and chocolate. Remove from the heat, then stir in the bananas, eggs, flour and baking powder until smooth. Spoon into a greased and lined 900 g/2 lb loaf tin (pan) and bake in a preheated oven at 150°C/300°F/gas mark 3 for 1 hour until springy to the touch. Leave to cool in the tin for 5 minutes before turning out to finish cooling on a wire rack.

Chocolate and Almond Cake

Makes one 20 cm/8 in cake

100 g/4 oz/½ cup butter or margarine,
  softened
100 g/4 oz/½ cup caster (superfine)
  sugar
2 eggs, lightly beaten
2.5 ml/½ tsp almond essence (extract)
100 g/4 oz/1 cup self-raising
  (self-rising) flour
25 g/1 oz/¼ cup cocoa (unsweetened
  chocolate) powder
2.5 ml/½ tsp baking powder
45 ml/3 tbsp ground almonds
60 ml/4 tbsp milk
Icing (confectioners') sugar
  for dusting

*C*ream together the butter or margarine and sugar until light and fluffy. Gradually beat in the eggs and almond essence, then fold in the flour, cocoa and baking powder. Stir in the ground almonds and enough of the milk to make a soft dropping consistency. Spoon the mixture into a greased and lined 20 cm/8 in cake tin (pan) and bake in a preheated oven at 200°C/400°F/gas mark 6 for 15–20 minutes until well risen and springy to the touch. Serve dusted with icing sugar.

Iced Almond Chocolate Cake

Makes one 23 cm/9 in cake

225 g/8 oz/2 cups plain (semi-sweet) chocolate
225 g/8 oz/1 cup butter or margarine, softened
225 g/8 oz/1 cup caster (superfine) sugar
5 eggs, separated
225 g/8 oz/2 cups self-raising (self-rising) flour
100 g/4 oz/1 cup ground almonds
For the icing (frosting):
175 g/6 oz/1 cup icing (confectioners') sugar
25 g/1 oz/¼ cup cocoa (unsweetened chocolate) powder
30 ml/2 tbsp Cointreau
30 ml/2 tbsp water
Blanched almonds to decorate

Melt the chocolate in a heatproof bowl set over a pan of gently simmering water. Leave to cool slightly. Cream together the butter or margarine and sugar until light and fluffy. Beat in the egg yolks, then pour in the melted chocolate. Fold in the flour and ground almonds. Beat the egg whites until stiff, then gradually fold into the chocolate mixture. Spoon into a greased and lined loose-bottomed 23 cm/9 in cake tin (pan) and bake in a preheated oven at 180°C/350°F/ gas mark 4 for 1¼ hours until well risen and springy to the touch. Leave to cool.

To make the icing, mix together the icing sugar and cocoa and make a well in the centre. Warm the Cointreau and water, then gradually mix enough of the liquid into the icing sugar to make a spreadable icing. Smooth over the cake and mark a pattern in the icing before it cools. Decorate with almonds.

Chocolate Angel Cake

Makes one 900 g/2 lb cake

6 egg whites
A pinch of salt
5 ml/1 tsp cream of tartar
450 g/1 lb/2 cups caster (superfine) sugar
2.5 ml/½ tsp lemon juice
A few drops of vanilla essence (extract)
100 g/4 oz/1 cup plain (all-purpose) flour
50 g/2 oz/½ cup cocoa (unsweetened chocolate) powder
5 ml/1 tsp baking powder
For the icing (frosting):
175 g/6 oz/1 cup icing (confectioners') sugar, sifted
5 ml/1 tsp cocoa (unsweetened chocolate) powder
A few drops of vanilla essence (extract)
30 ml/2 tbsp milk

Beat the egg whites and salt until they form soft peaks. Add the cream of tartar and beat until stiff. Fold in the sugar, lemon juice and vanilla essence. Mix together the flour, cocoa and baking powder, then fold it into the mixture. Spoon into a greased and lined 900 g/2 lb loaf tin (pan) and bake in a preheated oven at 180°C/350°F/gas mark 4 for 1 hour until firm. Remove from the pan immediately and leave to cool on a wire rack.

To make the icing, beat together all the icing ingredients until smooth, adding the milk a little at a time. Drizzle over the cooled cake.

American Chocolate Cake

Makes one 23 cm/9 in cake

175 g/6 oz/1½ cups plain
  (all-purpose) flour
45 ml/3 tbsp cocoa (unsweetened
  chocolate) powder
5 ml/1 tsp bicarbonate of soda
  (baking soda)
225 g/8 oz/1 cup caster (superfine)
  sugar
75 ml/5 tbsp oil
15 ml/1 tbsp white wine vinegar
5 ml/1 tsp vanilla essence (extract)
250 ml/8 fl oz/1 cup cold water
For the icing (frosting):
50 g/2 oz/¼ cup cream cheese
30 ml/2 tbsp butter or margarine
2.5 ml/½ tsp vanilla essence (extract)
175 g/6 oz/1 cup icing (confectioners')
  sugar, sifted

Mix together the dry ingredients and make a well in the centre. Pour in the oil, wine vinegar and vanilla essence and mix well. Stir in the cold water and mix again until smooth. Pour into a greased 23 cm/9 in baking tin (pan) and bake in a preheated oven at 180°C/350°F/ gas mark 4 for 30 minutes. Leave to cool.

To make the icing, beat together the cream cheese, butter or margarine and vanilla essence until light and fluffy. Gradually beat in the icing sugar until smooth. Spread over the top of the cake.

Chocolate Apple Cake

Makes one 20 cm/8 in cake

2 cooking (tart) apples
Lemon juice
100 g/4 oz/½ cup butter or margarine,
  softened
225 g/8 oz/1 cup caster (superfine)
  sugar
2 eggs, lightly beaten
5 ml/1 tsp vanilla essence (extract)
250 g/9 oz/2¼ cups plain
  (all-purpose) flour
25 g/1 oz/¼ cup cocoa (unsweetened
  chocolate) powder
5 ml/1 tsp baking powder
5 ml/1 tsp bicarbonate of soda
  (baking soda)
150 ml/¼ pt/⅔ cup milk
For the icing (frosting):
450 g/1 lb/2⅔ cups icing
  (confectioners') sugar, sifted
25 g/1 oz/¼ cup cocoa (unsweetened
  chocolate) powder
50 g/2 oz/¼ cup butter or margarine
75 ml/5 tbsp milk

Peel, core and finely chop the apples, then sprinkle with a little lemon juice. Cream together the butter or margarine and sugar until light and fluffy. Gradually beat in the eggs and vanilla essence, then fold in the flour, cocoa, baking powder and bicarbonate of soda alternately with the milk until everything is well blended. Stir in the chopped apples. Spoon into a greased and lined 20 cm/8 in cake tin (pan) and bake in a preheated oven at 180°C/350°F/gas mark 4 for 45 minutes until a skewer inserted in the centre comes out clean. Leave to cool in the tin for 10 minutes, then turn out on to a wire rack to finish cooling.

To make the icing, beat together the icing sugar, cocoa and butter or margarine, adding just enough milk to make the mixture smooth and creamy. Spread over the top and sides of the cake and mark into patterns with a fork.

Chocolate Brownie Cake

Makes one 38 × 25 cm/ 15 × 10 in cake

100 g/4 oz/¹⁄₂ cup butter or margarine
100 g/4 oz/¹⁄₂ cup lard (shortening)
250 ml/8 fl oz/1 cup water
25 g/1 oz/¹⁄₄ cup cocoa (unsweetened chocolate) powder
225 g/8 oz/2 cups plain (all-purpose) flour
450 g/1 lb/2 cups caster (superfine) sugar
120 ml/4 fl oz/¹⁄₂ cup buttermilk
2 eggs, beaten
5 ml/1 tsp bicarbonate of soda (baking soda)
A pinch of salt
5 ml/1 tsp vanilla essence (extract)

Melt the butter or margarine, lard, water and cocoa in a small pan. Mix the flour and sugar in a bowl, pour in the melted mixture and blend well. Stir in the remaining ingredients and beat until well blended. Spoon into a greased and floured Swiss roll tin (jelly roll pan) and bake in a preheated oven at 200°C/400°F/gas mark 6 for 20 minutes until springy to the touch.

Chocolate and Buttermilk Cake

Makes one 23 cm/9 in cake

225 g/8 oz/2 cups self-raising (self-rising) flour
350 g/12 oz/1¹⁄₂ cups caster (superfine) sugar
5 ml/1 tsp bicarbonate of soda (baking soda)
2.5 ml/¹⁄₂ tsp salt
100 g/4 oz/¹⁄₂ cup butter or margarine
250 ml/8 fl oz/1 cup buttermilk
2 eggs
50 g/2 oz/¹⁄₂ cup cocoa (unsweetened chocolate) powder
American Velvet Frosting (page 233)

Mix together the flour, sugar, bicarbonate of soda and salt. Rub in the butter or margarine until the mixture resembles breadcrumbs, then beat in the buttermilk, eggs and cocoa and continue to beat until smooth. Spoon the mixture into two greased and lined 23 cm/9 in sandwich tins (pans) and bake in a preheated oven at 180°C/350°F/gas mark 4 for 30 minutes until a skewer inserted in the centre comes out clean. Sandwich together with half the American Velvet Frosting and cover the cake with the remainder. Leave to set.

Chocolate Chip and Almond Cake

Makes one 20 cm/8 in cake

175 g/6 oz/³⁄₄ cup butter or margarine, softened
175 g/6 oz/³⁄₄ cup caster (superfine) sugar
3 eggs, lightly beaten
225 g/8 oz/2 cups self-raising (self-rising) flour
50 g/2 oz/¹⁄₂ cup ground almonds
100 g/4 oz/1 cup chocolate chips
30 ml/2 tbsp milk
25 g/1 oz/¹⁄₄ cup flaked (slivered) almonds

Cream together the butter or margarine and sugar until light and fluffy. Gradually beat in the eggs, then fold in the flour, ground almonds and chocolate chips. Blend in enough of the milk to give a dropping consistency, then stir in the flaked almonds. Spoon into a greased and lined 20 cm/8 in cake tin (pan) and bake in a preheated oven at 180°C/350°F/gas mark 4 for 1 hour until a skewer inserted in the centre comes out clean. Cool in the tin for 5 minutes, then turn out on to a wire rack to finish cooling.

Chocolate Cream Cake

Makes one 18 cm/7 in cake

4 eggs
100 g/4 oz/½ cup caster (superfine) sugar
60 g/2½ oz/⅔ cup plain (all-purpose) flour
25 g/1 oz/¼ cup drinking chocolate powder
150 ml/¼ pt/⅔ cup double (heavy) cream

Whisk together the eggs and sugar until light and fluffy. Fold in the flour and drinking chocolate. Spoon the mixture into two greased and lined 18 cm/7 in sandwich tins (pans) and bake in a preheated oven at 200°C/400°F/gas mark 6 for 15 minutes until springy to the touch. Cool on a wire rack. Whip the cream until stiff, then sandwich the cakes together with the cream.

Chocolate Cake with Dates

Makes one 20 cm/8 in cake

25 g/1 oz/1 square plain (semi-sweet) chocolate
175 g/6 oz/1 cup stoned (pitted) dates, chopped
5 ml/1 tsp bicarbonate of soda (baking soda)
375 ml/13 fl oz/1½ cups boiling water
175 g/6 oz/¾ cup butter or margarine, softened
225 g/8 oz/1 cup caster (superfine) sugar
2 eggs, beaten
175 g/6 oz/1½ cups plain (all-purpose) flour
2.5 ml/½ tsp salt
50 g/2 oz/¼ cup granulated sugar
100 g/4 oz/1 cup plain (semi-sweet) chocolate chips

Mix together the chocolate, dates, bicarbonate of soda and boiling water and stir until the chocolate has melted. Cream together the butter or margarine and sugar until light and fluffy. Gradually beat in the eggs. Fold in the flour and salt alternately with the chocolate mixture and stir until well blended. Spoon into a greased and floured 20 cm/8 in square cake tin (pan). Mix the granulated sugar and chocolate chips and sprinkle over the top. Bake in a preheated oven at 160°C/325°F/gas mark 3 for 45 minutes until a skewer inserted in the centre comes out clean.

Family Chocolate Cake

Makes one 23 cm/9 in cake

100 g/4 oz/½ cup butter or margarine, softened
175 g/6 oz/¾ cup caster (superfine) sugar
2 eggs, lightly beaten
5 ml/1 tsp vanilla essence (extract)
225 g/8 oz/2 cups plain (all-purpose) flour
45 ml/3 tbsp cocoa (unsweetened chocolate) powder
10 ml/2 tsp baking powder
2.5 ml/½ tsp bicarbonate of soda (baking soda)
A pinch of salt
150 ml/8 fl oz/1 cup water

Cream together the butter or margarine and sugar until light and fluffy. Gradually beat in the eggs and vanilla essence, then fold in the flour, cocoa, baking powder, bicarbonate of soda and salt alternately with the water until you have a smooth batter. Spoon into a greased and lined 23 cm/9 in cake tin (pan) and bake in a preheated oven at 220°C/425°F/gas mark 7 for 20–25 minutes until well risen and springy to the touch.

24

Devil's Food Cake with Marshmallow Icing

Makes one 18 cm/7 in cake

100 g/4 oz/½ cup butter or margarine, softened
100 g/4 oz/½ cup caster (superfine) sugar
2 eggs, lightly beaten
75 g/3 oz/⅓ cup self-raising (self-rising) flour
15 ml/1 tbsp cocoa (unsweetened chocolate) powder
A pinch of salt
For the icing (frosting):
100 g/4 oz marshmallows
30 ml/2 tbsp milk
2 egg whites
25 g/1 oz/2 tbsp caster (superfine) sugar
Grated chocolate to decorate

Cream together the butter or margarine and sugar until light and fluffy. Gradually beat in the eggs, then fold in the flour, cocoa and salt. Spoon the mixture into two greased and lined 18 cm/7 in sandwich tins (pans) and bake in a preheated oven at 180°C/350°F/gas mark 4 for 25 minutes until well risen and springy to the touch. Leave to cool.

Melt the marshmallows with the milk over a low heat, stirring occasionally, then leave to cool. Beat the egg whites until stiff, then fold in the sugar and beat again until stiff and glossy. Fold into the marshmallow mixture and leave to set slightly. Sandwich the cakes together with one-third of the marshmallow icing, then spread the remainder over the top and sides of the cake and decorate with grated chocolate.

Dreamy Chocolate Cake

Makes one 23 cm/9 in cake

225 g/8 oz/2 cups plain (semi-sweet) chocolate
30 ml/2 tbsp instant coffee powder
45 ml/3 tbsp water
4 eggs, separated
150 g/5 oz/⅔ cup butter or margarine, diced
A pinch of salt
100 g/4 oz/½ cup caster (superfine) sugar
50 g/2 oz/½ cup cornflour (cornstarch)
For the decoration:
150 ml/¼ pt/⅔ cup double (heavy) cream
25 g/1 oz/3 tbsp icing (confectioners') sugar
175 g/6 oz/1½ cups walnuts, chopped

Melt the chocolate, coffee and water together in a heatproof bowl set over a pan of gently simmering water. Remove from the heat and gradually beat in the egg yolks. Stir in the butter a piece at a time until melted into the mixture. Beat together the egg whites and salt until they form soft peaks. Carefully add the sugar and beat until stiff. Beat in the cornflour. Fold a spoonful of the mixture into the chocolate, then fold the chocolate into the remaining egg whites. Spoon into a greased and lined 23 cm/9 in cake tin (pan) and bake in a preheated oven at 180°C/350°F/gas mark 4 for 45 minutes until well risen and just springy to the touch. Remove from the oven and leave to cool slightly before removing from the tin; the cake will crack and sink. Leave to cool completely.

Beat the cream until stiff, then beat in the sugar. Spread some of the cream round the edge of the cake and press in the chopped nuts to decorate. Spread or pipe the remaining cream on top.

Floataway Chocolate Cake

Makes one 23 × 30 cm/
9 × 12 in cake

2 eggs, separated
350 g/12 oz/1½ cups caster (superfine) sugar
200 g/7 oz/1¾ cups self-raising (self-rising) flour
2.5 ml/½ tsp bicarbonate of soda (baking soda)
2.5 ml/½ tsp salt
60 ml/4 tbsp cocoa (unsweetened chocolate) powder
75 ml/5 tbsp oil
250 ml/8 fl oz/1 cup buttermilk

Beat the egg whites until stiff. Gradually beat in 100 g/4 oz/½ cup of the sugar and beat until stiff and glossy. Mix together the remaining sugar, the flour, bicarbonate of soda, salt and cocoa. Beat in the egg yolks, oil and buttermilk. Carefully fold in the egg whites. Spoon into a greased and floured 23 × 32 cm/ 9 × 12 in cake tin (pan) and bake in a preheated oven at 180°C/350°F/gas mark 4 for 40 minutes until a skewer inserted in the centre comes out clean.

Hazelnut and Chocolate Cake

Makes one 25 cm/10 in cake

100 g/4 oz/1 cup hazelnuts
175 g/6 oz/¾ cup caster (superfine) sugar
175 g/6 oz/1½ cups plain (all-purpose) flour
50 g/2 oz/½ cup cocoa (unsweetened chocolate) powder
5 ml/1 tsp baking powder
A pinch of salt
2 eggs, lightly beaten
2 egg whites
175 ml/6 fl oz/¾ cup oil
60 ml/4 tbsp cold strong black coffee

Spread the hazelnuts in a baking tin (pan) and bake in a preheated oven at 180°C/350°F/gas mark 4 for 15 minutes until browned. Rub briskly in a tea towel (dish cloth) to remove the skins, then finely chop the nuts in a food processor with 15 ml/1 tbsp of the sugar. Mix the nuts with the flour, cocoa, baking powder and salt. Beat together the eggs and egg whites until frothy. Add in the remaining sugar a little at a time and continue to beat until pale. Gradually beat in the oil, then the coffee. Stir into the dry ingredients, then spoon into a greased and lined 25 cm/10 in loose-bottomed cake tin (pan) and bake in a preheated oven at 180°C/350°F/gas mark 4 for 30 minutes until springy to the touch.

Chocolate Fudge Cake

Makes one 900 g/2 lb cake

60 ml/4 tbsp cocoa (unsweetened chocolate) powder
100 g/4 oz/½ cup butter or margarine
120 ml/4 fl oz/½ cup oil
250 ml/8 fl oz/1 cup water
350 g/12 oz/1½ cups caster (superfine) sugar
225 g/8 oz/2 cups self-raising (self-rising) flour
2 eggs, beaten
120 ml/4 fl oz/½ cup milk
2.5 ml/½ tsp bicarbonate of soda (baking soda)
5 ml/1 tsp vanilla essence (extract)
For the icing (frosting):
60 ml/4 tbsp cocoa (unsweetened chocolate) powder
100 g/4 oz/½ cup butter or margarine
60 ml/4 tbsp evaporated milk
450 g/1 lb/2⅔ cups icing (confectioners') sugar, sifted
5 ml/1 tsp vanilla essence (extract)
100 g/4 oz/1 cup plain (semi-sweet) chocolate

Put the cocoa, butter or margarine, oil and water into a pan and bring to the boil. Remove from the heat and stir in the sugar and flour. Beat together the eggs, milk, bicarbonate of soda and vanilla essence, then add to the mixture in the pan. Pour into a greased and lined 900 g/ 2 lb loaf tin (pan) and bake in a preheated oven at 180°C/350°F/gas mark 4 for 1¼ hours until well risen and springy to the touch. Turn out and cool on a wire rack.

To make the icing, bring all the ingredients to the boil in a medium-sized pan. Beat until smooth, then pour over the cake while still warm. Leave to set.

Chocolate Gâteau

Makes one 23 cm/9 in cake

150 g/5 oz/1¼ cups plain (semi-sweet) chocolate
150 g/5 oz/⅔ cup butter or margarine, softened
150 g/5 oz/⅔ cup caster (superfine) sugar
75 g/3 oz/¾ cup ground almonds
3 eggs, separated
100 g/4 oz/1 cup plain (all-purpose) flour
For the filling and topping:
300 ml/½ pt/1¼ cups double (heavy) cream
200 g/7 oz/1¼ cups plain (semi-sweet) chocolate, chopped
Crumbled chocolate flake

Melt the chocolate in a heatproof bowl over a pan of gently simmering water. Beat together the butter or margarine and sugar, then fold in the chocolate, almonds and egg yolks. Whisk the egg whites until they form soft peaks, then fold them into the mixture using a metal spoon. Carefully fold in the flour. Spoon into a greased 23 cm/9 in cake tin (pan) and bake in a preheated oven at 180°C/350°F/gas mark 4 for 40 minutes until springy to the touch.

Meanwhile, bring the cream to the boil, then add the chopped chocolate and stir until melted. Leave to cool. When the cake is cooked and cooled, slice horizontally and sandwich together with half the chocolate cream. Spread the remainder on top and decorate with crumbled chocolate flake.

Italian Chocolate Cake

Makes one 23 cm/9 in cake

100 g/4 oz/½ cup butter or margarine
225 g/8 oz/1 cup soft brown sugar
30 ml/2 tbsp cocoa (unsweetened chocolate) powder
3 eggs, well beaten
75 g/3 oz/¾ cup plain (semi-sweet) chocolate
150 ml/4 fl oz/½ cup boiling water
400 g/14 oz/3½ cups plain (all-purpose) flour
5 ml/1 tsp baking powder
A pinch of salt
10 ml/2 tsp vanilla essence (extract)
175 ml/6 fl oz/¾ cup single (light) cream
150 ml/¼ pt/⅔ cup double (heavy) cream

Cream together the butter or margarine, sugar and cocoa. Gradually beat in the eggs. Melt the chocolate in the boiling water, then add to the mixture. Stir in the flour, baking powder and salt. Beat in the vanilla essence and single cream. Spoon into two greased and lined 23 cm/9 in cake tins (pans) and bake in a preheated oven at 180°C/350°F/gas mark 4 for 25 minutes until well risen and springy to the touch. Leave to cool in the tins for 5 minutes, then turn out on to a wire rack to finish cooling. Whisk the double cream until stiff, then use to sandwich the cakes together.

Iced Hazelnut Chocolate Cake

Makes one 23 cm/9 in cake

150 g/5 oz/1¼ cups hazelnuts, skinned
225 g/8 oz/1 cup granulated sugar
15 ml/1 tbsp instant coffee powder
60 ml/4 tbsp water
175 g/6 oz/1½ cups plain (semi-sweet)
   chocolate, broken up
5 ml/1 tsp almond essence (extract)
100 g/4 oz/½ cup butter or margarine,
   softened
8 eggs, separated
45 ml/3 tbsp digestive biscuit
   (Graham cracker) crumbs
For the icing (frosting):
175 g/6 oz/1½ cups plain (semi-sweet)
   chocolate, broken up
60 ml/4 tbsp water
15 ml/1 tbsp instant coffee powder
225 g/8 oz/1 cup butter or margarine,
   softened
3 egg yolks
175 g/6 oz/1 cup icing (confectioners')
   sugar
Grated chocolate to decorate
   (optional)

Toast the hazelnuts in a dry pan until lightly browned, shaking the pan occasionally, then grind until fairly fine. Set aside 45 ml/3 tbsp for the icing. Dissolve the sugar and coffee in the water over a low heat, stirring for 3 minutes. Remove from the heat and stir in the chocolate and almond essence. Stir until melted and smooth, then leave to cool slightly. Cream together the butter or margarine until light and fluffy, then gradually beat in the egg yolks. Stir in the hazelnuts and biscuit crumbs. Beat the egg whites until stiff, then fold them into the mixture. Spoon into two greased and lined 23 cm/9 in cake tins (pans) and bake in a preheated oven at 180°C/350°F/gas mark 4 for 25 minutes until the cake begins to shrink away from the sides of the tin and feels springy to the touch.

To make the icing, melt the chocolate, water and coffee over a low heat, stirring until smooth. Leave to cool. Cream the butter or margarine until light and fluffy. Gradually beat in the egg yolks, then the chocolate mixture. Beat in the icing sugar. Chill until of a spreadable consistency.

Sandwich the cakes together with half the icing, then spread half the remainder round the sides of the cake and press the reserved hazelnuts round the sides. Cover the top of the cake with a thin layer of icing and pipe rosettes of icing round the edge. Decorate with grated chocolate, if liked.

Italian Chocolate and Brandy Cream Cake

Makes one 23 cm/9 in cake

400 g/14 oz/3½ cups plain
   (semi-sweet) chocolate
400 ml/14 fl oz/1¾ cups double
   (heavy) cream
600 ml/1 pt/2½ cups cold strong black
   coffee
75 ml/5 tbsp brandy or Amaretto
400 g/14 oz sponge finger biscuits

Melt the chocolate in a heatproof bowl set over a pan of gently simmering water. Remove from the heat and leave to cool. Meanwhile, beat the cream until stiff. Beat the chocolate into the cream. Mix together the coffee and brandy or Amaretto. Dip one-third of the sponge fingers in the mixture to moisten them and use to line a foil-lined, loose-bottomed 23 cm/9 in cake tin (pan). Spread with half the cream mixture. Moisten and add another layer of sponge fingers, then the remaining cream and finally the remaining biscuits. Chill thoroughly before removing from the tin to serve.

Chocolate Layer Cake

Makes one 20 cm/8 in cake

*75 g/3 oz/³⁄₄ cup plain (semi-sweet)
chocolate*
*175 g/6 oz/³⁄₄ cup butter or margarine,
softened*
*175 g/6 oz/³⁄₄ cup caster (superfine)
sugar*
3 eggs, lightly beaten
*150 g/5 oz/1¼ cups self-raising
(self-rising) flour*
*25 g/1 oz/¼ cup cocoa (unsweetened
chocolate) powder*
For the icing (frosting):
*175 g/6 oz/1 cup icing (confectioners')
sugar*
*50 g/2 oz/½ cup cocoa (unsweetened
chocolate) powder*
*175 g/6 oz/³⁄₄ cup butter or margarine,
softened*
Grated chocolate to decorate

Melt the chocolate in a heatproof bowl set over a pan of gently simmering water. Leave to cool slightly. Beat together the butter or margarine and sugar until light and fluffy. Gradually beat in the eggs, then fold in the flour and cocoa and the melted chocolate. Spoon the mixture into a greased and lined 20 cm/8 in cake tin (pan) and bake in a preheated oven at 180°C/350°F/gas mark 4 for 1¼ hours until springy to the touch. Leave to cool.

To make the icing, beat together the icing sugar, cocoa and butter or margarine until you have a spreadable icing. When the cake is cold, slice horizontally into three and use two-thirds of the icing to sandwich the three layers together. Spread the remaining icing on the top, mark into a pattern with a fork, and decorate with grated chocolate.

Moist Chocolate Cake

Makes one 20 cm/8 in cake

*200 g/7 oz/1³⁄₄ cups plain
(all-purpose) flour*
*30 ml/2 tbsp cocoa (unsweetened
chocolate) powder*
*5 ml/1 tsp bicarbonate of soda
(baking soda)*
5 ml/1 tsp baking powder
*150 g/5 oz/²⁄₃ cup caster (superfine)
sugar*
30 ml/2 tbsp golden (light corn) syrup
2 eggs, lightly beaten
150 ml/¼ pt/²⁄₃ cup oil
150 ml/¼ pt/²⁄₃ cup milk
*150 ml/¼ pt/²⁄₃ cup double (heavy) or
whipping cream, whipped*

Beat all the ingredients except the cream to a batter. Pour into two greased and lined 20 cm/8 in cake tins (pans) and bake in a preheated oven at 160°C/325°F/gas mark 3 for 35 minutes until well risen and springy to the touch. Leave to cool, then sandwich together with whipped cream.

Mocha Cake

Makes one 23 × 30 cm/
9 × 12 in cake

450 g/1 lb/2 cups caster (superfine)
sugar
225 g/8 oz/2 cups plain
(all-purpose) flour
75 g/3 oz/³⁄₄ cup cocoa (unsweetened
chocolate) powder
10 ml/2 tsp bicarbonate of soda
(baking soda)
5 ml/1 tsp baking powder
A pinch of salt
120 ml/4 fl oz/¹⁄₂ cup oil
250 ml/8 fl oz/1 cup hot black coffee
250 ml/8 fl oz/1 cup milk
2 eggs, lightly beaten

Mix together the dry ingredients and make a well in the centre. Stir in the remaining ingredients and mix just until the dry ingredients have been absorbed. Spoon into a greased and lined 23 × 30 cm/9 × 12 in cake tin (pan) and bake in a preheated oven at 180°C/350°F/gas mark 4 for 35–40 minutes until a skewer inserted in the centre comes out clean.

Mud Pie

Makes one 20 cm/8 in cake

225 g/8 oz/2 cups plain (semi-sweet)
chocolate
225 g/8 oz/1 cup butter or margarine
225 g/8 oz/1 cup caster (superfine)
sugar
4 eggs, lightly beaten
15 ml/1 tbsp cornflour (cornstarch)

Melt the chocolate and butter or margarine in a heatproof bowl set over a pan of gently simmering water. Remove from the heat and stir in the sugar until dissolved, then beat in the eggs and cornflour. Spoon into a greased and lined 20 cm/8 in cake tin (pan) and stand the tin in a roasting tray containing enough hot water to come half-way up the sides of the tin. Bake in a preheated oven at 180°C/350°F/gas mark 4 for 1 hour. Remove from the tray of water and leave to cool in the tin, then chill until ready to turn out and serve.

Crunchy-based Mississippi Mud Pie

Makes one 23 cm/9 in cake

75 g/3 oz/³⁄₄ cup ginger biscuit (cookie)
crumbs
75 g/3 oz/³⁄₄ cup digestive biscuit
(Graham crackers) crumbs
50 g/2 oz/¹⁄₄ cup butter or margarine,
melted
300 g/11 oz marshmallows
90 ml/6 tbsp milk
2.5 ml/¹⁄₂ tsp grated nutmeg
60 ml/4 tbsp rum or brandy
20 ml/4 tsp strong black coffee
450 g/l lb/4 cups plain (semi-sweet)
chocolate
450 ml/³⁄₄ pt/2 cups double (heavy)
cream

Blend the biscuit crumbs into the melted butter and press into the base of a greased 23 cm/9 in loose-bottomed cake tin (pan). Chill.
Melt the marshmallows with the milk and nutmeg over a low heat. Remove from the heat and leave to cool. Mix in the rum or brandy and coffee. Meanwhile, melt three-quarters of the chocolate in a heatproof bowl set over a pan of gently simmering water. Remove from the heat and leave to cool. Whip the cream until stiff. Fold the chocolate and the cream into the marshmallow mixture. Spoon into the base and smooth the top. Cover the clingfilm (plastic wrap) and chill for 2 hours until set.
Melt the remaining chocolate in a heatproof bowl set over a pan of gently simmering water. Spread the chocolate

thinly over a baking (cookie) sheet and chill until almost set. Scrape a sharp knife across the chocolate to cut it into curls and use to decorate the top of the cake.

Chocolate Nut Cake

Makes one 20 cm/8 in cake

175 g/6 oz/1½ cups ground almonds
175 g/6 oz/¾ cup caster (superfine)
sugar
4 eggs, separated
5 ml/1 tsp vanilla essence (extract)
175 g/6 oz/1½ cups plain (semi-sweet)
chocolate, grated
15 ml/1 tbsp chopped mixed nuts

Stir together the ground almonds and sugar, then beat in the egg yolks, vanilla essence and chocolate. Whisk the egg whites until very stiff, then fold into the chocolate mixture using a metal spoon. Spoon into a greased and lined 20 cm/8 in cake tin (pan) and sprinkle with the chopped nuts. Bake in a pre-heated oven at 190°C/375°F/gas mark 5 for 25 minutes until well risen and springy to the touch.

Rich Chocolate Cake

Makes one 900 g/2 lb cake

200 g/7 oz/1¾ cups plain
(semi-sweet) chocolate
15 ml/1 tbsp strong black coffee
225 g/8 oz/1 cup butter or margarine,
softened
225 g/8 oz/1 cup granulated sugar
4 eggs
225 g/8 oz/2 cups plain
(all-purpose) flour
5 ml/1 tsp baking powder

Melt the chocolate with the coffee in a heatproof bowl set over a pan of gently simmering water. Meanwhile, cream together the butter or margarine and sugar until light and fluffy. Gradually add the eggs, beating well after each addition. Stir in the melted chocolate, then fold in the flour and baking powder. Spoon the mixture into a greased and lined 900 g/2 lb loaf tin (pan) and bake in a preheated oven at 190°C/375°F/gas mark 5 for about 1 hour until a skewer inserted in the centre comes out clean. If necessary, cover the top with foil or greaseproof (waxed) paper for the last 10 minutes of cooking to prevent over-browning.

Chocolate, Nut and Cherry Cake

Makes one 20 cm/8 in cake

225 g/8 oz/1 cup butter or margarine,
softened
225 g/8 oz/1 cup caster (superfine)
sugar
4 eggs
A few drops of vanilla essence
(extract)
225 g/8 oz/2 cups rye flour
225 g/8 oz/2 cups ground hazelnuts
45 ml/3 tbsp cocoa (unsweetened
chocolate) powder
10 ml/2 tsp ground cinnamon
5 ml/1 tsp baking powder
900 g/2 lb stoned (pitted) cherries
Icing (confectioners') sugar for
dusting

Cream together the butter or margarine and sugar until pale and fluffy. Gradually beat in the eggs, one at a time, then stir in the vanilla essence. Mix together the flour, nuts, cocoa, cinnamon and baking powder, then fold into the mixture and mix to a soft dough. Roll out the dough on a lightly floured surface to a 20 cm/8 in round and press gently into a greased loose-bottomed cake tin (pan). Spoon the cherries on top. Bake in a preheated oven at 200°C/400°F/gas mark 6 for 30 minutes until springy to the touch. Remove from the tin to cool, then dust with icing sugar before serving.

31

Chocolate Rum Cake

Makes one 20 cm/8 in cake

100 g/4 oz/1 cup plain (semi-sweet)
chocolate
15 ml/1 tbsp rum
3 eggs
100 g/4 oz/½ cup caster (superfine)
sugar
25 g/1 oz/¼ cup cornflour (cornstarch)
50 g/2 oz/½ cup self-raising
(self-rising) flour

Melt the chocolate with the rum in a heatproof bowl set over a pan of gently simmering water. Whisk together the eggs and sugar until light and fluffy, then fold in the cornflour and flour. Stir in the chocolate mixture. Spoon into a greased and lined 20 cm/8 in cake tin (pan) and bake in a preheated oven at 190°C/375°F/gas mark 5 for 10–15 minutes until springy to the touch.

Chocolate Sandwich

Makes one 20 cm/8 in cake

100 g/4 oz/1 cup plain (all-purpose)
flour
10 ml/2 tsp baking powder
A pinch of bicarbonate of soda
(baking soda)
50 g/2 oz/½ cup cocoa (unsweetened
chocolate) powder
225 g/8 oz/1 cup caster (superfine)
sugar
120 ml/4 fl oz/½ cup corn oil
120 ml/4 fl oz/½ cup milk
150 ml/¼ pt/⅔ cup double (heavy)
cream
100 g/4 oz/1 cup plain (semi-sweet)
chocolate

Mix together the flour, baking powder, bicarbonate of soda and cocoa. Stir in the sugar. Mix the oil and milk and blend into the dry ingredients until smooth. Spoon into two greased and lined 20 cm/8 in sandwich tins (pans) and bake in a preheated oven at 180°C/350°F/gas mark 3 for 40 minutes until springy to the touch. Turn out on to a wire rack to cool.

Whip the cream until stiff. Reserve 30 ml/2 tbsp and use the rest to sandwich the cakes together. Melt the chocolate and reserved cream in a heatproof bowl set over a pan of gently simmering water. Spoon over the top of the cake and leave to set.

Carob and Nut Cake

Makes one 18 cm/7 in cake

175 g/6 oz/¾ cup butter or margarine,
softened
100 g/4 oz/½ cup soft brown sugar
4 eggs, separated
75 g/3 oz/¾ cup plain (all-purpose)
flour
25 g/1 oz/¼ cup carob powder
A pinch of salt
Finely grated rind and juice of
1 orange
175 g/6 oz carob bars
100 g/4 oz/1 cup chopped mixed nuts

Cream 100 g/4 oz/½ cup of the butter or margarine with the sugar until light and fluffy. Gradually beat in the egg yolks, then fold in the flour, carob powder, salt, orange rind and 15 ml/1 tbsp of the orange juice. Spoon the mixture into two greased and lined 18 cm/7 in cake tins (pans) and bake in a preheated oven at 180°C/350°F/gas mark 4 for 20 minutes until springy to the touch. Remove from the tins and leave to cool.

Melt the carob with the remaining orange juice in a heatproof bowl set over a pan of gently simmering water. Remove from the heat and beat in the remaining butter or margarine. Leave to cool slightly, stirring occasionally. Sandwich the cooled cakes together with half the icing and spread the remainder on top. Mark into a pattern with a fork and sprinkle with the nuts to decorate.

Carob Christmas Log

Makes one 20 cm/8 in roll

3 large eggs
100 g/4 oz/⅓ cup clear honey
75 g/3 oz/¾ cup wholemeal
  (wholewheat) flour
25 g/1 oz/¼ cup carob powder
20 ml/4 tsp hot water
  For the filling:
175 g/6 oz/¾ cup cream cheese
A few drops of vanilla essence
  (extract)
5 ml/1 tsp coffee granules, dissolved in
  a little hot water
30 ml/2 tbsp clear honey
15 ml/1 tbsp carob powder

Whisk together the eggs and honey until thick. Fold in the flour and carob, then the hot water. Spoon into a greased and lined 30 × 20 cm/12 × 8 in Swiss roll tin (jelly roll pan) and bake in a preheated oven at 220°C/425°F/gas mark 7 for 15 minutes until springy to the touch. Turn out on to a piece of greaseproof (waxed) paper and trim the edges. Roll up from the short end, using the paper to help, and leave until cold.

To make the filling, beat all the ingredients together. Unroll the cake and remove the paper. Spread half the filling over the cake, almost to the edges, then roll up again. Spread the remaining filling over the top and mark into a bark pattern with the tines of a fork.

Teatime Favourites

*T*he old favourites are sometimes the best, and here are some popular childhood cakes – and a few from even further back in time – for you to enjoy, plus, I confess, some other delicious cakes that didn't seem to fit into any other category!

Caraway Seed Cake

Makes one 18 cm/7 in cake

225 g/8 oz/1 cup butter or margarine, softened
225 g/8 oz/1 cup caster (superfine) sugar
4 eggs, separated
225 g/8 oz/2 cups self-raising (self-rising) flour
25 g/1 oz/¼ cup caraway seeds
2.5 ml/½ tsp ground cinnamon
2.5 ml/½ tsp grated nutmeg

Cream together the butter or margarine and sugar until pale and fluffy. Beat the egg yolks and add them to the mixture, then fold in the flour, seeds and spices. Beat the egg whites until stiff, then fold them into the mixture. Spoon the mixture into a greased and lined 18 cm/7 in cake tin (pan) and bake in a preheated oven at 180°C/350°F/gas mark 4 for 1 hour until a skewer inserted in the centre comes out clean.

Almond Rice Cake

Makes one 20 cm/8 in cake

225 g/8 oz/1 cup butter or margarine, softened
225 g/8 oz/1 cup caster (superfine) sugar
3 eggs, beaten
100 g/4 oz/1 cup plain (all-purpose) flour
75 g/3 oz/¾ cup self-raising (self-rising) flour
75 g/3 oz/¾ cup ground rice
2.5 ml/½ tsp almond essence (extract)

Cream together the butter or margarine and sugar until light and fluffy. Beat in the eggs a little at a time. Fold in the flours and ground rice and stir in the almond essence. Spoon into a greased and lined 20 cm/8 in cake tin (pan) and bake in a preheated oven at 150°C/300°F/gas mark 2 for 1¼ hours until springy to the touch. Cool in the tin for 10 minutes before turning out on to a wire rack to finish cooling.

Ale Cake

Makes one 20 cm/8 in cake

225 g/8 oz/1 cup butter or margarine, softened
225 g/8 oz/1 cup soft brown sugar
2 eggs, lightly beaten
350 g/12 oz/3 cups wholemeal (wholewheat) flour
10 ml/2 tsp baking powder
5 ml/1 tsp ground mixed (apple-pie) spice
150 ml/¼ pt/⅔ cup brown ale
175 g/6 oz/1 cup currants
175 g/6 oz/1 cup sultanas (golden raisins)
50 g/2 oz/⅓ cup raisins
100 g/4 oz/1 cup chopped mixed nuts
Grated rind of 1 large orange

Cream together the butter or margarine and sugar until light and fluffy. Gradually beat in the eggs, beating well after each addition. Mix together the flour, baking powder and spice and gradually fold into the creamed mixture alternating with the brown ale, then fold

34

in the fruit, nuts and orange rind. Spoon into a greased and lined 20 cm/8 in cake tin (pan) and bake in a preheated oven at 150°C/300°F/gas mark 2 for 2¼ hours until a skewer inserted in the centre comes out clean. Leave to cool in the tin for 30 minutes, then turn out on to a wire rack to finish cooling.

Ale and Date Cake

Makes one 23 cm/9 in cake

225 g/8 oz/1 cup butter or margarine,
  softened
450 g/1 lb/2 cups soft brown sugar
2 eggs, lightly beaten
450 g/1 lb/4 cups plain (all-purpose)
  flour
175 g/6 oz/1 cup stoned (pitted) dates,
  chopped
100 g/4 oz/1 cup chopped mixed nuts
10 ml/2 tsp bicarbonate of soda
  (baking soda)
5 ml/1 tsp ground cinnamon
5 ml/1 tsp ground mixed (apple-pie)
  spice
2.5 ml/½ tsp salt
500 ml/17 fl oz/2¼ cups beer or lager

Cream together the butter or margarine and sugar until light and fluffy. Gradually beat in the eggs, then fold in the dry ingredients alternately with the beer until you have a soft mixture. Spoon into a greased and lined 23 cm/9 in cake tin (pan) and bake in a preheated oven at 180°C/350°F/gas mark 4 for 1 hour until a skewer inserted in the centre comes out clean. Leave to cool in the tin for 10 minutes, then turn out on to a wire rack to finish cooling.

Battenburg Cake

Makes one 18 cm/7 in cake

175 g/6 oz/¾ cup butter or margarine,
  softened
175 g/6 oz/¾ cup caster (superfine)
  sugar
3 eggs, lightly beaten
225 g/8 oz/2 cups self-raising
  (self-rising) flour
A few drops of vanilla essence
  (extract)
A few drops of raspberry essence
  (extract)
For the icing (frosting):
15 ml/1 tbsp raspberry jam
  (conserve), sieved (strained)
225 g/8 oz Almond Paste (page 228)
A few glacé (candied) cherries

Cream together the butter or margarine and sugar. Gradually beat in the eggs, then fold in the flour and vanilla essence. Divide the mixture in half and stir the raspberry essence into one half. Grease and line an 18 cm/7 in square cake tin (pan) and divide the tin in half by folding greaseproof (waxed) paper down the centre of the tin. Pour each mixture into one half of the tin and bake in a preheated oven at 180°C/350°F/gas mark 4 for about 50 minutes until springy to the touch. Cool on a wire rack.

Trim the edges of the cake and cut each piece in half lengthways. Sandwich together a pink and a vanilla piece on the bottom and a vanilla and a pink on the top, using some of the jam to fix them together. Brush the outside of the cake with the remaining jam. Roll out the almond paste into a rectangle about 18 × 38 cm/7 × 15 in. Press round the outside of the cake and trim the edges. Decorate the top with glacé cherries.

Bread Pudding Cake

Makes one 23 cm/9 in cake

225 g/8 oz/8 thick slices bread
300 ml/½ pt/1¼ cups milk
350 g/12 oz/2 cups dried mixed fruit
  (fruit cake mix)
50 g/2 oz/¼ cup chopped mixed
  (candied) peel
1 apple, peeled, cored and grated
45 ml/3 tbsp soft brown sugar
30 ml/2 tbsp marmalade
45 ml/3 tbsp self-raising (self-rising)
  flour
2 eggs, lightly beaten
5 ml/1 tsp lemon juice
10 ml/2 tsp ground cinnamon
100 g/4 oz/½ cup butter or margarine,
  melted

Soak the bread in the milk until very soft. Mix in all the remaining ingredients except the butter or margarine. Stir in half the butter or margarine, then spoon the mixture into a greased 23 cm/9 in square cake tin (pan) and pour the remaining butter or margarine over the top. Bake in a preheated oven at 150°C/300°F/gas mark 3 for 1½ hours, then increase the oven temperature to 180°C/350°F/gas mark 4 and bake for a further 30 minutes. Leave to cool in the tin.

English Buttermilk Cake

Makes one 20 cm/8 in cake

75 g/3 oz/⅓ cup butter or margarine
75 g/3 oz/⅓ cup lard (shortening)
450 g/l lb/4 cups plain (all-purpose)
  flour
100 g/4 oz/½ cup caster (superfine)
  sugar
175 g/6 oz/1 cup chopped mixed
  (candied) peel
100 g/4 oz/⅔ cup raisins
30 ml/2 tbsp marmalade

250 ml/8 fl oz/1 cup buttermilk or
  sour milk
5 ml/1 tsp bicarbonate of soda
  (baking soda)

Rub the butter or margarine and lard into the flour until the mixture resembles breadcrumbs. Stir in the flour, sugar, mixed peel and raisins. Warm the marmalade slightly so that it blends easily into the milk, then blend in the bicarbonate of soda and mix into the cake mixture to form a soft dough. Spoon into a greased and lined 20 cm/8 in cake tin (pan) and bake in a preheated oven at 160°C/325°F/gas mark 3 for 1 hour. Reduce the oven temperature to 150°C/300°F/gas mark 2 and bake for a further 45 minutes until golden brown and springy to the touch. Leave to cool in the tin for 10 minutes before turning out on to a wire rack to finish cooling.

Caramel Cake

Makes one 23 cm/9 in cake

400 g/14 oz/1 large can condensed
  milk
225 g/8 oz/1 cup granulated sugar
250 ml/8 fl oz/1 cup boiling water
5 ml/1 tsp vanilla essence (extract)
225 g/8 oz/1 cup butter or margarine,
  softened
225 g/8 oz/1 cup caster (superfine)
  sugar
5 eggs, separated
450 g/1 lb/4 cups plain (all-purpose)
  flour
15 ml/1 tbsp baking powder
A pinch of salt
150 ml/¼ pt/⅔ cup double (heavy)
  cream
100 g/4 oz/1 cup chocolate, grated
  or cut into curls

Place the unopened can of condensed milk in a pan and cover with water, then bring to the boil, cover and simmer

36

for 3 hours, topping up with boiling water as necessary. The milk will turn into a caramel. Leave to cool before opening.

Melt the granulated sugar in a heavy-based pan over a low heat until melted and light golden. Remove from the heat and stir in the water, being careful as it may spit. Stir until blended, then leave to cool. Add the vanilla essence.

Cream together the butter or margarine and caster sugar until light and fluffy. Gradually beat in the egg yolks, then fold in the flour, baking powder and salt alternately with the sugar and water mixture. Whisk the egg whites until stiff, then fold them into the mixture using a metal spoon. Spoon into two greased and lined 23 cm/9 in cake tins (pans) and bake in a preheated oven at 180°C/350°F/gas mark 4 for 30 minutes until golden brown and springy to the touch. Leave to cool, then cut horizontally into three layers.

Remove the caramel from the can and beat until slightly soft. Sandwich the cakes together with the caramel. Whip the cream until stiff, then pile on to the top of the cake and sprinkle with grated chocolate or chocolate curls. To make the curls, scrape a sharp knife down the edge of a block of chocolate so that the mixture comes away in curls.

Golden Cinnamon and Nutmeg Cake

Makes one 20 cm/8 in cake

100 g/4 oz/½ cup butter or margarine, softened
100 g/4 oz/½ cup soft brown sugar
2 eggs
100 g/4 oz/1 cup plain (all-purpose) flour
50 g/2 oz/½ cup ground rice
5 ml/1 tsp baking powder
For the topping:
50 g/2 oz/¼ cup soft brown sugar
5 ml/1 tsp ground cinnamon
2.5 ml/½ tsp grated nutmeg

Cream together the butter or margarine and sugar until light and fluffy. Beat in the eggs, beating well between each addition. Fold in the flour, ground rice and baking powder and spoon into a greased 20 cm/8 in cake tin (pan). Mix together the topping ingredients and sprinkle over the cake. Bake in a preheated oven at 180°C/350°F/gas mark 4 for 40 minutes until a skewer inserted in the centre comes out clean. Leave to cool in the tin before turning out.

Coffee Cake

Makes one 20 cm/8 in cake

100 g/4 oz/½ cup butter or margarine, softened
100 g/4 oz/½ cup caster (superfine) sugar
2 eggs, lightly beaten
2.5 ml/½ tsp coffee essence (extract) or strong black coffee
150 g/5 oz/1¼ cups self-raising (self-rising) flour
2.5 ml/½ tsp baking powder
Coffee Butter Icing (page 230)
30 ml/2 tbsp chopped mixed nuts (optional)

Cream together the butter or margarine and sugar until light and fluffy. Gradually beat in the eggs and coffee essence, then fold in the flour and baking powder. Spoon into two greased and lined 20 cm/8 in sandwich tins (pans) and bake in a preheated oven at 160°C/325°F/gas mark 3 for 20 minutes until springy to the touch. Leave to cool in the tins for 4 minutes, then turn out on to a wire rack to finish cooling. Sandwich the cakes together with half the butter icing, then spread the remainder on top and mark into patterns with a fork. Sprinkle with nuts, if liked.

Coffee Streusel Cake

Makes one 20 cm/8 in cake

50 g/2 oz/¼ cup butter or margarine, softened
100 g/4 oz/½ cup caster (superfine) sugar
1 egg, lightly beaten
10 ml/2 tsp coffee essence (extract)
100 g/4 oz/1 cup self-raising (self-rising) flour
A pinch of salt
75 g/3 oz/½ cup sultanas (golden raisins)
60 ml/4 tbsp milk
For the topping:
50 g/2 oz/¼ cup butter or margarine
30 ml/2 tbsp plain (all-purpose) flour
75 g/3 oz/⅓ cup soft brown sugar
10 ml/2 tsp ground cinnamon
50 g/2 oz/½ cup chopped mixed nuts

Cream together the butter or margarine and sugar until light and fluffy. Gradually beat in the egg and coffee essence, then fold in the flour and salt. Stir in the sultanas and enough milk to make a soft dropping consistency.

To make the topping, rub the butter or margarine into the flour, sugar and cinnamon until the mixture resembles breadcrumbs. Stir in the nuts. Sprinkle half the topping over the base of a greased and lined 20 cm/8 in cake tin (pan). Spoon in the cake mixture and sprinkle with the remaining topping. Bake in a preheated oven at 220°C/425°F/gas mark 7 for 15 minutes until well risen and springy to the touch.

Farmhouse Dripping Cake

Makes one 18 cm/7 in cake

225 g/8 oz/1⅓ cups dried mixed fruit (fruit cake mix)
75 g/3 oz/⅓ cup beef dripping (shortening)
150 g/5 oz/⅔ cup soft brown sugar
250 ml/8 fl oz/1 cup water
225 g/8 oz/2 cups wholemeal (wholewheat) flour
5 ml/1 tsp baking powder
2.5 ml/½ tsp bicarbonate of soda (baking soda)
5 ml/1 tsp ground cinnamon
A pinch of grated nutmeg
A pinch of ground cloves

Bring the fruit, dripping, sugar and water to the boil in a heavy-based pan and simmer for 10 minutes. Leave to cool. Mix the remaining ingredients in a bowl, then pour in the melted mixture and blend together gently. Spoon into a greased and lined 18 cm/7 in cake tin (pan) and bake in a preheated oven at 180°C/350°F/gas mark 4 for 1½ hours until well risen and shrinking away from the sides of the tin.

American Gingerbread with Lemon Sauce

Makes one 20 cm/8 in cake

225 g/8 oz/1 cup caster (superfine) sugar
50 g/2 oz/¼ cup butter or margarine, melted
30 ml/2 tbsp black treacle (molasses)
2 egg whites, lightly beaten
225 g/8 oz/2 cups plain (all-purpose) flour
5 ml/1 tsp bicarbonate of soda (baking soda)
5 ml/1 tsp ground cinnamon
2.5 ml/½ tsp ground cloves
1.5 ml/¼ tsp ground ginger
A pinch of salt
250 ml/8 fl oz/1 cup buttermilk
For the sauce:
100 g/4 oz/½ cup caster (superfine) sugar
30 ml/2 tbsp cornflour (cornstarch)

A pinch of salt
A pinch of grated nutmeg
250 ml/8 fl oz/1 cup boiling water
15 g/½ oz/1 tbsp butter or margarine
30 ml/2 tbsp lemon juice
2.5 ml/½ tsp finely grated lemon rind

Mix together the sugar, butter or margarine and treacle. Stir in the egg whites. Mix together the flour, bicarbonate of soda, spices and salt. Stir the flour mixture and the buttermilk alternately into the butter and sugar mixture until well blended. Spoon into a greased and floured 20 cm/8 in cake tin (pan) and bake in a preheated oven at 200°C/400°F/gas mark 6 for 35 minutes until a skewer inserted in the centre comes out clean. Leave to cool in the tin for 5 minutes before turning out on to a wire rack to finish cooling. The cake can be served cold or warm.

To make the sauce, mix the sugar, cornflour, salt, nutmeg and water in a small pan over a low heat and stir until well blended. Simmer, stirring, until the mixture is thick and clear. Stir in the butter or margarine and lemon juice and rind and cook until blended. Pour over the gingerbread to serve.

Coffee Gingerbread

Makes one 20 cm/8 in cake

200 g/7 oz/1¾ cups self-raising
(self-rising) flour
10 ml/2 tsp ground ginger
10 ml/2 tsp instant coffee granules
100 ml/4 fl oz/½ cup hot water
100 g/4 oz/½ cup butter or margarine
75 g/3 oz/¼ cup golden (light corn)
syrup
50 g/2 oz/¼ cup soft brown sugar
2 eggs, beaten

Mix together the flour and ginger. Dissolve the coffee in the hot water. Melt together the margarine, syrup and sugar, then mix into the dry ingredients.

Mix in the coffee and eggs. Pour into a greased and lined 20 cm/8 in cake tin (pan) and bake in a preheated oven at 180°C/350°F/gas mark 4 for 40–45 minutes until well risen and springy to the touch.

Ginger Cream Cake

Makes one 20 cm/8 in cake

175 g/6 oz/¾ cup butter or margarine,
softened
150 g/5 oz/⅔ cup soft brown sugar
3 eggs, lightly beaten
175 g/6 oz/1½ cups self-raising
(self-rising) flour
15 ml/1 tbsp ground ginger
For the filling:
150 ml/¼ pt/⅔ cup double (heavy)
cream
15 ml/1 tbsp icing (confectioners')
sugar, sifted
5 ml/1 tsp ground ginger

Cream together the butter or margarine and sugar until light and fluffy. Gradually add the eggs, then the flour and ginger and mix together well. Spoon into two greased and lined 20 cm/8 in sandwich tins (pans) and bake in a preheated oven at 180°C/350°F/gas mark 4 for 25 minutes until well risen and springy to the touch. Leave to cool.

Whip the cream with the sugar and ginger until stiff, then use to sandwich the cakes together.

Liverpool Ginger Cake

Makes one 20 cm/8 in cake

100 g/4 oz/½ cup butter or margarine
100 g/4 oz/½ cup demerara sugar
30 ml/2 tbsp golden (light corn) syrup
225 g/8 oz/2 cups plain
  (all-purpose) flour
2.5 ml/½ tsp bicarbonate of soda
  (baking soda)
10 ml/2 tsp ground ginger
2 eggs, beaten
225 g/8 oz/1⅓ cups sultanas
  (golden raisins)
50 g/2 oz/½ cup crystallised (candied)
  ginger, chopped

Melt the butter or margarine with the sugar and syrup over a low heat. Remove from the heat and stir in the dry ingredients and egg and mix well. Stir in the sultanas and ginger. Spoon into a greased and lined 20 cm/8 in square cake tin (pan) and bake in a preheated oven at 150°C/300°F/gas mark 3 for 1½ hours until springy to the touch. The cake may sink a little in the centre. Leave to cool in the tin.

Oatmeal Gingerbread

Makes one 35 × 23 cm/ 14 × 9 in cake

225 g/8 oz/2 cups wholemeal
  (wholewheat) flour
75 g/3 oz/¾ cup rolled oats
5 ml/1 tsp bicarbonate of soda
  (baking soda)
5 ml/1 tsp cream of tartar
15 ml/1 tbsp ground ginger
225 g/8 oz/1 cup butter or margarine
225 g/8 oz/1 cup soft brown sugar

Mix together the flour, oats, bicarbonate of soda, cream of tartar and ginger in a bowl. Rub in the butter or margarine until the mixture resembles breadcrumbs. Stir in the sugar. Press the mixture down firmly into a greased 35 × 23 cm/14 × 9 in cake tin (pan) and bake in a preheated oven at 160°C/325°F/ gas mark 3 for 30 minutes until golden brown. Cut into squares while still warm and leave in the tin to cool completely.

Orange Gingerbread

Makes one 23 cm/9 in cake

450 g/1 lb/4 cups plain (all-purpose)
  flour
5 ml/1 tsp ground cinnamon
2.5 ml/½ tsp ground ginger
2.5 ml/½ tsp bicarbonate of soda
  (baking soda)
175 g/6 oz/¾ cup butter or margarine
175 g/6 oz/¾ cup caster (superfine)
  sugar
75 g/3 oz/½ cup glacé (candied)
  orange peel, chopped
Grated rind and juice of ½ large
  orange
175 g/6 oz/½ cup golden (light corn)
  syrup, warmed
2 eggs, lightly beaten
A little milk

Mix together the flour, spices and bicarbonate of soda, then rub in the butter or margarine until the mixture resembles breadcrumbs. Stir in the sugar, orange peel and rind, then make a well in the centre. Mix in the orange juice and warmed syrup, then stir in the eggs until you have a soft, dropping consistency, adding a little milk if necessary. Beat well, then spoon into a greased 23 cm/9 in square cake tin (pan) and bake in a preheated oven at 160°C/325°F/gas mark 3 for 1 hour until well risen and springy to the touch.

Sticky Gingerbread

Makes one 25 cm/10 in cake

275 g/10 oz/2½ cups plain (all-purpose) flour
10 ml/2 tsp ground cinnamon
5 ml/1 tsp bicarbonate of soda (baking soda)
100 g/4 oz/½ cup butter or margarine
175 g/6 oz/½ cup golden (light corn) syrup
175 g/6 oz/½ cup black treacle (molasses)
100 g/4 oz/½ cup soft brown sugar
2 eggs, beaten
150 ml/¼ pt/⅔ cup hot water

Mix together the flour, cinnamon and bicarbonate of soda. Melt the butter or margarine with the syrup, treacle and sugar and pour into the dry ingredients. Add the eggs and water and mix well. Pour into a greased and lined 25 cm/10 in square cake tin (pan). Bake in a preheated oven at 180°C/350°F/gas mark 4 for 40–45 minutes until well risen and springy to the touch.

Wholemeal Gingerbread

Makes one 18 cm/7 in cake

100 g/4 oz/1 cup plain (all-purpose) flour
100 g/4 oz/1 cup wholemeal (wholewheat) flour
50 g/2 oz/¼ cup soft brown sugar
50 g/2 oz/⅓ cup sultanas (golden raisins)
10 ml/2 tsp ground ginger
5 ml/1 tsp ground cinnamon
5 ml/1 tsp bicarbonate of soda (baking soda)
A pinch of salt
100 g/4 oz/½ cup butter or margarine
30 ml/2 tbsp golden (light corn) syrup
30 ml/2 tbsp black treacle (molasses)
1 egg, lightly beaten
150 ml/¼ pt/⅔ cup milk

Mix together the dry ingredients. Melt the butter or margarine with the syrup and treacle and stir into the dry ingredients with the egg and milk. Spoon into a greased and lined 18 cm/7 in cake tin (pan) and bake in a preheated oven at 160°C/325°F/gas mark 3 for 1 hour until just springy to the touch.

Honey and Almond Cake

Makes one 20 cm/8 in cake

250 g/9 oz carrots, grated
65 g/2½ oz almonds, finely chopped
2 eggs
100 g/4 oz/⅓ cup clear honey
60 ml/4 tbsp oil
150 ml/¼ pt/⅔ cup milk
100 g/4 oz/1 cup wholemeal (wholewheat) flour
25 g/1 oz/¼ cup plain (all-purpose) flour
10 ml/2 tsp ground cinnamon
2.5 ml/½ tsp bicarbonate of soda (baking soda)
A pinch of salt
Lemon Glacé Icing (page 231)
A few flaked (slivered) almonds to decorate

Mix together the carrots and nuts. Beat the eggs in a separate bowl, then mix in the honey, oil and milk. Stir into the carrots and nuts, then fold in the dry ingredients. Spoon into a greased and lined 20 cm/8 in cake tin (pan) and bake in a preheated oven at 150°C/300°F/gas mark 2 for 1–1¼ hours until well risen and springy to the touch. Leave to cool in the tin before turning out. Drizzle with the lemon glacé icing, then decorate with flaked almonds.

41

Lemon-iced Cake

Makes one 18 cm/7 in cake

100 g/4 oz/½ cup butter or margarine, softened
100 g/4 oz/½ cup caster (superfine) sugar
2 eggs
100 g/4 oz/1 cup plain (all-purpose) flour
50 g/2 oz/½ cup ground rice
2.5 ml/½ tsp baking powder
Grated rind and juice of 1 lemon
100 g/4 oz/⅔ cup icing (confectioners') sugar, sifted

Cream together the butter or margarine and sugar until light and fluffy. Mix in the eggs one at a time, beating well after each addition. Combine the flour, ground rice, baking powder and lemon rind, then fold into the mixture. Spoon into a greased and lined 18 cm/7 in cake tin (pan) and bake in a preheated oven at 180°C/350°F/gas mark 4 for 1 hour until springy to the touch. Remove from the tin and leave to cool.

Mix together the icing sugar with a little of the lemon juice until smooth. Spoon over the cake and leave to set.

Iced Tea Ring

Serves 4–6

150 ml/¼ pt/⅔ cup warm milk
2.5 ml/½ tsp dried yeast
25 g/1 oz/2 tbsp caster (superfine) sugar
25 g/1 oz/2 tbsp butter or margarine
225 g/8 oz/2 cups strong plain (bread) flour
1 egg, beaten
For the filling:
50 g/2 oz/¼ cup butter or margarine, softened
50 g/2 oz/¼ cup ground almonds
50 g/2 oz/¼ cup soft brown sugar

For the topping:
100 g/4 oz/⅔ cup icing (confectioners') sugar, sifted
15 ml/1 tbsp warm water
30 ml/2 tbsp flaked (slivered) almonds

Pour the milk on to the yeast and sugar and mix together. Leave in a warm place until frothy. Rub the butter or margarine into the flour. Stir in the yeast mixture and the egg and beat well. Cover the bowl with oiled clingfilm (plastic wrap) and leave in a warm place for 1 hour. Knead again, then shape into a rectangle about 30 × 23 cm/12 × 9 in. Spread the butter or margarine for the filling over the dough and sprinkle with ground almonds and sugar. Roll up into a long sausage and shape into a ring, sealing the edges with a little water. Snip two-thirds of the way through the roll at about 3 cm/1½ in intervals and place on a greased baking (cookie) sheet. Leave in a warm place for 20 minutes. Bake in a preheated oven at 200°C/425°F/gas 7 for 15 minutes. Reduce the oven temperature to 180°C/350°F/gas 4 for a further 15 minutes.

Meanwhile, blend together the icing sugar and water to make a glacé icing. When cool, spread over the cake and decorate with flaked almonds.

Lardy Cake

Makes one 23 × 18 cm/9 × 7 in cake

15 g/½ oz fresh yeast or 20 ml/4 tsp dried yeast
5 ml/1 tsp caster (superfine) sugar
300 ml/½ pt/1¼ cups warm water
150 g/5 oz/⅔ cup lard (shortening)
450 g/1 lb/4 cups strong (bread) flour
A pinch of salt
100 g/4 oz/⅔ cup sultanas (golden raisins)
100 g/4 oz/⅔ cup clear honey

Mix the yeast with the sugar and a little of the warm water and leave in a warm place for 20 minutes until frothy.

Rub 25 g/1 oz/2 tbsp of the lard into the flour and salt and make a well in the centre. Pour in the yeast mixture and the remaining warm water and mix to a stiffish dough. Knead until smooth and springy. Place in an oiled bowl, cover with oiled clingfilm (plastic wrap) and leave in a warm place for about 1 hour until doubled in size.

Dice the remaining lard. Knead the dough again, then roll out to a rectangle about 35 × 23 cm/14 × 9 in. Cover the top two-thirds of the dough with one-third of the lard, one-third of the sultanas and one-quarter of the honey. Fold the plain third of the pastry up over the filling, then fold the top third down over that. Press the edges together to seal, then give the pastry one quarter turn so the fold is on your left. Roll out and repeat the process twice more to use up all the lard and sultanas. Place on a greased baking (cookie) sheet and mark a criss-cross pattern on the top with a knife. Cover and leave in a warm place for 40 minutes.

Bake in a preheated oven at 220°C/425°F/gas mark 7 for 40 minutes. Drizzle the top with the remaining honey, then leave to cool.

Caraway Seed Lardy Cake

Makes one 23 × 18 cm/9 × 7 in cake

450 g/1 lb Basic White Loaf dough (page 325)
175 g/6 oz/¾ cup lard (shortening), cut into pieces
175 g/6 oz/¾ cup caster (superfine) sugar
15 ml/1 tbsp caraway seeds

Prepare the dough, then roll it out on a lightly floured surface to a rectangle about 35 × 23 cm/14 × 9 in. Dot the top two-thirds of the dough with half the lard and half the sugar, then fold up the plain third of the dough, and fold the top one-third down over that. Give the dough a quarter turn so the fold is on your left, then roll out again and sprinkle in the same way with the remaining lard and sugar and the caraway seeds. Fold again, then shape to fit a baking tin (pan) and score the top into diamond shapes. Cover with oiled clingfilm (plastic wrap) and leave in a warm place for about 30 minutes until doubled in size.

Bake in a preheated oven at 200°C/400°F/gas mark 6 for 1 hour. Leave to cool in the tin for 15 minutes so that the fat soaks into the dough, then turn out on to a wire rack to cool completely.

Marble Cake

Makes one 20 cm/8 in cake

175 g/6 oz/¾ cup butter or margarine, softened
175 g/6 oz/¾ cup caster (superfine) sugar
3 eggs, lightly beaten
225 g/8 oz/2 cups self-raising (self-rising) flour
A few drops of almond essence (extract)
A few drops of green food colouring
A few drops of red food colouring

Cream together the butter or margarine and sugar until light and fluffy. Gradually beat in the eggs, then fold in the flour. Divide the mixture into three. Add the almond essence to one-third, the green food colouring to one-third, and the red food colouring to the remaining third. Drop large spoonfuls of the three mixtures alternately into a greased and lined 20 cm/8 in cake tin (pan) and bake in a preheated oven at 180°C/350°F/gas mark 4 for 45 minutes until well risen and springy to the touch.

Lincolnshire Layer Cake

Makes one 20 cm/8 in cake

175 g/6 oz/³⁄₄ cup butter or margarine
350 g/12 oz/3 cups plain
  (all-purpose) flour
A pinch of salt
150 ml/¹⁄₄ pt/²⁄₃ cup milk
15 ml/1 tbsp dried yeast
For the filling:
225 g/8 oz/1¹⁄₃ cups sultanas
  (golden raisins)
225 g/8 oz/1 cup soft brown sugar
25 g/1 oz/2 tbsp butter or margarine
2.5 ml/¹⁄₂ tsp ground allspice
1 egg, separated

Rub half the butter or margarine into the flour and salt until the mixture resembles breadcrumbs. Warm the remaining butter or margarine with the milk until hand-hot, then mix a little to a paste with the yeast. Stir the yeast mixture and the remaining milk and butter into the flour mixture and knead to a soft dough. Place in an oiled bowl, cover and leave in a warm place for about 1 hour until doubled in size. Meanwhile, place all the filling ingredients except the egg white in a pan over a low heat and leave until melted.

Roll out a quarter of the dough to a 20 cm/8 in circle and spread with one-third of the filling. Repeat with the remaining quantities of dough and filling, topping with a circle of dough. Brush the edges with egg white and seal together. Bake in a preheated oven at 190°C/375°F/gas mark 5 for 20 minutes. Brush the top with egg white, then return to the oven for a further 30 minutes until golden.

Loaf Cake

Makes one 900 g/2 lb cake

175 g/6 oz/³⁄₄ cup butter or margarine,
  softened
275 g/10 oz/1¹⁄₄ cups caster (superfine)
  sugar
Grated rind and juice of ¹⁄₂ lemon
120 ml/4 fl oz/¹⁄₂ cup milk
275 g/10 oz/2¹⁄₄ cups self-raising
  (self-rising) flour
5 ml/1 tsp salt
5 ml/1 tsp baking powder
3 eggs
Icing (confectioners') sugar, sifted,
  for dusting

Cream together the butter or margarine, sugar and lemon rind until light and fluffy. Stir in the lemon juice and milk, then blend in the flour, salt and baking powder and mix until smooth. Gradually add the eggs, beating well after each addition. Spoon the mixture into a greased and lined 900 g/2 lb loaf tin (pan) and bake in a preheated oven at 150°F/300°F/gas mark 2 for 1¹⁄₄ hours until springy to the touch. Leave to cool in the tin for 10 minutes before turning out to finish cooling on to a wire rack. Serve sprinkled with icing sugar.

Marmalade Cake

Makes one 18 cm/7 in cake

175 g/6 oz/³⁄₄ cup butter or margarine,
  softened
175 g/6 oz/³⁄₄ cup caster (superfine)
  sugar
3 eggs, separated
300 g/10 oz/2¹⁄₂ cups self-raising
  (self-rising) flour
45 ml/3 tbsp thick marmalade
50 g/2 oz/¹⁄₃ cup chopped mixed
  (candied) peel
Grated rind of 1 orange
45 ml/3 tbsp water

For the icing (frosting):
*100 g/4 oz/⅔ cup icing (confectioners')
sugar, sifted
Juice of 1 orange
A few slices of crystallised (candied)
orange*

Cream together the butter or margarine and sugar until light and fluffy. Gradually beat in the egg yolks, then 15 ml/1 tbsp of the flour. Fold in the marmalade, mixed peel, orange rind and water, then fold in the remaining flour. Whisk the egg whites until stiff, then fold them into the mixture using a metal spoon. Spoon into a greased and lined 18 cm/7 in cake tin (pan) and bake in a preheated oven at 180°C/350°F/gas mark 4 for 1¼ hours until well risen and springy to the touch. Leave to cool in the tin for 5 minutes, then turn out on to a wire rack to finish cooling.

To make the icing, place the icing sugar in a bowl and make a well in the centre. Gradually work in enough orange juice to give a spreading consistency. Spoon over the cake and down the sides and leave to set. Decorate with crystallised orange slices.

Poppy Seed Cake

Makes one 20 cm/8 in cake

*250 ml/8 fl oz/1 cup milk
100 g/4 oz/1 cup poppy seeds
225 g/8 oz/1 cup butter or margarine,
softened
225 g/8 oz/1 cup soft brown sugar
3 eggs, separated
100 g/4 oz/1 cup plain (all-purpose)
flour
100 g/4 oz/1 cup wholemeal
(wholewheat) flour
5 ml/1 tsp baking powder*

Bring the milk to the boil in a small pan with the poppy seeds, then remove from the heat, cover and leave to soak for 30 minutes. Cream together the butter or margarine and sugar until pale and fluffy. Gradually beat in the egg yolks, then fold in the flours and baking powder. Stir in the poppy seeds and milk. Whisk the egg whites until stiff, then fold them into the mixture using a metal spoon. Spoon into a greased and lined 20 cm/8 in cake tin (pan) and bake in a preheated oven at 180°C/350°F/gas mark 4 for 1 hour until a skewer inserted in the centre comes out clean. Leave to cool in the tin for 10 minutes before turning out to finish cooling on a wire rack.

Plain Yoghurt Cake

Makes one 23 cm/9 in cake

*150 g/5 oz plain yoghurt
150 ml/¼ pt/⅔ cup oil
225 g/8 oz/1 cup caster (superfine)
sugar
225 g/8 oz/2 cups self-raising
(self-rising) flour
10 ml/2 tsp baking powder
2 eggs, beaten*

Mix together all the ingredients until smooth, then spoon into a greased and lined 23 cm/9 in cake tin (pan). Bake in a preheated oven at 160°C/325°F/gas mark 3 for 1¼ hours until springy to the touch. Leave to cool in the tin.

Prunes and Custard Cake

Makes one 23 cm/9 in cake

For the filling:
150 g/5 oz/⅔ cup stoned (pitted) prunes, coarsely chopped
120 ml/4 fl oz/½ cup orange juice
50 g/2 oz/¼ cup caster (superfine) sugar
30 ml/2 tbsp cornflour (cornstarch)
175 ml/6 fl oz/¾ cup milk
2 egg yolks
Finely grated rind of 1 orange
For the cake:
175 g/6 oz/¾ cup butter or margarine, softened
225 g/8 oz/1 cup caster (superfine) sugar
3 eggs, lightly beaten
200 g/7 oz/1¾ cups plain (all-purpose) flour
10 ml/2 tsp baking powder
2.5 ml/½ tsp grated nutmeg
75 ml/5 tbsp orange juice

Make the filling first. Soak the prunes in the orange juice for at least two hours.

Mix the sugar and cornflour to a paste with a little of the milk. Bring the remaining milk to the boil in a pan. Pour over the sugar and cornflour and blend well, then return to the rinsed-out pan and beat in the egg yolks. Add the orange rind and stir over a very low heat until thickened, but do not allow the custard to boil. Stand the pan in a bowl of cold water and stir the custard occasionally as it cools.

To make the cake, cream together the butter or margarine and sugar until light and fluffy. Gradually beat in the eggs, then fold in the flour, baking powder and nutmeg alternately with the orange juice. Spoon half the batter into a greased 23 cm/9 in cake tin (pan), then spread the custard over the top, leaving a gap round the edge. Spoon the prunes and soaking juice over the custard, then cover with the remaining cake mixture, making sure the cake mixture seals in the filling at the sides and the filling is completely covered. Bake in a preheated oven at 200°C/400°F/gas mark 6 for 35 minutes until golden brown and shrinking away from the sides of the tin. Leave to cool in the tin before turning out.

Raspberry Ripple Cake with Chocolate Icing

Makes one 20 cm/8 in cake

175 g/6 oz/¾ cup butter or margarine, softened
175 g/6 oz/¾ cup caster (superfine) sugar
3 eggs, lightly beaten
225 g/8 oz/2 cups self-raising (self-rising) flour
100 g/4 oz raspberries
For the icing (frosting) and decoration:
White Chocolate Butter Icing (page 230)
100 g/4 oz/1 cup plain (semi-sweet) chocolate

Cream together the butter or margarine and sugar until light and fluffy. Gradually beat in the eggs, then fold in the flour. Purée the raspberries, then rub through a sieve (strainer) to remove the pips. Stir the purée into the cake mixture, just so it marbles through the mixture and is not mixed in. Spoon into a greased and lined 20 cm/8 in cake tin (pan) and bake in a preheated oven at 180°C/350°F/gas mark 4 for 45 minutes until well risen and springy to the touch. Transfer to a wire rack to cool.

Spread the butter icing over the cake and roughen the surface with a fork. Melt the chocolate in a heatproof bowl set over a pan of gently simmering water. Spread over a baking (cookie) sheet and leave until almost set. Scrape the flat of a sharp knife across the chocolate to make curls. Use to decorate the top of the cake.

Sand Cake

Makes one 20 cm/8 in cake

75 g/3 oz/⅓ cup butter or margarine,
  softened
75 g/3 oz/⅓ cup caster (superfine)
  sugar
2 eggs, lightly beaten
100 g/4 oz/1 cup cornflour
  (cornstarch)
25 g/1 oz/¼ cup plain (all-purpose)
  flour
5 ml/1 tsp baking powder
50 g/2 oz/½ cup chopped mixed nuts

Cream together the butter or margarine and sugar until light and fluffy. Gradually beat in the eggs, then fold in the cornflour, flour and baking powder. Spoon the mixture into a greased 20 cm/ 8 in square cake tin (pan) and sprinkle with the chopped nuts. Bake in a preheated oven at 180°C/350°F/gas mark 4 for 1 hour until springy to the touch.

Seed Cake

Makes one 18 cm/7 in cake

100 g/4 oz/½ cup butter or margarine,
  softened
100 g/4 oz/½ cup caster (superfine)
  sugar
2 eggs, lightly beaten
225 g/8 oz/2 cups plain
  (all-purpose) flour
25 g/1 oz/¼ cup caraway seeds
5 ml/1 tsp baking powder
A pinch of salt
45 ml/3 tbsp milk

Cream together the butter or margarine and sugar until light and fluffy. Gradually beat in the eggs, then fold in the flour, caraway seeds, baking powder and salt. Stir in enough of the milk to make a dropping consistency. Spoon into a greased and lined 18 cm/7 in cake tin (pan) and bake in a preheated oven at

200°C/400°F/gas mark 6 for 1 hour until springy to the touch and beginning to shrink away from the sides of the tin.

Spiced Ring Cake

Makes one 23 cm/9 in ring

1 apple, peeled, cored and grated
30 ml/2 tbsp lemon juice
25 g/8 oz/1 cup soft brown sugar
5 ml/1 tsp ground ginger
5 ml/1 tsp ground cinnamon
2.5 ml/½ tsp ground mixed
  (apple-pie) spice
225 g/8 oz/⅔ cup golden (light corn)
  syrup
250 ml/8 fl oz/1 cup oil
10 ml/2 tsp baking powder
400 g/14 oz/3½ cups plain
  (all-purpose) flour
10 ml/2 tsp bicarbonate of soda
  (baking soda)
250 ml/8 fl oz/1 cup hot strong tea
1 egg, beaten
Icing (confectioners') sugar, sifted,
  for dusting

Mix together the apple and lemon juice. Stir in the sugar and spices, then the syrup and oil. Add the baking powder to the flour and the bicarbonate of soda to the hot tea. Stir these alternately into the mixture, then mix in the egg. Spoon into a greased and lined 23 cm/9 in deep ring cake tin (pan) and bake in a preheated oven at 180°C/350°F/gas mark 4 for 1 hour until springy to the touch. Leave to cool in the tin for 10 minutes, then turn out on to a wire rack to finish cooling. Serve dusted with icing sugar.

47

Spicy Layer Cake

Makes one 23 cm/9 in cake

100 g/4 oz/½ cup butter or margarine,
softened
100 g/4 oz/½ cup granulated sugar
100 g/4 oz/½ cup soft brown sugar
2 eggs, beaten
175 g/6 oz/1½ cups plain
(all-purpose) flour
5 ml/1 tsp baking powder
5 ml/1 tsp ground cinnamon
2.5 ml/½ tsp bicarbonate of soda
(baking soda)
2.5 ml/½ tsp ground mixed
(apple-pie) spice
A pinch of salt
200 ml/7 fl oz/scant 1 cup canned
evaporated milk
Lemon Butter Icing (page 230)

Cream together the butter or margarine and sugars until light and fluffy. Gradually beat in the eggs, then fold in the dry ingredients and the evaporated milk and blend to a smooth mixture. Spoon into two greased and lined 23 cm/9 in cake tins (pans) and bake in a preheated oven at 180°C/350°F/gas mark 4 for 30 minutes until springy to the touch. Leave to cool, then sandwich together with lemon butter icing.

Sugar and Cinnamon Cake

Makes one 23 cm/9 in cake

175 g/6 oz/1½ cups self-raising
(self-rising) flour
10 ml/2 tsp baking powder
A pinch of salt
175 g/6 oz/¾ cup caster (superfine)
sugar
50 g/2 oz/¼ cup butter or margarine,
melted
1 egg, lightly beaten
120 ml/4 fl oz/½ cup milk
2.5 ml/½ tsp vanilla essence (extract)

For the topping:
50 g/2 oz/¼ cup butter or margarine,
melted
50 g/2 oz/¼ cup soft brown sugar
2.5 ml/½ tsp ground cinnamon

Beat together all the cake ingredients until smooth and well blended. Spoon into a greased 23 cm/9 in cake tin (pan) and bake in a preheated oven at 180°C/350°F/gas mark 4 for 25 minutes until golden. Brush the warm cake with the butter. Mix together the sugar and cinnamon and sprinkle over the top. Return the cake to the oven for a further 5 minutes.

Victorian Tea Cake

Makes one 20 cm/8 in cake

225 g/8 oz/1 cup butter or margarine,
softened
225 g/8 oz/1 cup caster (superfine)
sugar
225 g/8 oz/2 cups self-raising
(self-rising) flour
25 g/1 oz/¼ cup cornflour (cornstarch)
30 ml/2 tbsp caraway seeds
5 eggs, separated
Granulated sugar for sprinkling

Cream together the butter or margarine and sugar until pale and fluffy. Fold in the flour, cornflour and caraway seeds. Beat the egg yolks, then mix them into the mixture. Whisk the egg whites until stiff, then gently fold them into the mixture using a metal spoon. Spoon into a greased and lined 20 cm/8 in cake tin (pan) and sprinkle with sugar. Bake in a preheated oven at 180°C/350°F/gas mark 4 for 1½ hours until golden brown and beginning to shrink away from the sides of the tin.

Fruit Cakes

*T*his section includes not just traditional fruit cakes made with sultanas, currants and raisins, but also delicious cakes containing apple, apricots, pineapple and other fruity ingredients.

All-in-one Fruit Cake

Makes one 20 cm/8 in cake

175 g/6 oz/¾ cup butter or margarine, softened
175 g/6 oz/¾ cup soft brown sugar
3 eggs
15 ml/1 tbsp golden (light corn) syrup
100 g/4 oz/½ cup glacé (candied) cherries
100 g/4 oz/⅔ cup sultanas (golden raisins)
100 g/4 oz/⅔ cup raisins
225 g/8 oz/2 cups self-raising (self-rising) flour
10 ml/2 tsp ground mixed (apple-pie) spice

*P*lace all the ingredients in a bowl and beat together until well blended, or process in a food processor. Spoon into a greased and lined 20 cm/8 in cake tin (pan) and bake in a preheated oven at 160°C/325°F/gas mark 3 for 1½ hours until a skewer inserted in the centre comes out clean. Leave in the tin for 5 minutes, then turn out on to a wire rack to finish cooling.

All-in-one Pan Fruit Cake

Makes one 20 cm/8 in cake

350 g/12 oz/2 cups dried mixed fruit (fruit cake mix)
100 g/4 oz/½ cup butter or margarine
100 g/4 oz/½ cup soft brown sugar
150 ml/¼ pt/⅔ cup water
2 large eggs, beaten
225 g/8 oz/2 cups self-raising (self-rising) flour

5 ml/1 tsp ground mixed (apple-pie) spice

*P*ut the fruit, butter or margarine, sugar and water in a pan, bring to the boil, then simmer gently for 15 minutes. Leave to cool. Stir in spoonfuls of the eggs alternately with the flour and mixed spice and mix well. Spoon into a greased 20 cm/8 in cake tin (pan) and bake in a preheated oven at 140°C/275°F/gas mark 1 for 1–1½ hours until a skewer inserted in the centre comes out clean.

Australian Fruit Cake

Makes one 900 g/2 lb cake

100 g/4 oz/½ cup butter or margarine
225 g/8 oz/1 cup soft brown sugar
250 ml/8 fl oz/1 cup water
350 g/12 oz/2 cups dried mixed fruit (fruit cake mix)
5 ml/1 tsp bicarbonate of soda (baking soda)
10 ml/2 tsp ground mixed (apple-pie) spice
5 ml/1 tsp ground ginger
100 g/4 oz/1 cup self-raising (self-rising) flour
100 g/4 oz/1 cup plain (all-purpose) flour
1 egg, beaten

*B*ring all the ingredients except the flours and egg to the boil in a pan. Remove from the heat and leave to cool. Mix in the flours and egg. Place the mixture in a greased and lined 900 g/2 lb loaf tin (pan) and bake in a preheated oven at 160°C/325°F/gas mark 3 for 1 hour until well risen and a skewer inserted in the centre comes out clean.

American Rich Cake

Makes one 25 cm/10 in cake

225 g/8 oz/1⅓ cups currants
100 g/4 oz/1 cup blanched almonds
15 ml/1 tbsp orange flower water
45 ml/3 tbsp dry sherry
1 large egg yolk
2 eggs
350 g/12 oz/1½ cups butter or
  margarine, softened
175 g/6 oz/¾ cup caster (superfine)
  sugar
A pinch of ground mace
A pinch of ground cinnamon
A pinch of ground cloves
A pinch of ground ginger
A pinch of grated nutmeg
30 ml/2 tbsp brandy
225 g/8 oz/2 cups plain
  (all-purpose) flour
50 g/2 oz/½ cup chopped mixed
  (candied) peel

Soak the currants in hot water for 15 minutes, then drain well. Grind the almonds with the orange flower water and 15 ml/1 tbsp of the sherry until fine. Beat together the egg yolk and eggs. Cream together the butter or margarine and sugar, then stir in the almond mixture and the eggs and beat until white and thick. Add the spices, the remaining sherry and the brandy. Stir in the flour, then mix in the currants and mixed peel. Spoon into a greased 25 cm/10 in cake tin and bake in a preheated oven at 180°C/350°F/gas mark 4 for about 1 hour until a skewer inserted in the centre comes out clean.

Carob Fruit Cake

Makes one 18 cm/7 in cake

450 g/1 lb/2⅔ cups raisins
300 ml/½ pt/1¼ cups orange juice
175 g/6 oz/¾ cup butter or margarine,
  softened
3 eggs, lightly beaten
225 g/8 oz/2 cups plain
  (all-purpose) flour
75 g/3 oz/¾ cup carob powder
10 ml/2 tsp baking powder
Grated rind of 2 oranges
50 g/2 oz/½ cup walnuts, chopped

Soak the raisins in the orange juice overnight. Blend together the butter or margarine and eggs until smooth. Gradually mix in the raisins and orange juice and the remaining ingredients. Spoon into a greased and lined 18 cm/7 in cake tin (pan) and bake in a preheated oven at 180°C/350°F/gas mark 4 for 30 minutes, then reduce the oven temperature to 160°C/325°F/gas mark 3 for a further 1¼ hours until a skewer inserted in the centre comes out clean. Leave to cool in the tin for 10 minutes before turning out on to a wire rack to finish cooling.

Coffee Fruit Cake

Makes one 25 cm/10 in cake

450 g/1 lb/2 cups caster (superfine)
  sugar
450 g/1 lb/2 cups stoned (pitted)
  dates, chopped
450 g/1 lb/2⅔ cups raisins
450 g/1 lb/2⅔ cups sultanas
  (golden raisins)
100 g/4 oz/½ cup glacé (candied)
  cherries, chopped
100 g/4 oz/1 cup chopped mixed nuts
450 ml/¾ pt/2 cups strong black coffee
120 ml/4 fl oz/½ cup oil
100 g/4 oz/⅓ cup golden (light corn)
  syrup
10 ml/2 tsp ground cinnamon
5 ml/1 tsp grated nutmeg
A pinch of salt
10 ml/2 tsp bicarbonate of soda
  (baking soda)
15 ml/1 tbsp water
2 eggs, lightly beaten
450 g/1 lb/4 cups plain (all-purpose)
  flour
120 ml/4 fl oz/½ cup sherry or brandy

Bring all the ingredients except the bicarbonate of soda, water, eggs, flour and sherry or brandy to the boil in a heavy-based pan. Boil for 5 minutes, stirring continuously, then remove from the heat and leave to cool.

Blend the bicarbonate of soda with the water and add to the fruit mixture with the eggs and flour. Spoon into a greased and lined 25 cm/10 in cake tin (pan) and tie a double layer of greaseproof (waxed) paper round the outside to stand above the top of the tin. Bake in a preheated oven at 160°C/325°F/gas mark 3 for 1 hour. Reduce the oven temperature to 150°C/300°F/gas mark 2 and bake for a further 1 hour. Reduce the oven temperature to 140°C/275°F/gas mark 1 and bake for a third hour. Reduce the oven temperature again to 120°C/250°F/ gas mark ½ and bake for a final hour, covering the top of the cake with greaseproof (waxed) paper if it begins to brown too much. When cooked, a skewer inserted in the centre will come out clean and the cake will begin to shrink away from the sides of the tin. Sprinkle with the sherry or brandy and leave to cool in the tin for 15 minutes, then turn out on to a wire rack to finish cooling.

Cornish Heavy Cake

Makes one 900 g/2 lb cake

350 g/12 oz/3 cups plain
  (all-purpose) flour
2.5 ml/½ tsp salt
175 g/6 oz/¾ cup lard (shortening)
75 g/3 oz/⅓ cup caster (superfine)
  sugar
175 g/6 oz/1 cup currants
A little chopped mixed (candied) peel
  (optional)
About 150 ml/¼ pt/⅔ cup mixed milk
  and water
1 egg, beaten

Place the flour and salt in a bowl, then rub in the lard until the mixture resembles breadcrumbs. Stir in the remaining dry ingredients. Gradually add enough milk and water to make a stiff dough. It will not take very much. Roll out on to a greased baking (cookie) sheet to about 1 cm/½ in thick. Glaze with beaten egg. Draw a criss-cross pattern on the top with the tip of a knife. Bake in a preheated oven at 160°C/325°F/gas mark 3 for about 20 minutes until golden. Allow to cool, then cut into squares.

Currant Cake

Makes one 23 cm/9 in cake

225 g/8 oz/1 cup butter or margarine
300 g/11 oz/1½ cups caster (superfine)
   sugar
A pinch of salt
100 ml/3½ fl oz/6½ tbsp boiling water
3 eggs
400 g/14 oz/3½ cups plain
   (all-purpose) flour
175 g/6 oz/1 cup currants
50 g/2 oz/½ cup chopped mixed
   (candied) peel
100 ml/3½ fl oz/6½ tbsp cold water
15 ml/1 tbsp baking powder

Place the butter or margarine, sugar and salt in a bowl, pour over the boiling water and allow to stand until softened. Beat rapidly until light and creamy. Gradually add the eggs, then mix in the flour, currants and mixed peel alternately with the cold water. Stir in the baking powder. Spoon the batter into a greased 23 cm/9 in cake tin (pan) and bake in a preheated oven at 180°C/350°F/ gas mark 4 for 30 minutes. Reduce the oven temperature to 150°C/300°F/gas mark 2 and bake for a further 40 minutes until a skewer inserted in the centre comes out clean. Leave to cool in the tin for 10 minutes before turning out to finish cooling on a wire rack.

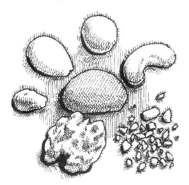

Dark Fruit Cake

Makes one 25 cm/10 in cake

225 g/8 oz/1 cup chopped mixed glacé
   (candied) fruits
350 g/12 oz/2 cups stoned (pitted)
   dates, chopped
225 g/8 oz/1⅓ cups raisins
225 g/8 oz/1 cup glacé (candied)
   cherries, chopped
100 g/4 oz/½ cup glacé (candied)
   pineapple, chopped
100 g/4 oz/1 cup chopped mixed nuts
225 g/8 oz/2 cups plain
   (all-purpose) flour
5 ml/1 tsp bicarbonate of soda
   (baking soda)
5 ml/1 tsp ground cinnamon
2.5 ml/½ tsp allspice
1.5 ml/¼ tsp ground cloves
1.5 ml/¼ tsp salt
225 g/8 oz/1 cup lard (shortening)
225 g/8 oz/1 cup soft brown sugar
3 eggs
175 g/6 oz/½ cup black treacle
   (molasses)
2.5 ml/½ tsp vanilla essence (extract)
120 ml/4 fl oz/½ cup buttermilk

Mix together the fruit and nuts. Mix together the flour, bicarbonate of soda, spices and salt and stir 50 g/2 oz/ ½ cup into the fruit. Cream together the lard and sugar until light and fluffy. Gradually add the eggs, beating well after each addition. Stir in the treacle and vanilla essence. Stir in the buttermilk alternately with the remaining flour mixture and beat until smooth. Stir in the fruit. Spoon into a greased and lined 25 cm/10 in cake tin (pan) and bake in a preheated oven at 140°C/275°F/gas mark 1 for 2½ hours until a skewer inserted in the centre comes out clean. Leave to cool in the tin for 10 minutes, then turn out on to a wire rack to finish cooling.

Cut-and-come-again Cake

Makes one 20 cm/8 in cake

275 g/10 oz/1⅔ cups dried mixed fruit
  (fruit cake mix)
100 g/4 oz/½ cup butter or margarine
150 ml/¼ pt/⅔ cup water
1 egg, beaten
225 g/8 oz/2 cups plain
  (all-purpose) flour
A pinch of salt
100 g/4 oz/½ cup caster (superfine)
  sugar

Put the fruit, butter or margarine and water in a pan and simmer for 20 minutes. Allow to cool. Add the egg, then gradually stir in the flour, salt and sugar. Spoon into a greased 20 cm/8 in cake tin (pan) and bake in a preheated oven at 160°C/325°F/gas mark 3 for 1¼ hours until a skewer inserted in the centre comes out clean.

Dundee Cake

Makes one 20 cm/8 in cake

225 g/8 oz/1 cup butter or margarine,
  softened
225 g/8 oz/1 cup caster (superfine)
  sugar
4 large eggs
225 g/8 oz/2 cups plain
  (all-purpose) flour
A pinch of salt
350 g/12 oz/2 cups currants
350 g/12 oz/2 cups sultanas
  (golden raisins)
175 g/6 oz/1 cup chopped mixed
  (candied) peel
100 g/4 oz/1 cup glacé (candied)
  cherries, quartered
Grated rind of ½ lemon
50 g/2 oz whole almonds, blanched

Cream together the butter and sugar until pale and light. Beat in the eggs one at a time, beating well between each addition. Fold in the flour and salt. Stir in

the fruit and lemon rind. Chop half the almonds and add them to the mixture. Spoon into a greased and lined 20 cm/8 in cake tin (pan) and tie a band of brown paper round the outside of the tin so that it is about 5 cm/2 in taller than the tin. Split the reserved almonds and arrange them in concentric circles on the top of the cake. Bake in a preheated oven at 150°C/300°F/gas mark 2 for 3½ hours until a skewer inserted in the centre comes out clean. Check after 2½ hours and if the cake begins to brown too much on the top, cover with damp greaseproof (waxed) paper and reduce the oven temperature to 140°C/275°F/gas mark 1 for the final hour of cooking.

Eggless Overnight Fruit Cake

Makes one 20 cm/8 in cake

50 g/2 oz/¼ cup butter or margarine
225 g/8 oz/2 cups self-raising
  (self-rising) flour
5 ml/1 tsp bicarbonate of soda
  (baking soda)
5 ml/1 tsp grated nutmeg
5 ml/1 tsp ground mixed (apple-pie)
  spice
A pinch of salt
225 g/8 oz/1⅓ cups dried mixed fruit
  (fruit cake mix)
100 g/4 oz/½ cup soft brown sugar
250 ml/8 fl oz/1 cup milk

Rub the butter or margarine into the flour, bicarbonate of soda, spices and salt until the mixture resembles breadcrumbs. Mix in the fruit and sugar, then stir in the milk until all the ingredients are well blended. Cover and leave overnight.

Spoon the mixture into a greased and lined 20 cm/8 in cake tin (pan) and bake in a preheated oven at 180°C/350°F/gas mark 4 for 1¾ hours until a skewer inserted in the centre comes out clean.

Foolproof Fruit Cake

Makes one 23 cm/9 in cake

225 g/8 oz/1 cup butter or margarine
200 g/7 oz/scant 1 cup caster
  (superfine) sugar
175 g/6 oz/1 cup currants
175 g/6 oz/1 cup sultanas
  (golden raisins)
50 g/2 oz/½ cup chopped mixed
  (candied) peel
75 g/3 oz/½ cup stoned (pitted) dates,
  chopped
5 ml/1 tsp bicarbonate of soda
  (baking soda)
200 ml/7 fl oz/scant 1 cup water
75 g/2 oz/¼ cup glacé (candied)
  cherries, chopped
100 g/4 oz/1 cup chopped mixed nuts
60 ml/4 tbsp brandy or sherry
300 g/11 oz/2¾ cups plain
  (all-purpose) flour
5 ml/1 tsp baking powder
A pinch of salt
2 eggs, lightly beaten

Melt the butter or margarine, then stir in the sugar, currants, sultanas, mixed peel and dates. Mix the bicarbonate of soda with a little of the water and stir into the fruit mixture with the remaining water. Bring to the boil, then simmer gently for 20 minutes, stirring occasionally. Cover and leave to stand overnight.

Grease and line a 23 cm/9 in cake tin (pan) and tie a double layer of greaseproof (waxed) or brown paper to stand above the top of the tin. Stir the glacé cherries, nuts and brandy or sherry into the mixture, then stir in the flour, baking powder and salt. Stir in the eggs. Spoon into the prepared cake tin and bake in a preheated oven at 160°C/325°F/gas mark 3 for 1 hour. Reduce the oven temperature to 140°C/275°F/gas mark 1 and bake for a further 1 hour. Reduce the oven temperature

again to 120°C/250°F/gas mark ½ and bake for a further 1 hour until a skewer inserted in the centre comes out clean. Cover the top of the cake with a circle of greaseproof or brown paper towards the end of the cooking time if it is over-browning. Allow to cool in the tin for 30 minutes, then turn out on to a wire rack to finish cooling.

Ginger Fruit Cake

Makes one 18 cm/7 in cake

100 g/4 oz/½ cup butter or margarine,
  softened
100 g/4 oz/½ cup caster (superfine)
  sugar
2 eggs, lightly beaten
30 ml/2 tbsp milk
225 g/8 oz/2 cups self-raising
  (self-rising) flour
5 ml/1 tsp baking powder
10 ml/2 tsp ground mixed
  (apple-pie) spice
5 ml/1 tsp ground ginger
100 g/4 oz/⅔ cup raisins
100 g/4 oz/⅔ cup sultanas
  (golden raisins)

Cream together the butter or margarine and sugar until light and fluffy. Gradually blend in the eggs and milk, then fold in the flour, baking powder and spices, then the fruit. Spoon the mixture into a greased and lined 18 cm/7 in cake tin (pan) and bake in a preheated oven at 160°C/325°F/gas mark 3 for 1¼ hours until well risen and golden brown.

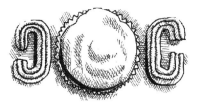

Farmhouse Honey Fruit Cake

Makes one 20 cm/8 in cake

175 g/6 oz/³⁄₄ cup butter or margarine,
softened
175 g/6 oz/¹⁄₂ cup clear honey
Grated rind of 1 lemon
3 eggs, lightly beaten
225 g/8 oz/2 cups wholemeal
(wholewheat) flour
10 ml/2 tsp baking powder
5 ml/1 tsp ground mixed (apple-pie)
spice
100 g/4 oz/³⁄₄ cup raisins
100 g/4 oz/³⁄₄ cup sultanas
(golden raisins)
100 g/4 oz/³⁄₄ cup currants
50 g/2 oz/¹⁄₃ cup ready-to-eat dried
apricots, chopped
50 g/2 oz/¹⁄₃ cup chopped mixed
(candied) peel
25 g/1 oz/¹⁄₄ cup ground almonds
25 g/1 oz/¹⁄₄ cup almonds

Cream together the butter or margarine, honey and lemon rind until light and fluffy. Gradually add the eggs, then fold in the flour, baking powder and mixed spice. Stir in the fruit and ground almonds. Spoon into a greased and lined 20 cm/8 in cake tin (pan) and make a slight hollow in the centre. Arrange the almonds around the top edge of the cake. Bake in a preheated oven at 160°C/325°F/gas mark 3 for 2–2½ hours until a skewer inserted in the centre comes out clean. Cover the top of the cake with greaseproof (waxed) paper towards the end of the cooking time if it is over-browning. Leave to cool in the tin for 10 minutes before turning out on to a wire rack to finish cooling.

Genoa Cake

Makes one 23 cm/9 in cake

225 g/8 oz/1 cup butter or margarine,
softened
100 g/4 oz/¹⁄₂ cup caster (superfine)
sugar
4 eggs, separated
5 ml/1 tsp almond essence (extract)
5 ml/1 tsp grated orange rind
225 g/8 oz/1¹⁄₃ cups raisins, chopped
100 g/4 oz/³⁄₄ cup currants, chopped
100 g/4 oz/³⁄₄ cup sultanas (golden
raisins), chopped
50 g/2 oz/¹⁄₄ cup glacé (candied)
cherries, chopped
50 g/2 oz/¹⁄₃ cup chopped mixed
(candied) peel
100 g/4 oz/1 cup ground almonds
25 g/1 oz/¹⁄₄ cup almonds
350 g/12 oz/3 cups plain
(all-purpose) flour
10 ml/2 tsp baking powder
5 ml/1 tsp ground cinnamon

Cream together the butter or margarine and sugar, then beat in the egg yolks, almond essence and orange rind. Mix the fruit and nuts with a little of the flour until coated, then stir in spoonfuls of the flour, baking powder and cinnamon alternately with spoonfuls of the fruit mixture until everything is well blended. Whisk the egg whites until stiff, then fold them into the mixture. Spoon into a greased and lined 23 cm/9 in cake tin (pan) and bake in a preheated oven at 190°C/375°F/gas mark 5 for 30 minutes, then reduce the oven temperature to 160°C/325°F/gas mark 3 for a further 1½ hours until springy to the touch and a skewer inserted in the centre comes out clean. Leave to cool in the tin.

Glacé Fruit Cake

Makes one 23 cm/9 in cake

225 g/8 oz/1 cup butter or margarine,
  softened
225 g/8 oz/1 cup caster (superfine)
  sugar
4 eggs, lightly beaten
45 ml/3 tbsp brandy
250 g/9 oz/1¼ cups plain
  (all-purpose) flour
2.5 ml/½ tsp baking powder
A pinch of salt
225 g/8 oz/1 cup mixed glacé
  (candied) fruit such as cherries,
  pineapple, oranges, figs, sliced
100 g/4 oz/⅔ cup raisins
100 g/4 oz/⅔ cup sultanas (golden
  raisins)
75 g/3 oz/½ cup currants
50 g/2 oz/½ cup chopped mixed nuts
Grated rind of 1 lemon

Cream together the butter or mar-garine and sugar until light and fluffy. Gradually mix in the eggs and brandy. In a separate bowl, stir together the remaining ingredients until the fruit is well coated with flour. Stir into the mixture and blend well. Spoon into a greased 23 cm/9 in cake tin (pan) and bake in a preheated oven at 180°C/350°F/gas mark 4 for 30 minutes. Reduce the oven temperature to 150°C/300°F/gas mark 3 and bake for a further 50 minutes until a skewer inserted in the centre comes out clean.

Guinness Fruit Cake

Makes one 23 cm/9 in cake

225 g/8 oz/1 cup butter or margarine
225 g/8 oz/1 cup soft brown sugar
300 ml/½ pt/1¼ cups Guinness
  or stout
225 g/8 oz/1⅓ cups raisins
225 g/8 oz/1⅓ cups sultanas
  (golden raisins)
225 g/8 oz/1⅓ cups currants
100 g/4 oz/⅔ cup chopped mixed
  (candied) peel
550 g/1¼ lb/5 cups plain
  (all-purpose) flour
2.5 ml/½ tsp bicarbonate of soda
  (baking soda)
5 ml/1 tsp ground mixed (apple-pie)
  spice
2.5 ml/½ tsp grated nutmeg
3 eggs, lightly beaten

Bring the butter or margarine, sugar and Guinness to the boil in a small pan over a low heat, stirring until well blended. Mix in the fruit and mixed peel, bring to the boil, then simmer for 5 minutes. Remove from the heat and leave to cool.

Mix together the flour, bicarbonate of soda and spices and make a well in the centre. Add the cool fruit mixture and the eggs and mix together until well blended. Spoon into a greased and lined 23 cm/9 in cake tin (pan) and bake in a preheated oven 160°C/325°F/gas mark 3 for 2 hours until a skewer inserted in the centre comes out clean. Leave to cool in the tin for 20 minutes, then turn out on to a wire rack to finish cooling.

Mincemeat Cake

Makes one 20 cm/8 in cake

225 g/8 oz/2 cups self-raising
  (self-rising) flour
350 g/12 oz/2 cups mincemeat
75 g/3 oz/½ cup dried mixed fruit
  (fruit cake mix)
3 eggs
150 g/5 oz/⅔ cup soft margarine
150 g/5 oz/⅔ cup soft brown sugar

Mix together all the ingredients until well blended. Turn into a greased and lined 20 cm/8 in cake tin and bake in a preheated oven at 160°C/325°F/gas mark 3 for 1¾ hours until well risen and firm to the touch.

Oat and Apricot Fruit Cake

Makes one 20 cm/8 in cake

175 g/6 oz/³⁄₄ cup butter or margarine,
  softened
50 g/2 oz/¼ cup soft brown sugar
30 ml/2 tbsp clear honey
3 eggs, beaten
175 g/6 oz/¹⁄₄ cups wholemeal
  (wholewheat) flour
50 g/2 oz/½ cup oat flour
10 ml/2 tsp baking powder
250 g/9 oz/1½ cups dried mixed fruit
  (fruit cake mix)
50 g/2 oz/¹⁄₃ cup ready-to-eat dried
  apricots, chopped
Grated rind and juice of 1 lemon

Cream the butter or margarine and sugar with the honey until light and fluffy. Gradually beat in the eggs alternately with the flours and baking powder. Stir in the dried fruit and lemon juice and rind. Spoon into a greased and lined 20 cm/8 in cake tin (pan) and bake in a preheated oven at 180°C/350°F/ gas mark 4 for 1 hour. Reduce the oven temperature to 160°C/325°F/gas mark 3 and bake for a further 30 minutes until a skewer inserted in the centre comes out clean. Cover the top with baking parchment if the cake begins to brown too quickly.

Overnight Fruit Cake

Makes one 20 cm/8 in cake

450 g/1 lb/4 cups plain (all-purpose)
  flour
225 g/8 oz/1¹⁄₃ cups currants
225 g/8 oz/1¹⁄₃ cups sultanas
  (golden raisins)
225 g/8 oz/1 cup soft brown sugar
50 g/2 oz/¹⁄₃ cup chopped mixed
  (candied) peel
175 g/6 oz/³⁄₄ cup lard (shortening)
15 ml/1 tbsp golden (light corn) syrup

10 ml/2 tsp bicarbonate of soda
  (baking soda)
15 ml/1 tbsp milk
300 ml/½ pt/1¼ cups water

Mix together the flour, fruits, sugar and peel. Melt together the lard and syrup and stir into the mixture. Dissolve the bicarbonate of soda in the milk and stir into the cake mixture with the water. Spoon into a greased 20 cm/8 in cake tin (pan), cover and leave to stand overnight.

Bake the cake in a preheated oven at 160°C/375°F/gas mark 3 for 1¾ hours until a skewer inserted in the centre comes out clean.

Raisin and Spice Cake

Makes one 900 g/2 lb loaf

225 g/8 oz/1 cup soft brown sugar
300 ml/½ pt/1¼ cups water
100 g/4 oz/½ cup butter or margarine
15 ml/1 tbsp black treacle (molasses)
175 g/6 oz/1 cup raisins
5 ml/1 tsp ground cinnamon
2. 5 ml/½ tsp grated nutmeg
2.5 ml/½ tsp allspice
225 g/8 oz/2 cups plain
  (all-purpose) flour
5 ml/1 tsp baking powder
5 ml/1 tsp bicarbonate of soda
  (baking soda)

Melt the sugar, water, butter or margarine, treacle, raisins and spices in a small pan over a medium heat, stirring continuously. Bring to the boil and simmer for 5 minutes. Remove from the heat and beat in the remaining ingredients. Spoon the mixture into a greased and lined 900 g/2 lb loaf tin (pan) and bake in a preheated oven at 180°C/ 350°F/gas mark 4 for 50 minutes until a skewer inserted in the centre comes out clean.

Richmond Cake

Makes one 15 cm/6 in cake

225 g/8 oz/2 cups plain
(all-purpose) flour
A pinch of salt
75 g/3 oz/⅓ cup butter or margarine
100 g/4 oz/½ cup caster (superfine)
sugar
2.5 ml/½ tsp baking powder
100 g/4 oz/⅔ cup currants
2 eggs, beaten
A little milk

Place the flour and salt in a bowl and rub in the butter or margarine until the mixture resembles breadcrumbs. Stir in the sugar, baking powder and currants. Add the eggs and enough milk to mix to a stiff batter. Turn into a greased and lined 15 cm/6 in cake tin. Bake in a preheated oven at 190°C/375°F/gas mark 5 for about 45 minutes until a skewer inserted into the centre comes out clean. Leave to cool on a wire rack.

Saffron Fruit Cake

Makes two 450 g/1 lb cakes

2.5 ml/½ tsp saffron strands
Warm water
15 g/½ oz fresh yeast or 20 ml/
4 tsp dried yeast
900 g/2 lb/8 cups plain (all-purpose)
flour
225 g/8 oz/1 cup caster (superfine)
sugar
2.5 ml/½ tsp ground mixed
(apple-pie) spice
A pinch of salt
100 g/4 oz/½ cup lard (shortening)
100 g/4 oz/½ cup butter or margarine
300 ml/½ pt/1¼ cups warm milk
350 g/12 oz/2 cups dried mixed fruit
(fruit cake mix)
50g/2 oz/⅓ cup chopped mixed
(candied) peel

Chop the saffron strands and soak in 45 ml/3 tbsp of warm water overnight.

Mix the yeast with 30 ml/2 tbsp of the flour, 5 ml/1 tsp of the sugar and 75 ml/5 tbsp of warm water and leave in a warm place for 20 minutes until frothy.

Mix together the remaining flour and sugar with the spice and salt. Rub in the lard and butter or margarine until the mixture resembles breadcrumbs, then make a well in the centre. Add the yeast mixture, the saffron and saffron liquid, the warm milk, fruit and mixed peel and mix to a soft dough. Place in an oiled bowl, cover with clingfilm (plastic wrap) and leave in a warm place for 3 hours.

Shape into two loaves, place in two greased 450 g/1 lb loaf tins (pans) and bake in a preheated oven at 220°C/450°F/gas mark 7 for 40 minutes until well risen and golden brown.

Soda Fruit Cake

Makes one 450 g/1 lb cake

225 g/8 oz/2 cups plain
  (all-purpose) flour
1.5 ml/¼ tsp salt
A pinch of bicarbonate of soda
  (baking soda)
50 g/2 oz/¼ cup butter or margarine
50 g/2 oz/¼ cup caster (superfine)
  sugar
100 g/4 oz/⅔ cup dried mixed fruit
  (fruit cake mix)
150 ml/¼ pt/⅔ cup sour milk or milk
  with 5 ml/1 tsp lemon juice
5 ml/1 tsp black treacle (molasses)

Mix together the flour, salt and bicarbonate of soda in a bowl. Rub in the butter or margarine until the mixture resembles breadcrumbs. Stir in the sugar and fruit and mix well. Heat the milk and treacle until the treacle has melted, then add to the dry ingredients and mix to a stiff batter. Spoon into a greased 450 g/1 lb loaf tin (pan) and bake in a preheated oven at 190°C/375°F/gas mark 5 for about 45 minutes until golden.

Speedy Fruit Cake

Makes one 20 cm/8 in cake

450 g/1 lb/2⅔ cups mixed dried fruit
  (fruit cake mix)
225 g/8 oz/1 cup soft brown sugar
100 g/4 oz/½ cup butter or margarine
150 ml/¼ pt/⅔ cup water
2 eggs, beaten
225 g/8 oz/2 cups self-raising
  (self-rising) flour

Bring the fruit, sugar, butter or margarine and water to the boil, then cover and simmer gently for 15 minutes. Leave to cool. Beat in the eggs and flour, then spoon the mixture into a greased and lined 20 cm/8 in cake tin and bake in a preheated oven at 150°C/300°F/gas

mark 3 for 1½ hours until browned on top and shrinking away from the sides of the tin.

Hot Tea Fruit Cake

Makes one 900 g/2 lb cake

450 g/1 lb/2½ cups dried mixed fruit
  (fruit cake mix)
300 ml/½ pt/1¼ cups hot black tea
350 g/10 oz/1¼ cups soft brown sugar
350 g/10 oz/2½ cups self-raising
  (self-rising) flour
1 egg, beaten

Place the fruit in the hot tea and leave to soak overnight. Stir in the sugar, flour and egg and turn into a greased and lined 900 g/2 lb loaf tin (pan). Bake in a preheated oven at 160°C/325°F/gas mark 3 for 2 hours until well risen and golden brown.

Cold Tea Fruit Cake

Makes one 15 cm/6 in cake

100 g/4 oz/½ cup butter or margarine
225 g/8 oz/1⅓ cups dried mixed fruit
  (fruit cake mix)
250 ml/8 fl oz/1 cup cold black tea
225 g/8 oz/2 cups self-raising
  (self-rising) flour
100 g/4 oz/½ cup caster (superfine)
  sugar
5 ml/1 tsp bicarbonate of soda
  (baking soda)
1 large egg

Melt the butter or margarine in a saucepan, add the fruit and tea and bring to the boil. Simmer for 2 minutes, then allow to cool. Stir in the remaining ingredients and mix well. Spoon into a greased and lined 15 cm/6 in cake tin and bake in a preheated oven at 160°C/325°F/gas mark 3 for 1¼–1½ hours until firm to the touch. Leave to cool, then serve sliced and spread with butter.

Sugar-free Fruit Cake

Makes one 20 cm/8 in cake

4 dried apricots
60 ml/4 tbsp orange juice
250 ml/8 fl oz/1 cup stout
100 g/4 oz/⅔ cup sultanas
 (golden raisins)
100 g/4 oz/⅔ cup raisins
50 g/2 oz/¼ cup currants
50 g/2 oz/¼ cup butter or margarine
225 g/8 oz/2 cups self-raising
 (self-rising) flour
75 g/3 oz/¾ cup chopped mixed nuts
10 ml/2 tsp ground mixed
 (apple-pie) spice
5 ml/1 tsp instant coffee powder
3 eggs, lightly beaten
15 ml/1 tbsp brandy or whisky

Soak the apricots in the orange juice until soft, then chop. Place in a pan with the stout, dried fruit and butter or margarine, bring to the boil, then simmer for 20 minutes. Leave to cool.

Mix together the flour, nuts, spice and coffee. Blend in the stout mixture, eggs and brandy or whisky. Spoon the mixture into a greased and lined 20 cm/8 in cake tin and bake in a preheated oven at 180°C/350°F/gas mark 4 for 20 minutes. Reduce the oven temperature to 150°C/300°F/gas mark 2 and bake for a further 1½ hours until a skewer inserted in the centre comes out clean. Cover the top with greaseproof (waxed) paper towards the end of the cooking time if it is over-browning. Leave to cool in the tin for 10 minutes before turning out on to a wire rack to finish cooling.

Tiny Fruit Cakes

Makes 48

100 g/4 oz/½ cup butter or margarine,
 softened
225 g/8 oz/1 cup soft brown sugar
2 eggs, lightly beaten
175 g/6 oz/1 cup stoned (pitted) dates,
 chopped
50 g/2 oz/½ cup chopped mixed nuts
15 ml/1 tbsp grated orange rind
225 g/8 oz/2 cups plain
 (all-purpose) flour
5 ml/1 tsp bicarbonate of soda
 (baking soda)
2.5 ml/½ tsp salt
150 ml/¼ pt/⅔ cup buttermilk
6 glacé (candied) cherries, sliced
Orange Fruitcake Glaze (page 237)

Cream the butter or margarine and sugar until light and fluffy. Beat in the eggs a little at a time. Stir in the dates, nuts and orange rind. Mix together the flour, bicarbonate of soda and salt. Add to the mixture alternately with the buttermilk and beat until well combined. Spoon into greased 5 cm/2 in muffin tins (pans) and decorate with the cherries. Bake in a preheated oven at 190°C/375°F/gas mark 5 for 20 minutes until a skewer inserted in the centre comes out clean. Transfer to a cooling rack and leave until just warm, then brush with the orange glaze.

Vinegar Fruit Cake

Makes one 23 cm/9 in cake

225 g/8 oz/1 cup butter or margarine
450 g/1 lb/4 cups plain (all-purpose) flour
225 g/8 oz/1⅓ cups sultanas (golden raisins)
100 g/4 oz/⅔ cup raisins
100 g/4 oz/⅔ cup currants
225 g/8 oz/1 cup soft brown sugar
5 ml/1 tsp bicarbonate of soda (baking soda)
300 ml/½ pt/1¼ cups milk
45 ml/3 tbsp malt vinegar

Rub the butter or margarine into the flour until the mixture resembles breadcrumbs. Stir in the fruit and sugar and make a well in the centre. Mix together the bicarbonate of soda, milk and vinegar – the mixture will froth. Stir into the dry ingredients until well blended. Spoon the mixture into a greased and lined 23 cm/9 in cake tin (pan) and bake in a preheated oven at 200°C/400°F/gas mark 6 for 25 minutes. Reduce the oven temperature to 160°C/325°F/gas mark 3 and bake for a further 1½ hours until golden and firm to the touch. Leave to cool in the tin for 5 minutes, then turn out on to a wire rack to finish cooling.

Virginia Whiskey Cake

Makes one 450 g/1 lb cake

100 g/4 oz/½ cup butter or margarine, softened
50 g/2 oz/¼ cup caster (superfine) sugar
3 eggs, separated
175 g/6 oz/1½ cups plain (all-purpose) flour
5 ml/1 tsp baking powder
A pinch of grated nutmeg
A pinch of ground mace

120 ml/4 fl oz/½ cup port
30 ml/2 tbsp brandy
100 g/4 oz/⅔ cup dried mixed fruit (fruit cake mix)
120 ml/4 fl oz/½ cup whiskey

Cream together the butter and sugar until smooth. Mix in the egg yolks. Mix together the flour, baking powder and spices and stir into the mixture. Stir in the port, brandy and dried fruit. Whisk the egg whites until they form soft peaks, then fold them in to the mixture. Spoon into a greased 450 g/1 lb loaf tin (pan) and bake in a preheated oven at 160°C/325°F/gas mark 3 for 1 hour until a skewer inserted in the centre comes out clean. Leave to cool in the tin, then pour the whiskey over the cake and leave in the tin for 24 hours before cutting.

Welsh Fruit Cake

Makes one 23 cm/9 in cake

50 g/2 oz/¼ cup butter or margarine
50 g/2 oz/¼ cup lard (shortening)
225 g/8 oz/2 cups plain (all-purpose) flour
A pinch of salt
10 ml/2 tsp baking powder
100 g/4 oz/½ cup demerara sugar
175 g/6 oz/1 cup dried mixed fruit (fruit cake mix)
Grated rind and juice of ½ lemon
1 egg, lightly beaten
30 ml/2 tbsp milk

Rub the butter or margarine and lard into the flour, salt and baking powder until the mixture resembles breadcrumbs. Stir in the sugar, fruit and lemon rind and juice, then mix in the egg and milk and knead to a soft dough. Shape into a greased and lined 23 cm/9 in square baking tin (pan) and bake in a preheated oven at 200°C/400°F/gas mark 6 for 20 minutes until risen and golden brown.

White Fruit Cake

Makes one 23 cm/9 in cake

100 g/4 oz/½ cup butter or margarine,
  softened
225 g/8 oz/1 cup caster (superfine)
  sugar
5 eggs, lightly beaten
350 g/12 oz/2 cups dried mixed fruit
350 g/12 oz/2 cups sultanas
  (golden raisins)
100 g/4 oz/⅔ cup stoned (pitted) dates,
  chopped
100 g/4 oz/½ cup glacé (candied)
  cherries, chopped
100 g/4 oz/½ cup glacé (candied)
  pineapple, chopped
100 g/4 oz/1 cup chopped mixed nuts
225 g/8 oz/2 cups plain
  (all-purpose) flour
10 ml/2 tsp baking powder
2.5 ml/½ tsp salt
60 ml/4 tbsp pineapple juice

Cream together the butter or margarine and sugar until light and fluffy. Gradually add the eggs, beating well after each addition. Mix together all the fruit, the nuts and a little of the flour until the ingredients are well coated in flour. Mix the baking powder and salt into the remaining flour, then stir it into the egg mixture alternately with the pineapple juice until evenly blended. Stir in the fruit and mix well. Spoon into a greased and lined 23 cm/9 in cake tin (pan) and bake in a preheated oven at 140°C/275°F/ gas mark 1 for about 2½ hours until a skewer inserted in the centre comes out clean. Leave to cool in the tin for 10 minutes before turning out on to a wire rack to finish cooling.

Apple Cake

Makes one 20 cm/8 in cake

175 g/6 oz/1½ cups self-raising
  (self-rising) flour
5 ml/1 tsp baking powder
A pinch of salt
150 g/5 oz/⅔ cup butter or margarine
150 g/5 oz/⅔ cup caster (superfine)
  sugar
1 egg, beaten
175 ml/6 fl oz/¾ cup milk
3 eating (dessert) apples, peeled, cored
  and sliced
2.5 ml/½ tsp ground cinnamon
15 ml/1 tbsp clear honey

Mix together the flour, baking power and salt. Rub in the butter or margarine until the mixture resembles breadcrumbs, then stir in the sugar. Mix in the egg and milk. Pour the mixture into a greased and lined 20 cm/8 in cake tin (pan) and press the apple slices gently into the top. Sprinkle with the cinnamon and drizzle with the honey. Bake in a preheated oven at 200°C/400°F/gas mark 6 for 45 minutes until golden and firm to the touch.

Crunchy-topped Spiced Apple Cake

Makes one 20 cm/8 in cake

75 g/3 oz/⅓ cup butter or margarine
175 g/6 oz/1½ cups self-raising
    (self-rising) flour
50 g/2 oz/¼ cup caster (superfine)
    sugar
1 egg
75 ml/5 tbsp water
3 eating (dessert) apples, peeled, cored
    and cut into wedges
For the topping:
75 g/3 oz/⅓ cup demerara sugar
10 ml/2 tsp ground cinnamon
25 g/1 oz/2 tbsp butter or margarine

Rub the butter or margarine into the flour until the mixture resembles breadcrumbs. Stir in the sugar, then mix in the egg and water to make a soft dough. Add a little more water if the mixture is too dry. Spread the dough in a 20 cm/8 in cake tin (pan) and press the apples into the dough. Sprinkle with the demerara sugar and cinnamon and dot with the butter or margarine. Bake in a preheated oven at 180°C/350°F/gas mark 4 for 30 minutes until golden brown and firm to the touch.

American Apple Cake

Makes one 20 cm/8 in cake

50 g/2 oz/¼ cup butter or margarine,
    softened
225 g/8 oz/1 cup soft brown sugar
1 egg, lightly beaten
5 ml/1 tsp vanilla essence (extract)
100 g/4 oz/1 cup plain (all-purpose)
    flour
2.5 ml/½ tsp baking powder
2.5 ml/½ tsp bicarbonate of soda
    (baking soda)
2.5 ml/½ tsp salt

2.5 ml/½ tsp ground cinnamon
2.5 ml/½ tsp grated nutmeg
450 g/1 lb eating (dessert) apples,
    peeled, cored and diced
25 g/1 oz/¼ cup almonds, chopped

Cream the butter or margarine and sugar until light and fluffy. Gradually beat in the egg and vanilla essence. Mix together the flour, baking powder, bicarbonate of soda, salt and spices and beat into the mixture until blended. Stir in the apples and nuts. Spoon into a greased and lined 20 cm/8 in square baking tin (pan) and bake in a preheated oven at 180°C/350°F/gas mark 4 for 45 minutes until a skewer inserted in the centre comes out clean.

Apple Purée Cake

Makes one 900 g/2 lb cake

100 g/4 oz/½ cup butter or margarine,
    softened
225 g/8 oz/1 cup soft brown sugar
2 eggs, lightly beaten
225 g/8 oz/2 cups plain
    (all-purpose) flour
5 ml/1 tsp ground cinnamon
2.5 ml/½ tsp grated nutmeg
100 g/4 oz/1 cup apple purée (sauce)
5 ml/1 tsp bicarbonate of soda
    (baking soda)
30 ml/2 tbsp hot water

Cream together the butter or margarine and sugar until light and fluffy. Gradually blend in the eggs. Stir in the flour, cinnamon, nutmeg and apple purée. Mix the bicarbonate of soda with the hot water and stir it into the mixture. Spoon into a greased 900 g/2 lb loaf tin (pan) and bake in a preheated oven at 180°C/350°F/gas mark 4 for 1¼ hours until a skewer inserted in the centre comes out clean.

Cider Apple Cake

Makes one 20 cm/8 in cake

*100 g/4 oz/½ cup butter or margarine,
softened
150 g/5 oz/⅔ cup caster (superfine)
sugar
3 eggs
225 g/8 oz/2 cups self-raising
(self-rising) flour
5 ml/1 tsp ground mixed (apple-pie)
spice
5 ml/1 tsp bicarbonate of soda
(baking soda)
5 ml/1 tsp baking powder
150 ml/¼ pt/⅔ cup dry cider
2 cooking (tart) apples, peeled, cored
and sliced
75 g/3 oz/⅓ cup demerara sugar
100 g/4 oz/1 cup chopped mixed nuts*

Blend together the butter or margarine,
sugar, eggs, flour, spice, bicarbonate of
soda, baking powder and 120 ml/4 fl oz/
½ cup of the cider until well mixed,
adding the remaining cider if necessary to
create a smooth batter. Spoon half the
mixture into a greased and lined 20 cm/
8 in cake tin (pan) and cover with half the
apple slices. Mix together the sugar and
nuts and spread half over the apples.
Spoon in the remaining cake mixture and
top with the remaining apples and the rest
of the sugar and nut mixture. Bake in a
preheated oven at 180°C/350°F/gas mark
4 for 1 hour until golden brown and firm
to the touch.

Apple and Cinnamon Cake

Makes one 23 cm/9 in cake

*100 g/4 oz/½ cup butter or margarine
100 g/4 oz/½ cup caster (superfine)
sugar
1 egg, lightly beaten
100 g/4 oz/1 cup plain (all-purpose)
flour
5 ml/1 tsp baking powder
30 ml/2 tbsp milk (optional)
2 large cooking (tart) apples, peeled,
cored and sliced
30 ml/2 tbsp caster (superfine) sugar
5 ml/1 tsp ground cinnamon
25 g/1 oz/¼ cup almonds, chopped
30 ml/2 tbsp demerara sugar*

Cream together the butter or margarine and sugar until light and fluffy.
Gradually beat in the egg, then fold in the
flour and baking powder. The mixture
should be quite stiff; if it is too stiff, stir in
a little milk. Spoon half the mixture into a
greased and lined 23 cm/9 in loose-
bottomed cake tin (pan). Arrange the
apple slices on top. Mix together the sugar
and cinnamon and sprinkle with the
almonds over the apples. Top with the
remaining cake mixture and sprinkle with
demerara sugar. Bake in a preheated oven
at 180°C/350°F/gas mark 4 for 30–35
minutes until a skewer inserted in the
centre comes out clean.

Spanish Apple Cake

Makes one 23 cm/9 in cake

175 g/6 oz/³⁄₄ cup butter or margarine
6 Cox's eating (dessert) apples, peeled,
  cored and cut into segments
30 ml/2 tbsp apple brandy
175 g/6 oz/³⁄₄ cup caster (superfine)
  sugar
150 g/5 oz/1¼ cups plain
  (all-purpose) flour
10 ml/2 tsp baking powder
5 ml/1 tsp ground cinnamon
3 eggs, lightly beaten
45 ml/3 tbsp milk
For the glaze:
60 ml/4 tbsp apricot jam (conserve),
  sieved (strained)
15 ml/1 tbsp apple brandy
5 ml/1 tsp cornflour (cornstarch)
10 ml/2 tsp water

Melt the butter or margarine in a large frying pan (skillet) and fry the apple pieces over a low heat for 10 minutes, stirring once to coat in the butter. Remove from the heat. Chop one-third of the apples and add the apple brandy, then mix in the sugar, flour, baking powder and cinnamon. Add the eggs and milk and spoon the mixture into a greased and floured 23 cm/9 in loose-bottomed cake tin (pan). Arrange the remaining apple slices on top. Bake in a preheated oven at 180°C/350°F/gas mark 4 for 45 minutes until well risen and golden brown, and starting to shrink away from the sides of the tin.

To make the glaze, warm the jam and brandy together. Mix the cornflour to a paste with the water and stir into the jam and brandy. Cook for a few minutes, stirring, until clear. Brush over the warm cake and leave to cool for 30 minutes. Remove the sides of the cake tin, warm the glaze again, and brush over a second time. Leave to cool.

Apple and Sultana Cake

Makes one 20 cm/8 in cake

350 g/12 oz/3 cups self-raising
  (self-rising) flour
A pinch of salt
2.5 ml/½ tsp ground cinnamon
225 g/8 oz/1 cup butter or margarine
175 g/6 oz/³⁄₄ cup caster (superfine)
  sugar
100 g/4 oz/²⁄₃ cup sultanas
  (golden raisins)
450 g/1 lb cooking (tart) apples,
  peeled, cored and finely chopped
2 eggs
A little milk

Mix together the flour, salt and cinnamon, then rub in the butter or margarine until the mixture resembles breadcrumbs. Stir in the sugar. Make a well in the centre and add the sultanas, apples and eggs and mix well, adding a little milk to make a stiff mixture. Spoon into a greased 20 cm/8 in cake tin and bake in a preheated oven at 180°C/350°F/gas mark 4 for about 1½–2 hours until firm to the touch. Serve hot or cold.

Apple Upside-down Cake

Makes one 23 cm/9 in cake

2 eating (dessert) apples, peeled, cored
and thinly sliced
75 g/3 oz/⅓ cup soft brown sugar
45 ml/3 tbsp raisins
30 ml/2 tbsp lemon juice
For the cake:
200 g/7 oz/1¾ cups plain
(all-purpose) flour
50 g/2 oz/¼ cup caster (superfine)
sugar
10 ml/2 tsp baking powder
5 ml/1 tsp bicarbonate of soda
(baking soda)
5 ml/1 tsp ground cinnamon
A pinch of salt
120 ml/4 fl oz/½ cup milk
50 g/2 oz/½ cup apple purée (sauce)
75 ml/5 tbsp oil
1 egg, lightly beaten
5 ml/1 tsp vanilla essence (extract)

Mix together the apples, sugar, raisins and lemon juice and arrange in the base of a greased 23 cm/9 in cake tin (pan). Mix together the dry cake ingredients and make a well in the centre. Mix together the milk, apple sauce, oil, egg and vanilla essence and stir into the dry ingredients until just blended. Spoon into the cake tin and bake in a preheated oven at 180°C/350°F/gas mark 4 for 40 minutes until the cake is golden and shrinking away from the sides of the tin. Leave to cool in the tin for 10 minutes, then carefully invert on to a plate. Serve warm or cold.

Apricot Loaf Cake

Makes one 900 g/2 lb loaf

225 g/8 oz/1 cup butter or margarine,
softened
225 g/8 oz/1 cup caster (superfine)
sugar
2 eggs, well beaten
6 ripe apricots, stoned (pitted),
skinned and mashed
300 g/11 oz/2¾ cups plain
(all-purpose) flour
5 ml/1 tsp bicarbonate of soda
(baking soda)
A pinch of salt
75 g/3 oz/¾ cup almonds, chopped

Cream together the butter or margarine and sugar. Gradually beat in the eggs, then stir in the apricots. Beat in the flour, bicarbonate of soda and salt. Stir in the nuts. Spoon into a greased and floured 900 g/2 lb loaf tin (pan) and bake in a preheated oven at 180°C/350°F/gas mark 4 for 1 hour until a skewer inserted in the centre comes out clean. Leave to cool in the tin before turning out.

Apricot and Ginger Cake

Makes one 18 cm/7 in cake

100 g/4 oz/1 cup self-raising
(self-rising) flour
100 g/4 oz/½ cup soft brown sugar
10 ml/2 tsp ground ginger
100 g/4 oz/½ cup butter or margarine,
softened
2 eggs, lightly beaten
100 g/4 oz/⅔ cup ready-to-eat dried
apricots, chopped
50 g/2 oz/⅓ cup raisins

Beat together the flour, sugar, ginger, butter or margarine and eggs to a soft mixture. Stir in the apricots and raisins. Spoon the mixture into a greased and lined 18 cm/7 in cake tin (pan) and bake in a preheated oven at 180°C/350°F/gas mark 4 for 30 minutes until a skewer inserted in the centre comes out clean.

Tipsy Apricot Cake

Makes one 20 cm/8 in cake

120 ml/4 fl oz/½ cup brandy or rum
120 ml/4 fl oz/½ cup orange juice
225 g/8 oz/1⅓ cups ready-to-eat dried
   apricots, chopped
100 g/4 oz/⅔ cup sultanas
   (golden raisins)
175 g/6 oz/¾ cup butter or margarine,
   softened
45 ml/3 tbsp clear honey
4 eggs, separated
175 g/6 oz/1½ cups self-raising
   (self-rising) flour
10 ml/2 tsp baking powder

Bring the brandy or rum and orange juice to the boil with the apricots and sultanas. Stir well, then remove from the heat and leave to stand until cool. Cream together the butter or margarine and honey, then gradually mix in the egg yolks. Fold in the flour and baking powder. Whisk the egg whites until stiff, then fold them gently into the mixture. Spoon into a greased and lined 20 cm/8 in cake tin and bake in a preheated oven at 180°C/350°F/gas mark 4 for 1 hour until a skewer inserted in the centre comes out clean. Leave to cool in the tin.

Banana Cake

Makes one 23 × 33 cm/
9 × 13 in cake

4 ripe bananas, mashed
2 eggs, lightly beaten
350 g/12 oz/1½ cups caster (superfine)
   sugar
120 ml/4 fl oz/½ cup oil
5 ml/1 tsp vanilla essence (extract)
50 g/2 oz/½ cup chopped mixed nuts
225 g/8 oz/2 cups plain
   (all-purpose) flour
10 ml/2 tsp bicarbonate of soda
   (baking soda)
5 ml/1 tsp salt

Cream together the bananas, eggs, sugar, oil and vanilla. Add the remaining ingredients and stir until just mixed. Spoon into a 23 × 33 cm/9 × 13 in cake tin (pan) and bake in a preheated oven at 180°C/350°F/gas mark 4 for 45 minutes until a skewer inserted in the centre comes out clean.

Crunchy-topped Banana Cake

Makes one 23 cm/9 in cake

100 g/4 oz/½ cup butter or margarine,
   softened
300 g/11 oz/1⅓ cups caster (superfine)
   sugar
2 eggs, lightly beaten
175 g/6 oz/1½ cups plain
   (all-purpose) flour
2.5 ml/½ tsp salt
1.5 ml/½ tsp grated nutmeg
5 ml/1 tsp bicarbonate of soda
   (baking soda)
75 ml/5 tbsp milk
A few drops of vanilla essence
   (extract)
4 bananas, mashed
For the topping:
50 g/2 oz/¼ cup demerara sugar
50 g/2 oz/2 cups cornflakes, crushed
2.5 ml/½ tsp ground cinnamon
25 g/1 oz/2 tbsp butter or margarine

Beat together the butter or margarine and sugar until light and fluffy. Gradually beat in the eggs, then fold in the flour, salt and nutmeg. Mix the bicarbonate of soda into the milk and vanilla essence and stir into the mixture with the bananas. Spoon into a greased and lined 23 cm/9 in square cake tin (pan).

To make the topping, mix together the sugar, cornflakes and cinnamon and rub in the butter or margarine. Sprinkle over the cake and bake in a preheated oven at 180°C/350°F/gas mark 4 for 45 minutes until firm to the touch.

Banana Sponge

Makes one 23 cm/9 in cake

*100 g/4 oz/½ cup butter or margarine,
softened*
*100 g/4 oz/½ cup caster (superfine)
sugar*
2 eggs, beaten
2 large ripe bananas, mashed
*225 g/8 oz/1 cup self-raising
(self-rising) flour*
45 ml/3 tbsp milk
For the filling and topping:
225 g/8 oz/1 cup cream cheese
*30 ml/2 tbsp soured (dairy sour)
cream*
100 g/4 oz dried banana chips

Cream together the butter or margarine and sugar until pale and fluffy. Gradually add the eggs, then stir in the bananas and flour. Mix in the milk until the mixture has a dropping consistency. Spoon into a greased and lined 23 cm/9 in cake tin and bake in a preheated oven at 180°C/350°F/gas mark 4 for about 30 minutes until a skewer inserted in the centre comes out clean. Turn out on to a wire rack and leave to cool, then cut in half horizontally.

To make the topping, beat together the cream cheese and soured cream and use half the mixture to sandwich together the two halves of the cake. Spread the remaining mixture on top and decorate with the banana chips.

High-fibre Banana Cake

Makes one 18 cm/7 in cake

*100 g/4 oz/½ cup butter or margarine,
softened*
50 g/2 oz/¼ cup soft brown sugar
2 eggs, lightly beaten
*100 g/4 oz/1 cup wholemeal
(wholewheat) flour*
10 ml/2 tsp baking powder
2 bananas, mashed
For the filling:
*225 g/8 oz/1 cup curd (smooth
cottage) cheese*
5 ml/1 tsp lemon juice
15 ml/1 tbsp clear honey
1 banana, sliced
*Icing (confectioners') sugar, sifted,
for dusting*

Cream together the butter or margarine and sugar until light and fluffy. Gradually beat in the eggs, then fold in the flour and baking powder. Gently stir in the bananas. Spoon the mixture into two greased and lined 18 cm/7 in cake tins (pans) and bake in a preheated oven for 30 minutes until firm to the touch. Leave to cool.

To make the filling, beat together the cream cheese, lemon juice and honey and spread over one of the cakes. Arrange the banana slices on top, then cover with the second cake. Serve dusted with icing sugar.

68

Banana and Lemon Cake

Makes one 18 cm/7 in cake

100 g/4 oz/½ cup butter or margarine,
  softened
175 g/6 oz/¾ cup caster (superfine)
  sugar
2 eggs, lightly beaten
225 g/8 oz/2 cups self-raising
  (self-rising) flour
2 bananas, mashed
For the filling and topping:
75 ml/5 tbsp lemon curd
2 bananas, sliced
45 ml/3 tbsp lemon juice
100 g/4 oz/⅔ cup icing (confectioners')
  sugar, sifted

Cream together the butter or margarine and sugar until light and fluffy.
Gradually beat in the eggs, beating well
after each addition, then fold in the flour
and bananas. Spoon the mixture into two
greased and lined 18 cm/7 in sandwich
tins and bake in a preheated oven at
180°C/350°F/gas mark 4 for 30 minutes.
Turn out and leave to cool.

Sandwich the cakes together with the
lemon curd and half the banana slices.
Sprinkle the remaining banana slices with
15 ml/1 tbsp of lemon juice. Mix the
remaining lemon juice with the icing
sugar to make a stiff icing (frosting).
Smooth the icing over the cake and
decorate with the banana slices.

Blender Banana Chocolate Cake

Makes one 20 cm/8 in cake

225 g/8 oz/2 cups self-raising
  (self-rising) flour
2.5 ml/½ tsp baking powder
40 g/1½ oz/3 tbsp drinking chocolate
  powder
2 eggs
60 ml/4 tbsp milk

150 g/5 oz/⅔ cup caster (superfine)
  sugar
100 g/4 oz/½ cup soft margarine
2 ripe bananas, chopped

Mix together the flour, baking powder
and drinking chocolate. Blend the
remaining ingredients in a blender or
food processor for about 20 seconds – the
mixture will look curdled. Pour into the
dry ingredients and mix well. Turn into a
greased and lined 20 cm/8 in cake tin and
bake in a preheated oven at 180°C/350°F/
gas mark 4 for about 1 hour until a skewer
inserted in the centre comes out clean.
Turn out on to a wire rack to cool.

Banana and Peanut Cake

Makes one 900 g/2 lb cake

275 g/10 oz/2½ cups plain
  (all-purpose) flour
225 g/8 oz/1 cup caster (superfine)
  sugar
100 g/4 oz/1 cup peanuts, finely
  chopped
15 ml/1 tbsp baking powder
A pinch of salt
2 eggs, separated
6 bananas, mashed
Grated rind and juice of 1 small
  lemon
50 g/2 oz/¼ cup butter or margarine,
  melted

Mix together the flour, sugar, nuts,
baking powder and salt. Beat the egg
yolks and stir them into the mixture with
the bananas, lemon rind and juice and
butter or margarine. Whisk the egg whites
until stiff, then fold into the mixture.
Spoon into a greased 900 g/2 lb loaf tin
(pan) and bake in a preheated oven at
180°C/350°F/gas mark 4 for 1 hour until a
skewer inserted in the centre comes out
clean.

All-in-one Banana and Raisin Cake

Makes one 900 g/2 lb cake

450 g/1 lb ripe bananas, mashed
50 g/2 oz/½ cup chopped mixed nuts
120 ml/4 fl oz/½ cup sunflower oil
100 g/4 oz/⅔ cup raisins
75 g/3 oz/¾ cup rolled oats
150 g/5 oz/1¼ cups wholemeal
   (wholewheat) flour
1.5 ml/¼ tsp almond essence (extract)
A pinch of salt

Mix together all the ingredients together to a soft, moist mixture. Spoon into a greased and lined 900 g/2 lb loaf tin (pan) and bake in a preheated oven at 190°C/375°F/gas mark 5 for 1 hour until golden brown and a skewer inserted in the centre comes out clean. Cool in the tin for 10 minutes before turning out.

Banana and Whisky Cake

Makes one 25 cm/10 in cake

225 g/8 oz/1 cup butter or margarine,
   softened
450 g/1 lb/2 cups soft brown sugar
3 ripe bananas, mashed
4 eggs, lightly beaten
175 g/6 oz/1½ cups pecan nuts,
   coarsely chopped
225 g/8 oz/1⅓ cups sultanas
   (golden raisins)
350g/12 oz/3 cups plain
   (all-purpose) flour
15 ml/1 tbsp baking powder
5 ml/1 tsp ground cinnamon
2.5 ml/½ tsp ground ginger
2.5 ml/½ tsp grated nutmeg
150 ml/¼ pint/⅔ cup whisky

Cream together the butter or margarine and sugar until light and fluffy.

Mix in the bananas, then gradually beat in the eggs. Mix the nuts and sultanas with a large spoonful of flour, then, in a separate bowl, mix the remaining flour with the baking powder and spices. Stir the flour into the creamed mixture alternately with the whisky. Fold in the nuts and sultanas. Spoon the mixture into an ungreased 25 cm/10 in cake tin (pan) and bake in a preheated oven at 180°C/350°F/gas mark 4 for 1¼ hours until springy to the touch. Leave to cool in the tin for 10 minutes before turning out on to a wire rack to finish cooling.

Blueberry Cake

Makes one 23 cm/9 in cake

175 g/6 oz/¾ cup caster (superfine)
   sugar
60 ml/4 tbsp oil
1 egg, lightly beaten
120 ml/4 fl oz/½ cup milk
225 g/8 oz/2 cups plain
   (all-purpose) flour
10 ml/2 tsp baking powder
2.5 ml/½ tsp salt
225 g/8 oz blueberries
For the topping:
50 g/2 oz/¼ cup butter or margarine,
   melted
100 g/4 oz/½ cup granulated sugar
50 g/2 oz/¼ cup plain (all-purpose)
   flour
2.5 ml/½ tsp ground cinnamon

Beat together the sugar, oil and egg until well blended and pale. Stir in the milk, then mix in the flour, baking powder and salt. Fold in the blueberries. Spoon the mixture into a greased and floured 23 cm/9 in cake tin. Mix together the topping ingredients and sprinkle over the mixture. Bake in a preheated oven at 190°C/375°F/gas mark 5 for 50 minutes until a skewer inserted in the centre comes out clean. Serve warm.

Cherry Cobblestone Cake

Makes one 900 g/2 lb cake

175 g/6 oz/³⁄₄ cup butter or margarine,
  softened
175 g/6 oz/³⁄₄ cup caster (superfine)
  sugar
3 eggs, beaten
225 g/8 oz/2 cups plain
  (all-purpose) flour
2.5 ml/½ tsp baking powder
100 g/4 oz/²⁄₃ cup sultanas (golden
  raisins)
150 g/5 oz/²⁄₃ cup glacé (candied)
  cherries, quartered
225 g/8 oz fresh cherries, stoned
  (pitted) and halved
30 ml/2 tbsp apricot jam (conserve)

Beat the butter or margarine until soft, then beat in the sugar. Mix in the eggs, then the flour, baking powder, sultanas and glacé cherries. Spoon into a greased 900 g/2 lb loaf tin (pan) and bake in a preheated oven at 160°C/325°F/gas mark 3 for 2½ hours. Leave in the tin for 5 minutes, then turn out on to a wire rack to finish cooling.

Arrange the cherries in a row on the top of the cake. Bring the apricot jam to the boil in a small pan, then sieve (strain) it and brush over the top of the cake to glaze.

Cherry and Coconut Cake

Makes one 20 cm/8 in cake

350 g/12 oz/3 cups self-raising
  (self-rising) flour
175 g/6 oz/³⁄₄ cup butter or margarine
225 g/8 oz/1 cup glacé (candied)
  cherries, quartered
100 g/4 oz/1 cup desiccated
  (shredded) coconut

175 g/6 oz/³⁄₄ cup caster (superfine)
  sugar
2 large eggs, lightly beaten
200 ml/7 fl oz/scant 1 cup milk

Place the flour in a bowl and rub in the butter or margarine until the mixture resembles breadcrumbs. Toss the cherries in the coconut, then add them to the mixture with the sugar and mix together lightly. Add the eggs and most of the milk. Beat well, adding extra milk if necessary to give a soft dropping consistency. Turn into a greased and lined 20 cm/8 in cake tin. Bake in a preheated oven at 180°C/350°F/gas mark 4 for 1½ hours until a skewer inserted in the centre comes out clean.

Cherry and Sultana Cake

Makes one 900 g/2 lb cake

100 g/4 oz/½ cup butter or margarine,
  softened
100 g/4 oz/½ cup caster (superfine)
  sugar
3 eggs, lightly beaten
100 g/4 oz/½ cup glacé (candied)
  cherries
350 g/12 oz/2 cups sultanas
  (golden raisins)
175 g/6 oz/1½ cups plain
  (all-purpose) flour
A pinch of salt

Cream together the butter or margarine and sugar until light and fluffy. Gradually add the eggs. Toss the cherries and sultanas in a little of the flour to coat, then fold the remaining flour into the mixture with the salt. Stir in the cherries and sultanas. Spoon the mixture into a greased and lined 900 g/2 lb loaf tin (pan) and bake in a preheated oven at 160°C/325°F/gas mark 3 for 1½ hours until a skewer inserted in the centre comes out clean.

Iced Cherry and Walnut Cake

Makes one 18 cm/7 in cake

*100 g/4 oz/½ cup butter or margarine,
  softened*
*100 g/4 oz/½ cup caster (superfine)
  sugar*
2 eggs, lightly beaten
15 ml/1 tbsp clear honey
*150 g/5 oz/1¼ cups self-raising
  (self-rising) flour*
5 ml/1 tsp baking powder
A pinch of salt
For the decoration:
*225 g/8 oz/1⅓ cups icing
  (confectioners') sugar, sifted*
30 ml/2 tbsp water
A few drops of red food colouring
4 glacé (candied) cherries, halved
4 walnut halves

Cream together the butter or margarine and sugar until light and fluffy. Gradually beat in the eggs and honey, then fold in the flour, baking powder and salt. Spoon the mixture into a greased and lined 18 cm/8 in cake tin (pan) and bake in a preheated oven at 190°C/375°F/gas mark 5 for 20 minutes until well risen and firm to the touch. Leave to cool.

Place the icing sugar in a bowl and gradually beat in enough of the water to make a spreadable icing (frosting). Spread most over the top of the cake. Colour the remaining icing with a few drops of food colour, adding a little more icing sugar if this makes the icing too thin. Pipe or trickle the red icing across the cake to divide it into wedges, then decorate with the glacé cherries and walnuts.

Damson Cake

Makes one 20 cm/8 in cake

*100 g/4 oz/½ cup butter or margarine,
  softened*
75 g/3 oz/⅓ cup soft brown sugar
2 eggs, lightly beaten
*225 g/8 oz/2 cups self-raising
  (self-rising) flour*
*450 g/1 lb damsons, stoned (pitted)
  and halved*
50 g/2 oz/½ cup chopped mixed nuts.

Cream together the butter or margarine and sugar until light and fluffy, then gradually add the eggs, beating well after each addition. Fold in the flour and the damsons. Spoon the mixture into a greased and lined 20 cm/8 in cake tin (pan) and sprinkle with the nuts. Bake in a preheated oven at 190°C/375°F/gas mark 5 for 45 minutes until firm to the touch. Allow to cool in the tin for 10 minutes before turning out on to a wire rack to finish cooling.

Date and Walnut Cake

Makes one 23 cm/9 in cake

300 ml/½ pt/1¼ cups boiling water
*225 g/8 oz/1⅓ cups dates, stoned
  (pitted) and chopped*
*5 ml/1 tsp bicarbonate of soda
  (baking soda)*
*75 g/3 oz/⅓ cup butter or margarine,
  softened*
*225 g/8 oz/1 cup caster (superfine)
  sugar*
1 egg, beaten
*275 g/10 oz/2½ cups plain
  (all-purpose) flour*
A pinch of salt
2.5 ml/½ tsp baking powder
50 g/2 oz/½ cup walnuts, chopped
For the topping:
50 g/2 oz/¼ cup soft brown sugar
25 g/1 oz/2 tbsp butter or margarine
30 ml/2 tbsp milk
A few walnut halves to decorate

Put the water, dates and bicarbonate of soda in a bowl and leave to stand for 5 minutes. Cream together the butter or margarine and sugar until soft, then stir in the egg with the water and dates. Mix together the flour, salt and baking powder, then fold into the mixture with the walnuts. Turn into a greased and lined 23 cm/9 in cake tin (pan) and bake in a preheated oven at 180°C/350°F/gas mark 4 for 1 hour until firm. Cool on a wire rack.

To make the topping, blend the sugar, butter and milk until smooth. Spread over the cake and decorate with the walnut halves.

Lemon Cake

Makes one 20 cm/8 in cake

175 g/6 oz/³⁄₄ cup butter or margarine, softened
175 g/6 oz/³⁄₄ cup caster (superfine) sugar
2 eggs, beaten
225 g/8 oz/2 cups self-raising (self-rising) flour
Juice and grated rind of 1 lemon
60 ml/4 tbsp milk

Cream together the butter or margarine and 100 g/4 oz/½ cup of the sugar. Add the eggs a little at a time, then fold in the flour and grated lemon rind. Stir in enough of the milk to give a soft consistency. Turn the mixture into a greased and lined 20 cm/8 in cake tin and bake in a preheated oven at 180°C/350°F/gas mark 4 for 1 hour until risen and golden. Dissolve the remaining sugar in the lemon juice. Prick the hot cake all over with a fork and pour over the juice mixture. Leave to cool.

Orange and Almond Cake

Makes one 20 cm/8 in cake

4 eggs, separated
100 g/4 oz/½ cup caster (superfine) sugar
Grated rind of 1 orange
50 g/2 oz/½ cup almonds, finely chopped
50 g/2 oz/½ cup ground almonds
For the syrup:
100 g/4 oz/½ cup caster (superfine) sugar
300 ml/½ pt/1¼ cups orange juice
15 ml/1 tbsp orange liqueur (optional)
1 cinnamon stick

Beat together the egg yolks, sugar, orange rind, almonds and ground almonds. Beat the egg whites until stiff, then fold them into the mixture. Spoon into a greased and floured 20 cm/8 in loose-bottomed cake tin (pan) and bake in a preheated oven at 180°C/350°F/gas mark 4 for 45 minutes until firm to the touch. Prick all over with a skewer and leave to cool.

Meanwhile, dissolve the sugar in the orange juice and liqueur, if using, over a low heat with the cinnamon stick, stirring occasionally. Bring to the boil and boil until reduced to a thin syrup. Discard the cinnamon. Spoon the warm syrup over the cake and leave to soak in.

Oaty Loaf Cake

Makes one 900 g/2 lb cake

100 g/4 oz/1 cup oatmeal
300 ml/½ pt/1¼ cups boiling water
100 g/4 oz/½ cup butter or margarine,
softened
225 g/8 oz/1 cup soft brown sugar
225 g/8 oz/1 cup caster (superfine)
sugar
2 eggs, lightly beaten
175 g/6 oz/1½ cups plain
(all-purpose) flour
10 ml/2 tsp baking powder
5 ml/1 tsp bicarbonate of soda
(baking soda)
5 ml/1 tsp ground cinnamon

Soak the oatmeal in the boiling water. Cream together the butter or margarine and sugars until light and fluffy. Gradually beat in the eggs, then fold in the flour, baking powder, bicarbonate of soda and cinnamon. Finally, fold in the oatmeal mixture and stir until well blended. Spoon into a greased and lined 900 g/2 lb loaf tin (pan) and bake in a preheated oven at 180°C/350°F/gas mark 4 for about 1 hour until firm to the touch.

Sharp Frosted Mandarin Cake

Makes one 20 cm/8 in cake

175 g/6 oz/¾ cup soft tub margarine
250 g/9 oz/generous 1 cup caster
(superfine) sugar
225 g/8 oz/2 cups self-raising (self-
rising) flour
5 ml/1 tsp baking powder
3 eggs
Finely grated rind and juice of 1 small
orange
300 g/11 oz/1 medium can of
mandarin oranges, well drained
Finely grated rind and juice of ½
lemon

Blend the margarine, 175 g/6 oz/¾ cup of the sugar, the flour, baking powder, eggs, orange rind and juice in a food processor or beat with an electric beater until smooth. Roughly chop the mandarins and fold in. Spoon into a greased and lined 20 cm/8 in cake tin (pan). Smooth the surface. Bake in a preheated oven at 180°C/350°F/gas mark 4 for 1 hour 10 minutes or until a skewer inserted in the centre comes out clean. Cool for 5 minutes, then remove from the tin and place on a wire rack. Meanwhile mix the remaining sugar with the lemon rind and juice to a paste. Spread over the top and leave to cool.

Orange Cake

Makes one 20 cm/8 in cake

175 g/6 oz/¾ cup butter or margarine,
softened
175 g/6 oz/¾ cup caster (superfine)
sugar
2 eggs, beaten
225 g/8 oz/2 cups self-raising
(self-rising) flour
Juice and grated rind of 1 orange
60 ml/4 tbsp milk

Cream together the butter or margarine and 100 g/4 oz/½ cup of the sugar. Add the eggs a little at a time, then fold in the flour and grated orange rind. Stir in enough milk to give a soft consistency. Turn the mixture into a greased and lined 20 cm/8 in cake tin (pan) and bake in a preheated oven at 180°C/350°F/gas mark 4 for 1 hour until risen and golden. Dissolve the remaining sugar in the orange juice. Prick the hot cake all over with a fork and pour over the juice mixture. Leave to cool.

Orange and Marsala Cake

Makes one 23 cm/9 in cake

175 g/6 oz/1 cup sultanas (golden raisins)
120 ml/4 fl oz/½ cup Marsala
175 g/6 oz/¾ cup butter or margarine, softened
100 g/4 oz/½ cup soft brown sugar
225 g/8 oz/1 cup caster (superfine) sugar
3 eggs, lightly beaten
Finely grated rind of 1 orange
5 ml/1 tsp orange flower water
275 g/10 oz/2½ cups plain (all-purpose) flour
10 ml/2 tsp bicarbonate of soda (baking soda)
A pinch of salt
375 ml/13 fl oz/1½ cups buttermilk
Orange Liqueur Icing (page 231)

Soak the sultanas in the Marsala overnight.
Cream together the butter or margarine and sugars until light and fluffy. Gradually beat in the eggs, then mix in the orange rind and orange flower water. Fold in the flour, bicarbonate of soda and salt alternately with the buttermilk. Stir in the soaked sultanas and Marsala. Spoon into two greased and lined 23 cm/9 in cake tins (pans) and bake in a preheated oven at 180°C/350°F/gas mark 4 for 35 minutes until springy to the touch and starting to shrink away from the sides of the tins. Leave to cool in the tins for 10 minutes before turning out on to a wire rack to finish cooling.
Sandwich the cakes together with half the orange liqueur icing, then spread the remaining icing on top.

Peach and Pear Cake

Makes one 23 cm/9 in cake

175 g/6 oz/¾ cup butter or margarine, softened
150 g/5 oz/⅔ cup caster (superfine) sugar
2 eggs, lightly beaten
75 g/3 oz/¾ cup wholemeal (wholewheat) flour
75 g/3 oz/¾ cup plain (all-purpose) flour
10 ml/2 tsp baking powder
15 ml/1 tbsp milk
2 peaches, stoned (pitted), skinned and chopped
2 pears, peeled, cored and chopped
30 ml/2 tbsp icing (confectioners') sugar, sifted

Cream together the butter or margarine and sugar until light and fluffy. Gradually beat in the eggs, then fold in the flours and baking powder, adding the milk to give the mixture a dropping consistency. Fold in the peaches and pears. Spoon the mixture into a greased and lined 23 cm/9 in cake tin (pan) and bake in a preheated oven at 190°C/375°F/gas mark 5 for 1 hour until well risen and springy to the touch. Leave to cool in the tin for 10 minutes before turning out on to a wire rack to finish cooling. Dust with icing sugar before serving.

Peach Cake

Makes one 23 cm/9 in cake

100 g/4 oz/½ cup butter or margarine, softened
225 g/8 oz/1 cup caster (superfine) sugar
3 eggs, separated
450 g/1 lb/4 cups plain (all-purpose) flour
A pinch of salt
5 ml/1 tsp bicarbonate of soda (baking soda)
120 ml/4 fl oz/½ cup milk
225 g/8 oz/⅔ cup peach jam (conserve)

Cream together the butter or margarine and sugar. Gradually beat in the egg yolks, then fold in the flour and salt. Mix the bicarbonate of soda with the milk, then mix into the cake mixture, followed by the jam. Whisk the egg whites until stiff, then fold into the mixture. Spoon in to two greased and lined 23 cm/9 in cake tins (pans) and bake in a preheated oven at 180°C/350°F/gas mark 4 for 25 minutes until well risen and springy to the touch.

Moist Pineapple Cake

Makes one 20 cm/8 in cake

100 g/4 oz/½ cup butter or margarine
350 g/12 oz/2 cups dried mixed fruit (fruit cake mix)
225 g/8 oz/1 cup soft brown sugar
5 ml/1 tsp ground mixed (apple-pie) spice
5 ml/1 tsp bicarbonate of soda (baking soda)
425 g/15 oz/1 large tin unsweetened crushed pineapple, drained
225 g/8 oz/2 cups self-raising (self-rising) flour
2 eggs, beaten

Place all the ingredients except the flour and eggs in a pan and heat gently to boiling point, stirring well. Boil steadily for 3 minutes, then allow the mixture to cool completely. Stir in the flour, then gradually stir in the eggs. Turn the mixture into a greased and lined 20 cm/8 in cake tin and bake in a preheated oven at 180°C/350°F/gas mark 4 for 1½–1¾ hours until well risen and firm to the touch. Allow to cool in the tin.

Pineapple and Cherry Cake

Makes one 20 cm/8 in cake

100 g/4 oz/½ cup butter or margarine, softened
100 g/4 oz/1 cup caster (superfine) sugar
2 eggs, beaten
225 g/8 oz/2 cups self-raising (self-rising) flour
2.5 ml/½ tsp baking powder
2.5 ml/½ tsp ground cinnamon
175 g/6 oz/1 cup sultanas (golden raisins)
25 g/1 oz/2 tbsp glacé (candied) cherries
400 g/14 oz/1 large can pineapple, drained and chopped
30 ml/2 tbsp brandy or rum
Icing (confectioners') sugar, sifted, for dusting

Cream together the butter or margarine and sugar until light and fluffy. Gradually beat in the eggs, then fold in the flour, baking powder and cinnamon. Gently stir in the remaining ingredients. Spoon the mixture into a greased and lined 20 cm/8 in cake tin (pan) and bake in a preheated oven at 160°C/325°F/gas mark 3 for 1½ hours until a skewer inserted in the centre comes out clean. Leave to cool, then serve dusted with icing sugar.

Natal Pineapple Cake

Makes one 23 cm/9 in cake

50 g/2 oz/¼ cup butter or margarine
100 g/4 oz/½ cup caster (superfine)
  sugar
1 egg, lightly beaten
150 g/5 oz/1¼ cups self-raising
  (self-rising) flour
A pinch of salt
120 ml/4 fl oz/½ cup milk
For the topping:
100 g/4 oz fresh or canned pineapple,
  coarsely grated
1 eating (dessert) apple, peeled, cored
  and coarsely grated
120 ml/4 fl oz/½ cup orange juice
15 ml/1 tbsp lemon juice
100 g/4 oz/½ cup caster (superfine)
  sugar
5 ml/1 tsp ground cinnamon

Melt the butter or margarine, then beat in the sugar and egg until frothy. Stir in the flour and salt alternately with the milk to make a batter. Spoon into a greased and lined 23 cm/9 in cake tin (pan) and bake in a preheated oven at 180°C/350°F/gas mark 4 for 25 minutes until golden and springy.

Bring all the topping ingredients to the boil, then simmer for 10 minutes. Spoon over the warm cake and grill (broil) until the pineapple begins to brown. Cool before serving warm or cold.

Pineapple Upside-down

Makes one 20 cm/8 in cake

175 g/6 oz/¾ cup butter or margarine,
  softened
175 g/6 oz/¾ cup soft brown sugar
400 g/14 oz/1 large can pineapple
  slices, drained and juice reserved
4 glacé (candied) cherries, halved
2 eggs
100 g/4 oz/1 cup self-raising
  (self-rising) flour

Cream 75 g/3 oz/⅓ cup of the butter or margarine with 75 g/3 oz/⅓ cup of the sugar until light and fluffy and spread over the base of a greased 20 cm/8 in cake tin (pan). Arrange the pineapple slices on top and dot with the cherries, rounded-side down. Cream together the remaining butter or margarine and sugar, then gradually beat in the eggs. Fold in the flour and 30 ml/2 tbsp of the reserved pineapple juice. Spoon over the pineapple and bake in a preheated oven at 180°C/350°F/gas mark 4 for 45 minutes until firm to the touch. Leave to cool in the tin for 5 minutes, then carefully remove from the tin and invert on to a wire rack to cool.

Pineapple and Walnut Cake

Makes one 23 cm/9 in cake

225 g/8 oz/1 cup butter or margarine,
  softened
225 g/8 oz/1 cup caster (superfine)
  sugar
5 eggs
350 g/12 oz/3 cups plain
  (all-purpose) flour
100 g/4 oz/1 cup walnuts, coarsely
  chopped
100 g/4 oz/⅔ cup glacé (candied)
  pineapple, chopped
A little milk

Cream together the butter or margarine and sugar until light and fluffy. Gradually beat in the eggs, then fold in the flour, nuts and pineapple, adding just enough milk to give a dropping consistency. Spoon into a greased and lined 23 cm/9 in cake tin (pan) and bake in a preheated oven at 150°C/300°F/ gas mark 2 for 1½ hours until a skewer inserted in the centre comes out clean.

Raspberry Cake

Makes one 20 cm/8 in cake

100 g/4 oz/½ cup butter or margarine,
 softened
200 g/7 oz/scant 1 cup caster
 (superfine) sugar
2 eggs, lightly beaten
250 ml/8 fl oz/1 cup soured
 (dairy sour) cream
5 ml/1 tsp vanilla essence (extract)
250 g/9 oz/2¼ cups plain
 (all-purpose) flour
5 ml/1 tsp baking powder
5 ml/1 tsp bicarbonate of soda
 (baking soda)
5 ml/1 tsp cocoa (unsweetened
 chocolate) powder
2.5 ml/½ tsp salt
100 g/4 oz fresh or thawed frozen
 raspberries
For the topping:
30 ml/2 tbsp caster (superfine) sugar
5 ml/1 tsp ground cinnamon

Cream together the butter or margarine and sugar. Gradually beat in the eggs, then the soured cream and vanilla essence. Fold in the flour, baking powder, bicarbonate of soda, cocoa and salt. Fold in the raspberries. Spoon into a greased 20 cm/8 in cake tin (pan). Mix together the sugar and cinnamon and sprinkle over the top of the cake. Bake in a preheated oven at 200°C/400°F/gas mark 4 for 35 minutes until golden brown and a skewer in the centre comes out clean. Sprinkle with the sugar mixed with the cinnamon.

Rhubarb Cake

Makes one 20 cm/8 in cake

225 g/8 oz/2 cups wholemeal
 (wholewheat) flour
10 ml/2 tsp baking powder
10 ml/2 tsp ground cinnamon
45 ml/3 tbsp clear honey
175 g/6 oz/1 cup sultanas
 (golden raisins)

2 eggs
150 ml/¼ pt/⅔ cup milk
225 g/8 oz rhubarb, chopped
30 ml/2 tbsp demerara sugar

Blend all the ingredients except the rhubarb and sugar. Stir in the rhubarb and spoon into a greased and floured 20 cm/8 in cake tin (pan). Sprinkle with the sugar. Bake in a preheated oven at 180°C/350°F/gas mark 4 for 45 minutes until firm. Leave to cool in the tin for 10 minutes before turning out.

Rhubarb-honey Cake

Makes two 450 g/1 lb cakes

250 g/9 oz/⅔ cup clear honey
120 ml/4 fl oz/½ cup oil
1 egg, lightly beaten
15 ml/1 tbsp bicarbonate of soda
 (baking soda)
150 ml/¼ pt/⅔ cup plain yoghurt
75 ml/5 tbsp water
350 g/12 oz/3 cups plain
 (all-purpose) flour
10 ml/2 tsp salt
350 g/12 oz rhubarb, finely chopped
5 ml/1 tsp vanilla essence (extract)
50 g/2 oz/½ cup chopped mixed nuts
For the topping:
75 g/3 oz/⅓ cup soft brown sugar
5 ml/1 tsp ground cinnamon
15 ml/1 tbsp butter or margarine,
 melted

Mix together the honey and oil, then beat in the egg. Mix the bicarbonate of soda into the yoghurt and water until dissolved. Mix the flour and salt and add to the honey mixture alternately with the yoghurt. Stir in the rhubarb, vanilla essence and nuts. Pour into two greased and lined 450 g/1 lb loaf tins (pans). Mix together the topping ingredients and sprinkle over the cakes. Bake in a preheated oven at 160°C/325°F/gas mark 3 for 1 hour until just firm to the touch and golden on top. Leave to cool in the tins for 10 minutes, then turn out on to a wire rack to finish cooling.

Vegetable and Nut Cakes

Carrot cake is usually the first to spring to mind when you think about making a cake with vegetables, and there are plenty of delicious variations here. But there are also lots of other vegetables that can be used to make interesting cakes.

Beetroot Cake

Makes one 20 cm/8 in cake

250 g/9 oz/1¼ cups plain
   (all-purpose) flour
15 ml/1 tbsp baking powder
5 ml/1 tsp ground cinnamon
A pinch of salt
150 ml/8 fl oz/1 cup oil
300 g/11 oz/1⅓ cups caster (superfine)
   sugar
3 eggs, separated
150 g/5 oz raw beetroot, peeled and
   coarsely grated
150 g/5 oz carrots, coarsely grated
100 g/4 oz/1 cup chopped mixed nuts

Mix together the flour, baking powder, cinnamon and salt. Beat in the oil and sugar. Beat in the eggs yolks, beetroot, carrots and nuts. Whisk the egg whites until stiff, then fold into the mixture using a metal spoon. Spoon the mixture into a greased and lined 20 cm/8 in cake tin (pan) and bake in a preheated oven at 180°C/350°F/gas mark 4 for 1 hour until springy to the touch.

Carrot and Banana Cake

Makes one 20 cm/8 in cake

175 g/6 oz carrots, grated
2 bananas, mashed
75 g/3 oz/½ cup sultanas (golden
   raisins)
50 g/2 oz/½ cup chopped mixed nuts
175 g/6 oz/1½ cups self-raising
   (self-rising) flour
5 ml/1 tsp baking powder
5 ml/1 tsp ground mixed (apple-pie)
   spice
Juice and grated rind of 1 orange
2 eggs, beaten
75 g/3 oz/½ cup light muscovado sugar
100 ml/3½ fl oz/scant ½ cup sunflower
   oil

Mix together all the ingredients until well blended. Spoon into a greased and lined 20 cm/8 in cake tin (pan) and bake in a preheated oven at 180°C/350°F/ gas mark 4 for 1 hour until a skewer inserted in the centre comes out clean.

Carrot and Apple Cake

Makes one 23 cm/9 in cake

250 g/9 oz/2¼ cups self-raising
(self-rising) flour
5 ml/1 tsp bicarbonate of soda
(baking soda)
5 ml/1 tsp ground cinnamon
175 g/6 oz/¾ cup soft brown sugar
Finely grated rind of 1 orange
3 eggs
200 ml/7 fl oz/scant 1 cup oil
150 g/5 oz eating (dessert) apples,
peeled, cored and grated
150 g/5 oz carrots, grated
100 g/4 oz/⅔ cup ready-to-eat dried
apricots, chopped
100 g/4 oz/1 cup pecan nuts or
walnuts, chopped

Mix together the flour, bicarbonate of soda and cinnamon, then stir in the sugar and orange rind. Beat the eggs into the oil, then stir in the apple, carrots and two-thirds of the apricots and nuts. Fold in the flour mixture and spoon into a greased and lined 23 cm/9 in cake tin (pan). Sprinkle with the remaining chopped apricots and nuts. Bake in a preheated oven at 180°C/350°F/gas mark 4 for 30 minutes until springy to the touch. Leave to cool slightly in the tin, then turn out on to a wire rack to finish cooling.

Carrot and Cinnamon Cake

Makes one 20 cm/8 in cake

100 g/4 oz/1 cup wholemeal
(wholewheat) flour
100 g/4 oz/1 cup plain (all-purpose)
flour
15 ml/1 tbsp ground cinnamon
5 ml/1 tsp grated nutmeg
10 ml/2 tsp baking powder
100 g/4 oz/½ cup butter or margarine
100 g/4 oz/⅓ cup clear honey
100 g/4 oz/½ cup soft brown sugar
225 g/8 oz carrots, grated

Mix together the flours, cinnamon, nutmeg and baking powder in a bowl. Melt the butter or margarine with the honey and sugar, then mix into the flour. Stir in the carrots and combine well. Spoon into a greased and lined 20 cm/8 in cake tin (pan) and bake in a preheated oven at 160°C/325°F/gas mark 3 for 1 hour until a skewer inserted in the centre comes out clean. Leave to cool in the tin for 10 minutes, then turn out on to a wire rack to finish cooling.

Carrot and Courgette Cake

Makes one 23 cm/9 in cake

2 eggs
175 g/6 oz/¾ cup soft brown sugar
100 g/4 oz carrots, grated
50 g/2 oz courgettes (zucchini), grated
75 ml/5 tbsp oil
225 g/8 oz/2 cups self-raising
(self-rising) flour
2.5 ml/½ tsp baking powder
5 ml/1 tsp ground mixed (apple-pie)
spice
Cream Cheese Icing (page 230)

Mix together the eggs, sugar, carrots, courgettes and oil. Stir in the flour, baking powder and mixed spice and mix to a smooth batter. Spoon into a greased and lined 23 cm/9 in cake tin (pan) and bake in a preheated oven at 180°C/350°F/gas mark 4 for 30 minutes until a skewer inserted in the centre comes out clean. Leave to cool, then spread with cream cheese icing.

Carrot and Ginger Cake

Makes one 20 cm/8 in cake

175 g/6 oz/³⁄₄ cup butter or margarine
100 g/4 oz/¹⁄₃ cup golden (light corn)
  syrup
120 ml/4 fl oz/¹⁄₂ cup water
100 g/4 oz/¹⁄₂ cup soft brown sugar
150 g/5 oz carrots, coarsely grated
5 ml/1 tsp bicarbonate of soda
  (baking soda)
200 g/7 oz/1³⁄₄ cups plain
  (all-purpose) flour
100 g/4 oz/1 cup self-raising
  (self-rising) flour
5 ml/1 tsp ground ginger
A pinch of salt
For the icing (frosting):
175 g/6 oz/1 cup icing (confectioners')
  sugar, sifted
5 ml/1 tsp butter or margarine,
  softened
30 ml/2 tbsp lemon juice

Melt the butter or margarine with the syrup, water and sugar, then bring to the boil. Remove from the heat and stir in the carrots and bicarbonate of soda. Leave to cool. Mix in the flours, ginger and salt, spoon into a greased 20 cm/8 in cake tin (pan) and bake in a preheated oven at 180°C/350°F/gas mark 4 for 45 minutes until well risen and springy to the touch. Turn out and leave to cool.

Mix the icing sugar with the butter or margarine and enough lemon juice to make a spreadable icing. Cut the cake in half horizontally, then use half the icing to sandwich the cake together and pipe or spread the remainder on top.

Carrot and Nut Cake

Makes one 18 cm/7 in cake

2 large eggs, separated
150 g/5 oz/²⁄₃ cup caster (superfine)
  sugar
225 g/8 oz carrots, grated
150 g/5 oz/1¹⁄₄ cups chopped mixed
  nuts
10 ml/2 tsp grated lemon rind
50 g/2 oz/¹⁄₂ cup plain (all-purpose)
  flour
2.5 ml/¹⁄₂ tsp baking powder

Whisk together the egg yolks and sugar until thick and creamy. Stir in the carrots, nuts and lemon rind, then fold in the flour and baking powder. Whisk the egg whites until they form soft peaks, then fold into the mixture. Turn into a greased 19 cm/7 in square cake tin (pan). Bake in a preheated oven at 180°C/350°F/gas mark 4 for 40–45 minutes until a skewer inserted into the centre comes out clean.

Carrot, Orange and Nut Cake

Makes one 20 cm/8 in cake

100 g/4 oz/¹⁄₂ cup butter or margarine,
  softened
100 g/4 oz/¹⁄₂ cup soft brown sugar
5 ml/1 tsp ground cinnamon
5 ml/1 tsp grated orange rind
2 eggs, lightly beaten
15 ml/1 tbsp orange juice
100 g/4 oz carrots, finely grated
50 g/2 oz/¹⁄₂ cup chopped mixed nuts
225 g/8 oz/2 cups self-raising
  (self-rising) flour
5 ml/1 tsp baking powder

Cream together the butter or margarine, sugar, cinnamon and orange rind until light and fluffy. Gradually beat in the eggs and orange juice, then fold in the carrots, nuts, flour and baking powder. Spoon into a greased and lined 20 cm/8 in cake tin (pan) and bake in a preheated oven at 180°C/350°F/gas mark 4 for 45 minutes until springy to the touch.

Carrot, Pineapple and Coconut Cake

Makes one 25 cm/10 in cake

3 eggs
350 g/12 oz/1½ cups caster (superfine)
sugar
300 ml/½ pt/1¼ cups oil
5 ml/1 tsp vanilla essence (extract)
225 g/8 oz/2 cups plain
(all-purpose) flour
5 ml/1 tsp bicarbonate of soda
(baking soda)
10 ml/2 tsp ground cinnamon
5 ml/1 tsp salt
225 g/8 oz carrots, grated
100 g/4 oz canned pineapple, drained
and crushed
100 g/4 oz/1 cup desiccated
(shredded) coconut
100 g/4 oz/1 cup chopped mixed nuts
Icing (confectioners') sugar, sifted,
for sprinkling

Beat together the eggs, sugar, oil and vanilla essence. Mix together the flour, bicarbonate of soda, cinnamon and salt and gradually beat into the mixture. Fold in the carrots, pineapple, coconut and nuts. Spoon into a greased and floured 25 cm/10 in cake tin (pan) and bake in a preheated oven at 160°C/325°F/gas mark 3 for 1¼ hours until a skewer inserted in the centre comes out clean. Leave to cool in the tin for 10 minutes before turning out on to a wire rack to finish cooling. Sprinkle with icing sugar before serving.

Carrot and Pistachio Cake

Makes one 23 cm/9 in cake

100 g/4 oz/½ cup butter or margarine,
softened
100 g/4 oz/½ cup caster (superfine)
sugar
2 eggs
225 g/8 oz/2 cups plain
(all-purpose) flour
5 ml/1 tsp bicarbonate of soda
(baking soda)
5 ml/1 tsp ground cardamom
225 g/8 oz carrots, grated
50 g/2 oz/½ cup pistachio nuts,
chopped
50 g/2 oz/½ cup ground almonds
100 g/4 oz/⅔ cup sultanas
(golden raisins)

Cream together the butter or margarine and sugar until light and fluffy. Gradually beat in the eggs, beating well after each addition, then fold in the flour, bicarbonate of soda and cardamom. Stir in the carrots, nuts, ground almonds and raisins. Spoon the mixture into a greased and lined 23 cm/9 in cake tin (pan) and bake in a preheated oven at 180°C/350°F/gas mark 4 for 40 minutes until well risen, golden and springy to the touch.

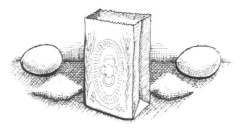

Carrot and Walnut Cake

Makes one 23 cm/9 in cake

200 ml/7 fl oz/scant 1 cup oil
4 eggs
225 g/8 oz/⅔ cup clear honey
225 g/8 oz/2 cups wholemeal
(wholewheat) flour
10 ml/2 tsp baking powder
2.5 ml/½ tsp bicarbonate of soda
(baking soda)
A pinch of salt
5 ml/1 tsp vanilla essence (extract)
175 g/6 oz carrots, coarsely grated
175 g/6 oz/1 cup raisins
100 g/4 oz/1 cup walnuts, finely
chopped

Blend together the oil, eggs and honey. Gradually mix in all the remaining ingredients and beat until well blended. Spoon into a greased and floured 23 cm/ 9 in cake tin (pan) and bake in a preheated oven at 180°C/350°F/gas mark 4 for 1 hour until a skewer inserted in the centre comes out clean.

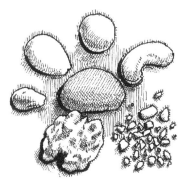

Spiced Carrot Cake

Makes one 18 cm/7 in cake

175 g/6 oz/1 cup dates
120 ml/4 fl oz/½ cup water
175 g/6 oz/¾ cup butter or margarine,
softened
2 eggs, lightly beaten
225 g/8 oz/2 cups self-raising
(self-rising) flour
175 g/6 oz carrots, finely grated
25 g/1 oz/¼ cup ground almonds
Grated rind of 1 orange
2.5 ml/½ tsp ground mixed
(apple-pie) spice
2.5 ml/½ tsp ground cinnamon
2.5 ml/½ tsp ground ginger
For the icing (frosting):
350 g/12 oz/1½ cups quark
25 g/1 oz/2 tbsp butter or margarine,
softened
Grated rind of 1 orange

Place the dates and water in a small pan, bring to the boil, then simmer for 10 minutes until soft. Remove and discard the stones (pits), then chop the dates finely. Mix together the dates and the liquid, the butter or margarine and the eggs until creamy. Fold in all the remaining cake ingredients. Spoon the mixture into a greased and lined 18 cm/7 in cake tin (pan) and bake in a preheated oven at 180°C/350°F/gas mark 4 for 1 hour until a skewer inserted in the centre comes out clean. Leave to cool in the tin for 10 minutes before turning out on to a wire rack to finish cooling.

To make the icing, beat together all the ingredients until you have a spreadable consistency, adding a little more orange juice or water if necessary. Slice the cake in half horizontally, sandwich the layers together with half the icing and spread the remainder on top.

Carrot and Brown Sugar Cake

Makes one 18 cm/7 in cake

5 eggs, separated
200 g/7 oz/scant 1 cup soft brown
  sugar
15 ml/1 tbsp lemon juice
300 g/10 oz carrots, grated
225 g/8 oz/2 cups ground almonds
25 g/1 oz/¼ cup wholemeal
  (wholewheat) flour
5 ml/1 tsp ground cinnamon
25 g/1 oz/2 tbsp butter or margarine,
  melted
25 g/1 oz/2 tbsp caster (superfine)
  sugar
30 ml/2 tbsp single (light) cream
75 g/3 oz/¾ cup chopped mixed nuts

Beat the egg yolks until frothy, beat in the sugar until smooth, then beat in the lemon juice. Stir in one-third of the carrots, then one-third of the almonds and continue in this way until they are all combined. Stir in the flour and cinnamon. Whisk the egg whites until stiff, then fold them into the mixture using a metal spoon. Turn into a greased and lined deep 18 cm/7 in cake tin (pan) and bake in a preheated oven at 180°C/350°F/gas mark 4 for 1 hour. Cover the cake loosely with greaseproof (waxed) paper and reduce the oven temperature to 160°C/325°F/gas mark 3 for a further 15 minutes or until the cake shrinks slightly from the sides of the tin and the centre is still moist. Leave the cake in the tin until just warm, then turn out to finish cooling.

Combine the melted butter or margarine, sugar, cream and nuts, pour over the cake and cook under a medium grill (broiler) until golden brown.

Courgette and Marrow Cake

Makes one 20 cm/8 in cake

225 g/8 oz/1 cup caster (superfine)
  sugar
2 eggs, beaten
120 ml/4 fl oz/½ cup oil
100 g/4 oz/1 cup plain (all-purpose)
  flour
5 ml/1 tsp baking powder
2.5 ml/½ tsp bicarbonate of soda
  (baking soda)
2.5 ml/½ tsp salt
100 g/4 oz courgettes (zucchini),
  grated
100 g/4 oz crushed pineapple
50 g/2 oz/½ cup walnuts, chopped
5 ml/1 tsp vanilla essence (extract)

Beat together the sugar and eggs until pale and well blended. Beat in the oil and then the dry ingredients. Stir in the courgettes, pineapple, walnuts and vanilla essence. Spoon into a greased and floured 20 cm/8 in cake tin (pan) and bake in a preheated oven at 180°C/350°F/gas mark 4 for 1 hour until a skewer inserted in the centre comes out clean. Leave to cool in the tin for 30 minutes before turning out on to a wire rack to finish cooling.

Courgette and Orange Cake

Makes one 25 cm/10 in cake

225 g/8 oz/1 cup butter or margarine,
  softened
450 g/1 lb/2 cups soft brown sugar
4 eggs, lightly beaten
275 g/10 oz/2½ cups plain
  (all-purpose) flour
15 ml/1 tbsp baking powder
2.5 ml/½ tsp salt
5 ml/1 tsp ground cinnamon
2.5 ml/½ tsp grated nutmeg
A pinch of ground cloves
Grated rind and juice of 1 orange
225 g/8 oz/2 cups courgettes
  (zucchini), grated

Cream together the butter or margarine and sugar until light and fluffy. Gradually beat in the eggs, then fold in the flour, baking powder, salt and spices alternately with the orange rind and juice. Stir in the courgettes. Spoon into a greased and lined 25 cm/10 in cake tin (pan) and bake in a preheated oven at 180°C/350°F/gas mark 4 for 1 hour until golden brown and springy to the touch. If the top begins to over-brown towards the end of baking, cover with greaseproof (waxed) paper.

Spiced Courgette Cake

Makes one 25 cm/10 in cake

350 g/12 oz/3 cups plain
  (all-purpose) flour
10 ml/2 tsp baking powder
7.5 ml/1½ tsp ground cinnamon
5 ml/1 tsp bicarbonate of soda
  (baking soda)
2.5 ml/½ tsp salt
8 egg whites
450 g/1 lb/2 cups caster (superfine)
  sugar
100 g/4 oz/1 cup apple purée (sauce)
120 ml/4 fl oz/½ cup buttermilk
15 ml/1 tbsp vanilla essence (extract)
5 ml/1 tsp finely grated orange rind
350 g/12 oz/3 cups courgettes
  (zucchini), grated
75 g/3 oz/¾ cup walnuts, chopped
For the topping:
100 g/4 oz/½ cup cream cheese
25 g/1 oz/2 tbsp butter or margarine,
  softened
5 ml/1 tsp finely grated orange rind
10 ml/2 tsp orange juice
350 g/12 oz/2 cups icing
  (confectioners') sugar, sifted

Mix together the dry ingredients. Beat the egg whites until they form soft peaks. Slowly beat in the sugar, then the apple purée, buttermilk, vanilla essence and orange rind. Fold in the flour mixture, then the courgettes and walnuts. Spoon into a greased and floured 25 cm/10 in cake tin (pan) and bake in a preheated oven at 150°C/300°F/gas mark 2 for 1 hour until a skewer inserted in the centre comes out clean. Leave to cool in the tin.

Beat together all the topping ingredients until smooth, adding enough sugar to make a spreadable consistency. Spread over the cooled cake.

Pumpkin Cake

Makes one 23 × 33 cm/
9 × 13 in cake

450 g/1 lb/2 cups caster (superfine)
  sugar
4 eggs, beaten
375 ml/13 fl oz/1½ cups oil
350 g/12 oz/3 cups plain
  (all-purpose) flour
15 ml/1 tbsp baking powder
10 ml/2 tsp bicarbonate of soda
  (baking soda)
10 ml/2 tsp ground cinnamon
2.5 ml/½ tsp ground ginger
A pinch of salt
225 g/8 oz diced cooked pumpkin
100 g/4 oz/1 cup walnuts, chopped

Beat together the sugar and eggs until well blended, then beat in the oil. Mix in the remaining ingredients. Spoon into a greased and floured 23 × 33 cm/ 9 × 13 in baking tin (pan) and bake in a preheated oven at 180°C/350°F/gas mark 4 for 1 hour until a skewer inserted in the centre comes out clean.

Fruited Pumpkin Cake

Makes one 20 cm/8 in cake

100 g/4 oz/½ cup butter or margarine,
softened
150 g/5 oz/⅔ cup soft brown sugar
2 eggs, lightly beaten
225 g/8 oz cold cooked pumpkin
30 ml/2 tbsp golden (light corn) syrup
225 g/8 oz 1/⅓ cups dried mixed fruit
(fruit cake mix)
225 g/8 oz/2 cups self-raising
(self-rising) flour
50 g/2 oz/½ cup bran

Cream together the butter or margarine and sugar until light and fluffy.
Gradually beat in the eggs, then fold in the
remaining ingredients. Spoon into a
greased and lined 20 cm/8 in cake tin
(pan) and bake in a preheated oven
at 160°C/325°F/gas mark 3 for 1¼ hours
until a skewer inserted in the centre
comes out clean.

Spiced Pumpkin Roll

Makes one 30 cm/12 in roll

75 g/3 oz/¾ cup plain (all-purpose)
flour
5 ml/1 tsp bicarbonate of soda
(baking soda)
5 ml/1 tsp ground ginger
2.5 ml/½ tsp grated nutmeg
10 ml/2 tsp ground cinnamon
A pinch of salt
1 egg
225 g/8 oz/1 cup caster (superfine)
sugar
100 g/4 oz cooked pumpkin, diced
5 ml/1 tsp lemon juice
4 egg whites
50 g/2 oz/½ cup walnuts, chopped
50 g/2 oz/⅓ cup icing (confectioners')
sugar, sifted
For the filling:
175 g/6 oz/1 cup icing (confectioners')
sugar, sifted

100 g/4 oz/½ cup cream cheese
2.5 ml/½ tsp vanilla essence (extract)

Mix together the flour, bicarbonate of
soda, spices and salt. Beat the egg
until thick and pale, then beat in the sugar
until the mixture is pale and creamy. Stir
in the pumpkin and lemon juice. Fold in
the flour mixture. In a clean bowl, beat
the egg whites until stiff. Fold into the
cake mix and spread in a greased and
lined 30 × 12 cm/12 × 8 in Swiss roll tin
(jelly roll pan) and sprinkle the walnuts
over the top. Bake in a preheated oven at
190°C/375°F/gas mark 5 for 10 minutes
until springy to the touch. Sift the icing
sugar over a clean tea towel (dish cloth)
and turn the cake out on to the towel.
Remove the lining paper and roll up the
cake and towel, then leave to cool.

To make the filling, gradually beat the
sugar into the cream cheese and vanilla
essence until you have a spreadable
mixture. Unroll the cake and spread the
filling over the top. Roll up the cake again
and chill before serving sprinkled with a
little more icing sugar.

Rhubarb and Honey Cake

Makes two 450 g/1 lb cakes

250 g/9 oz/¾ cup clear honey
100 ml/4 fl oz/½ cup oil
1 egg
5 ml/1 tsp bicarbonate of soda
(baking soda)
60 ml/4 tbsp water
350 g/12 oz/3 cups wholemeal
(wholewheat) flour
10 ml/2 tsp salt
350 g/12 oz rhubarb, finely chopped
5 ml/1 tsp vanilla essence (extract)
50 g/2 oz/½ cup chopped mixed nuts
(optional)
For the topping:
75 g/3 oz/⅓ cup muscovado sugar
5 ml/1 tsp ground cinnamon
15 g/½ oz/1 tbsp butter or margarine,
softened

Mix together the honey and oil. Add the egg and beat well. Add the bicarbonate of soda to the water and leave to dissolve. Mix together the flour and salt. Add to the honey mixture alternately with the bicarbonate of soda mixture. Stir in the rhubarb, vanilla essence and nuts, if using. Pour into two greased 450 g/1 lb loaf tins (pans). Mix together the topping ingredients and spread over the cake mixture. Bake in a preheated oven at 180°C/350°F/gas mark 4 for 1 hour until springy to the touch.

Sweet Potato Cake

Makes one 23 cm/9 in cake

300 g/11 oz/2¾ cups plain (all-purpose) flour
15 ml/1 tbsp baking powder
5 ml/1 tsp ground cinnamon
5 ml/1 tsp grated nutmeg
A pinch of salt
350 g/12 oz/1¾ cups caster (superfine) sugar
375 ml/13 fl oz/1½ cups oil
60 ml/4 tbsp boiled water
4 eggs, separated
225 g/8 oz sweet potatoes, peeled and coarsely grated
100 g/4 oz/1 cup chopped mixed nuts
5 ml/1 tsp vanilla essence (extract)
For the icing (frosting):
225 g/8 oz/1⅓ cups icing (confectioners') sugar, sifted
50 g/2 oz/¼ cup butter or margarine, softened
250 g/9 oz/1 medium tub cream cheese
50 g/2 oz/½ cup chopped mixed nuts
A pinch of ground cinnamon for sprinkling

Mix together the flour, baking powder, cinnamon, nutmeg and salt. Beat together the sugar and oil, then add the boiling water and beat until well blended. Add the egg yolks and flour mixture and mix until well blended. Stir in the sweet potatoes, nuts and vanilla essence. Beat the egg whites until stiff, then fold into the mixture. Spoon into two greased and floured 23 cm/9 in cake tins (pans) and bake in a preheated oven at 180°C/350°F/gas mark 4 for 40 minutes until springy to the touch. Leave to cool in the tins for 5 minutes, then turn out on to a wire rack to finish cooling.

Mix together the icing sugar, butter or margarine and half the cream cheese. Spread half the remaining cream cheese over one cake, then spread the icing over the cheese. Sandwich the cakes together. Spread the remaining cream cheese over the top and sprinkle the nuts and cinnamon over the top before serving.

Italian Almond Cake

Makes one 20 cm/8 in cake

1 egg
150 ml/¼ pt/⅔ cup milk
2.5 ml/½ tsp almond essence (extract)
45 ml/3 tbsp butter, melted
350 g/12 oz/3 cups plain (all-purpose) flour
100 g/4 oz/½ cup caster (superfine) sugar
10 ml/2 tsp baking powder
2.5 ml/½ tsp salt
1 egg white
100 g/4 oz/1 cup almonds, chopped

Beat the egg in a bowl, then gradually add the milk, almond essence and melted butter, beating all the time. Add the flour, sugar, baking powder and salt and continue mixing until smooth. Spoon in to a greased and lined 20 cm/8 in cake tin (pan). Whisk the egg white until frothy, then brush generously over the top of the cake and sprinkle with the almonds. Bake in a preheated oven at 220°C/425°F/gas mark 7 for 25 minutes until golden brown and springy to the touch.

Almond and Coffee Torte

Makes one 23 cm/9 in cake

8 eggs, separated
175 g/6 oz/¾ cup caster (superfine)
  sugar
60 ml/4 tbsp strong black coffee
175 g/6 oz/1½ cups ground almonds
45 ml/3 tbsp semolina (cream of
  wheat)
100 g/4 oz/1 cup plain
  (all-purpose) flour

Beat the egg yolks and sugar until very
thick and creamy. Add the coffee,
ground almonds and semolina and beat
well. Fold in the flour. Beat the egg whites
until stiff, then fold into the mixture.
Spoon into a greased 23 cm/9 in cake tin
(pan) and bake in a preheated oven at
180°C/350°F/gas mark 4 for 45 minutes
until springy to the touch.

Almond and Honey Cake

Makes one 20 cm/8 in cake

225 g/8 oz carrots, grated
75 g/3 oz/¾ cup almonds, chopped
2 eggs, beaten
100 ml/4 fl oz/½ cup clear honey
60 ml/4 tbsp oil
150 ml/¼ pt/⅔ cup milk
150 g/5 oz/1¼ cups wholemeal
  (wholewheat) flour
10 ml/2 tsp salt
10 ml/2 tsp bicarbonate of soda
  (baking soda)
15 ml/1 tbsp ground cinnamon

Mix together the carrots and nuts.
Beat the eggs with the honey, oil and
milk, then stir into the carrot mixture.
Mix together the flour, salt, bicarbonate of
soda and cinnamon and stir into the
carrot mixture. Spoon the mixture into a
greased and lined 20 cm/8 in square cake
tin (pan) and bake in a preheated oven at
150°C/300°F/gas mark 2 for 1¼ hours

until a skewer inserted in the centre
comes out clean. Leave to cool in the tin
for 10 minutes before turning out.

Almond and Lemon Cake

Makes one 23 cm/9 in cake

25 g/1 oz/¼ cup flaked (slivered)
  almonds
100 g/4 oz/½ cup butter or margarine,
  softened
100 g/4 oz/½ cup soft brown sugar
2 eggs, beaten
100 g/4 oz/1 cup self-raising
  (self-rising) flour
Grated rind of 1 lemon
For the syrup:
75 g/3 oz/⅓ cup caster (superfine)
  sugar
45–60 ml/3–4 tbsp lemon juice

Grease and line a 23 cm/9 in cake tin
(pan) and sprinkle the almonds over
the base. Cream together the butter and
brown sugar. Beat in the eggs one at a
time, then fold in the flour and lemon
rind. Spoon into the prepared tin and
level the surface. Bake in a preheated oven
at 180°C/350°F/gas mark 4 for 20–25
minutes until well risen and springy to
the touch.
Meanwhile, heat the caster sugar and
lemon juice in a pan, stirring occasionally,
until the sugar has dissolved. Remove the
cake from the oven and leave to cool for
2 minutes, then turn out on to a wire rack
with the base uppermost. Spoon over the
syrup, then leave to cool completely.

Almond Cake with Orange

Makes one 20 cm/8 in cake

225 g/8 oz/1 cup butter or margarine, softened
225 g/8 oz/1 cup caster (superfine) sugar
4 eggs, separated
225 g/8 oz/2 cups plain (all-purpose) flour
10 ml/2 tsp baking powder
50 g/2 oz/½ cup ground almonds
5 ml/1 tsp grated orange rind

Cream together the butter or margarine and sugar until light and fluffy. Beat in the egg yolks, then fold in the flour, baking powder, ground almonds and orange rind. Whisk the egg whites until stiff, then fold into the mixture using a metal spoon. Spoon into a greased and lined 20 cm/8 in cake tin (pan) and bake in a preheated oven at 180°C/350°F/gas mark 4 for 1 hour until a skewer inserted in the centre comes out clean.

Rich Almond Cake

Makes one 18 cm/7 in cake

100 g/4 oz/½ cup butter or margarine, softened
150 g/5 oz/⅔ cup caster (superfine) sugar
3 eggs, lightly beaten
75 g/3 oz/¾ cup ground almonds
50 g/2 oz/½ cup plain (all-purpose) flour
A few drops of almond essence (extract)

Cream together the butter or margarine and sugar until light and fluffy. Gradually beat in the eggs, then fold in the ground almonds, flour and almond essence. Spoon into a greased and lined 18 cm/7 in cake tin (pan) and bake in a preheated oven at 180°C/350°F/gas mark 4 for 45 minutes until springy to the touch.

Swedish Macaroon Cake

Makes one 23 cm/9 in cake

100 g/4 oz/1 cup ground almonds
75 g/3 oz/⅓ cup granulated sugar
5 ml/1 tsp baking powder
2 large egg whites, whisked

Mix together the almonds, sugar and baking powder. Stir in the egg whites until the mixture is thick and smooth. Spoon into a greased and lined 23 cm/9 in sandwich tin (pan) and bake in a preheated oven at 160°C/325°F/gas mark 3 for 20–25 minutes until risen and golden. Turn out very carefully from the tin as the cake is fragile.

Coconut Loaf

Makes one 450 g/1 lb loaf

100 g/4 oz/1 cup self-raising (self-rising) flour
225 g/8 oz/1 cup caster (superfine) sugar
100 g/4 oz/1 cup desiccated (shredded) coconut
1 egg
120 ml/4 fl oz/½ cup milk
A pinch of salt

Mix all the ingredients together well and spoon into a greased and lined 450 g/1 lb loaf tin (pan). Bake in a preheated oven at 180°C/350°F/gas mark 4 for about 1 hour until golden and springy to the touch.

89

Coconut Cake

Makes one 23 cm/9 in cake

75 g/3 oz/⅓ cup butter or margarine
150 ml/¼ pt/⅔ cup milk
2 eggs, lightly beaten
225 g/8 oz/1 cup caster (superfine)
    sugar
150 g/5 oz/1¼ cups self-raising
    (self-rising) flour
A pinch of salt
    For the topping:
100 g/4 oz/½ cup butter or margarine
75 g/3 oz/¾ cup desiccated (shredded)
    coconut
60 ml/4 tbsp clear honey
45 ml/3 tbsp milk
50 g/2 oz/¼ cup soft brown sugar

Melt the butter or margarine in the milk, then leave to cool slightly. Beat together the eggs and caster sugar until light and frothy, then beat in the butter and milk mixture. Stir in the flour and salt to make a fairly thin mixture. Spoon into a greased and lined 23 cm/9 in cake tin (pan) and bake in a preheated oven at 180°C/350°F/gas mark 4 for 40 minutes until golden brown and springy to the touch.

Meanwhile, bring the topping ingredients to the boil in a pan. Turn out the warm cake and spoon over the topping mixture. Place under a hot grill (broiler) for a few minutes until the topping just begins to brown.

Golden Coconut Cake

Makes one 20 cm/8 in cake

100 g/4 oz/½ cup butter or margarine,
    softened
200 g/7 oz/scant 1 cup caster
    (superfine) sugar
200 g/7 oz/1¾ cups plain
    (all-purpose) flour
10 ml/2 tsp baking powder
A pinch of salt

175 ml/6 fl oz/¾ cup milk
3 egg whites
    For the filling and topping:
150 g/5 oz/1¼ cups desiccated
    (shredded) coconut
200 g/7 oz/scant 1 cup caster
    (superfine) sugar
120 ml/4 fl oz/½ cup milk
120 ml/4 fl oz/½ cup water
3 egg yolks

Cream together the butter or margarine and sugar until light and fluffy. Stir the flour, baking powder and salt into the mixture alternately with the milk and water until you have a smooth batter. Beat the egg whites until stiff, then fold into the batter. Spoon the mixture into two greased 20 cm/8 in cake tins (pans) and bake in a preheated oven at 180°C/350°F/gas mark 4 for 25 minutes until springy to the touch. Leave to cool.

Mix together the coconut, sugar, milk and egg yolks in a small pan. Heat over a gentle heat for a few minutes until the eggs are cooked, stirring continuously. Leave to cool. Sandwich the cakes together with half the coconut mixture, then spoon the rest on top.

Coconut Layer Cake

Makes one 9 × 18 cm/3½ × 7 in cake

100 g/4 oz/½ cup butter or margarine,
    softened
175 g/6 oz/¾ cup caster (superfine)
    sugar
3 eggs
175 g/6 oz/1½ cups plain
    (all-purpose) flour
5 ml/1 tsp baking powder
175 g/6 oz/1 cup sultanas (golden
    raisins)
120 ml/4 fl oz/½ cup milk
6 plain biscuits (cookies), crushed
100 g/4 oz/½ cup soft brown sugar
100 g/4 oz/1 cup desiccated
    (shredded) coconut

Cream together the butter or margarine and caster sugar until light and fluffy. Gradually beat in two of the eggs, then fold in the flour, baking powder and sultanas alternately with the milk. Spoon half the mixture into a greased and lined 450 g/1 lb loaf tin (pan). Mix together the remaining egg with the biscuit crumbs, brown sugar and coconut and sprinkle into the tin. Spoon in the remaining mixture and bake in a preheated oven at 180°C/350°F/gas mark 4 for 1 hour. Leave to cool in the tin for 30 minutes, then turn out on to a wire rack to finish cooling.

Coconut and Lemon Cake

Makes one 20 cm/8 in cake

100 g/4 oz/½ cup butter or margarine, softened
75 g/3 oz/⅓ cup soft brown sugar
Grated rind of 1 lemon
1 egg, beaten
A few drops of almond essence (extract)
350 g/12 oz/3 cups self-raising (self-rising) flour
60 ml/4 tbsp raspberry jam (conserve)
For the topping:
1 egg, beaten
75 g/3 oz/⅓ cup soft brown sugar
225 g/8 oz/2 cups desiccated (shredded) coconut

Cream together the butter or margarine, sugar and lemon rind until light and fluffy. Gradually beat in the egg and almond essence, then fold in the flour. Spoon the mixture into a greased and lined 20 cm/8 in cake tin (pan). Spoon the jam over the mixture. Beat together the topping ingredients and spread over the mixture. Bake in a preheated oven at 180°C/350°F/gas mark 4 for 30 minutes until springy to the touch. Leave to cool in the tin.

Coconut New Year Cake

Makes one 18 cm/7 in cake

100 g/4 oz/½ cup butter or margarine, softened
100 g/4 oz/½ cup caster (superfine) sugar
2 eggs, lightly beaten
75 g/3 oz/¾ cup plain (all-purpose) flour
45 ml/3 tbsp desiccated (shredded) coconut
30 ml/2 tbsp rum
A few drops of almond essence (extract)
A few drops of lemon essence (extract)

Cream together the butter and sugar until light and fluffy. Gradually beat in the eggs, then fold in the flour and coconut. Stir in the rum and essences. Spoon into a greased and lined 18 cm/7 in cake tin (pan) and level the surface. Bake in a preheated oven at 190°C/375°F/gas mark 5 for 45 minutes until a skewer inserted in the centre comes out clean. Leave to cool in the tin.

91

Coconut and Sultana Cake

Makes one 23 cm/9 in cake

100 g/4 oz/½ cup butter or margarine,
softened
175 g/6 oz/¾ cup caster (superfine)
sugar
2 eggs, lightly beaten
175 g/6 oz/1½ cups plain
(all-purpose) flour
5 ml/1 tsp baking powder
A pinch of salt
175 g/6 oz/1 cup sultanas (golden
raisins)
120 ml/4 fl oz/½ cup milk
For the filling:
1 egg, lightly beaten
50 g/2 oz/½ cup plain biscuit (cookie)
crumbs
100 g/4 oz/½ cup soft brown sugar
100 g/4 oz/1 cup desiccated
(shredded) coconut

Cream together the butter or margarine and caster sugar until light and
fluffy. Gradually mix in the eggs. Fold in
the flour, baking powder, salt and sultanas
with enough of the milk to make a soft
dropping consistency. Spoon half the
mixture into a greased 23 cm/9 in cake tin
(pan). Mix together the filling ingredients
and spoon over the mixture, then top
with the remaining cake mix. Bake in a
preheated oven at 180°C/350°F/gas mark
4 for 1 hour until springy to the touch and
beginning to shrink away from the sides
of the tin. Leave to cool in the tin before
turning out.

Crunchy-topped Nut Cake

Makes one 23 cm/9 in cake

225 g/8 oz/1 cup butter or margarine,
softened
225 g/8 oz/1 cup caster (superfine)
sugar
2 eggs, lightly beaten

225 g/8 oz/2 cups plain
(all-purpose) flour
2.5 ml/½ tsp bicarbonate of soda
(baking soda)
2.5 ml/½ tsp cream of tartar
200 ml/7 fl oz/scant 1 cup milk
For the topping:
100 g/4 oz/1 cup chopped mixed nuts
100 g/4 oz/½ cup soft brown sugar
5 ml/1 tsp ground cinnamon

Cream together the butter or margarine and caster sugar until light and
fluffy. Gradually beat in the eggs, then fold
in the flour, bicarbonate of soda and
cream of tartar alternately with the milk.
Spoon into a greased and lined 23 cm/9 in
cake tin (pan). Mix together the nuts,
brown sugar and cinnamon and sprinkle
over the top of the cake. Bake in a
preheated oven at 180°C/350°F/gas mark
4 for 40 minutes until golden brown and
shrinking away from the sides of the tin.
Leave to cool in the tin for 10 minutes,
then turn out on to a wire rack to finish
cooling.

Mixed Nut Cake

Makes one 23 cm/9 in cake

100 g/4 oz/½ cup butter or margarine,
softened
225 g/8 oz/1 cup caster (superfine)
sugar
1 egg, beaten
225 g/8 oz/2 cups self-raising
(self-rising) flour
10 ml/2 tsp baking powder
A pinch of salt
250 ml/8 fl oz/1 cup milk
5 ml/1 tsp vanilla essence (extract)
2.5 ml/½ tsp lemon essence (extract)
100 g/4 oz/1 cup chopped mixed nuts

Cream together the butter or
margarine and sugar until light and
fluffy. Gradually beat in the egg. Mix
together the flour, baking powder and salt

and add to the mixture alternately with the milk and essences. Fold in the nuts. Spoon into two greased and lined 23 cm/9 in cake tins (pans) and bake in a preheated oven at 180°F/350°F/gas mark 4 for 40 minutes until a skewer inserted in the centre comes out clean.

Greek Nut Cake

Makes one 25 cm/10 in cake

100 g/4 oz/¹⁄₂ cup butter or margarine, softened
225 g/8 oz/1 cup caster (superfine) sugar
3 eggs, lightly beaten
250 g/9 oz/2¹⁄₄ cups plain (all-purpose) flour
225 g/8 oz/2 cups walnuts, ground
10 ml/2 tsp baking powder
5 ml/1 tsp ground cinnamon
1.5 ml/¹⁄₄ tsp ground cloves
A pinch of salt
75 ml/5 tbsp milk
For the honey syrup:
175 g/6 oz/³⁄₄ cup caster (superfine) sugar
75 g/3 oz/¹⁄₄ cup clear honey
15 ml/1 tbsp lemon juice
250 ml/8 fl oz/1 cup boiling water

Cream together the butter or margarine and sugar until light and fluffy. Gradually beat in the eggs, then fold in the flour, walnuts, baking powder, spices and salt. Add the milk and mix until smooth. Spoon into a greased and floured 25 cm/10 in cake tin (pan) and bake in a preheated oven at 180°C/350°F/ gas mark 4 for 40 minutes until springy to the touch. Leave to cool in the tin for 10 minutes, then transfer to a wire rack.

To make the syrup, mix together the sugar, honey, lemon juice and water and heat until dissolved. Prick the warm cake all over with a fork, then spoon over the honey syrup.

Iced Walnut Cake

Makes one 18 cm/7 in cake

100 g/4 oz/¹⁄₂ cup butter or margarine, softened
100 g/4 oz/¹⁄₂ cup caster (superfine) sugar
2 eggs, lightly beaten
100 g/4 oz/1 cup self-raising (self-rising) flour
100 g/4 oz/1 cup walnuts, chopped
A pinch of salt
For the icing (frosting):
450 g/1 lb/2 cups granulated sugar
150 ml/¹⁄₄ pt/³⁄₃ cup water
2 egg whites
A few walnut halves to decorate

Cream together the butter or margarine and caster sugar until light and fluffy. Gradually beat in the eggs, then fold in the flour, nuts and salt. Spoon the mixture into two greased and lined 18 cm/7 in cake tins (pans) and bake in a preheated oven at 180°C/350°F/gas mark 4 for 25 minutes until well risen and springy to the touch. Leave to cool.

Dissolve the granulated sugar in the water over a low heat, stirring continuously, then bring to the boil and continue to boil, without stirring, until a drop of the mixture forms a soft ball when dropped into cold water. Meanwhile, whisk the egg whites in a clean bowl until stiff. Pour the syrup on to the egg white and whisk until the mixture is thick enough to coat the back of a spoon. Sandwich the cakes together with a layer of the icing, then spread the rest over the top and sides of the cake and decorate with walnut halves.

Walnut Cake with Chocolate Cream

Makes one 18 cm/7 in cake

3 eggs
75 g/3 oz/⅓ cup soft brown sugar
50 g/2 oz/½ cup wholemeal
  (wholewheat) flour
25 g/1 oz/¼ cup cocoa (unsweetened
  chocolate) powder
  For the icing (frosting):
150 g/5 oz/1¼ cups plain
  (semi-sweet) chocolate
225 g/8 oz/1 cup low-fat cream cheese
45 ml/3 tbsp icing (confectioners')
  sugar, sifted
75 g/3 oz/¾ cup walnuts, chopped
15 ml/1 tbsp brandy (optional)
Grated chocolate to garnish

Whisk together the eggs and brown sugar until pale and thick. Fold in the flour and cocoa. Spoon the mixture into two greased and lined 18 cm/7 in sandwich tins (pans) and bake in a preheated oven at 190°C/375°F/gas mark 5 for 15–20 minutes until well risen and springy to the touch. Remove from the tins and leave to cool.

Melt the chocolate in a heatproof bowl set over a pan of gently simmering water. Remove from the heat and stir in the cream cheese and icing sugar, then stir in the nuts and brandy, if using. Sandwich the cakes together with most of the filling and spread the remainder on top. Garnish with the grated chocolate.

Walnut Cake with Honey and Cinnamon

Makes one 23 cm/9 in cake

225 g/8 oz/2 cups plain
  (all-purpose) flour
10 ml/2 tsp baking powder
5 ml/1 tsp bicarbonate of soda
  (baking soda)
5 ml/1 tsp ground cinnamon
A pinch of salt
100 g/4 oz/1 cup plain yoghurt
75 ml/5 tbsp oil
100 g/4 oz/⅓ cup clear honey
1 egg, lightly beaten
5 ml/1 tsp vanilla essence (extract)
  For the filling:
50 g/2 oz/½ cup chopped walnuts
225 g/8 oz/1 cup soft brown sugar
10 ml/2 tsp ground cinnamon
30 ml/2 tbsp oil

Mix together the dry ingredients for the cake and make a well in the centre. Whisk together the remaining cake ingredients and blend into the dry ingredients. Mix together the ingredients for the filling. Spoon half the cake mixture into a greased and floured 23 cm/9 in cake tin (pan) and sprinkle with half the filling. Add the remaining cake mixture, then the remaining filling. Bake in a preheated oven at 180°C/350°F/ gas mark 4 for 30 minutes until well risen and golden brown and beginning to shrink away from the sides of the pan.

Traybakes

*E*_{asy} *to make – especially in larger quantities for local fêtes or similar events – you can make a traybake very quickly, then simply cut it into squares or bars.*

Almond and Honey Bars

Makes 10

15 g/½ oz fresh yeast or 20 ml/4 tsp dried yeast
45 ml/3 tbsp caster (superfine) sugar
120 ml/4 fl oz/½ cup warm milk
300 g/11 oz/2¾ cups plain (all-purpose) flour
A pinch of salt
1 egg, lightly beaten
50 g/2 oz/¼ cup butter or margarine, softened
300 ml/½ pt/1¼ cups double (heavy) cream
30 ml/2 tbsp icing (confectioners') sugar, sifted
45 ml/3 tbsp clear honey
300 g/11 oz/2¾ cups flaked (slivered) almonds

Mix the yeast, 5 ml/1 tsp of the caster sugar and a little of the milk and leave in a warm place for 20 minutes until frothy. Mix the remaining sugar with the flour and salt and make a well in the centre. Gradually blend in the egg, butter or margarine, yeast mixture and remaining warm milk and mix to a soft dough. Knead on a lightly floured surface until smooth and elastic. Place in an oiled bowl, cover with oiled clingfilm (plastic wrap) and leave in a warm place for 45 minutes until doubled in size.

Knead the dough again, then roll out and place in a 30 × 20 cm/12 × 8 in greased cake tin (pan), prick all over with a fork, cover and leave in a warm place for 10 minutes.

Put 120 ml/4 fl oz/½ cup of the cream, the icing sugar and honey in a small pan

and bring to the boil. Remove from the heat and mix in the almonds. Spread over the dough, then bake in a preheated oven at 200°C/400°F/gas mark 6 for 20 minutes until golden and springy to the touch, covering with greaseproof (waxed) paper if the top begins to brown too much before the end of cooking. Turn out and leave to cool.

Cut the cake in half horizontally. Whip the remaining cream until stiff and spread over the bottom half of the cake. Top with the almond-covered half of the cake and cut into bars.

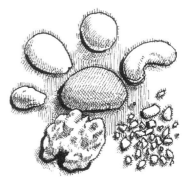

95

Apple and Blackcurrant Crumble Bars

Makes 12

175 g/6 oz/1½ cups plain
(all-purpose) flour
5 ml/1 tsp baking powder
A pinch of salt
175 g/6 oz/¾ cup butter or margarine
225 g/8 oz/1 cup soft brown sugar
100 g/4 oz/1 cup rolled oats
450 g/1 lb cooking (tart) apples,
peeled, cored and sliced
30 ml/2 tbsp cornflour (cornstarch)
10 ml/2 tsp ground cinnamon
2.5 ml/½ tsp grated nutmeg
2.5 ml/½ tsp ground allspice
225 g/8 oz blackcurrants

Mix the flour, baking powder and salt, then rub in the butter or margarine. Stir in the sugar and oats. Spoon half into the base of a greased and lined 25 cm/9 in square cake tin (pan). Mix the apples, cornflour and spices and spread over. Top with the blackcurrants. Spoon over the remaining mixture and level the top. Bake in a preheated oven at 180°C/350°F/gas mark 4 for 30 minutes until springy. Leave to cool, then cut into bars.

Apricot and Oatmeal Bars

Makes 24

75 g/3 oz/½ cup dried apricots
25 g/1 oz/3 tbsp sultanas
(golden raisins)
250 ml/8 fl oz/1 cup water
5 ml/1 tsp lemon juice
150 g/5 oz/⅔ cup soft brown sugar
50 g/2 oz/½ cup desiccated (shredded)
coconut
50 g/2 oz/½ cup plain (all-purpose)
flour
2.5 ml/½ tsp bicarbonate of soda
(baking soda)

100 g/4 oz/1 cup rolled oats
50 g/2 oz/¼ cup butter, melted

Place the apricots, sultanas, water, lemon juice and 30 ml/2 tbsp of the brown sugar in a small pan and stir over a low heat until thick. Stir in the coconut and leave to cool. Mix the flour, bicarbonate of soda, oats and the remaining sugar, then blend in the melted butter. Press half the oat mixture into the base of a greased 20 cm/8 in square baking tin (pan), then spread the apricot mixture on top. Cover with the remaining oat mixture and press down lightly. Bake in a preheated oven at 180°C/350°F/gas mark 4 for 30 minutes until golden. Leave to cool, then cut into bars.

Apricot Crunchies

Makes 16

100 g/4 oz/⅔ cup ready-to-eat dried
apricots
120 ml/4 fl oz/½ cup orange juice
100 g/4 oz/½ cup butter or margarine
75 g/3 oz/¾ cup wholemeal
(wholewheat) flour
75 g/3 oz/¾ cup rolled oats
75 g/3 oz/⅓ cup demerara sugar

Soak the apricots in the orange juice for at least 30 minutes until soft, then drain and chop. Rub the butter or margarine into the flour until the mixture resembles breadcrumbs. Stir in the oats and sugar. Press half the mixture into a greased 30 × 20 cm/12 × 8 in Swiss roll tin (jelly roll pan) and sprinkle with the apricots. Spread the remaining mixture on top and press down gently. Bake in a preheated oven at 180°C/350°F/gas mark 4 for 25 minutes until golden brown. Leave to cool in the tin before turning out and cutting into bars.

Photograph opposite: Lemon and Strawberry Roulade (page 18)

96

Nutty Banana Bars

Makes about 14

50 g/2 oz/¼ cup butter or margarine, softened
75 g/3 oz/⅓ cup caster (superfine) or soft brown sugar
2 large bananas, chopped
175 g/6 oz/1½ cups plain (all-purpose) flour
7.5 ml/1½ tsp baking powder
2 eggs, beaten
50 g/2 oz/½ cup walnuts, roughly chopped

Cream together the butter or margarine and sugar. Mash the bananas and stir into the mixture. Mix the flour and baking powder. Add the flour, eggs and nuts to the bananas mixture and beat well. Spoon into a greased and lined 18 × 28 cm/7 × 11 in cake tin, level the surface and bake in a preheated oven at 160°C/325°F/gas mark 3 for 30–35 minutes until springy to the touch. Leave to cool for a few minutes in the tin, then turn out on to a wire rack to finish cooling. Cut into about 14 bars.

American Brownies

Makes about 15

2 large eggs
225 g/8 oz/1 cup caster (superfine) sugar
50 g/2 oz/¼ cup butter or margarine, melted
2.5 ml/½ tsp vanilla essence (extract)
75 g/3 oz/¾ cup plain (all-purpose) flour
45 ml/3 tbsp cocoa (unsweetened chocolate) powder
2.5 ml/½ tsp baking powder
A pinch of salt
50 g/2 oz/½ cup walnuts, roughly chopped

Whisk together the eggs and sugar until thick and creamy. Beat in the butter and vanilla essence. Sift in the flour, cocoa, baking powder and salt and fold into the mixture with the walnuts. Turn into a well greased 20 cm/8 in square cake tin (pan). Bake in a preheated oven at 180°C/350°F/gas mark 4 for 40–45 minutes until springy to the touch. Leave in the tin for 10 minutes, then cut into squares and transfer to a wire rack while still warm.

Chocolate Fudge Brownies

Makes about 16

225 g/8 oz/1 cup butter or margarine
175 g/6 oz/¾ cup granulated sugar
350 g/12 oz/3 cups self-raising (self-rising) flour
30 ml/2 tbsp cocoa (unsweetened chocolate) powder
For the icing (frosting):
175 g/6 oz/1 cup icing (confectioners') sugar, sifted
30 ml/2 tbsp cocoa (unsweetened chocolate) powder
Boiling water

Melt the butter or margarine, then stir in the granulated sugar. Stir in the flour and cocoa. Press into a lined 18 × 28 cm/7 × 11 in baking tin (pan). Bake in a preheated oven at 180°C/350°F/gas mark 4 for about 20 minutes until springy to the touch.

To make the icing, sift the icing sugar and cocoa into a bowl and add a drop of boiling water. Stir until well blended, adding a drop or so more water if necessary. Ice the brownies while still warm (but not hot), then leave to cool before cutting into squares.

Photograph opposite: Chocolate Fudge Cake (page 26)

Walnut and Chocolate Brownies

Makes 12

50 g/2 oz/½ cup plain (semi-sweet) chocolate
75 g/3 oz/⅓ cup butter or margarine
225 g/8 oz/1 cup caster (superfine) sugar
75 g/3 oz/¾ cup plain (all-purpose) flour
75 g/3 oz/¾ cup walnuts, chopped
50 g/2 oz/½ cup chocolate chips
2 eggs, beaten
2.5 ml/½ tsp vanilla essence (extract)

Melt the chocolate and butter or margarine in a heatproof bowl set over a pan of gently simmering water. Remove from the heat and stir in the remaining ingredients. Spoon into a greased and lined 20 cm/8 in cake tin (pan) and bake in a preheated oven at 180°C/350°F/gas mark 4 for 30 minutes until a skewer inserted in the centre comes out clean. Leave to cool in the tin, then cut into squares.

Butter Bars

Makes 16

100 g/4 oz/½ cup butter or margarine, softened
100 g/4 oz/½ cup caster (superfine) sugar
1 egg, separated
100 g/4 oz/1 cup plain (all-purpose) flour
25 g/1 oz/¼ cup chopped mixed nuts

Cream together the butter or margarine and sugar until light and fluffy. Blend in the egg yolk, then stir in the flour and nuts to make a fairly stiff mixture. If it is too stiff, add a little milk; if it is runny, stir in a little more flour. Spoon the dough into a greased 30 × 20 cm/12 × 8 in Swiss roll tin (jelly roll pan). Beat the egg white until frothy and spread over the mixture. Bake in a preheated oven at 180°C/350°F/gas mark 4 for 30 minutes until golden. Leave to cool, then cut into bars.

Cherry Toffee Traybake

Makes 12

100 g/4 oz/1 cup almonds
225 g/8 oz/1 cup glacé (candied) cherries, halved
225 g/8 oz/1 cup butter or margarine, softened
225 g/8 oz/1 cup caster (superfine) sugar
3 eggs, beaten
100 g/4 oz/1 cup self-raising (self-rising) flour
50 g/2 oz/½ cup ground almonds
5 ml/1 tsp baking powder
5 ml/1 tsp almond essence (extract)

Sprinkle the almonds and cherries over the base of a greased and lined 20 cm/8 in cake tin (pan). Melt 50 g/2 oz/¼ cup of the butter or margarine with 50 g/2 oz/¼ cup of the sugar, then pour it over the cherries and nuts. Beat the remaining butter or margarine and sugar until light and fluffy, then beat in the eggs and mix in the flour, ground almonds, baking powder and almond essence. Spoon the mixture into the tin and level the top. Bake in a preheated oven at 160°C/325°F/gas mark 3 for 1 hour. Leave to cool in the tin for a few minutes, then invert carefully on to a wire rack, scraping any of the topping off the lining paper if necessary. Leave to cool completely before cutting.

98

Chocolate Chip Traybake

Makes 24

100 g/4 oz/½ cup butter or margarine, softened
100 g/4 oz/½ cup soft brown sugar
50 g/2 oz/¼ cup caster (superfine) sugar
1 egg
5 ml/1 tsp vanilla essence (extract)
100 g/4 oz/1 cup plain (all-purpose) flour
2.5 ml/½ tsp bicarbonate of soda (baking soda)
A pinch of salt
100 g/4 oz/1 cup chocolate chips

Cream together the butter or margarine and sugars until light and fluffy, then gradually add the egg and vanilla essence. Stir in the flour, bicarbonate of soda and salt. Stir in the chocolate chips. Spoon into a greased and floured 25 cm/12 in square baking tin (pan) and bake in a pre-heated oven at 190°C/375°F/gas mark 2 for 15 minutes until golden brown. Leave to cool, then cut into squares.

Cinnamon Crumble Layer

Makes 12

For the base:
100 g/4 oz/½ cup butter or margarine, softened
30 ml/2 tbsp clear honey
2 eggs, lightly beaten
100 g/4 oz/1 cup plain (all-purpose) flour
For the crumble:
75 g/3 oz/⅓ cup butter or margarine
75 g/3 oz/¾ cup plain (all-purpose) flour
75 g/3 oz/¾ cup rolled oats
5 ml/1 tsp ground cinnamon
50 g/2 oz/¼ cup demerara sugar

Cream together the butter or margarine and honey until light and fluffy. Gradually beat in the eggs, then fold in the flour. Spoon half the mixture into a greased 20 cm/8 in square cake tin (pan) and level the surface.

To make the crumble, rub the butter or margarine into the flour until the mixture resembles breadcrumbs. Stir in the oats, cinnamon and sugar. Spoon half the crumble into the tin, then top with the remaining cake mix, then the remaining crumble. Bake in a preheated oven at 190°C/375°F/gas mark 5 for about 35 minutes until a skewer inserted in the centre comes out clean. Leave to cool, then cut into bars.

Gooey Cinnamon Bars

Makes 16

225 g/8 oz/2 cups plain (all-purpose) flour
10 ml/2 tsp baking powder
225 g/8 oz/1 cup soft brown sugar
15 ml/1 tbsp melted butter
250 ml/8 fl oz/1 cup milk
30 ml/2 tbsp demerara sugar
10 ml/2 tsp ground cinnamon
25 g/1 oz/2 tbsp butter, chilled and diced

Mix together the flour, baking powder and sugar. Stir in the melted butter and milk and blend together well. Press the mixture into two 23 cm/9 in square cake tins (pans). Sprinkle the tops with the demerara sugar and cinnamon, then press pieces of butter over the surface. Bake in a preheated oven at 180°C/350°F/gas mark 4 for 30 minutes. The butter will make holes in the mixture and go gooey as it cooks.

Coconut Bars

Makes 16

75 g/3 oz/⅓ cup butter or margarine
100 g/4 oz/1 cup plain (all-purpose)
  flour
30 ml/2 tbsp caster (superfine) sugar
2 eggs
100 g/4 oz/½ cup soft brown sugar
A pinch of salt
175 g/6 oz/1½ cups desiccated
  (shredded) coconut
50 g/2 oz/½ cup chopped mixed nuts
Orange Icing (page 230)

Rub the butter or margarine into the flour until the mixture resembles breadcrumbs. Stir in the sugar and press into an ungreased 23 cm/9 in square baking tin (pan). Bake in a preheated oven at 190°C/350°F/gas mark 4 for 15 minutes until just set.

Blend together the eggs, brown sugar and salt, then stir in the coconut and nuts and spread over the base. Bake for 20 minutes until set and golden. Ice with orange icing when cool. Cut into bars.

Coconut and Jam Sandwich Bars

Makes 16

25 g/1 oz/2 tbsp butter or margarine
175 g/6 oz/1½ cups self-raising
  (self-rising) flour
225 g/8 oz/1 cup caster (superfine)
  sugar
2 egg yolks
75 ml/5 tbsp water
175 g/6 oz/1½ cups desiccated
  (shredded) coconut
4 egg whites
50 g/2 oz/½ cup plain (all-purpose)
  flour
100 g/4 oz/⅓ cup strawberry jam
  (conserve)

Rub the butter or margarine into the self-raising flour, then stir in 50 g/ 2 oz/¼ cup of the sugar. Beat together the egg yolks and 45 ml/3 tbsp of the water and stir into the mixture. Press into the base of a greased 30 × 20 cm/12 × 8 in Swiss roll tin (jelly roll pan) and prick with a fork. Bake in a preheated oven at 180°C/350°F/gas mark 4 for 12 minutes. Leave to cool.

Place the coconut, the remaining sugar and water and one egg white in a pan and stir over a low heat until the mixture becomes lumpy without letting it brown. Leave to cool. Mix in the plain flour. Whisk the remaining egg whites until stiff, then fold into the mixture. Spread the jam over the base, then spread with the coconut topping. Bake in the oven for 30 minutes until golden brown. Leave to cool in the tin before cutting into bars.

Date and Apple Traybake

Makes 12

1 cooking (tart) apple, peeled, cored
  and chopped
225 g/8 oz/1⅓ cups stoned (pitted)
  dates, chopped
150 ml/¼ pt/⅔ cup water
350 g/12 oz/3 cups rolled oats
175 g/6 oz/¾ cup butter or margarine,
  melted
45 ml/3 tbsp demerara sugar
5 ml/1 tsp ground cinnamon

Place the apples, dates and water in a pan and simmer gently for about 5 minutes until the apples are soft. Leave to cool. Mix together the oats, butter or margarine, sugar and cinnamon. Spoon half into a greased 20 cm/8 in square cake tin (pan) and level the surface. Top with the apple and date mixture, then cover with the remaining oat mixture and level the surface. Press down gently. Bake in a preheated oven at 190°C/375°F/gas mark 5 for about 30 minutes until golden brown. Leave to cool, then cut into bars.

Date Slices

Makes 12

225 g/8 oz/1⅓ cups stoned (pitted) dates, chopped
30 ml/2 tbsp clear honey
30 ml/2 tbsp lemon juice
225 g/8 oz/1 cup butter or margarine
225 g/8 oz/2 cups wholemeal (wholewheat) flour
225 g/8 oz/2 cups rolled oats
75 g/3 oz/⅓ cup soft brown sugar

Simmer the dates, honey and lemon juice over a low heat for a few minutes until the dates are soft. Rub the butter or margarine into the flour and oats until the mixture resembles breadcrumbs, then stir in the sugar. Spoon half the mixture into a greased and lined 20 cm/8 in square cake tin (pan). Spoon the date mixture over the top, then finish with the remaining cake mixture. Press down firmly. Bake in a preheated oven at 190°C/375°F/gas mark 5 for 35 minutes until springy to the touch. Leave to cool in the tin, cutting into slices while still warm.

Grandma's Date Bars

Makes 16

100 g/4 oz/½ cup butter or margarine, softened
225 g/8 oz/1 cup soft brown sugar
2 eggs, lightly beaten
175 g/6 oz/1½ cups plain (all-purpose) flour
2.5 ml/½ tsp bicarbonate of soda (baking soda)
5 ml/1 tsp ground cinnamon
A pinch of ground cloves
A pinch of grated nutmeg
175 g/6 oz/1 cup stoned (pitted) dates, chopped

Cream together the butter or margarine and sugar until light and fluffy. Gradually add the eggs, beating well after each addition. Stir in the remaining ingredients until well blended. Spoon into a greased and floured 23 cm/9 in square baking tin (pan) and bake in a preheated oven at 180°C/350°F/gas mark 4 for 25 minutes until a skewer inserted in the centre comes out clean. Leave to cool, then cut into bars.

Date and Oatmeal Bars

Makes 16

175 g/6 oz/1 cup stoned (pitted) dates, chopped
15 ml/1 tbsp clear honey
30 ml/2 tbsp water
225 g/8 oz/2 cups wholemeal (wholewheat) flour
100 g/4 oz/1 cup rolled oats
100 g/4 oz/½ cup soft brown sugar
150 g/5 oz/⅔ cup butter or margarine, melted

Simmer the dates, honey and water in a small pan until the dates are soft. Mix together the flour, oats and sugar, then blend in the melted butter or margarine. Press half the mixture into a greased 18 cm/7 in square cake tin (pan), sprinkle with the date mixture, then top with the remaining oat mixture and press down gently. Bake in a preheated oven at 180°C/350°F/gas mark 4 for 1 hour until firm and golden. Leave to cool in the tin, cutting into bars while still warm.

Date and Walnut Bars

Makes 12

100 g/4 oz/½ cup butter or margarine,
    softened
150 g/5 oz/⅔ cup caster (superfine)
    sugar
1 egg, lightly beaten
100 g/4 oz/1 cup self-raising
    (self-rising) flour
225 g/8 oz/1⅓ cups stoned (pitted)
    dates, chopped
100 g/4 oz/1 cup walnuts, chopped
15 ml/1 tbsp milk (optional)
100 g/4 oz/1 cup plain (semi-sweet)
    chocolate

Cream together the butter or
margarine and sugar until light and
fluffy. Mix in the egg, then the flour, dates
and walnuts, adding a little of the milk if
the mixture is too stiff. Spoon into a
greased 30 × 20 cm/12 × 8 in Swiss roll
tin (jelly roll pan) and bake in a preheated
oven at 180°C/350°F/gas mark 4 for 30
minutes until springy to the touch. Leave
to cool.

Melt the chocolate in a heatproof bowl
set over a pan of gently simmering water.
Spread over the mixture and leave to cool
and set. Cut into bars with a sharp knife.

Fig Bars

Makes 16

225 g/8 oz fresh figs, chopped
30 ml/2 tbsp clear honey
15 ml/1 tbsp lemon juice
225 g/8 oz/2 cups wholemeal
    (wholewheat) flour
225 g/8 oz/2 cups rolled oats
225 g/8 oz/1 cup butter or margarine
75 g/3 oz/⅓ cup soft brown sugar

Simmer the figs, honey and lemon juice
over a low heat for 5 minutes. Allow to
cool slightly. Mix together the flour and
oats, then rub in the butter or margarine
and stir in the sugar. Press half the

mixture into a greased 20 cm/8 in square
cake tin (pan), then spoon the fig mixture
over the top. Cover with the remaining
cake mixture and press down firmly. Bake
in a preheated oven at 180°C/350°F/gas
mark 4 for 30 minutes until golden
brown. Leave in the tin to cool, then cut
into slices while still warm.

Flapjacks

Makes 16

75 g/3 oz/⅓ cup butter or margarine
50 g/2 oz/3 tbsp golden (light corn)
    syrup
100 g/4 oz/½ cup soft brown sugar
175 g/6 oz/1½ cups rolled oats

Melt the butter or margarine with the
syrup and sugar, then stir in the
oats. Press into a greased 20 cm/8 in
square tin and bake in a preheated oven at
180°C/350°F/gas mark 4 for about 20
minutes until lightly golden. Leave to cool
slightly before cutting into bars, then
leave in the tin to cool completely before
turning out.

Cherry Flapjacks

Makes 16

75 g/3 oz/⅓ cup butter or margarine
50 g/2 oz/3 tbsp golden (light corn)
    syrup
100 g/4 oz/½ cup soft brown sugar
175 g/6 oz/1½ cups rolled oats
100 g/4 oz/1 cup glacé (candied)
    cherries, chopped

Melt the butter or margarine with the
syrup and sugar, then stir in the oats
and cherries. Press into a greased 20 cm/
8 in square cake tin (pan) and bake in a
preheated oven at 180°C/350°F/gas mark
4 for about 20 minutes until lightly
golden. Leave to cool slightly before
cutting into bars, then leave in the tin to
cool completely before turning out.

Chocolate Flapjacks

Makes 16

75 g/3 oz/⅓ cup butter or margarine
50 g/2 oz/3 tbsp golden (light corn) syrup
100 g/4 oz/½ cup soft brown sugar
175 g/6 oz/1½ cups rolled oats
100 g/4 oz/1 cup chocolate chips

Melt the butter or margarine with the syrup and sugar, then stir in the oats and chocolate chips. Press into a greased 20 cm/8 in square cake tin (pan) and bake in a preheated oven at 180°C/350°F/gas mark 4 for about 20 minutes until lightly golden. Leave to cool slightly before cutting into bars, then leave in the tin to cool completely before turning out.

Fruit Flapjacks

Makes 16

75 g/3 oz/⅓ cup butter or margarine
100 g/4 oz/½ cup soft brown sugar
50 g/2 oz/3 tbsp golden (light corn) syrup
175 g/6 oz/1½ cups rolled oats
75 g/3 oz/½ cup raisins, sultanas or other dried fruit

Melt the butter or margarine with the sugar and syrup, then stir in the oats and raisins. Press into a greased 20 cm/8 in square cake tin (pan) and bake in a preheated oven at 180°C/350°F/gas mark 4 for about 20 minutes until lightly golden. Leave to cool slightly before cutting into bars, then leave in the tin to cool completely before turning out.

Fruit and Nut Flapjacks

Makes 16

75 g/3 oz/⅓ cup butter or margarine
100 g/4 oz/⅓ cup clear honey
50 g/2 oz/⅓ cup raisins
50 g/2 oz/½ cup walnuts, chopped
175 g/6 oz/1½ cups rolled oats

Melt the butter or margarine with the honey over a low heat. Stir in the raisins, walnuts and oats and mix together well. Spoon into a greased 23 cm/9 in square cake tin (pan) and bake in a preheated oven at 180°C/350°F/gas mark 4 for 25 minutes. Leave to cool in the tin, cutting into bars while still warm.

Ginger Flapjacks

Makes 16

75 g/3 oz/⅓ cup butter or margarine
100 g/4 oz/½ cup soft brown sugar
50 g/2 oz/3 tbsp syrup from a jar of stem ginger
175 g/6 oz/1½ cups rolled oats
4 pieces stem ginger, finely chopped

Melt the butter or margarine with the sugar and syrup, then stir in the oats and ginger. Press into a greased 20 cm/8 in square cake tin (pan) and bake in a preheated oven at 180°C/350°F/gas mark 4 for about 20 minutes until lightly golden. Leave to cool slightly before cutting into bars, then leave in the tin to cool completely before turning out.

Nutty Flapjacks

Makes 16

75 g/3 oz/⅓ cup butter or margarine
50 g/2 oz/3 tbsp golden (light corn)
syrup
100 g/4 oz/½ cup soft brown sugar
175 g/6 oz/1½ cups rolled oats
100 g/4 oz/1 cup chopped mixed nuts

Melt the butter or margarine with the syrup and sugar, then stir in the oats and nuts. Press into a greased 20 cm/8 in square cake tin (pan) and bake in a preheated oven at 180°C/350°F/gas mark 4 for about 20 minutes until lightly golden. Leave to cool slightly before cutting into bars, then leave in the tin to cool completely before turning out.

Sharp Lemon Shortbread

Makes 16

100 g/4 oz/1 cup plain (all-purpose)
flour
100 g/4 oz/½ cup butter or margarine,
softened
75 g/3 oz/½ cup icing (confectioners')
sugar, sifted
2.5 ml/½ tsp baking powder
A pinch of salt
30 ml/2 tbsp lemon juice
10 ml/2 tsp grated lemon rind

Blend together the flour, butter, or margarine, icing sugar and baking powder to a paste. Press into a greased 20 cm/8 in square cake tin (pan) and bake in a preheated oven at 180°C/350°F/gas mark 4 for 20 minutes.

Mix together the remaining ingredients and spoon over the hot base, reduce the oven temperature to 160°C/325°F/gas mark 3 and return to the oven for a further 25 minutes until golden. Leave to cool, then cut into squares.

Mocha and Coconut Squares

Makes 20

1 egg
100 g/4 oz/½ cup caster (superfine)
sugar
100 g/4 oz/1 cup plain (all-purpose)
flour
10 ml/2 tsp baking powder
A pinch of salt
75 ml/5 tbsp milk
75 g/3 oz/⅓ cup butter or margarine,
melted
15 ml/1 tbsp cocoa (unsweetened
chocolate) powder
2.5 ml/½ tsp vanilla essence (extract)
For the topping:
75 g/3 oz/½ cup icing (confectioners')
sugar, sifted
50 g/2 oz/¼ cup butter or margarine,
melted
45 ml/3 tbsp hot strong black coffee
15 ml/1 tbsp cocoa (unsweetened
chocolate) powder
2.5 ml/½ tsp vanilla essence (extract)
25 g/1 oz/¼ cup desiccated (shredded)
coconut

Beat together the eggs and sugar until light and fluffy. Stir in the flour, baking powder and salt alternately with the milk and melted butter or margarine. Stir in the cocoa and vanilla essence. Spoon the mixture into a greased 20 cm/8 in square cake tin (pan) and bake in a preheated oven at 200°C/400°F/gas mark 6 for 15 minutes until well risen and springy to the touch.

To make the topping, mix together the icing sugar, butter or margarine, coffee, cocoa and vanilla essence. Spread over the warm cake and sprinkle with coconut. Leave to cool in the tin, then turn out and cut into squares.

Hello Dolly Cookies

Makes 16

100 g/4 oz/½ cup butter or margarine
100 g/4 oz/1 cup digestive biscuit
(Graham cracker) crumbs
100 g/4 oz/1 cup chocolate chips
100 g/4 oz/1 cup desiccated
(shredded) coconut
100 g/4 oz/1 cup walnuts, chopped
400 g/14 oz/1 large can condensed
milk

Melt the butter or margarine and stir in the biscuit crumbs. Press the mixture into the base of a greased and foil-lined 28 × 18 cm/11 × 7 in cake tin (pan). Sprinkle with the chocolate chips, then the coconut and, finally, the walnuts. Pour the condensed milk over the top and bake in a preheated oven at 180°C/350°F/ gas mark 4 for 25 minutes. Cut into bars while still warm, then leave to cool completely.

Nut and Chocolate Coconut Bars

Makes 12

75 g/3 oz/¾ cup milk chocolate
75 g/3 oz/¾ cup plain (semi-sweet)
chocolate
75 g/3 oz/⅓ cup crunchy peanut butter
75 g/3 oz/¾ cup digestive biscuit
(Graham cracker) crumbs
75 g/3 oz/¾ cup walnuts, crushed
75 g/3 oz/¾ cup desiccated (shredded)
coconut
75 g/3 oz/¾ cup white chocolate

Melt the milk chocolate in a heatproof bowl set over a pan of gently simmering water. Spread over the base of a 23 cm/7 in square cake tin (pan) and leave to set.

Gently melt the plain chocolate and peanut butter over a low heat, then stir in the biscuit crumbs, walnuts and coconut.

Spread over the set chocolate and chill until set.

Melt the white chocolate in a heatproof bowl set over a pan of gently simmering water. Drizzle over the biscuits in a pattern, then leave to set before cutting into bars.

Nutty Squares

Makes 12

75 g/3 oz/¾ cup plain (semi-sweet)
chocolate
50 g/2 oz/¼ cup butter or margarine
100 g/4 oz/½ cup caster (superfine)
sugar
2 eggs
5 ml/1 tsp vanilla essence (extract)
75 g/3 oz/¾ cup plain (all-purpose)
flour
2.5 ml/½ tsp baking powder
100 g/4 oz/1 cup chopped mixed nuts

Melt the chocolate in a heatproof bowl over a pan of gently simmering water. Stir in the butter until melted, then stir in the sugar. Remove from the heat and beat in the eggs and vanilla essence. Fold in the flour, baking powder and nuts. Spoon the mixture into a greased 25 cm/10 in square cake tin (pan) and bake in a preheated oven at 180°C/350°F/ gas mark 4 for 15 minutes until golden. Cut into small squares while still warm.

Orange Pecan Slices

Makes 16

375 g/13 oz/3¼ cups plain
  (all-purpose) flour
275 g/10 oz/1¼ cups caster (superfine)
  sugar
5 ml/1 tsp baking powder
75 g/3 oz/⅓ cup butter or margarine
2 eggs, beaten
175 ml/6 fl oz/¾ cup milk
200 g/7 oz/1 small can mandarins,
  drained and coarsely chopped
100 g/4 oz/1 cup pecan nuts, chopped
Finely grated rind of 2 oranges
10 ml/2 tsp ground cinnamon

Mix together 325 g/12 oz/3 cups of the flour, 225 g/8 oz/1 cup of the sugar and the baking powder. Melt 50 g/2 oz/ ¼ cup of the butter or margarine and stir in the eggs and milk. Mix the liquid gently into the dry ingredients until smooth. Fold in the mandarins, pecan nuts and orange rind. Pour into a greased and lined 30 × 20 cm/12 × 8 in baking tin (pan). Rub together the remaining flour, sugar, butter and the cinnamon and sprinkle over the cake. Bake in a preheated oven at 180°C/350°F/gas mark 4 for 40 minutes until golden. Leave to cool in the tin, then cut into about 16 slices.

Parkin

Makes 16 squares

100 g/4 oz/½ cup lard (shortening)
100 g/4 oz/½ cup butter or margarine
75 g/3 oz/⅓ cup soft brown sugar
100 g/4 oz/⅓ cup golden (light corn)
  syrup
100 g/4 oz/⅓ cup black treacle
  (molasses)
10 ml/2 tsp bicarbonate of soda
  (baking soda)
150 ml/¼ pt/⅔ cup milk
225 g/8 oz/2 cups wholemeal
  (wholewheat) flour

225 g/8 oz/2 cups oatmeal
10 ml/2 tsp ground ginger
2.5 ml/½ tsp salt

Melt together the lard, butter or margarine, sugar, syrup and treacle in a pan. Dissolve the bicarbonate of soda in the milk and stir into the pan with the remaining ingredients. Spoon into a greased and lined 20 cm/8 in square cake tin (pan) and bake in a preheated oven at 160°C/325°F/gas mark 3 for 1 hour until firm. It may sink in the middle. Leave to cool, then store in an airtight container for a few days before cutting into squares and serving.

Peanut Butter Bars

Makes 16

100 g/4 oz/1 cup butter or margarine
175 g/6 oz/1¼ cups plain (all-
  purpose) flour
175 g/6 oz/¾ cup soft brown sugar
75 g/3 oz/⅓ cup peanut butter
A pinch of salt
1 small egg yolk, beaten
2.5 ml/½ tsp vanilla essence (extract)
100 g/4 oz/1 cup plain (semi-sweet)
  chocolate
50 g/2 oz/2 cups puffed rice cereal

Rub the butter or margarine into the flour until the mixture resembles breadcrumbs. Stir in the sugar, 30 ml/ 2 tbsp of the peanut butter and the salt. Stir in the egg yolk and vanilla essence and mix until well blended. Press into a 25 cm/10 in square cake tin (pan). Bake in a preheated oven at 160°C/325°F/gas mark 3 for 30 minutes until risen and springy to the touch.
  Melt the chocolate in a heatproof bowl over a pan of gently simmering water. Remove from the heat and stir in the remaining peanut butter. Stir in the cereal and mix well until coated in the chocolate mixture. Spoon over the cake and level the surface. Leave to cool, then chill and cut into bars.

Picnic Slices

Makes 12

225 g/8 oz/2 cups plain (semi-sweet) chocolate
50 g/2 oz/¼ cup butter or margarine, softened
100 g/4 oz/½ cup caster sugar
1 egg, lightly beaten
100 g/4 oz/1 cup desiccated (shredded) coconut
50 g/2 oz/⅓ cup sultanas (golden raisins)
50 g/2 oz/¼ cup glacé (candied) cherries, chopped

Melt the chocolate in a heatproof bowl set over a pan of gently simmering water. Pour into the base of a greased and lined 30 × 20 cm/12 × 8 in Swiss roll tin (jelly roll pan). Cream together the butter or margarine and sugar until light and fluffy. Gradually add the egg, then mix in the coconut, sultanas and cherries. Spread over the chocolate and bake in a preheated oven at 150°C/300°F/gas mark 3 for 30 minutes until golden brown. Leave to cool, then cut into bars.

Pineapple and Coconut Bars

Makes 20

1 egg
100 g/4 oz/½ cup caster (superfine) sugar
75 g/3 oz/¾ cup plain (all-purpose) flour
5 ml/1 tsp baking powder
A pinch of salt
75 ml/5 tbsp water
For the topping:
200 g/7 oz/1 small can pineapple, drained and chopped
25 g/1 oz/2 tbsp butter or margarine
50 g/2 oz/¼ cup caster (superfine) sugar
1 egg yolk
25 g/1 oz/¼ cup desiccated (shredded) coconut
5 ml/1 tsp vanilla essence (extract)

Beat together the egg and sugar until light and pale. Fold in the flour, baking powder and salt alternately with the water. Spoon into a greased and floured 18 cm/7 in square cake tin (pan) and bake in a preheated oven at 200°C/400°F/gas mark 6 for 20 minutes until well risen and springy to the touch. Spoon the pineapple over the warm cake. Warm the remaining topping ingredients in a small pan over a low heat, stirring continuously until well blended without allowing the mixture to boil. Spoon over the pineapple, then return the cake to the oven for a further 5 minutes until the topping turns golden brown. Leave to cool in the tin for 10 minutes, then turn out on to a wire rack to finish cooling before cutting into bars.

Plum Yeast Cake

Makes 16

*15 g/½ oz fresh yeast or 20 ml/4 tsp
dried yeast*
*50 g/2 oz/¼ cup caster (superfine)
sugar*
150 ml/¼ pt/⅔ cup warm milk
*50 g/2 oz/¼ cup butter or margarine,
melted*
1 egg
1 egg yolk
*250 g/9 oz/2¼ cups plain
(all-purpose) flour*
5 ml/1 tsp finely grated lemon rind
*675 g/1½ lb plums, quartered and
stoned (pitted)*
*Icing (confectioners') sugar, sifted, for
dusting*
Ground cinnamon

Mix the yeast with 5 ml/1 tsp of the sugar and a little of the warm milk and leave in a warm place for 20 minutes until frothy. Whisk the remaining sugar and milk with the melted butter or margarine, the egg and egg yolk. Mix together the flour and lemon rind in a bowl and make a well in the centre. Gradually beat in the yeast mixture and the egg mixture to form a soft dough. Beat until the dough is very smooth and bubbles are beginning to form on the surface. Press gently into a greased and floured 25 cm/10 in square cake tin (pan). Arrange the plums close together over the top of the dough. Cover with oiled clingfilm (plastic wrap) and leave in a warm place for 1 hour until doubled in size. Place in a preheated oven at 200°C/400°F/gas mark 6, then immediately reduce the oven temperature to 190°C/375°F/gas mark 5 and bake for 45 minutes. Reduce the oven temperature again to 180°C/350°F/gas mark 4 and bake for a further 15 minutes until golden brown. Dust the cake with icing sugar and cinnamon while still hot, then leave to cool and cut into squares.

American Pumpkin Bars

Makes 20

2 eggs
*175 g/6 oz/¾ cup caster (superfine)
sugar*
120 ml/4 fl oz/½ cup oil
225 g/8 oz cooked, diced pumpkin
*100 g/4 oz/1 cup plain (all-purpose)
flour*
5 ml/1 tsp baking powder
5 ml/1 tsp ground cinnamon
*2.5 ml/½ tsp bicarbonate of soda
(baking soda)*
*50 g/2 oz/⅓ cup sultanas (golden
raisins)*
Cream Cheese Icing (page 230)

Beat the eggs until light and fluffy, then beat in the sugar and oil and stir in the pumpkin. Beat in the flour, baking powder, cinnamon and bicarbonate of soda until well blended. Stir in the sultanas. Spoon the mixture into a greased and floured 30 × 20 cm/12 × 8 in Swiss roll tin (jelly roll pan) and bake in a preheated oven at 180°C/350°F/gas mark 4 for 30 minutes until a skewer inserted in the centre comes out clean. Leave to cool, then spread with cream cheese icing and cut into bars.

Quince and Almond Bars

Makes 16

450 g/1 lb quinces
50 g/2 oz/¼ cup lard (shortening)
50 g/2 oz/¼ cup butter or margarine
*100 g/4 oz/1 cup plain (all-purpose)
flour*
30 ml/2 tbsp caster (superfine) sugar
About 30 ml/2 tbsp water
For the filling:
*75 g/3 oz/⅓ cup butter or margarine,
softened*
*100 g/4 oz/½ cup caster (superfine)
sugar*
2 eggs

A few drops of almond essence (extract)
100 g/4 oz/1 cup ground almonds
25 g/1 oz/¼ cup plain (all-purpose) flour
50 g/2 oz/½ cup flaked (slivered) almonds

Peel, core and slice the quinces thinly. Place in a pan and just cover with water. Bring to the boil and simmer for about 15 minutes until soft. Drain off any excess water.

Rub the lard and butter or margarine into the flour until the mixture resembles breadcrumbs. Stir in the sugar. Add just enough water to mix to a soft dough, then roll out on a lightly floured surface and use to line the base and sides of a 30 × 20 cm/12 × 8 in Swiss roll tin (jelly roll pan). Prick all over with a fork. Using a slotted spoon, arrange the quinces over the pastry.

Cream together the butter or margarine and sugar, then gradually beat in the eggs and almond essence. Fold in the ground almonds and flour and spoon over the quinces. Sprinkle the slivered almonds over the top and bake in a preheated oven at 180°C/350°F/gas mark 4 for 45 minutes until firm and golden brown. Cut into squares when cool.

Raisin Bars

Makes 12

175 g/6 oz/1 cup raisins
250 ml/8 fl oz/1 cup water
75 ml/5 tbsp oil
225 g/8 oz/1 cup caster (superfine) sugar
1 egg, lightly beaten
200 g/7 oz/1¾ cups plain (all-purpose) flour
1.5 ml/¼ tsp salt
5 ml/1 tsp bicarbonate of soda (baking soda)
5 ml/1 tsp ground cinnamon

2.5 ml/½ tsp grated nutmeg
2.5 ml/½ tsp ground allspice
A pinch of ground cloves
50 g/2 oz/½ cup chocolate chips
50 g/2 oz/½ cup walnuts, chopped
30 ml/2 tbsp icing (confectioners') sugar, sifted

Bring the raisins and water the boil, then add the oil, remove from the heat and leave to cool slightly. Stir in the caster sugar and egg. Mix together the flour, salt, bicarbonate of soda and spices. Blend with the raisin mixture, then stir in the chocolate chips and walnuts. Spoon into a greased 30 cm/12 in square cake tin (pan) and bake in a preheated oven at 190°C/375°F/gas mark 5 for 25 minutes until the cake begins to shrink away from the sides of the tin. Leave to cool before dusting with icing sugar and cutting into bars.

Raspberry Oat Squares

Makes 12

175 g/6 oz/¾ cup butter or margarine
225 g/8 oz/2 cups self-raising (self-rising) flour
5 ml/1 tsp salt
175 g/6 oz/1½ cups rolled oats
175 g/6 oz/¾ cup caster (superfine) sugar
300 g/11 oz/1 medium can raspberries, drained

Rub the butter or margarine into the flour and salt, then stir in the oats and sugar. Press half the mixture into a greased 25 cm/10 in square baking tin (pan). Scatter the raspberries over the top and cover with the remaining mixture, pressing down well. Bake in a preheated oven at 200°C/400°F/gas mark 6 for 20 minutes. Leave to cool slightly in the tin before cutting into squares.

Shortbread Cinnamon Meringues

Makes 24

75 g/3 oz/½ cup icing (confectioners')
  sugar, sifted
100 g/4 oz/1 cup plain (all-purpose)
  flour
100 g/4 oz/½ cup butter or margarine,
  softened
1 egg
225 g/8 oz/⅔ cup jam (fruit conserve)
2 egg whites
100 g/4 oz/½ cup caster (superfine)
  sugar
2.5 ml/½ tsp ground cinnamon

Blend together the icing sugar, flour, butter or margarine and egg. Press the mixture into the bottom of a greased 25 cm/12 in square cake tin (pan) and bake in a preheated oven at 180°C/350°F/ gas mark 4 for 10 minutes. Remove from the oven and spread the jam over the top. Beat the egg whites until they hold soft peaks, then beat in the caster sugar and cinnamon until the mixture is firm and glossy. Spread over the jam and return to the oven for 25 minutes until golden brown. Leave to cool, then cut into squares.

Strawberry and Coconut Traybake

Makes 16

For the pastry (paste):
50 g/2 oz/¼ cup lard (shortening)
50 g/2 oz/¼ cup butter or margarine
200 g/7 oz/1¾ cups plain
  (all-purpose) flour
About 15 ml/1 tbsp water
225 g/8 oz/⅔ cup strawberry jam
  (conserve)
For the filling:
175 g/6 oz/¾ cup butter or margarine,
  softened

175 g/6 oz/¾ cup caster (superfine)
  sugar
3 eggs, lightly beaten
15 ml/1 tbsp plain (all-purpose) flour
Grated rind of 1 lemon
225 g/8 oz/2 cups desiccated
  (shredded) coconut

To make the pastry, rub the lard and butter or margarine into the flour until the mixture resembles breadcrumbs. Mix in enough water to form a dough, roll out on a lightly floured surface and use to line the base and sides of a 30 × 20 cm/12 × 8 in Swiss roll tin (jelly roll pan). Prick all over with a fork. Reserve the trimmings. Spread the pastry with jam.

To make the filling, cream together the butter or margarine and sugar until light and fluffy. Gradually beat in the eggs, then fold in the flour and lemon rind. Stir in the coconut. Spread over the jam, sealing the edges to the pastry. Roll out the pastry trimmings and make a lattice pattern over the top of the traybake. Bake in a preheated oven at 190°C/375°F/gas mark 5 for 30 minutes until golden. Cut into squares when cool.

Brown Sugar and Banana Bars

Makes 12

75 g/3 oz/⅓ cup butter or margarine
225 g/8 oz/1 cup soft brown sugar
1 large egg, lightly beaten
150 g/5 oz/1¼ cups plain
  (all-purpose) flour
5 ml/1 tsp baking powder
A pinch of salt
100 g/4 oz/1 cup chocolate chips
50 g/2 oz/½ cup dried banana chips,
  coarsely chopped

Melt the butter or margarine, then remove from the heat and stir in the sugar. Leave to cool until lukewarm.

Gradually beat in the egg, then stir in the remaining ingredients to make a fairly stiff batter. If it is too stiff, stir in a little milk. Spoon into a greased 18 cm/ 7 in square cake tin (pan) and bake in a preheated oven at 140°C/275°F/gas mark 1 for 1 hour until crisp on top. Leave in the tin until lukewarm, then cut into bars and lift out to finish cooling on a wire rack. The mixture will be quite sticky until it cools.

Sunflower and Nut Bars

Makes 18

150 g/5 oz/⅔ cup butter or margarine
45 ml/3 tbsp clear honey
A few drops of almond essence
(extract)
275 g/10 oz/2½ cups rolled oats
25 g/1 oz/¼ cup flaked (slivered)
almonds
25 g/1 oz/2 tbsp sunflower seeds
25 g/1 oz/2 tbsp sesame seeds
50 g/2 oz/⅓ cup raisins

Melt the butter or margarine with the honey, then stir in all the remaining ingredients and mix well. Spoon into a greased 20 cm/8 in square cake tin (pan) and level the surface. Press the mixture down gently. Bake in a preheated oven at 190°C/375°F/gas mark 5 for 20 minutes. Leave to cool slightly, then cut into bars and remove from the tin when cold.

Toffee Squares

Makes 16

75 g/3 oz/¾ cup plain
(all-purpose) flour
50 g/2 oz/¼ cup butter or margarine,
softened
25 g/1 oz/2 tbsp soft brown sugar
A pinch of salt
1.5 ml/¼ tsp bicarbonate of soda
(baking soda)
30 ml/2 tbsp milk

For the topping:
75 g/3 oz/⅓ cup butter or margarine
75 g/3 oz/⅓ cup soft brown sugar
25 g/1 oz/¼ cup chocolate chips

Blend together all the cake ingredients, adding just enough milk to make a soft dropping consistency. Press into a greased 23 cm/9 in square cake tin (pan) and bake in a preheated oven at 180°C/ 350°F/gas mark 4 for 15 minutes until golden brown.

To make the topping, melt the butter or margarine and sugar in a small pan, bring to the boil, then simmer for 2 minutes, stirring continuously. Pour over the base and return to the oven for 5 minutes. Sprinkle with the chocolate chips and leave them to soften into the topping as the cake cools. Cut into bars.

Toffee Traybake

Makes 16

100 g/4 oz/½ cup butter or margarine,
softened
100 g/4 oz/½ cup soft brown sugar
1 egg yolk
50 g/2 oz/½ cup plain (all-purpose)
flour
50 g/2 oz/½ cup rolled oats
For the topping:
100 g/4 oz/1 cup plain (semi-sweet)
chocolate
25 g/1 oz/2 tbsp butter or margarine
30 ml/2 tbsp chopped walnuts

Beat together the butter or margarine, sugar and egg yolk until smooth. Stir in the flour and oats. Press into a greased 30 × 20 cm/12 × 8 in Swiss roll tin (jelly roll pan) and bake in a preheated oven at 190°C/375°F/gas mark 5 for 20 minutes.

To make the topping, melt the chocolate and butter or margarine in a heatproof bowl set over a pan of gently simmering water. Spread over the mixture and sprinkle with the walnuts. Leave to cool slightly, then cut into bars and leave to cool in the tin.

Cheesecakes

*T*here are two basic types of cheesecake: chilled and baked. The former tend to be lighter in texture and often have a crushed biscuit base. Baked cheesecakes have a heavier texture and richer flavour. Most plain cheesecakes go particularly well with fruit, so you can top almost any of these cakes with a purée of fresh or cooked fruits.

Apricot Cheesecake

Makes one 23 cm/9 in cake

*225 g/8 oz/2 cups ginger biscuit
(cookie) crumbs*
30 ml/2 tbsp soft brown sugar
*50 g/2 oz/¼ cup butter or margarine,
melted*
For the filling:
15 g/½ oz/1 tbsp powdered gelatine
*225 g/8 oz/1 cup caster (superfine)
sugar*
*250 ml/8 fl oz/1 cup syrup from the
can of apricots*
90 ml/6 tbsp brandy or apricot brandy
45 ml/3 tbsp lemon juice
4 eggs, separated
450 g/1 lb/2 cups soft cream cheese
250 ml/8 fl oz/1 cup whipping cream
For the topping:
*400 g/14 oz/1 large can apricot halves
in syrup, drained and syrup
reserved*
90 ml/6 tbsp apricot brandy
30 ml/2 tbsp cornflour (cornstarch)

Stir the biscuit crumbs and brown sugar into the melted butter and press into the base of a 23 cm/9 in loose-bottomed cake tin (pan). Bake in a preheated oven at 160°C/335°F/gas mark 3 for 10 minutes. Remove and leave to cool.

To make the filling, blend the gelatine and half the sugar into the apricot syrup, brandy and lemon juice. Cook over a low heat for about 10 minutes, stirring continuously, until thickened. Stir in the egg yolks. Remove from the heat and leave to cool slightly. Beat the cheese until smooth. Slowly mix the gelatine mixture into the cheese and chill until slightly thickened. Whisk the egg whites until they form soft peaks, then gradually beat in the remaining sugar until the mixture is stiff and glossy. Beat the cream until stiff. Fold the two mixtures into the cheese and spoon into the baked base. Chill for several hours until firm.

Arrange the apricot halves on top of the cheesecake. Heat the brandy and cornflour together, stirring until thick and clear. Leave to cool slightly, then spoon over the apricots to glaze.

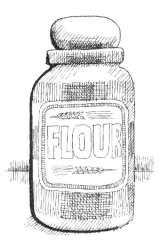

Avocado Cheesecake

Makes one 20 cm/8 in cake

225 g/8 oz/2 cups digestive biscuit
(Graham cracker) crumbs
75 g/3 oz/⅓ cup butter or margarine,
melted
For the filling:
10 ml/2 tsp powdered gelatine
30 ml/2 tbsp water
2 ripe avocados
Juice of ½ lemon
Grated rind of 1 lemon
100 g/4 oz/½ cup cream cheese
75 g/3 oz/⅓ cup caster (superfine)
sugar
2 egg whites
300 ml/½ pt/1¼ cups whipping or
double (heavy) cream

Mix together the biscuit crumbs and melted butter or margarine and press into the base and sides of a greased 20 cm/8 in loose-bottomed cake tin (pan). Chill.

Sprinkle the gelatine over the water in a bowl and leave until spongy. Stand the bowl in a pan of hot water and leave until dissolved. Leave to cool slightly. Peel and stone (pit) the avocados and mash the flesh with the lemon juice and rind. Beat in the cheese and sugar. Stir in the dissolved gelatine. Whisk the egg whites until stiff, then fold them into the mixture using a metal spoon. Whip half the cream until stiff, then fold it into the mixture. Spoon over the biscuit base and chill until set.

Whip the remaining cream until stiff, then pipe it decoratively on top of the cheesecake.

Banana Cheesecake

Makes one 20 cm/8 in cake

75 g/3 oz/⅓ cup butter or margarine,
melted
175 g/6 oz/1½ cups digestive biscuit
(Graham cracker) crumbs
For the filling:
2 bananas, mashed
350 g/12 oz/1½ cups firm tofu
100 g/4 oz/½ cup cottage cheese
Grated rind and juice of 1 lemon
Lemon slices to garnish

Mix together the butter or margarine and biscuit crumbs and press into the base of a greased 20 cm/8 in loose-bottomed cake tin (pan). Beat together all the topping ingredients and spoon over the base. Chill for 4 hours before serving garnished with lemon slices.

Light Caribbean Cheesecake

Makes one 20 cm/8 in cake

75 g/3 oz/⅓ cup butter or margarine
175 g/6 oz/1¾ cups plain
(all-purpose) flour
A pinch of salt
30 ml/2 tbsp cold water
400 g/14 oz/1 large can pineapple,
drained and chopped
150 g/5 oz/⅔ cup cottage cheese
2 eggs, separated
15 ml/1 tbsp rum

Rub the butter or margarine into the flour and salt until the mixture resembles breadcrumbs. Mix in enough water to make a pastry (paste). Roll out and use to line a 20 cm/8 in flan ring. Mix together the pineapple, cheese, egg yolks and rum. Whisk the egg whites until stiff, then fold them into the mixture. Spoon into the case (shell). Bake in a preheated oven at 200°C/400°F/gas mark 6 for 20 minutes. Allow to cool in the tin before turning out.

Black Cherry Cheesecake

__Makes one 20 cm/8 in cake__

75 g/3 oz/⅓ cup butter or margarine, melted
175 g/6 oz/1½ cups digestive biscuit (Graham cracker) crumbs
For the filling:
350 g/12 oz/1½ cups firm tofu
100 g/4 oz/½ cup cottage cheese
Grated rind and juice of 1 lemon
400 g/14 oz/1 large can black cherries, drained

Mix together the butter or margarine and biscuit crumbs and press into the base of a greased 20 cm/8 in loose-bottomed cake tin (pan). Beat together the tofu, cheese, lemon juice and rind, then stir in the cherries. Spoon over the base. Chill for 4 hours before serving.

Coconut and Apricot Cheesecake

__Makes one 20 cm/8 in cake__

For the crust:
200 g/7 oz/1¾ cups desiccated (shredded) coconut
75 g/3 oz/⅓ cup butter or margarine, melted
For the filling:
120 ml/4 fl oz/½ cup condensed milk
30 ml/2 tbsp lemon juice
250 g/9 oz/1 tub cream cheese
120 ml/4 fl oz/½ cup double (heavy) cream
For the topping:
5 ml/1 tsp powdered gelatine
30 ml/2 tbsp water
100 g/4 oz/⅓ cup apricot jam (conserve), sieved (strained)
30 ml/2 tbsp caster (superfine) sugar

Toast the coconut in a dry frying pan (skillet) until golden. Stir in the butter or margarine, then press the mixture firmly into a 20 cm/8 in pie dish. Chill.

Mix together the condensed milk and lemon juice, then stir in the cream cheese. Whip the cream until stiff, then fold it into the mixture. Spoon into the coconut base.

Mix the gelatine and water in a small pan over a very low heat and stir in the jam and sugar for a few minutes until clear and well blended. Spoon over the filling, then leave to cool and chill until set.

Cranberry Cheesecake

__Makes one 23 cm/9 in cake__

100 g/4 oz/1 cup digestive biscuit (Graham cracker) crumbs
50 g/2 oz/¼ cup butter or margarine, melted
225 g/8 oz cranberries, rinsed and drained
150 ml/¼ pt/⅔ cup water
150 g/5 oz/⅔ cup caster (superfine) sugar
15 g/½ oz/1 tbsp powdered gelatine
60 ml/4 tbsp water
225 g/8 oz/1 cup cream cheese
175 g/6 oz/¾ cup Ricotta cheese
5 ml/1 tsp vanilla essence (extract)

Mix together the biscuit crumbs and melted butter and press into the base of a greased 23 cm/9 in spring-form cake tin (pan). Chill.

Place the cranberries, 150 ml/¼ pt/⅔ cup of water and sugar in a pan and bring to the boil. Boil for 10 minutes, stirring occasionally. Sprinkle the gelatine over the 60 ml/4 tbsp of water in a bowl and leave until spongy. Stand the bowl in a pan of hot water and leave until dissolved. Stir the gelatine into the cranberry mixture, remove from the heat and leave to cool slightly. Mix in the cheeses and vanilla essence. Spoon the mixture into the base and spread evenly. Chill for several hours until firm.

Ginger Cheesecake

Makes one 900 g/2 lb cake

275 g/10 oz/2½ cups ginger biscuit (cookie) crumbs
100 g/4 oz/½ cup butter or margarine, melted
225 g/8 oz/1 cup cream cheese
150 ml/¼ pt/⅔ cup double (heavy) cream
100 g/4 oz/½ cup caster (superfine) sugar
15 ml/1 tbsp chopped stem ginger
15 ml/1 tbsp brandy or ginger syrup
2 eggs, separated
Juice of 1 lemon
15 g/½ oz/1 tbsp powdered gelatine

Stir the biscuits into the butter. Mix together the cream cheese, cream, sugar, ginger and brandy or ginger syrup. Beat in the egg yolks. Put the lemon juice into a small pan and sprinkle over the gelatine. Leave to soak for a few minutes, then dissolve over a gentle heat. Do not boil. Whisk the egg whites into soft peaks. Stir 15 ml/1 tbsp thoroughly into the cheese mixture. Carefully fold in the remainder. Pour half the mixture into a lightly greased 900 g/2 lb loaf tin (pan). Sprinkle evenly with half the biscuit mixture. Add another layer of the remaining cheese and biscuit mixtures. Chill for several hours. Dip the tin in boiling water for a few seconds, then cover with a plate and turn out ready to serve.

Ginger and Lemon Cheesecake

Makes one 20 cm/8 in cake

175 g/6 oz/1½ cups gingernut biscuit (cookie) crumbs
50 g/2 oz/¼ cup butter or margarine, melted
15 g/½ oz/1 tbsp gelatine
30 ml/2 tbsp cold water
2 lemons
100 g/4 oz/½ cup cottage cheese
100 g/4 oz/½ cup cream cheese
50 g/2 oz/¼ cup caster (superfine) sugar
150 ml/¼ pt/⅔ cup plain yoghurt
150 ml/¼ pt/⅔ cup double (heavy) cream

Stir the biscuit crumbs into the butter or margarine. Press the mixture into the base of a 20 cm/8 in loose-bottomed flan ring. Sprinkle the gelatine on the water, then dissolve over a pan of hot water. Pare three strips of rind from one lemon. Grate the remaining rind of both lemons. Quarter the lemons, remove the pips and skin and purée the flesh in a food processor or blender. Add the cheese and mix. Add the sugar, yoghurt and cream and mix again. Mix in the gelatine. Pour over the base and chill until set. Decorate with the lemon rind.

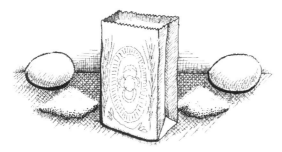

115

Hazelnut and Honey Cheesecake

Makes one 23 cm/9 in cake

175 g/6 oz/1½ cups digestive biscuit
(Graham cracker) crumbs
75 g/3 oz/⅓ cup butter or margarine,
melted
100 g/4 oz/1 cup hazelnuts
225 g/8 oz/1 cup cream cheese
60 ml/4 tbsp clear honey
2 eggs, separated
15 g/½ oz/1 tbsp powdered gelatine
30 ml/2 tbsp water
250 ml/8 fl oz/1 cup double (heavy)
cream

Mix together the biscuit crumbs and butter and press into the base of a 23 cm/9 in loose-bottomed flan tin. Reserve a few hazelnuts for decoration and grind the remainder. Mix with the cream cheese, honey and egg yolks and beat well. Meanwhile, sprinkle the gelatine on the water and leave to stand until spongy. Place the bowl in a pan of hot water and stir until melted. Stir into the cheese mixture with the cream. Whisk the egg whites until stiff and gently fold them into the mixture. Spoon over the base and chill until set. Garnish with the whole hazelnuts.

Gooseberry and Ginger Cheesecake

Makes one 23 cm/9 in cake

3 pieces stem ginger, thinly sliced
50 g/2 oz/¼ cup granulated sugar
75 ml/5 tbsp water
225 g/8 oz gooseberries
50 g/2 oz/½ pack lime-flavoured jelly
(jello)
15 g/½ oz/1 tbsp powdered gelatine
Grated rind and juice of ½ lemon
225 g/ 8 oz/1 cup cream cheese
75 g/3 oz/⅓ cup caster (superfine)
sugar
2 eggs, separated
300 ml/½ pt/1¼ cups double (heavy)
cream
75 g/3 oz/⅓ cup butter or margarine,
melted
175 g/6 oz/1½ cups ginger biscuit
(cookie) crumbs

Grease and line a 23 cm/9 in loose-bottomed flan ring. Arrange the stem ginger around the edge of the base. Dissolve the granulated sugar in the water in a pan, then bring to the boil. Add the gooseberries and simmer gently for about 15 minutes until just tender. Lift the gooseberries out of the syrup with a slotted spoon and arrange in the centre of the prepared tin. Measure the syrup and make up to 275 ml/9 fl oz/scant 1 cup with water. Return to a low heat and stir in the jelly until dissolved. Remove from the heat and leave until beginning to set. Spoon over the gooseberries and chill until set.

Sprinkle the gelatine over 45 ml/ 3 tbsp of the lemon juice in a bowl and leave until spongy. Stand the bowl in a pan of hot water and leave until dissolved. Beat the cream cheese with the lemon rind, caster sugar, egg yolks, gelatine and half the cream. Whip the remaining cream until thick, then fold it into the mixture. Whisk the egg whites until stiff, then lightly fold them in. Spoon into the tin and chill until set.

Mix together the butter or margarine and biscuit crumbs and sprinkle over the cheesecake. Press down lightly to firm the base. Chill until firm.

Dip the base of the tin in hot water for a few seconds, run a knife around the edge of the cheesecake, then turn out on to a serving plate.

Light Lemon Cheesecake

Makes one 20 cm/8 in cake

For the base:
50 g/2 oz/¼ cup butter or margarine
50 g/2 oz/¼ cup caster (superfine)
sugar
100 g/4 oz/1 cup digestive biscuit
(Graham cracker) crumbs
For the filling:
225 g/8 oz/1 cup full-fat soft cheese
2 eggs, separated
100 g/4 oz/½ cup caster (superfine)
sugar
Grated rind of 3 lemons
150 ml/¼ pt/⅔ cup double (heavy)
cream
Juice of 1 lemon
45 ml/3 tbsp water
15 g/½ oz/1 tbsp powdered gelatine
For the topping:
45 ml/3 tbsp lemon curd

To make the base, melt the butter or margarine and sugar over a gentle heat. Stir in the biscuit crumbs. Press into the base of a 20 cm/8 in cake tin (pan) and chill in the fridge.

To make the filling, soften the cheese in a large mixing bowl. Beat in the egg yolks, half the sugar, the lemon rind and cream. Put the lemon juice, water and gelatine in a bowl and dissolve over a pan of hot water. Beat into the cheese mixture and leave until on the point of setting. Whisk the egg whites until stiff, then whisk in the remaining caster sugar. Fold lightly but thoroughly into the cheese mixture. Spoon on to the base and smooth the surface. Chill for 3–4 hours until set. Spread with lemon curd to finish.

Lemon Muesli Cheesecake

Makes one 20 cm/8 in cake

175 g/6 oz/generous 1 cup muesli
75 g/3 oz/⅓ cup butter or margarine,
melted
Finely grated rind and juice of
2 lemons
15 g/½ oz/1 tbsp powdered gelatine
225 g/8 oz/1 cup cream cheese
150 ml/¼ pt/⅔ cup plain yoghurt
60 ml/4 tbsp clear honey
2 egg whites

Stir the muesli into the butter or margarine and press into the base of a greased 20 cm/8 in loose-bottomed flan tin (pan). Chill until set.

Make the lemon juice up to 150 ml/¼ pt/⅔ cup with water. Sprinkle the gelatine over and leave to stand until soft. Stand the bowl in a pan of hot water and heat gently until the gelatine has dissolved. Mix together the lemon rind, cheese, yoghurt and honey, then stir in the gelatine. Whisk the egg whites until they form stiff peaks, then gently fold into the cheesecake mixture. Spoon over the base and chill until firm.

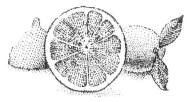

117

Mandarin Cheesecake

Makes one 20 cm/8 in cake

200 g/7 oz/1¾ cups digestive biscuit (Graham cracker) crumbs
75 g/3 oz/⅓ cup butter or margarine, melted
For the topping:
275 g/10 oz/1 large can mandarins, drained
15 g/½ oz/1 tbsp powdered gelatine
30 ml/2 tbsp hot water
150 g/5 oz/⅔ cup cottage cheese
150 ml/¼ pt/⅔ cup plain yoghurt

Mix together the biscuit crumbs and butter or margarine and press into the base of a 20 cm/8 in loose-bottomed flan ring. Chill. Crush the mandarins with the back of a spoon. Sprinkle the gelatine on the water in a small bowl and leave until spongy. Place the bowl in a pan of boiling water and leave until dissolved. Mix together the mandarins, cottage cheese, and yoghurt. Stir in the gelatine. Spoon the filling mixture over the base and chill until set.

Lemon and Nut Cheesecake

Makes one 20 cm/8 in cake

For the base:
225 g/8 oz/2 cups digestive biscuit (Graham cracker) crumbs
25 g/1 oz/2 tbsp caster (superfine) sugar
5 ml/1 tsp ground cinnamon
50 g/2 oz/¼ cup butter or margarine, melted
For the filling:
15 g/½ oz/1 tbsp powdered gelatine
30 ml/2 tbsp cold water
2 eggs, separated
100 g/4 oz/½ cup caster (superfine) sugar
350 g/12 oz/1½ cups full-fat soft cheese

Grated rind and juice of 1 lemon
150 ml/¼ pt/⅔ cup double (heavy) cream
25 g/1 oz/¼ cup chopped mixed nuts

Stir in the biscuit crumbs, sugar and cinnamon into the butter or margarine. Press over the base and sides of a 20 cm/8 in loose-bottomed flan tin (pan). Chill.
To make the filling, dissolve the gelatine in the water in a small bowl. Stand the bowl in a pan of hot water and stir until the gelatine dissolves. Remove from the heat and leave to cool slightly. Beat together the egg yolks and sugar. Stand the bowl over a pan of gently simmering water and continue to beat until the mixture is thick and light. Remove from the heat and beat until lukewarm. Fold in the cheese, lemon rind and juice. Whip the cream until stiff, then fold it into the mixture with the nuts. Carefully stir in the gelatine. Whisk the egg whites until stiff, then fold them into the mixture. Spoon into the base and chill for several hours or overnight before serving.

Lime Cheesecake

Serves 8

For the base:
40 g/1½ oz/2 tbsp clear honey
50 g/2 oz/¼ cup demerara sugar
225 g/8 oz/2 cups rolled oats
100 g/4 oz/½ cup butter or margarine, melted
For the filling:
225 g/8 oz/1 cup quark
250 ml/8 fl oz/1 cup plain yoghurt
2 eggs, separated
50 g/2 oz/¼ cup caster (superfine) sugar
Grated rind and juice of 2 limes
15 g/½ oz/1 tbsp powdered gelatine
30 ml/2 tbsp boiling water

Stir the honey, demerara sugar and oats into the butter or margarine. Press into the base of a greased 20 cm/8 in cake tin (pan).

To make the filling, mix together the quark, yoghurt, egg yolks, sugar and lime rind. Sprinkle the gelatine on the lime juice and hot water and leave until dissolved. Warm over a bowl of hot water until transparent, then stir into the mixture and stir gently until beginning to set. Whisk the egg whites until they form soft peaks, then fold into the mixture. Spoon over the prepared base and leave to set.

St Clement's Cheesecake

Makes one 20 cm/8 in cake

50 g/2 oz/¼ cup butter or margarine
100 g/4 oz/1 cup digestive biscuit
   (Graham cracker) crumbs
2 eggs, separated
A pinch of salt
100 g/4 oz/½ cup caster (superfine)
   sugar
45 ml/3 tbsp orange juice
45 ml/3 tbsp lemon juice
15 g/½ oz/1 tbsp gelatine
30 ml/2 tbsp cold water
350 g/12 oz/1½ cups cottage cheese,
   sieved
150 ml/¼ pt/⅔ cup double (heavy)
   cream, whipped
1 orange, peeled and sliced

Rub a 20 cm/8 in loose-bottomed cake tin (pan) with the butter and sprinkle with the biscuit crumbs. Beat the egg yolks with the salt and half the sugar until thick and creamy. Put into a bowl with the orange and lemon juices and stir over a pan of hot water until the mixture begins to thicken and will coat the back of a spoon. Dissolve the gelatine in the cold water and heat gently until syrupy. Stir into the fruit juice mixture, then leave to cool, stirring occasionally. Stir in the cottage cheese and cream. Whisk the egg whites until stiff, then fold in the remaining sugar. Fold into the cheesecake mixture and pour into the cake tin. Chill until firm. Turn out and sprinkle with any loose crumbs. Serve decorated with orange slices.

Pashka

Makes one 23 cm/9 in cake

450 g/1 lb/2 cups cream cheese
100 g/4 oz/½ cup butter or margarine,
   softened
150 g/5 oz/⅔ cup caster (superfine)
   sugar
150 ml/¼ pt/⅔ cup soured (dairy sour)
   cream
175 g/6 oz/1 cup sultanas
   (golden raisins)
50 g/2 oz/¼ cup glacé (candied)
   cherries
100 g/4 oz/1 cup almonds
50 g/2 oz/⅓ cup chopped mixed
   (candied) peel

Mix together the cheese, butter or margarine, sugar and soured cream until well blended. Stir in the remaining ingredients. Spoon into a savarin mould, cover and chill overnight. Dip the mould in a pan of hot water for a few seconds, run a knife around the rim of the mould and invert the cheesecake on to a plate. Chill before serving.

Light Pineapple Cheesecake

Makes one 25 cm/10 in cake

225 g/8 oz/1 cup butter or margarine
225 g/8 oz/2 cups digestive biscuit
  (Graham cracker) crumbs
450 g/1 lb/2 cups quark
1 egg, beaten
5 ml/1 tsp almond essence (extract)
15 ml/1 tbsp caster (superfine) sugar
25 g/1 oz/¼ cup ground almonds
100 g/4 oz canned pineapple, chopped

Melt half the butter or margarine and stir in the biscuit crumbs. Press into the base of a 25 cm/10 in flan dish and leave to cool. Cream the remaining butter or margarine with the quark, egg, almond essence, sugar and ground almonds. Stir in the pineapple. Spread over the biscuit base and chill for 2 hours.

Pineapple Cheesecake

Makes one 20 cm/8 in cake

75 g/3 oz/⅓ cup butter or margarine,
  melted
175 g/6 oz/1½ cups digestive biscuit
  (Graham cracker) crumbs
15 g/½ oz/1 tbsp powdered gelatine
425 g/15 oz/1 large can pineapple in
  natural juice, drained and juice
  reserved
3 eggs, separated
75 g/3 oz/⅓ cup caster (superfine)
  sugar
150 ml/¼ pt/⅔ cup single (light) cream
150 ml/¼ pt/⅔ cup double (heavy)
  cream
225 g/8 oz/2 cups Cheddar cheese,
  grated
150 ml/¼ pt/⅔ cup milk
150 ml/¼ pt/⅔ cup whipping cream

Mix the butter or margarine with the biscuit crumbs and press into the base of a 20 cm/8 in loose-bottomed flan ring. Chill until firm.

Sprinkle the gelatine over 30 ml/2 tbsp of the reserved pineapple juice in a bowl and leave until spongy. Reserve a little of the pineapple for decoration, then chop the remainder and arrange over the biscuit base. Stand the bowl in a pan of hot water and leave until dissolved. Whisk together the egg yolks, sugar and 150 ml/¼ pt/⅔ cup of the reserved pineapple juice in a heatproof bowl set over a pan of gently simmering water until the mixture is thick and trails off the whisk in ribbons. Remove from the heat. Whip together the single and double creams until thick, stir in the cheese and milk, then fold into the egg mixture with the gelatine. Leave to cool. Whisk the egg whites until stiff, then gently fold into the mixture. Spoon over the pineapple and chill until set.

Whip the whipping cream and pipe rosettes round the top of the cake, then decorate with the reserved pineapple.

Raisin Cheesecake

Serves 8

For the base:
100 g/4 oz/½ cup butter or margarine
40 g/1½ oz/2 tbsp clear honey
50 g/2 oz/¼ cup demerara sugar
225 g/8 oz/2 cups rolled oats
For the filling:
225 g/8 oz/1 cup cottage cheese
150 ml/¼ pt/⅔ cup plain yoghurt
150 ml/¼ pt/⅔ cup soured (dairy sour)
  cream
50 g/2 oz/⅓ cup raisins
15 g/½ oz/1 tbsp powdered gelatine
60 ml/4 tbsp boiling water

Melt the butter or margarine, then stir in the honey, sugar and oats. Press into the base of a greased 20 cm/8 in cake tin (pan).

To make the filling, sieve the cottage cheese into a bowl and mix with the yoghurt and soured cream. Stir in the raisins. Sprinkle the gelatine on the hot water and leave until dissolved. Warm over a bowl of hot water until transparent, then stir into the mixture and stir gently until beginning to set. Spoon over the prepared base and leave to set.

Raspberry Cheesecake
Makes one 15 cm/6 in cake

75 g/3 oz/⅓ cup butter or margarine, melted
175 g/6 oz/1½ cups digestive biscuit (Graham cracker) crumbs
3 eggs, separated
300 ml/½ pt/1¼ cups milk
25 g/1 oz/2 tbsp caster (superfine) sugar
15 g/½ oz/1 tbsp gelatine
30 ml/2 tbsp cold water
225 g/8 oz/1 cup cream cheese, lightly beaten
Grated rind and juice of ½ lemon
450 g/1 lb raspberries

Mix together the butter or margarine and biscuits and press into the base of a loose-bottomed 15 cm/6 in cake tin (pan). Chill while making the filling.

Whisk the egg yolks, then pour into a pan with the milk and heat gently, stirring continuously, until the custard thickens. Remove from the heat and stir in the sugar. Sprinkle the gelatine on the hot water and leave until dissolved. Warm over a bowl of hot water until transparent, then stir into the cheese with the custard, lemon rind and juice. Whisk the egg whites until stiff, then fold into the mixture and spoon over the base. Chill to set. Decorate with the raspberries just before serving.

Sicilian Cheesecake
Makes one 25 cm/10 in cake

900 g/2 lb/4 cups Ricotta cheese
100 g/4 oz/⅔ cup icing (confectioners') sugar
5 ml/1 tsp grated orange rind
100 g/4 oz/1 cup plain (semi-sweet) chocolate, grated
275 g/10 oz chopped mixed fruit
275 g/10 oz sponge finger biscuits (cookies) or sponge cake, sliced
175 ml/6 fl oz/¾ cup rum

Beat the Ricotta with half the sugar and the orange rind. Reserve 15 ml/1 tbsp of the chocolate and fruit for decoration, then fold the remainder into the mixture. Line a 25 cm/10 in cake tin (pan) with clingfilm (plastic wrap). Dip the biscuits or sponge into the rum to moisten, then use most of them to line the bottom and sides of the tin. Spread the cheese mixture inside. Dip the remaining biscuits in the rum and use to cover the cheese mixture. Cover with clingfilm (plastic wrap) and press down. Chill for 1 hour until firm. Turn out, using the clingfilm to help, dust with the remaining icing sugar and decorate with the reserved chocolate and fruit.

121

Glazed Yoghurt Cheesecake

Makes one 23 cm/9 in cake

For the base:
2 eggs
75 g/3 oz/¼ cup clear honey
100 g/4 oz/1 cup wholemeal
(wholewheat) flour
10 ml/2 tsp baking powder
A few drops of vanilla essence
(extract)
For the filling:
25 g/1 oz/2 tbsp powdered gelatine
30 ml/2 tbsp caster (superfine) sugar
75 ml/5 tbsp water
225 g/8 oz/1 cup plain yoghurt
225 g/8 oz/1 cup soft cream cheese
75 g/3 oz/¼ cup clear honey
250 ml/8 fl oz/1 cup whipping cream
For the topping:
100 g/4 oz raspberries
45 ml/3 tbsp jam (conserve)
15 ml/1 tbsp water

To make the base, whisk the eggs and honey until fluffy. Gradually work in the flour, baking powder and vanilla essence to make a smooth dough. Roll out on a lightly floured surface and place in the base of a greased 23 cm/9 in loose-bottomed cake tin (pan). Bake in a preheated oven at 200°C/400°F/gas mark 6 for 20 minutes. Remove from the oven and leave to cool.

To make the filling, dissolve the gelatine and sugar in the water in a small bowl, then leave the mixture in a pan of hot water until transparent. Remove from the water and leave to cool slightly. Beat together the yoghurt, cream cheese and honey until well blended. Whisk the cream until stiff. Fold the cream into the yoghurt mixture, then fold in the gelatine. Spoon over the base and leave to set.

Arrange the raspberries in an attractive pattern over the top. Melt the jam with the water, then push through a sieve (strainer). Brush over the top of the cheesecake and chill before serving.

Strawberry Cheesecake

Makes one 20 cm/8 in cake

100 g/4 oz/1 cup digestive biscuit
(Graham cracker) crumbs
25 g/1 oz/2 tbsp demerara sugar
50 g/2 oz/¼ cup butter or margarine,
melted
15 ml/1 tbsp powdered gelatine
45 ml/3 tbsp water
350 g/12 oz/1½ cups cottage cheese
50 g/2 oz/¼ cup caster (superfine)
sugar
Grated rind and juice of 1 lemon
2 eggs, separated
300 ml/½ pt/1¼ cups single (light)
cream
100 g/4 oz strawberries, sliced
120 ml/4 fl oz/½ cup double (heavy)
cream, whipped

Mix together the biscuit crumbs, demerara sugar and butter or margarine and press into the base of a 20 cm/8 in loose-bottomed flan tin (pan). Chill until firm.

Sprinkle the gelatine on the water and leave until spongy. Stand the bowl in a pan of hot water and leave until transparent. Mix together the cheese, caster sugar, lemon rind and juice, egg yolks and single cream. Beat in the gelatine. Whisk the egg whites until stiff, then fold into the cheese mixture. Spoon over the base and chill until set.

Arrange the strawberries over the top of the cheesecake and pipe the cream round the edge to decorate.

Sultana and Brandy Cheesecake

Makes one 20 cm/8 in cake

100 g/4 oz/²⁄₃ cup sultanas
(golden raisins)
45 ml/3 tbsp brandy
100 g/4 oz/½ cup butter or margarine,
softened
100 g/4 oz/½ cup soft brown sugar
75 g/3 oz/¾ cup plain (all-purpose)
flour
75 g/3 oz/¾ cup ground almonds
2 eggs, separated
225 g/8 oz/1 cup cream cheese
100 g/4 oz/½ cup curd (smooth
cottage) cheese
A few drops of vanilla essence
(extract)
150 ml/¼ pt/²⁄₃ cup double (heavy)
cream

Put the sultanas in a bowl with the brandy and leave to soak until plump. Cream together the butter or margarine and 50 g/2 oz/¼ cup of sugar until pale and fluffy. Mix in the flour and ground almonds and blend together to a dough. Press into a greased 20 cm/8 in loose-bottomed cake tin (pan) and bake in a preheated oven at 180°C/350°F/gas mark 4 for 12 minutes until browned. Leave to cool.

Beat the egg yolks with half the remaining sugar. Beat in the cheeses, vanilla essence, sultanas and brandy. Whip the cream until stiff, then fold into the mixture. Whisk the egg whites until stiff, then whisk in the remaining sugar and beat again until stiff and glossy. Fold into the cheese mixture. Spoon over the cooked base and chill for several hours until set.

Baked Cheesecake

Makes one 20 cm/8 in cake

50 g/2 oz/¼ cup butter or margarine,
melted
225 g/8 oz/2 cups digestive biscuit
(Graham cracker) crumbs
225 g/8 oz/1 cup cottage cheese
100 g/4 oz/½ cup caster (superfine)
sugar
3 eggs, separated
25 g/1 oz/¼ cup cornflour (cornstarch)
2.5 ml/½ tsp vanilla essence (extract)
400 ml/14 fl oz/1¾ cups soured (dairy
sour) cream

Blend together the butter or margarine and biscuit crumbs and press into the base of a greased 20 cm/8 in loose-bottomed flan tin (pan). Mix together all the remaining ingredients except the egg whites. Beat the egg whites until stiff, then fold into the mixture and spoon over the biscuit base. Bake in a preheated oven at 150°C/300°F/gas mark 3 for 1½ hours. Turn off the oven and open the door slightly. Leave the cheesecake in the oven until cool.

Baked Cheesecake Bars

Makes 16

75 g/3 oz/⅓ cup butter or margarine
100 g/4 oz/1 cup plain (all-purpose)
flour
75 g/3 oz/⅓ cup soft brown sugar
50 g/2 oz/½ cup chopped pecan nuts
225 g/8 oz/1 cup cream cheese
50 g/2 oz/¼ cup caster (superfine)
sugar
1 egg
30 ml/2 tbsp milk
5 ml/1 tsp lemon juice
2.5 ml/½ tsp vanilla essence (extract)

Rub the butter or margarine into the flour until the mixture resembles breadcrumbs. Stir in the brown sugar and nuts. Press all but 100 g/4 oz/1 cup of the mixture into a greased 20 cm/8 in cake tin (pan). Bake in a preheated oven at 180°C/350°F/gas mark 4 for 15 minutes until lightly browned.

Beat together the cream cheese and caster sugar until smooth. Beat in the egg, milk, lemon juice and vanilla essence. Spread the mixture over the cake in the pan and sprinkle with the reserved butter and nut mixture. Bake for a further 30 minutes until just set and lightly golden on top. Leave to cool, then chill and serve cold.

American Cheesecake

Makes one 23 cm/9 in cake

175 g/6 oz/1½ cups digestive biscuit
(Graham cracker) crumbs
15 ml/1 tbsp caster (superfine) sugar
50 g/2 oz/¼ cup butter or margarine,
melted
For the filling:
450 g/1 lb/2 cups cream cheese
450 g/1 lb/2 cups cottage cheese
250 g/9 oz/generous 1 cup caster
(superfine) sugar
10 ml/2 tsp vanilla essence (extract)
5 eggs, separated
400 ml/14 fl oz/1 large can evaporated
milk
120 ml/4 fl oz/½ cup double (heavy)
cream
30 ml/2 tbsp plain (all-purpose) flour
A pinch of salt
15 ml/1 tbsp lemon juice

Mix the biscuit crumbs and sugar into the melted butter and press into the base of a 23 cm/9 in loose-bottomed cake tin (pan).

To make the filling, mix together the cheeses, then stir in the sugar and vanilla essence. Blend in the egg yolks, followed by the evaporated milk, cream, flour, salt and lemon juice. Whisk the egg whites until stiff, then carefully fold into the mixture. Spoon into the cake tin and bake in a preheated oven at 180°C/350°F/gas mark 4 for 45 minutes. Leave to cool slowly, then chill before serving.

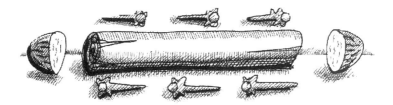

Baked Dutch Apple Cheesecake

Makes one 20 cm/8 in cake

100 g/4 oz/½ cup butter or margarine
175 g/6 oz/1½ cups digestive biscuit
(Graham cracker) crumbs
2 eating (dessert) apples, peeled, cored
and sliced
100 g/4 oz/⅔ cup sultanas
(golden raisins)
225 g/8 oz/2 cups Gouda cheese,
grated
25 g/1 oz/¼ cup plain (all-purpose)
flour
75 ml/5 tbsp single (light) cream
2.5 ml/½ tsp ground mixed
(apple-pie) spice
Grated rind and juice of 1 lemon
3 eggs, separated
100 g/4 oz/¾ cup caster (superfine)
sugar
2 red-skinned apples, cored and sliced
30 ml/2 tbsp apricot jam (conserve),
sieved (strained)

Melt half the butter or margarine and stir in the biscuit crumbs. Press the mixture into the base of a loose-bottomed 20 cm/8 in cake tin (pan). Melt the remaining butter and fry (sauté) the eating apples until soft and golden. Drain off any excess fat, allow to cool slightly, then spread over the biscuit base and sprinkle with the sultanas.

Mix together the cheese, flour, cream, mixed spice and lemon juice and rind. Mix together the egg yolks and sugar and stir into the cheese mixture until well blended. Whisk the egg whites until stiff, then fold into the mixture. Turn into the prepared tin and bake in a preheated oven at 180°C/350°F/gas mark 4 for 40 minutes until firm in the centre. Leave to cool in the tin.

Arrange the apple slices in circles around the top of the cake. Warm the jam and brush it over the apples to glaze.

Baked Apricot and Hazelnut Cheesecake

Makes one 18 cm/7 in cake

75 g/3 oz/⅓ cup butter or margarine
100 g/4 oz/1 cup plain (all-purpose)
flour
100 g/4 oz/½ cup caster (superfine)
sugar
25 g/1 oz/¼ cup ground hazelnuts
30 ml/2 tbsp cold water
100 g/4 oz/⅔ cup ready-to-eat dried
apricots, chopped
Grated rind and juice of 1 lemon
100 g/4 oz/½ cup curd (smooth
cottage) cheese
100 g/4 oz/½ cup cream cheese
25 g/1 oz/¼ cup cornflour (cornstarch)
2 eggs, separated
15 ml/1 tbsp icing (confectioners')
sugar

Rub the butter or margarine into the flour until the mixture resembles breadcrumbs. Stir in half the sugar and the hazelnuts, then add enough of the water to make a firm pastry (paste). Roll out and use to line a greased 18 cm/7 in loose-bottomed flan ring. Spread the apricots over the base. Purée the lemon rind and juice and the cheeses in a food processor or blender. Blend in the remaining sugar, the cornflour and the egg yolks until smooth and creamy. Whisk the egg whites until stiff, then fold into the mixture and spread it over the flan. Bake in a preheated oven at 180°C/350°F/gas 4 for 30 minutes until well risen and golden brown. Allow to cool slightly, then sift the icing sugar over the top and serve warm or cold.

Apricot and Orange Baked Cheesecake

Serves 8

For the pastry (paste):
75 g/3 oz/⅓ cup butter or margarine
175 g/6 oz/1½ cups plain
 (all-purpose) flour
A pinch of salt
30 ml/2 tbsp water
For the filling:
225 g/8 oz/1 cup curd (smooth
 cottage) cheese
75 ml/5 tbsp milk
2 eggs, separated
30 ml/2 tbsp clear honey
3 drops of orange essence (extract)
Grated rind of 1 orange
25 g/1 oz/¼ cup plain (all-purpose)
 flour
75 g/3 oz/½ cup apricot halves,
 chopped

Rub the butter or margarine into the flour and salt until the mixture resembles breadcrumbs. Gradually stir in enough of the water to make a soft dough. Roll out on a lightly floured surface and use to line a greased 20 cm/8 in flan ring. Line with greaseproof (waxed) paper and baking beans and bake blind in a preheated oven at 200°C/400°F/gas mark 6 for 10 minutes, then remove the paper and beans, reduce the oven temperature to 190°C/375°F/gas mark 5 and bake the case (pie shell) for a further 5 minutes. Meanwhile, mix together the cheese, milk, egg yolks, honey, orange essence, orange rind and flour until smooth. Whisk the egg whites until they form soft peaks, then fold them into the mixture. Spoon into the case and sprinkle the apricots on top. Bake in the preheated oven for 20 minutes until just firm.

Apricot and Ricotta Baked Cheesecake

Makes one 23 cm/9 in cake

100 g/4 oz/½ cup butter or margarine
225 g/8 oz/2 cups digestive biscuit
 (Graham cracker) crumbs
75 g/3 oz/⅓ cup caster (superfine)
 sugar
5 ml/1 tsp ground cinnamon
900 g/2 lb/4 cups Ricotta cheese
30 ml/2 tbsp plain (all-purpose) flour
2.5 ml/½ tsp vanilla essence (extract)
Grated rind of 1 lemon
3 egg yolks
350 g/12 oz apricots, stoned (pitted)
 and halved
50 g/2 oz/½ cup flaked (slivered)
 almonds

Melt the butter, then stir in the biscuit crumbs, 30 ml/2 tbsp of the sugar and the cinnamon. Press the mixture into a greased 23 cm/9 in loose-bottomed cake tin (pan). Beat the Ricotta cheese with the remaining sugar, the flour, vanilla essence and lemon rind for 2 minutes. Gradually whisk in the egg yolks until the mixture is smooth. Spoon half the filling over the biscuit base. Spread the apricots over the filling, sprinkle with almonds, then spoon the remaining filling over the top. Bake in a preheated oven at 180°C/350°F/gas mark 4 for 15 minutes until firm to the touch. Leave to cool, then chill.

Boston Cheesecake

Makes one 23 cm/9 in cake

225 g/8 oz/2 cups plain biscuit
(cookie) crumbs
50 g/2 oz/¼ cup caster (superfine)
sugar
2.5 ml/½ tsp ground cinnamon
A pinch of grated nutmeg
75 g/3 oz/⅓ cup butter or margarine,
melted
For the filling:
4 eggs, separated
225 g/8 oz/1 cup caster (superfine)
sugar
250 ml/8 fl oz/1 cup soured (dairy
sour) cream
5 ml/1 tsp vanilla essence (extract)
30 ml/2 tbsp plain (all-purpose) flour
A pinch of salt
450 g/1 lb/2 cups cream cheese

Mix the biscuit crumbs, sugar, cinnamon and nutmeg into the melted butter, then press into the base and sides of a 23 cm/9 in loose-bottomed flan tin (pan). Beat the egg yolks until thick and creamy. Whisk the egg whites until stiff, fold in 50 g/2 oz/¼ cup of the sugar, then continue to beat until stiff and glossy. Mix the soured cream and vanilla essence into the egg yolks, then stir in the remaining sugar, the flour and salt. Carefully stir in the cheese, then fold in the egg whites. Spoon into the base and bake in a preheated oven at 160°C/325°F/gas mark 3 for 1 hour until just firm to the touch. Leave to cool, then chill before serving.

Baked Caribbean Cheesecake

Makes one 23 cm/9 in cake

For the base:
100 g/4 oz/1 cup plain (all-purpose)
flour
25 g/1 oz/¼ cup ground almonds
25 g/1 oz/2 tbsp soft brown sugar
50 g/2 oz/¼ cup butter or margarine,
melted and cooled
1 egg
15 ml/1 tbsp milk
For the filling:
75 g/3 oz/½ cup raisins
15–30 ml/1–2 tbsp rum (to taste)
225 g/8 oz/1 cup curd (smooth
cottage) cheese
50 g/2 oz/¼ cup butter or margarine
25 g/1 oz/¼ cup ground almonds
50 g/2 oz/¼ cup caster (superfine)
sugar
2 eggs

To make the base, mix together the flour, almonds and brown sugar. Work in the butter or margarine, egg and milk and mix to a softish dough. Roll out and shape into the base of a greased 23 cm/9 in cake tin (pan), prick all over with a fork and bake in a preheated oven at 190°C/375°F/gas mark 5 for 10 minutes until light golden.

To make the filling, soak the raisins in the rum until plump. Mix together the cheese, butter, ground almonds and caster sugar. Mix in the eggs, then fold in the raisins and rum to taste. Spoon over the base and bake in the preheated oven for 10 minutes until golden and just firm to the touch.

Baked Chocolate Cheesecake

Makes one 23 cm/9 in cake

For the base:
100 g/4 oz/1 cup ginger biscuit
(cookie) crumbs
15 ml/1 tbsp sugar
50 g/2 oz/¼ cup butter, melted
For the filling:
175 g/6 oz/1½ cups plain
(semi-sweet) chocolate
225 g/8 oz/1 cup caster (superfine)
sugar
30 ml/2 tbsp cocoa (unsweetened
chocolate) powder
450 g/1 lb/2 cups cream cheese
120 ml/4 fl oz/½ cup soured (dairy
sour) cream
5 ml/1 tsp vanilla essence (extract)
4 eggs, lightly beaten

To make the base, mix the biscuits and sugar into the melted butter and press into the base of a greased 23 cm/9 in loose-bottomed cake tin (pan). To make the filling, melt the chocolate with half the sugar and the cocoa in a heatproof bowl set over a pan of gently simmering water. Remove from the heat and leave to cool slightly. Beat the cheese until light, then gradually mix in the remaining sugar, the soured cream and vanilla essence. Gradually beat in the eggs, then stir in the chocolate mixture and spoon over the prepared base. Bake in a preheated oven at 180°C/350°F/gas mark 4 for 40 minutes until firm to the touch.

Chocolate and Nut Cheesecake

Makes one 23 cm/9 in cake

For the base:
100 g/4 oz/1 cup digestive biscuit
(Graham cracker) crumbs
100 g/4 oz/½ cup caster (superfine)
sugar
50 g/2 oz/¼ cup butter, melted
For the filling:
175 g/6 oz/1½ cups plain
(semi-sweet) chocolate
50 g/2 oz/¼ cup caster (superfine)
sugar
30 ml/2 tbsp cocoa (unsweetened
chocolate) powder
450 g/1 lb/2 cups cream cheese
25 g/1 oz/¼ cup ground almonds
120 ml/4 fl oz/½ cup soured (dairy
sour) cream
5 ml/1 tsp almond essence (extract)
4 eggs, lightly beaten

To make the base, mix the biscuit crumbs and 100 g/4 oz/½ cup of the sugar into the melted butter and press into the base of a greased 23 cm/9 in loose-bottomed cake tin (pan). To make the filling, melt the chocolate with the sugar and cocoa in a heatproof bowl set over a pan of gently simmering water. Remove from the heat and leave to cool slightly. Beat the cheese until light, then gradually mix in the remaining sugar, the ground almonds, soured cream and almond essence. Gradually beat in the eggs, then stir in the chocolate mixture and spoon over the prepared base. Bake in a preheated oven at 180°C/350°F/gas mark 4 for 40 minutes until firm to the touch.

Photograph opposite: Battenburg Cake (page 35)

German Cheesecake

Makes one 23 cm/9 in cake

For the base
25 g/1 oz/2 tbsp butter or margarine
225 g/8 oz/2 cups plain
(all-purpose) flour
2.5 ml/½ tsp baking powder
50 g/2 oz/¼ cup caster (superfine)
sugar
1 egg yolk
15 ml/1 tbsp milk
For the filling:
900 g/2 lb/4 cups cottage cheese
225 g/8 oz/1 cup caster (superfine)
sugar
50 g/2 oz/¼ cup butter or margarine,
melted
250 ml/8 fl oz/1 cup double (heavy)
cream
5 ml/1 tsp vanilla essence (extract)
4 eggs, lightly beaten
175 g/6 oz/1 cup sultanas (golden
raisins)
15 ml/1 tbsp cornflour (cornstarch)
A pinch of salt

To make the base, rub the butter or margarine into the flour and baking powder, then stir in the sugar and make a well in the centre. Mix in the egg yolk and milk and blend together to a fairly soft dough. Press into the base of a 23 cm/9 in square cake tin (pan).

To make the filling, drain any excess liquid from the cottage cheese, then stir in the sugar, melted butter, cream and vanilla essence. Stir in the eggs. Toss the sultanas in the cornflour and salt until coated, then stir them into the mixture. Spoon over the base and bake in a preheated oven at 230°C/450°F/gas mark 8 for 10 minutes. Reduce the oven temperature to 190°C/375°F/gas mark 5 and bake for a further 1 hour until firm to the touch. Leave to cool in the tin, then chill.

Irish Cream Liqueur Cheesecake

Makes one 23 cm/9 in cake

For the base:
225 g/8 oz/2 cups digestive biscuit
(Graham cracker) crumbs
50 g/2 oz/½ cup ground almonds
100 g/4 oz/½ cup caster (superfine)
sugar
100 g/4 oz/½ cup butter or margarine,
melted
For the filling:
900 g/2 lb/4 cups cream cheese
225 g/8 oz/1 cup caster (superfine)
sugar
5 ml/1 tsp vanilla essence (extract)
175 ml/6 fl oz/¾ cup Irish cream
liqueur
3 eggs
For the topping:
250 ml/8 fl oz/1 cup soured
(dairy sour) cream
60 ml/4 tbsp Irish cream liqueur
50 g/2 oz/¼ cup caster (superfine)
sugar

To make the base, mix the biscuit crumbs, almonds and sugar with the melted butter or margarine and press into the base and sides of a 23 cm/9 in springform cake tin (pan). Chill.

To make the filling, beat the cream cheese and sugar until smooth. Blend in the vanilla essence and liqueur. Gradually blend in the eggs. Spoon into the base and bake in a preheated oven at 180°C/350°F/gas mark 4 for 40 minutes.

To make the topping, whip together the cream, liqueur and sugar until thick. Spoon over the top of the cheesecake and spread evenly. Return the cheesecake to the oven for a further 5 minutes. Leave to cool, then chill before serving.

Photograph opposite: Farmhouse Honey Fruit Cake (page 55) and Tiny Fruit Cakes (page 60)

American Lemon and Nut Cheesecake

Makes one 20 cm/8 in cake

For the base:
225 g/8 oz/2 cups digestive biscuit (Graham cracker) crumbs
25 g/1 oz/2 tbsp caster (superfine) sugar
5 ml/1 tsp ground cinnamon
50 g/2 oz/¼ cup butter or margarine, melted

For the filling:
2 eggs, separated
100 g/4 oz/½ cup caster sugar
350 g/12 oz/1½ cups full-fat soft cheese
Grated rind and juice of 1 lemon
150 ml/¼ pt/⅔ cup double (heavy) cream
25 g/1 oz/¼ cup chopped mixed nuts

To make the base, stir in the crumbs, sugar and cinnamon into the butter or margarine. Press over the base and sides of a 20 cm/8 in loose-bottomed flan tin (pan). Chill.

To make the filling, beat together the egg yolks and sugar until thick. Fold in the cheese, lemon rind and juice. Whip the cream until stiff, then fold it into the mixture. Whisk the egg whites until stiff, then fold into the mixture. Spoon into the base and bake in a preheated oven at 160°C/325°F/gas mark 3 for 45 minutes. Sprinkle with the nuts and return to the oven for a further 20 minutes. Turn off the oven and leave the cheesecake in the oven to cool, then chill before serving.

Orange Cheesecake

Makes one 23 cm/9 in cake

For the base:
100 g/4 oz/1 cup crushed wafer biscuits (cookies)
2.5 ml/½ tsp ground cinnamon
15 ml/1 tbsp egg white

For the filling:
450 g/1 lb/2 cups cottage cheese
225 g/8 oz/1 cup cream cheese
75 g/3 oz/⅓ cup caster (superfine) sugar
15 ml/1 tbsp plain (all-purpose) flour
30 ml/2 tbsp orange juice
10 ml/2 tsp grated orange rind
5 ml/1 tsp vanilla essence (extract)
1 large orange, cut into sections and membranes removed
100 g/4 oz strawberries, sliced

To make the base, mix together the crusted wafers and cinnamon. Whisk the egg whites until foamy, then mix into the crumbs. Press the mixture into the base of a loose-bottomed 23 cm/9 in flan tin (pan). Bake in a preheated oven at 180°C/350°F/gas mark 4 for 10 minutes. Remove from the oven and leave to cool. Reduce the oven temperature to 150°C/300°F/gas mark 2.

To make the filling, mix together the cheeses, sugar, flour, orange juice and rind and vanilla essence until smooth. Spoon over the base and bake in the preset oven for 35 minutes until firm. Leave to cool, then chill until set. Decorate with the oranges and strawberries.

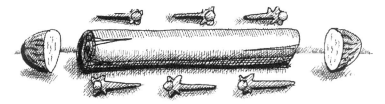

Ricotta Cheesecake

Makes one 23 cm/9 in cake

For the base:
25 g/1 oz/2 tbsp caster (superfine) sugar
5 ml/1 tsp grated lemon rind
100 g/4 oz/1 cup plain (all-purpose) flour
A few drops of vanilla essence (extract)
1 egg yolk
25 g/1 oz/2 tbsp butter or margarine
For the topping:
750 g/1½ lb/3 cups Ricotta cheese
225 g/8 oz/1 cup caster (superfine) sugar
120 ml/4 fl oz/½ cup double (heavy) cream
45 ml/3 tbsp plain (all-purpose) flour
5 ml/1 tsp vanilla essence (extract)
5 eggs, separated
150 g/5 oz raspberries or strawberries

To make the base, beat together the sugar, lemon rind and flour, then add the vanilla essence, egg yolk and butter or margarine. Continue to beat until the mixture forms a dough. Press half the dough into a greased 23 cm/9 in spring-form cake tin (pan) and bake in a preheated oven at 200°C/400°F/gas mark 6 for 8 minutes. Reduce the oven temperature to 180°C/350°F/gas mark 4. Leave to cool, then press the remaining mixture round the sides of the tin.

To make the topping, beat the Ricotta cheese until creamy. Mix in the sugar, cream, flour, vanilla essence and egg yolks. Whisk the egg whites until stiff, then fold into the mixture. Spoon into the crust and bake in the preheated oven for 1 hour. Leave to cool in the tin, then chill before arranging the fruit on top to serve.

Baked Cheese and Soured Cream Layer Cheesecake

Makes one 23 cm/9 in cake

50 g/2 oz/¼ cup butter or margarine, softened
50 g/2 oz/¼ cup caster (superfine) sugar
1 egg
350 g/12 oz/3 cups plain (all-purpose) flour
For the filling:
675 g/1½ lb/3 cups cream cheese
15 ml/1 tbsp lemon juice
5 ml/1 tsp grated lemon rind
175 g/6 oz/¾ cup caster (superfine) sugar
3 eggs
250 ml/8 fl oz/1 cup soured (dairy sour) cream
5 ml/1 tsp vanilla essence (extract)

To make the base, cream together the butter or margarine and sugar until light and fluffy. Gradually beat in the egg, then fold in the flour to make a pastry (paste). Roll out and use to line a greased 23 cm/9 in cake tin (pan) and bake in a preheated oven at 220°C/425°F/gas mark 7 for 5 minutes.

To make the filling, mix together the cream cheese, lemon juice and rind. Reserve 30 ml/2 tbsp of the sugar, then mix the rest into the cheese. Gradually add the eggs, then spoon the mixture on to the base. Bake in the preheated oven for 10 minutes, then reduce the oven temperature to 150°C/300°F/gas mark 2 and bake for a further 30 minutes. Mix together the soured cream, reserved sugar and vanilla essence. Spoon over the cake and return to the oven and bake for a further 10 minutes. Leave to cool, then chill before serving.

Light Baked Cheesecake with Sultanas

Makes one 18 cm/7 in cake

75 g/3 oz/⅓ cup butter or margarine,
  melted
100 g/4 oz/1 cup rolled oats
50 g/2 oz/⅓ cup sultanas
  (golden raisins)
For the filling:
50 g/2 oz/¼ cup butter or margarine,
  softened
250 g/9 oz/generous 1 cup quark
2 eggs
25 g/1 oz/3 tbsp sultanas
  (golden raisins)
25 g/1 oz/¼ cup ground almonds
Juice and grated rind of 1 lemon
45 ml/3 tbsp plain yoghurt

Mix together the butter or margarine, oats and sultanas. Press into the base of a greased 18 cm/7 in cake tin (pan) and bake in a preheated oven at 180°C/350°F/gas mark 4 for 10 minutes. Beat together the filling ingredients and spoon over the base. Bake for a further 45 minutes. Leave to cool in the tin before turning out.

Light Baked Vanilla Cheesecake

Makes one 23 cm/9 in cake

175 g/6 oz/1½ cups digestive biscuit
  (Graham cracker) crumbs
225 g/8 oz/1 cup caster (superfine)
  sugar
5 egg whites
50 g/2 oz/¼ cup butter or margarine,
  melted
225 g/8 oz/1 cup cream cheese
225 g/8 oz/1 cup cottage cheese
120 ml/4 fl oz/½ cup milk
30 ml/2 tbsp plain (all-purpose) flour
5 ml/1 tsp vanilla essence (extract)
A pinch of salt

Mix together the biscuit crumbs and 50 g/2 oz/¼ cup of the sugar. Lightly beat one egg white and stir it into the butter or margarine, then mix with the biscuit crumb mixture. Press into the base and sides of a 23 cm/9 in loose-bottomed flan tin (pan) and leave to set.

To make the filling, beat together the cream cheese and cottage cheese, then stir in the remaining sugar, the milk, flour, vanilla essence and salt. Beat the remaining egg whites until stiff, then fold into the mixture. Spoon into the base and bake in a preheated oven at 180°C/350°F/gas mark 4 for 1 hour until set in the centre. Leave to cool in the tin for 30 minutes before turning out on to a wire rack to finish cooling. Chill until ready to serve.

Baked White Chocolate Cheesecake

Makes one 18 cm/7 in cake

225 g/8 oz/2 cups plain (semi-sweet)
  chocolate digestive biscuit
  (Graham cracker) crumbs
50 g/2 oz/¼ cup butter or margarine,
  melted
300 g/11 oz/2¾ cups white chocolate
400 g/14 oz/1¾ cups cream cheese
150 ml/¼ pt/⅔ cup soured (dairy sour)
  cream
2 eggs, lightly beaten
5 ml/1 tsp vanilla essence (extract)

Stir the biscuit crumbs into the butter or margarine and press into the base of an 18 cm/7 in loose-bottomed cake tin (pan). Melt the white chocolate in a heatproof bowl set over a pan of gently simmering water. Remove from the heat and stir in the cream cheese, cream, eggs and vanilla essence. Spread the mixture over the base and level the top. Bake in a preheated oven at 160°C/325°F/gas mark 3 for 1 hour until firm to the touch. Leave to cool in the tin.

White Chocolate and Hazelnut Cheesecake

Makes one 23 cm/9 in cake

225 g/8 oz chocolate wafer biscuits (cookies)
100 g/4 oz/1 cup ground hazelnuts
30 ml/2 tbsp soft brown sugar
5 ml/1 tsp ground cinnamon
225 g/8 oz/1 cup butter or margarine
450 g/1 lb/4 cups white chocolate
900 g/2 lb/4 cups cream cheese
4 eggs
1 egg yolk
5 ml/1 tsp vanilla essence (extract)

Grind or crush the wafers and mix with half the hazelnuts, the sugar and cinnamon. Set aside 45 ml/3 tbsp of the mixture for the topping. Melt 90 ml/6 tbsp of the butter or margarine and mix with the remaining wafer mixture. Press into the base and sides of a greased 23 cm/9 in loose-bottomed flan tin (pan) and chill while you make the filling.

Melt the chocolate in a heatproof bowl set over a pan of gently simmering water. Remove from the heat and leave to cool slightly. Beat the cheese until light and fluffy. Gradually beat in the eggs and egg yolk, then beat in the remaining butter and the melted chocolate. Stir in the vanilla essence and remaining hazelnuts and beat until smooth. Spoon the filling into the crumb base. Bake in a preheated oven at 150°C/300°F/gas mark 2 for 1¼ hours. Sprinkle the top with the reserved wafer biscuit and nut mixture and return to the oven for a further 15 minutes. Leave to cool, then chill before serving.

White Chocolate and Wafer Cheesecake

Makes one 23 cm/9 in cake

225 g/8 oz chocolate wafer biscuits (cookies)
30 ml/2 tbsp caster (superfine) sugar
5 ml/1 tsp ground cinnamon
225 g/8 oz/1 cup butter or margarine
450 g/1 lb/4 cups white chocolate
900 g/2 lb/4 cups cream cheese
4 eggs
1 egg yolk
5 ml/1 tsp vanilla essence (extract)

Grind or crush the wafers and mix with the sugar and cinnamon. Set aside 45 ml/3 tbsp of the mixture for topping. Melt 90 ml/6 tbsp of the butter or margarine and mix with the remaining wafer mixture. Press into the base and sides of a greased 23 cm/9 in loose-bottomed flan tin (pan) and chill.

To make the filling, melt the chocolate in a heatproof bowl set over a pan of gently simmering water. Remove from the heat and leave to cool slightly. Beat the cheese until light and fluffy. Gradually beat in the eggs and egg yolk, then beat in the remaining butter and the melted chocolate. Stir in the vanilla essence and beat until smooth. Spoon the filling into the crumb base. Bake in a preheated oven at 150°C/300°F/gas mark 2 for 1¼ hours. Sprinkle the top with the reserved wafer biscuit mixture and return to the oven for a further 15 minutes. Leave to cool, then chill before serving.

Pastries

*L*ots of cakes can be made with a pastry (paste) base, or use pastry as their main component. You can buy excellent pastry of all kinds from the chill cabinet or freezer at your local supermarket, or you can make your own.

Shortcrust Pastry

Shortcrust pastry (basic pie crust) is the most versatile pastry (paste) and can be used for all kinds of applications, mainly tarts and pies. It is usually baked at 200°C/400°F/gas mark 6.

Makes 350 g/12 oz

225 g/8 oz/2 cups plain
(all-purpose) flour
2.5 ml/½ tsp salt
50 g/2 oz/¼ cup lard (shortening)
50 g/2 oz/½ cup butter or margarine
30–45 ml/2–3 tbsp cold water

Mix together the flour and salt in a bowl, then rub in the lard and butter or margarine until the mixture resembles breadcrumbs. Sprinkle the water evenly over the mixture, then mix it in with a round-bladed knife until the pastry begins to form large lumps. Press together gently with your fingers until the pastry forms a ball. Roll out on a lightly floured surface until smooth, but do not over-handle. Wrap in clingfilm (plastic wrap) and chill for 30 minutes before use.

Shortcrust Pastry with Oil

Similar to shortcrust pastry (basic pie crust), this is more crumbly and must be used as soon as it is made. It is usually baked at 200°C/400°F/gas mark 6.

Makes 350 g/12 oz

75 ml/5 tbsp oil
65 ml/2½ fl oz/4½ tbsp cold water
225 g/8 oz/2 cups plain
(all-purpose) flour
A pinch of salt

Beat together the oil and water in a bowl until blended. Gradually add the flour and salt, mixing with a round-bladed knife until a dough forms. Turn out on a lightly floured surface and knead gently until smooth. Wrap in clingfilm (plastic wrap) and chill for 30 minutes before use.

Rich Shortcrust Pastry

This is used for sweet tarts and flans as it is richer than ordinary shortcrust pastry (basic pie crust). It is usually baked at 200°C/400°F/gas mark 6.

Makes 350 g/12 oz

150 g/5 oz/1¼ cups plain
(all-purpose) flour
A pinch of salt
75 g/3 oz/⅓ cup unsalted (sweet)
butter or margarine
1 egg yolk
10 ml/2 tsp caster (superfine) sugar
45–60 ml/3–4 tbsp cold water

Mix together the flour and salt in a bowl, then rub in the butter or margarine until the mixture resembles breadcrumbs. Beat together the egg yolk, sugar and 10 ml/2 tsp of the water in a small bowl, then stir into the flour with a round-bladed knife, adding enough extra water to make a soft dough. Press into a ball, turn on to a lightly floured surface and knead gently until smooth. Wrap in clingfilm (plastic wrap) and chill for 30 minutes before use.

American Shortbread Pastry

A sticky pastry (paste) that gives a crisper finish, ideal for use with fruit. It is usually baked at 200°C/400°F/gas mark 6.

Makes 350 g/12 oz

175 g/6 oz/³⁄₄ cup butter or margarine, softened
225 g/8 oz/2 cups self-raising (self-rising) flour
2.5 ml/½ tsp salt
45 ml/3 tbsp cold water

Beat the butter or margarine until soft. Gradually beat in the flour, salt and water and mix to a sticky dough. Cover with clingfilm (plastic wrap) and chill for 30 minutes. Roll out between lightly floured sheets of baking parchment.

Cheese Pastry

A shortcrust pastry (paste) for savoury tarts or baked goods. It is usually baked at 200°C/400°F/gas mark 6.

Makes 350 g/12 oz

100 g/4 oz/1 cup plain (all-purpose) flour
A pinch of salt
A pinch of cayenne
50 g/2 oz/¼ cup butter or margarine
50 g/2 oz/½ cup Cheddar cheese, grated
1 egg yolk
30 ml/2 tbsp cold water

Mix together the flour, salt and cayenne in a bowl, then rub in the butter or margarine until the mixture resembles breadcrumbs. Stir in the cheese, then mix in the egg yolk and enough of the water to make a firm dough. Turn out on a lightly floured surface and knead gently until blended. Wrap in clingfilm (plastic wrap) and chill for 30 minutes before use.

Choux Pastry

A light pastry (paste) which puffs up to three times its unbaked size during cooking. Ideal for piped cream cakes and pastries. It is usually baked at 200°C/400°F/gas mark 6.

Makes 350 g/12 oz

50 g/2 oz/¼ cup unsalted (sweet) butter
150 ml/¼ pt/⅔ cup milk and water in equal quantities, mixed
75 g/3 oz/⅓ cup plain (all-purpose) flour
2 eggs, lightly beaten

Melt the butter in the milk and water in a pan over a low heat. Bring quickly to the boil, the remove from heat. Tip in all the flour and beat just until the mixture comes away from the sides of the pan. Leave to cool slightly. Gradually beat in the eggs, a little at a time, until the mixture is smooth and glossy.

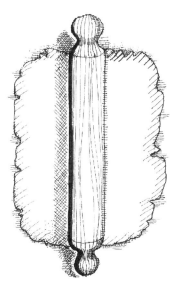

Flaky Pastry

Flaky pastry (paste) is used for delicate pastries such as cream horns. It should only be made in cool conditions. It is usually baked at 220°C/425°F/gas mark 7.

Makes 450 g/1 lb

*225 g/8 oz/2 cups plain
(all-purpose) flour
2. 5 ml/½ tsp salt
75 g/3 oz/⅓ cup lard (shortening)
75 g/3 oz/⅓ cup butter or margarine
5 ml/1 tsp lemon juice
100 ml/3½ fl oz/6½ tbsp iced water*

Mix together the flour and salt in a bowl. Blend together the lard and butter or margarine, then shape into a block and cut into quarters. Rub one quarter of the fat into the flour until the mixture resembles breadcrumbs. Add the lemon juice and enough of the water to mix to a soft dough with a round-bladed knife. Cover with clingfilm (plastic wrap) and chill for 20 minutes.

Roll out the pastry on a lightly floured surface to about 5 mm/¼ in thick. Chop the next quarter of fat and dot all over two-thirds of the pastry, leaving a gap round the edge. Fold the unbuttered third of the pastry over the fat, then fold the buttered third down over that. Press round all the joins with your fingers to seal. Cover with clingfilm and chill for 20 minutes.

Place the dough on the surface with the join on the right. Roll out as before, then dot with the third quarter of the fat. Fold, seal and chill as before.

Place the dough on the surface with the join on the left. Roll out as before, then dot with the final quarter of the fat. Fold, seal and chill as before.

Roll out the pastry to 5 mm/¼ in thick, then fold again. Cover with clingfilm and chill for 20 minutes before use.

Puff Pastry

Puff pastry (paste) should rise to about six times its height once baked and can be used for all kinds of light cakes requiring a fluffy pastry. It is usually baked at 230°C/450°F/gas mark 8.

Makes 450 g/1 lb

*225 g/8 oz/2 cups plain
(all-purpose) flour
5 ml/1 tsp salt
225 g/8 oz/1 cup butter or margarine
2.5 ml/½ tsp lemon juice
150 ml/¼ pt/⅔ cup iced water*

Mix together the flour and salt in a bowl. Cut 50 g/2 oz/¼ cup of the butter or margarine into pieces, then rub into the flour until the mixture resembles breadcrumbs. Add the lemon juice and water and mix with a round-bladed knife to a soft dough. Turn the dough on to a lightly floured surface and knead gently until smooth. Shape into a ball and cut a deep cross in the centre, cutting about three-quarters of the way through the pastry (paste). Open out the flaps and roll the pastry so that the centre remains thicker than the edges. Place the remaining butter or margarine on the centre of the pastry, fold the flaps over to cover it and seal the edges. Roll out the pastry to a 40 × 20 cm/16 × 8 in rectangle, being careful not to let the butter leak out. Fold the bottom one-third of the pastry up to the centre, then fold the top one-third over that. Press the edges together to seal, then give the pastry one quarter turn. Cover with clingfilm (plastic wrap) and chill for 20 minutes. Repeat the rolling, folding and chilling 6 times in all. Cover with clingfilm and chill for 30 minutes before use.

Rough Puff Pastry

Easier to make than puff pastry (paste), with a light texture, this is best served warm rather than cold. It is usually baked at 220°C/425°F/gas mark 7.

Makes 450 g/1 lb

225 g/8 oz/2 cups plain (all-purpose) flour
5 ml/1 tsp salt
175 g/6 oz/¾ cup butter or margarine, chilled and diced
5 ml/1 tsp lemon juice
150 ml/¼ pt/⅔ cup iced water

Mix together all the ingredients with a round-bladed knife to form a soft dough. Turn on to a lightly floured surface and carefully roll out to a 30 × 10 cm/12 × 4 in rectangle about 2 cm/¾ in thick. Fold the bottom one-third of the pastry up to the centre, then the top one-third down the over the top. Turn the pastry so that the join is on the left and seal the edges with your fingertips. Roll out to a slightly larger rectangle about 1 cm/½ in thick. Fold into thirds in the same way, seal the edges and give the pastry a quarter turn. Cover with clingfilm (plastic wrap) and chill for 20 minutes. Repeat this rolling, folding and turning four times in all, chilling after every two turns. Wrap in clingfilm and chill for 20 minutes before use.

Pâte Sucrée

A thin, sweet pastry (paste) with a melting texture, excellent for tart cases (pie shells). It is usually baked blind at 180°C/350°F/gas mark 4.

Makes 350 g/12 oz

100 g/4 oz/1 cup plain (all-purpose) flour
A pinch of salt
50 g/2 oz/¼ cup butter or margarine, softened
50 g/2 oz/¼ cup caster (superfine) sugar
2 egg yolks

Sift the flour and salt on to a cool work surface and make a well in the centre. Place the butter or margarine, sugar and egg yolks in the centre and work together, gradually working in the flour with your fingertips until you have a soft, smooth dough. Cover with clingfilm (plastic wrap) and chill for 30 minutes before use.

Choux Cream Buns

Makes 16

50 g/2 oz/¼ cup unsalted (sweet) butter
150 ml/¼ pt/⅔ cup milk and water in equal quantities, mixed
75 g/3 oz/⅓ cup plain (all-purpose) flour
2 eggs, beaten
150 ml/¼ pt/⅔ cup double (heavy) cream
Icing (confectioners') sugar, sifted, for dusting

Melt the butter with the milk and water in a pan, then bring to the boil. Remove from the heat, tip in all the flour and beat until the mixture comes away from the sides of the pan. Gradually beat in the eggs a little at a time until blended. Pipe or place spoonfuls of the dough on a dampened baking (cookie) sheet and bake in a preheated oven at 200°C/400°F/gas mark 6 for 20 minutes, depending on size, until golden. Make a slit in the side of each cake to allow the steam to escape, then leave to cool on a wire rack. Whip the cream until stiff, then pipe it into the centre of the choux buns. Serve dusted with icing sugar.

Cheesy Mandarin Puffs

Makes 16

For the pastry (paste):
50 g/2 oz/¼ cup butter
150 ml/¼ pt/⅔ cup water
75 g/3 oz/¾ cup plain (all-purpose) flour
2 eggs, beaten
For the filling:
300 ml/½ pt/1¼ cups double (heavy) cream
75 g/3 oz/¾ cup Cheddar cheese, grated
10 ml/2 tsp orange liqueur
300 g/11 oz/1 medium can mandarins, drained

Melt the butter with the water in a pan, then bring to the boil. Remove from the heat, tip in all the flour and beat until the mixture comes away from the sides of the pan. Gradually beat in the eggs, a little at a time, until blended. Pipe or place spoonfuls of the dough on a dampened baking (cookie) sheet and bake in a preheated oven at 200°C/400°F/gas mark 6 for 20 minutes, depending on size, until golden. Make a slit in the side of each cake to allow the steam to escape, then leave to cool on a wire rack.

Whip half the cream until stiff, then stir in the cheese and liqueur. Pipe into the choux puffs and press a few mandarins into each one. Pile the puffs on a large dish and serve with the remaining cream.

Chocolate Éclairs

Makes 10

225 g/8 oz Choux Pastry (page 135)
For the filling:
150 ml/¼ pt/⅔ cup double (heavy) cream
5 ml/1 tsp caster (superfine) sugar
5 ml/1 tsp icing (confectioners') sugar
A few drops of vanilla essence (extract)
For the sauce:
50 g/2 oz /½ cup plain (semi-sweet) chocolate
15 g/½ oz/1 tbsp butter or margarine
20 ml/4 tsp water
25 g/1 oz/3 tbsp icing (confectioners') sugar

Spoon the pastry into an icing (piping) bag fitted with a plain 2 cm/¾ in nozzle (tip) and pipe into 10 lengths on to a lightly greased baking (cookie) sheet, spaced well apart. Bake in a preheated oven at 190°C/375°F/gas mark 5 for 30 minutes until the éclairs are well risen and golden brown. Place on a wire rack and slit one side to let the steam escape. Leave to cool.

To make the filling, whip the cream with the sugars and vanilla essence. Spoon into the éclairs.

To make the sauce, melt the chocolate, butter or margarine and water in a small pan over a low heat, stirring continuously. Beat in the icing sugar and spread over the top of the éclairs.

138

Profiteroles

Makes 20

225 g/8 oz Choux Pastry (page 135)
For the filling:
*150 ml/¼ pt/⅔ cup double (heavy)
    cream*
5 ml/1 tsp caster (superfine) sugar
5 ml/1 tsp icing (confectioners') sugar
*A few drops of vanilla essence
    (extract)*
For the sauce:
*50 g/2 oz/½ cup plain (semi-sweet)
    chocolate, grated*
*25 g/1 oz/2 tbsp caster (superfine)
    sugar*
300 ml/½ pt 1¼ cups milk
15 ml/1 tbsp cornflour (cornstarch)
*A few drops of vanilla essence
    (extract)*

Spoon the pastry into an icing (piping) bag fitted with a plain 2 cm/¾ in nozzle (tip) and pipe about 20 tiny balls on to a lightly greased baking (cookie) sheet, spaced well apart. Bake in a preheated oven at 190°C/375°F/gas mark 5 for 25 minutes until the profiteroles are well risen and golden brown. Place on a wire rack and slit each one to let the steam escape. Leave to cool.

To make the filling, whip the cream with the sugars and vanilla essence. Spoon into the profiteroles. Arrange them in a tall mound in a serving dish.

To make the sauce, put the chocolate and sugar in a bowl with all but 15 ml/1 tbsp of the milk. Mix the reserved milk with the cornflour. Heat the milk, chocolate and sugar gently until the chocolate melts, stirring occasionally. Stir in the cornflour mixture and bring to the boil. Boil for 3 minutes, stirring. Add the vanilla essence. Strain into a warm jug. Pour the hot sauce over the profiteroles, or leave to cool and then pour over the pastries.

Almond and Peach Pastry

Makes one 23 cm/9 in cake

250 g/12 oz Puff Pastry (page 136)
225 g/8 oz/2 cups ground almonds
*175 g/6 oz/¾ cup caster (superfine)
    sugar*
2 eggs
5 ml/1 tsp lemon juice
15 ml/1 tbsp Amaretto
*450 g/1 lb peaches, stoned (pitted)
    and halved*
*Extra caster (superfine) sugar for
    dusting*
*50 g/2 oz/½ cup flaked (slivered)
    almonds*

Roll out the pastry on a lightly floured surface to form two rectangles about 5 mm/¼ in thick. Place one on a dampened baking (cookie) sheet. Blend together the ground almonds, sugar, one egg, the lemon juice and Amaretto and mix to a paste. Roll out the paste to a similar-sized rectangle and place on top of the pastry. Arrange the peaches, cut-side down, on the almond paste. Separate the remaining egg and brush the edges of the pastry with a little of the beaten yolk. Fold the remaining rectangle of pastry in half lengthways. Cut slits every 1 cm/½ in from the fold to within 1 cm/½ in of the opposite edge. Unfold the pastry and place over the peaches, pressing the edges together to seal. Flute the edges with a knife. Chill for 30 minutes. Brush with the remaining beaten yolk and bake in a preheated oven at 220°C/425°F/gas mark 7 for 20 minutes until well risen. Brush with the egg white, dredge with caster sugar and sprinkle with the flaked almonds. Return to the oven for a further 10 minutes until golden brown.

Apple Windmills

Makes 6

225 g/8 oz Puff Pastry (page 136)
1 large eating (dessert) apple
15 ml/1 tbsp lemon juice
30 ml/2 tbsp apricot jam (conserve),
 sieved (strained)
15 ml/1 tbsp water

Roll out the pastry and cut into 13 cm/5 in squares. Make four 5 cm/ 2 in cuts on the diagonal lines of the pastry squares in from the edge towards the centre. Moisten the centre of the squares, and press one point from each corner into the centre to make a windmill. Peel, core and thinly slice the apple and toss in the lemon juice. Arrange the apple slices on the centre of the windmills and bake in a preheated oven at 220°C/ 425°F/gas mark 7 for 10 minutes until puffed and golden. Heat the jam with the water until well blended, then brush over the apples and pastry to glaze. Leave to cool.

Cream Horns

Makes 10

450 g/1 lb Puff Pastry (page 136) or
 Flaky Pastry (page 136)
1 egg yolk
15 ml/1 tbsp milk
300 ml/½ pt/1¼ cups double (heavy)
 cream
50 g/2 oz/⅓ cup icing (confectioners')
 sugar, sifted, plus extra for dusting

Roll out the pastry to a 50 × 30 cm/ 20 × 12 in rectangle, trim the edges, then cut lengthways into 2.5 cm/1 in strips. Mix the egg yolk with the milk and brush the pastry carefully with the mixture, making sure that no egg gets on to the underside of the pastry or it will stick to the moulds. Twist each strip in a spiral round a metal horn mould, overlapping the edges of the pastry strips.

Brush again with egg yolk and milk and place on a baking (cookie) sheet with the end underneath. Bake in a preheated oven at 200°C/400°F/gas mark 6 for 15 minutes until golden. Leave to cool for 3 minutes, then remove the moulds from the pastry while it is still warm. Leave to cool. Whip the cream with the icing sugar until stiff, then pipe into the cream horns. Dust with a little more icing sugar.

Feuilleté

Makes 6

225 g/8 oz Puff Pastry (page 136)
100 g/4 oz raspberries
120 ml/4 fl oz/½ cup double (heavy)
 cream
60 ml/4 tbsp icing (confectioners')
 sugar
A few drops of water
A few drops of red food colouring

Roll out the pastry to 5 mm/¼ in thick on a lightly floured surface and neaten the edges into a rectangle. Place on an ungreased baking (cookie) sheet and bake in a preheated oven at 220°C/425°F/ gas mark 7 for 10 minutes until well risen and golden. Leave to cool.

Cut the pastry horizontally into two layers. Wash, drain and dry the fruit carefully. Whip the cream until stiff. Spread over the bottom layer of the pastry, top with the fruit, then place the top layer of pastry on top. Place the icing sugar in a bowl and gradually add enough water to make a thick icing. Spread most of the icing over the top of the cake. Colour the remaining icing with a little food colouring, adding a little more icing sugar if it becomes too runny. Pipe or drizzle in lines on the white icing, then run a cocktail stick (toothpick) across the lines to create a feathered effect. Serve immediately.

Ricotta-filled Pastries

Makes 16

350 g/12 oz Puff Pastry (page 136)
1 egg white
10 ml/2 tsp caster (superfine) sugar
For the filling:
150 ml/¼ pt/⅔ cup double (heavy) or
  whipping cream
100 g/4 oz/½ cup Ricotta cheese
30 ml/2 tbsp caster (superfine) sugar
45 ml/3 tbsp chopped mixed peel
Icing (confectioners') sugar for
  dusting

Roll out the pastry (paste) thinly on a lightly floured surface and cut into four 18 cm/7 in circles. Cut each circle into quarters, place on a lightly greased baking (cookie) sheet and chill for 30 minutes.

Whisk the egg white until frothy, then stir in the sugar. Brush over the pastry and bake in a preheated oven for 10 minutes until risen and golden. Transfer to a wire rack and make a slit in the triangles in which to spoon the filling. Leave to cool.

To make the filling, whip the cream until stiff. Soften the Ricotta in a bowl, then stir in the cream, sugar and fruit. Pipe or spoon the filling into the pastries and serve at once, dusted with icing sugar.

Walnut Puffs

Makes 18

200 g/7 oz/1¾ cups walnuts, coarsely
  ground
75 g/3 oz/⅓ cup caster (superfine)
  sugar
30 ml/2 tbsp anis liqueur or Pernod
25 g/1 oz/2 tbsp butter or margarine,
  softened
450 g/1 lb Puff Pastry (page 136)
1 egg, beaten

Mix together the walnuts, sugar, liqueur and butter or margarine. Roll out the pastry (paste) on a lightly floured surface to a 60 × 30 cm/24 × 12 in rectangle (or you can roll out half the pastry at a time). Cut into 18 squares and divide the walnut mixture between the squares. Brush the edges of the squares with beaten egg, fold over and seal into sausage shapes with the join underneath and twist the ends like a sweet wrapper. Arrange on a greased baking (cookie) sheet and brush with beaten egg. Bake in a preheated oven at 230°C/450°F/gas mark 8 for 10 minutes until puffed and golden brown. Eat warm on the day they are baked.

Danish Pastry

Makes 450 g/1 lb

450 g/1 lb/4 cups plain (all-purpose)
    flour
5 ml/1 tsp salt
25 g/1 oz/2 tbsp caster (superfine)
    sugar
5 ml/1 tsp ground cardamom
50 g/2 oz fresh yeast or 75 ml/5 tbsp
    dried yeast
250 ml/8 fl oz/1 cup milk
1 egg, beaten
300 g/10 oz/1¼ cups butter, sliced

Sift together the flour, salt, sugar and cardamom into a bowl. Cream the yeast with a little of the milk and stir into the flour with the remaining milk and the egg. Mix to a dough and knead until smooth and shiny.

Roll out the pastry (paste) on a lightly floured surface to a 56 × 30 cm/ 22 × 12 in rectangle about 1 cm/½ in thick. Arrange the butter slices over the centre third of the dough, leaving a gap around the edges. Fold over a third of the dough to cover the butter, then fold over the remaining third. Press the ends together with your fingertips, then chill for 15 minutes. Roll out to the same size again, fold into thirds and chill for 15 minutes. Repeat the process once more. Place the dough in a floured plastic bag and leave to rest for 15 minutes before using.

Danish Birthday Pretzel

Serves 8

50 g/2 oz fresh yeast
50 g/2 oz/¼ cup granulated sugar
450 g/1 lb/4 cups plain (all-purpose)
    flour
250 ml/8 fl oz/1 cup milk
1 egg
200 g/7 oz/scant 1 cup butter, chilled
    and sliced

For the filling:

100 g/4 oz/1 cup chopped almonds
100 g/4 oz/½ cup butter or margarine
100 g/4 oz/½ cup caster (superfine)
    sugar
Beaten egg to glaze
25 g/1 oz/¼ cup blanched almonds,
    coarsely chopped
15 ml/1 tbsp demerara sugar

Cream the yeast with the sugar. Place the flour in a bowl. Whisk together the milk and egg and add to the flour with the yeast. Mix to a dough, cover and leave in a cold place for 1 hour. Roll out the pastry (paste) to 56 × 30 cm/22 × 12 in. Arrange the butter in the middle third of the dough, avoiding the edges. Fold one-third of the dough over the butter, then fold over the other third and press the edges together. Chill for 15 minutes. Roll out, fold and chill three more times.

Mix together the remaining ingredients, except the egg, almonds and sugar, until smooth.

Roll out the pastry into a long strip about 3 mm/⅛ in thick and 10 cm/4 in wide. Spread the filling down the centre, moisten the edges and press them together over the filling. Shape into a pretzel shape on a greased baking (cookie) sheet and leave to stand for 15 minutes in a warm place. Brush with beaten egg and sprinkle with the blanched almonds and demerara sugar. Bake in a preheated oven at 230°C/450°F/gas mark 8 for 15–20 minutes until risen and golden.

Danish Pastry Snails

Makes 16

100 g/4 oz/½ cup unsalted (sweet)
    butter, softened
60 ml/4 tbsp icing (confectioners')
    sugar
45 ml/3 tbsp currants
½ quantity Danish Pastry (page 142)
15 ml/1 tbsp ground cinnamon
Glacé Icing (page 231)

To make the filling, cream together the butter and icing sugar until smooth, then stir in the currants. Roll out the pastry to a rectangle about 40 × 15 cm/16 × 6 in. Spread with the butter filling and sprinkle with cinnamon. Roll up from the short end to make a Swiss (jelly) roll shape. Cut into 16 slices and place on a baking (cookie) sheet. Leave in a warm place for 15 minutes. Bake in a preheated oven at 230°C/450°F/gas mark 8 for 10–15 minutes until golden. Leave to cool, then decorate with glacé icing.

Danish Pastry Plaits

Makes 16

½ quantity Danish Pastry (page 142)
1 egg, beaten
25 g/1 oz/3 tbsp currants
Glacé Icing (page 231)

Divide the pastry into six equal portions and shape each one into a long roll. Moisten the ends of the rolls and press them together in threes, then plait the lengths together, sealing the ends. Cut into 10 cm/4 in lengths and place on a baking (cookie) sheet. Leave in a warm place for 15 minutes. Brush with beaten egg and sprinkle with currants. Bake in a preheated oven at 230°C/450°F/gas mark 8 for 10–15 minutes until well risen and golden brown. Leave to cool, then ice with glacé icing.

Danish Pastry Windmills

Makes 16

25 g/1 oz/¼ cup ground almonds
25 g/1 oz/3 tbsp icing (confectioners')
  sugar
A little egg white
½ quantity Danish Pastry (page 142)

To make the filling, grind the almonds and icing sugar together, then gradually blend in enough egg white to make a firm, smooth mixture. Roll out the pastry and cut into 10 cm/4 in squares. Cut diagonally from the corners to within 1 cm/½ in of the centre. Place a spoonful of the filling in the centre of each windmill, then bring four of the corners into the centre like a windmill and press into the filling. Place on a baking (cookie) sheet and leave in a warm place for 15 minutes. Brush with the remaining egg white and bake in a preheated oven at 230°C/450°F/gas mark 8 for 10–15 minutes until risen and golden.

Almond Pastries

Makes 24

450 g/1 lb/2 cups caster (superfine)
  sugar
450 g/1 lb/4 cups ground almonds
6 eggs, lightly beaten
5 ml/1 tsp vanilla essence (extract)
75 g/3 oz/¾ cup pine nuts

Mix together the sugar, ground almonds, eggs and vanilla essence until well blended. Spoon into a greased and lined 30 × 23 cm/12 × 9 in baking tray and sprinkle with the pine nuts. Bake in a preheated oven at 180°C/350°F/gas mark 4 for 1½ hours until browned and firm to the touch. Cut into squares.

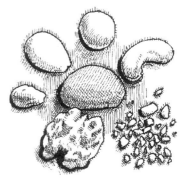

Tarts

*O*pen tarts make wonderful desserts or can be served as cakes at tea time. You can make the base with sponge, pastry, or crushed biscuits to suit the recipe you are making.

Basic Sponge Tart Case

Makes one 23 cm/9 in case (shell)

2 eggs
200 g/7 oz/scant 1 cup caster
(superfine) sugar
5 ml/1 tsp vanilla essence (extract)
150 g/5 oz/1¼ cups plain
(all-purpose) flour
5 ml/1 tsp baking powder
A pinch of salt
120 ml/4 fl oz/½ cup milk
50 g/2 oz/¼ cup butter or margarine

Beat together the eggs, sugar and vanilla essence, then mix in the flour, baking powder and salt. Bring the milk and butter or margarine to the boil in a small pan, then pour into the cake mixture and blend well. Spoon into a greased 23 cm/9 in shaped flan tin (pan) and bake in a preheated oven at 180°C/350°F/gas mark 4 for 30 minutes until lightly golden. Turn out on to a wire rack to cool.

Almond Tart

Makes one 20 cm/8 in tart

175 g/6 oz Shortcrust Pastry
(page 134)
For the filling:
50 g/2 oz/¼ cup butter or margarine,
softened
2 eggs, beaten
50 g/2 oz /½ cup self-raising
(self-rising) flour
75 g/3 oz/¾ cup ground almonds
A few drops of almond essence
(extract)
45 ml/3 tbsp orange juice
400 g/14 oz/1 large can peaches or
apricots, well drained
15 ml/1 tbsp flaked (slivered)
almonds

Roll out the pastry (paste) and use to line a greased 20 cm/8 in flan tin (pan). Prick the base with a fork. Beat together the butter or margarine and eggs until light. Gradually mix in the flour, ground almonds, almond essence and orange juice. Purée the peaches or apricots in a food processor, or rub through a sieve (strainer). Spread the purée over the pastry, then spoon the almond mixture on top. Sprinkle with the flaked almonds and bake in a preheated oven at 190°C/375°F/gas mark 5 for 40 minutes until springy to the touch.

Eighteenth-century Apple and Orange Tart

Makes one 18 cm/7 in tart

For the pastry (paste):
100 g/4 oz/1 cup plain (all-purpose) flour
25 g/1 oz/2 tbsp caster (superfine) sugar
50 g/2 oz/¼ cup butter or margarine
1 egg yolk
For the filling:
75 g/3 oz/⅓ cup butter or margarine, softened
75 g/3 oz/⅓ cup caster (superfine) sugar
4 egg yolks
25 g/1 oz/3 tbsp chopped mixed (candied) peel
Grated rind of 1 large orange
1 eating (dessert) apple

To make the pastry, mix together the flour and sugar in a bowl, then rub in the butter or margarine until the mixture resembles breadcrumbs. Blend in the egg yolks and mix lightly to a dough. Wrap in clingfilm (plastic wrap) and chill for 30 minutes before using. Roll out the pastry and use to line a greased 18 cm/7 in flan ring.

To make the filling, cream together the butter or margarine and sugar until light and fluffy, then mix in the egg yolks, mixed peel and orange rind. Spoon over the pastry. Peel, core and grate the apple and spread over the flan. Bake in a preheated oven at 180°C/350°F/gas mark 4 for 30 minutes.

German Apple Tart

Makes one 20 cm/8 in tart

For the pastry (paste):
100 g/4 oz/1 cup self-raising (self-rising) flour
50 g/2 oz/¼ cup soft brown sugar
25 g/1 oz/¼ cup ground almonds
75 g/3 oz/⅓ cup butter or margarine
5 ml/1 tsp lemon juice
1 egg yolk
For the filling:
450 g/1 lb cooking (tart) apples, peeled, cored and sliced
75 g/3 oz/⅓ cup soft brown sugar
Grated rind of 1 lemon
5 ml/1 tsp lemon juice
For the topping:
50 g/2 oz/¼ cup butter or margarine
50 g/2 oz/½ cup plain (all-purpose) flour
5 ml/1 tsp ground cinnamon
150 g/5 oz/⅔ cup soft brown sugar

To make the pastry, mix together the flour, sugar and almonds, then rub in the butter or margarine until the mixture resembles breadcrumbs. Stir in the lemon juice and egg yolk and mix to a dough. Press into the base of a greased 20 cm/8 in cake tin (pan). Mix together the filling ingredients and spread over the base. To make the topping, rub the butter or margarine into the flour and cinnamon, then stir in the sugar and spread over the filling. Bake in a preheated oven at 180°C/350°F/gas mark 4 for 1 hour until golden.

Honeyed Apple Tart

Makes one 20 cm/8 in tart

For the pastry (paste):
75 g/3 oz/⅓ cup butter or margarine
175 g/6 oz/1½ cups wholemeal
(wholewheat) flour
A pinch of salt
5 ml/1 tsp clear honey
1 egg yolk
30 ml/2 tbsp cold water
For the filling:
900 g/2 lb cooking (tart) apples
30 ml/2 tbsp water
75 ml/5 tbsp clear honey
Grated rind and juice of 1 lemon
25 g/1 oz/2 tbsp butter or margarine
2.5 ml/½ tsp ground cinnamon
2 eating (dessert) apples

To make the pastry, rub the butter or margarine into the flour and salt until the mixture resembles breadcrumbs. Stir in the honey. Beat the egg yolk with a little of the water and stir into the mixture, adding enough additional water to make a soft dough. Wrap in clingfilm (plastic wrap) and chill for 30 minutes.

To make the filling, peel, core and slice the cooking apples and simmer gently with the water until soft. Add 45 ml/ 3 tbsp of the honey, the lemon rind, butter or margarine and cinnamon and cook, uncovered, until reduced to a purée. Allow to cool.

Roll out the pastry on a lightly floured surface and use to line a 20 cm/8 in flan ring. Prick all over with a fork, cover with greaseproof (waxed) paper and fill with baking beans. Bake in a preheated oven at 200°C/400°F/gas mark 6 for 10 minutes. Remove the paper and beans. Reduce the oven temperature to 190°C/375°F/gas mark 5. Spoon the apple purée into the case. Core the eating apples without peeling them, then slice them thinly. Arrange in neatly overlapping circles on top of the purée. Bake in the preheated

oven for 30 minutes until the apples are cooked and lightly browned.

Place the remaining honey in a pan with the lemon juice and heat gently until the honey dissolves. Spoon over the cooked flan to glaze.

Apple and Mincemeat Tart

Makes one 18 cm/7 in tart

175 g/6 oz Shortcrust Pastry
(page 134)
1 medium cooking (tart) apple,
peeled, cored and grated
175 g/6 oz/½ cup mincemeat
150 ml/¼ pt/⅔ cup double (heavy)
cream
25 g/1 oz/¼ cup almonds, chopped
and toasted

Roll out the pastry (paste) and use to line an 18 cm/7 in flan ring. Prick all over with a fork. Stir the apple into the mincemeat and spread over the base. Bake in a preheated oven at 200°C/400°F/gas mark 6 for 15 minutes. Reduce the oven temperature to 160°C/325°F/gas mark 3 and bake for a further 10 minutes. Leave to cool. Whip the cream until stiff, then spread over the top of the flan, sprinkle with the almonds and serve at once.

Apple and Sultana Tart

Makes one 20 cm/8 in tart

100 g/4 oz/½ cup butter or margarine
225 g/8 oz/2 cups wholemeal
(wholewheat) flour
30 ml/2 tbsp cold water
450 g/1 lb cooking (tart) apples,
peeled, cored and sliced
15 ml/1 tbsp lemon juice
50 g/2 oz/⅓ cup sultanas (golden
raisins)
50 g/2 oz/¼ cup soft brown sugar

Rub the butter or margarine into the flour until the mixture resembles breadcrumbs. Add enough of the cold water to mix to a pastry (paste). Roll out and use to line a greased 20 cm/8 in flan ring. Toss the apples in the lemon juice and arrange in the pastry case. Sprinkle with the sultanas and sugar. Roll out the pastry trimmings and make a lattice over the top of the filling. Bake in a preheated oven at 190°C/375°F/gas mark 5 for 30 minutes.

Apricot and Coconut Meringue Tart

Serves 8

4 eggs, separated
100 g/4 oz/½ cup butter or margarine, softened
175 g/3 oz/⅓ cup clear honey
225 g/8 oz/2 cups wholemeal (wholewheat) flour
A pinch of salt
450 g/1 lb fresh apricots, halved and stoned (pitted)
100 g/4 oz/½ cup caster (superfine) sugar
175 g/6 oz/1½ cups desiccated (shredded) coconut

Whisk together the egg yolks, butter or margarine and honey until well blended. Mix in the flour and salt until smooth and firm. Roll out the pastry (paste) on a lightly floured surface to about 1 cm/½ in thick and transfer to a greased baking (cookie) sheet. Cover with the apricot halves, cut side down and bake in a preheated oven at 200°C/400°C/ gas mark 6 for 15 minutes.

Whisk the egg whites until stiff. Add half the sugar and continue to whisk again until stiff and shiny. Fold in the remaining sugar and the coconut. Spread the meringue mixture over the apricots and return to the oven for a further 30 minutes until lightly golden. Cut into squares while still warm.

Bakewell Tart

Makes one 18 cm/7 in tart

For the pastry (paste):
50 g/2 oz/¼ cup butter or margarine
100 g/4 oz/1 cup plain (all-purpose) flour
30 ml/2 tbsp water
For the filling:
100 g/4 oz/⅓ cup strawberry jam (conserve)
50 g/2 oz/¼ cup butter or margarine, softened
50 g/2 oz/¼ cup caster (superfine) sugar
1 egg, lightly beaten
A few drops of almond essence (extract)
25 g/1 oz/¼ cup self-raising (self-rising) flour
25 g/1 oz/3 tbsp ground almonds
50 g/2 oz/½ cup flaked (slivered) almonds

To make the pastry, rub the butter or margarine into the flour until the mixture resembles breadcrumbs. Stir in just enough water to mix to a pastry. Roll out and use to line a greased 18 cm/7 in flan tin. Spread with the jam. To make the filling, cream together the butter or margarine and sugar, then beat in the egg and almond essence. Stir in the flour and ground almonds. Spoon over the jam and level the surface. Sprinkle with the flaked almonds. Bake in a preheated oven at 190°C/375°F/gas 5 for 20 minutes.

Banoffee Fudge Pie

Serves 4

250 g/9 oz Shortcrust Pastry
  (page 134)
75 g/3 oz/⅓ cup butter or margarine
50 g/2 oz/¼ cup soft brown sugar
30 ml/2 tbsp milk
250 ml/8 fl oz/1 cup condensed milk
3–4 bananas, thickly sliced
Lemon juice
300 ml/½ pt/1¼ cups double (heavy)
  cream

Roll out the pastry and use to line a 23 cm/9 in deep loose-bottomed flan tin (pan). Cover with baking parchment and fill with baking beans and bake blind in a preheated oven at 200°C/400°F/gas 6 for about 10 minutes. Remove the paper and beans and bake for a further 5 minutes until light golden.

Meanwhile, heat the butter and sugar in a pan and stir until dissolved. Bring to the boil and boil for 1 minute, stirring continuously. Remove from the heat and stir in the milk and condensed milk. Return to the boil for 2 minutes or until the mixture is golden and very thick, stirring continuously. Arrange the bananas in the pastry case and sprinkle with a little lemon juice. Cover completely with the fudge and leave to cool. Chill for 45 minutes until set. Whip the cream and pile on top of the pie. Decorate with extra banana, sprinkled with lemon juice, if you wish. Serve within 2–3 hours.

Welsh Blackberry Turnover

Makes one 20 cm/8 in tart

225 g/8 oz blackberries
225 g/8 oz Shortcrust Pastry (page
  134)
A little milk to glaze
25 g/1 oz/2 tbsp butter or margarine,
  diced
50 g/2 oz/¼ cup soft brown sugar

Wash and trim the fruit. Roll out the pastry (paste) to a 23 cm/9 in circle and place on a greased baking (cookie) sheet. Cover half the pastry with the fruit, avoiding the edges. Fold loosely in half, brush the top with milk and bake in a preheated oven at 190°C/375°F/gas mark 5 for 40 minutes. Remove from the oven and carefully lift the lid, just enough to allow you to dot the fruit with the butter or margarine and sprinkle with the sugar.

Brandy or Rum Tart

Makes one 20 cm/8 in tart

225 g/8 oz/1 cup stoned (pitted) dates,
  chopped
250 ml/8 fl oz/1 cup boiling water
2.5 ml/½ tsp bicarbonate of soda
  (baking soda)
100 g/4 oz/½ cup butter or margarine,
  softened
175 g/6 oz/¾ cup caster (superfine)
  sugar
2 eggs
175 g/6 oz/1½ cups plain
  (all-purpose) flour
2.5 ml/½ tsp baking powder
2.5 ml/½ tsp ground ginger
A pinch of salt
50 g/2 oz/½ cup chopped mixed nuts
50 g/2 oz/½ cup biscuit (cookie)
  crumbs
For the syrup:
450 g/1 lb/2 cups soft brown sugar
250 ml/8 fl oz/1 cup boiling water
15 g/½ oz/1 tbsp butter or margarine
5 ml/1 tsp ground cinnamon
60 ml/4 tbsp brandy or rum

Mix together the dates, 200 ml/7 fl oz/scant 1 cup of the boiling water and the bicarbonate of soda, stir well and leave to stand. Cream together the butter or margarine, sugar and remaining boiling water until light and fluffy. Gradually beat in the eggs, then fold in the flour, baking powder, ginger and salt. Stir in the nuts, biscuit crumbs and date mixture. Spoon into a greased and lined 20 cm/8 in square cake tin (pan) and bake in a preheated oven at 190°C/375°F/gas mark 5 for 30 minutes until golden brown and springy to the touch.

To make the syrup, bring the all the ingredients except the brandy or rum to the boil in a pan. Simmer for 5 minutes, then leave to cool. Stir in the brandy, then spoon the syrup over the hot tart. Cool to lukewarm before serving.

Butter Tarts

Makes 12

225 g/8 oz Shortcrust Pastry (page 134)
50 g/2 oz/¼ cup butter or margarine, melted
175 g/6 oz/¾ cup soft brown sugar
45 ml/3 tbsp single (light) cream
100 g/4 oz/⅔ cup sultanas (golden raisins)
1 egg, lightly beaten
5 ml/1 tsp vanilla essence (extract)

Roll out the pastry (paste) and use to line 12 greased tartlet tins (patty pans) and prick with a fork. Mix together all the remaining ingredients and spoon into the tins. Bake in a preheated oven at 180°C/350°F/gas mark 4 for 25 minutes.

Coconut Tart

Makes one 23 cm/9 in tart

150 g/5 oz/⅔ cup butter or margarine
50 g/2 oz/¼ cup soft brown sugar
75 ml/5 tbsp clear honey
45 ml/3 tbsp milk
75 g/3 oz/¾ cup desiccated (shredded) coconut
1 Basic Sponge Tart Case (page 144)

Bring all the filling ingredients to the boil, stirring continuously. Spoon into the tart case (pie shell) and place under a hot grill (broiler) for a few minutes to brown the top.

Custard Tarts

Makes 12

225 g/8 oz Shortcrust Pastry (page 134)
15 ml/1 tbsp caster (superfine) sugar
1 egg, lightly beaten
150 ml/¼ pt/⅔ cup warm milk
A pinch of salt
Grated nutmeg for sprinkling

Roll out the pastry and use to line 12 deep tartlet tins (patty pans). Mix the sugar into the egg, then gradually stir in the warm milk and salt. Pour the mixture into the pastry cases (pie shells) and sprinkle with nutmeg. Bake in a preheated oven at 200°C/400°F/gas mark 6 for 20 minutes. Leave to cool in the tins.

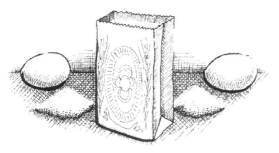

Danish Custard Tartlets

Makes 8

200 g/7 oz/scant 1 cup butter or
margarine
250 g/9 oz/2¼ cups plain
(all-purpose) flour
50 g/2 oz/⅓ cup icing (confectioners')
sugar, sifted
2 egg yolks
1 quantity Danish Custard Filling
(page 236)

Rub the butter or margarine into the flour and sugar until the mixture resembles breadcrumbs. Work in the egg yolks until well blended. Cover with clingfilm (plastic wrap) and chill for 1 hour. Roll out two-thirds of the pastry (paste) and use to line greased tartlet tins (patty pans). Fill with the custard filling. Roll out the remaining pastry and cut out lids for the tarts. Moisten the edges and press them together to seal. Bake in a preheated oven at 200°C/400°F/gas mark 6 for 15–20 minutes until golden. Leave to cool in the tins.

Fruit Tartlets

Makes 12

75 g/3 oz/⅓ cup butter or margarine,
diced
175 g/6 oz/1½ cups plain
(all-purpose) flour
45 ml/3 tbsp caster (superfine) sugar
10 ml/2 tsp finely grated orange rind
1 egg yolk
15 ml/1 tbsp water
175 g/6 oz/¾ cup cream cheese
15 ml/1 tbsp milk
350 g/12 oz mixed fruit such as halved
seedless grapes, mandarin
segments, sliced strawberries,
blackberries or raspberries
45 ml/3 tbsp apricot jam (conserve),
sieved (strained)
15 ml/1 tbsp water

Rub the butter or margarine into the flour until the mixture resembles breadcrumbs. Stir in 30 ml/2 tbsp of the sugar and half the orange rind. Add the egg yolk and just enough of the water to mix to a soft dough. Wrap in clingfilm (plastic wrap) and chill for 30 minutes. Roll out the pastry (paste) to 3mm/⅛ in thick on a lightly floured surface and use to line 12 barquette (boat-shaped) or tartlet moulds. Cover with greaseproof (waxed) paper, fill with baking beans and bake in a preheated oven at 190°C/375°F/gas mark 5 for 10 minutes. Remove the paper and beans and bake for a further 5 minutes until golden. Leave to cool in the tins for 5 minutes, then turn out on to a wire rack to finish cooling.

Beat the cheese with the milk, the remaining sugar and orange rind until smooth. Spoon into the pastry cases (pie shells) and arrange the fruit on top. Heat the jam and water in a small pan until well blended, then brush over the fruit to glaze. Chill before serving.

Genoese Tart

Makes one 23 cm/9 in tart

100 g/4 oz Puff Pastry (page 136)
50 g/2 oz/¼ cup butter or margarine,
softened
75 g/3 oz/⅓ cup caster (superfine)
sugar
75 g/3 oz/¾ cup almonds, chopped
3 eggs, separated
2.5 ml/½ tsp vanilla essence (extract)
100 g/4 oz/1 cup plain (all-purpose)
flour
100 g/4 oz/⅔ cup icing (confectioners')
sugar, sifted
Juice of ½ lemon

Roll out the pastry on a lightly floured surface and use to line a 23 cm/9 in cake tin (pan). Prick all over with a fork. Cream together the butter or margarine and caster sugar until light and fluffy. Gradually beat in the almonds, egg yolks and vanilla essence. Fold in the flour. Beat the egg whites until stiff, then fold into the mixture. Spoon into the pastry case (pie shell) and bake in a preheated oven at 190°C/375°F/gas mark 5 for 30 minutes. Allow to cool for 5 minutes. Blend the icing sugar with the lemon juice and spread over the top of the tart.

Ginger Tart

Makes one 23 cm/9 in tart

225 g/8 oz/⅔ cup golden (light corn) syrup
250 ml/8 fl oz/1 cup boiling water
2.5 ml/½ tsp ground ginger
60 ml/4 tbsp finely chopped crystallised (candied) ginger
30 ml/2 tbsp cornflour (cornstarch)
15 ml/1 tbsp custard powder
1 Basic Sponge Tart Case (page 144)

Bring the syrup, water and ground ginger to the boil, then stir in the crystallised ginger. Mix together the cornflour and custard powder to a paste with a little water, then stir it into the ginger mixture and cook over a low heat for a few minutes, stirring continuously. Spoon the filling into the tart case (shell) and leave to cool and set.

Jam Tarts

Makes 12

225 g/8 oz Shortcrust Pastry (page 134)
175 g/6 oz/½ cup firm or whole fruit jam (conserve)

Roll out the pastry (paste) and use to line a greased bun tin (patty pan). Divide the jam between the tarts and bake in a preheated oven at 200°C/400°F/gas mark 6 for 15 minutes.

Pecan Tart

Makes one 23 cm/9 in tart

225 g/8 oz Shortcrust Pastry (page 134)
50 g/2 oz/½ cup pecan nuts
3 eggs
225 g/8 oz/⅔ cup golden (light corn) syrup
75 g/3 oz/⅓ cup soft brown sugar
2.5 ml/½ tsp vanilla essence (extract)
A pinch of salt

Roll out the pastry (paste) on a lightly floured surface and use to line a greased 23 cm/9 in flan dish. Cover with greaseproof (waxed) paper, fill with baking beans and bake blind in a preheated oven at 190°C/375°F/gas mark 5 for 10 minutes. Remove the paper and beans.

Arrange the pecans in an attractive pattern in the pastry case (pie shell). Beat the eggs until light and frothy. Beat in the syrup, then the sugar and continue beating until the sugar has dissolved. Add the vanilla essence and salt and beat until smooth. Spoon the mixture into the case and bake in the preheated oven for 10 minutes. Reduce the oven temperature to 180°C/350°F/gas mark 4 and bake for a further 30 minutes until golden. Leave to cool and set before serving.

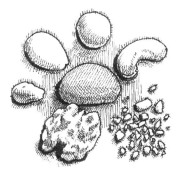

Pecan and Apple Tart

Makes one 23 cm/9 in tart

2 eggs
350 g/12 oz/1½ cups caster (superfine)
  sugar
50 g/2 oz/½ cup plain (all-purpose)
  flour
10 ml/2 tsp baking powder
A pinch of salt
100 g/4 oz cooking (tart) apples,
  peeled, cored and diced
100 g/4 oz/1 cup pecan nuts or
  walnuts
150 ml/¼ pt/⅔ cup whipped cream

Beat the eggs until pale and frothy. Stir in all the remaining ingredients, except the cream, one at a time in the order listed. Spoon into a greased and lined 23 cm/9 in cake tin (pan) and bake in a preheated oven at 160°C/325°F/ gas 3 for about 45 minutes until well risen and golden brown. Serve with the cream.

Gainsborough Tart

Makes one 20 cm/8 in tart

25 g/1 oz/2 tbsp butter or margarine
2.5 ml/½ tsp baking powder
50 g/2 oz/¼ cup caster (superfine)
  sugar
100 g/4 oz/1 cup desiccated
  (shredded) coconut
50 g/2 oz/¼ cup glacé (candied)
  cherries, chopped
2 eggs, beaten

Melt the butter, then mix in the remaining ingredients and spoon into a greased and lined 20 cm/8 in cake tin (pan). Bake in a preheated oven at 180°C/350°F/gas mark 4 for 30 minutes until springy to the touch.

Lemon Tart

Makes one 25 cm/10 in tart

225 g/8 oz Shortcrust Pastry
  (page 134)
100 g/4 oz/½ cup butter or margarine
4 eggs
Grated rind and juice of 2 lemons
100 g/4 oz/½ cup caster (superfine)
  sugar
250 ml/8 fl oz/1 cup double (heavy)
  cream
Mint leaves to decorate

Roll out the pastry (paste) on a lightly floured surface and use to line a 25 cm/10 in flan tin (pan). Prick the base with a fork. Cover with greaseproof (waxed) paper and fill with baking beans. Bake in a preheated oven at 200°C/ 400°F/gas mark 6 for 10 minutes. Remove the paper and beans and return to the oven for a further 5 minutes until the base is dry. Reduce the oven temperature to 160°C/325°F/gas mark 3.

Melt the butter or margarine, then leave to cool for 1 minute. Whisk the eggs with the lemon rind and juice. Whisk in the butter, sugar and cream. Pour into the pastry base and bake at the reduced temperature for 20 minutes. Leave to cool, then chill before serving, decorated with mint leaves.

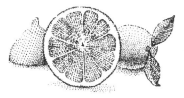

Lemon Tartlets

Makes 12

225 g/8 oz/1 cup butter or margarine,
  softened
75 g/3 oz/½ cup icing (confectioners')
  sugar, sifted
175 g/6 oz/1½ cups plain
  (all-purpose) flour
50 g/2 oz/½ cup cornflour (cornstarch)
5 ml/1 tsp grated lemon rind
  For the topping:
30 ml/2 tbsp lemon curd
30 ml/2 tbsp icing (confectioners')
  sugar, sifted

Blend together all the cake ingredients until soft. Spoon into a piping bag and pipe decoratively into 12 paper cases placed in a bun tin (patty pan). Bake in a preheated oven at 180°C/350°F/gas mark 4 for 20 minutes until pale golden. Leave to cool slightly, then place a spoonful of lemon curd on top of each cake and dust with icing sugar.

Orange Tart

Makes one 23 cm/9 in tart

1 Basic Sponge Tart Case (page 144)
400 ml/14 fl oz/1¾ cups orange juice
150 g/5 oz/⅔ cup caster (superfine)
  sugar
30 ml/2 tbsp custard powder
15 g/½ oz/1 tbsp butter or margarine
15 ml/1 tbsp grated orange rind
A few candied orange slices (optional)

Prepare the basic sponge tart case (shell). While it is cooking, mix 250 ml/8 fl oz/1 cup of the orange juice with the sugar, custard powder and butter or margarine. Bring the mixture to the boil over a low heat and simmer gently until transparent and thick. Stir in the orange rind. As soon as the flan case comes out of the oven, spoon over the remaining orange juice, then spoon the orange filling

into the flan and leave to cool and set. Decorate with candied orange slices, if liked.

Pear Tart

Makes one 20 cm/8 in tart

1 quantity Pâte Sucrée (page 137)
  For the filling:
150 ml/¼ pt/⅔ cup double (heavy)
  cream
2 eggs
50 g/2 oz/¼ cup caster (superfine)
  sugar
5 pears
  For the glaze:
75 ml/5 tbsp redcurrant jelly
  (clear conserve)
30 ml/2 tbsp water
A squeeze of lemon juice

Roll out the pâte sucrée and use to line a 20 cm/8 in flan tin (pan). Cover with greaseproof (waxed) paper and fill with baking beans and bake in a preheated oven at 190°C/375°F/gas mark 5 for 12 minutes. Remove from the oven, remove the paper and beans and leave to cool.

To make the filling, mix together the cream, eggs and sugar. Peel and core the pears and cut in half lengthways. Place cut side down, and slice almost through to the centre of the pears, but still leaving them intact. Arrange in the tart case (shell). Pour over the cream mixture and bake in a preheated oven at 190°C/375°F/gas mark 4 for 45 minutes, covering with greaseproof (waxed) paper if it browns before the cream is set. Leave to cool.

To make the glaze, melt the jelly, water and lemon juice in a small pan until blended. Brush over the fruit while the glaze is hot, then leave to set. Serve the same day.

Pear and Almond Tart

Makes one 20 cm/8 in tart

For the pastry (paste):
100 g/4 oz/1 cup plain (all-purpose) flour
50 g/2 oz/½ cup ground almonds
50 g/2 oz/¼ cup caster (superfine) sugar
75 g/3 oz/⅓ cup butter or margarine, diced and softened
1 egg yolk
A few drops of almond essence (extract)
For the filling:
1 egg yolk
50 g/2 oz/¼ cup caster (superfine) sugar
50 g/2 oz/½ cup ground almonds
30 ml/2 tbsp pear-flavoured liqueur or other liqueur to taste
3 large pears
For the custard:
3 eggs
25 g/1 oz/2 tbsp caster (superfine) sugar
300 ml/½ pt/1¼ cups single (light) cream

To make the pastry, mix together the flour, almonds and sugar in a bowl and make a well in the centre. Add the butter or margarine, egg yolk and vanilla essence and gradually work the ingredients together until you have a soft dough. Wrap in clingfilm (plastic wrap) and chill for 45 minutes. Roll out on a floured surface and use to line a greased and lined 20 cm/8 in flan tin (pan). Cover with greaseproof (waxed) paper and fill with baking beans and bake blind in a preheated oven at 200°C/400°F/gas mark 6 for 15 minutes. Remove the paper and beans.

To make the filling, beat together the egg yolk and sugar. Stir in the almonds and liqueur and spoon the mixture into the pastry case (pie shell). Peel, core and halve the pears, then arrange them flat side down on the filling.

To make the custard, beat together the eggs and sugar until pale and fluffy. Stir in the cream. Cover the pears with the custard and bake in a preheated oven at 180°C/350°F/gas mark 4 for about 15 minutes until the custard is just set.

Royal Raisin Tart

Makes one 20 cm/8 in tart

For the pastry (paste):
100 g/4 oz/½ cup butter or margarine
225 g/8 oz/2 cups plain (all-purpose) flour
A pinch of salt
45 ml/3 tbsp cold water
For the filling:
50 g/2 oz/½ cup cake crumbs
175 g/6 oz/1 cup raisins
1 egg yolk
5 ml/1 tsp grated lemon rind
For the topping:
225 g/8 oz/1⅓ cups icing (confectioners') sugar, sifted
1 egg white
5 ml/1 tsp lemon juice
To finish:
45 ml/3 tbsp redcurrant jelly (clear conserve)

To make the pastry, rub the butter or margarine into the flour and salt until the mixture resembles breadcrumbs. Mix in enough cold water to make a pastry. Wrap in clingfilm (plastic wrap) and chill for 30 minutes.

Roll out the pastry and use to line a 20 cm/8 in square cake tin (pan). Mix together the filling ingredients and spoon over the base, levelling the top. Beat the topping ingredients together and spread over the cake. Beat the redcurrant jelly until smooth, then pipe a trellis design over the top of the cake. Bake in a preheated oven at 190°C/375°F/gas mark 5 for 30 minutes, then reduce the oven temperature to 180°C/350°F/gas mark 4 and bake for a further 10 minutes.

Raisin and Soured Cream Tart

Makes one 23 cm/9 in tart

225 g/8 oz Shortcrust Pastry (page 134)
30 ml/2 tbsp plain (all-purpose) flour
2 eggs, lightly beaten
60 ml/4 tbsp caster (superfine) sugar
250 ml/8 fl oz/1 cup soured (dairy sour) cream
225 g/8 oz/1⅓ cups raisins
60 ml/4 tbsp rum or brandy
A few drops of vanilla essence (extract)

Roll out the pastry (paste) to 5mm/¼ in thick on a lightly floured surface. Mix together the flour, eggs, sugar and cream, then stir in the raisins, rum or brandy and vanilla essence. Spoon the mixture into the pastry case and bake in a preheated oven at 200°C/400°F/gas mark 6 for 20 minutes. Reduce the oven temperature to 180°C/350°F/gas mark 4 and bake for a further 5 minutes until just set.

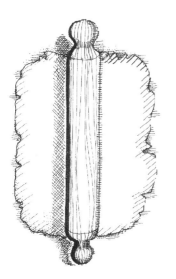

Strawberry Tart

Makes one 20 cm/8 in tart

1 quantity Pâte Sucrée (page 137)
For the filling:
5 egg yolks
175 g/6 oz/¾ cup caster (superfine) sugar
75 g/3 oz/¾ cup cornflour (cornstarch)
1 vanilla pod (bean)
450 ml/¾ pt/2 cups milk
15 g/½ oz/1 tbsp butter or margarine
550 g/1¼ lb strawberries, halved
For the glaze:
75 ml/5 tbsp redcurrant jelly (clear conserve)
30 ml/2 tbsp water
A squeeze of lemon juice

Roll out the pastry (paste) and use to line a 20 cm/8 in flan tin (pan). Cover with greaseproof (waxed) paper and fill with baking beans and bake in a preheated oven at 190°C/375°F/gas mark 5 for 12 minutes. Remove from the oven, remove the paper and beans and leave to cool.

To make the filling, beat together the egg yolks and sugar until the mixture is pale and fluffy and trails from the whisk in ribbons. Beat in the cornflour. Place the vanilla pod in the milk and bring to the boil. Remove the vanilla pod. Gradually beat into the egg mixture. Pour the mixture into a clean pan and bring to the boil, stirring continuously, then cook, still stirring, for 3 minutes. Remove from the heat and stir in the butter or margarine until melted. Cover with buttered greaseproof (waxed) paper and leave to cool.

Spoon the custard into the pastry case (pie shell) and arrange the strawberries attractively on the top. To make the glaze, melt the jelly, water and lemon juice until blended. Brush over the fruit while the glaze is hot, then leave to set. Serve the same day.

Treacle Tart

Makes one 20 cm/8 in tart

75 g/3 oz/⅓ cup butter or margarine
175 g/6 oz/1½ cups plain
  (all-purpose) flour
15 ml/1 tbsp caster (superfine) sugar
1 egg yolk
30 ml/2 tbsp water
225 g/8 oz/⅔ cup golden (light corn)
  syrup
50 g/2 oz/1 cup fresh breadcrumbs
5 ml/1 tsp lemon juice

Rub the butter or margarine into the flour until the mixture resembles breadcrumbs. Stir in the sugar, then add the egg yolk and water and mix to a pastry (paste). Wrap in clingfilm (plastic wrap) and chill for 30 minutes.

Roll out the pastry and use to line a 20 cm/8 in flan tin (pan). Warm the syrup, then mix it with the breadcrumbs and lemon juice. Spoon the filling into the pastry case and bake in a preheated oven at 180°C/350°F/gas mark 4 for 35 minutes until bubbling.

Walnut and Treacle Tart

Makes one 20 cm/8 in tart

225 g/8 oz Shortcrust Pastry
  (page 134)
100 g/4 oz/½ cup butter or margarine,
  softened
50 g/2 oz/¼ cup soft brown sugar
2 eggs, beaten
175 g/6 oz/½ cup golden (light corn)
  syrup, warmed
100 g/4 oz/1 cup walnuts, finely
  chopped
Grated rind of 1 lemon
Juice of ½ lemon

Roll out the pastry (paste) and use to line a greased 20 cm/8 in cake tin (pan). Cover with greaseproof (waxed) paper and fill with baking beans and bake in a preheated oven at 200°C/400°F/gas mark 6 for 10 minutes. Remove from the oven and remove the paper and beans. Reduce the oven temperature to 180°C/350°F/gas mark 4.

Beat together the butter or margarine and sugar until pale and fluffy. Gradually beat in the eggs, then stir in the syrup, walnuts, lemon rind and juice. Spoon into the pastry case (pie shell) and bake in the oven for 45 minutes until browned and crisp.

International Cakes

Amish Shoo-fly Cake
Makes one 23 × 30 cm cake

225 g/8 oz/1 cup butter or margarine,
softened
225 g/8 oz/2 cups plain
(all-purpose) flour
225 g/8 oz/2 cups wholemeal
(wholewheat) flour
450 g/1 lb/2 cups soft brown sugar
350 g/12 oz/1 cup black treacle
(molasses)
10 ml/2 tsp bicarbonate of soda
(baking soda)
450 ml/³⁄₄ pt/2 cups boiling water

Rub the butter or margarine into the flours until the mixture resembles breadcrumbs. Stir in the sugar. Set aside 100 g/4 oz/1 cup of the mixture for the topping. Mix together the treacle, bicarbonate of soda and water and stir into the flour mixture just until the dry ingredients have been absorbed. Spoon into a greased and floured 23 × 30 cm/ 9 × 12 in cake tin (pan) and sprinkle with the reserved mixture. Bake in a preheated oven at 180°C/350°F/gas mark 4 for 35 minutes until a skewer inserted in the centre comes out clean. Serve warm.

Boston Custard Slice
Makes one 23 cm/9 in cake

100 g/4 oz/½ cup butter or margarine,
softened
225 g/8 oz/1 cup caster (superfine)
sugar
2 eggs, lightly beaten
2.5 ml/½ tsp vanilla essence (extract)
175 g/6 oz/1½ cups self-raising
(self-rising) flour
5 ml/1 tsp baking powder
A pinch of salt
60 ml/4 tbsp milk
Custard Filling (page 236)

Cream together the butter or margarine and sugar until light and fluffy. Gradually add the eggs and vanilla essence, beating well after each addition. Mix together the flour, baking powder and salt and add to the mixture alternately with the milk. Spoon into a greased and floured 23 cm/9 in cake tin (pan) and bake in a preheated oven at 180°C/350°F/gas mark 4 for 30 minutes until firm to the touch. When cool, cut the cake horizontally and sandwich the two halves together with the custard filling.

American White Mountain Cake

Makes one 23 cm/9 in cake

225 g/8 oz/1 cup butter or margarine, softened
450 g/1 lb/2 cups caster (superfine) sugar
3 eggs, lightly beaten
350 g/12 oz/3 cups self-raising (self-rising) flour
15 ml/1 tbsp baking powder
1.5 ml/¼ tsp salt
250 ml/8 fl oz/1 cup milk
5 ml/1 tsp vanilla essence (extract)
5 ml/1 tsp almond essence (extract)
For the lemon filling:
45 ml/3 tbsp cornflour (cornstarch)
75 g/3 oz/⅓ cup caster (superfine) sugar
1.5 ml/¼ tsp salt
300 ml/½ pt/1¼ cups milk
25 g/1 oz/2 tbsp butter or margarine
90 ml/6 tbsp lemon juice
5 ml/1 tsp grated lemon rind
For the frosting:
350 g/12 oz/1½ cups caster (superfine) sugar
A pinch of salt
2 egg whites
75 ml/5 tbsp cold water
15 ml/1 tbsp golden (light corn) syrup
5 ml/1 tsp vanilla essence (extract)
175 g/6 oz/1½ cups desiccated (shredded) coconut

Cream together the butter or margarine and sugar until light and fluffy. Gradually beat in the eggs. Mix together the flour, baking powder and salt, then add to the creamed mixture alternately with the milk and essences. Spoon the mixture into three greased and lined 23 cm/9 in cake tins (pans) and bake in a preheated oven at 180°C/350°F/gas mark 4 for 30 minutes until a skewer inserted into the centre comes out clean. Leave to cool.

To make the filling, mix together the cornflour, sugar and salt, then whisk in the milk until blended. Add the butter or margarine in pieces and whisk over a low heat for about 2 minutes until thick. Stir in the lemon juice and rind. Leave to cool and chill.

To make the frosting, mix together all the ingredients except the vanilla essence and coconut in a heatproof bowl set over a pan of gently simmering water. Beat for about 5 minutes until stiff. Stir in the vanilla essence and beat for a further 2 minutes.

To assemble the cake, spread the base layer with half the lemon filling and sprinkle with 25 g/1 oz/¼ cup of coconut. Repeat with the second layer. Spread the frosting over the top and sides of the cake and sprinkle with the remaining coconut.

American Buttermilk Cake

Makes one 23 cm/9 in cake

100 g/4 oz/½ cup butter or margarine, softened
225 g/8 oz/1 cup caster (superfine) sugar
2 eggs, lightly beaten
5 ml/1 tsp grated lemon rind
5 ml/1 tsp vanilla essence (extract)
225 g/8 oz/2 cups self-raising (self-rising) flour
5 ml/1 tsp baking powder
5 ml/1 tsp bicarbonate of soda (baking soda)
A pinch of salt
250 ml/8 fl oz/1 cup buttermilk
Lemon Filling (page 237)

Cream together the butter or margarine and sugar until light and fluffy. Gradually beat in the eggs, then stir in the lemon rind and vanilla essence. Mix together the flour, baking powder, bicarbonate of soda and salt and add to the mixture alternately with the buttermilk. Beat well until smooth. Spoon the mixture into two greased and floured 23 cm/9 in cake tins (pans) and bake in a preheated oven at 180°C/350°F/gas mark 4 for 25 minutes until firm to the touch. Leave to cool in the tins for 5 minutes before turning out on to a wire rack to finish cooling. When cool, sandwich together with the lemon filling.

Caribbean Ginger and Rum Cake

Makes one 20 cm/8 in cake

50 g/2 oz/¼ cup butter or margarine
120 ml/4 fl oz/½ cup black treacle (molasses)
1 egg, lightly beaten
60 ml/4 tbsp rum
100 g/4 oz/1 cup self-raising (self-rising) flour
10 ml/2 tsp ground ginger
75 g/3 oz/⅓ cup soft brown sugar
25 g/1 oz crystallised (candied) ginger, chopped

Melt the butter or margarine with the treacle over a low heat, then leave to cool slightly. Stir in the remaining ingredients to make a soft batter. Spoon into a greased and lined 20 cm/8 in ring tin (pan) and bake in a preheated oven at 200°C/400°F/gas mark 6 for 20 minutes until well risen and firm to the touch.

Sachertorte

Makes one 20 cm/8 in cake

200 g/7 oz/1¾ cups plain (semi-sweet) chocolate
8 eggs, separated
100 g/4 oz/½ cup unsalted (sweet) butter, melted
2 egg whites
A pinch of salt
150 g /5 oz/⅔ cup caster (superfine) sugar
A few drops of vanilla essence (extract)
100 g/4 oz/1 cup plain (all-purpose) flour
For the icing (frosting):
150 g/5 oz/1¼ cups plain (semi-sweet) chocolate
250 ml/8 fl oz/1 cup single (light) cream
175 g/6 oz/¾ cup caster (superfine) sugar
A few drops of vanilla essence (extract)
1 egg, beaten
100 g/4 oz/⅓ cup apricot jam (conserve), sieved (strained)

Melt the chocolate in a heatproof bowl set over a pan of gently simmering water. Remove from the heat. Lightly beat the egg yolks with the butter, then stir into the melted chocolate. Whisk all the egg whites and the salt until stiff, then gradually add the sugar and vanilla essence and continue to beat until the mixture stands in stiff peaks. Gradually fold into the chocolate mixture, then fold in the flour. Spoon the mixture into two greased and lined 20 cm/8 in cake tins (pans) and bake in a preheated oven at 180°C/350°F/gas mark 4 for 45 minutes until a skewer inserted in the centre comes out clean. Turn out on to a wire rack and leave to cool.

To make the icing, melt the chocolate with the cream, sugar and vanilla essence over a medium heat until well blended, then simmer for 5 minutes without stirring. Mix a few spoonfuls of the chocolate mixture with the egg, then stir into the chocolate and cook for 1 minute, stirring. Remove from the heat and leave to cool to room temperature.

Sandwich the cakes together with the apricot jam. Cover the whole cake with the chocolate icing, smoothing the surface with a palette knife or spatula. Leave to cool, then chill for several hours until the icing hardens.

Caribbean Rum Fruit Cake

Makes one 20 cm/8 in cake

450 g/1 lb/2⅔ cups dried mixed fruit
(fruit cake mix)
225 g/8 oz/1⅓ cups sultanas (golden
raisins)
100 g/4 oz/⅔ cup raisins
100 g/4 oz/⅔ cup currants
50 g/2 oz/¼ cup glacé (candied)
cherries
300 ml/½ pt/1¼ cups red wine
225 g/8 oz/1 cup butter or margarine,
softened
225 g/8 oz/1 cup soft brown sugar
5 eggs, lightly beaten
10 ml/2 tsp black treacle (molasses)
225 g/8 oz/2 cups plain
(all-purpose) flour
50 g/2 oz/½ cup ground almonds
5 ml/1 tsp ground cinnamon
5 ml/1 tsp grated nutmeg
5 ml/1 tsp vanilla essence (extract)
300 ml/½ pt/1¼ cups rum

Place all the fruit and the wine in a pan and bring to the boil. Reduce the heat to minimum, cover and leave for 15 minutes, then remove from the heat and leave to cool. Cream together the butter or margarine and sugar until light and fluffy, then gradually mix in the eggs and treacle. Fold in the dry ingredients. Stir in the fruit mixture, vanilla essence and 45 ml/3 tbsp of the rum. Spoon into a greased and lined 20 cm/8 in cake tin (pan) and bake in a preheated oven at 160°C/325°F/gas mark 3 for 3 hours until well risen and a skewer inserted in the centre comes out clean. Leave to cool in the tin for 10 minutes, then turn out on to a wire rack to finish cooling. Pierce the top of the cake with a fine skewer and spoon over the remaining rum. Wrap in foil and leave to mature for as long as possible.

Danish Butter Cake

Makes one 23 cm/9 in cake

225 g/8 oz/1 cup butter or margarine,
diced
175 g/6 oz/1½ cups plain
(all-purpose) flour
40 g/1½ oz fresh yeast or 60 ml/4 tbsp
dried yeast
15 ml/1 tbsp granulated sugar
1 egg, beaten
½ quantity Danish Custard Filling
(page 236)
60 ml/4 tbsp icing (confectioners')
sugar, sifted
45 ml/3 tbsp currants

Rub 100 g/4 oz/½ cup of the butter or margarine into the flour. Cream together the yeast and granulated sugar, then add it to the flour and butter with the egg and mix to a smooth dough. Cover and leave in a warm place for about 1 hour until doubled in size.

Turn out on to a floured surface and knead well. Roll out one-third of the dough and use to line the base of a greased 23 cm/9 in loose-bottomed cake tin (pan). Spread the custard filling over the dough.

Roll out the remaining dough to a rectangle about 5 mm/¼ in thick. Cream together the remaining butter or margarine and the icing sugar, then mix in the currants. Spread over the dough, leaving a gap around the edges, then roll up the dough from the shorter side. Cut into slices and arrange on top of the custard filling. Cover and leave in a warm place to rise for about 1 hour. Bake in a preheated oven at 230°C/450°F/gas mark 8 for 25–30 minutes until well risen and golden on top.

Photograph opposite: **Spiced Carrot Cake (page 83)**

160

Danish Cardamom Cake

Makes one 900 g/2 lb cake

225 g/8 oz/1 cup butter or margarine,
  softened
225 g/8 oz/1 cup caster (superfine)
  sugar
3 eggs
350 g/12 oz/3 cups plain
  (all-purpose) flour
10 ml/2 tsp baking powder
10 cardamom seeds, ground
150 ml/¼ pt/⅔ cup milk
45 ml/3 tbsp raisins
45 ml/3 tbsp chopped mixed
  (candied) peel

Cream together the butter or margarine and sugar until light and fluffy. Add the eggs, a little at a time, beating well after each addition. Fold in the flour, baking powder and cardamom. Gradually stir in the milk, raisins and mixed peel. Spoon into a greased and lined 900 g/2 lb loaf tin (pan) and bake in a preheated oven at 190°C/375°F/ gas mark 5 for 50 minutes until a skewer inserted in the centre comes out clean.

Photograph opposite: Cherry Toffee
Traybake (page 98) and Shortbread
Cinnamon Meringues (page 110)

Gâteau Pithiviers

Makes one 25 cm/10 in cake

100 g/4 oz/½ cup butter or margarine,
  softened
100 g/4 oz/½ cup caster (superfine)
  sugar
1 egg
1 egg yolk
100 g/4 oz/1 cup ground almonds
30 ml/2 tbsp rum
400 g/14 oz Puff Pastry (page 136)
  For the glaze:
1 egg, beaten
30 ml/2 tbsp icing (confectioners')
  sugar

Beat together the butter or margarine and sugar until light and fluffy. Beat in the egg and egg yolk, then beat in the almonds and rum. Roll out half the pastry (paste) on a lightly floured surface and cut into a 23 cm/9 in circle. Place on a dampened baking (cookie) sheet and spread the filling over the pastry to within 1 cm/½ in of the edge. Roll out the remaining pastry and cut into a 25 cm/ 10 in circle. Cut a 1 cm/½ in ring off the edge of this circle. Brush the edge of the pastry base with water and press the ring round the edge, gently pushing it to fit. Brush with water and press the second circle over the top, sealing the edges. Seal and flute the edges. Brush the top with beaten egg, then mark a pattern of radial cuts on the top with the blade of a knife. Bake in a preheated oven at 220°C/425°F/gas mark 7 for 30 minutes until risen and golden brown. Sift the icing sugar over the top and return to the oven for a further 5 minutes until shiny. Serve warm or cold.

Galette des Rois

Makes one 18 cm/7 in cake

250 g/9 oz/2¼ cups plain
(all-purpose) flour
5 ml/1 tsp salt
200 g/7 oz/scant 1 cup unsalted
(sweet) butter, diced
175 ml/6 fl oz/¾ cup water
1 egg
1 egg white

Place the flour and salt in a bowl and make a well in the centre. Add 75 g/ 3 oz/⅓ cup of the butter, the water and whole egg and mix to a soft dough. Cover and leave to stand for 30 minutes.

Roll out the dough into a long rectangle on a lightly floured surface. Dot two-thirds of the dough with one-third of the remaining butter. Fold the uncovered pastry up over the butter, then fold the remaining pastry over the top. Seal the edges and chill for 10 minutes. Roll out the dough again and repeat with half the remaining butter. Chill, roll out and add the remaining butter, then chill for a final 10 minutes.

Roll out the dough into a 2.5 cm/1 in thick circle about 18 cm/7 in in diameter. Place on a greased baking (cookie) sheet, brush with egg white and leave to stand for 15 minutes. Bake in a preheated oven at 180°C/350°F/gas mark 4 for 15 minutes until well risen and golden brown.

Crème Caramel

Makes one 15 cm/6 in cake

For the caramel:
100 g/4 oz/½ cup caster (superfine)
sugar
150 ml/¼ pt/⅔ cup water
For the custard:
600 ml/1 pt/2½ cups milk
4 eggs, lightly beaten
15 ml/1 tbsp caster (superfine) sugar
1 orange

To make the caramel, place the sugar and water in a small pan and dissolve over a low heat. Bring to the boil, then boil without stirring for about 10 minutes until the syrup turns a rich golden brown. Pour into a 15 cm/6 in soufflé dish and tilt the dish so the caramel flows over the base.

To make the custard, warm the milk, then pour it on to the eggs and sugar and whisk thoroughly. Pour into the dish. Stand the dish in a baking tin (pan) with hot water to half-way up the sides of the dish. Bake in a preheated oven at 170°C/325°F/gas mark 3 for 1 hour until set. Leave until cold before turning out on to a serving plate. Peel the orange and slice horizontally, then cut each slice in half. Arange around the caramel to decorate.

Gugelhopf

Makes one 20 cm/8 in cake

25 g/1 oz fresh yeast or 40 ml/
2½ tbsp dried yeast
120 ml/4 fl oz/½ cup warm milk
100 g/4 oz/⅔ cup raisins
15 ml/1 tbsp rum
450 g/1 lb/4 cups strong plain (bread)
flour
5 ml/1 tsp salt
A pinch of grated nutmeg
100 g/4 oz/½ cup caster (superfine)
sugar
Grated rind of 1 lemon
175 g/6 oz/¾ cup butter or margarine,
softened
3 eggs
100 g/4 oz/1 cup blanched almonds
Icing (confectioners') sugar for
dusting

Blend the yeast with a little of the warm milk and leave in a warm place for 20 minutes until frothy. Place the raisins in a bowl, sprinkle with the rum and leave to soak. Place the flour, salt and nutmeg in a bowl and stir in the sugar and lemon rind.

Make a well in the centre, pour in the yeast mixture, the remaining milk, the butter or margarine and the eggs and work together to make a dough. Place in an oiled bowl, cover with oiled clingfilm (plastic wrap) and leave in a warm place for 1 hour until doubled in size. Generously butter a 20 cm/8 in gugelhopf tin (fluted tube pan) and place the almonds around the base. Knead the raisins and rum into the risen dough and mix well. Spoon the mixture into the tin, cover and leave in a warm place for 40 minutes until the dough has almost doubled in volume and reached to the top of the tin. Bake in a preheated oven at 200°C/400°F/gas mark 6 for 45 minutes until a skewer inserted in the centre comes out clean. Cover with a double layer of greaseproof (waxed) paper towards the end of the cooking if the cake is over-browning. Turn out and leave to cool, then dust with icing sugar.

Luxury Chocolate Gugelhopf

Makes one 20 cm/8 in cake

25 g/1 oz fresh yeast or
*   40 ml/2½ tbsp dried yeast*
120 ml/4 fl oz/½ cup warm milk
50 g/2 oz/⅓ cup raisins
50 g/2 oz/⅓ cup currants
25 g/1 oz/3 tbsp chopped mixed
*   (candied) peel*
15 ml/1 tbsp rum
450 g/1 lb/4 cups strong plain (bread)
*   flour*
5 ml/1 tsp salt
5 ml/1 tsp ground allspice
A pinch of ground ginger
100 g/4 oz/½ cup caster (superfine)
*   sugar*
Grated rind of 1 lemon
175 g/6 oz/¾ cup butter or margarine,
*   softened*
3 eggs

For the topping:
60 ml/4 tbsp apricot jam (conserve),
*   sieved (strained)*
30 ml/2 tbsp water
100 g/4 oz/1 cup plain (semi-sweet)
*   chocolate*
50 g/2 oz/½ cup flaked (slivered)
*   almonds, toasted*

Blend the yeast with a little of the warm milk and leave in a warm place for 20 minutes until frothy. Place the raisins, currants and mixed peel in a bowl, sprinkle with the rum and leave to soak. Place the flour, salt and spices in a bowl and stir in the sugar and lemon rind. Make a well in the centre, pour in the yeast mixture, the remaining milk and the eggs and work together to make a dough. Place in an oiled bowl, cover with oiled clingfilm (plastic wrap) and leave in a warm place for 1 hour until doubled in size. Knead the fruit and rum into the risen dough and mix well. Spoon the mixture into a well-buttered 20 cm/8 in gugelhopf tin (fluted tube pan), cover and leave in a warm place for 40 minutes until the dough has almost doubled in volume and reached to the top of the tin. Bake in a preheated oven at 200°C/400°F/gas mark 6 for 45 minutes until a skewer inserted in the centre comes out clean. Cover with a double layer of greaseproof (waxed) paper towards the end of the cooking if the cake is becoming too brown. Turn out and leave to cool.

Heat the jam with the water, stirring until well blended. Brush over the cake. Melt the chocolate in a heatproof bowl set over a pan of gently simmering water. Spread over the cake and press the flaked almonds around the base before the chocolate sets.

Stollen

Makes three 350 g/12 oz cakes

15 g/½ oz fresh yeast or 20 ml/4 tsp
  dried yeast
15 ml/1 tbsp caster (superfine) sugar
120 ml/4 fl oz/½ cup warm water
25 g/1 oz/¼ cup strong plain (bread)
  flour
For the fruit dough:
450 g/1 lb/4 cups strong plain (bread)
  flour
5 ml/1 tsp salt
75 g/3 oz/⅓ cup demerara sugar
1 egg, lightly beaten
225 g/8 oz/1⅓ cups raisins
30 ml/2 tbsp rum
50 g/2 oz/⅓ cup chopped mixed
  (candied) peel
50 g/2 oz/½ cup ground almonds
5 ml/1 tsp ground cinnamon
100 g/4 oz/½ cup butter or margarine,
  melted
175 g/6 oz Almond Paste (page 228)
For the glaze:
1 egg, lightly beaten
75 g/3 oz/⅓ cup caster (superfine)
  sugar
90 ml/6 tbsp water
50 g/2 oz/½ cup flaked (slivered)
  almonds
Icing (confectioners') sugar for
  dusting

To make the yeast mixture, mix the yeast and sugar to a paste with the warm water and flour. Leave in a warm place for 20 minutes until frothy.

To make the fruit dough, place the flour and salt in a bowl, stir in the sugar and make a well in the centre. Add the egg with the yeast mixture and mix to a smooth dough. Add the raisins, rum, mixed peel, ground almonds and cinnamon and knead until well blended and smooth. Place in an oiled bowl, cover with oiled clingfilm (plastic wrap) and leave in a warm place for 30 minutes.

Divide the dough into thirds and roll out into rectangles about 1 cm/½ in thick. Brush the butter over the top. Divide the almond paste into thirds and roll into sausage shapes. Place one in the centre of each rectangle and fold the pastry over the top. Turn over with the seam underneath and place on a greased baking (cookie) sheet. Brush with egg, cover with oiled clingfilm (plastic wrap) and leave in a warm place for 40 minutes until doubled in size.

Bake in a preheated oven at 220°C/425°F/gas mark 7 for 30 minutes until golden brown.

Meanwhile, boil the sugar with the water for 3 minutes until you have a thick syrup. Brush the top of each stollen with the syrup and sprinkle with flaked almonds and icing sugar.

Almond Stollen

Makes two 450 g/1 lb loaves

15 g/½ oz fresh yeast or 20 ml/
  4 tsp dried yeast
50 g/2 oz/¼ cup caster (superfine)
  sugar
300 ml/½ pt/1¼ cups warm milk
1 egg
Grated rind of 1 lemon
A pinch of grated nutmeg
450 g/1 lb/4 cups plain (all-purpose)
  flour
A pinch of salt
100 g/4 oz/⅔ cup chopped mixed
  (candied) peel
175 g/6 oz/1½ cups almonds, chopped
50 g/2 oz/¼ cup butter or margarine,
  melted
75 g/3 oz/½ cup icing (confectioners')
  sugar, sifted, for dusting

Blend the yeast with 5 ml/1 tsp of the sugar and a little of the warm milk and leave in a warm place for 20 minutes until frothy. Beat the egg with the remaining sugar, the lemon rind and nutmeg, then beat into the yeast mixture with the flour, salt and remaining warm milk and mix to a soft dough. Place in an oiled bowl, cover with oiled clingfilm (plastic wrap) and leave in a warm place for 30 minutes.

Knead in the mixed peel and almonds, cover again and leave in a warm place for 30 minutes until doubled in size.

Divide the dough into halves. Roll one half into a 30 cm/12 in sausage shape. Press the rolling pin into the centre to make a dip, then fold over one side lengthways and press down gently. Repeat with the other half. Place both on a greased and lined baking (cookie) sheet, cover with oiled clingfilm (plastic wrap) and leave in a warm place for 25 minutes until doubled in size. Bake in a preheated oven at 200°C/400°F/gas mark 6 for 1 hour until golden and a skewer inserted in the centre comes out clean. Brush the warm loaves generously with the melted butter and sprinkle with the icing sugar.

Pistachio Nut Stollen

Makes two 450 g/1 lb loaves

15 g/½ oz fresh yeast or 20 ml/ 4 tsp dried yeast
50 g/2 oz/¼ cup caster (superfine) sugar
300 ml/½ pt/1¼ cups warm milk
1 egg
Grated rind of 1 lemon
A pinch of grated nutmeg
450 g/1 lb/4 cups plain (all-purpose) flour
A pinch of salt
100 g/4 oz/⅔ cup chopped mixed (candied) peel
100 g/4 oz/1 cup pistachio nuts, chopped
100 g/4 oz Almond Paste (page 228)
15 ml/1 tbsp maraschino liqueur
50 g/2 oz/⅓ cup icing (confectioners') sugar, sifted

For the topping:
50 g/2 oz/¼ cup butter or margarine, melted
75 g/3 oz/½ cup icing (confectioners') sugar, sifted, for dusting

Blend the yeast with 5 ml/1 tsp of the sugar and a little of the warm milk and leave in a warm place for 20 minutes until frothy. Beat the egg with the remaining sugar, the lemon rind and nutmeg, then beat into the yeast mixture with the flour, salt and remaining warm milk and mix to a soft dough. Place in an oiled bowl, cover with oiled clingfilm (plastic wrap) and leave in a warm place for 30 minutes.

Knead in the mixed peel and pistachio nuts, cover again and leave in a warm place for 30 minutes until doubled in size. Work the almond paste, liqueur and icing sugar to a paste, roll out to 1 cm/½ in thick and cut into cubes. Work into the dough so that the cubes remain whole.

Divide the dough into halves. Roll one half into a 30 cm/12 in sausage shape. Press the rolling pin into the centre to make a dip, then fold over one side lengthways and press down gently. Repeat with the second half. Place both on a greased and lined baking (cookie) sheet, cover with oiled clingfilm (plastic wrap) and leave in a warm place for 25 minutes until doubled in size. Bake in a preheated oven at 200°C/400°F/gas mark 6 for 1 hour until golden and a skewer inserted in the centre comes out clean. Brush the warm loaves generously with the melted butter and dust with the icing sugar.

Baklava

Makes 24

450 g/1 lb/2 cups caster (superfine) sugar
300 ml/½ pt/1¼ cups water
5 ml/1 tsp lemon juice
30 ml/2 tbsp rose water
350 g/12 oz/1½ cups unsalted (sweet) butter, melted
450 g/1 lb filo pastry (paste)
675 g/1½ lb/6 cups almonds, finely chopped

To make the syrup, dissolve the sugar in the water over a low heat, stirring occasionally. Add the lemon juice and bring to the boil. Boil for 10 minutes until syrupy, then add the rose water and leave to cool, then chill.

Brush a large roasting tin with melted butter. Layer half the sheets of filo in the tin, brushing each one with butter. Fold up the edges to hold in the filling. Spread the almonds over the top. Continue to layer the remaining pastry, brushing each sheet with melted butter. Brush the top generously with butter. Cut the pastry into lozenge shapes about 5 cm/2 in wide. Bake in a preheated oven at 180°C/350°F/gas mark 4 for 25 minutes until crisp and golden. Pour the cool syrup over the top, then leave to cool.

Hungarian Stressel Whirls

Makes 16

25 g/1 oz fresh yeast or 40 ml/2½ tbsp dried yeast
15 ml/1 tbsp soft brown sugar
300 ml/½ pt/1¼ cups warm water
15 ml/1 tbsp butter or margarine
450 g/1 lb/4 cups wholemeal (wholewheat) flour
15 ml/1 tbsp milk powder (non-fat dry milk)
5 ml/1 tsp ground mixed (apple-pie) spice

2.5 ml/½ tsp salt
1 egg
175 g/6 oz/1 cup currants
100 g/4 oz/⅔ cup sultanas (golden raisins)
50 g/2 oz/⅓ cup raisins
50 g/2 oz/⅓ cup chopped mixed (candied) peel
For the topping:
75 g/3 oz/¾ cup wholemeal (wholewheat) flour
50 g/2 oz/¼ cup butter or margarine, melted
75 g/3 oz/⅓ cup soft brown sugar
25 g/1 oz/¼ cup sesame seeds
For the filling:
50 g/2 oz/¼ cup soft brown sugar
50 g/2 oz/¼ cup butter or margarine, softened
50 g/2 oz/½ cup ground almonds
2.5 ml/½ tsp grated nutmeg
25 g/2 oz/⅓ cup stoned (pitted) prunes, chopped
1 egg, beaten

Mix together the yeast and sugar with a little of the warm water and leave in a warm place for 10 minutes until frothy. Rub the butter or margarine into the flour, then stir in the milk powder, mixed spice and salt and make a well in the centre. Stir in the egg, the yeast mixture and the remaining warm water and mix to a dough. Knead until smooth and elastic. Knead in the currants, sultanas, raisins and mixed peel. Place in an oiled bowl, cover with oiled clingfilm (plastic wrap) and leave in warm place for 1 hour.

Mix together the topping ingredients until crumbly. To make the filling, cream together the butter or margarine and sugar, then mix in the almonds and nutmeg. Roll out the dough to a large rectangle about 1 cm/½ in thick. Spread with the filling and sprinkle with the prunes. Roll up like a Swiss (jelly) roll, brushing the edges with egg to seal together. Cut into 2.5 cm/1 in slices and arrange in a greased, shallow baking tin (pan). Brush with egg and sprinkle with the topping mixture. Cover and leave in a warm place to rise for 30 minutes. Bake in a preheated oven at 220°C/425°F/gas mark 7 for 30 minutes.

Panforte

Makes one 23 cm/9 in cake

175 g/6 oz/³⁄₄ cup granulated sugar
175 g/6 oz/¹⁄₂ cup clear honey
100 g/4 oz/²⁄₃ cup dried figs, chopped
100 g/4 oz/²⁄₃ cup chopped mixed (candied) peel
50 g/2 oz/¹⁄₄ cup glacé cherries (candied), chopped
50 g/2 oz/¹⁄₄ cup glacé (candied) pineapple, chopped
175 g/6 oz/1¹⁄₂ cups blanched almonds, coarsely chopped
100 g/4 oz/1 cup walnuts, coarsely chopped
100 g/4 oz/1 cup hazelnuts, coarsely chopped
50 g/2 oz/¹⁄₂ cup plain (all-purpose) flour
25 g/1 oz/¹⁄₄ cup cocoa (unsweetened chocolate) powder
5 ml/1 tsp ground cinnamon
A pinch of grated nutmeg
15 ml/1 tbsp icing (confectioners') sugar, sifted

Dissolve the granulated sugar in the honey in a pan over a low heat. Bring to the boil and boil for 2 minutes until you have a thick syrup. Mix together the fruit and nuts and stir in the flour, cocoa and spices. Stir in the syrup. Spoon the mixture into a greased 23 cm/9 in sandwich tin (pan) lined with rice paper. Bake in a preheated oven at 180°C/350°F/gas mark 4 for 45 minutes. Leave to cool in the tin for 15 minutes, then turn out on to a wire rack to cool. Sprinkle with the icing sugar before serving.

Pasta Ribbon Cake

Makes one 23 cm/9 in cake

300 g/11 oz/2³⁄₄ cups plain (all-purpose) flour
50 g/2 oz/¹⁄₄ cup butter or margarine, melted
3 eggs, beaten
A pinch of salt
225 g/8 oz/2 cups almonds, chopped
200 g/7 oz/scant 1 cup caster (superfine) sugar
Grated rind and juice of 1 lemon
90 ml/6 tbsp kirsch

Place the flour in a bowl and make a well in the centre. Stir in the butter, eggs and salt and mix to a soft dough. Roll out thinly and cut into narrow ribbons. Mix together the almonds, sugar and lemon rind. Grease a 23 cm/9 in cake tin (pan) and sprinkle with flour. Arrange a layer of the pasta ribbons in the base of the tin, sprinkle with a little of the almond mixture and drizzle with a little of the kirsch. Continue layering, ending with a layer of pasta. Cover with buttered greaseproof (waxed) paper and bake at 180°C/350°F/gas mark 4 for 1 hour. Turn out carefully and serve warm or cold.

Italian Rice Cake with Grand Marnier

Makes one 20 cm/8 in cake

1.5 litres/2½ pts/6 cups milk
A pinch of salt
350 g/12 oz/1½ cups arborio or other medium-grain rice
Grated rind of 1 lemon
60 ml/4 tbsp caster (superfine) sugar
3 eggs
25 g/1 oz/2 tbsp butter or margarine
1 egg yolk
30 ml/2 tbsp chopped mixed (candied) peel
225 g/8 oz/2 cups slivered (flaked) almonds, toasted
45 ml/3 tbsp Grand Marnier
30 ml/2 tbsp dried breadcrumbs

Bring the milk and salt to the boil in a heavy pan, add the rice and lemon rind, cover and simmer for 18 minutes, stirring occasionally. Remove from the heat and stir in the sugar, eggs and butter or margarine and leave until lukewarm. Beat in the egg yolk, mixed peel, nuts and Grand Marnier. Grease a 20 cm/8 in cake tin (pan) and sprinkle with the breadcrumbs. Spoon the mixture into the tin and bake in a preheated oven at 150°C/300°F/gas mark 2 for 45 minutes until a skewer inserted in the centre comes out clean. Leave to cool in the tin, then turn out and serve warm.

Sicilian Sponge Cake

Makes one 23 × 9 cm/ 7 × 3½ in cake

450 g/1 lb Madeira Cake (page 11)
For the filling:
450 g/1 lb/2 cups Ricotta cheese
50 g/2 oz/¼ cup caster (superfine) sugar
30 ml/2 tbsp double (heavy) cream
30 ml/2 tbsp chopped mixed (candied) peel

15 ml/1 tbsp chopped almonds
30 ml/2 tbsp orange-flavoured liqueur
50 g/2 oz /½ cup plain (semi-sweet) chocolate, grated
For the icing (frosting):
350 g/12 oz/3 cups plain (semi-sweet) chocolate
175 ml/6 fl oz/¾ cup strong black coffee
225 g/8 oz/1 cup unsalted (sweet) butter or margarine

Cut the cake lengthways into 1 cm/½ in slices. To make the filling, press the Ricotta through a sieve (strainer), then beat until smooth. Beat in the sugar, cream, mixed peel, almonds, liqueur and chocolate. Arrange layers of cake and Ricotta mixture in a foil-lined 450 g/1 lb loaf tin (pan), finishing with a layer of cake. Fold the foil over the top and chill for 3 hours until firm.

To make the icing, melt the chocolate and coffee in a heatproof bowl set over a pan of gently simmering water. Beat in the butter or margarine and continue to beat until the mixture is smooth. Leave to cool until thick.

Remove the cake from the foil and place on a serving plate. Pipe or spread the icing over the top and sides of the cake and mark into patterns with a fork, if liked. Chill until firm.

Italian Ricotta Cake

Makes one 25 cm/10 in cake

For the sauce:
225 g/8 oz raspberries
250 ml/8 fl oz/1 cup water
50 g/2 oz/¼ cup caster (superfine) sugar
30 ml/2 tbsp cornflour (cornstarch)
For the filling:
450 g/1 lb/ 2 cups Ricotta cheese
225 g/8 oz/1 cup cream cheese
75 g/3 oz/⅓ cup caster (superfine) sugar

5 ml/1 tsp vanilla essence (extract)
Grated rind of 1 lemon
Grated rind of 1 orange
One 25 cm/10 in Angel Food Cake
(page 8)

To make the sauce, purée the ingredients until smooth, then pour into a small pan and cook over a medium heat, stirring, until the sauce thickens and just comes to the boil. Strain and discard the seeds, if you prefer. Cover and chill.

To make the filling, beat together all the ingredients until well mixed.

Cut the cake horizontally into three layers and sandwich them together with two-thirds of the filling, spreading the remainder on the top. Cover and chill until ready to serve with the sauce poured over the top.

Italian Vermicelli Cake

Makes one 23 cm/9 in cake

225 g/8 oz vermicelli
4 eggs, separated
200 g/7 oz/scant 1 cup caster
(superfine) sugar
225 g/8 oz Ricotta cheese
2.5 ml/½ tsp ground cinnamon
2.5 ml/½ tsp ground cloves
A pinch of salt
50 g/2 oz/½ cup plain (all-purpose)
flour
50 g/2 oz/⅓ cup raisins
45 ml/3 tbsp clear honey
Single (light) or double (heavy) cream
to serve

Bring a large pan of water to the boil, add the pasta and boil for 2 minutes. Drain and rinse under cold water. Beat the egg yolks with the sugar until pale and fluffy. Beat in the Ricotta, cinnamon, cloves and salt, then fold in the flour. Stir in the raisins and pasta. Beat the egg whites until they form soft peaks, then fold into the cake mixture. Pour into a greased and lined 23 cm/9 in cake tin

(pan) and bake in a preheated oven at 200°C/400°F/gas mark 6 for 1 hour until golden. Heat the honey gently and pour it over the warm cake. Serve warm with cream.

Italian Walnut and Mascarpone Cake

Makes one 23 cm/9 in cake

450 g/1 lb Puff Pastry (page 136)
175 g/6 oz/¾ cup Mascarpone cheese
50 g/2 oz/¼ cup caster (superfine)
sugar
30 ml/2 tbsp apricot jam (conserve)
3 egg yolks
50 g/2 oz/½ cup walnuts, chopped
100 g/4 oz/⅔ cup chopped mixed
(candied) peel
Finely grated rind of 1 lemon
Icing (confectioners') sugar, sifted,
for dusting

Roll out the pastry and use half to line a greased 23 cm/9 in flan tin (pan). Beat the Mascarpone with the sugar, jam and 2 egg yolks. Reserve 15 ml/1 tbsp of the nuts for decoration, then fold the remainder into the mixture with the mixed peel and lemon rind. Spoon into the pastry case (pie shell). Cover the filling with the remaining pastry (paste), then dampen and seal the edges together. Beat the remaining egg yolk and brush over the top. Bake in a preheated oven at 200°C/400°F/gas mark 6 for 35 minutes until risen and golden brown. Sprinkle with the reserved walnuts and dust with icing sugar.

Dutch Apple Cake

Serves 8

150 g/5 oz/⅔ cup butter or margarine
225 g/8 oz/2 cups plain
  (all-purpose) flour
5 ml/1 tsp baking powder
2 eggs, separated
10 ml/2 tsp lemon juice
900 g/2 lb unpeeled cooking (tart)
  apples, cored and sliced
175 g/6 oz/1 cup ready-to-eat dried
  apricots, quartered
100 g/4 oz/⅔ cup raisins
30 ml/2 tbsp water
5 ml/1 tsp ground cinnamon
50 g/2 oz/½ cup ground almonds

Rub the butter or margarine into the flour and baking powder until the mixture resembles breadcrumbs. Add the egg yolks and 5 ml/1 tsp of the lemon juice and mix to a soft dough. Roll out two-thirds of the pastry (paste) and use to line a greased 23 cm/9 in cake tin (pan).

Place the apple slices, apricots and raisins in a pan with the remaining lemon juice and the water. Simmer gently for 5 minutes, then drain. Spoon the fruit into the pastry case. Mix together the cinnamon and ground almonds and sprinkle over the top. Roll out the remaining pastry and make a lid for the cake. Seal the edge with a little water and brush the top with egg white. Bake in a preheated oven at 180°C/350°F/gas mark 4 for about 45 minutes until firm and golden.

Norwegian Plain Cake

Makes one 25 cm/10 in cake

225 g/8 oz/1 cup butter or margarine,
  softened
275 g/10 oz/1¼ cups caster (superfine)
  sugar
5 eggs
175 g/6 oz/1½ cups plain
  (all-purpose) flour
7.5 ml/1½ tsp baking powder
A pinch of salt
5 ml/1 tsp almond essence (extract)

Cream the butter or margarine and sugar until well blended. Gradually add the eggs, beating well after each addition. Beat in the flour, baking powder, salt and almond essence until smooth. Spoon into an ungreased 25 cm/10 in cake tin (pan) and bake in a preheated oven at 160°C/320°F/gas mark 3 for 1 hour until firm to the touch. Leave to cool in the tin for 10 minutes before turning out on to a wire rack to finish cooling.

Norwegian Kransekake

Makes one 25 cm/10 in cake

450 g/1 lb/4 cups ground almonds
100 g/4 oz/1 cup ground bitter
  almonds
450 g/1 lb/2⅔ cups icing
  (confectioners') sugar
3 egg whites
  For the icing (frosting):
75 g/3 oz/½ cup icing (confectioners')
  sugar
½ egg white
2.5 ml/½ tsp lemon juice

Mix together the almonds and icing sugar in a pan. Stir in one egg white, then place the mixture over a low heat until it is lukewarm. Remove from the heat and mix in the remaining egg whites. Spoon the mixture into a piping bag with a 1 cm/½ in fluted nozzle (tip) and pipe a spiral 25 cm/10 in in diameter on a greased baking (cookie) sheet. Continue to pipe into spirals, each one 5 mm/¼ in smaller than the last, until you have a 5 cm/2 in circle. Bake in a preheated oven at 150°C/300°F/gas mark 2 for about 15 minutes until light brown. While they are still warm, place them one on top of the other to make a tower.

Mix together the icing ingredients and pipe zig-zag lines all over the cake through a fine nozzle.

Portuguese Coconut Cakes

Makes 12

4 eggs, separated
450 g/1 lb/2 cups caster (superfine)
* sugar*
450 g/1 lb/4 cups desiccated
* (shredded) coconut*
100 g/4 oz/1 cup rice flour
50 ml/2 fl oz/3½ tbsp rose water
1.5 ml/¼ tsp ground cinnamon
1.5 ml/¼ tsp ground cardamom
A pinch of ground cloves
A pinch of grated nutmeg
25 g/1 oz/¼ cup flaked (slivered)
* almonds*

Beat together the egg yolks and sugar until pale. Stir in the coconut, then fold in the flour. Stir in the rose water and spices. Whisk the egg whites until stiff, then fold into the mixture. Pour into a greased 25 cm/10 in square baking tin (pan) and sprinkle the almonds over the top. Bake in a preheated oven at 180°C/350°F/gas mark 4 for 50 minutes until a skewer inserted in the centre comes out clean. Leave to cool in the tin for 10 minutes, then cut into squares.

Scandinavian Tosca Cake

Makes one 23 cm/9 in cake

2 eggs
150 g/5 oz/⅔ cup soft brown sugar
50 g/2 oz/¼ cup butter or margarine,
* melted*
10 ml/2 tsp grated orange rind
150 g/5 oz/1¼ cups plain
* (all-purpose) flour*
7.5 ml/1½ tsp baking powder
60 ml/4 tbsp double (heavy) cream
For the topping:
50 g/2 oz/¼ cup butter or margarine
50 g/2 oz/¼ cup caster (superfine)
* sugar*
100 g/4 oz/1 cup almonds, chopped
15 ml/1 tbsp double (heavy) cream
30 ml/2 tbsp plain (all-purpose) flour

Whisk together the eggs and sugar until light and fluffy. Stir in the butter or margarine and orange rind, then fold in the flour and baking powder. Stir in the cream. Spoon the mixture into a greased and lined 23 cm/9 in cake tin (pan) and bake in a preheated oven at 180°C/350°C/gas mark 4 for 20 minutes.

To make the topping, heat the ingredients in a pan, stirring until well blended, and bring to boiling point. Pour over the cake. Increase the oven temperature to 200°C/400°F/gas mark 6 and return the cake to the oven for a further 15 minutes until golden brown.

South African Hertzog Cookies

Makes 12

75 g/3 oz/³⁄₄ cup plain (all-purpose) flour
15 ml/1 tbsp caster (superfine) sugar
5 ml/1 tsp baking powder
A pinch of salt
40 g/1½ oz/3 tbsp butter or margarine
1 large egg yolk
5 ml/1 tsp milk
For the filling:
30 ml/2 tbsp apricot jam (conserve)
1 large egg white
100 g/4 oz/½ cup caster (superfine) sugar
50 g/2 oz/½ cup desiccated (shredded) coconut

Mix together the flour, sugar, baking powder and salt. Rub in the butter or margarine until the mixture resembles breadcrumbs. Mix in the egg yolk and enough milk to make a soft dough. Knead well. Roll out the dough on a lightly floured surface, cut into circles with a biscuit (cookie) cutter and use to line greased bun tins (patty pans). Place a spoonful of jam in the centre of each one.

To make the filling, beat the egg white until stiff, then beat in the sugar until stiff and glossy. Stir in the coconut. Spoon the filling into the pastry cases (pie shells), making sure it covers the jam. Bake in a preheated oven at 180°C/350°F/gas mark 4 for 20 minutes until golden. Allow to cool in the tins for 5 minutes before turning out on to a wire rack to finish cooling.

Basque Cake

Makes one 25 cm/10 in cake

For the filling:
50 g/2 oz/¼ cup caster (superfine) sugar
25 g/1 oz/¼ cup cornflour (cornstarch)
2 egg yolks
300 ml/½ pt/1¼ cups milk
½ vanilla pod (bean)
A little icing (confectioners') sugar
For the cake:
275 g/10 oz/1¼ cups butter or margarine, softened
175 g/5 oz/¾ cup caster (superfine) sugar
3 eggs
5 ml/1 tsp vanilla essence (extract)
450 g/1 lb/4 cups plain (all-purpose) flour
10 ml/2 tsp baking powder
A pinch of salt
15 ml/1 tbsp brandy
Icing (confectioners') sugar for dusting

To make the filling, beat half the caster sugar with the cornflour, egg yolks and a little of the milk. Bring the remaining milk and sugar to the boil with the vanilla pod, then slowly pour in the sugar and egg mixture, whisking continuously. Bring to the boil and cook for 3 minutes, beating all the time. Pour into a bowl, sprinkle with icing sugar to prevent a skin forming and leave to cool.

To make the cake, cream together the butter or margarine and caster sugar until light and fluffy. Gradually beat in the eggs and vanilla essence alternately with spoonfuls of flour, baking powder and salt, then fold in the remaining flour. Transfer the mixture to a piping bag with a plain 1 cm/½ in nozzle (tip) and pipe half the mixture in a spiral in the base of a greased and floured 25 cm/10 in cake tin (pan). Pipe a circle on top round the edge to form a lip to contain the filling. Discard the vanilla pod from the filling, stir in the brandy and whisk until smooth, then spoon over the cake mixture. Pipe the remaining cake mixture in a spiral over the top. Bake in a preheated oven at 190°C/375°F/gas mark 5 for 50 minutes until golden brown and firm to the touch. Leave to cool, then dust with icing sugar.

Gâteaux and Special Occasion Cakes

*T*he very word gâteau conjures up something rather special, but while some of these cakes take a little more effort, others are spectacular without involving too much hard work. This chapter also includes those traditional cakes for special times of the year.

Almond and Cream Cheese Prism

Makes one 23 cm/9 in cake

200 g/7 oz/1¾ cups butter or margarine, softened
100 g/4 oz/½ cup caster (superfine) sugar
1 egg
200 g/7 oz/scant 1 cup cream cheese
5 ml/1 tsp lemon juice
2.5 ml/½ tsp ground cinnamon
75 ml/5 tbsp brandy
90 ml/6 tbsp milk
30 Nice biscuits (cookies)
For the icing (frosting):
60 ml/4 tbsp caster sugar
30 ml/2 tbsp cocoa (unsweetened chocolate) powder
100 g/4 oz/1 cup plain (semi-sweet) chocolate
60 ml/4 tbsp water
50 g/2 oz/¼ cup butter or margarine
100 g/4 oz/1 cup flaked (slivered) almonds

*C*ream together the butter or margarine and sugar until light and fluffy. Beat in the egg, cream cheese, lemon juice and cinnamon. Lay a large sheet of foil on a work surface. Mix the brandy and milk. Dip 10 biscuits in the brandy mixture and arrange on the foil in a rectangle two biscuits high by five biscuits long. Spread the cheese mixture over the biscuits. Dip the remaining biscuits in the brandy and milk and place on top of the mixture to make a long triangular shape. Fold in the foil and chill overnight.

To make the icing, bring the sugar, cocoa, chocolate and water to the boil in a small pan and boil for 3 minutes. Remove from the heat and beat in the butter. Leave to cool slightly. Remove the foil from the cake and spread the chocolate mixture over the top While still warm press on the almonds. Chill until set.

173

Black Forest Gâteau

Makes one 18 cm/7 in cake

175 g/6 oz/³⁄₄ cup butter or margarine, softened
175 g/6 oz/³⁄₄ cup caster (superfine) sugar
3 eggs, lightly beaten
150 g/5 oz/1¼ cups self-raising (self-rising) flour
25 g/1 oz/¼ cup cocoa (unsweetened chocolate) powder
10 ml/2 tsp baking powder
90 ml/6 tbsp cherry jam (conserve)
100 g/4 oz/1 cup plain (semi-sweet) chocolate, finely grated
400 g/14 oz/1 large can black cherries, drained and juice reserved
150 ml/¼ pt/²⁄₃ cup double (heavy) cream, whipped
10 ml/2 tsp arrowroot

Cream together the butter or margarine and sugar until light and fluffy. Gradually beat in the eggs, then work in the flour, cocoa and baking powder. Divide the mixture between two greased and lined 18 cm/7 in sandwich tins (pans) and bake in a preheated oven at 180°C/350°F/gas mark 4 for 25 minutes until firm to the touch. Leave to cool.

Sandwich the cakes together with some of the jam and spread the remainder over the sides of the cake. Press the grated chocolate over the sides of the cake. Arrange the cherries attractively over the top. Pipe the cream around the top edge of the cake. Warm the arrowroot with a little of the cherry juice and brush over the fruit to glaze.

Chocolate and Almond Gâteau

Makes one 23 cm/9 in cake

100 g/4 oz/1 cup plain (semi-sweet) chocolate
100 g/4 oz/½ cup butter or margarine, softened
150 g/5 oz/²⁄₃ cup caster (superfine) sugar
3 eggs, separated
50 g/2 oz/½ cup ground almonds
100 g/4 oz/1 cup plain (all-purpose) flour
For the filling:
225 g/8 oz/2 cups plain (semi-sweet) chocolate
300 ml/½ pt/1¼ cups double (heavy) cream
75 g/3 oz/¼ cup raspberry jam (conserve)

Melt the chocolate in a heatproof bowl set over a pan of gently simmering water. Cream together the butter or margarine and sugar, then stir in the chocolate and the egg yolks. Fold in the ground almonds and flour. Whisk the egg whites until stiff, then fold them into the mixture. Spoon into a greased and lined 23 cm/9 in cake tin (pan) and bake in a preheated oven at 180°C/350°F/gas mark 4 for 40 minutes until firm to the touch. Leave to cool, then slice the cake in half horizontally.

To make the filling, melt the chocolate and cream in a heatproof bowl set over a pan of gently simmering water. Stir until smooth, then leave to cool, stirring occasionally. Sandwich the cakes together with the jam and half the chocolate cream, then spread the remaining cream over the top and sides of the cake and leave to set.

174

Chocolate Cheesecake Gâteau

Makes one 23 cm/9 in cake

For the base:
25 g/1 oz/2 tbsp caster (superfine) sugar
175 g/6 oz/1½ cups digestive biscuit (Graham cracker) crumbs
75 g/3 oz/⅓ cup butter or margarine, melted
For the filling:
100 g/4 oz/1 cup plain (semi-sweet) chocolate
300 g/10 oz/1¼ cups cream cheese
3 eggs, separated
45 ml/3 tbsp cocoa (unsweetened chocolate) powder
25 g/1 oz/¼ cup plain (all-purpose) flour
50g /2 oz/¼ cup soft brown sugar
150 ml/¼ pt/⅔ cup soured (dairy sour) cream
50 g/2 oz/¼ cup caster (superfine) sugar
For decoration:
100 g/4 oz/1 cup plain (semi-sweet) chocolate
25 g/1 oz/2 tbsp butter or margarine
120 ml/4 fl oz/½ cup double (heavy) cream
6 glacé (candied) cherries

To make the base, stir the sugar and biscuit crumbs into the melted butter and press into the base and sides of a greased 23 cm/9 in springform cake tin (pan).

To make the filling, melt the chocolate in a heatproof bowl set over a pan of gently simmering water. Leave to cool slightly. Beat the cheese with the egg yolks, cocoa, flour, brown sugar and soured cream, then blend in the melted chocolate. Whisk the egg whites until they form soft peaks, then add the caster sugar and whisk again until stiff and glossy.

Fold into the mixture using a metal spoon and spoon over the base, levelling the surface. Bake in a preheated oven at 160°C/325°F/gas mark 3 for 1½ hours. Turn off the oven and leave the cake to cool in the oven with the door ajar. Chill until firm, then remove from the tin.

To decorate, melt the chocolate and butter or margarine in a heatproof bowl set over a pan of gently simmering water. Remove from the heat and leave to cool slightly, then stir in the cream. Swirl the chocolate over the top of the cake in patterns, then decorate with the glacé cherries.

Chocolate Fudge Gâteau

Makes one 20 cm/8 in cake

75 g/3 oz/³⁄₄ cup plain (semi-sweet)
  chocolate, chopped
200 ml/7 fl oz/scant 1 cup milk
225 g/8 oz/1 cup dark brown sugar
75 g/3 oz/¹⁄₃ cup butter or margarine,
  softened
2 eggs, lightly beaten
2.5 ml/¹⁄₂ tsp vanilla essence (extract)
150 g/5 oz/1¹⁄₄ cups plain
  (all-purpose) flour
25 g/1 oz/¹⁄₄ cup cocoa (unsweetened
  chocolate) powder
5 ml/1 tsp bicarbonate of soda
  (baking soda)
For the icing (frosting):
100 g/4 oz/1 cup plain (semi-sweet)
  chocolate
100 g/4 oz/¹⁄₂ cup butter or margarine,
  softened
225 g/8 oz/1¹⁄₃ cups icing
  (confectioners') sugar, sifted
Chocolate flakes or curls to decorate

Melt together the chocolate, milk and 75 g/3 oz/¹⁄₃ cup of the sugar in a pan, then leave to cool slightly. Cream together the butter and the remaining sugar until light and fluffy. Gradually beat in the eggs and vanilla essence, then stir in the chocolate mixture. Gently fold in the flour, cocoa and bicarbonate of soda. Spoon the mixture into two greased and lined 20 cm/8 in sandwich tins (pans) and bake in a preheated oven at 180°C/350°F/ gas mark 4 for 30 minutes until springy to the touch. Leave to cool in the tins for 3 minutes, then turn out on to a wire rack to finish cooling.

To make the icing, melt the chocolate in a heatproof bowl set over a pan of gently simmering water. Beat together the butter or margarine and sugar until soft, then stir in the melted chocolate. Sandwich the cakes together with one-third of the icing, then spread the rest over the top and sides of the cake.

Decorate the top with crumbled flakes or make curls by scraping a sharp knife along the side of a bar of chocolate.

Carob Mint Gâteau

Makes one 20 cm/8 in cake

3 eggs
50 g/2 oz/¹⁄₄ cup caster (superfine)
  sugar
75 g/3 oz/¹⁄₃ cup self-raising
  (self-rising) flour
25 g/1 oz/¹⁄₄ cup carob powder
150 ml/¹⁄₄ pt/²⁄₃ cup whipping cream
A few drops of peppermint essence
  (extract)
50 g/2 oz/¹⁄₂ cup chopped mixed nuts

Beat the eggs until pale. Beat in the sugar and continue until the mixture is pale and creamy and trails off the whisk in ribbons. This may take 15–20 minutes. Mix together the flour and carob powder and fold into the egg mixture. Spoon into two greased and lined 20 cm/18 in cake tins (pans) and bake in a preheated oven at 180°C/350°F/gas mark 4 for 15 minutes until springy to the touch. Cool.

Whip the cream to soft peaks, stir in the essence and nuts. Slice each cake in half horizontally and sandwich all the cakes together with the cream.

Iced Coffee Gâteau

Makes one 18 cm/7 in cake

225 g/8 oz/1 cup butter or margarine
100 g/4 oz/¹⁄₂ cup caster (superfine)
  sugar
2 eggs, lightly beaten
100 g/4 oz/1 cup self-raising
  (self-rising) flour
A pinch of salt
30 ml/2 tbsp coffee essence (extract)
100 g/4 oz/1 cup flaked (slivered)
  almonds
225 g/8 oz/1¹⁄₃ cups icing
  (confectioners') sugar, sifted

Cream together half the butter or margarine and the caster sugar until light and fluffy. Gradually beat in the eggs, then fold in the flour, salt and 15 ml/ 1 tbsp of the coffee essence. Spoon the mixture into two greased and lined 18 cm/7 in sandwich tins (pans) and bake in a preheated oven at 180°C/350°F/gas mark 4 for 25 minutes until firm to the touch. Leave to cool. Place the almonds in a dry frying pan (skillet) and toast over a medium heat, shaking the pan continuously, until golden.

Beat the remaining butter or margarine until soft, then gradually beat in the icing sugar and the remaining coffee essence until you have a spreading consistency. Sandwich the cakes together with one-third of the icing (frosting). Spread half the remaining icing round the sides of the cake and press the toasted almonds into the icing. Spread the remainder over the top of the cake and mark into patterns with a fork.

Coffee and Walnut Ring Gâteau

Makes one 23 cm/9 in cake

For the cake:
15 ml/1 tbsp instant coffee powder
15 ml/1 tbsp milk
100 g/4 oz/1 cup self-raising (self-rising) flour
5 ml/1 tsp baking powder
100 g/4 oz/½ cup butter or margarine, softened
100 g/4 oz/½ cup caster (superfine) sugar
2 eggs, lightly beaten
For the filling:
45 ml/3 tbsp apricot jam (conserve), sieved (strained)
15 ml/1 tbsp water
10 ml/2 tsp instant coffee powder
30 ml/2 tbsp milk
100 g/4 oz/⅔ cup icing (confectioners') sugar, sifted

50 g/2 oz/¼ cup butter or margarine, softened
50 g/2 oz/½ cup walnuts, chopped
For the icing (frosting):
30 ml/2 tbsp instant coffee powder
90 ml/6 tbsp milk
450 g/1 lb/2⅔ cups icing (confectioners') sugar, sifted
50 g/2 oz/¼ cup butter or margarine
A few walnut halves to decorate

To make the cake, dissolve the coffee in the milk, then mix into the remaining cake ingredients and beat until everything is well blended. Spoon into a greased 23 cm/9 in ring mould (tube pan) and bake in a preheated oven at 160°C/325°F/gas mark 3 for 40 minutes until springy to the touch. Leave to cool in the tin for 5 minutes, then turn out on to a wire rack to finish cooling. Cut the cake in half horizontally.

To make the filling, heat the jam and water until well blended, then brush over the cut surfaces of the cake. Dissolve the coffee in the milk, then mix into the icing sugar with the butter or margarine and nuts and beat until you have a spreadable consistency. Sandwich together the two halves of the cake with the filling.

To make the icing, dissolve the coffee in the milk in a heatproof bowl set over a pan of gently simmering water. Add the icing sugar and butter or margarine and beat until smooth. Remove from the heat and leave to cool and thicken to coating consistency, beating occasionally. Spoon the icing over the cake, decorate with walnut halves and leave to set.

Danish Chocolate and Custard Gâteau

Makes one 23 cm/9 in cake

4 eggs, separated
175 g/6 oz/1 cup icing (confectioners')
  sugar, sifted
Grated rind of ½ lemon
60 g/2½ oz/⅔ cup plain (all-purpose)
  flour
60 g/2½ oz/⅔ cup potato flour
2.5 ml/½ tsp baking powder
  For the filling:
45 ml/3 tbsp caster (superfine) sugar
15 ml/1 tbsp cornflour (cornstarch)
300 ml/½ pt/1¼ cups milk
3 egg yolks, beaten
50 g/2 oz/½ cup chopped mixed nuts
150 ml/¼ pt/⅔ cup double (heavy)
  cream
  For the topping:
100 g/4 oz/1 cup plain (semi-sweet)
  chocolate
30 ml/2 tbsp double (heavy) cream
25 g/1 oz/¼ cup white chocolate,
  grated or sliced into curls

Beat the egg yolks into the icing sugar and lemon rind. Stir in the flours and baking powder. Whisk the egg whites until stiff, then fold into the mixture using a metal spoon. Spoon into a greased and lined 23 cm/9 in cake tin (pan) and bake in a preheated oven at 190°C/375°F/gas mark 5 for 20 minutes until golden brown and springy to the touch. Leave to cool in the tin for 5 minutes, then turn out on to a wire rack to finish cooling. Slice the cake horizontally into three layers.

To make the filling, blend the sugar and cornflour to a paste with a little of the milk. Bring the remaining milk just to the boil, then pour on to the cornflour mixture and blend well. Return to the rinsed-out pan and stir continuously over a very gentle heat until the custard thickens. Beat in the egg yolks over a very low heat without allowing the custard to boil. Leave to cool slightly, then stir in the nuts. Whip the cream until stiff, then fold into the custard. Sandwich the layers together with the custard.

To make the topping, melt the chocolate with the cream in a heatproof bowl set over a pan of gently simmering water. Spread over the top of the cake and decorate with grated white chocolate.

Fruit Gâteau

Makes one 20 cm/8 in cake

1 cooking (tart) apple, peeled, cored
  and chopped
25 g/1 oz/¼ cup dried figs, chopped
25 g/1 oz/¼ cup raisins
75 g/3 oz/⅓ cup butter or margarine,
  softened
2 eggs
175 g/6 oz/1½ cups wholemeal
  (wholewheat) flour
5 ml/1 tsp baking powder
30 ml/2 tbsp skimmed milk
15 ml/1 tbsp gelatine
30 ml/2 tbsp water
400 g/14 oz/1 large can chopped
  pineapple, drained
300 ml/½ pt/1¼ cups fromage frais
150 ml/¼ pt/⅔ cup whipping cream

Mix together the apple, figs, raisins and butter or margarine. Beat in the eggs. Fold in the flour and baking powder and enough of the milk to mix to a soft mixture. Spoon into a greased 20 cm/8 in cake tin (pan) and bake in a preheated oven at 180°C/350°F/gas mark 4 for 30 minutes until firm to the touch. Remove from the tin and cool on a wire rack.

To make the filling, sprinkle the gelatine on the water in a small bowl and leave until spongy. Stand the bowl in a pan of hot water and leave until dissolved. Leave to cool slightly. Stir into the pineapple, fromage frais and cream and chill until set. Cut the cake in half horizontally and sandwich together with the cream.

178

Fruit Savarin

Makes one 20 cm/8 in cake

15 g/½ oz fresh yeast or
20 ml/4 tsp dried yeast
45 ml/3 tbsp warm milk
100 g/4 oz/1 cup strong plain (bread)
flour
A pinch of salt
5 ml/1 tsp sugar
2 eggs, beaten
50 g/2 oz/¼ cup butter or margarine,
softened
For the syrup:
225 g/8 oz/1 cup caster (superfine)
sugar
300 ml/½ pt/1¼ cups water
45 ml/3 tbsp kirsch
For the filling:
2 bananas
100 g/4 oz strawberries, sliced
100 g/4 oz raspberries

Blend together the yeast and milk, then work in 15 ml/1 tbsp of the flour. Leave to stand until frothy. Add the remaining flour, the salt, sugar, eggs and butter and beat until you have a soft dough. Spoon into a greased and floured 20 cm/8 in savarin or ring mould (tube pan) and leave in a warm place for about 45 minutes until the mixture almost reaches the top of the tin. Bake in a preheated oven for 30 minutes until golden and shrinking away from the sides of the tin. Turn out on to a wire rack over a tray and prick all over with a skewer.

While the savarin is cooking, make the syrup. Dissolve the sugar in the water over a low heat, stirring occasionally. Bring to the boil and simmer without stirring for 5 minutes until syrupy. Stir in the kirsch. Spoon the hot syrup over the savarin until saturated. Leave to cool.

Thinly slice the bananas and mix with the other fruit and the syrup that has dripped into the tray. Place the savarin on a plate and spoon the fruit into the centre just before serving.

Ginger Layer Cake

Makes one 18 cm/7 in cake

100 g/4 oz/1 cup self-raising
(self-rising) flour
5 ml/1 tsp baking powder
100 g/4 oz/½ cup butter or margarine,
softened
100 g/4 oz/½ cup caster (superfine)
sugar
2 eggs
For the filling and decoration:
150 ml/¼ pt/⅔ cup whipping or
double (heavy) cream
100 g/4 oz/⅓ cup ginger marmalade
4 ginger biscuits (cookies), crushed
A few pieces of crystallised (candied)
ginger

Beat together all the cake ingredients until well blended. Spoon into two greased and lined 18 cm/7 in sandwich tins (pans) and bake in a preheated oven at 160°C/325°F/gas mark 3 for 25 minutes until golden brown and springy to the touch. Leave to cool in the tins for 5 minutes, then turn out on to a wire rack to finish cooling. Cut each cake in half horizontally.

To make the filling, whip the cream until stiff. Spread the base layer of one cake with half the marmalade and place the second layer on top. Spread with half the cream and top with the next layer. Spread that with the remaining marmalade and top with the final layer. Spread the remaining cream on top and decorate with the biscuit crumbs and crystallised ginger.

Grape and Peach Gâteau

Makes one 20 cm/8 in cake

4 eggs
100 g/4 oz/½ cup caster (superfine)
sugar
75 g/6 oz/1½ cups plain
(all-purpose) flour
A pinch of salt
For the filling and decoration:
100 g/14 oz/1 large can peaches in
syrup
450 ml/¾ pt/2 cups double (heavy)
cream
50 g/2 oz/¼ cup caster (superfine)
sugar
A few drops of vanilla essence
(extract)
100 g/4 oz/1 cup hazelnuts, chopped
100 g/4 oz seedless(pitless) grapes
A sprig of fresh mint

Beat together the eggs and sugar until the mixture is thick and pale and trails off the whisk in ribbons. Sift in the flour and salt and fold in gently until combined. Spoon into a greased and lined 20 cm/8 in springform cake tin (pan) and bake in a preheated oven at 180°C/350°F/gas mark 4 for 30 minutes until a skewer inserted in the centre comes out clean. Leave to cool in the tin for 5 minutes, then turn out on to a wire rack to finish cooling. Cut the cake in half horizontally.

Drain the peaches and reserve 90 ml/6 tbsp of the syrup. Thinly slice half the peaches and chop the remainder. Whip the cream with the sugar and vanilla essence until thick. Spread half the cream over the bottom layer of the cake, sprinkle with the chopped peaches and replace the top of the cake. Spread the remaining cream round the sides and over the top of the cake. Press the chopped nuts round the sides. Arrange the sliced peaches around the edge of the top of the cake and the grapes in the centre. Decorate with a sprig of mint.

Lemon Gâteau

Makes one 18 cm/7 in cake

For the cake:
100 g/4 oz/½ cup butter or margarine,
softened
100 g/4 oz/½ cup caster (superfine)
sugar
2 eggs, lightly beaten
100 g/4 oz/1 cup self-raising
(self-rising) flour
A pinch of salt
Grated rind and juice of 1 lemon
For the icing (frosting):
100 g/4 oz/½ cup butter or margarine,
softened
225 g/8 oz/1⅓ cups icing
(confectioners') sugar, sifted
100 g/4 oz/⅓ cup lemon curd
Icing flowers for decoration

To make the cake, cream together the butter or margarine and sugar until light and fluffy. Gradually beat in the eggs, then fold in the flour, salt and lemon rind. Spoon the mixture into two greased and lined 18 cm/7 in sandwich tins (pans) and bake in a preheated oven at 180°C/350°F/gas mark 4 for 25 minutes until firm to the touch. Leave to cool.

To make the icing, beat the butter or margarine until soft, then beat in the icing sugar and lemon juice to make a spreadable consistency. Sandwich the cakes together with the lemon curd and spread three-quarters of the icing over the top and sides of the cake, marking into patterns with a fork. Place the rest of the icing in a piping bag with a star nozzle (tip) and pipe rosettes round the top of the cake. Decorate with icing flowers.

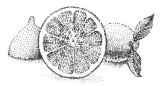

Marron Gâteau

Makes one 25 cm/10 in cake

425 g/15 oz/1 large can chestnut purée
6 eggs, separated
5 ml/1 tsp vanilla essence (extract)
5 ml/1 tsp ground cinnamon
350 g/12 oz/2 cups icing
   (confectioners') sugar, sifted
100 g/4 oz/1 cup plain (all-purpose)
   flour
5 ml/1 tsp powdered gelatine
30 ml/2 tbsp water
15 ml/1 tbsp rum
300 ml/½ pt/1¼ cups double (heavy)
   cream
90 ml/6 tbsp apricot jam (conserve),
   sieved (strained)
30 ml/2 tbsp water
450 g/1 lb/4 cups plain (semi-sweet)
   chocolate, broken into pieces
100 g/4 oz Almond Paste (page 228)
30 ml/2 tbsp chopped pistachio nuts

Sieve the chestnut purée and stir until smooth, then divide in half. Mix one half with the egg yolks, vanilla essence, cinnamon and 50 g/2 oz/⅓ cup of the icing sugar. Whisk the egg whites until stiff, then gradually whisk in 175 g/6 oz/1 cup of the icing sugar until the mixture forms stiff peaks. Fold into the egg yolk and chestnut mixture. Fold in the flour and spoon into a greased and lined 25 cm/10 in cake tin (pan). Bake in a preheated oven at 180°C/350°F/gas mark 4 for 45 minutes until springy to the touch. Leave to cool, then cover and leave overnight.

Sprinkle the gelatine over the water in a bowl and leave until spongy. Stand the bowl in a pan of hot water and leave until dissolved. Leave to cool slightly. Mix the remaining chestnut purée with the remaining icing sugar and the rum. Whip the cream until stiff, then fold into the purée with the dissolved gelatine. Cut the cake horizontally into three and sandwich together with the chestnut purée. Trim the edges, then chill for 30 minutes.

Boil the jam with the water until well blended, then brush over the top and sides of the cake. Melt the chocolate in a heatproof bowl set over a pan of gently simmering water. Shape the almond paste into 16 chestnut shapes. Dip the base into the melted chocolate, then into the pistachio nuts. Spread the remaining chocolate over the top and sides of the cake and smooth the surface with a palette knife. Arrange the almond-paste chestnuts round the edge while the chocolate is still warm, and mark into 16 slices. Leave to cool and set.

Millefeuille

Makes one 23 cm/9 in cake

225 g/8 oz Puff Pastry (page 136)
150 ml/¼ pt/⅔ cup double (heavy) or
   whipping cream
45 ml/3 tbsp raspberry jam (conserve)
Icing (confectioners') sugar, sifted

Roll out the pastry (paste) to about 3 mm/⅛ in thick and cut into three equal rectangles. Place on a dampened baking (cookie) sheet and bake in a preheated oven at 200°C/400°F/gas mark 6 for 10 minutes until golden. Cool on a wire rack. Whip the cream until stiff. Spread the jam over the top of two of the pastry rectangles. Sandwich together the rectangles with the cream, topping with any remaining cream. Serve sprinkled with icing sugar.

Orange Gâteau

Makes one 18 cm/7 in cake

225 g/8 oz/1 cup butter or margarine,
softened
100 g/4 oz/½ cup caster (superfine)
sugar
2 eggs, lightly beaten
100 g/4 oz/1 cup self-raising
(self-rising) flour
A pinch of salt
Grated rind and juice of 1 orange
225 g/8 oz/1⅓ cups icing
(confectioners') sugar, sifted
Glacé (candied) orange slices to
decorate

Cream together half the butter or
margarine and the caster sugar until
light and fluffy. Gradually beat in the eggs,
then fold in the flour, salt and orange
rind. Spoon the mixture into two greased
and lined 18 cm/7 in sandwich tins (pans)
and bake in a preheated oven at 180°C/
350°F/gas mark 4 for 25 minutes until
firm to the touch. Leave to cool.

Beat the remaining butter or margarine until soft, then beat in the icing
sugar and orange juice to make a
spreadable consistency. Sandwich the
cakes together with one-third of the icing
(frosting), then spread the remainder over
the top and sides of the cake, marking
into patterns with a fork. Decorate with
glacé orange slices.

Four-tier Orange Marmalade Gâteau

Makes one 23 cm/9 in cake

For the cake:
200 ml/7 fl oz/scant 1 cup water
25 g/1 oz/2 tbsp butter or margarine
4 eggs, lightly beaten
300 g/11 oz/1⅓ cups caster (superfine)
sugar
5 ml/1 tsp vanilla essence (extract)
300 g/11 oz/2¾ cups plain
(all-purpose) flour

10 ml/2 tsp baking powder
A pinch of salt
For the filling:
30 ml/2 tbsp plain (all-purpose) flour
30 ml/2 tbsp cornflour (cornstarch)
15 ml/1 tbsp caster (superfine) sugar
2 eggs, separated
450 ml/¾ pt/2 cups milk
5 ml/1 tsp vanilla essence (extract)
120 ml/4 fl oz/½ cup sweet sherry
175 g/6 oz/½ cup orange marmalade
120 ml/4 fl oz/½ cup double (heavy)
cream
100 g/4 oz peanut brittle, crushed

To make the cake, bring the water to
the boil with the butter or margarine.
Beat together the eggs and sugar until pale
and frothy, then continue to beat until the
mixture is very light. Beat in the vanilla
essence, sprinkle with flour, baking
powder and salt and pour in the boiling
butter and water mixture. Mix together
just until blended. Spoon into two
greased and floured 23 cm/9 in sandwich
tins (pans) and bake in a preheated oven
at 180°C/350°F/gas mark 4 for 25 minutes
until golden brown and springy to the
touch. Leave to cool in the tins for 3
minutes, then turn out on to a wire rack
to finish cooling. Cut each cake in half
horizontally.

To make the filling, mix together the
flour, cornflour, sugar and egg yolks to a
paste with a little of the milk. Bring the
remaining milk to the boil in a pan, then
pour it into the mixture and whisk until
smooth. Return to the rinsed-out pan and
bring to the boil over a low heat, stirring
continuously until thick. Remove from
the heat and stir in the vanilla essence,
then leave to cool slightly. Whisk the egg
whites until stiff, then fold in.

Sprinkle the sherry over the four cake
layers, spread three with marmalade, then
spread the custard over the top. Assemble
the layers together into a four-tiered
sandwich. Whip the cream until stiff and
spoon over the top of the cake. Sprinkle
with the peanut brittle.

Pecan and Date Gâteau

Makes one 23 cm/9 in cake

For the cake:
250 ml/8 fl oz/1 cup boiling water
450 g/1 lb/2 cups stoned (pitted)
  dates, finely chopped
2.5 ml/½ tsp bicarbonate of soda
  (baking soda)
225 g/8 oz/1 cup butter or margarine,
  softened
225 g/8 oz/1 cup caster (superfine)
  sugar
3 eggs
100 g/4 oz/1 cup chopped pecan nuts
5 ml/1 tsp vanilla essence (extract)
350 g/12 oz/3 cups plain
  (all-purpose) flour
10 ml/2 tsp ground cinnamon
5 ml/1 tsp baking powder
For the icing (frosting):
120 ml/4 fl oz/½ cup water
30 ml/2 tbsp cocoa (unsweetened
  chocolate) powder
10 ml/2 tsp instant coffee powder
100 g/4 oz/½ cup butter or margarine
400 g/14 oz/2⅓ cups icing
  (confectioners') sugar, sifted
50 g/2 oz/½ cup pecan nuts, finely
  chopped

To make the cake, pour the boiling water over the dates and bicarbonate of soda and leave to stand until cool. Cream together the butter or margarine and caster sugar until light and fluffy. Gradually beat in the eggs, then stir in the nuts, vanilla essence and dates. Fold in the flour, cinnamon and baking powder. Spoon into two greased 23 cm/9 in sandwich tins (pans) and bake in a preheated oven at 180°C/350°F/gas mark 4 for 30 minutes until springy to the touch. Turn out on to a wire rack to cool.

To make the icing, boil the water, cocoa and coffee in a small pan until you have a thick syrup. Leave to cool. Cream together the butter or margarine and the icing sugar until soft, then beat in the syrup.

Sandwich the cakes together with one-third of the icing. Spread half the remaining icing round the sides of the cake, then press on the chopped pecans. Spread most of the remaining icing over the top and pipe a few icing rosettes.

Plum and Cinnamon Gâteau

Makes one 23 cm/9 in cake

350 g/12 oz/1½ cups butter or
  margarine, softened
175 g/6 oz/¾ cup caster (superfine)
  sugar
3 eggs
150 g/5 oz/1¼ cups self-raising
  (self-rising) flour
5 ml/1 tsp baking powder
5 ml/1 tsp ground cinnamon
350 g/12 oz/2 cups icing
  (confectioners') sugar, sifted
5 ml/1 tsp finely grated orange rind
100 g/4 oz/1 cup hazelnuts, coarsely
  ground
300 g/11 oz/1 medium can plums,
  drained

Cream together half the butter or margarine and the caster sugar until light and fluffy. Gradually beat in the eggs, then fold in the flour, baking powder and cinnamon. Spoon into a greased and lined 23 cm/9 in square cake tin (pan) and bake in a preheated oven at 180°C/350°F/gas mark 4 for 40 minutes until a skewer inserted in the centre comes out clean. Remove from the tin and leave to cool.

Beat the remaining butter or margarine until soft, then mix in the icing sugar and grated orange rind. Cut the cake in half horizontally, then sandwich the two halves together with two-thirds of the icing. Spread most of the remaining icing over the top and sides of the cake. Press the nuts round the sides of the cake and arrange the plums attractively on top. Pipe the remaining icing decoratively round the top edge of the cake.

Prune Layer Gâteau

Makes one 25 cm/10 in cake

For the cake:
225 g/8 oz/1 cup butter or margarine
300 g/10 oz/2¼ cups caster (superfine) sugar
3 eggs, separated
450 g/1 lb/4 cups plain (all-purpose) flour
5 ml/1 tsp baking powder
5 ml/1 tsp bicarbonate of soda (baking soda)
5 ml/1 tsp ground cinnamon
5 ml/1 tsp grated nutmeg
2.5 ml/½ tsp ground cloves
A pinch of salt
250 ml/8 fl oz/1 cup single (light) cream
225 g/8 oz/1⅓ cups stoned (pitted) cooked prunes, finely chopped
For the filling:
250 ml/8 fl oz/1 cup single (light) cream
100 g/4 oz/½ cup caster (superfine) sugar
3 egg yolks
225 g/8 oz/1⅓ cups stoned (pitted)cooked prunes
30 ml/2 tbsp grated orange rind
5 ml/1 tsp vanilla essence (extract)
50 g/2 oz/½ cup chopped mixed nuts

To make the cake, cream together the butter or margarine and sugar. Gradually beat in the egg yolks, then fold in the flour, baking powder, bicarbonate of soda, spices and salt. Fold in the cream and prunes. Whisk the egg whites until stiff, then fold them in to the mixture. Spoon into three greased and floured 25 cm/10 in sandwich tins (pans) and bake in a preheated oven at 180°C/350°F/ gas mark 4 for 25 minutes until well risen and springy to the touch. Leave to cool.

Mix together all the filling ingredients except the nuts until well blended. Place in a pan and cook over a low heat until thickened, stirring continuously. Spread one-third of the filling over the base cake and sprinkle with one-third of the nuts. Place the second cake on top and cover with half the remaining icing and half the remaining nuts. Place the final cake on top and spread the remaining icing and nuts over the top.

Rainbow-stripe Cake

Makes one 18 cm/7 in cake

For the cake:
100 g/4 oz/½ cup butter or margarine, softened
225 g/8 oz/1 cup caster (superfine) sugar
3 eggs, separated
225 g/8 oz/2 cups plain (all-purpose) flour
A pinch of salt
120 ml/4 fl oz/½ cup milk, plus a little extra
5 ml/1 tsp cream of tartar
2.5 ml/½ tsp bicarbonate of soda (baking soda)
A few drops of lemon essence (extract)
A few drops of red food colouring
10 ml/2 tsp cocoa (unsweetened chocolate) powder
For the filling and icing (frosting):
225 g/8 oz/1⅓ cups icing (confectioners') sugar, sifted
50 g/2 oz/¼ cup butter or margarine, softened
10 ml/2 tsp hot water
5 ml/1 tsp milk
2.5 ml/½ tsp vanilla essence (extract)
Coloured sugar strands to decorate

To make the cake, cream together the butter or margarine and sugar until light and fluffy. Gradually beat in the egg yolks, then fold in the flour and salt alternately with the milk. Mix the cream of tartar and bicarbonate of soda with a little extra milk, then stir into the mixture.

Whisk the egg whites until stiff, then fold into the mixture using a metal spoon. Divide the mixture into three equal portions. Stir the lemon essence into the first bowl, the red food colouring into the second bowl, and the cocoa into the third bowl. Spoon the mixtures into greased and lined 18 cm/7 in cake tins (pans) and bake in a preheated oven at 180°C/350°F/gas mark 4 for 25 minutes until golden brown and springy to the touch. Leave to cool in the tins for 5 minutes, then turn out on to a wire rack to finish cooling.

To make the icing, place the icing sugar in a bowl and make a well in the centre. Gradually beat in the butter or margarine, water, milk and vanilla essence until you have a spreadable mixture. Sandwich together the cakes with one-third of the mixture, then spread the remainder over the top and sides of the cake, roughing up the surface with a fork. Sprinkle with top with coloured sugar strands.

Gâteau St-Honoré

Makes one 25 cm/10 in cake

For the choux pastry (paste):
50 g/2 oz/¼ cup unsalted (sweet)
  butter or margarine
150 ml/¼ pt/⅔ cup milk
A pinch of salt
50 g/2 oz/½ cup plain (all-purpose)
  flour
2 eggs, lightly beaten
225 g/8 oz Puff Pastry (page 136)
1 egg yolk
For the caramel:
225 g/6 oz/¾ cup caster (superfine)
  sugar
90 ml/6 tbsp water
For the filling and decoration:
5 ml/1 tsp powdered gelatine
15 ml/1 tbsp water
1 quantity Vanilla Cream Icing
  (page 191)
3 egg whites

175 g/6 oz/¾ cup caster (superfine)
  sugar
90 ml/6 tbsp water

To make the choux pastry (paste), melt the butter with the milk and salt over a low heat. Bring rapidly to the boil, then remove from the heat and quickly stir in the flour and mix just until the pastry comes away from the sides of the pan. Leave to cool slightly, then very gradually beat in the eggs and continue to beat until smooth and glossy.

Roll out the puff pastry to a 26 cm/10½ in circle, place on a greased baking (cookie) sheet and prick with a fork. Transfer the choux pastry to a piping bag with a plain 1 cm/½ in nozzle (tip) and pipe a circle round the edge of the puff pastry. Pipe a second circle half-way in towards the centre. On a separate greased baking sheet, pipe the remaining choux pastry into small balls. Brush all the pastry with egg yolk and bake in a preheated oven at 220°C/425°F/gas mark 7 for 12 minutes for the choux balls and 20 minutes for the base until golden and puffed.

To make the caramel, dissolve the sugar in the water, then boil without stirring for about 8 minutes to 160°C/320°F until you have a light caramel. Brush the outside ring with caramel, a little at a time. Dip the top half of the balls into the caramel, then press them on to the outside pastry ring.

To make the filling, sprinkle the gelatine over the water in a bowl and leave until spongy. Stand the bowl in a pan of hot water and leave until dissolved. Leave to cool slightly, then stir in the vanilla cream. Whisk the egg whites until stiff. Meanwhile, boil the sugar and water to 120°C/250°F or until a drop in cold water forms a hard ball. Gradually whisk into the egg whites, then continue to whisk until cool. Stir into the custard. Pipe the custard into the centre of the cake and chill before serving.

Strawberry Choux Gâteau

Makes one 23 cm/9 in cake

50 g/2 oz/¼ cup butter or margarine
150 ml/¼ pt/⅔ cup water
75 g/3 oz/⅓ cup plain (all-purpose) flour
A pinch of salt
2 eggs, lightly beaten
50 g/2 oz/⅓ cup icing (confectioners') sugar, sifted
300 ml/½ pt/1¼ cups double (heavy) cream, whipped
225 g/8 oz strawberries, halved
25 g/1 oz/¼ cup flaked (slivered) almonds

Place the butter or margarine and water in a pan and bring slowly to the boil. Remove from the heat and quickly beat in the flour and salt. Gradually beat in the eggs until the dough is shiny and comes away from the sides of the pan. Place spoonfuls of the mixture in a circle on a greased baking (cookie) sheet to build up a circular ring cake and bake in a preheated oven at 220°C/425°F/gas mark 7 for 30 minutes until golden. Leave to cool. Slice the cake in half horizontally. Beat the icing sugar into the cream. Sandwich the halves together with the cream, strawberries and almonds.

Strawberry Fruit Gâteau

Makes one 20 cm/8 in cake

1 cooking (tart) apple, peeled, cored and chopped
25 g/1 oz/3 tbsp dried figs, chopped
25 g/1 oz/3 tbsp raisins
75 g/3 oz/⅓ cup butter or margarine
2 eggs
175 g/6 oz/1½ cups plain (all-purpose) flour
5 ml/1 tsp baking powder
30 ml/2 tbsp milk
225 g/8 oz strawberries, sliced
225 g/8 oz/1 cup fromage frais

Purée the apples, figs, raisins and butter or margarine until light and fluffy. Beat in the eggs, then fold in the flour, baking powder and enough of the milk to mix to a soft dough. Spoon into a greased 20 cm/8 in loose-bottomed cake tin (pan) and bake in a preheated oven at 180°C/350°F/gas mark 4 for 30 minutes until firm to the touch. Remove from the tin and leave to cool. Cut the cake in half horizontally. Sandwich together with the strawberries and fromage frais.

186

Spanish Malaga-soaked Cake

Makes one 23 cm/9 in cake

8 eggs
700 g/1½ lb/3 cups granulated sugar
350 g/12 oz/3 cups plain
   (all-purpose) flour
300 ml/½ pt/1¼ cups water
350 g/12 oz/1½ cups soft brown sugar
400 ml/14 fl oz/1¾ cups Malaga or
   fortified wine
Ground cinnamon

Beat the eggs and half the granulated sugar in a heatproof bowl set over a pan of gently simmering water until a thick syrup forms. Gradually add flour, whisking continuously. Spoon into a greased and floured 23 cm/9 in square cake tin (pan) and bake in a preheated oven at 190°C/375°F/gas mark 5 for 45 minutes until springy to the touch. Leave to cool in the tin for 5 minutes before turning out on to a wire rack to finish cooling.

Meanwhile, heat the water in a pan and add the remaining granulated sugar and the brown sugar. Simmer over a medium heat for about 25 minutes until you have a clear, thick syrup. Remove from the heat and leave to cool. Thoroughly mix in the Malaga or wine. Pour the syrup over the cake and serve sprinkled with cinnamon.

Christmas Cake

Makes one 23 cm/9 in cake

350 g/12 oz/1½ cups butter or
   margarine, softened
350 g/12 oz/1½ cups soft brown sugar
6 eggs
450 g/1 lb/4 cups plain (all-purpose)
   flour
A pinch of salt
5 ml/1 tsp ground mixed (apple-pie)
   spice
225 g/8 oz/1⅓ cups raisins
450 g/1 lb/2⅔ cups sultanas
   (golden raisins)
225 g/8 oz/1⅓ cups currants
175 g/6 oz/1 cup chopped mixed
   (candied) peel
50 g/2 oz/¼ cup glacé (candied)
   cherries, chopped
100 g/4 oz/1 cup almonds, chopped
30 ml/2 tbsp black treacle (molasses)
45 ml/3 tbsp brandy
Almond paste (page 228)
Royal icing (page 228)

Cream together the butter or margarine and sugar until soft, then beat in the eggs one at a time. Fold in the flour, salt and spice, then mix in all the remaining ingredients. Spoon into a greased and lined 23 cm/9 in cake tin and bake at 140°C/275°F/gas mark 1 for 6½ hours until a skewer inserted in the centre comes out clean. Leave to cool completely, then wrap in foil and store in an airtight container for at least three weeks before covering with almond paste and decorating with royal icing, if liked.

Strawberry Mousse Gâteau

Makes one 23 cm/9 in cake

For the cake:
100 g/4 oz/1 cup self-raising
(self-rising) flour
100 g/4 oz/½ cup butter or margarine,
softened
100 g/4 oz/½ cup caster (superfine)
sugar
2 eggs
For the mousse:
15 ml/1 tbsp powdered gelatine
30 ml/2 tbsp water
450 g/1 lb strawberries
3 eggs, separated
75 g/3 oz/⅓ cup caster (superfine)
sugar
5 ml/1 tsp lemon juice
300 ml/½ pt/1¼ cups double (heavy)
cream
30 ml/2 tbsp flaked (slivered)
almonds, lightly toasted

Beat together the cake ingredients until smooth. Spoon into a greased and lined 23 cm/9 in cake tin (pan) and bake in a preheated oven at 190°C/375°F/gas mark 5 for 25 minutes until golden brown and firm to the touch. Remove from the tin and leave to cool.

To make the mousse, sprinkle the gelatine over the water in a bowl and leave until spongy. Stand the bowl in a pan of hot water and leave until dissolved. Leave to cool slightly. Meanwhile, purée 350 g/12 oz of the strawberries, then rub through a sieve (strainer) to discard the pips. Beat the egg yolks and sugar until pale and thick and the mixture trails off the whisk in ribbons. Stir in the purée, lemon juice and gelatine. Whip the cream until stiff, then fold half into the mixture. With a clean whisk and bowl, whisk the egg whites until stiff, then fold into the mixture.

Cut the sponge in half horizontally and place one half in the base of a clean cake tin (pan) lined with clingfilm (plastic wrap). Slice the remaining strawberries and arrange over the sponge, then top with the flavoured cream, and finally the second layer of cake. Press down very gently. Chill until set.

To serve, invert the gâteau on to a serving plate and remove the clingfilm (plastic wrap). Decorate with the remaining cream and garnish with the almonds.

Yule Log

Makes one

3 eggs
100 g/4 oz/½ cup caster (superfine)
sugar
100 g/4 oz/1 cup plain (all-purpose)
flour
50 g/2 oz/½ cup plain (semi-sweet)
chocolate, grated
15 ml/1 tbsp hot water
Caster (superfine) sugar for rolling
For the icing (frosting):
175 g/6 oz/¾ cup butter or margarine,
softened
350 g/12 oz/2 cups icing
(confectioners') sugar, sifted
30 ml/2 tbsp warm water
30 ml/2 tbsp cocoa (unsweetened
chocolate) powder
To decorate:
Holly leaves and robin (optional)

Beat together the eggs and sugar in a heatproof bowl set over a pan of gently simmering water. Continue to beat until the mixture is stiff and trails off the whisk in ribbons. Remove from the heat and beat until cool. Fold in half the flour, then the chocolate, then the remaining flour, then stir in the water. Spoon into a greased and lined Swiss roll tin (jelly roll pan) and bake in a preheated oven at 220°C/425°F/gas mark 7 for about 10 minutes until firm to the touch. Sprinkle a large sheet of greaseproof (waxed) paper with caster sugar. Turn the cake out of the tin on to the paper and trim the edges. Cover with another sheet of paper and roll up loosely from the short edge.

To make the icing, cream together the butter or margarine and icing sugar, then beat in the water and cocoa. Unroll the cold cake, remove the paper and spread the cake with half the icing. Roll it up again, then ice with the remaining icing, marking it with a fork to look like a log. Sift a little icing sugar over the top and decorate as liked.

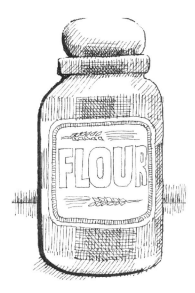

Easter Bonnet Cake

Makes one 20 cm/8 in cake

75 g/3 oz/⅓ cup muscovado sugar
3 eggs
75 g/3 oz/¾ cup self-raising (self-rising) flour
15 ml/1 tbsp cocoa (unsweetened chocolate) powder
15 ml/1 tbsp warm water
For the filling:
50 g/2 oz/¼ cup butter or margarine, softened
75 g/3 oz/½ cup icing (confectioners') sugar, sifted
For the topping:
100 g/4 oz/1 cup plain (semi-sweet) chocolate
25 g/1 oz/2 tbsp butter or margarine
Ribbon or sugar flowers (optional)

Beat together the sugar and eggs in a heatproof bowl set over a pan of gently simmering water. Continue to beat until the mixture is thick and creamy. Leave to stand for a few minutes, then remove from the heat and beat again until the mixture leaves a trail when the whisk is removed. Fold in the flour and cocoa, then stir in the water. Spoon the mixture into a greased and lined 20 cm/8 in cake tin (pan) and a greased and lined 15 cm/6 in cake tin. Bake in a preheated oven at 200°C/400°F/gas mark 6 for 15–20 minutes until well risen and firm to the touch. Leave to cool on a wire rack.

To make the filling, cream together the margarine and icing sugar. Use to sandwich the smaller cake on top of the larger one.

To make the topping, melt the chocolate and butter or margarine in a heatproof bowl set over a pan of gently simmering water. Spoon the topping over the cake and spread with a knife dipped in hot water so that it is completely covered. Decorate round the brim with a ribbon or sugar flowers.

Easter Simnel Cake

Makes one 20 cm/8 in cake

225 g/8 oz/1 cup butter or margarine,
softened
225 g/8 oz/1 cup soft brown sugar
Grated rind of 1 lemon
4 eggs, beaten
225 g/8 oz/2 cups plain
(all-purpose) flour
5 ml/1 tsp baking powder
2.5 ml/½ tsp grated nutmeg
50 g/2 oz/½ cup cornflour (cornstarch)
100 g/4 oz/⅔ cup sultanas (golden
raisins)
100 g/4 oz/⅔ cup raisins
75 g/3 oz/½ cup currants
100 g/4 oz/½ cup glacé (candied)
cherries, chopped
25 g/1 oz/¼ cup ground almonds
450 g/1 lb Almond Paste (page 228)
30 ml/2 tbsp apricot jam (conserve)
1 egg white, beaten

Cream together the butter or margarine, sugar and lemon rind until pale and fluffy. Gradually beat in the eggs, then fold in the flour, baking powder, nutmeg and cornflour. Stir in the fruit and almonds. Spoon half the mixture into a greased and lined 20 cm/8 in deep cake tin (pan). Roll out half the almond paste to a circle the size of the cake and place on top of the mixture. Fill with the remaining mixture and bake in a preheated oven at 160°C/325°F/gas mark 3 for 2–2½ hours until golden brown. Leave to cool in the tin. When cool, turn out and wrap in greaseproof (waxed) paper. Store in an airtight container for up to three weeks if possible to mature.

To finish the cake, brush the top with the jam. Roll out three-quarters of the remaining almond paste to a 20 cm/8 in circle, neaten the edges and place on top of the cake. Roll the remaining almond paste into 11 balls (to represent the disciples without Judas). Brush the top of the cake with beaten egg white and arrange the balls around the edge of the cake, then brush them with egg white. Place under a hot grill (broiler) for a minute or so to brown it slightly.

Twelfth Night Cake

Makes one 20 cm/8 in cake

225 g/8 oz/1 cup butter or margarine,
softened
225 g/8 oz/1 cup soft brown sugar
4 eggs, beaten
225 g/8 oz/2 cups plain
(all-purpose) flour
5 ml/1 tsp ground mixed (apple-pie)
spice
175 g/6 oz/1 cup sultanas
(golden raisins)
100 g/4 oz/⅔ cup raisins
75 g/3 oz/½ cup currants
50 g/2 oz/¼ cup glacé (candied)
cherries
50 g/2 oz/⅓ cup chopped mixed
(candied) peel
30 ml/2 tbsp milk
12 candles to decorate

Cream together the butter or margarine and sugar until pale and fluffy. Gradually beat in the eggs, then fold in the flour, mixed spice, fruit and peel and mix until well blended, adding a little milk if necessary to achieve a soft mixture. Spoon into a greased and lined 20 cm/8 in cake tin (pan) and bake in a preheated oven at 180°C/350°F/gas mark 4 for 2 hours until a skewer inserted in the centre comes out clean. Leave to cool, then decorate with 12 candles.

190

Children's Party Cake Ideas

*T*his is not really a book about special occasion cakes, it is about everyday baking, but sometimes all you need is the inspiration of a few ideas to help you make a cake which is just that bit different. And these ideas are so easy, you might even be tempted to make them for an ordinary teatime.

The Basic Butter Cake (below) gives a firm cake that is easy to cut and shape. For the toppings, try using Vanilla Cream Icing (below), Fondant Icing (page 229) or even ready-roll icing. And there are lots of ideas for shaping and decoration.

This one chapter gives you everything you need. Just remember to keep it simple, add a little imagination and go for overall effect rather than perfect detail – it is going to be cut and eaten by children after all! What are you waiting for?

Basic Butter Cake

Makes one 20 cm/8 in cake

100 g/4 oz/½ cup butter or margarine, softened
100 g/4 oz/½ cup caster (superfine) sugar
2 eggs, lightly beaten
2.5 ml/½ tsp vanilla essence (extract)
175 g/6 oz/1½ cups self-raising (self-rising) flour
75 ml/5 tbsp milk

Blend together the butter or margarine and sugar until pale and fluffy. Gradually beat in the eggs and vanilla essence, then fold in the flour and enough of the milk to make a smooth mixture. Spoon the mixture into a greased and lined 20 cm/8 in cake tin (pan) and bake in a preheated oven at 190°C/375°F/ gas mark 5 for 35 minutes until well risen and firm to the touch.

Vanilla Cream Icing

Makes enough to cover one 20 cm/8 in cake

100 g/4 oz/½ cup butter or margarine, at room temperature
250 g/9 oz/1½ cups icing (confectioners') sugar, sifted
5 ml/1 tsp vanilla essence (extract)
25 ml/1½ tbsp milk
A few drops of food colouring (optional)

Beat the butter or margarine until soft, then gradually add the icing sugar until the mixture begins to stiffen. Mix in the vanilla essence and milk, then continue to add the icing sugar until you have a workable icing (frosting). If you want to colour the icing, work in a few drops of food colouring and reduce the amount of milk slightly. If the icing becomes too soft, simply sift in a little more icing sugar.

Quick and Easy Decoration Ideas

You need quick and easy ideas for decoration? No problem! For simplicity and speed, you can't beat Butter Icing (page 229) – so why not try some of these instant ideas:

- chocolate butter icing (frosting) sprinkled with coconut, piped with whipped cream and sprinkled with grated chocolate
- coloured butter icing sprinkled with sugar strands and dotted with silver dragees
- coloured butter icing dotted with Smarties (M&Ms) or mini-marshmallows
- vanilla butter icing sprinkled in Dalmatian spots with chocolate vermicelli
- butter icing sprinkled with desiccated (shredded) coconut
- orange butter icing striped with thin strips of liquorice
- icing dotted with chocolate chips, icing flowers or jelly sweets
- icing piped into rosettes through a star nozzle

If you prefer to use Fondant Icing, you can either make your own (page 229), or buy ready-to-roll icing. Lightly spread the cake with sieved (strained) apricot jam, roll out the icing on a surface lightly dusted with icing (confectioners') sugar and use to cover the cake.

And don't forget that you can arrange your child's favourite little plastic toy figures – space men, cowboys, teddy bears or ponies – on a cake for instant effect! Think simple and effective and you can't go wrong.

Cut the 'wasted' pieces of cake into small squares or shapes, spread some icing on the top, decorate with a chocolate sweet or vermicelli and serve as little cakes.

Photograph opposite: Apricot Cheesecake (page 112)

Number Shape Cakes

You do not need to hire the special tins to bake number-shaped cakes. You can bake and shape them yourself quite simply. Use the quantities of Basic Butter Cake (page 191) indicated and if you are using more than one tin, divide the mixture between the tins so that the mixture is at the same level in each. Once cooked and cut, spread the edges of the cake with sieved (strained) apricot jam or Vanilla Cream Icing (page 191) to stick the pieces together. Ice with Vanilla Cream or butter icing (pages 229–30) and decorate to suit the birthday child.

Number 1 Cake

1 quantity of Basic Butter Cake (page 191)

Bake the cake mixture in two 450 g/1 lb loaf tins for 35 minutes until golden brown and firm to the touch.

Number 3 Cake

2 quantities of Basic Butter Cake (page 191)

Bake the cake mixture in two 20 cm/8 in ring moulds (tube pans) until golden brown and firm to the touch.

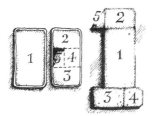

Number 2 Cake

2 quantities of Basic Butter Cake (page 191)

Bake the cake mixture in a 30 × 20 cm/12 × 8 in Swiss roll tin (jelly roll pan) until golden brown and firm to the touch.

Number 4 Cake

1 quantity of Basic Butter Cake (page 191)

Bake the cake mixture in a 25 × 20 cm/10 × 8 in cake tin (pan) until golden brown and firm to the touch.

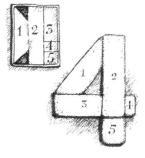

Photograph opposite: **Apple Windmills (page 140) and Walnut and Treacle Tart (page 156)**

Number 5 Cake

*2 quantities of Basic Butter Cake
(page 191)*

Bake the cake mixture in a 20 cm/8 in ring mould (tube pan) and a 18 cm/7 in square cake tin (pan) until golden brown and firm to the touch.

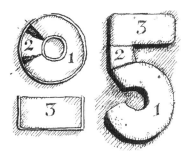

Number 7 Cake

*1 quantity of Basic Butter Cake
(page 191)*

Bake the cake mixture in two 900 g/2 lb loaf tins (pans) until golden brown and firm to the touch.

Number 6 Cake

*1 quantity of Basic Butter Cake
(page 191)*

Bake the cake mixture in one 18 cm/7 in ring mould (tube pan) and one 900 g/2 lb loaf tin (pan) until golden brown and firm to the touch.

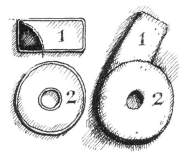

Number 8 Cake

*2 quantities of Basic Butter Cake
(page 191)*

Bake the cake mixture in two 20 cm/8 in ring moulds (tube pans) until golden brown and firm to the touch.

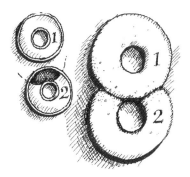

Number 9 Cake

1 quantity of Basic Butter Cake
(page 191)

Bake the cake mixture in one 18 cm/ 7 in ring mould (tube pans) and one 900 g/2 lb loaf tin (pan) until golden brown and firm to the touch.

Number 10 Cake

2 quantities of Basic Butter Cake
(page 191)

Bake the cake mixture in one 18 cm/ 7 in ring mould (tube pan) and one 25 × 20 cm/10 × 8 in cake tin (pan) until golden brown and firm to the touch.

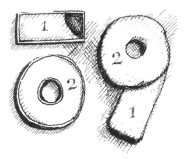

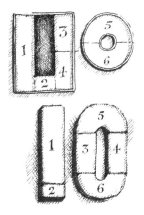

Funny Face Cakes

Make a Basic Butter Cake (page 191) in a 20 cm/8 in cake tin (pan). Use Vanilla Cream Icing (page 191) or Fondant Icing (page 229), coloured to suit the face you have chosen, then decorate with small amounts of coloured royal icing (frosting) to make up the remaining shapes, with biscuits (cookies), decorations or sweets. Stick layers of royal icing together with a little egg white or water. The illustrations are designed to inspire your imagination.

Cat

Bake a little of the cake mixture in a small square tin and cut to make two triangular ears to stick to the top of the cake. Ice in suitable colours and use jelly sweets for eyes and liquorice for whiskers.

Clown

Use a white base for the icing (frosting). Small jelly or chocolate sweets make good eyes and noses, while thin wafer biscuits can make eye or cheek shapes. Liquorice is always good for sharp lines and outlines. Jelly-lip sweets couldn't be easier to make a jolly smile, or you can cut wafer biscuits or pipe icing in a separate colour. Hair can be piped icing, or you could curl strands of paper ribbon by pulling them across the blade of some scissors. A party hat, cut in half, completes the effect.

Lion

Use half the icing to ice the cake in a yellow-brown, then colour the remaining icing in a darker shade and pipe the mane on to the board. Make the features fierce or friendly with marshmallow and chocolate sweet eyes, liquorice whiskers and a chocolate biscuit nose. Cut marshmallows to make teeth, if you wish.

Dog

Shape the cake to create two floppy ears and ice in suitable colours. Use marshmallow and fruit gum eyes, a wafer-biscuit tongue and a liquorice smile.

Mouse

Bake a little of the cake mixture in a square tin to make into ears to shape and fix to the top of the cake. Cover with cake with a suitable colour butter icing, then sprinkle with desiccated (shredded) coconut. Add jelly-sweet eyes, long liquorice whiskers and marshmallow teeth.

Masked Warriors

Use colours to suit your child's favourite character and copy the shapes from a picture to get the details right. Fondant Icing (page 229) is the easiest type to use for cutting out distinctive shapes.

Nurse

Cut shapes from Fondant Icing (page 229) to lay over the base icing. Roll thin strands of icing for the hair.

Monsters

Colour the monster any way you like and let your imagination run riot. Try marshmallow or icing teeth, liquorice hair and even jelly-sweet spots.

Pig

Bake a little of the cake mixture in a ramekin dish (custard cup). Cut it in half horizontally and attach the circle to the front of the cake to make a snout. Cut the remaining half into little ears to fix to the top. Ice in pink, then add chocolate-sweet nostrils and little black sweet eyes.

Pirate

Use fondant icing shapes or liquorice for a moustache, red liquorice or jelly sweets for the mouth and jelly sweets for the other features. Pipe some hair – unless you want a bald pirate! – in a suitably coloured icing and cut a hat out of paper. Use a gold-wrapped chocolate coin for an earring and pipe on a scar for a really wicked effect.

Sheep

Pipe the cake in white icing (frosting) through a very fine nozzle (tip), or use a potato rice to squeeze the icing in swirls all over the cake. Add tiny biscuit ears, sweets for the nose and eyes and a liquorice smile.

Rabbit

Bake a little of the cake mixture in a 450 g/1 lb loaf tin (pan) and shape into long ears. Ice in a suitable colour, then sprinkle with desiccated (shredded) coconut, masking the inside of the ears and the eyes. Make long liquorice whiskers, a pink biscuit nose and marshmallow teeth.

Leopard

Ice the cake in a yellow butter icing (frosting) and sprinkle chocolate vermicelli in little patches over the cake. Add twinkling sweet eyes and a wide or a wicked smile.

Teddy

Make the cake in an 18 cm/7 in cake tin (pan) and two small cake tins so that you have nice large ears. Shape the edges and sandwich them together. A happy face from liquorice or jelly sweets and wafer biscuits for the inside of the ears are then all you need. Add a paper bow tie (or even a real one) if you like.

Easy Cake Shapes

Use the quantity of Basic Butter Cake (page 191) indicated, cut out the shape and sandwich them together with Butter Icing (page 229) or a little sieved (strained) apricot jam (conserve) before icing wih Vanilla Cream Icing (page 191), Fondant Icing (page 229) or ready-roll icing.

Boat

Use one quantity of Basic Butter Cake (page 191) baked in a 450 g/1 lb loaf tin (pan) and a small quantity baked in a second loaf tin. Shape the bottom of the main cake piece to make the boat, then cut and fix pieces on the top to finish. Once iced, use cocktails sticks (toothpicks) and thread for the rails, little sweets for the portholes and liquorice for the ropes.

Butterfly

Use one quantity of Basic Butter Cake (page 191) baked in a 23 cm/9 in square cake tin (pan). Cut across diagonally, then slice a triangle off each corner and place the large shapes together to form the wings. Use chocolate flakes for the body, liquorice for the antennae and ice patterns on to the wings or decorate with colourful sweets.

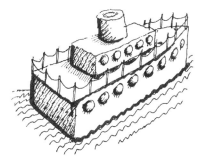

Cat

Bake two quantities of Basic Butter Cake (page 191) in a greased 20 cm/8 in cake tin, a 10 cm/4 in cake tin and a 10 cm/4 in square tin. Trim where the large and small cakes are placed together to make the neck, and cut the small square cake to make ears and a tail. Once iced (frosted), use liquorice for the whiskers and sweets for the features.

Sheep

Use one Swiss Roll (page 14), then bake one quantity of Basic Butter Cake (page 191) in a 600 ml/1 pt/2½ cup pudding basin. Shape the round cake into a head and cut legs from the trimmings. Cover the head and legs in smooth Butter Icing (page 229), then squeeze the remaining icing (frosting) through a potato ricer or garlic press to make the fleece. Use sweets for the features.

House

Make two quantities of Basic Butter Cake (page 191) and bake in a 20 cm/8 in square, deep cake tin (pan) and a 20 × 10 cm/8 × 4 in rectangular tin. Cut the smaller cake to make two triangular pieces for the roof. Cover with Butter Icing (page 229) or ready-to-roll icing (frosting) and decorate with sweets.

Train

Use one Swiss Roll (page 14) and one quantity of Basic Butter Cake (page 191) baked in one 450 g/1 lb loaf tin (pan) and one 10 cm/4 in square cake tin. Top with Fondant (page 229) or Butter Icing (page 229), then use orange-chocolate biscuits for the wheels; biscuits or icing (frosting) shapes for the windows; sweets for lights and coloured liquorice or sweets for the features. A little whipped cream on the top makes the steam.

Microwave Cakes and Bakes

With microwave baking, you do not achieve the same look as with conventional baking, but you can cook cakes and biscuits in a fraction of the time, and if you choose your recipes carefully you can still achieve delicious and eye-catching results. Times are based on a 650-watt oven, and remember that some recipes will continue to cook after they have been removed from the oven, so do not overbake. Microwave cakes do not always keep as well as conventionally baked cakes.

Microwave Apple Cake

Makes one 23 cm/ 9 in square

100 g/4 oz/½ cup butter or margarine, softened
100 g/4 oz/½ cup soft brown sugar
30 ml/2 tbsp golden (light corn) syrup
2 eggs, lightly beaten
225 g/8 oz/2 cups self-raising (self-rising) flour
10 ml/2 tsp ground mixed (apple-pie) spice
120 ml/4 fl oz/½ cup milk
2 cooking (tart) apples, peeled, cored and thinly sliced
15 ml/1 tbsp caster (superfine) sugar
5 ml/1 tsp ground cinnamon

Cream together the butter or margarine, brown sugar and syrup until pale and fluffy. Gradually beat in the eggs. Fold in the flour and mixed spice, then stir in the milk until you have a soft consistency. Stir in the apples. Spoon into a greased and base-lined 23 cm/9 in microwave ring mould (tube pan) and microwave on Medium for 12 minutes until firm. Allow to stand for 5 minutes, then turn out upside-down and sprinkle with the caster sugar and cinnamon.

Microwave Applesauce Cake

Makes one 20 cm/8 in cake

100 g/4 oz/½ cup butter or margarine, softened
175 g/6 oz/¾ cup soft brown sugar
1 egg, lightly beaten
175 g/6 oz/1½ cups plain (all-purpose) flour
2.5 ml/½ tsp baking powder
A pinch of salt
2.5 ml/½ tsp ground allspice
1.5 ml/¼ tsp grated nutmeg
1.5 ml/¼ tsp ground cloves
300 ml/½ pt/1¼ cups unsweetened apple purée (sauce)
75 g/3 oz/½ cup raisins
Icing (confectioner's) sugar for dusting

Cream together the butter or margarine and brown sugar until light and fluffy. Gradually beat in the egg, then fold in the flour, baking powder, salt and spices alternately with the apple purée and raisins. Spoon into a greased and floured 20 cm/8 in square microwave dish and microwave on High for 12 minutes. Leave to cool in the dish, then cut into squares and dust with icing sugar.

Microwave Apple and Walnut Cake

Makes one 20 cm/8 in cake

175 g/6 oz/³⁄₄ cup butter or margarine, softened
100 g/4 oz/½ cup caster (superfine) sugar
3 eggs, lightly beaten
30 ml/2 tbsp golden (light corn) syrup
Grated rind and juice of 1 lemon
175 g/6 oz/1½ cups self-raising (self-rising) flour
50 g/2 oz/½ cup walnuts, chopped
1 eating (dessert) apple, peeled, cored and chopped
100 g/4 oz/⅔ cup icing (confectioner's) sugar
30 ml/2 tbsp lemon juice
15 ml/1 tbsp water
Walnut halves to decorate

Cream together the butter or margarine and caster sugar until light and fluffy. Gradually add the eggs, then the syrup, lemon rind and juice. Fold in the flour, chopped nuts and apple. Spoon into a greased 20 cm/8 in round microwave dish and microwave on High for 4 minutes. Remove from the oven and cover with foil. Leave to cool. Mix the icing sugar with the lemon juice and enough of the water to form a smooth icing (frosting). Spread over the cake and decorate with walnut halves.

Microwave Carrot Cake

Makes one 18 cm/7 in cake

100 g/4 oz/½ cup butter or margarine, softened
100 g/4 oz/½ cup soft brown sugar
2 eggs, beaten
Grated rind and juice of 1 orange
2.5 ml/½ tsp ground cinnamon
A pinch of grated nutmeg
100 g/4 oz carrots, grated

100 g/4 oz/1 cup self-raising (self-rising) flour
25 g/1 oz/¼ cup ground almonds
25 g/1 oz/2 tbsp caster (superfine) sugar
For the topping:
100 g/4 oz/½ cup cream cheese
50 g/2 oz/⅓ cup icing (confectioners') sugar, sifted
30 ml/2 tbsp lemon juice

Cream together the butter and sugar until light and fluffy. Gradually beat in the eggs, then stir in the orange juice and rind, the spices and carrots. Fold in the flour, almonds and sugar. Spoon into a greased and lined 18 cm/7 in cake dish and cover with clingfilm (plastic wrap). Microwave on High for 8 minutes until a skewer inserted in the centre comes out clean. Remove the clingfilm and leave to stand for 8 minutes before turning out on to a wire rack to finish cooling. Beat the topping ingredients together, then spread over the cooled cake.

Microwave Carrot, Pineapple and Nut Cake

Makes one 20 cm/8 in cake

225 g/8 oz/1 cup caster (superfine) sugar
2 eggs
120 ml/4 fl oz/½ cup oil
1.5 ml/¼ tsp salt
5 ml/1 tsp bicarbonate of soda (baking soda)
100 g/4 oz/1 cup self-raising (self-rising) flour
5 ml/1 tsp ground cinnamon
175 g/6 oz carrots, grated
75 g/3 oz/¾ cup walnuts, chopped
225 g/8 oz crushed pineapple with its juice
For the icing (frosting):
15 g/½ oz/1 tbsp butter or margarine
50 g/2 oz/¼ cup cream cheese

10 ml/2 tsp lemon juice
Icing (confectioners') sugar, sifted

Line a large ring mould (tube pan) with baking parchment. Cream together the sugar, eggs and oil. Gently stir in the dry ingredients until well combined. Stir in the remaining cake ingredients. Pour the mixture into the prepared mould, stand it on a rack or upturned plate and microwave on High for 13 minutes or until just set. Leave to stand for 5 minutes, then turn out on to a rack to cool.

Meanwhile, make the icing. Put the butter or margarine, cream cheese and lemon juice in a bowl and microwave on High for 30–40 seconds. Gradually beat in enough icing sugar to make a thick consistency and beat until fluffy. When the cake is cold, spread over the icing.

Microwave Spiced Bran Cakes

Makes 15

75 g/3 oz/¾ cup All Bran cereal
250 ml/8 fl oz/1 cup milk
175 g/6 oz/1½ cups plain
   (all-purpose) flour
75 g/3 oz/⅓ cup caster (superfine)
   sugar
10 ml/2 tsp baking powder
10 ml/2 tsp ground mixed
   (apple-pie) spice
A pinch of salt
60 ml/4 tbsp golden (light corn) syrup
45 ml/3 tbsp oil
1 egg, lightly beaten
75 g/3 oz/½ cup raisins
15 ml/1 tbsp grated orange rind

Soak the cereal in the milk for 10 minutes. Mix together the flour, sugar, baking powder, mixed spice and salt, then mix into the cereal. Stir in the syrup, oil, egg, raisins and orange rind. Spoon into paper cases (cupcake papers) and microwave five cakes at a time on High for 4 minutes. Repeat for the remaining cakes.

Microwave Banana and Passion Fruit Cheesecake

Makes one 23 cm/9 in cake

100 g/4 oz/½ cup butter or margarine,
   melted
175 g/6 oz/1½ cups ginger biscuit
   (cookie) crumbs
250 g/9 oz/generous 1 cup cream
   cheese
175 ml/6 fl oz/¾ cup soured
   (dairy sour) cream
2 eggs, lightly beaten
100 g/4 oz/½ cup caster (superfine)
   sugar
Grated rind and juice of 1 lemon
150 ml/¼ pt/⅔ cup whipping cream
1 banana, sliced
1 passion fruit, chopped

Mix together the butter or margarine and biscuit crumbs and press into the base and sides of a 23 cm/9 in microwave flan dish. Microwave on High for 1 minute. Leave to cool.

Beat together the cream cheese and soured cream until smooth, then beat in the egg, sugar and lemon juice and rind. Spoon into the base and spread evenly. Cook on Medium for 8 minutes. Leave to cool.

Whip the cream until stiff, then spread over the case. Top with banana slices and spoon the passion fruit flesh over the top.

Microwave Baked Orange Cheesecake

Makes one 20 cm/8 in cake

50 g/2 oz/¼ cup butter or margarine
12 digestive biscuits (Graham crackers), crushed
100 g/4 oz/½ cup caster (superfine) sugar
225 g/8 oz/1 cup cream cheese
2 eggs
30 ml/2 tbsp concentrated orange juice
15 ml/1 tbsp lemon juice
150 ml/¼ pt/⅔ cup soured (dairy sour) cream
A pinch of salt
1 orange
30 ml/2 tbsp apricot jam (conserve)
150 ml/¼ pt/⅔ cup double (heavy) cream

Melt the butter or margarine in a 20 cm/8 in microwave flan dish on High for 1 minute. Stir in the biscuit crumbs and 25 g/1 oz/2 tbsp of the sugar and press over the base and sides of the dish. Cream the cheese with the remaining sugar and the eggs, then stir in the orange and lemon juices, soured cream and salt. Spoon into the case (shell) and microwave on High for 2 minutes. Leave to stand for 2 minutes, then microwave on High for a further 2 minutes. Leave to stand for 1 minute, then microwave on High for 1 minute. Leave to cool.

Peel the orange and remove the segments from the membrane, using a sharp knife. Melt the jam and brush over the top of the cheesecake. Whip the cream and pipe round the edge of the cheesecake, then decorate with the orange segments.

Microwave Pineapple Cheesecake

Makes one 23 cm/9 in cake

100 g/4 oz/½ cup butter or margarine, melted
175 g/6 oz/1½ cups digestive biscuit (Graham cracker) crumbs
250 g/9 oz/generous 1 cup cream cheese
2 eggs, lightly beaten
5 ml/1 tsp grated lemon rind
30 ml/2 tbsp lemon juice
75 g/3 oz/⅓ cup caster (superfine) sugar
400 g/14 oz/1 large can pineapple, drained and crushed
150 ml/¼ pt/⅔ cup double (heavy) cream

Mix together the butter or margarine and biscuit crumbs and press into the base and sides of a 23 cm/9 in microwave flan dish. Microwave on High for 1 minute. Leave to cool.

Beat together the cream cheese, eggs, lemon rind and juice and sugar until smooth. Stir in the pineapple and spoon into the base. Microwave on Medium for 6 minutes until firm. Leave to cool.

Whip the cream until stiff, then pile on top of the cheesecake.

Microwave Cherry and Nut Loaf

Makes one 900 g/2 lb loaf

*175 g/6 oz/³⁄₄ cup butter or margarine,
softened
175 g/6 oz/³⁄₄ cup soft brown sugar
3 eggs, beaten
225 g/8 oz/2 cups plain
(all-purpose) flour
10 ml/2 tsp baking powder
A pinch of salt
45 ml/3 tbsp milk
75 g/3 oz/¹⁄₃ cup glacé (candied)
cherries
75 g/3 oz/³⁄₄ cup chopped mixed nuts
25 g/1 oz/3 tbsp icing (confectioners')
sugar, sifted*

Cream together the butter or margarine and brown sugar until light
and fluffy. Gradually beat in the eggs, then
fold in the flour, baking powder and salt.
Stir in enough of the milk to make a soft
consistency, then stir in the cherries and
nuts. Spoon into a greased and lined
900 g/2 lb microwave loaf dish and
sprinkle with the sugar. Microwave on
High for 7 minutes. Leave to stand for
5 minutes, then turn out on to a wire rack
to finish cooling.

Microwave Chocolate Cake

Makes one 18 cm/7 in cake

*225 g/8 oz/1 cup butter or margarine,
softened
175 g/6 oz/³⁄₄ cup caster (superfine)
sugar
150 g/5 oz/1¹⁄₄ cups self-raising
(self-rising) flour
50 g/2 oz/¹⁄₄ cup cocoa (unsweetened
chocolate) powder
5 ml/1 tsp baking powder
3 eggs, beaten
45 ml/3 tbsp milk*

Mix together all the ingredients and
spoon into a greased and lined
18 cm/7 in microwave dish. Microwave
on High for 9 minutes until just firm to
the touch. Leave to cool in the dish for
5 minutes, then turn out on to a wire rack
to finish cooling.

Microwave Chocolate Almond Cake

Makes one 20 cm/8 in cake

For the cake:
100 g/4 oz/½ cup butter or margarine, softened
100 g/4 oz/½ cup caster (superfine) sugar
2 eggs, lightly beaten
100 g/4 oz/1 cup self-raising (self-rising) flour
50 g/2 oz/½ cup cocoa (unsweetened chocolate) powder
50 g/2 oz/½ cup ground almonds
150 ml/¼ pt/⅔ cup milk
60 ml/4 tbsp golden (light corn) syrup
For the icing (frosting):
100 g/4 oz/1 cup plain (semi-sweet) chocolate
25 g/1 oz/2 tbsp butter or margarine
8 whole almonds

To make the cake, cream together the butter or mar-garine and sugar until light and fluffy. Gradually beat in the eggs, then fold in the flour and cocoa, followed by the ground almonds. Stir in the milk and syrup and beat until light and soft. Spoon into a 20 cm/8 in microwave dish lined with clingfilm (plastic wrap) and microwave on High for 4 minutes. Remove from the oven, cover the top with foil and leave to cool slightly, then turn out on to a wire rack to finish cooling.

To make the icing, melt the chocolate and butter or margarine on High for 2 minutes. Beat well. Half-dip the almonds in the chocolate, then leave to set on a piece of greaseproof (waxed) paper. Pour the remaining icing over the cake and spread over the top and down the sides. Decorate with the almonds and leave to set.

Microwave Double Chocolate Brownies

Makes 8

150 g/5 oz/1¼ cups plain (semi-sweet) chocolate, coarsely chopped
75 g/3 oz/⅓ cup butter or margarine
175 g/6 oz/¾ cup soft brown sugar
2 eggs, lightly beaten
150 g/5 oz/1¼ cups plain (all-purpose) flour
2.5 ml/½ tsp baking powder
2.5 ml/½ tsp vanilla essence (extract)
30 ml/2 tbsp milk

Melt 50 g/2 oz/½ cup of the chocolate with the butter or margarine on High for 2 minutes. Beat in the sugar and eggs, then stir in the flour, baking powder, vanilla essence and milk until smooth. Spoon into a greased 20 cm/8 in square microwave dish and microwave on High for 7 minutes. Leave to cool in the dish for 10 minutes. Melt the remaining chocolate on High for 1 minute, then spread over the top of the cake and leave to cool. Cut into squares.

Microwave Chocolate Date Bars

Makes 8

50 g/2 oz/⅓ cup stoned (pitted) dates, chopped
60 ml/4 tbsp boiling water
65 g/2½ oz/⅓ cup butter or margarine, softened
225 g/8 oz/1 cup caster (superfine) sugar
1 egg
100 g/4 oz/1 cup plain (all-purpose) flour
10 ml/2 tsp cocoa (unsweetened chocolate) powder
2.5 ml/½ tsp baking powder

A pinch of salt
25 g/1 oz/¼ cup chopped mixed nuts
100 g/4 oz/1 cup plain (semi-sweet)
chocolate, finely chopped

Mix the dates with the boiling water and leave to stand until cool. Cream together the butter or margarine with half the sugar until light and fluffy. Gradually work in the egg, then alternately fold in the flour, cocoa, baking powder and salt and the date mixture. Spoon into a greased and floured 20 cm/8 in square microwave dish. Mix the remaining sugar with the nuts and chocolate and sprinkle over the top, pressing down lightly. Microwave on High for 8 minutes. Leave to cool in the dish before cutting into squares.

Microwave Chocolate Squares

Makes 16

For the cake:
50 g/2 oz/¼ cup butter or margarine
5 ml/1 tsp caster (superfine) sugar
75 g/3 oz/¾ cup plain (all-purpose)
flour
1 egg yolk
15 ml/1 tbsp water
175 g/6 oz/1½ cups plain (semi-sweet)
chocolate, grated
or finely chopped
For the topping:
50g /2 oz/¼cup butter or margarine
50 g/2 oz/¼ cup caster (superfine)
sugar
1 egg
2.5 ml/½ tsp vanilla essence (extract)
100 g/4 oz/1 cup walnuts, chopped

To make the cake, soften the butter or margarine and work in the sugar, flour, egg yolk and water. Spread the mixture evenly in a 20 cm/8 in square microwave dish and microwave on High for 2 minutes. Sprinkle over the chocolate and microwave on High for 1 minute. Spread evenly over the base and leave until hardened.

To make the topping, microwave the butter or margarine on High for 30 seconds. Stir in the remaining topping ingredients and spread over the chocolate. Microwave on High for 5 minutes. Leave to cool, then cut into squares.

Microwave Quick Coffee Cake

Makes one19 cm/7 in cake

For the cake:
225 g/8 oz/1 cup butter or margarine,
softened
225 g/8 oz/1 cup caster (superfine)
sugar
225 g/8 oz/2 cups self-raising
(self-rising) flour
5 eggs
45 ml/3 tbsp coffee essence (extract)
For the icing (frosting):
30 ml/2 tbsp coffee essence (extract)
175 g/6 oz/¾ cup butter or margarine
Icing (confectioners') sugar, sifted
Walnut halves to decorate

Mix together all the cake ingredients until well blended. Divided between two 19 cm/7 in microwave cake containers and cook each one on high for 5–6 minutes. Remove from the microwave and leave to cool.

Blend together the icing ingredients, sweetening to taste with icing sugar. When cool, sandwich the cakes together with half the icing and spread the rest on top. Decorate with walnut halves.

207

Microwave Christmas Cake

Makes one 23 cm/9 in cake

*150 g/5 oz/⅔ cup butter or margarine,
  softened*
150 g/5 oz/⅔ cup soft brown sugar
3 eggs
30 ml/2 tbsp black treacle (molasses)
*225 g/8 oz/2 cups self-raising
  (self-rising) flour*
*10 ml/2 tsp ground mixed
  (apple-pie) spice*
2. 5 ml/½ tsp grated nutmeg
*2.5 ml/½ tsp bicarbonate of soda
  (baking soda)*
*450 g/1 lb/2⅔ cups mixed dried fruit
  (fruit cake mix)*
*50 g/2 oz/¼ cup glacé (candied)
  cherries*
50 g/2 oz/½ cup chopped mixed peel
50 g/2 oz/½ cup chopped mixed nuts
30 ml/2 tbsp brandy
*Additional brandy to mature the cake
  (optional)*

Cream together the butter or margarine and sugar until light and fluffy. Gradually beat in the eggs and treacle, then fold in the flour, spices and bicarbonate of soda. Gently stir in the fruit, mixed peel and nuts, then stir in the brandy. Spoon into a base-lined 23 cm/9 in microwave dish and microwave on Low for 45–60 minutes. Leave to cool in the dish for 15 minutes before turning out on to a wire rack to finish cooling.

When cool, wrap the cake in foil and store in a cool, dark place for 2 weeks. If liked, pierce the top of the cake several times with a thin skewer and sprinkle over some additional brandy, then re-wrap and store the cake. You can do this several times to create a richer cake.

Microwave Crumb Cake

Makes one 20 cm/8 in cake

*300 g/10 oz/1¼ cups caster (superfine)
  sugar*
*225 g/8 oz/2 cups plain
  (all-purpose) flour*
10 ml/2 tsp baking powder
5 ml/1 tsp ground cinnamon
*100 g/4 oz/½ cup butter or margarine,
  softened*
2 eggs, lightly beaten
100 ml/3½ fl oz/6½ tbsp milk

Mix together the sugar, flour, baking powder and cinnamon. Work in the butter or margarine, then set aside a quarter of the mixture. Mix together the eggs and milk and beat into the larger portion of cake mix. Spoon the mixture into a greased and floured 20 cm/8 in microwave dish and sprinkle with the reserved crumble mix. Microwave on High for 10 minutes. Leave to cool in the dish.

Microwave Date Bars

Makes 12

*150 g/5 oz/1¼ cups self-raising
  (self-raising) flour*
*175 g/6 oz/¾ cup caster (superfine)
  sugar*
*100 g/4 oz/1 cup desiccated
  (shredded) coconut*
*100 g/4 oz/⅔ cups stoned (pitted)
  dates, chopped*
50 g/2 oz/½ cup chopped mixed nuts
*100 g/4 oz/½ cup butter or margarine,
  melted*
1 egg, lightly beaten
*Icing (confectioners') sugar for
  dusting*

Mix together the dry ingredients. Stir in the butter or margarine and egg and mix to a firm dough. Press into the base of a 20 cm/8 in square microwave dish and microwave on Medium for 8 minutes until just firm. Leave in the dish for 10 minutes, then cut into bars and turn out on to a wire rack to finish cooling.

Microwave Fig Bread

Makes one 675 g/1½ lb loaf

100 g/4 oz/2 cups bran
50 g/2 oz/¼ cup soft brown sugar
45 ml/3 tbsp clear honey
100 g/4 oz/⅔ cup dried figs, chopped
50 g/2 oz/½ cup hazelnuts, chopped
300 ml/½ pt/1¼ cups milk
100 g/4 oz/1 cup wholemeal
  (wholewheat) flour
10 ml/2 tsp baking powder
A pinch of salt

Mix together all the ingredients to a stiff dough. Shape into a microwave loaf dish and level the surface. Cook on High for 7 minutes. Leave to cool in the dish for 10 minutes, then turn out on to a wire rack to finish cooling.

Microwave Flapjacks

Makes 24

175 g/6 oz/¾ cup butter or margarine, softened
50 g/2 oz/¼ cup caster (superfine) sugar
50 g/2 oz/¼ cup soft brown sugar
90 ml/6 tbsp golden (light corn) syrup
A pinch of salt
275 g/10 oz/2½ cups rolled oats

Mix together the butter or margarine and sugars in a large bowl and cook on High for 1 minute. Add the remaining ingredients and stir well. Spoon the mixture into a greased 18 cm/7 in microwave dish and press down lightly. Cook on High for 5 minutes. Leave to cool slightly, then cut into squares.

Microwave Fruit Cake

Makes one 18 cm/7 in cake

175 g/6 oz/¾ cup butter or margarine, softened
175 g/6 oz/¾ cup caster (superfine) sugar
Grated rind of 1 lemon
3 eggs, beaten
225 g/8 oz/2 cups plain
  (all-purpose) flour
5 ml/1 tsp ground mixed (apple-pie) spice
225 g/8 oz/1⅓ cups raisins
225 g/8 oz/1⅓ cups sultanas
  (golden raisins)
50 g/2 oz/¼ cup glacé (candied) cherries
50 g/2 oz/½ cup chopped mixed nuts
15 ml/1 tbsp golden (light corn) syrup
45 ml/3 tbsp brandy

Cream together the butter or margarine and sugar until light and fluffy. Mix in the lemon rind, then gradually beat in the eggs. Fold in the flour and mixed spice, then mix in the remaining ingredients. Spoon into a greased and lined 18 cm/7 in round microwave dish and microwave on Low for 35 minutes until a skewer inserted in the centre comes out clean. Leave to cool in the dish for 10 minutes, then turn out on to a wire rack to finish cooling.

Microwave Fruit and Coconut Squares

Makes 8

50 g/2 oz/¼ cup butter or margarine
9 digestive biscuits (Graham crackers), crushed
50 g/2 oz/½ cup desiccated (shredded) coconut
100 g/4 oz/⅔ cup chopped mixed (candied) peel
50 g/2 oz/⅓ cup stoned (pitted) dates, chopped
15 ml/1 tbsp plain (all-purpose) flour
25 g/1 oz/2 tbsp glacé (candied) cherries, chopped
100 g/4 oz/1 cup walnuts, chopped
150 ml/¼ pt/⅔ cup condensed milk

Melt the butter or margarine in a 20 cm/8 in square microwave dish on High for 40 seconds. Stir in the biscuit crumbs and spread evenly over the base of the dish. Sprinkle with the coconut, then with the mixed peel. Mix the dates with the flour, cherries and nuts and sprinkle over the top, then pour over the milk. Microwave on High for 8 minutes. Leave to cool in the dish, then cut into squares.

Microwave Fudge Cake

Makes one 20 cm/8 in cake

150 g/5 oz/1¼ cups plain (all-purpose) flour
5 ml/1 tsp baking powder
A pinch of bicarbonate of soda (baking soda)
A pinch of salt
300 g/10 oz/1¼ cups caster (superfine) sugar
50 g/2 oz/¼ cup butter or margarine, softened
250 ml/8 fl oz/1 cup milk
A few drops of vanilla essence (extract)
1 egg

100 g/4 oz/1 cup plain (semi-sweet) chocolate, chopped
50 g/2 oz/½ cup chopped mixed nuts
Chocolate Butter Icing (page 229)

Mix together the flour, baking powder, bicarbonate of soda and salt. Stir in the sugar, then beat in the butter or margarine, milk and vanilla essence until smooth. Beat in the egg. Microwave three-quarters of the chocolate on High for 2 minutes until melted, then beat into the cake mixture until creamy. Stir in the nuts. Spoon the mixture into two greased and floured 20 cm/8 in microwave dishes and microwave each one separately for 8 minutes. Remove from the oven, cover with foil and leave to cool for 10 minutes, then turn out on to a wire rack to finish cooling. Sandwich together with half the butter icing (frosting), then spread the remaining icing over the top and decorate with the reserved chocolate.

Microwave Gingerbread

Makes one 20 cm/8 in cake

50 g/2 oz/¼ cup butter or margarine
75 g/3 oz/¼ cup black treacle (molasses)
15 ml/1 tbsp caster (superfine) sugar
100 g/4 oz/1 cup plain (all-purpose) flour
5 ml/1 tsp ground ginger
2.5 ml/½ tsp ground mixed (apple-pie) spice
2.5 ml/½ tsp bicarbonate of soda (baking soda)
1 egg, beaten

Place the butter or margarine in a bowl and microwave on High for 30 seconds. Stir in the treacle and sugar and microwave on High for 1 minute. Stir in the flour, spices and bicarbonate of soda. Beat in the egg. Spoon the mixture into a greased 1.5 litre/2½ pint/6 cup dish and microwave on High for 4 minutes. Cool in the dish for 5 minutes, then turn out on to a wire rack to finish cooling.

Microwave Ginger Bars

Makes 12

For the cake:
150 g/5 oz/⅔ cup butter or margarine,
softened
50 g/2 oz/¼ cup caster (superfine)
sugar
100 g/4 oz/1 cup plain (all-purpose)
flour
2.5 ml/½ tsp baking powder
5 ml/1 tsp ground ginger
For the topping:
15 g/½ oz/1 tbsp butter or margarine
15 ml/1 tbsp golden (light corn) syrup
A few drops of vanilla essence
(extract)
5 ml/1 tsp ground ginger
50 g/2 oz/⅓ cup icing (confectioners')
sugar

To make the cake, cream together the butter or mar-garine and sugar until light and fluffy. Stir in the flour, baking powder and ginger and mix to a smooth dough. Press into a 20 cm/8 in square microwave dish and microwave on Medium for 6 minutes until just firm.

To make the topping, melt the butter or margarine and syrup. Stir in the vanilla essence, ginger and icing sugar and whisk until thick. Spread evenly over the warm cake. Leave to cool in the dish, then cut into bars or squares.

Microwave Golden Cake

Makes one 20 cm/8 in cake

For the cake:
100 g/4 oz/½ cup butter or margarine,
softened
100 g/4 oz/½ cup caster (superfine)
sugar
2 eggs, lightly beaten
A few drops of vanilla essence
(extract)
225 g/8 oz/2 cups plain
(all-purpose) flour
10 ml/2 tsp baking powder
A pinch of salt
60 ml/4 tbsp milk
For the icing (frosting):
50 g/2 oz/¼ cup butter or margarine,
softened
100 g/4 oz/⅔ cup icing (confectioner's)
sugar
A few drops of vanilla essence
(extract) (optional)

To make the cake, cream together the butter or margarine and sugar until light and fluffy. Gradually beat in the eggs, then fold in the flour, baking powder and salt. Stir in enough of the milk to give a soft, dropping consistency. Spoon into two greased and floured 20 cm/8 in microwave dishes and cook each cake separately on High for 6 minutes. Remove from the oven, cover with foil and leave to cool for 5 minutes, then turn out on to a wire rack to finish cooling.

To make the icing, beat the butter or margarine until soft, then beat in the icing sugar and vanilla essence, if liked. Sandwich the cakes together with half the icing, then spread the remainder over the top.

Microwave Honey and Hazelnut Cake

Makes one 18 cm/7 in cake

150 g/5 oz/⅔ cup butter or margarine, softened
100 g/4 oz/½ cup soft brown sugar
45 ml/3 tbsp clear honey
3 eggs, beaten
225 g/8 oz/2 cups self-raising (self-rising) flour
100 g/4 oz/1 cup ground hazelnuts
45 ml/3 tbsp milk
Butter Icing (page 229)

Cream together the butter or margarine, sugar and honey until light and fluffy. Gradually beat in the eggs, then fold in the flour and hazelnuts and enough of the milk to give a soft consistency. Spoon into an 18 cm/7 in microwave dish and cook on Medium for 7 minutes. Leave to cool in the dish for 5 minutes, then turn out on to a wire rack to finish cooling. Cut the cake in half horizontally, then sandwich together with butter icing (frosting).

Microwave Chewy Muesli Bars

Makes about 10

100 g/4 oz/½ cup butter or margarine
175 g/6 oz/½ cup clear honey
50 g/2 oz/⅓ cup ready-to-eat dried apricots, chopped
50 g/2 oz/⅓ cup stoned (pitted) dates, chopped
75 g/3 oz/¾ cup chopped mixed nuts
100 g/4 oz/1 cup rolled oats
100 g/4 oz/½ cup soft brown sugar
1 egg, beaten
25 g/1 oz/2 tbsp self-raising (self-rising) flour

Place the butter or margarine and honey in a bowl and cook on High for 2 minutes. Mix in all the remaining ingredients. Spoon into a 20 cm/8 in microwave baking tray and microwave on High for 8 minutes. Leave to cool slightly, then cut into squares or slices.

Microwave Nut Cake

Makes one 20 cm/8 in cake

150 g/5 oz/1¼ cups plain (all-purpose) flour
A pinch of salt
5 ml/1 tsp ground cinnamon
75 g/3 oz/⅓ cup soft brown sugar
75 g/3 oz/⅓ cup caster (superfine) sugar
75 ml/5 tbsp oil
25 g/1 oz/¼ cup walnuts, chopped
5 ml/1 tsp baking powder
2.5 ml/½ tsp bicarbonate of soda (baking soda)
1 egg
150 ml/¼ pt/⅔ cup soured milk

Mix together the flour, salt and half the cinnamon. Stir in the sugars, then beat in the oil until well mixed. Remove 90 ml/6 tbsp of the mixture and stir it into the nuts and remaining cinnamon. Add the baking powder, bicarbonate of soda, egg and milk to the bulk of the mixture and beat until smooth. Spoon the main mixture into a greased and floured 20 cm/8 in microwave dish and sprinkle the nut mixture over the top. Microwave on High for 8 minutes. Leave to cool in the dish for 10 minutes and serve warm.

Microwave Orange Juice Cake

Makes one 20 cm/8 in cake

250 g/9 oz/2¼ cups plain
(all-purpose) flour
225 g/8 oz/1 cup granulated sugar
15 ml/1 tbsp baking powder
2.5 ml/½ tsp salt
60 ml/4 tbsp oil
250 ml/8 fl oz/2 cups orange juice
2 eggs, separated
100 g/4 oz/½ cup caster (superfine)
sugar
Orange Butter Icing (page 230)
Orange Glacé Icing (page 231)

Mix together the flour, granulated sugar, baking powder, salt, oil and half the orange juice and beat until well blended. Beat in the egg yolks and remaining orange juice until light and soft. Whisk the egg whites until stiff, then add half the caster sugar and beat until thick and glossy. Fold in the remaining sugar, then fold the egg whites into the cake mixture. Spoon into two greased and floured 20 cm/8 in microwave dishes and microwave each one separately on High for 6–8 minutes. Remove from the oven, cover with foil and leave to cool for 5 minutes, then turn out on to a wire rack to finish cooling. Sandwich the cakes together with orange butter icing (frosting) and spread the orange glacé icing over the top.

Microwave Pavlova

Makes one 23 cm/9 in cake

4 egg whites
225 g/8 oz/1 cup caster (superfine)
sugar
2.5 ml/½ tsp vanilla essence (extract)
A few drops of wine vinegar
150 ml/¼ pt/⅔ cup whipping cream
1 kiwi fruit, sliced
100 g/4 oz strawberries, sliced

Beat the egg whites until they form soft peaks. Sprinkle in half the sugar and beat well. Gradually add the rest of the sugar, the vanilla essence and vinegar and beat until dissolved. Spoon the mixture into to a 23 cm/9 in circle on a piece of baking parchment. Microwave on High for 2 minutes. Leave to stand in the microwave with the door open for 10 minutes. Remove from the oven, tear off the backing paper and leave to cool. Whip the cream until stiff and spread over the top of the meringue. Arrange the fruit attractively on top.

Microwave Shortcake

Makes one 20 cm/8 in cake

225 g/8 oz/2 cups plain
(all-purpose) flour
15 ml/1 tbsp baking powder
50 g/2 oz/¼ cup caster (superfine)
sugar
100 g/4 oz/½ cup butter or margarine
75 ml/5 tbsp single (light) cream
1 egg

Mix together the flour, baking powder and sugar, then rub in the butter or margarine until the mixture resembles breadcrumbs. Mix together the cream and egg, then work into the flour mixture until you have a soft dough. Press into a greased 20 cm/8 in microwave dish and microwave on High for 6 minutes. Leave to stand for 4 minutes, then turn out and finish cooling on a wire rack.

Microwave Strawberry Shortcake

Makes one 20 cm/8 in cake

900 g/2 lb strawberries, thickly sliced
225 g/8 oz/1 cup caster (superfine)
  sugar
225 g/8 oz/2 cups plain
  (all-purpose) flour
15 ml/1 tbsp baking powder
175 g/6 oz/³⁄₄ cup butter or margarine
75 ml/5 tbsp single (light) cream
1 egg
150 ml/¹⁄₄ pt/²⁄₃ cup double (heavy)
  cream, whipped

Mix the strawberries with 175 g/
6 oz/³⁄₄ cup of the sugar, then chill
for at least 1 hour.

Mix together the flour, baking powder
and remaining sugar, then rub in 100 g/
4 oz/¹⁄₂ cup of the butter or margarine
until the mixture resembles breadcrumbs.
Mix together the single cream and egg,
then work into the flour mixture until
you have a soft dough. Press into a greased
20 cm/8 in microwave dish and
microwave on High for 6 minutes. Leave
to stand for 4 minutes, then turn out and
split through the centre while still warm.
Leave to cool.

Spread both cut surfaces with the
remaining butter or margarine. Spread
one-third of the whipped cream over the
base, then cover with three-quarters of
the strawberries. Top with a further one-
third of the cream, then place the second
shortcake on top. Top with the remaining
cream and strawberries.

Microwave Sponge Cake

Makes one 18 cm/7 in cake

150 g/5 oz/1¹⁄₄ cups self-raising
  (self-rising) flour
100 g/4 oz/¹⁄₂ cup butter or margarine
100 g/4 oz/¹⁄₂ cup caster (superfine)
  sugar
2 eggs
30 ml/2 tbsp milk

Beat together all the ingredients until
smooth. Spoon into a base-lined 18
cm/7 in microwave dish and microwave
on Medium for 6 minutes. Leave to cool
in the dish for 5 minutes, then turn out on
to a wire rack to finish cooling.

Microwave Sultana Bars

Makes 12

175 g/6 oz/³⁄₄ cup butter or margarine
100 g/4 oz/¹⁄₂ cup caster (superfine)
  sugar
15 ml/1 tbsp golden (light corn) syrup
75 g/3 oz/¹⁄₂ cup sultanas
  (golden raisins)
5 ml/1 tsp grated lemon rind
225 g/8 oz/2 cups self-raising
  (self-rising) flour
For the icing (frosting):
175 g/6 oz/1 cup icing (confectioners')
  sugar
30 ml/2 tbsp lemon juice

Microwave the butter or margarine,
caster sugar and syrup on Medium
for 2 minutes. Stir in the sultanas and
lemon rind. Fold in the flour. Spoon into
a greased and lined 20 cm/8 in square
microwave dish and microwave on
Medium for 8 minutes until just firm.
Leave to cool slightly.

Place the icing sugar in a bowl and
make a well in the centre. Gradually mix
in the lemon juice to make a smooth
icing. Spread over the cake while still just
warm, then leave to cool completely.

Microwave Chocolate Biscuits

Makes 24

225 g/8 oz/1 cup butter or margarine, softened
100 g/4 oz/½ cup dark brown sugar
5 ml/1 tsp vanilla essence (extract)
225 g/8 oz/2 cups self-raising (self-rising) flour
50 g/2 oz/½ cup drinking chocolate powder

Cream together the butter, sugar and vanilla essence until light and fluffy. Gradually mix in the flour and chocolate and mix to a smooth dough. Shape into walnut-sized balls, arrange six at a time on a greased microwave baking (cookie) sheet and flatten slightly with a fork. Microwave each batch on High for 2 minutes, until all the biscuits (cookies) are cooked. Leave to cool on a wire rack.

Microwave Coconut Cookies

Makes 24

50 g/2 oz/¼ cup butter or margarine, softened
75 g/3 oz/⅓ cup caster (superfine) sugar
1 egg, lightly beaten
2.5 ml/½ tsp vanilla essence (extract)
75 g/3 oz/¾ cup plain (all-purpose) flour
25 g/1 oz/¼ cup desiccated (shredded) coconut
A pinch of salt
30 ml/2 tbsp strawberry jam (conserve)

Beat together the butter or margarine and sugar until light and fluffy. Stir in the egg and vanilla essence alternately with the flour, coconut and salt and mix to a smooth dough. Shape into walnut-sized balls and arrange six at a time on a greased microwave baking (cookie) sheet, then press lightly with a fork to flatten

slightly. Microwave on High for 3 minutes until just firm. Transfer to a wire rack and place a spoonful of jam on the centre of each cookie. Repeat with the remaining cookies.

Microwave Florentines

Makes 12

50 g/2 oz/¼ cup butter or margarine
50 g/2 oz/¼ cup demerara sugar
15 ml/1 tbsp golden (light corn) syrup
50 g/2 oz/¼ cup glacé (candied) cherries
75 g/3 oz/¾ cup walnuts, chopped
25 g/1 oz/3 tbsp sultanas (golden raisins)
25 g/1 oz/¼ cup flaked (slivered) almonds
30 ml/2 tbsp chopped mixed (candied) peel
25 g/1 oz/¼ cup plain (all-purpose) flour
100 g/4 oz/1 cup plain (semi-sweet) chocolate, broken up (optional)

Microwave the butter or margarine, sugar and syrup on High for 1 minute until melted. Stir in the cherries, walnuts, sultanas and almonds, then mix in the mixed peel and flour. Place teaspoonfuls of the mixture, well apart, on greaseproof (waxed) paper and cook four at a time on High for 1½ minutes each batch. Neaten the edges with a knife, leave to cool on the paper for 3 minutes, then transfer to a wire rack to finish cooling. Repeat with the remaining biscuits. If liked, melt the chocolate in a bowl for 30 seconds and spread over one side of the florentines, then leave to set.

Microwave Hazelnut and Cherry Biscuits

Makes 24

100 g/4 oz/½ cup butter or margarine, softened
100 g/4 oz/½ cup caster (superfine) sugar
1 egg, beaten
175 g/6 oz/1½ cups plain (all-purpose) flour
50 g/2 oz/½ cup ground hazelnuts
100 g/4 oz/½ cup glacé (candied) cherries

Cream together the butter or margarine and sugar until light and fluffy. Gradually beat in the egg, then fold in the flour, hazelnuts and cherries. Place spoonfuls well spaced out on microwave baking (cookie) sheets and microwave eight biscuits (cookies) at a time on High for about 2 minutes until just firm.

Microwave Sultana Biscuits

Makes 24

225 g/8 oz/2 cups plain (all-purpose) flour
5 ml/1 tsp ground mixed (apple-pie) spice
175 g/6 oz/¾ cup butter or margarine, softened
100 g/4 oz/⅔ cup sultanas (golden raisins)
175 g/6 oz/¾ cup demerara sugar

Mix together the flour and mixed spice, then blend in the butter or margarine, sultanas and 100 g/4 oz/½ cup of the sugar to make a soft dough. Roll into two sausage shapes about 18 cm/7 in long and roll in the remaining sugar. Cut into slices and arrange six at a time on a greased microwave baking (cookie) sheet and microwave on High for 2 minutes. Leave to cool on a wire rack and repeat with the remaining biscuits (cookies).

Microwave Banana Bread

Makes one 450 g/1 lb loaf

75 g/3 oz/⅓ cup butter or margarine, softened
175 g/6 oz/¾ cup caster (superfine) sugar
2 eggs, lightly beaten
200 g/7 oz/1¾ cups plain (all-purpose) flour
10 ml/2 tsp baking powder
2.5 ml/½ tsp bicarbonate of soda (baking soda)
A pinch of salt
2 ripe bananas
15 ml/1 tbsp lemon juice
60 ml/4 tbsp milk
50 g/2 oz/½ cup walnuts, chopped

Cream together the butter or margarine and sugar until light and fluffy. Gradually beat in the eggs, then fold in the flour, baking powder, bicarbonate of soda and salt. Mash the bananas with the lemon juice, then fold into the mixture with the milk and walnuts. Spoon into a greased and floured 450 g/1 lb microwave loaf tin (pan) and microwave on High for 12 minutes. Remove from the oven, cover with foil and leave to cool for 10 minutes, then turn out on to a wire rack to finish cooling.

Microwave Cheese Bread

Makes one 450 g/1 lb loaf

50 g/2 oz/¼ cup butter or margarine
250 ml/8 fl oz/1 cup milk
2 eggs, lightly beaten
225 g/8 oz/2 cups plain
(all-purpose) flour
10 ml/2 tsp baking powder
10 ml/2 tsp mustard powder
2.5 ml/½ tsp salt
175 g/6 oz/1½ cups Cheddar cheese,
grated

Melt the butter or margarine in a small bowl on High for 1 minute. Stir in the milk and eggs. Mix together the flour, baking powder, mustard, salt and 100 g/4 oz/1 cup of the cheese. Stir in the milk mixture until well blended. Spoon into a microwave loaf tin (pan) and microwave on High for 9 minutes. Sprinkle with the remaining cheese, cover with foil and leave to stand for 20 minutes.

Microwave Walnut Loaf

Makes one 450 g/1 lb loaf

225 g/8 oz/2 cups plain
(all-purpose) flour
300 g/10 oz/1¼ cups caster (superfine)
sugar
5 ml/1 tsp baking powder
A pinch of salt
100 g/4 oz/½ cup butter or margarine,
softened
150 ml/¼ pt/⅔ cup milk
2.5 ml/½ tsp vanilla essence (extract)
4 egg whites
50 g/2 oz/½ cup walnuts, chopped

Mix together the flour, sugar, baking powder and salt. Beat in the butter or margarine, then the milk and vanilla essence. Beat in the egg whites until creamy, then fold in the nuts. Spoon into a greased and floured 450 g/1 lb microwave loaf tin (pan) and microwave on High for 12 minutes. Remove from the oven, cover with foil and leave to cool for 10 minutes, then turn out on to a wire rack to finish cooling.

No-bake Cakes and Bars

When time runs out completely or you are short of ingredients in your store cupboard, there are still some tasty treats you can create for the tea table.

No-bake Amaretti Cake

Makes one 20 cm/8 in cake

100 g/4 oz/½ cup butter or margarine
175 g/6 oz/1½ cups plain (semi-sweet) chocolate
75 g/3 oz Amaretti biscuits (cookies), coarsely crushed
175 g/6 oz/1½ cups walnuts, chopped
50 g/2 oz/½ cup pine nuts
75 g/3 oz/⅓ cup glacé (candied) cherries, chopped
30 ml/2 tbsp Grand Marnier
225 g/8 oz/1 cup Mascarpone cheese

Melt the butter or margarine and chocolate in a heatproof bowl set over a pan of gently simmering water. Remove from the heat and stir in the biscuits, nuts and cherries. Spoon into a sandwich tin (pan) lined with clingfilm (plastic wrap) and press down gently. Chill for 1 hour until set. Turn out on to a serving plate and remove the clingfilm. Beat the Grand Marnier into the Mascarpone and spoon over the base.

American Crispy Rice Bars

Makes about 24 bars

50 g/2 oz/¼ cup butter or margarine
225 g/8 oz white marshmallows
5 ml/1 tsp vanilla essence (extract)
150 g/5 oz/5 cups puffed rice cereal

Melt the butter or margarine in a large pan over a low heat. Add the marshmallows and cook, stirring continuously, until the marshmallows have melted and the mixture is syrupy. Remove from the heat and add the vanilla essence. Stir in the rice cereal until evenly coated. Press into a 23 cm/9 in square tin (pan) and cut into bars. Leave to set.

Apricot Squares

Makes 12

50 g/2 oz/¼ cup butter or margarine
175 g/6 oz/1 small can evaporated milk
15 ml/1 tbsp clear honey
45 ml/3 tbsp apple juice
50 g/2 oz/¼ cup soft brown sugar
50 g/2 oz/⅓ cup sultanas (golden raisins)
225 g/8 oz/1⅓ cups ready-to-eat dried apricots, chopped
100 g/4 oz/1 cup desiccated (shredded) coconut
225 g/8 oz/2 cups rolled oats

Melt the butter or margarine with the milk, honey, apple juice and sugar. Stir in the remaining ingredients. Press into a greased 25 cm/12 in baking tin (pan) and chill before cutting into squares.

Apricot Swiss Roll Cake

Makes one 23 cm/9 in cake

*400 g/14 oz/1 large can apricot halves,
drained and juice reserved*
50 g/2 oz/½ cup custard powder
*75 g/3 oz/¼ cup apricot jelly (clear
conserve)*
*75 g/3 oz/½ cup ready-to-eat dried
apricots, chopped*
*400 g/14 oz/1 large can condensed
milk*
225 g/8 oz/1 cup cottage cheese
45 ml/3 tbsp lemon juice
1 Swiss Roll (page 14), sliced

Make up the apricot juice with water to make 500 ml/17 fl oz/2¼ cups. Mix the custard powder to a paste with a little of the liquid, then bring the remainder to the boil. Stir in the custard paste and apricot jelly and simmer until thick and shiny, stirring continuously. Mash the canned apricots and add to the mixture with the dried apricots. Leave to cool, stirring occasionally.

Beat together the condensed milk, cottage cheese and lemon juice until well blended, then stir into the jelly mixture. Line a 23 cm/9 in cake tin (pan) with clingfilm (plastic wrap) and arrange the Swiss (jelly) roll slices over the base and sides of the tin. Spoon in the cake mixture and chill until set. Turn out carefully when ready to serve.

Broken Biscuit Cakes

Makes 12

100 g/4 oz/½ cup butter or margarine
30 ml/2 tbsp caster (superfine) sugar
15 ml/1 tbsp golden (light corn) syrup
*30 ml/2 tbsp cocoa (unsweetened
chocolate) powder*
*225 g/8 oz/2 cups broken biscuit
(cookie) crumbs*
*50 g/2 oz/⅓ cup sultanas (golden
raisins)*

Melt the butter or margarine with the sugar and syrup without allowing the mixture to boil. Stir in the cocoa, biscuits and sultanas. Press into a greased 25 cm/10 in baking tin (pan), leave to cool, then chill until firm. Cut into squares.

No-bake Buttermilk Cake

Makes one 23 cm/9 in cake

30 ml/2 tbsp custard powder
*100 g/4 oz/½ cup caster (superfine)
sugar*
450 ml/¾ pt/2 cups milk
175 ml/6 fl oz/¾ cup buttermilk
25 g/1 oz/2 tbsp butter or margarine
*400 g/12 oz plain biscuits (cookies),
crushed*
120 ml/4 fl oz/½ cup whipping cream

Blend the custard powder and sugar to a paste with a little of the milk. Bring the remaining milk to the boil. Stir it into the paste, then return the whole mixture to the pan and stir over a low heat for about 5 minutes until thickened. Stir in the buttermilk and butter or margarine. Spoon layers of crushed biscuits and custard mixture into a 23 cm/9 in cake tin (pan) lined with clingfilm (plastic wrap), or into a glass dish. Press down gently and chill until set. Whip the cream until stiff, then pipe rosettes of cream on the top of the cake. Either serve from the dish, or lift out carefully to serve.

Chestnut Slice

Makes one 900 g/2 lb loaf

225 g/8 oz/2 cups plain (semi-sweet)
   chocolate
100 g/4 oz/½ cup butter or margarine,
   softened
100 g/4 oz/½ cup caster (superfine)
   sugar
450 g/1 lb/1 large can unsweetened
   chestnut purée
25 g/1 oz/¼ cup rice flour
A few drops of vanilla essence
   (extract)
150 ml/¼ pt/⅔ cup whipping cream,
   whipped
Grated chocolate to decorate

Melt the plain chocolate in a heatproof bowl over a pan of gently simmering water. Cream together the butter or margarine and sugar until light and fluffy. Beat in the chestnut purée, chocolate, rice flour and vanilla essence. Turn into a greased and lined 900 g/2 lb loaf tin (pan) and chill until firm. Decorate with whipped cream and grated chocolate before serving.

Chestnut Sponge Cake

Makes one 900 g/2 lb cake

For the cake:
400 g/14 oz/1 large can sweetened
   chestnut purée
100 g/4 oz/½ cup butter or margarine,
   softened
1 egg
A few drops of vanilla essence
   (extract)
30 ml/2 tbsp brandy
24 sponge finger biscuits (cookies)
For the glaze:
30 ml/2 tbsp cocoa (unsweetened
   chocolate) powder
15 ml/1 tbsp caster (superfine) sugar
30 ml/2 tbsp water
For the butter cream:
100 g/4 oz/½ cup butter or margarine,
   softened
100 g/4 oz/⅔ cup icing (confectioners')
   sugar, sifted
15 ml/1 tbsp coffee essence (extract)

To make the cake, blend together the chestnut purée, butter or margarine, egg, vanilla essence and 15 ml/1 tbsp of the brandy and beat until smooth. Grease and line a 900 g/2 lb loaf tin (pan) and line the base and sides with the sponge fingers. Sprinkle the remaining brandy over the biscuits and spoon the chestnut mixture into the centre. Chill until firm.

Lift out of the tin and remove the lining paper. Dissolve the glaze ingredients in a heatproof bowl set over a pan of gently simmering water, stirring until smooth. Leave to cool slightly, then brush most of the glaze over the top of the cake. Cream together the butter cream ingredients until smooth, then pipe into swirls around the edge of the cake. Drizzle with the reserved glaze to finish.

Chocolate and Almond Bars

Makes 12

175 g/6 oz/1½ cups plain (semi-sweet) chocolate, chopped
3 eggs, separated
120 ml/4 fl oz/½ cup milk
10 ml/2 tsp powdered gelatine
120 ml/4 fl oz/½ cup double (heavy) cream
45 ml/3 tbsp caster (superfine) sugar
60 ml/4 tbsp flaked (slivered) almonds, toasted

Melt the chocolate in a heatproof bowl set over a pan of gently simmering water. Remove from the heat and beat in the egg yolks. Boil the milk in a separate pan, then whisk in the gelatine. Stir into the chocolate mixture, then stir in the cream. Beat the egg whites until stiff, then add the sugar and beat again until stiff and glossy. Fold into the mixture. Spoon into a greased and lined 450 g/1 lb loaf tin (pan), sprinkle with the toasted almonds and leave to cool, then chill for at least 3 hours until set. Turn over and cut into thick slices to serve

Chocolate Crisp Cake

Makes one 450 g/1 lb loaf

150 g/5 oz/⅔ cup butter or margarine
30 ml/2 tbsp golden (light corn) syrup
175 g/6 oz/1½ cups digestive biscuit (Graham cracker) crumbs
50 g/2 oz/2 cups puffed rice cereal
25 g/1 oz/3 tbsp sultanas (golden raisins)
25 g/1 oz/2 tbsp glacé (candied) cherries, chopped
225 g/8 oz/2 cups chocolate chips
30 ml/2 tbsp water
175 g/6 oz/1 cup icing (confectioners') sugar, sifted

Melt 100 g/4 oz/½ cup of the butter or margarine with the syrup, then remove from the heat and stir in the biscuit crumbs, cereal, sultanas, cherries and three-quarters of the chocolate chips. Spoon into a greased and lined 450 g/1 lb loaf tin (pan) and smooth the top. Chill until firm. Melt the remaining butter or margarine with the remaining chocolate and the water. Stir in the icing sugar and mix until smooth. Remove the cake from the tin and halve lengthways. Sandwich together with half the chocolate icing (frosting), place on a serving plate, then pour over the remaining icing. Chill before serving.

Chocolate Crumb Squares

Makes about 24

225 g/8 oz digestive biscuits (Graham crackers)
100 g/4 oz/½ cup butter or margarine
25 g/1 oz/2 tbsp caster (superfine) sugar
15 ml/1 tbsp golden (light corn) syrup
45 ml/3 tbsp cocoa (unsweetened chocolate) powder
200 g/7 oz/1¾ cups chocolate cake covering

Place the biscuits in a plastic bag and crush with a rolling pin. Melt the butter or margarine in a pan, then stir in the sugar and syrup. Remove from the heat and stir in the biscuit crumbs and cocoa. Turn into a greased and lined 18 cm/7 in square cake tin and press down evenly. Leave to cool, then chill in the fridge until set.
Melt the chocolate in a heatproof bowl set over a pan of gently simmering water. Spread over the biscuit, marking into lines with a fork while setting. Cut into squares when firm.

Chocolate Fridge Cake

Makes one 450 g/1 lb cake

100 g/4 oz/½ cup soft brown sugar
100 g/4 oz/½ cup butter or margarine
50 g/2 oz/½ cup drinking chocolate
powder
25 g/1 oz/¼ cup cocoa (unsweetened
chocolate) powder
30 ml/2 tbsp golden (light corn) syrup
150 g/5 oz digestive biscuits (Graham
crackers) or rich tea biscuits
50 g/2 oz/¼ cup glacé (candied)
cherries or mixed nuts and raisins
100 g/4 oz/1 cup milk chocolate

Place the sugar, butter or margarine, drinking chocolate, cocoa and syrup in a pan and warm gently until the butter has melted, stirring well. Remove from the heat and crumble in the biscuits. Stir in the cherries or nuts and raisins and spoon into a 450 g/1 lb loaf tin (pan). Leave in the fridge to cool.

Melt the chocolate in a heatproof bowl over a pan of gently simmering water. Spread over the top of the cooled cake and slice when set.

Chocolate and Fruit Cake

Makes one 18 cm/7 in cake

100 g/4 oz/½ cup butter or margarine,
melted
100 g/4 oz/½ cup soft brown sugar
225 g/8 oz/2 cups digestive biscuit
(Graham cracker) crumbs
50 g/2 oz/⅓ cup sultanas
(golden raisins)
45 ml/3 tbsp cocoa (unsweetened
chocolate) powder
1 egg, beaten
A few drops of vanilla essence
(extract)

Mix the butter or margarine and sugar, then stir in the remaining ingredients and beat well. Spoon into a greased 18 cm/7 in sandwich tin (pan) and smooth the surface. Chill until set.

Chocolate and Ginger Squares

Makes 24

100 g/4 oz/½ cup butter or margarine
100 g/4 oz/½ cup soft brown sugar
30 ml/2 tbsp cocoa (unsweetened
chocolate) powder
1 egg, lightly beaten
225 g/8 oz/2 cups ginger biscuit
(cookie) crumbs
15 ml/1 tbsp chopped crystallised
(candied) ginger

Melt the butter or margarine, then stir in the sugar and cocoa until well blended. Mix in the egg, biscuit crumbs and ginger. Press into a Swiss roll tin (jelly roll pan) and chill until firm. Cut into squares.

Luxury Chocolate and Ginger Squares

Makes 24

100 g/4 oz/½ cup butter or margarine
100 g/4 oz/½ cup soft brown sugar
30 ml/2 tbsp cocoa (unsweetened
chocolate) powder
1 egg, lightly beaten
225 g/8 oz/2 cups ginger biscuit
(cookie) crumbs
15 ml/1 tbsp chopped crystallised
(candied) ginger
100 g/4 oz/1 cup plain (semi-sweet)
chocolate

Melt the butter or margarine, then stir in the sugar and cocoa until well blended. Mix in the egg, biscuit crumbs and ginger. Press into a Swiss roll tin (jelly roll pan) and chill until firm.

Melt the chocolate in a heatproof bowl set over a pan of gently simmering water. Spread over the cake and leave to set. Cut into squares when the chocolate is almost hard.

Honey Chocolate Cookies

Makes 12

225 g/8 oz/1 cup butter or margarine
30 ml/2 tbsp clear honey
90 ml/6 tbsp carob or cocoa
(unsweetened chocolate) powder
225 g/8 oz/2 cups sweet biscuit
(cookie) crumbs

Melt the butter or margarine, honey and carob or cocoa powder in a pan until well blended. Mix in the biscuit crumbs. Spoon into a greased 20 cm/8 in square cake tin (pan) and leave to cool, then cut into squares.

Chocolate Layer Cake

Makes one 450 g/1 lb cake

300 ml/½ pt/1¼ cups double (heavy)
cream
225 g/8 oz/2 cups plain (semi-sweet)
chocolate, broken up
5 ml/1 tsp vanilla essence (extract)
20 plain biscuits (cookies)

Heat the cream in a pan over a low heat until almost boiling. Remove from the heat and add the chocolate, stir, cover and leave for 5 minutes. Stir in the vanilla essence and mix until well blended, then chill until the mixture begins to thicken.

Line a 450g /1 lb loaf tin (pan) with clingfilm (plastic wrap). Spread a layer of chocolate on the bottom, then arrange a few biscuits in a layer on top. Continue layering the chocolate and biscuits until you have used them up. Finish with a layer of chocolate. Cover with clingfilm and chill for at least 3 hours. Turn out the cake and remove the clingfilm.

Nice Chocolate Bars

Makes 12

100 g/4 oz/½ cup butter or margarine
30 ml/2 tbsp golden (light corn) syrup
30 ml/2 tbsp cocoa (unsweetened
chocolate) powder
225 g/8 oz/1 packet Nice or plain
biscuits (cookies), roughly crushed
100 g/4 oz/1 cup plain (semi-sweet)
chocolate, diced

Melt the butter or margarine and syrup, then remove from the heat and stir in the cocoa and crushed biscuits. Spread the mixture in a 23 cm/9 in square cake tin (pan) and level the surface. Melt the chocolate in a heatproof bowl over a pan of gently simmering water and spread over the top. Leave to cool slightly, then cut into bars or squares and chill until set.

Chocolate Praline Squares

Makes 12

100 g/4 oz/½ cup butter or margarine
30 ml/2 tbsp caster (superfine) sugar
15 ml/1 tbsp golden (light corn) syrup
15 ml/1 tbsp drinking chocolate
powder
225 g/8 oz digestive biscuits (Graham
crackers), crushed
200 g/7 oz/1¾ cups plain (semi-sweet)
chocolate
100 g/4 oz/1 cup chopped mixed nuts

Melt the butter or margarine, sugar, syrup and drinking chocolate in a pan. Bring to the boil, then boil for 40 seconds. Remove from the heat and stir in the biscuits and nuts. Press into a greased 28 × 18 cm/11 × 7 in cake tin (pan). Melt the chocolate in a heatproof bowl over a pan of gently simmering water. Spread over the biscuits and leave to cool, then chill for 2 hours before cutting into squares.

Coconut Crunchies

Makes 12

100 g/4 oz/1 cup plain (semi-sweet)
chocolate
30 ml/2 tbsp milk
30 ml/2 tbsp golden (light corn) syrup
100 g/4 oz/4 cups puffed rice cereal
50 g/2 oz/½ cup desiccated (shredded)
coconut

Melt the chocolate, milk and syrup in a pan. Remove from the heat and stir in the cereal and coconut. Spoon into paper cake cases (cupcake papers) and leave to set.

Crunch Bars

Makes 12

175 g/6 oz/¾ cup butter or margarine
50 g/2 oz/¼ cup soft brown sugar
30 ml/2 tbsp golden (light corn) syrup
45 ml/3 tbsp cocoa (unsweetened
chocolate) powder
75 g/3 oz/½ cup raisins or sultanas
(golden raisins)
350 g/12 oz/3 cups oat crunch cereal
225 g/8 oz/2 cups plain (semi-sweet)
chocolate

Melt the butter or margarine with the sugar, syrup and cocoa. Stir in the raisins or sultanas and the cereal. Press the mixture into a greased 25 cm/12 in baking tin (pan). Melt the chocolate in a heatproof bowl over a pan of gently simmering water. Spread over the bars and leave to cool, then chill before cutting into bars.

Coconut and Raisin Crunchies

Makes 12

100 g/4 oz/1 cup white chocolate
30 ml/2 tbsp milk
30 ml/2 tbsp golden (light corn) syrup
175 g/6 oz/6 cups puffed rice cereal
50 g/2 oz/⅓ cup raisins

Melt the chocolate, milk and syrup in a pan. Remove from the heat and stir in the cereal and raisins. Spoon into paper cake cases (cupcake papers) and leave to set.

Coffee Milk Squares

Makes 20

25 g/1 oz/2 tbsp powdered gelatine
75 ml/5 tbsp cold water
225 g/8 oz/2 cups plain biscuit
(cookie) crumbs
50 g/2 oz/¼ cup butter or margarine,
melted
400 g/14 oz/1 large can evaporated
milk
150 g/5 oz/⅔ cup caster (superfine)
sugar
400 ml/14 fl oz/1¾ cups strong black
coffee, ice cold
Whipped cream and crystallised
(candied) orange slices to decorate

Sprinkle the gelatine over the water in a bowl and leave until spongy. Stand the bowl in a pan of hot water and leave until dissolved. Leave to cool slightly. Stir the biscuit crumbs into the melted butter and press into the base and sides of a greased 30 × 20 cm/12 × 8 in rectangular cake tin (pan). Beat the evaporated milk until thick, then gradually beat in the sugar, followed by the dissolved gelatine and the coffee. Spoon over the base and chill until set. Cut into squares and decorate with piped whipped cream and crystallised (candied) orange slices.

Photograph opposite: **Baklava (page 166)**

224

No-bake Fruit Cake

Makes one 23 cm/9 in cake

450 g/1 lb/2⅔ cups dried mixed fruit (fruit cake mix)
450 g/1 lb plain biscuits (cookies), crushed
100 g/4 oz/½ cup butter or margarine, melted
100 g/4 oz/½ cup soft brown sugar
400 g/14 oz/1 large can condensed milk
5 ml/1 tsp vanilla essence (extract)

Mix together all the ingredients until well blended. Spoon into a greased 23 cm/9 in cake tin (pan) lined with clingfilm (plastic wrap) and press down. Chill until firm.

Fruity Squares

Makes about 12

100 g/4 oz/½ cup butter or margarine
100 g/4 oz/½ cup soft brown sugar
400 g/14 oz/1 large can condensed milk
5 ml/1 tsp vanilla essence (extract)
250 g/9 oz/1½ cups dried mixed fruit (fruit cake mix)
100 g/4 oz/½ cup glacé (candied) cherries
50 g/2 oz/½ cup chopped mixed nuts
400 g/14 oz plain biscuits (cookies), crushed

Melt the butter or margarine and sugar over a low heat. Stir in the condensed milk and vanilla essence and remove from the heat. Mix in the remaining ingredients. Press into a greased Swiss roll tin (jelly roll pan) and chill for 24 hours until firm. Cut into squares.

Photograph opposite: **Strawberry Mousse Gâteau (page 188)**

Fruit and Fibre Crackles

Makes 12

100 g/4 oz/1 cup plain (semi-sweet) chocolate
50 g/2 oz/¼ cup butter or margarine
15 ml/1 tbsp golden (light corn) syrup
100 g/4 oz/1 cup fruit and fibre breakfast cereal

Melt the chocolate in a heatproof bowl over a pan of gently simmering water. Beat in the butter or margarine and syrup. Stir in the cereal. Spoon into paper cake cases (cupcake papers) and leave to cool and set.

Nougat Layer Cake

Makes one 900 g/2 lb cake

15 g/½ oz/1 tbsp powdered gelatine
100 ml/3½ fl oz/6½ tbsp water
1 packet trifle sponges
225 g/8 oz/1 cup butter or margarine, softened
50 g/2 oz/¼ cup caster (superfine) sugar
400 g/14 oz/1 large can condensed milk
5 ml/1 tsp lemon juice
5 ml/1 tsp vanilla essence (extract)
5 ml/1 tsp cream of tartar
100 g/4 oz/⅔ cup dried mixed fruit (fruit cake mix), chopped

Sprinkle the gelatine over the water in a small bowl, then stand the bowl in a pan of hot water until the gelatine is transparent. Cool slightly. Line a 900 g/2 lb loaf tin (pan) with foil so that the foil will cover the top of the tin, then arrange half the trifle sponges on the base. Beat together the butter or margarine and sugar until creamy, then beat in all the remaining ingredients. Spoon into the tin and arrange the remaining trifle sponges on top. Cover with foil and put a weight on the top. Chill until firm.

Milk and Nutmeg Squares

Makes 20

For the base:
225 g/8 oz/2 cups plain biscuit (cookie) crumbs
30 ml/2 tbsp soft brown sugar
2.5 ml/½ tsp grated nutmeg
100 g/4 oz/½ cup butter or margarine, melted
For the filling:
1.2 litres/2 pts/5 cups milk
25 g/1 oz/2 tbsp butter or margarine
2 eggs, separated
225 g/8 oz/1 cup caster (superfine) sugar
100 g/4 oz/1 cup cornflour (cornstarch)
50 g/2 oz/½ cup plain (all-purpose) flour
5 ml/1 tsp baking powder
A pinch of grated nutmeg
Grated nutmeg for sprinkling

To make the base, mix the biscuit crumbs, sugar and nutmeg into the melted butter or margarine and press into the base of a greased 30 × 20 cm/12 × 8 in cake tin (pan).

To make the filling, bring 1 litre/1¾ pts/4¼ cups of the milk to the boil in a large pan. Add the butter or margarine. Beat the egg yolks with the remaining milk. Mix in the sugar, cornflour, flour, baking powder and nutmeg. Beat a little of the boiling milk into the egg yolk mixture until blended to a paste, then mix the paste into the boiling milk, stirring continuously over a low heat for a few minutes until thickened. Remove from the heat. Beat the egg whites until stiff, then fold them into the mixture. Spoon over the base and sprinkle generously with nutmeg. Leave to cool, then chill and cut into squares before serving.

Muesli Crunch

Makes about 16 squares

400 g/14 oz/3½ cups plain (semi-sweet) chocolate
45 ml/3 tbsp golden (light corn) syrup
25 g/1 oz/2 tbsp butter or margarine
About 225 g/8 oz/⅔ cup muesli

Melt together half the chocolate, the syrup and butter or margarine. Gradually stir in enough muesli to make a stiff mixture. Press into a greased Swiss roll tin (jelly roll pan). Melt the remaining chocolate and smooth over the top. Chill in the fridge before cutting into squares.

Orange Mousse Squares

Makes 20

25 g/1 oz/2 tbsp powdered gelatine
75 ml/5 tbsp cold water
225 g/8 oz/2 cups plain biscuit (cookie) crumbs
50 g/2 oz/¼ cup butter or margarine, melted
400 g/14 oz/1 large can evaporated milk
150 g/5 oz/⅔ cup caster (superfine) sugar
400 ml/14 fl oz/1¾ cups orange juice
Whipped cream and chocolate sweets to decorate

Sprinkle the gelatine over the water in a bowl and leave until spongy. Stand the bowl in a pan of hot water and leave until dissolved. Leave to cool slightly. Stir the biscuit crumbs into the melted butter and press on to the base and sides of a greased 30 × 20 cm/12 × 8 in shallow cake tin (pan). Beat the milk until thick, then gradually beat in the sugar, followed by the dissolved gelatine and the orange juice. Spoon over the base and chill until set. Cut into squares and decorate with piped whipped cream and chocolate sweets.

Peanut Squares

Makes 18

225 g/8 oz/2 cups plain biscuit
(cookie) crumbs
100 g/4 oz/½ cup butter or margarine,
melted
225 g/8 oz/1 cup crunchy peanut
butter
25 g/1 oz/2 tbsp glacé (candied)
cherries
25 g/1 oz/3 tbsp currants

Mix together all the ingredients until well blended. Press into a greased 25 cm/12 in baking tin (pan) and chill until firm, then cut into squares.

Peppermint Caramel Cakes

Makes 16

400 g/14 oz/1 large can condensed
milk
600 ml/1 pt/2½ cups milk
30 ml/2 tbsp custard powder
225 g/8 oz/2 cups digestive biscuit
(Graham cracker) crumbs
100 g/4 oz/1 cup peppermint
chocolate, broken into pieces

Place the unopened can of condensed milk in a pan filled with sufficient water to cover the can. Bring to the boil, cover and simmer for 3 hours, topping up with boiling water as necessary. Leave to cool, then open the can and remove the caramel.

Heat 500 ml/17 fl oz/2¼ cups of the milk with the caramel, bring to the boil and stir together until melted. Mix the custard powder to a paste with the remaining milk, then stir it into the pan and continue to simmer until thickened, stirring continuously. Sprinkle half the biscuit crumbs over the base of a greased 20 cm/8 in square cake tin (pan), then spoon half the caramel custard on top and sprinkle with half the chocolate. Repeat the layers, then leave to cool. Chill, then cut into portions to serve.

Rice Cookies

Makes 24

175 g/6 oz/½ cup clear honey
225 g/8 oz/1 cup granulated sugar
60 ml/4 tbsp water
350 g/12 oz/1 box puffed rice cereal
100 g/4 oz/1 cup roasted peanuts

Melt the honey, sugar and water in a large pan, then leave to cool for 5 minutes. Stir in the cereal and peanuts. Roll into balls, place in paper cake cases (cupcake papers) and leave until cool and set.

Rice and Chocolate Toffette

Makes 225 g/8 oz

50 g/2 oz/¼ cup butter or margarine
30 ml/2 tbsp golden (light corn) syrup
30 ml/2 tbsp cocoa (unsweetened
chocolate) powder
60 ml/4 tbsp caster (superfine) sugar
50 g/2 oz/½ cup ground rice

Melt the butter and syrup. Stir in the cocoa and sugar until dissolved, then stir in the ground rice. Bring gently to the boil, reduce the heat and simmer gently for 5 minutes, stirring continuously. Spoon into a greased and lined 20 cm/8 in square tin (pan) and leave to cool slightly. Cut into squares, then leave to cool completely before lifting out of the tin.

Icings and Fillings

Use these various icings (frostings) and fillings to decorate your favourite cakes.

Almond Paste

Covers the top and sides
of one 23 cm/9 in cake

225 g/8 oz/2 cups ground almonds
225 g/8 oz/1⅓ cups icing
(confectioners') sugar, sifted
225 g/8 oz/1 cup caster (superfine)
sugar
2 eggs, lightly beaten
10 ml/2 tsp lemon juice
A few drops of almond essence
(extract)

Beat together the almonds and sugars. Gradually blend in the remaining ingredients until you have a smooth paste. Wrap in clingfilm (plastic wrap) and chill before use.

Sugar-free Almond Paste

Covers the top and sides
of one 15 cm/6 in cake

100 g/4 oz/1 cup ground almonds
50 g/2 oz/½ cup fructose
25 g/1 oz/¼ cup cornflour (cornstarch)
1 egg, lightly beaten

Blend together all the ingredients until you have a smooth paste. Wrap in clingfilm (plastic wrap) and chill before using.

Royal Icing

Covers the top and sides
of one 20 cm/8 in cake

5 ml/1 tsp lemon juice
2 egg whites
450 g/1 lb/2⅔ cups icing
(confectioners') sugar, sifted
5 ml/1 tsp glycerine (optional)

Mix together the lemon juice and egg whites and gradually beat in the icing sugar until the icing (frosting) is smooth and white and will coat the back of a spoon. A few drops of glycerine will prevent the icing from becoming too brittle. Cover with a damp cloth and leave to stand for 20 minutes to allow any air bubbles to rise to the surface.

Icing of this consistency can be poured on to the cake and smoothed with a knife dipped in hot water. For piping, mix in extra icing sugar so that the icing is stiff enough to stand in peaks.

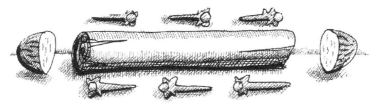

Sugar-free Icing

Makes enough to cover one
15 cm/6 in cake

50 g/2 oz/⅓ cup fructose
A pinch of salt
1 egg white
2.5 ml/½ tsp lemon juice

Process the fructose powder in a food processor until it is as fine as icing sugar. Blend in the salt. Transfer to a heatproof bowl and whisk in the egg white and lemon juice. Place the bowl over a pan of gently simmering water and continue to whisk until stiff peaks form. Remove from the heat and whisk until cool.

Fondant Icing

Makes enough to cover one
20 cm/8 in cake

450 g/1 lb/2 cups caster (superfine) or
lump sugar
150 ml/¼ pt/⅔ cup water
15 ml/1 tbsp liquid glucose or
2.5 ml/½ tsp cream of tartar

Dissolve the sugar in the water in a large, heavy-based pan over a low heat. Wipe down the sides of the pan with a brush dipped in cold water to prevent crystals forming. Dissolve the cream of tartar in a little water, then stir into the pan. Bring to the boil and boil steadily to 115°C/242°F when a drop of icing forms a soft ball when dropped into cold water. Slowly pour the syrup into a heatproof bowl and leave until a skin forms. Beat the icing with a wooden spoon until it becomes opaque and firm. Knead until smooth. Warm in a heatproof bowl over a pan of hot water to soften, if necessary, before use.

Butter Icing

Makes enough to fill and cover one
20 cm/8 in cake

100 g/4 oz/½ cup butter or margarine,
softened
225 g/ 8 oz/1⅓ cups icing
(confectioners') sugar, sifted
30 ml/2 tbsp milk

Beat the butter or margarine until soft. Gradually beat in the icing sugar and milk until well blended.

Chocolate Butter Icing

Makes enough to fill and cover one
20 cm/8 in cake

30 ml/2 tbsp cocoa (unsweetened
chocolate) powder
15 ml/1 tbsp boiling water
100 g/4 oz/½ cup butter or margarine,
softened
225 g/8 oz/1⅓ cups icing
(confectioners') sugar, sifted
15 ml/1 tbsp milk

Mix the cocoa to a paste with the boiling water, then leave to cool. Beat the butter or margarine until soft. Gradually beat in the icing sugar, milk and cocoa mixture until well blended.

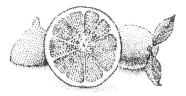

229

White Chocolate Butter Icing

Makes enough to fill and cover one 20 cm/8 in cake

100 g/4 oz/1 cup white chocolate
100 g/4 oz/½ cup butter or margarine, softened
225 g/8 oz/1⅓ cups icing (confectioners') sugar, sifted
15 ml/1 tbsp milk

Melt the chocolate in a heatproof bowl set over a pan of gently simmering water, then leave to cool slightly. Beat the butter or margarine until soft. Gradually beat in the icing sugar, milk and chocolate until well blended.

Coffee Butter Icing

Makes enough to fill and cover one 20 cm/8 in cake

100 g/4 oz/½ cup butter or margarine, softened
225 g/8 oz/1⅓ cups icing (confectioners') sugar, sifted
15 ml/1 tbsp milk
15 ml/1 tbsp coffee essence (extract)

Beat the butter or margarine until soft. Gradually beat in the icing sugar, milk and coffee essence until well blended.

Lemon Butter Icing

Makes enough to fill and cover one 20 cm/8 in cake

100 g/4 oz/½ cup butter or margarine, softened
225 g/8 oz/1⅓ cups icing (confectioners') sugar, sifted
30 ml/2 tbsp lemon juice
Grated rind of 1 lemon

Beat the butter or margarine until soft. Gradually beat in the icing sugar, lemon juice and rind until well blended.

Orange Butter Icing

Makes enough to fill and cover one 20 cm/8 in cake

100 g/4 oz/½ cup butter or margarine, softened
225 g/8 oz/1⅓ cups icing (confectioners') sugar, sifted
30 ml/2 tbsp orange juice
Grated rind of 1 orange

Beat the butter or margarine until soft. Gradually beat in the icing sugar, orange juice and rind until well blended.

Cream Cheese Icing

Makes enough to cover one 25 cm/9 in cake

75 g/3 oz/⅓ cup cream cheese
30 ml/2 tbsp butter or margarine
350 g/12 oz/2 cups icing (confectioners') sugar, sifted
5 ml/1 tsp vanilla essence (extract)

Beat together the cheese and butter or margarine until light and fluffy. Gradually beat in the icing sugar and vanilla essence until you have a smooth, creamy icing.

Orange Icing

Makes enough to cover one 25 cm/9 in cake

250 g/9 oz/1½ cups icing (confectioners') sugar, sifted
30 ml/2 tbsp butter or margarine, softened
A few drops of almond essence (extract)
60 ml/4 tbsp orange juice

Place the icing sugar in a bowl and blend in the butter or margarine and the almond essence. Gradually blend in enough of the orange juice to make a stiff icing.

Orange Liqueur Icing

Makes enough to cover one
20 cm/8 in cake

100 g/4 oz/½ cup butter or margarine,
softened
450 g/1 lb/2⅔ cups icing
(confectioners') sugar, sifted
60 ml/4 tbsp orange liqueur
15 ml/1 tbsp grated orange rind

Cream together the butter or margarine and sugar until light and fluffy. Beat in enough of the orange liqueur to give a spreadable consistency, then stir in the orange rind.

Glacé Icing

Makes enough to cover one
20 cm/8 in cake

100 g/4 oz/⅔ cup icing (confectioners')
sugar, sifted
25–30 ml/1½–2 tbsp water
A few drops of food colouring
(optional)

Place the sugar in a bowl and mix in the water a little at a time until the icing is smooth. Colour with a few drops of food colouring, if liked. The icing will turn opaque if spread over cold cakes or transparent if spread over warm cakes.

Coffee Glacé Icing

Makes enough to cover one
20 cm/8 in cake

100 g/4 oz/⅔ cup icing (confectioners')
sugar, sifted
25–30 ml/1½–2 tbsp very strong black
coffee

Place the sugar in a bowl and mix in the coffee a little at a time until the icing is smooth.

Lemon Glacé Icing

Makes enough to cover one
20 cm/8 in cake

100 g/4 oz/⅔ cup icing (confectioners')
sugar, sifted
25–30 ml/1½–2 tbsp lemon juice
Finely grated rind of 1 lemon

Place the sugar in a bowl and mix in the lemon juice and rind a little at a time until the icing is smooth.

Orange Glacé Icing

Makes enough to cover one
20 cm/8 in cake

100 g/4 oz/⅔ cup icing (confectioners')
sugar, sifted
25–30 ml/1½–2 tbsp orange juice
Finely grated rind of 1 orange

Place the sugar in a bowl and mix in the orange juice and rind a little at a time until the icing is smooth.

Rum Glacé Icing

Makes enough to cover one
20 cm/8 in cake

100 g/4 oz/⅔ cup icing (confectioners')
sugar, sifted
25–30 ml/1½–2 tbsp rum

Place the sugar in a bowl and mix in the rum a little at a time until the icing is smooth.

Vanilla Glacé Icing

Makes enough to cover one
20 cm/8 in cake

*100 g/4 oz/⅔ cup icing (confectioners')
sugar, sifted*
25 ml/1½ tbsp water
*A few drops of vanilla essence
(extract)*

Place the sugar in a bowl and mix in the water and vanilla essence a little at a time until the icing is smooth.

Boiled Chocolate Icing

Makes enough to cover one
23 cm/9 in cake

*275 g/10 oz/1¼ cups caster (superfine)
sugar*
*100 g/4 oz/1 cup plain (semi-sweet)
chocolate*
*50 g/2 oz/¼ cup cocoa (unsweetened
chocolate) powder*
120 ml/4 fl oz/½ cup water

Bring all the ingredients to the boil, stirring until well blended. Boil over a medium heat to 108°C/220°F or when a long thread forms when pulled between two teaspoons. Pour into a wide bowl and beat until thick and glossy.

Chocolate-coconut Topping

Makes enough to cover one
23 cm/9 in cake

*175 g/6 oz/1½ cups plain
(semi-sweet) chocolate*
90 ml/6 tbsp boiling water
*225 g/8 oz/2 cups desiccated
(shredded) coconut*

Purée the chocolate and water in a blender or food processor, then add the coconut and process until smooth. Sprinkle over plain cakes while still warm.

Fudge Topping

Makes enough to cover one
23 cm/9 in cake

50 g/2 oz/¼ cup butter or margarine
*45 ml/3 tbsp cocoa (unsweetened
chocolate) powder*
60 ml/4 tbsp milk
*425 g/15 oz/2½ cups icing
(confectioners') sugar, sifted*
5 ml/1 tsp vanilla essence (extract)

Melt the butter or margarine in a small pan, then stir in the cocoa and milk. Bring to the boil, stirring continuously, then remove from the heat. Gradually stir in the sugar and vanilla essence and beat until smooth.

Sweet Cream Cheese Topping

Makes enough to cover one
30 cm/12 in cake

100 g/4 oz/½ cup cream cheese
25 g/1 oz/2 tbsp butter or margarine, softened
350 g/12 oz/2 cups icing (confectioners') sugar, sifted
5 ml/1 tsp vanilla essence (extract)
30 ml/2 tbsp clear honey (optional)

Beat together the cream cheese and butter or margarine until lightly and fluffy. Gradually beat in the sugar and vanilla essence until smooth. Sweeten with a little honey, if liked.

American Velvet Frosting

Makes enough to cover two
23 cm/9 in cakes

175 g/6 oz/1½ cups plain (semi-sweet) chocolate
120 ml/4 fl oz/½ cup soured (dairy sour) cream
5 ml/1 tsp vanilla essence (extract)
A pinch of salt
400 g/14 oz/2⅓ cups icing (confectioners') sugar, sifted

Melt the chocolate in a heatproof bowl over a pan of gently simmering water. Remove from the heat and stir in the cream, vanilla essence and salt. Gradually beat in the sugar until smooth.

Butter Frosting

Makes enough to cover one
23 cm/9 in cake

50 g/2 oz/¼ cup butter or margarine, softened
250 g/9 oz/1½ cups icing (confectioners') sugar, sifted
5 ml/1 tsp vanilla essence (extract)
30 ml/2 tbsp single (light) cream

Cream the butter or margarine until soft, then gradually blend in the sugar, the vanilla essence and cream until smooth and creamy.

Caramel Frosting

Makes enough to fill and cover one
23 cm/9 in cake

100 g/4 oz/½ cup butter or margarine
225 g/8 oz/1 cup soft brown sugar
60 ml/4 tbsp milk
350 g/12 oz/2 cups icing (confectioners') sugar, sifted

Melt the butter or margarine and sugar over a low heat, stirring continuously until blended. Stir in the milk and bring to the boil. Remove from the heat and leave to cool. Beat in the icing sugar until you have a spreading consistency.

Lemon Frosting

Makes enough to cover one
23 cm/9 in cake

25 g/1 oz/2 tbsp butter or margarine
5 ml/1 tsp grated lemon rind
30 ml/2 tbsp lemon juice
250 g/9 oz/1½ cups icing (confectioners') sugar, sifted

Cream together the butter or margarine and lemon rind until light and fluffy. Gradually beat in the lemon juice and sugar until smooth.

Coffee Buttercream Frosting

Makes enough to fill and cover one
23 cm/9 in cake

1 egg white
75 g/3 oz/⅓ cup butter or margarine,
  softened
30 ml/2 tbsp hot milk
5 ml/1 tsp vanilla essence (extract)
15 ml/1 tbsp instant coffee granules
A pinch of salt
350g/12 oz/2 cups icing
  (confectioners') sugar, sifted

Blend together the egg white, butter or margarine, hot milk, vanilla essence, coffee and salt. Gradually mix in the icing sugar until smooth.

Lady Baltimore Frosting

Makes enough to fill and cover one
23 cm/9 in cake

50 g/2 oz/⅓ cup raisins, chopped
50 g/2 oz/¼ cup glacé (candied)
  cherries, chopped
50 g/2 oz/½ cup pecan nuts, chopped
25 g/1 oz/3 tbsp dried figs, chopped
2 egg whites
350 g/12 oz/1½ cups caster (superfine)
  sugar
A pinch of cream of tartar
75 ml/5 tbsp cold water
A pinch of salt
5 ml/1 tsp vanilla essence (extract)

Mix together the raisins, cherries, nuts and figs. Beat the egg whites, sugar, cream of tartar, water and salt in a heatproof bowl set over a pan of gently simmering water for about 5 minutes until stiff peaks form. Remove from the heat and beat in the vanilla essence. Mix the fruits into one-third of the frosting and use to fill the cake, then spread the remainder over the top and sides of the cake.

White Frosting

Makes enough to cover one
23 cm/9 in cake

225 g/8 oz/1 cup granulated sugar
1 egg white
30 ml/2 tbsp water
15 ml/1 tbsp golden (light corn) syrup

Beat together the sugar, egg white and water in a heatproof bowl set over a pan of gently simmering water. Continue to beat for up to 10 minutes until the mixture thickens and forms stiff peaks. Remove from the heat and add the syrup. Continue to beat until of a spreading consistency.

Creamy White Frosting

Makes enough to fill and cover one
23 cm/9 in cake

75 ml/5 tbsp single (light) cream
5 ml/1 tsp vanilla essence (extract)
75 g/3 oz/⅓ cup cream cheese
10 ml/2 tsp butter or margarine,
  softened
A pinch of salt
350 g/12 oz/2 cups icing
  (confectioners') sugar, sifted

Blend together the cream, vanilla essence, cream cheese, butter or margarine and salt until smooth. Gradually work in the icing sugar until smooth.

Fluffy White Frosting

Makes enough to fill and cover one
23 cm/9 in cake

2 egg whites
350 g/12 oz/1½ cups caster (superfine)
  sugar
A pinch of cream of tartar
75 ml/5 tbsp cold water
A pinch of salt
5 ml/1 tsp vanilla essence (extract)

Beat together together the egg whites, sugar, cream of tartar, water and salt in a heatproof bowl set over a pan of gently simmering water for about 5 minutes until stiff peaks form. Remove from the heat and beat in the vanilla essence. Use to sandwich together the cake, then spread the remainder over the top and sides of the cake.

Brown Sugar Frosting

Makes enough to cover one
23 cm/9 in cake

225 g/8 oz/1 cup soft brown sugar
1 egg white
30 ml/2 tbsp water
5 ml/1 tsp vanilla essence (extract)

Beat together the sugar, egg white and water in a heatproof bowl set over a pan of gently simmering water. Continue to beat for up to 10 minutes until the mixture thickens and forms stiff peaks. Remove from the heat and add the vanilla essence. Continue to beat until of a spreading consistency.

Vanilla Buttercream Frosting

Makes enough to fill and cover one
23 cm/9 in cake

1 egg white
75 g/3 oz/⅓ cup butter or margarine,
  softened
30 ml/2 tbsp hot milk
5 ml/1 tsp vanilla essence (extract)
A pinch of salt
350 g/12 oz/2 cups icing
  (confectioners') sugar, sifted

Blend together the egg white, butter or margarine, hot milk, vanilla essence and salt. Gradually mix in the icing sugar until smooth.

Vanilla Custard

Makes 600 ml/1 pt/2½ cups

100 g/4 oz/½ cup caster (superfine)
  sugar
50 g/2 oz/¼ cup cornflour (cornstarch)
4 egg yolks
600 ml/1 pt/2½ cups milk
1 vanilla pod (bean)
Icing (confectioners') sugar, sifted, for
  sprinkling

Whisk half the sugar with the cornflour and egg yolks until thoroughly blended. Bring the remaining sugar and the milk to the boil with the vanilla pod. Whisk the sugar mixture into the hot milk, then return to the boil, whisking continuously, and cook for 3 minutes until thickened. Pour into a bowl, sprinkle with icing sugar to prevent a skin forming and leave to cool. Beat again before use.

Custard Filling

Makes enough to fill one
23 cm/9 in cake

325 ml/11 fl oz/1⅓ cups milk
45 ml/3 tbsp cornflour (cornstarch)
60 g/2½ oz/⅓ cup caster (superfine)
sugar
1 egg
15 ml/1 tbsp butter or margarine
5 ml/1 tsp vanilla essence (extract)

Blend 30 ml/2 tbsp of milk with the cornflour, sugar and egg. Bring the remaining milk to just under boiling point in a small pan. Gradually stir the hot milk into the egg mixture. Rinse out the pan, then return the mixture to the pan and stir over a low heat until it thickens. Stir in the butter or margarine and vanilla essence. Cover with buttered greaseproof (waxed) paper and leave to cool.

Danish Custard Filling

Makes 750 ml/1¼ pts/3 cups

2 eggs
50 g/2 oz/¼ cup caster (superfine)
sugar
50 g/2 oz/½ cup plain (all-purpose)
flour
600 ml/1 pt/2½ cups milk
¼ vanilla pod (bean)

Beat together the eggs and sugar until thick. Gradually work in the flour. Bring the milk and vanilla pod to the boil. Remove the vanilla pod and stir the milk into the egg mixture. Return to the pan and simmer gently for 2–3 minutes, stirring continuously. Leave to cool before use.

Rich Danish Custard Filling

Makes 750 ml/1¼ pts/3 cups

4 egg yolks
30 ml/2 tbsp granulated sugar
25 ml/1½ tbsp plain (all-purpose)
flour
10 ml/2 tsp potato flour
450 ml/¾ pt/2 cups single (light)
cream
A few drops of vanilla essence
(extract)
150 ml/¼ pt/⅔ cup double (heavy)
cream, whipped

Blend together the egg yolks, sugar, flours and cream in a pan. Whisk over a medium heat until the mixture begins to thicken. Add the vanilla essence, then leave to cool. Fold in the whipped cream.

Crème Patissière

Makes 300 ml/½ pt/1¼ cups

2 eggs, separated
45 ml/3 tbsp cornflour (cornstarch)
300 ml/½ pt/1¼ cups milk
A few drops of vanilla essence
(extract)
50 g/2 oz/¼ cup caster (superfine)
sugar

Mix together the egg yolks, cornflour and milk in a small pan until well blended. Bring to the boil over a medium heat, then simmer for 2 minutes, stirring all the time. Stir in the vanilla essence and leave to cool.

Whisk the egg whites until stiff, then add half the sugar and whisk again until they form stiff peaks. Fold in the rest of the sugar. Whisk into the cream mixture and chill until ready to use.

Ginger Cream Filling

Makes enough to fill one
23 cm/9 in cake

100 g/4 oz/½ cup butter or margarine,
softened
450 g/1 lb/2⅔ cups icing
(confectioners') sugar, sifted
5 ml/1 tsp ground ginger
30 ml/2 tbsp milk
75 g/3 oz/¼ cup black treacle
(molasses)

Beat the butter or margarine with the sugar and ginger until light and creamy. Gradually beat in the milk and treacle until smooth and spreadable. If the filling is too thin, beat in a little more sugar.

Lemon Filling

Makes 250 ml/8 fl oz/1 cup

100 g/4 oz/½ cup caster (superfine)
sugar
30 ml/2 tbsp cornflour (cornstarch)
60 ml/4 tbsp lemon juice
15 ml/1 tbsp grated lemon rind
120 ml/4 fl oz/½ cup water
A pinch of salt
15 ml/1 tbsp butter or margarine

Mix together all the ingredients except the butter or margarine in a small pan over a low heat, stirring gently until the mixture is well blended. Bring to the boil and boil for 1 minute. Stir in the butter or margarine and leave to cool. Chill before using.

Chocolate Glaze

Makes enough to glaze one
25 cm/10 in cake

50 g/2 oz/½ cup plain (semi-sweet)
chocolate, chopped
50 g/2 oz/¼ cup butter or margarine
2.5 ml/½ tsp vanilla essence (extract)
75 ml/5 tbsp boiling water
350 g/12 oz/2 cups icing
(confectioners') sugar, sifted

Blend together all the ingredients in a blender or food processor until smooth, pushing the ingredients down as necessary. Use at once.

Fruitcake Glaze

Makes enough to glaze one
25 cm/10 in cake

75 ml/5 tbsp golden (light corn) syrup
60 ml/4 tbsp pineapple or orange juice

Combine the syrup and juice in a small pan and bring to a rolling boil. Remove from the heat and brush the mixture over the top and sides of a cooled cake. Allow to set. Bring the glaze to the boil again and brush a second coat over the cake.

Orange Fruitcake Glaze

Makes enough to glaze one
25 cm/10 in cake

50 g/2 oz/¼ cup caster (superfine)
sugar
30 ml/2 tbsp orange juice
10 ml/2 tsp grated orange rind

Combine the ingredients in a small pan and bring to the boil, stirring constantly. Remove from the heat and brush the mixture over the top and sides of a cooled cake. Allow to set. Bring the glaze to the boil again and brush a second coat over the cake.

Small Cakes

*P*erfect for children, quick to cook and interesting to serve, you can bake two or three varieties of small cake at the same time to make an attractive combination to serve to guests.

Almond Meringue Squares

Makes 12

225 g/8 oz Shortcrust Pastry
(page 134)
60 ml/4 tbsp raspberry jam (conserve)
2 egg whites
50 g/2 oz/½ cup ground almonds
100 g/4 oz/½ cup caster (superfine)
sugar
A few drops of almond essence
(extract)
25 g/1 oz/¼ cup flaked (slivered)
almonds

Roll out the pastry (paste) and use to line a greased 30 × 20 cm/12 × 8 in Swiss roll tin (jelly roll pan). Spread with the jam. Whisk the egg whites until stiff, then gently fold in the ground almonds, sugar and almond essence. Spread over the jam and sprinkle with the flaked almonds. Bake in a preheated oven at 180°C/350°F/gas mark 4 for 45 minutes until golden and crisp. Leave to cool, then cut into squares.

Angel Drops

Makes 24

50 g/2 oz/¼ cup butter or margarine,
softened
50 g/2 oz/¼ cup lard (shortening)
100 g/4 oz/½ cup caster (superfine)
sugar
1 small egg, beaten
A few drops of vanilla essence
(extract)
175 g/6 oz/1½ cups self-raising
(self-rising) flour

45 ml/3 tbsp rolled oats
50 g/2 oz/¼ cup glacé (candied)
cherries, halved

Cream together the butter or margarine, lard and sugar until light and fluffy. Beat in the egg and vanilla essence, then fold in the flour and mix to a firm dough. Break into small balls and roll in the oats. Place well apart on a greased baking (cookie) sheet and top each one with a cherry. Bake in a preheated oven at 180°C/350°F/gas mark 4 for 20 minutes until just firm. Leave to cool on the tray.

Almond Slices

Makes 12

100 g/4 oz/½ cup butter or margarine
225 g/8 oz/2 cups plain (all-purpose)
flour
5 ml/1 tsp baking powder
50 g/2 oz/¼ cup caster (superfine)
sugar
1 egg, separated
75 ml/5 tbsp raspberry jam (conserve)
100 g/4 oz/⅔ cup icing (confectioners')
sugar, sifted
100 g/4 oz/1 cup flaked (slivered)
almonds

Rub the butter or margarine into the flour and baking powder until the mixture resembles breadcrumbs. Stir in the sugar, then mix in the egg yolk and knead to a firm dough. Roll out on a lightly floured surface to fit a greased 30 × 20 cm/12 × 8 in Swiss roll tin (jelly roll pan). Press gently into the pan and lift the edges of the dough slightly to make a lip. Spread with the jam. Whisk the egg white until stiff, then gradually beat in the icing sugar. Spread over the jam and sprinkle with the almonds. Bake in a preheated oven at 160°C/325°F/gas mark 3 for 1 hour until golden brown and just firm. Leave to cool in the tin for 5 minutes, then cut into fingers and turn out on to a wire rack to finish cooling.

Bakewell Tartlets

Makes 24

For the pastry:
25 g/1 oz/2 tbsp lard (shortening)
25 g/1 oz/2 tbsp butter or margarine
100 g/4 oz/1 cup plain (all-purpose) flour
A pinch of salt
30 ml/2 tbsp water
45 ml/3 tbsp raspberry jam (conserve)
For the filling:
50 g/2 oz/¼ cup butter or margarine, softened
50 g/2 oz/¼ cup caster (superfine) sugar
1 egg, lightly beaten
25 g/1 oz/¼ cup self-raising (self-rising) flour
25 g/1 oz/¼ cup ground almonds
A few drops of almond essence (extract)

To make the pastry (paste), rub the lard and butter or margarine into the flour and salt until the mixture resembles breadcrumbs. Mix in enough of the water to make a soft pastry. Roll out thinly on a lightly floured surface, cut into 7.5 cm/ 3 in circles and use to line the sections of two greased bun tins (patty pans). Fill with jam.

To make the filling, cream together the butter or margarine and sugar, then gradually mix in the egg. Stir in the flour, ground almonds and almond essence. Spoon the mixture into the tarts, sealing the edges to the pastry so that the jam is completely covered. Bake in a preheated oven at 180°C/350°F/gas mark 4 for 20 minutes until golden brown.

Chocolate Butterfly Cakes

Makes about 12 cakes

For the cakes:
100 g/4 oz/½ cup butter or margarine, softened
100 g/4 oz/½ cup caster (superfine) sugar
2 eggs, lightly beaten
100 g/4 oz/1 cup self-raising (self-rising) flour
30 ml/2 tbsp cocoa (unsweetened chocolate) powder
A pinch of salt
30 ml/2 tbsp cold milk
For the icing (frosting):
50 g/2 oz/¼ cup butter or margarine, softened
100 g/4 oz/⅔ cup icing (confectioners') sugar, sifted
10 ml/2 tsp hot milk

To make the cakes, cream together the butter or margarine and sugar until pale and fluffy. Gradually mix in the eggs alternately with the flour, cocoa and salt, then add the milk so you have a soft mixture. Spoon into paper cake cakes (cupcake papers) or greased bun tins (patty pans) and bake in a preheated oven at 190°/375°F/gas mark 5 for 15–20 minutes until well risen and springy to the touch. Leave to cool. Slice off the tops of the cakes horizontally, then cut the tops in half vertically to make the butterfly 'wings'.

To make the icing, beat the butter or margarine until soft, then beat in half the icing sugar. Beat in the milk, then the remaining sugar. Divide the icing mixture between the cakes, then press the 'wings' into the tops of the cakes at an angle.

Coconut Cakes

Makes 12

100 g/4 oz Shortcrust Pastry
(page 134)
50 g/2 oz/¼ cup butter or margarine,
softened
50 g/2 oz/¼ cup caster (superfine)
sugar
1 egg, beaten
25 g/1 oz/2 tbsp rice flour
50 g/2 oz/½ cup desiccated (shredded)
coconut
1.5 ml/¼ tsp baking powder
60 ml/4 tbsp chocolate spread

Roll out the pastry (paste) and use to line the sections of a bun tin (patty pan). Cream together the butter or margarine and sugar, then beat in the egg and rice flour. Stir in the coconut and baking powder. Put a small spoonful of chocolate spread in the base of each pastry case (pie shell). Spoon the coconut mixture over the top and bake in a preheated oven at 200°C/400°F/gas mark 6 for 15 minutes until risen and golden.

Sweet Cupcakes

Makes 15

100 g/4 oz/½ cup butter or margarine,
softened
225 g/8 oz/1 cup caster (superfine)
sugar
2 eggs
5 ml/1 tsp vanilla essence (extract)
175 g/6 oz/1½ cups self-raising
(self-rising) flour
5 ml/1 tsp baking powder
A pinch of salt
75 ml/5 tbsp milk

Cream together the butter or margarine and sugar until light and fluffy. Gradually add the eggs and vanilla essence, beating well after each addition. Fold in the flour, baking powder and salt alternately with the milk, beating well. Spoon the mixture into paper cake cases (cupcake papers) and bake in a preheated oven at 190°C/375°F/gas mark 5 for 20 minutes until a skewer inserted in the centre comes out clean.

Coffee Dot Cakes

Makes 12

For the cakes:
100 g/4 oz/½ cup butter or margarine,
softened
100 g/4 oz/½ cup caster (superfine)
sugar
2 eggs, lightly beaten
100 g/4 oz/1 cup self-raising
(self-rising) flour
10 ml/2 tsp coffee essence (extract)
For the icing (frosting):
50 g/2 oz/¼ cup butter or margarine,
softened
100 g/4 oz/⅔ cup icing (confectioners')
sugar, sifted
A few drops of coffee essence (extract)
100 g/4 oz/1 cup chocolate chips

To make the cakes, cream together the butter or margarine and sugar until light and fluffy. Gradually beat in the eggs, then fold in the flour and coffee essence. Spoon the mixture into paper cake cases (cupcake papers) set in a bun tin (patty pan) and bake in a preheated oven at 180°C/350°F/gas mark 4 for 20 minutes until well risen and springy to the touch. Leave to cool.

To make the icing, beat the butter or margarine until soft, then beat in the icing sugar and coffee essence. Spread over the tops of the cakes and decorate with the chocolate chips.

Eccles Cakes

Makes 16

50 g/2 oz/¼ cup butter or margarine
50 g/2 oz/¼ cup soft brown sugar
225 g/8 oz/1⅓ cups currants
450 g/1 lb Puff Pastry (page 136) or
  Flaky Pastry (page 136)
A little milk
45 ml/3 tbsp caster (superfine) sugar

Melt the butter or margarine and brown sugar over a low heat, stirring well. Remove from the heat and stir in the currants. Leave to cool slightly. Roll out the pastry (paste) on a floured surface and cut into 16 circles. Divide the filling mixture between the circles, then fold the edges over to the centre, brushing with water to seal the edges together. Turn the cakes over and roll them lightly with a rolling pin to flatten them slightly. Cut three slits in the top of each one, brush with milk and sprinkle with the sugar. Place on a greased baking (cookie) sheet and bake in a preheated oven at 200°C/400°F/gas mark 6 for 20 minutes until golden.

Fairy Cakes

Makes about 12

100 g/4 oz/½ cup butter or margarine,
  softened
100 g/4 oz/½ cup caster (superfine)
  sugar
2 eggs, lightly beaten
100 g/4 oz/1 cup self-raising
  (self-rising) flour
A pinch of salt
30 ml/2 tsp milk
A few drops of vanilla essence
  (extract)

Cream togther the butter or margarine and sugar until pale and fluffy. Gradually mix in the eggs alternately with the flour and salt, then add the milk and vanilla essence to make a soft mixture. Spoon into paper cake cakes (cupcake papers) or greased bun tins (patty pans) and bake in a preheated oven at 190°C/375°F/gas mark 5 for 15–20 minutes until well risen and springy to the touch.

Feather-iced Fairy Cakes

Makes 12

50 g/2 oz/¼ cup butter or margarine,
  softened
50 g/2 oz/¼ cup caster (superfine)
  sugar
1 egg
50 g/2 oz/½ cup self-raising
  (self-rising) flour
100 g/4 oz/⅔ cup icing (confectioners')
  sugar
15 ml/1 tbsp warm water
A few drops of food colouring

Cream together the butter or margarine and sugar until pale and fluffy. Gradually beat in the egg, then fold in the flour. Divide the mixture between 12 paper cake cases (cupcake papers) set in bun tins (patty pans). Bake in a preheated oven at 160°C/325°F/gas mark 3 for 15–20 minutes until risen and springy to the touch. Leave to cool.

Blend together the icing sugar and warm water. Colour one-third of the icing (frosting) with food colouring of your choice. Spread the white icing over the cakes. Pipe the coloured icing in lines across the cake, then draw a knife point at right angles to the lines first one way, then in the other direction, to create a wavy pattern. Leave to set.

Genoese Fancies

Makes 12

3 eggs, lightly beaten
75 g/3 oz/⅓ cup caster (superfine)
  sugar
75 g/3 oz/¾ cup self-raising
  (self-rising) flour
A few drops of vanilla essence
  (extract)
25 g/1 oz/2 tbsp butter or margarine,
  melted and cooled
60 ml/4 tbsp apricot jam (conserve),
  sieved (strained)
60 ml/4 tbsp water
225 g/8 oz/1⅓ cups icing
  (confectioners') sugar, sifted
A few drops of pink and blue food
  colouring (optional)
Cake decorations

Place the eggs and caster sugar in a
heatproof bowl set over a pan of
gently simmering water. Whisk until the
mixture trails off the whisk in ribbons.
Fold in the flour and vanilla essence, then
stir in the butter or margarine. Pour
the mixture into a greased 30 × 20 cm/
12 × 8 in Swiss roll tin (jelly roll pan) and
bake in a preheated oven at 190°C/375°F/
gas mark 5 for 30 minutes. Leave to cool,
then cut into shapes. Warm the jam with
30 ml/2 tbsp of the water and brush over
the cakes.

Sift the icing sugar into a bowl. If you
wish to make the icing (frosting) different
colours, divide it into separate bowls and
make a well in the centre of each.
Gradually add a few drops of colour and
just enough of the remaining water to
mix to a fairly stiff icing. Spread over the
cakes and decorate as liked.

Almond Macaroons

Makes 16

Rice paper
100 g/4 oz/½ cup caster (superfine)
  sugar
50 g/2 oz/½ cup ground almonds
5 ml/1 tsp ground rice
A few drops of almond essence
  (extract)
1 egg white
8 blanched almonds, halved

Line a baking (cookie) sheet with rice
paper. Mix together all the ingredients,
except the blanched almonds, to a stiff
paste and beat well. Place spoonfuls of the
mixture on the baking (cookie) sheet and
top each one with an almond half. Bake in
a preheated oven at 150°C/325°F/gas
mark 3 for 25 minutes. Leave to cool on
the baking sheet, then cut or tear round
each one to release it from the rice paper
sheet.

Coconut Macaroons

Makes 16

2 egg whites
150 g/5 oz/⅔ cup caster (superfine)
  sugar
150 g/5 oz/1¼ cups desiccated
  (shredded) coconut
Rice paper
8 glacé (candied) cherries, halved

Beat the egg whites until stiff. Whisk in
the sugar until the mixture forms stiff
peaks. Fold in the coconut. Place the rice
paper on a baking (cookie) sheet and
place spoonfuls of the mixture on the
sheet. Place a cherry half on top of each
one. Bake in a preheated oven at 160°C/
325°F/gas mark 3 for 30 minutes until
firm. Leave on the rice paper to cool, then
cut or tear round each one to release it
from the rice paper sheet.

Lime Macaroons

Makes 12

100 g/4 oz Shortcrust Pastry
 (page 134)
60 ml/4 tbsp lime marmalade
2 egg whites
50 g/2 oz/¼ cup caster (superfine)
 sugar
25 g/1 oz/¼ cup ground almonds
10 ml/2 tsp ground rice
5 ml/1 tsp orange flower water

Roll out the pastry (paste) and use to line the sections of a bun tin (patty pan). Put a small spoonful of marmalade into each pastry case (pie shell). Whisk the egg whites until stiff. Whisk in the sugar until stiff and glossy. Fold in the almonds, rice and orange flower water. Spoon into the cases, covering the marmalade completely. Bake in a preheated oven at 180°C/350°F/gas mark 4 for 30 minutes until risen and golden brown.

Oaty Macaroons

Makes 24

175 g/6 oz/1½ cups rolled oats
175 g/6 oz/¾ cup muscovado sugar
120 ml/4 fl oz/½ cup oil
1 egg
2.5 ml/½ tsp salt
2.5 ml/½ tsp almond essence (extract)

Mix together the oats, sugar and oil and leave to stand for 1 hour. Beat in the egg, salt and almond essence. Place spoonfuls of the mixture on a greased baking (cookie) sheet and bake in a preheated oven at 160°C/325°F/gas mark 3 for 20 minutes until golden brown.

Madeleines

Makes 9

100 g/4 oz/½ cup butter or margarine,
 softened
100 g/4 oz/½ cup caster (superfine)
 sugar
2 eggs, lightly beaten
100 g/4 oz/1 cup self-raising
 (self-rising) flour
175 g/6 oz/½ cup strawberry or
 raspberry jam (conserve)
60 ml/4 tbsp water
50 g/2 oz/½ cup desiccated (shredded)
 coconut
5 glacé (candied) cherries, halved

Cream the butter or margarine until light, then beat in the sugar until light and fluffy. Gradually beat in the eggs, then fold in the flour. Spoon into nine greased dariole (castle pudding) moulds and stand them on a baking (cookie) sheet. Bake in a preheated oven at 190°C/375°F/ gas mark 5 for 20 minutes until well risen and golden brown. Leave to cool in the tins for 5 minutes, then turn out on to a wire rack to finish cooling.

Trim the tops of each cake to form a flat base. Sieve (strain) the jam and bring to the boil with the water in a small pan, stirring until well blended. Spread the coconut on a large sheet of greaseproof (waxed) paper. Push a skewer into the base of the first cake, brush with the jam glaze, then roll in the coconut until covered. Place on a serving plate. Repeat with the remaining cakes. Top with halved glacé cherries.

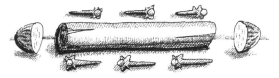

Marzipan Cakes

Makes about 12

450 g/1 lb/4 cups ground almonds
100 g/4 oz/²⁄₃ cup icing (confectioners')
   sugar, sifted
100 g/4 oz/½ cup caster (superfine)
   sugar
30 ml/2 tbsp water
3 egg whites
   For the icing (frosting):
100 g/4 oz/²⁄₃ cup icing (confectioners')
   sugar, sifted
1 egg white
2.5 ml/½ tsp vinegar

Mix together all the cake ingredients in a pan and heat gently, stirring, until the paste has absorbed all the liquid. Remove from the heat and leave to cool. Roll out on a lightly floured surface to 1 cm/½ in thick and cut into 3 cm/1½ in strips. Cut into 5 cm/2 in lengths, arrange on a greased baking (cookie) sheet and bake in a preheated oven at 150°C/300°F/gas mark 2 for 20 minutes until light brown on top. Leave to cool.

To make the icing, gradually stir the egg white and vinegar into the icing sugar until you have a smooth, thick icing. Drizzle the icing over the cakes.

Muffins

Makes 12

225 g/8 oz/2 cups plain
   (all-purpose) flour
100 g/4 oz/½ cup caster (superfine)
   sugar
10 ml/2 tsp baking powder
2.5 ml/½ tsp salt
1 egg, lightly beaten
250 ml/8 fl oz/1 cup milk
120 ml/4 fl oz/½ cup oil

Mix together the flour, sugar, baking powder and salt and make a well in the centre. Blend together the remaining ingredients and mix into the dry ingredients until just blended. Do not overmix. Spoon into muffin cases (papers) or greased muffin tins (pans) and bake in a preheated oven at 200°C/400°F/gas mark 6 for 20 minutes until well risen and springy to the touch.

Apple Muffins

Makes 12

225 g/8 oz/2 cups plain
   (all-purpose) flour
100 g/4 oz/½ cup caster (superfine)
   sugar
10 ml/2 tsp baking powder
2.5 ml/½ tsp salt
1 egg, lightly beaten
250 ml/8 fl oz/1 cup milk
120 ml/4 fl oz/½ cup oil
2 eating (dessert) apples, peeled, cored
   and chopped

Mix together the flour, sugar, baking powder and salt and make a well in the centre. Blend together the remaining ingredients and mix into the dry ingredients until just blended. Do not overmix. Spoon into muffin cases (papers) or greased muffin tins (pans) and bake in a preheated oven at 200°C/400°F/gas mark 6 for 20 minutes until well risen and springy to the touch.

Banana Muffins

Makes 12

225 g/8 oz/2 cups plain
   (all-purpose) flour
100 g/4 oz/½ cup caster (superfine)
   sugar
10 ml/2 tsp baking powder
2.5 ml/½ tsp salt
1 egg, lightly beaten
250 ml/8 fl oz/1 cup milk
120 ml/4 fl oz/½ cup oil
2 bananas, mashed

Mix together the flour, sugar, baking powder and salt and make a well in the centre. Blend together the remaining ingredients and mix into the dry ingredients until just blended. Do not overmix. Spoon into muffin cases (papers) or greased muffin tins (pans) and bake in a preheated oven at 200°C/400°F/gas mark 6 for 20 minutes until well risen and springy to the touch.

Blackcurrant Muffins

Makes 12

225 g/8 oz/2 cups self-raising (self-rising) flour
75 g/3 oz/⅓ cup caster (superfine) sugar
2 egg whites
75 g/3 oz blackcurrants
200 ml/7 fl oz/scant 1 cup milk
30 ml/2 tbsp oil

Mix together the flour and sugar. Lightly whisk the egg whites, then mix into the dry ingredients. Stir in the blackcurrants, milk and oil. Spoon into greased muffin tins (pans) and bake in a preheated oven at 200°C/400°F/gas mark 6 for 15–20 minutes until golden brown.

American Blueberry Muffins

Makes 12

150 g/5 oz/1¼ cups plain (all-purpose) flour
75 g/3 oz/¾ cup cornmeal
75 g/3 oz/⅓ cup caster (superfine) sugar
10 ml/2 tsp baking powder
A pinch of salt
1 egg, lightly beaten
75 g/3 oz/⅓ cup butter or margarine, melted
250 ml/8 fl oz/1 cup buttermilk
100 g/4 oz blueberries

Mix together the flour, cornmeal, sugar, baking powder and salt and make a well in the centre. Add the egg, butter or margarine and buttermilk and mix together until just combined. Stir in the blueberries or blackberries. Spoon into muffin cases (papers) and bake in a preheated oven at 200°C/400°F/gas mark 6 for 20 minutes until golden brown and springy to the touch.

Cherry Muffins

Makes 12

225 g/8 oz/2 cups plain (all-purpose) flour
100 g/4 oz/½ cup caster (superfine) sugar
100 g/4 oz/½ cup glacé (candied) cherries
10 ml/2 tsp baking powder
2.5 ml/½ tsp salt
1 egg, lightly beaten
250 ml/8 fl oz/1 cup milk
120 ml/4 fl oz/½ cup oil

Mix together the flour, sugar, cherries, baking powder and salt and make a well in the centre. Blend together the remaining ingredients and mix into the dry ingredients until just blended. Do not overmix. Spoon into muffin cases (papers) or greased muffin tins (pans) and bake in a preheated oven at 200°C/400°F/gas mark 6 for 20 minutes until well risen and springy to the touch.

Chocolate Muffins

Makes 10–12

*175 g/6 oz/1½ cups plain
(all-purpose) flour
40 g/1½ oz/⅓ cup cocoa (unsweetened
chocolate) powder
100 g/4 oz/½ cup caster (superfine)
sugar
10 ml/2 tsp baking powder
2.5 ml/½ tsp salt
1 large egg
250 ml/8 fl oz/1 cup milk
2.5 ml/½ tsp vanilla essence (extract)
120 ml/4 fl oz/½ cup sunflower or
vegetable oil*

Mix together the dry ingredients and make a well in the centre. Thoroughly mix together the egg, milk, vanilla essence and oil. Quickly stir the liquid into the dry ingredients just until they are all incorporated. Do not overmix; the mixture should be lumpy. Spoon into muffin cases (papers) or tins (pans) and bake in a preheated oven at 200°C/400°F/gas mark 6 for about 20 minutes until well risen and springy to the touch.

Chocolate Chip Muffins

Makes 12

*175 g/6 oz/1½ cups plain
(all-purpose) flour
100 g/4 oz/½ cup caster (superfine)
sugar
45 ml/3 tbsp cocoa (unsweetened
chocolate) powder
100 g/4 oz/1 cup chocolate chips
10 ml/2 tsp baking powder
2.5 ml/½ tsp salt
1 egg, lightly beaten
250 ml/8 fl oz/1 cup milk
120 ml/4 fl oz/½ cup oil
2.5 ml/½ tsp vanilla essence (extract)*

Mix together the flour, sugar, cocoa, chocolate chips, baking powder and salt and make a well in the centre. Blend together the remaining ingredients and mix into the dry ingredients until just blended. Do not overmix. Spoon into muffin cases (papers) or greased muffin tins (pans) and bake in a preheated oven at 200°C/400°F/gas mark 6 for 20 minutes until well risen and springy to the touch.

Cinnamon Muffins

Makes 12

*225 g/8 oz/2 cups plain
(all-purpose) flour
100 g/4 oz/½ cup caster (superfine)
sugar
10 ml/2 tsp baking powder
5 ml/1 tsp ground cinnamon
2.5 ml/½ tsp salt
1 egg, lightly beaten
250 ml/8 fl oz/1 cup milk
120 ml/4 fl oz/½ cup oil*

Mix together the flour, sugar, baking powder, cinnamon and salt and make a well in the centre. Blend together the remaining ingredients and mix into the dry ingredients until just blended. Do not overmix. Spoon into muffin cases (papers) or greased muffin tins (pans) and bake in a preheated oven at 200°C/400°F/gas mark 6 for 20 minutes until well risen and springy to the touch.

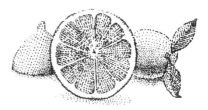

Cornmeal Muffins

Makes 12

50 g/2 oz/½ cup plain (all-purpose)
   flour
100 g/4 oz/1 cup cornmeal
5 ml/1 tsp baking powder
1 egg, separated
1 egg yolk
30 ml/2 tbsp corn oil
30 ml/2 tbsp milk

Mix together the flour, cornmeal and baking powder. Beat together the egg yolks, oil and milk, then stir into the dry ingredients. Whisk the egg white until stiff, then fold it into the mixture. Spoon into muffin cases (papers) or greased muffin tins (pans) and bake in a preheated oven at 200°C/400°F/gas mark 6 for about 20 minutes until golden.

Wholemeal Fig Muffins

Makes 10

100 g/4 oz/1 cup wholemeal
   (wholewheat) flour
5 ml/1 tsp baking powder
50 g/2 oz/½ cup rolled oats
50 g/2 oz/⅓ cup dried figs, chopped
45 ml/3 tbsp oil
75 ml/5 tbsp milk
15 ml/1 tbsp black treacle (molasses)
1 egg, lightly beaten

Mix together the flour, baking powder and oats, then stir in the figs. Warm the oil, milk and treacle together until blended, then stir into the dry ingredients with the egg and mix to a firm dough. Place spoonfuls of the mixture in muffin cases (papers) or greased muffin tins (pans) and bake in a preheated oven at 190°C/375°F/gas mark 5 for about 20 minutes until golden brown.

Fruit and Bran Muffins

Makes 8

100 g/4 oz/1 cup All Bran cereal
50 g/2 oz/½ cup plain (all-purpose)
   flour
2.5 ml/½ tsp baking powder
5 ml/1 tsp bicarbonate of soda
   (baking soda)
5 ml/1 tsp ground mixed (apple-pie)
   spice
50 g/2 oz/⅓ cup raisins
100 g/4 oz/1 cup apple purée (sauce)
5 ml/1 tsp vanilla essence (extract)
30 ml/2 tbsp milk

Mix together the dry ingredients and make a well in the centre. Stir in the raisins, apple purée and vanilla essence and enough of the milk to make a soft mixture. Spoon into muffin cases (papers) or greased muffin tins (pans) and bake in a preheated oven at 200°C/400°F/gas mark 6 for 20 minutes until well risen and golden brown.

Oat Muffins

Makes 20

100 g/4 oz/1 cup oatmeal
100 g/4 oz/1 cup oat flour
225 g/8 oz/2 cups wholemeal
   (wholewheat) flour
10 ml/2 tsp baking powder
50 g/2 oz/⅓ cup raisins (optional)
375 ml/13 fl oz/1½ cups milk
10 ml/2 tsp oil
2 egg whites

Mix together the oatmeal, flours and baking powder and stir in the raisins, if using. Stir in the milk and oil. Whisk the egg whites until stiff, then fold them into the mixture. Spoon into muffin cases (papers) or greased muffin tins (pans) and bake in a preheated oven at 190°C/375°F/gas mark 5 for about 25 minutes until golden.

Oatmeal Fruit Muffins

Makes 10

100 g/4 oz/1 cup wholemeal
(wholewheat) flour
100 g/4 oz/1 cup oatmeal
15 ml/1 tbsp baking powder
100 g/4 oz/²⁄₃ cup sultanas
(golden raisins)
50 g/2 oz/½ cup chopped mixed nuts
1 eating (dessert) apple, peeled, cored
and grated
45 ml/3 tbsp oil
30 ml/2 tbsp clear honey
15 ml/1 tbsp black treacle (molasses)
1 egg, lightly beaten
90 ml/6 tbsp milk

Mix together the flour, oatmeal and baking powder. Stir in the sultanas, nuts and apple. Warm the oil, honey and treacle together until melted, then stir into the mixture with the egg and enough milk to make a soft dropping consistency. Spoon into muffin cases (papers) or greased muffin tins (pans) and bake in a preheated oven at 190°C/375°F/gas mark 5 for about 25 minutes until golden.

Orange Muffins

Makes 12

100 g/4 oz/1 cup self-raising
(self-rising) flour
100 g/4 oz/½ cup soft brown sugar
1 egg, lightly beaten
120 ml/4 fl oz/½ cup orange juice
60 ml/4 tbsp oil
2.5 ml/½ tsp vanilla essence (extract)
25 g/1 oz/2 tbsp butter or margarine
30 ml/2 tbsp plain (all-purpose) flour
2.5 ml/½ tsp ground cinnamon

Mix together the self-raising flour and half the sugar in a bowl. Mix together the egg, orange juice, oil and vanilla essence, then stir into the dry ingredients until just blended. Do not overmix. Spoon into muffin cases (papers) or greased muffin tins (pans) and bake in a preheated oven at 200°C/ 400°F/gas mark 6 for 10 minutes.

Meanwhile, rub the butter or margarine for the topping into the plain flour, then mix in the remaining sugar and the cinnamon. Sprinkle over the muffins and return them to the oven for a further 5 minutes until golden brown.

Peachy Muffins

Makes 12

225 g/8 oz/2 cups plain
(all-purpose) flour
100 g/4 oz/½ cup caster (superfine)
sugar
10 ml/2 tsp baking powder
2.5 ml/½ tsp salt
1 egg, lightly beaten
175 ml/6 fl oz/¾ cup milk
120 ml/4 fl oz/½ cup oil
200 g/7 oz/1 small can peaches,
drained and chopped

Mix together the flour, sugar, baking powder and salt and make a well in the centre. Blend together the remaining ingredients and mix into the dry ingredients until just blended. Do not overmix. Spoon into muffin cases (papers) or greased muffin tins (pans) and bake in a preheated oven at 200°C/400°F/gas mark 6 for 20 minutes until well risen and springy to the touch.

Peanut Butter Muffins

Makes 12

225 g/8 oz/2 cups plain
  (all-purpose) flour
100 g/4 oz/½ cup soft brown sugar
10 ml/2 tsp baking powder
2.5 ml/½ tsp salt
1 egg, lightly beaten
250 ml/8 fl oz/1 cup milk
120 ml/4 fl oz/½ cup oil
45 ml/3 tbsp peanut butter

Mix together the flour, sugar, baking powder and salt and make a well in the centre. Blend together the remaining ingredients and mix into the dry ingredients until just blended. Do not overmix. Spoon into muffin cases (papers) or greased muffin tins (pans) and bake in a preheated oven at 200°C/400°F/gas mark 6 for 20 minutes until well risen and springy to the touch.

Pineapple Muffins

Makes 12

225 g/8 oz/2 cups plain
  (all-purpose) flour
100 g/4 oz/½ cup soft brown sugar
10 ml/2 tsp baking powder
2.5 ml/½ tsp salt
1 egg, lightly beaten
175 ml/6 fl oz/¾ cup milk
120 ml/4 fl oz/½ cup oil
200 g/7 oz/1 small can pineapple,
  drained and chopped
30 ml/2 tbsp demerara sugar

Mix together the flour, soft brown sugar, baking powder and salt and make a well in the centre. Blend together all the remaining ingredients except the demerara sugar and mix into the dry ingredients until just blended. Do not overmix. Spoon into muffin cases (papers) or greased muffin tins (pans) and sprinkle with the demerara sugar.

Bake in a preheated oven at 200°C/400°F/ gas mark 6 for 20 minutes until well risen and springy to the touch.

Raspberry Muffins

Makes 12

225 g/8 oz/2 cups plain
  (all-purpose) flour
100 g/4 oz/½ cup caster (superfine)
  sugar
10 ml/2 tsp baking powder
2.5 ml/½ tsp salt
200 g/7 oz raspberries
1 egg, lightly beaten
250 ml/8 fl oz/1 cup milk
120 ml/4 fl oz/½ cup vegetable oil

Mix together the flour, sugar, baking powder and salt. Stir in the raspberries and make a well in the centre. Mix together the egg, milk and oil and pour into the dry ingredients. Stir gently until all the dry ingredients are mixed in but the mixture is still lumpy. Do not overbeat. Spoon the mixture into muffin cases (papers) or greased muffin tins (pans) and bake in a preheated oven at 200°C/400°F/gas mark 6 for 20 minutes until well risen and springy to the touch.

Raspberry and Lemon Muffins

Makes 12

175 g/6 oz/1½ cups plain
(all-purpose) flour
50 g/2 oz/¼ cup granulated sugar
50 g/2 oz/¼ cup soft brown sugar
10 ml/2 tsp baking powder
5 ml/1 tsp ground cinnamon
A pinch of salt
1 egg, lightly beaten
100 g/4 oz/½ cup butter or margarine,
melted
120 ml/4 fl oz/½ cup milk
100 g/4 oz fresh raspberries
10 ml/2 tsp grated lemon rind
For the topping:
75 g/3 oz/½ cup icing (confectioners')
sugar, sifted
15 ml/1 tbsp lemon juice

Mix together the flour, granulated sugar, brown sugar, baking powder, cinnamon and salt in a bowl and make a well in the centre. Add the egg, butter or margarine and milk and blend until the ingredients are just combined. Stir in the raspberries and lemon rind. Spoon into muffin cases (papers) or greased muffin tins (pans) and bake in a preheated oven at 180°C/350°F/gas mark 4 for 20 minutes until golden brown and springy to the touch. Mix together the icing sugar and lemon juice for the topping and drizzle over the warm muffins.

Sultana Muffins

Makes 12

225 g/8 oz/2 cups plain
(all-purpose) flour
100 g/4 oz/½ cup caster (superfine)
sugar
100 g/4 oz/⅔ cup sultanas (golden
raisins)
10 ml/2 tsp baking powder
5 ml/1 tsp ground mixed (apple-pie)
spice
2.5 ml/½ tsp salt
1 egg, lightly beaten
250 ml/8 fl oz/1 cup milk
120 ml/4 fl oz/½ cup oil

Mix together the flour, sugar, sultanas, baking powder, mixed spice and salt and make a well in the centre. Mix in the remaining ingredients until just blended. Spoon into muffin cases (papers) or greased muffin tins (pans) and bake in a preheated oven at 200°C/400°F/gas mark 6 for 20 minutes until well risen and springy to the touch.

Treacle Muffins

Makes 12

225 g/8 oz/2 cups plain
(all-purpose) flour
100 g/4 oz/½ cup soft brown sugar
10 ml/2 tsp baking powder
2.5 ml/½ tsp salt
1 egg, lightly beaten
175 ml/6 fl oz/¾ cup milk
60 ml/4 tbsp black treacle (molasses)
120 ml/4 fl oz/½ cup oil

Mix together the flour, sugar, baking powder and salt and make a well in the centre. Mix in the remaining ingredients until just blended. Do not overmix. Spoon into muffin cases (papers) or greased muffin tins (pans) and bake in a preheated oven at 200°C/400°F/gas mark 6 for 20 minutes until well risen and springy to the touch.

Treacle and Oat Muffins

Makes 10

100 g/4 oz/1 cup plain (all-purpose)
 flour
175 g/6 oz/1½ cups rolled oats
100 g/4 oz/½ cup soft brown sugar
15 ml/1 tbsp baking powder
5 ml/1 tsp ground cinnamon
2.5 ml/½ tsp salt
1 egg, lightly beaten
120 ml/4 fl oz/½ cup milk
60 ml/4 tbsp black treacle (molasses)
75 ml/5 tbsp oil

Mix together the flour, oats, sugar, baking powder, cinnamon and salt and make a well in the centre. Blend together the remaining ingredients, then mix into the dry ingredients until just blended. Do not overmix. Spoon into muffin cases (papers) or greased muffins tins (pans) and bake in a preheated oven at 200°C/400°F/gas mark 6 for 15 minutes until well risen and springy to the touch.

Oat Toasties

Makes 8

225 g/8 oz/2 cups rolled oats
100 g/4 oz/1 cup wholemeal
 (wholewheat) flour
5 ml/1 tsp salt
5 ml/1 tsp baking powder
50 g/2 oz/¼ cup lard (shortening)
30 ml/2 tbsp cold water

Mix together the dry ingredients, then rub in the lard until the mixture resembles breadcrumbs. Stir in enough of the water to make a firm dough. Roll out on a lightly floured surface to an 18 cm/7 in circle and cut into eight wedges. Place on a greased baking (cookie) sheet and bake in a preheated oven at 180°C/350°F/gas mark 4 for 25 minutes. Serve with butter, jam or marmalade.

Strawberry Sponge Omelettes

Makes 18

5 egg yolks
75 g/3 oz/⅓ cup caster (superfine)
 sugar
A pinch of salt
Grated rind of ½ lemon
4 egg whites
40 g/1½ oz/⅓ cup cornflour
 (cornstarch)
40 g/1½ oz/⅓ cup plain (all-purpose)
 flour
40 g/1½ oz/3 tbsp butter or
 margarine, melted
300 ml/½ pt/1¼ cups whipping cream
225 g/8 oz strawberries
Icing (confectioners') sugar, sifted,
 for dusting

Beat the egg yolks with 25 g/1 oz/2 tbsp of the caster sugar until pale and thick, then beat in the salt and lemon rind. Whisk the egg whites until stiff, then add the remaining caster sugar and continue to beat until stiff and glossy. Fold into the egg yolks, then fold in the cornflour and flour. Stir in the melted butter or margarine. Transfer the mixture to a piping bag with a 1 cm/½ in plain nozzle (tip) and pipe into 15 cm/6 in circles on a greased and lined baking (cookie) sheet. Bake in a preheated oven at 220°C/425°F/gas mark 7 for 10 minutes until just coloured but not browned. Leave to cool.

Whip the cream until stiff. Pipe a thin layer over half of each circle, arrange the strawberries on top, then finish with more cream. Fold the top half of the 'omelettes' over the top. Dust with icing sugar and serve.

Peppermint Cakes

Makes 12

100 g/4 oz/½ cup butter or margarine, softened
100 g/4 oz/½ cup caster (superfine) sugar
2 eggs, lightly beaten
75 g/3 oz/¾ cup self-raising (self-rising) flour
10 ml/2 tsp cocoa (unsweetened chocolate) powder
A pinch of salt
225 g/8 oz/1⅓ cups icing (confectioners') sugar, sifted
30 ml/2 tbsp water
A few drops of green food colouring
A few drops of peppermint essence (extract)
Chocolate mints, halved, for decoration

Cream together the butter or margarine and sugar until light and fluffy, then gradually beat in the eggs. Fold in the flour, cocoa and salt. Spoon into greased bun tins (patty pans) and bake in a preheated oven at 200°C/400°F/gas mark 6 for 10 minutes until springy to the touch. Leave to cool.

Sift the icing sugar into a bowl and mix in 15 ml/1 tbsp of the water, then add the food colouring and peppermint essence to taste. Add more water if necessary to give a consistency that will coat the back of a spoon. Spread the icing on top of the cakes and decorate with chocolate mints.

Raisin Cakes

Makes 12

175 g/6 oz/1 cup raisins
250 ml/8 fl oz/1 cup water
5 ml/1 tsp bicarbonate of soda (baking soda)
100 g/4 oz/½ cup butter or margarine, softened
100 g/4 oz/½ cup soft brown sugar
1 egg, beaten
5 ml/1 tsp vanilla essence (extract)
200 g/7 oz/1¾ cups plain (all-purpose) flour
5 ml/1 tsp baking powder
A pinch of salt

Bring the raisins, water and bicarbonate of soda to the boil in a pan, then simmer gently for 3 minutes. Leave to cool until lukewarm. Cream together the butter or margarine and sugar until pale and fluffy. Gradually stir in the egg and vanilla essence. Stir into the raisin mixture, then mix in the flour, baking powder and salt. Spoon the mixture into muffin cases (papers) or greased muffin tins (pans) and bake in a preheated oven at 180°C/350°F/gas mark 4 for 12–15 minutes until well risen and golden brown.

Raisin Curls

Makes 24

225 g/8 oz/2 cups plain (all-purpose) flour
A pinch of ground mixed (apple-pie) spice
5 ml/1 tsp bicarbonate of soda (baking soda)
225 g/8 oz/1 cup caster (superfine) sugar
45 ml/3 tbsp ground almonds
225 g/8 oz/1 cup butter or margarine, melted
45 ml/3 tbsp raisins
1 egg, lightly beaten

Mix together the dry ingredients, then stir in the melted butter or margarine, followed by the raisins and egg. Mix well to a stiff paste. Roll out on a lightly floured surface to about 5 mm/¼ in thick and cut into strips 5 mm × 20 cm/ ¼ × 8 in. Moisten the top surface lightly with a little water, then roll up each strip from the short end. Place on a greased baking (cookie) sheet and bake in a preheated oven at 200°C/400°F/gas mark 6 for 15 minutes until golden.

Raspberry Buns

Makes 12 buns

225 g/8 oz/2 cups plain
(all-purpose) flour
7.5 ml/½ tbsp baking powder
2.5 ml/½ tsp ground mixed
(apple-pie) spice
A pinch of salt
75 g/3 oz/⅓ cup butter or margarine
75 g/3 oz/⅓ cup caster (superfine)
sugar, plus extra for sprinkling
1 egg
60 ml/4 tbsp milk
60 ml/4 tbsp raspberry jam (conserve)

Mix together the flour, baking powder, spice and salt, then rub in the butter or margarine until the mixture resembles breadcrumbs. Stir in the sugar. Mix in the egg and enough of the milk to make a stiff dough. Divide into 12 balls and place on a greased baking (cookie) sheet. Make a hole with a finger in the centre of each one and spoon in a little raspberry jam. Brush with milk and sprinkle with caster sugar. Bake in a preheated oven at 220°C/425°F/gas mark 7 for 10–15 minutes until golden. Top with a little more jam, if necessary.

Brown Rice and Sunflower Cakes

Makes 12

75 g/3 oz/³⁄₄ cup cooked brown rice
50 g/2 oz/½ cup sunflower seeds
25 g/1 oz/¼ cup sesame seeds
40 g/1½ oz/¼ cup raisins
40 g/1½ oz/¼ cup glacé (candied)
cherries, quartered
25 g/1 oz/2 tbsp soft brown sugar
15 ml/1 tbsp clear honey
75 g/3 oz/⅓ cup butter or margarine
5 ml/1 tsp lemon juice

Mix together the rice, seeds and fruit. Melt together the sugar, honey, butter or margarine and lemon juice and stir into the rice mixture. Spoon into 12 cake cases (cupcake papers) and bake in a preheated oven at 200°C/400°F/gas mark 6 for 15 minutes.

Rock Cakes

Makes 12

225 g/8 oz/2 cups plain
  (all-purpose) flour
A pinch of salt
10 ml/2 tsp baking powder
50 g/2 oz/¼ cup butter or margarine
50 g/2 oz/¼ cup lard (shortening)
100 g/4 oz/⅔ cup dried mixed fruit
  (fruit cake mix)
100 g/4 oz/½ cup demerara sugar
Grated rind of ½ lemon
1 egg
15–30 ml/1–2 tbsp milk

Mix together the flour, salt and baking powder, then rub in the butter or margarine and lard until the mixture resembles breadcrumbs. Stir in the fruit, sugar and lemon rind. Beat the egg with 15 ml/1 tbsp of the milk, add to the dry ingredients and mix to a stiff dough, adding extra milk if necessary. Place small piles of the mixture on a greased baking (cookie) sheet and bake in a preheated oven at 200°C/400°F/gas mark 6 for 15–20 minutes until golden brown.

Sugar-free Rock Cakes

Makes 12

75 g/3 oz/⅓ cup butter or margarine
175 g/6 oz/1¼ cups wholemeal
  (wholewheat) flour
50 g/2 oz/½ cup oat flour
10 ml/2 tsp baking powder
5 ml/1 tsp ground cinnamon
100 g/4 oz/⅔ cup sultanas
  (golden raisins)
Grated rind of 1 lemon
1 egg, lightly beaten
90 ml/6 tbsp milk

Rub the butter or margarine into the flours, baking powder and cinnamon until the mixture resembles breadcrumbs. Stir in the sultanas and lemon rind. Add the egg and enough of the milk to make a soft mixture. Place spoonfuls on a greased baking (cookie) sheet and bake in a preheated oven at 200°C/400°F/gas mark 6 for 15–20 minutes until golden.

Saffron Cakes

Makes 12

A pinch of ground saffron
75 ml/5 tbsp boiling water
75 ml/5 tbsp cold water
100 g/4 oz/½ cup butter or margarine,
  softened
225 g/8 oz/1 cup caster (superfine)
  sugar
2 eggs, lightly beaten
225 g/8 oz/2 cups plain
  (all-purpose) flour
10 ml/2 tsp baking powder
2.5 ml/½ tsp salt
175 g/6 oz/1 cup sultanas (golden
  raisins)
175 g/6 oz/1 cup chopped mixed
  (candied) peel

Soak the saffron in the boiling water for 30 minutes, then add the cold water. Cream together the butter or margarine and sugar until light and fluffy, then gradually beat in the eggs. Mix the flour with the baking powder and salt, then mix 50 g/2 oz/½ cup of the flour mixture with the sultanas and mixed peel. Stir the flour into the creamed mixture alternately with the saffron water, then fold in the fruit. Spoon into muffin cases (papers) or greased and floured muffin tins (pans) and bake in a preheated oven at 190°C/375°F/gas mark 5 for about 15 minutes until springy to the touch.

Rum Babas

Makes 8

100 g/4 oz/1 cup strong plain (bread)
flour
5 ml/1 tsp easy-blend dried yeast
A pinch of salt
45 ml/3 tbsp warm milk
2 eggs, lightly beaten
50 g/2 oz/¼ cup butter or margarine,
melted
25 g/1 oz/3 tbsp currants
   For the syrup:
250 ml/8 fl oz/1 cup water
75 g/3 oz/⅓ cup granulated sugar
20 ml/4 tsp lemon juice
60 ml/4 tbsp rum
   For the glaze and decoration:
60 ml/4 tbsp apricot jam (conserve),
sieved (strained)
15 ml/1 tbsp water
150 ml/¼ pt/⅔ cup whipping or
double (heavy) cream
4 glacé (candied) cherries, halved
A few strips of angelica, cut into
triangles

Stir together the flour, yeast and salt in a bowl and make a well in the centre. Mix together the milk, eggs and butter or margarine, then beat into the flour to make a smooth batter. Stir in the currants. Spoon the batter into eight greased and floured individual ring moulds (tube pans) so that it comes just one-third of the way up the moulds. Cover with oiled clingfilm (plastic wrap) and leave in a warm place for 30 minutes until the batter has risen to the top of the tins. Bake in a preheated oven at 200°C/400°F/gas mark 6 for 15 minutes until golden brown. Turn the tins upside down and leave to cool for 10 minutes, then ease the cakes out of the tins and place in a large shallow dish. Prick them all over with a fork.

To make the syrup, heat the water, sugar and lemon juice over a low heat, stirring until the sugar has dissolved.

Raise the heat and bring to the boil. Remove from the heat and stir in the rum. Spoon the hot syrup over the cakes and leave for 40 minutes to soak in.

Heat the jam and water over a low heat until well blended. Brush over the babas and arrange on a serving plate. Whip the cream and pipe into the centre of each cake. Decorate with cherries and angelica.

Sponge-ball Cakes

Makes 24

5 egg yolks
75 g/3 oz/⅓ cup caster (superfine)
sugar
7 egg whites
75 g/3 oz/¾ cup cornflour (cornstarch)
50 g/2 oz/½ cup plain (all-purpose)
flour

Beat the egg yolks with 15 ml/1 tbsp of the sugar until pale and thick. Whisk the egg whites until stiff, then whisk in the remaining sugar until thick and glossy. Fold in the cornflour, using a metal spoon. Fold half the egg yolks into the whites, using a metal spoon, then fold in the remaining yolks. Very gently fold in the flour. Transfer the mixture to a piping bag with a plain 2.5 cm/1 in nozzle (tip) and pipe into round cakes, well apart, on a greased and lined baking (cookie) sheet. Bake in a preheated oven at 200°C/400°F/gas mark 6 for 5 minutes, then reduce the oven temperature to 180°C/350°F/gas mark 4 for a further 10 minutes until golden brown and springy to the touch.

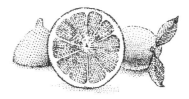

Chocolate Sponge Cakes

Makes 12

5 egg yolks
75 g/3 oz/⅓ cup caster (superfine)
   sugar
7 egg whites
75 g/3 oz/¾ cup cornflour (cornstarch)
50 g/2 oz/½ cup plain (all-purpose)
   flour
60 ml/4 tbsp apricot jam (conserve),
   sieved (strained)
30 ml/2 tbsp water
1 quantity Boiled Chocolate Icing
   (page 232)
150 ml/¼ pt/⅔ cup whipping cream

Beat the egg yolks with 15 ml/1 tbsp of the sugar until pale and thick. Whisk the egg whites until stiff, then whisk in the remaining sugar until thick and glossy. Fold in the cornflour, using a metal spoon. Fold half the egg yolks into the whites, using a metal spoon, then fold in the remaining yolks. Very gently fold in the flour. Transfer the mixture to a piping bag with a plain 2.5 cm/1 in nozzle (tip) and pipe into round cakes, well apart, on a greased and lined baking (cookie) sheet. Bake in a preheated oven at 200°C/400°F/ gas mark 6 for 5 minutes, then reduce the oven temperature to 180°C/350°F/gas mark 4 for a further 10 minutes until golden brown and springy to the touch. Transfer to a wire rack.

Boil the jam and water until thick and well blended, then brush over the tops of the cakes. Leave to cool. Dip the sponges in the chocolate icing, then leave to cool. Whip the cream until stiff, then sandwich pairs of cakes together with the cream.

Summer Snowballs

Makes 24

100 g/4 oz/½ cup butter or margarine,
   softened
100 g/4 oz/½ cup caster (superfine)
   sugar
5 ml/1 tsp vanilla essence (extract)
2 eggs, lightly beaten
225 g/8 oz/2 cups self-raising
   (self-rising) flour
120 ml/4 fl oz/½ cup milk
120 ml/4 fl oz/½ cup double (heavy)
   cream
25 g/1 oz/3 tbsp icing (confectioners')
   sugar, sifted
60 ml/4 tbsp apricot jam (conserve),
   sieved (strained)
30 ml/2 tbsp water
150 g/5 oz/1¼ cups desiccated
   (shredded) coconut

Cream together the butter or margarine and sugar until light and fluffy. Gradually beat in the vanilla essence and eggs, then fold in the flour alternately with the milk. Spoon the mixture into greased muffin tins (pans) and bake in a preheated oven at 180°C/350°F/gas mark 4 for 15 minutes until well risen and springy to the touch. Transfer to a wire rack to cool. Slice the tops off the muffins.

Whip the cream and icing sugar until stiff, then spoon a little on to the top of each muffin and replace the lid. Warm the jam with the water until blended, then brush over the top of the muffins and sprinkle generously with the coconut.

Photograph opposite: Dolly Mixture
Cake (pages 191–2)

Sponge Drops

Makes 12

3 eggs, beaten
100 g/4 oz/½ cup caster (superfine)
  sugar
2.5 ml/½ tsp vanilla essence (extract)
100 g/4 oz/1 cup plain (all-purpose)
  flour
5 ml/1 tsp baking powder
100 g/4 oz/⅓ cup raspberry jam
  (conserve)
150 ml/¼ pt/⅔ cup double (heavy)
  cream, whipped
Icing (confectioners') sugar, sifted, for
  dusting

Place the eggs, caster sugar and vanilla essence in a heatproof bowl set over a pan of simmering water and beat until the mixture thickens. Remove the bowl from the pan and stir in the flour and baking powder. Place small spoonfuls of the mixture on to a greased baking (cookie) sheet and bake in a preheated oven at 190°C/375°F/gas mark 5 for 10 minutes until golden. Transfer to a wire rack and leave to cool. Sandwich the drops together with jam and cream and sprinkle with icing sugar to serve.

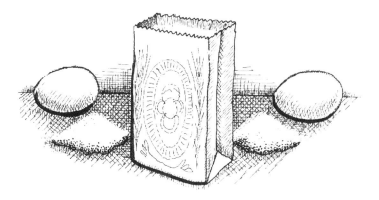

Photograph opposite: Chocolate
Butterfly Cakes (page 239) and
Feather-iced Fairy Cakes (page 241)

Meringues

*M*eringue cakes are simple to make if you follow a few basic rules. The eggs should be at room temperature before you start, and all your utensils must be absolutely clean and grease-free. Whisk the egg whites until they are just stiff; overbeating will not help your results. Meringues need to dry out very slowly in a cool oven. Recipes that are baked at a higher temperature are usually aiming for a crisp outside and a melting inside, rather than a meringue that is crisp all the way through.

Basic Meringues

Makes 6–8

2 egg whites
100 g/4 oz/½ cup caster (superfine) sugar

Whisk the egg whites in a clean, grease-free bowl until they begin to form soft peaks. Add half the sugar and continue to whisk until the mixture stands in stiff peaks. Lightly fold in the remaining sugar using a metal spoon. Line a baking (cookie) sheet with baking parchment and place 6–8 mounds of meringue on the sheet. Dry the meringues at the lowest possible setting in the oven for 2–3 hours. Cool on a wire rack.

Almond Meringues

Makes 12

2 egg whites
100 g/4 oz/½ caster (superfine) sugar
100 g/4 oz/1 cup ground almonds
A few drops of almond essence (extract)
12 almond halves to decorate

Whisk the egg whites until stiff. Add half the sugar and continue to whisk until the mixture forms stiff peaks. Fold in the remaining sugar, the ground almonds and the almond essence. Spoon the mixture into 12 rounds on a greased and lined baking (cookie) sheet and place an almond half on top of each one. Bake in a preheated oven at 130°C/250°F/gas mark ½ for 2–3 hours until crisp.

Spanish Almond Meringue Biscuits

Makes 16

225 g/8 oz/1 cup granulated sugar
225 g/8 oz/2 cups ground almonds
1 egg white
100 g/4 oz/1 cup whole almonds

Beat the sugar, ground almonds and egg white to a smooth dough. Shape into a ball and flatten the dough with a rolling pin. Cut into small rounds and place on a greased baking (cookie) sheet. Press a whole almond into the centre of each biscuit (cookie). Bake in a preheated oven at 160°C/325°F/gas mark 3 for 15 minutes.

Meringue Cuite Baskets

Makes 6

4 egg whites
225–250 g/8–9 oz/1⅓–1½ cups icing (confectioners') sugar, sifted
A few drops of vanilla essence (extract)

Whisk the egg whites in a clean, grease-free, heatproof bowl until frothy, then gradually whisk in the icing

258

sugar followed by the vanilla essence. Set the bowl over a pan of gently simmering water and whisk until the meringue holds its shape and leaves a thick trail when the whisk is lifted out. Line a baking (cookie) sheet with baking parchment and draw six 7.5 cm/3 in circles on the paper. Using half the meringue mixture, spoon a layer of meringue inside each circle. Place the remainder in a piping bag and pipe two layers of meringue round the edge of each base. Dry in a preheated oven at 150°C/300°F/gas mark 2 for about 45 minutes.

Almond Crisps

Makes 10

2 egg whites
100 g/4 oz/½ cup caster (superfine) sugar
75 g/3 oz/¾ cup ground almonds
25 g/1 oz/2 tbsp butter or margarine, softened
50 g/2 oz/⅓ cup icing (confectioners') sugar, sifted
10 ml/2 tsp cocoa (unsweetened chocolate) powder
50 g/2 oz/½ cup plain (semi-sweet) chocolate, melted

Whisk the egg whites until they form stiff peaks. Whisk in the caster sugar a little at a time. Fold in the ground almonds. Using a 1 cm/½ in piping nozzle (tip), pipe the mixture into 5 cm/2 in lengths on a lightly oiled baking (cookie) sheet. Bake in a preheated oven at 140°C/275°F/gas mark 1 for 1–1½ hours. Leave to cool.

Cream together the butter or margarine, icing sugar and cocoa. Sandwich pairs of biscuits (cookies) together with the filling. Melt the chocolate in a heatproof bowl over a pan of gently simmering water. Dip the ends of the meringues in the chocolate and leave to cool on a wire rack.

Spanish Almond and Lemon Meringues

Makes 30

150 g/5 oz/1¼ cups blanched almonds
2 egg whites
Grated rind of ½ lemon
200 g/7 oz/scant 1 cup caster (superfine) sugar
10 ml/2 tsp lemon juice

Toast the almonds in a preheated oven at 150°C/300°F/gas mark 2 for about 30 minutes until golden and aromatic. Chop one-third of the nuts coarsely and grind the remainder finely.

Whisk the egg whites until stiff. Fold in the lemon rind and two-thirds of the sugar. Add the lemon juice and whisk until stiff and shiny. Fold in the remaining sugar and the ground almonds. Fold in the chopped almonds. Place spoonfuls of the meringue on a greased and foil-lined baking (cookie) sheet and place in the preheated oven. Immediately reduce the oven temperature to 110°C/225°F/gas mark ¼ and bake for about 1½ hours until dry.

Chocolate-covered Meringues

Makes 4

2 egg whites
100 g/4 oz/½ cup caster (superfine) sugar
100 g/4 oz/1 cup plain (semi-sweet) chocolate
150 ml/¼ pt/⅔ cup double (heavy) cream, whipped

Whisk the egg whites in a clean, grease-free bowl until they begin to form soft peaks. Add half the sugar and continue to whisk until the mixture stands in stiff peaks. Lightly fold in the remaining sugar using a metal spoon. Line a baking (cookie) sheet with baking parchment and place eight mounds of meringue on the sheet. Dry the meringues at the lowest possible setting in the oven for 2–3 hours. Cool on a wire rack.

Melt the chocolate in a heatproof bowl set over a pan of gently simmering water. Leave to cool slightly. Carefully dip four of the meringues into the chocolate so that the outsides are coated. Leave to stand on greaseproof (waxed) paper until set. Sandwich one chocolate-covered meringue and one plain meringue together with cream then repeat with the remaining meringues.

Chocolate Mint Meringues

Makes 18

3 egg whites
100 g/4 oz/½ cup caster (superfine) sugar
75 g/3 oz/¾ cup chopped chocolate-covered mints

Beat the egg whites until stiff. Gradually beat in the sugar until the egg whites are stiff and shiny. Fold in the chopped mints. Drop small spoonfuls of the mixture on to a greased and lined baking (cookie) sheet and bake in a preheated oven at 140°C/275°F/gas mark 1 for 1½ hours until dry.

Chocolate Chip and Nut Meringues

Makes 12

2 egg whites
175 g/6 oz/¾ cup caster (superfine) sugar
50 g/2 oz/½ cup chocolate chips
25 g/1 oz/¼ cup walnuts, finely chopped

Preheat the oven to 190°C/375°F/gas mark 5. Beat the egg whites until they form soft peaks. Gradually add the sugar and beat until the mixture forms stiff peaks. Fold in the chocolate chips and walnuts. Drop spoonfuls of the mixture on to greased baking (cookie) sheets and place in the oven. Turn off the oven and leave until cool.

Hazelnut Meringues

Makes 12

100 g/4 oz/1 cup hazelnuts
2 egg whites
100 g/4 oz/½ cup caster (superfine) sugar
A few drops of vanilla essence (extract)

Reserve 12 nuts for decoration and crush the remainder. Whisk the egg whites until stiff. Add half the sugar and continue to whisk until the mixture forms stiff peaks. Fold in the remaining sugar, the ground hazelnuts and the vanilla essence. Spoon the mixture into 12 rounds on a greased and lined baking (cookie) sheet and place a reserved nut on the top of each one. Bake in a preheated oven at 130°C/250°F/gas mark ½ for 2–3 hours until crisp.

Meringue Layer Cake with Nuts

Makes one 23 cm/9 in cake

For the cake:
50 g/2 oz/¼ cup butter or margarine, softened
150 g/5 oz/⅔ cup caster (superfine) sugar
4 eggs, separated
100 g/4 oz/1 cup plain (all-purpose) flour
10 ml/2 tsp baking powder
A pinch of salt
60 ml/4 tbsp milk
5 ml/1 tsp vanilla essence (extract)
50 g/2 oz/½ cup pecan nuts, finely chopped
For the custard:
250 ml/8 fl oz/1 cup milk
50 g/2 oz/¼ cup caster (superfine) sugar
50 g/2 oz/½ cup plain (all-purpose) flour
1 egg
A pinch of salt
120 ml/4 fl oz/½ cup double (heavy) cream

To make the cake, beat the butter or margarine with 100 g/4 oz/½ cup of the sugar until light and fluffy. Gradually beat in the egg yolks, then fold in the flour, baking powder and salt alternately with the milk and vanilla essence. Spoon into two greased and lined 23 cm/9 in cake tins (pans) and level the surface. Whisk the egg whites until stiff, then fold in the remaining sugar and whisk again until stiff and glossy. Spread over the cake mixture and sprinkle with the nuts. Bake in a preheated oven at 150°C/300°F/gas mark 3 for 45 minutes until the meringue is dry. Transfer to a wire rack to cool.

To make the custard, blend a little of the milk with the sugar and flour. Bring the remaining milk to the boil in a pan, pour over the sugar mixture and whisk until blended. Return the milk to the rinsed-out pan and bring to the boil, stirring continuously, then simmer, stirring, until thickened. Remove from the heat and beat in the egg and salt and leave to cool slightly. Whip the cream until stiff, then fold into the mixture. Leave to cool. Sandwich the cakes together with the custard.

Hazelnut Macaroon Slices

Makes 20

175 g/6 oz/1½ cups hazelnuts, peeled
3 egg whites
225 g/8 oz/1 cup caster (superfine) sugar
5 ml/1 tsp vanilla essence (extract)
5 ml/1 tsp ground cinnamon
5 ml/1 tsp grated lemon rind
Rice paper

Roughly chop 12 of the hazelnuts, then pound the remainder until finely crushed. Whisk the egg whites until light and frothy. Gradually add the sugar and continue to beat until the mixture forms stiff peaks. Fold in the hazelnuts, vanilla essence, cinnamon and lemon rind. Drop heaped teaspoonfuls on to a baking (cookie) sheet lined with rice paper, then flatten into thin strips. Leave to set for 1 hour. Bake in a preheated oven at 180°C/350°F/gas mark 4 for 12 minutes until firm to the touch.

Meringue and Walnut Layer

Makes one 25 cm/10 in cake

100 g/4 oz/½ cup butter or margarine, softened
400 g/14 oz/1¾ cup caster (superfine) sugar
3 egg yolks
100 g/4 oz/1 cup plain (all-purpose) flour
10 ml/2 tsp baking powder
120 ml/4 fl oz/½ cup milk
100 g/4 oz/1 cup walnuts
4 egg whites
250 ml/8 fl oz/1 cup double (heavy) cream
5 ml/1 tsp vanilla essence (extract)
Cocoa (unsweetened chocolate) powder for dusting

Cream together the butter or margarine and 75 g/3 oz/⅓ cup of the sugar until light and fluffy. Gradually beat in the egg yolks, then fold in the flour and baking powder alternately with the milk. Spoon the dough into two greased and floured 25 cm/10 in cake tins (pans). Reserve a few walnut halves for decoration, chop the remainder finely and sprinkle over the cakes. Whisk the egg whites until stiff, then add the remaining sugar and whisk again until thick and glossy. Spread over the top of the cakes and bake in a preheated oven at 180°C/ 350°F/gas mark 4 for 25 minutes, covering the cake with greaseproof (waxed) paper towards the end of cooking if the meringue begins to brown too much. Allow to cool in the tins, then turn the cakes out with the meringue on the top.

Whip together the cream and vanilla essence until stiff. Sandwich the cakes together, meringue-side up, with half the cream and spread the remainder on top. Decorate with the reserved walnuts and sprinkle with sifted cocoa.

Meringue Mountains

Makes 6

2 eggs whites
100 g/4 oz/½ cup caster (superfine) sugar
150 ml/¼ pt/⅔ cup double (heavy) cream
350 g/12 oz strawberries, sliced
25 g/1 oz/¼ cup plain (semi-sweet) chocolate, grated

Beat the egg whites until stiff. Add half the sugar and beat until thick and glossy. Fold in the remaining sugar. Pipe six circles of meringue on to baking parchment on a baking (cookie) sheet. Bake in a preheated oven at 140°C/275°F/ gas mark 1 for 45 minutes until pale golden and crisp. The insides will remain fairly soft. Remove from the sheet and cool on a wire rack.

Whip the cream until stiff. Pipe or spoon half the cream over the meringue circles, top with the fruit, then decorate with the remaining cream. Sprinkle the grated chocolate over the top.

262

Raspberry Cream Meringues

Serves 6

2 egg whites
100 g/4 oz/½ cup caster (superfine) sugar
150 ml/¼ pt/⅔ cup double (heavy) cream
30 ml/2 tbsp icing (confectioners') sugar
225 g/8 oz raspberries

Whisk the egg whites in a clean, grease-free bowl until they begin to form soft peaks. Add half the sugar and continue to whisk until the mixture stands in stiff peaks. Lightly fold in the remaining sugar, using a metal spoon. Line a baking (cookie) sheet with baking parchment and pipe tiny swirls of meringue on to the sheet. Dry the meringues at the lowest possible setting in the oven for 2 hours. Cool on a wire rack.

Whip the cream with the icing sugar until stiff, then fold in the raspberries. Use to sandwich pairs of the meringues together and pile on to a serving plate.

Caramel Vacherin

Makes one 23 cm/9 in cake

4 egg whites
225 g/8 oz/1 cup soft brown sugar
50 g/2 oz/½ cup hazelnuts, chopped
300 ml/½ pt/1¼ cups double (heavy) cream
A few whole hazelnuts to decorate

Whisk the egg whites until they hold soft peaks. Gradually whisk in the sugar until stiff and glossy. Spoon the meringue into a piping bag fitted with a plain 1 cm/½ in nozzle (tip) and pipe two 23 cm/9 in spirals of meringue on to a greased and lined baking (cookie) sheet. Sprinkle with 15 ml/1 tbsp of chopped nuts and bake in a preheated oven at 120°C/250°F/gas mark ½ for 2 hours until crisp. Transfer to a wire rack to cool.

Whip the cream until stiff, then fold in the remaining nuts. Use most of the cream to sandwich the meringue rounds together, then decorate with the remaining cream and top with the whole hazelnuts.

Ratafia Cakes

Makes 16

3 egg whites
100 g/4 oz/1 cup ground almonds
225 g/8 oz/1 cup caster (superfine) sugar

Beat the egg whites until stiff. Fold in the almonds and half the sugar and beat again until stiff. Fold in the remaining sugar. Place small rounds on a greased and lined baking (cookie) sheet and bake in a preheated oven at 150°C/300°F/gas mark 2 for 50 minutes until dry and crisp at the edges.

Scones (Biscuits)

*S*cones are quick and easy to prepare and all sorts of flavourings and extra
ingredients can be added to the basic recipe to give you a wide variety. This
chapter contains oven-baked scones: you will find griddle scones in Griddle
Cakes and Breads on pages 272–80.

Simple Scones

Makes 10

225 g/8 oz/2 cups plain
  (all-purpose) flour
A pinch of salt
2.5 ml/½ tsp bicarbonate of soda
  (baking soda)
5 ml/1 tsp cream of tartar
50 g/2 oz/¼ cup butter or margarine,
  diced
30 ml/2 tbsp milk
30 ml/2 tbsp water

*M*ix together the flour, salt, bicarbonate of soda and cream of tartar.
Rub in the butter or margarine. Slowly
add the milk and water until you have a
soft dough. Knead quickly on a floured
surface until smooth, then roll out until
1 cm/½ in thick and cut into 5 cm/
2 in rounds with a biscuit (cookie) cutter.
Place the scones (biscuits) on a greased
baking (cookie) sheet and bake in a
preheated oven at 230°C/450°F/gas mark
8 for about 10 minutes until well risen
and golden brown.

Rich Egg Scones

Makes 12

50 g/2 oz/¼ cup butter or margarine
225 g/8 oz/2 cups self-raising
  (self-rising) flour
10 ml/2 tsp baking powder
25 g/1 oz/2 tbsp caster (superfine)
  sugar
1 egg, lightly beaten
100 ml/3½ fl oz/6½ tbsp milk

*R*ub the butter or margarine into the
flour and baking powder. Stir in the
sugar. Blend in the egg and milk until you
have a soft dough. Knead lightly on a
floured surface, then roll out to about
1 cm/½ in thick and cut into 5 cm/2 in
rounds with a biscuit (cookie) cutter.
Re-roll the trimmings and cut out. Place
the scones (biscuits) on a greased baking
(cookie) sheet and bake in a preheated
oven at 230°C/450°F/gas mark 8 for 10
minutes or until golden.

Apple Scones

Makes 12

225 g/8 oz/2 cups wholemeal
  (wholewheat) flour
20 ml/1½ tbsp baking powder
A pinch of salt
50 g/2 oz/¼ cup butter or margarine
30 ml/2 tbsp grated cooking (tart)
  apple
1 egg, beaten
150 ml/¼ pt/⅔ cup milk

*M*ix together the flour, baking powder
and salt. Rub in the butter or
margarine, then stir in the apple.
Gradually mix in enough of the egg and
milk to make a soft dough. Roll out on a
lightly floured surface to about 5 cm/2 in
thick and cut into rounds with a biscuit
(cookie) cutter. Place the scones (biscuits)
on a greased baking (cookie) sheet and
brush with any remaining egg. Bake in a
preheated oven at 200°C/400°F/gas mark
6 for 12 minutes until lightly browned.

Apple and Coconut Scones

Makes 12

50 g/2 oz/¼ cup butter or margarine
225 g/8 oz/2 cups self-raising
  (self-rising) flour
25 g/1 oz/2 tbsp caster (superfine)
  sugar
30 ml/2 tbsp desiccated (shredded)
  coconut
1 eating (dessert) apple, peeled, cored
  and chopped
150 ml/¼ pt/⅔ cup plain yoghurt
30 ml/2 tbsp milk

Rub the butter or margarine into the flour. Stir in the sugar, coconut and apple, then blend in the yoghurt to make a soft dough, adding a little of the milk if necessary. Roll out on a lightly floured surface to about 2.5 cm/1 in thick and cut into rounds with a biscuit (cookie) cutter. Place the scones (biscuits) on a greased baking (cookie) sheet and bake in a preheated oven at 220°C/425°F/gas mark 7 for 10–15 minutes until well risen and golden.

Apple and Date Scones

Makes 12

50 g/2 oz/¼ cup butter or margarine
225 g/8 oz/2 cups plain
  (all-purpose) flour
5 ml/1 tsp mixed (apple pie) spice
5 ml/1 tsp cream of tartar
2.5 ml/½ tsp bicarbonate of soda
  (baking soda)
25 g/1 oz/2 tbsp soft brown sugar
1 small cooking (tart) apple, peeled,
  cored and chopped
50 g/2 oz/⅓ cup stoned (pitted) dates,
  chopped
45 ml/3 tbsp milk

Rub the butter or margarine into the flour, mixed spice, cream of tartar and bicarbonate of soda. Stir in the sugar, apple and dates, then add the milk and mix to a soft dough. Knead lightly, then roll out on a floured surface to 2.5 cm/1 in thick and cut into rounds with a biscuit (cookie) cutter. Place the scones (biscuits) on a greased baking (cookie) sheet and bake in a preheated oven at 220°C/425°F/gas mark 7 for 12 minutes until risen and golden brown.

Barley Scones

Makes 12

175 g/6 oz/1½ cups barley flour
50 g/2 oz/½ cup plain (all-purpose)
  flour
A pinch of salt
2.5 ml/½ tsp bicarbonate of soda
  (baking soda)
2.5 ml/½ tsp cream of tartar
25 g/1 oz/2 tbsp butter or margarine
25 g/1 oz/2 tbsp soft brown sugar
100 ml/3½ fl oz/6½ tbsp milk
Egg yolk to glaze

Mix together the flours, salt, bicarbonate of soda and cream of tartar. Rub in the butter or margarine until the mixture resembles breadcrumbs, then stir in the sugar and enough of the milk to make a soft dough. Roll out on a lightly floured surface to 2 cm/¾ in thick and cut into rounds with a biscuit (cookie) cutter. Place the scones (biscuit) on a greased baking (cookie) sheet and brush with egg yolk. Bake in a preheated oven at 220°C/425°F/gas mark 7 for 10 minutes until golden.

Date Scones

Makes 12

*225 g/8 oz/2 cups wholemeal
(wholewheat) flour
2.5 ml/½ tsp bicarbonate of soda
(baking soda)
2.5 ml/½ tsp cream of tartar
2.5 ml/½ tsp salt
40 g/1½ oz/3 tbsp butter or margarine
15 ml/1 tbsp caster (superfine) sugar
100 g/4 oz/⅔ cup stoned (pitted) dates,
chopped
About 100 ml/3½ fl oz/6 ½ tbsp
buttermilk*

Mix together the flour, bicarbonate of soda, cream of tartar and salt. Rub in the butter or margarine, then stir in the sugar and dates and make a well in the centre. Gradually mix in just enough of the buttermilk to make a medium-soft dough. Roll out thickly and cut into triangles. Place the scones (biscuits) on a greased baking (cookie) sheet and bake in a preheated oven at 230°C/450°F/gas mark 8 for 20 minutes until golden.

Herby Scones

Makes 8

*175 g/6 oz/¾ cup butter or margarine
225 g/8 oz/2 cups strong plain (bread)
flour
15 ml/1 tsp baking powder
A pinch of salt
5 ml/1 tsp soft brown sugar
30 ml/2 tbsp dried mixed herbs
60 ml/4 tbsp milk or water
Milk for brushing*

Rub the butter or margarine into the flour, baking powder and salt until the mixture resembles breadcrumbs. Stir in the sugar and herbs. Add enough of the milk or water to make a soft dough. Roll out on a lightly floured surface to about 2 cm/¾ in thick and cut into rounds with a biscuit (cookie) cutter. Place the scones (biscuits) on a greased baking (cookie) sheet and brush the tops with milk. Bake in a preheated oven at 200°C/400°F/gas mark 6 for 10 minutes until well risen and golden brown.

Honey Scone Ring

Makes one 20 cm/8 in ring

For the dough:
*100 g/4 oz/½ cup butter or margarine
350 g/12 oz/3 cups self-raising
(self-rising) flour
A pinch of salt
1 egg
150 ml/¼ pt/⅔ cup milk*
For the filling:
*100 g/4 oz/½ cup butter or margarine,
softened
60 ml/4 tbsp clear honey
15 ml/1 tbsp demerara sugar*

To make the dough, rub the butter or margarine into the flour and salt until the mixture resembles breadcrumbs. Beat together the egg and milk, then mix enough into the flour mixture to make a soft dough. Roll out on a lightly floured surface to a 30 cm/12 in square.

To make the filling, cream together the butter or margarine and honey. Reserve 15 ml/1 tbsp of the mixture and spread the rest over the dough. Roll up like a Swiss (jelly) roll, then cut into eight slices. Arrange the slices in a greased 20 cm/8 in cake tin (pan), seven around the edge and one in the centre. Spread with the reserved honey mixture and sprinkle with sugar. Bake the scone (biscuit) in a preheated oven at 190°C/375°F/gas mark 5 for 30 minutes until golden brown. Leave to cool in the tin for 10 minutes before turning out on to a wire rack to finish cooling.

Muesli Scones

Makes 8 wedges

100 g/4 oz/1 cup muesli
150 ml/¼ pt/⅔ cup water
50 g/2 oz/¼ cup butter or margarine
100 g/4 oz/1 cup plain (all-purpose)
   or wholemeal (wholewheat) flour
10 ml/2 tsp baking powder
50 g/2 oz/⅓ cup raisins
1 egg, beaten

Soak the muesli in the water for 30 minutes. Rub the butter or margarine into the flour and baking powder until the mixture resembles breadcrumbs, then stir in the raisins and soaked muesli and mix to a soft dough. Shape into a 20 cm/8 in round and flatten on to a greased baking (cookie) sheet. Cut partially through into eight sections and brush with beaten egg. Bake in a preheated oven at 230°C/450°F/gas mark 8 for about 20 minutes until golden.

Orange and Raisin Scones

Makes 12

50 g/2 oz/¼ cup butter or margarine
225 g/8 oz/2 cups plain
   (all-purpose) flour
2.5 ml/½ tsp bicarbonate of soda
   (baking soda)
100 g/4 oz/⅔ cup raisins
5 ml/1 tsp grated orange rind
60 ml/4 tbsp orange juice
60 ml/4 tbsp milk
Milk to glaze

Rub the butter or margarine into the flour and bicarbonate of soda, then stir in the raisins and orange rind. Work in the orange juice and milk to make a soft dough. Roll out on a lightly floured surface to about 2.5 cm/1 in thick and cut into rounds with a biscuit (cookie) cutter. Place the scones (biscuits) on a greased

baking (cookie) sheet and brush the tops with milk. Bake in a preheated oven at 200°C/400°F/gas mark 6 for 15 minutes until lightly browned.

Pear Scones

Makes 12

50 g/2 oz/¼ cup butter or margarine
225 g/8 oz/2 cups self-raising
   (self-rising) flour
25 g/1 oz/2 tbsp caster (superfine)
   sugar
1 firm pear, peeled, cored and
   chopped
150 ml/¼ pt/⅔ cup plain yoghurt
30 ml/2 tbsp milk

Rub the butter or margarine into the flour. Stir in the sugar and the pear, then blend in the yoghurt to make a soft dough, adding a little of the milk if necessary. Roll out on a lightly floured surface to about 2.5 cm/1 in thick and cut into rounds with a biscuit (cookie) cutter. Place the scones (biscuits) on a greased baking (cookie) sheet and bake in a preheated oven at 230°C/450°F/gas mark 8 for 10–15 minutes until well risen and golden.

Potato Scones

Makes 12

50 g/2 oz/¼ cup butter or margarine
225 g/8 oz/2 cups self-raising
(self-rising) flour
A pinch of salt
175 g/6 oz/¾ cup cooked mashed
potato
60 ml/4 tbsp milk

Rub the butter or margarine into the flour and salt. Stir in the mashed potato and enough of the milk to make a soft dough. Roll out on a lightly floured surface to about 2.5 cm/1 in thick and cut into rounds with a biscuit (cookie) cutter. Place the scones (biscuits) on a lightly greased baking (cookie) sheet and bake in a preheated oven at 200°C/400°F/gas mark 6 for 15–20 minutes until lightly golden.

Raisin Scones

Makes 12

75 g/3 oz/½ cup raisins
225 g/8 oz/2 cups plain
(all-purpose) flour
2.5 ml/½ tsp salt
15 ml/1 tbsp baking powder
25 g/1 oz/2 tbsp caster (superfine)
sugar
50 g/2 oz/¼ cup butter or margarine
120 ml/4 fl oz/½ cup single (light)
cream
1 egg, beaten

Soak the raisins in hot water for 30 minutes, then drain. Mix together the dry ingredients, then rub in the butter or margarine. Stir in the cream and egg to make a soft dough. Divide into three balls, then roll out until about 1 cm/½ in thick and place on a greased baking (cookie) sheet. Cut each one into quarters. Bake the scones (biscuits) in a preheated oven at 230°C/450°F/gas mark 8 for about 10 minutes until golden brown.

Treacle Scones

Makes 10

225 g/8 oz/2 cups plain
(all-purpose) flour
10 ml/2 tsp baking powder
2.5 ml/½ tsp ground cinnamon
50 g/2 oz/¼ cup butter or margarine,
diced
25 g/1 oz/2 tbsp caster (superfine)
sugar
30 ml/2 tbsp black treacle (molasses)
150 ml/¼ pt/⅔ cup milk

Mix together the flour, baking powder and cinnamon. Rub in the butter or margarine, then stir in the sugar, treacle and enough of the milk to make a soft dough. Roll out to 1 cm/½ in thick and cut into 5 cm/2 in rounds with a biscuit (cookie) cutter. Place the scones (biscuits) on a greased baking tray and bake in a preheated oven at 220°C/425°F/gas mark 7 for 10–15 minutes until well risen and golden brown.

Treacle and Ginger Scones

Makes 12

400 g/14 oz/3½ cups plain
(all-purpose) flour
50 g/2 oz/½ cup rice flour
5 ml/1 tsp bicarbonate of soda
(baking soda)
2.5 ml/½ tsp cream of tartar
10 ml/2 tsp ground ginger
2.5 ml/½ tsp salt
10 ml/2 tsp caster (superfine) sugar
50 g/2 oz/¼ cup butter or margarine
30 ml/2 tbsp black treacle (molasses)
300 ml/½ pt/1¼ cups milk

Mix together the dry ingredients. Rub in the butter or margarine until the mixture resembles breadcrumbs. Stir in the treacle and enough of the milk to make a soft but not sticky dough. Knead gently on a lightly floured surface, roll out and cut into rounds with a 7.5 cm/ 3 in biscuit (cookie) cutter. Place the scones (biscuits) on a greased baking (cookie) sheet and brush with any remaining milk. Bake in a preheated oven at 220°C/425°F/gas mark 7 for 15 minutes until risen and golden brown.

Sultana Scones

Makes 12

225 g/8 oz/2 cups plain
(all-purpose) flour
A pinch of salt
2.5 ml/½ tsp bicarbonate of soda
(baking soda)
2.5 ml/½ tsp cream of tartar
50 g/2 oz/¼ cup butter or margarine
25 g/1 oz/2 tbsp caster (superfine)
sugar
50 g/2 oz/⅓ cup sultanas
(golden raisins)
7.5 ml/½ tbsp lemon juice
150 ml/¼ pt/⅔ cup milk

Mix together the flour, salt, bicarbonate of soda and cream of tartar. Rub in the butter or margarine until the mixture resembles breadcrumbs. Stir in the sugar and sultanas. Mix the lemon juice into the milk and gradually stir into the dry ingredients until you have a soft dough. Knead lightly, then roll out to about 1 cm/½ in thick and cut into 5 cm/ 2 in rounds with a biscuit (cookie) cutter. Place the scones (biscuits) on a greased baking (cookie) sheet and bake in a preheated oven at 230°C/450°F/gas mark 8 for about 10 minutes until well risen and golden brown.

Wholemeal Treacle Scones

Makes 12

100 g/4 oz/1 cup wholemeal
(wholewheat) flour
100 g/4 oz/1 cup plain (all-purpose)
flour
25 g/1 oz/2 tbsp caster (superfine)
sugar
2.5 ml/½ tsp cream of tartar
2.5 ml/½ tsp bicarbonate of soda
(baking soda)
5 ml/1 tsp mixed (apple pie) spice
50 g/2 oz/¼ cup butter or margarine
30 ml/2 tbsp black treacle (molasses)
100 ml/3½ fl oz/6½ tbsp milk

Mix together the dry ingredients, then rub in the butter or margarine. Warm the treacle, then mix it into the ingredients with enough of the milk to make a soft dough. Roll out on a lightly floured surface to 1 cm/½ in thick and cut into rounds with a biscuit (cookie) cutter. Arrange the scones (biscuits) on a greased and floured baking (cookie) sheet and brush with milk. Bake in a preheated oven at 190°C/375°F/gas mark 5 for 20 minutes.

269

Yoghurt Scones

Makes 12

200 g/7 oz/1¼ cups plain
(all-purpose) flour
25 g/1 oz/¼ cup rice flour
10 ml/2 tsp baking powder
A pinch of salt
15 ml/1 tbsp caster (superfine) sugar
50 g/2 oz/¼ cup butter or margarine
150 ml/¼ pt/⅔ cup plain yoghurt

Mix together the flours, baking powder, salt and sugar. Rub in the butter or margarine until the mixture resembles breadcrumbs. Stir in the yoghurt to make a soft but not sticky dough. Roll out on a floured surface to about 2 cm/¾ in thick and cut into 5 cm/2 in rounds with a biscuit (cookie) cutter. Place on a greased baking (cookie) sheet and bake in a preheated oven at 200°C/400°F/gas mark 6 for about 15 minutes until well risen and golden brown.

Cheese Scones

Makes 12

225 g/8 oz/2 cups plain
(all-purpose) flour
2.5 ml/½ tsp salt
15 ml/1 tbsp baking powder
50 g/2 oz/¼ cup butter or margarine
100 g/4 oz/1 cup Cheddar cheese,
grated
150 ml/¼ pt/⅔ cup milk

Mix together the flour, salt and baking powder. Rub in the butter or margarine until the mixture resembles breadcrumbs. Stir in the cheese. Gradually blend in the milk to make a soft dough. Knead lightly, then roll out to about 1 cm/½ in thick and cut into 5 cm/2 in rounds with a biscuit (cookie) cutter. Place the scones (biscuits) on a greased baking (cookie) sheet and bake in a preheated oven at 220°C/425°F/gas mark 7 for 12–15 minutes until well risen and golden on top. Serve warm or cold.

Wholemeal Herb Scones

Makes 12

100 g/4 oz/½ cup butter or margarine
175 g/6 oz/1¼ cups wholemeal
  (wholewheat) flour
50 g/2 oz/½ cup plain (all-purpose)
  flour
10 ml/2 tsp baking powder
30 ml/2 tbsp chopped fresh sage or
  thyme
150 ml/¼ pt/⅔ cup milk

Rub the butter or margarine into the flours and baking powder until the mixture resembles breadcrumbs. Stir in the herbs and enough of the milk to make a soft dough. Knead lightly, then roll out to about 1 cm/½ in thick and cut into 5 cm/2 in rounds with a biscuit (cookie) cutter. Place the scones (biscuits) on a greased baking (cookie) sheet and brush the tops with milk. Bake in a preheated oven at 220°C/425°F/gas mark 7 for 10 minutes until risen and golden brown.

Salami and Cheese Scones

Serves 4

50 g/2 oz/¼ cup butter or margarine
225 g/8 oz/2 cups self-raising
  (self-rising) flour
A pinch of salt
50 g/2 oz salami, chopped
75 g/3 oz/¾ cup Cheddar cheese,
  grated
75 ml/5 tbsp milk

Rub the butter or margarine into the flour and salt until the mixture resembles breadcrumbs. Stir in the salami and cheese, then add the milk and mix to a soft dough. Shape into a 20 cm/8 in round and flatten slightly. Place the scones (biscuits) on a greased baking (cookie) sheet and bake in a preheated oven at 220°C/425°F/gas mark 7 for 15 minutes until golden brown.

Wholemeal Scones

Makes 12

175 g/6 oz/1½ cups wholemeal
  (wholewheat) flour
50 g/2 oz/½ cup plain (all-purpose)
  flour
15 ml/1 tbsp baking powder
A pinch of salt
50 g/2 oz/¼ cup butter or margarine
50 g/2 oz/¼ cup caster (superfine)
  sugar
150 ml/¼ pt/⅔ cup milk

Mix together the flours, baking powder and salt. Rub in the butter or margarine until the mixture resembles breadcrumbs. Stir in the sugar. Gradually mix in the milk to make a soft dough. Knead lightly, then roll out to about 1 cm/½ in thick and cut into 5 cm/2 in rounds with a biscuit (cookie) cutter. Place the scones (biscuits) on a greased baking (cookie) sheet and bake in a preheated oven at 230°C/450°F/gas mark 8 for about 15 minutes until risen and golden brown. Serve warm.

271

Griddle Cakes and Breads

Some cakes, breads and biscuits (cookies) can be cooked on top of the oven, so although not strictly 'bakes', I think they still qualify for this collection. Here are some delicious scones, old-fashioned country breads and cakes. One advantage to most of them is that they can be cooked very quickly. Why not try making some for that lazy Sunday breakfast you've been promising yourself? Most of them are cooked on a griddle or in a frying pan (skillet), but there are a couple of fried (sautéed) and steamed recipes too.

Barbadian Conkies

Makes 12

350 g/12 oz pumpkin, grated
225 g/8 oz sweet potato, grated
1 large coconut, grated, or 225 g/8 oz
    2 cups desiccated (shredded)
    coconut
350 g/12 oz/1½ cups soft brown sugar
5 ml/1 tsp ground mixed (apple-pie)
    spice
5 ml/1 tsp grated nutmeg
5 ml/1 tsp salt
5 ml/1 tsp almond essence (extract)
100 g/4 oz/⅔ cup raisins
350 g/12 oz/3 cups cornmeal
100 g/4 oz/1 cup self-raising
    (self-rising) flour
175 g/6 oz/¾ cup butter or margarine,
    melted
300 ml/½ pt/1¼ cups milk

Mix together the pumpkin, sweet potato and coconut. Stir in the sugar, spices, salt and almond essence. Add the raisins, cornmeal and flour and mix well. Mix the melted butter or margarine with the milk and fold into the dry ingredients until well blended. Place about 60 ml/4 tbsp of the mixture into a square of foil, taking care not to overfill. Fold the foil into a parcel so that it is neatly wrapped and no mixture is left exposed. Repeat with the remaining mixture. Steam the conkies on a rack over a pan of boiling water for about 1 hour until firm and cooked. Serve hot or cold.

Deep-fried Christmas Biscuits

Makes 40

50 g/2 oz/¼ cup butter or margarine
100 g/4 oz/1 cup plain (all-purpose)
    flour
2.5 ml/½ tsp ground cardamom
25 g/1 oz/2 tbsp caster (superfine)
    sugar
15 ml/1 tbsp double (heavy) cream
5 ml/1 tsp brandy
1 small egg, beaten
Oil for deep-frying
Icing (confectioners') sugar for
    dusting

Rub the butter or margarine into the flour and cardamom until the mixture resembles breadcrumbs. Stir in the sugar, then add the cream and brandy and enough of the egg to make a fairly stiff mixture. Cover and leave in a cool place for 1 hour.

Roll out on a lightly floured surfaced to 5 mm/¼ in thick and cut into 10 × 2.5 cm/4 × 1 in strips with a pastry cutter. Cut a slit down the middle of each strip with a sharp knife. Pull one end of the strip through the slit to make a half-bow. Deep-fry the biscuits (cookies) in batches in hot oil for about 4 minutes until golden brown and puffed. Drain on kitchen paper (paper towels) and serve sprinkled with icing sugar.

Cornmeal Cakes

Makes 12

*100 g/4 oz/1 cup self-raising
(self-rising) flour*
100 g/4 oz/1 cup cornmeal
5 ml/1 tsp baking powder
*15 g/½ oz/1 tbsp caster (superfine)
sugar*
2 eggs
375 ml/13 fl oz/1½ cups milk
60 ml/4 tbsp oil
Oil for shallow-frying

Mix together the dry ingredients and make a well in the centre. Beat together the eggs, milk and measured oil, then beat into the dry ingredients. Heat a little oil in a large frying pan (skillet) and fry (sauté) 60 ml/4 tbsp of the batter until bubbles appear on the top. Turn over and brown on the other side. Remove from the pan and keep warm while you continue with the remaining batter. Serve warm.

Crumpets

Makes 8

*15 g/½ oz fresh yeast or 20 ml/
4 tsp dried yeast*
5 ml/1 tsp caster (superfine) sugar
300 ml/½ pt/1¼ cups milk
1 egg
*250 g/9 oz/2¼ cups plain
(all-purpose) flour*
5 ml/1 tsp salt
Oil for greasing

Mix the yeast and sugar with a little of the milk to a paste, then blend in the remaining milk and the egg. Stir the liquid into the flour and salt and mix to a creamy, thick batter. Cover and leave in a warm place for 30 minutes until doubled in size. Heat a griddle or heavy frying pan (skillet) and grease it lightly. Place 7.5 cm/3 in baking rings on the griddle.

(If you do not have baking rings, carefully cut the top and bottom off a small tin.) Pour cupfuls of the mixture into the rings and cook for about 5 minutes until the underside is browned and the top is pitted. Repeat with the remaining mixture. Serve toasted.

Doughnuts

Makes 16

300 ml/½ pt/1¼ cups warm milk
15 ml/1 tbsp dried yeast
*175 g/6 oz/¾ cup caster (superfine)
sugar*
*450 g/1 lb/4 cups strong plain (bread)
flour*
5 ml/1 tsp salt
50 g/2 oz/¼ cup butter or margarine
1 egg, beaten
Oil for deep-frying
5 ml/1 tsp ground cinnamon

Mix together the warm milk, yeast, 5 ml/1 tsp of the sugar and 100 g/ 4 oz/1 cup of the flour. Leave in a warm place for 20 minutes until frothy. Mix together the remaining flour, 50 g/2 oz/ ¼ cup of the sugar and the salt in a bowl and rub in the butter or margarine until the mixture resembles breadcrumbs. Mix in the egg and the yeast mixture and knead well to a smooth dough. Cover and leave in a warm place for 1 hour. Knead again and roll out to 2 cm/½ in thick. Cut into rings with an 8 cm/3 in cutter and cut out the centres with a 4 cm/1½ in cutter. Place on a greased baking (cookie) sheet and leave to rise for 20 minutes. Heat the oil until almost smoking, then deep-fry the doughnuts a few at a time for a few minutes until golden. Drain well. Place the remaining sugar and the cinnamon in a bag and shake the doughnuts in the bag until well coated.

Potato Doughnuts

Makes 24

15 ml/1 tbsp dried yeast
60 ml/4 tbsp warm water
25 g/1 oz/2 tbsp caster (superfine)
sugar
25 g/1 oz/2 tbsp lard (shortening)
1.5 ml/¼ tsp salt
75 g/3 oz/⅓ cup mashed potato
1 egg, beaten
120 ml/4 fl oz/½ cup milk, boiled
300 g/10 oz/2½ cups strong plain
(bread) flour
Oil for deep-frying
Granulated sugar for sprinkling

Dissolve the yeast in the warm water with a teaspoon of the sugar and leave until frothy. Mix together the lard, remaining sugar and the salt. Stir in the potato, yeast mixture, egg and milk, then gradually work in the flour and mix to a smooth dough. Turn out on to a floured surface and knead well. Place in a greased bowl, cover with clingfilm (plastic wrap) and leave in a warm place for about 1 hour until doubled in size.

Knead again, then roll out to 1 cm/½ in thick. Cut into rings with an 8 cm/3 in cutter, then cut out the centres with a 4 cm/1½ in cutter to make doughnut shapes. Leave to rise until doubled in size. Heat the oil and deep-fry the doughnuts until golden. Sprinkle with sugar and leave to cool.

Naan Bread

Makes 6

2.5 ml/½ tsp dried yeast
60 ml/4 tbsp warm water
350 g/12 oz/3 cups plain
(all-purpose) flour
10 ml/2 tsp baking powder
A pinch of salt
150 ml/¼ pt/⅔ cup plain yoghurt
Melted butter for brushing

Mix together the yeast and warm water and leave in a warm place for 10 minutes until frothy. Mix the yeast mixture into the flour, baking powder and salt, then work in the yoghurt to make a soft dough. Knead until no longer sticky. Place in an oiled bowl, cover and leave to rise for 8 hours.

Divide the dough into six pieces and roll into ovals about 5 mm/¼ in thick. Place on a greased baking (cookie) sheet and brush with melted butter. Grill (broil) under a medium grill (broiler) for about 5 minutes until slightly puffy, then turn and brush the other side with butter and grill for a further 3 minutes until lightly browned.

Oat Bannocks

Makes 4

100 g/4 oz/1 cup medium oatmeal
2.5 ml/½ tsp salt
A pinch of bicarbonate of soda
(baking soda)
10 ml/2 tsp oil
60 ml/4 tsp hot water

Mix the dry ingredients in a bowl and make a well in the centre. Stir in the oil and enough of the water to make a firm dough. Turn out on to a lightly floured surface and knead until smooth. Roll out to about 5 mm/¼ in thick, tidy the edges, then cut into quarters. Heat a griddle or heavy-based frying pan (skillet) and fry (sauté) the bannocks for about 20 minutes until the corners begin to curl. Turn over and cook the other side for 6 minutes.

274

Pikelets

Makes 8

10 ml/2 tsp fresh yeast or 5 ml/
  1 tsp dried yeast
5 ml/1 tsp caster (superfine) sugar
300 ml/½ pt/1¼ cups milk
1 egg
225 g/8 oz/2 cups plain
  (all-purpose) flour
5 ml/1 tsp salt
Oil for greasing

Mix the yeast and sugar with a little of the milk to a paste, then blend in the remaining milk and the egg. Stir the liquid into the flour and salt and mix to a thin batter. Cover and leave in a warm place for 30 minutes until doubled in size. Heat a griddle or heavy frying pan (skillet) and grease it lightly. Pour cupfuls of the mixture on to the griddle and cook for about 3 minutes until the underside is browned, then turn and cook for about 2 minutes on the other side. Repeat with the remaining mixture.

Easy Drop Scones

Makes 15

100 g/4 oz/1 cup self-raising
  (self-rising) flour
A pinch of salt
15 ml/1 tbsp caster (superfine) sugar
1 egg
150 ml/¼ pt/⅔ cup milk
Oil for greasing

Mix together the flour, salt and sugar and make a well in the centre. Drop in the egg and gradually work in the egg and milk until you have a smooth batter. Heat a large frying pan (skillet) and oil it lightly. When hot, place spoonfuls of batter in the pan so they form rounds. Cook for about 3 minutes until the scones (biscuits) are puffed and golden on the underside, then turn over and brown the other side. Serve hot or warm.

Maple Drop Scones

Makes 30

200 g/7 oz/1¾ cups self-raising
  (self-rising) flour
25 g/1 oz/¼ cup rice flour
10 ml/2 tsp baking powder
25 g/1 oz/2 tbsp caster (superfine)
  sugar
A pinch of salt
15 ml/1 tbsp maple syrup
1 egg, beaten
200 ml/7 fl oz/scant 1 cup milk
Sunflower oil
50 g/2 oz/¼ cup butter or margarine,
  softened
15 ml/1 tbsp finely chopped walnuts

Mix together the flours, baking powder, sugar and salt and make a well in the centre. Add the maple syrup, egg and half the milk and beat until smooth. Stir in the remaining milk to make a thick batter. Heat a little oil in a frying pan (skillet), then pour off the excess. Drop spoonfuls of the batter into the pan and fry (sauté) until the undersides are golden. Turn and fry the other sides. Remove from the pan and keep warm while you fry the remaining scones (biscuits). Mash the butter or margarine with the nuts and top the warm scones with the flavoured butter to serve.

Griddle Scones

Makes 12

225 g/8 oz/2 cups plain
   (all-purpose) flour
5 ml/1 tsp bicarbonate of soda
   (baking soda)
10 ml/2 tsp cream of tartar
2.5 ml/½ tsp salt
25 g/1 oz/2 tbsp lard (shortening)
   or butter
25 g/1 oz/2 tbsp caster (superfine)
   sugar
150 ml/¼ pt/⅔ cup milk
Oil for greasing

Mix together the flour, bicarbonate of soda, cream of tartar and salt. Rub in the lard or butter, then stir in the sugar. Gradually blend in the milk until you have a soft dough. Cut the dough in half and knead and shape each into a flat round about 1 cm/½ in thick. Cut each round into six. Heat a griddle or large frying pan (skillet) and oil lightly. When hot, place the scones (biscuits) in the pan and cook for about 5 minutes until golden on the underside, then turn over and cook on the other side. Leave to cool on a wire rack.

Cheesy Griddle Scones

Makes 12

25 g/1 oz/2 tbsp butter or margarine,
   softened
100 g/4 oz/½ cup cottage cheese
5 ml/1 tsp snipped fresh chives
2 eggs, beaten
40 g/1½ oz/⅓ cup plain (all-purpose)
   flour
15 g/½ oz/2 tbsp rice flour
5 ml/1 tsp baking powder
15 ml/1 tbsp milk
Oil for greasing

Beat together all the ingredients except the oil to make a thick batter. Heat a little oil in a frying pan (skillet), then drain off any excess. Fry (sauté) spoonfuls of the mixture until the undersides are golden. Turn the scones (biscuits) over and fry the other side. Remove from the pan and keep warm while you fry the remaining scones

Special Scotch Pancakes

Makes 12

100 g/4 oz/1 cup plain (all-purpose)
   flour
10 ml/2 tsp caster (superfine) sugar
5 ml/1 tsp cream of tartar
2.5 ml/½ tsp salt
2.5 ml/½ tsp bicarbonate of soda
   (baking soda)
1 egg
5 ml/1 tsp golden (light corn) syrup
120 ml/4 fl oz/½ cup warm milk
Oil for greasing

Mix together the dry ingredients and make a well in the centre. Beat the egg with the syrup and milk and mix into the flour mixture until you have a very thick batter. Cover and leave to stand for about 15 minutes until the mixture bubbles. Heat a large griddle or heavy-based frying pan (skillet) and grease it lightly. Drop small spoonfuls of the batter on to the griddle and cook one side for about 3 minutes until the underside is golden, then turn and cook the other side for about 2 minutes. Wrap the pancakes in a warm tea towel (dish cloth) while you cook the remaining batter. Serve fresh and buttered, toasted or fried (sautéed).

Fruit Scotch Pancakes

Makes 12

100 g/4 oz/1 cup plain (all-purpose)
    flour
10 ml/2 tsp caster (superfine) sugar
5 ml/1 tsp cream of tartar
2.5 ml/½ tsp salt
2.5 ml/½ tsp bicarbonate of soda
    (baking soda)
100 g/4 oz/⅔ cup raisins
1 egg
5 ml/1 tsp golden (light corn) syrup
120 ml/4 fl oz/½ cup warm milk
Oil for greasing

Mix together the dry ingredients and raisins and make a well in the centre. Beat the egg with the syrup and milk and mix into the flour mixture until you have a very thick batter. Cover and leave to stand for about 15 minutes until the mixture bubbles. Heat a large griddle or heavy-based frying pan (skillet) and grease it lightly. Drop small spoonfuls of the batter on to the griddle and cook one side for about 3 minutes until the underside is golden, then turn and cook the other side for about 2 minutes. Wrap the pancakes in a warm tea towel (dish cloth) while you cook the remainder. Serve fresh and buttered, toasted or fried (sautéed).

Orange Scotch Pancakes

Makes 12

100 g/4 oz/1 cup plain (all-purpose)
    flour
10 ml/2 tsp caster (superfine) sugar
5 ml/1 tsp cream of tartar
2.5 ml/½ tsp salt
2.5 ml/½ tsp bicarbonate of soda
    (baking soda)
10 ml/2 tsp grated orange rind
1 egg
5 ml/1 tsp golden (light corn) syrup
120 ml/4 fl oz/½ cup warm milk

A few drops of orange essence
    (extract)
Oil for greasing

Mix together the dry ingredients and orange rind and make a well in the centre. Beat the egg with the syrup, milk and orange essence and mix into the flour mixture until you have a very thick batter. Cover and leave to stand for about 15 minutes until the mixture bubbles. Heat a large griddle or heavy-based frying pan (skillet) and grease it lightly. Drop small spoonfuls of the batter on to the griddle and cook one side for about 3 minutes until the underside is golden, then turn and cook the other side for about 2 minutes. Wrap the pancakes in a warm tea towel (dish cloth) while you cook the remainder. Serve fresh and buttered, toasted or fried (sautéed).

Singing Hinny

Makes 12

225 g/8 oz/2 cups plain
    (all-purpose) flour
2.5 ml/½ tsp salt
2.5 ml/½ tsp baking powder
50 g/2 oz/¼ cup lard (shortening)
50 g/2 oz/¼ cup butter or margarine
100 g/4 oz/⅔ cup currants
120 ml/4 fl oz/½ cup milk
Oil for greasing

Mix together the dry ingredients, then rub in the lard and butter or margarine until the mixture resembles breadcrumbs. Stir in the currants and make a well in the centre. Mix in enough of the milk to make a stiff dough. Roll out on a lightly floured surface to about 1 cm/½ in thick and prick the top with a fork. Heat a griddle or heavy-based frying pan (skillet) and grease it lightly. Cook the cake for about 5 minutes until the underside is golden, then turn and cook the other side for about 4 minutes. Serve split and buttered.

Welsh Cakes

Serves 4

225 g/8 oz/2 cups plain
  (all-purpose) flour
5 ml/1 tsp baking powder
2.5 ml/½ tsp ground mixed
  (apple-pie) spice
50 g/2 oz/¼ cup butter or margarine
50 g/2 oz/¼ cup lard (shortening)
75 g/3 oz/⅓ cup caster (superfine)
  sugar
50 g/2 oz/⅓ cup currants
1 egg, beaten
30–45 ml/2–3 tbsp milk

Mix together the flour, baking powder and mixed spice in a bowl. Rub in the butter or margarine and lard until the mixture resembles breadcrumbs. Stir in the sugar and currants. Stir in the egg and enough of the milk to make a stiff dough. Roll out on a floured board to 5 mm/¼ in thick and cut into 7.5 cm/3 in rounds. Bake on a greased griddle for about 4 minutes on each side until golden brown.

Welsh Pancakes

Makes 12

175 g/6 oz/1½ cups plain
  (all-purpose) flour
2.5 ml/½ tsp cream of tartar
2.5 ml/½ tsp bicarbonate of soda
  (baking soda)
50 g/2 oz/¼ cup caster (superfine)
  sugar
25 g/1 oz/2 tbsp butter or margarine
1 egg, beaten
120 ml/4 fl oz/½ cup milk
2.5 ml/½ tsp vinegar
Oil for greasing

Mix together the dry ingredients and stir in the sugar. Rub in the butter or margarine and make a well in the centre. Mix in the egg and just enough of the milk to make a thin batter. Stir in the vinegar. Heat a griddle or heavy-based frying pan (skillet) and grease it lightly. Drop large spoonfuls of batter into the pan and fry (sauté) for about 3 minutes until golden on the underside. Turn and cook the other side for about 2 minutes. Serve hot and buttered.

Mexican Spiced Corn Bread

Makes 8 rolls

225 g/8 oz/2 cups self-raising
  (self-rising) flour
5 ml/1 tsp chilli powder
2.5 ml/½ tsp bicarbonate of soda
  (baking soda)
200 g/7 oz/1 small can creamed
  sweetcorn (corn)
15 ml/1 tbsp curry paste
250 ml/8 fl oz/1 cup plain yoghurt
Oil for shallow-frying

Mix together the flour, chilli powder and bicarbonate of soda. Stir in the remaining ingredients except the oil and mix to a soft dough. Turn out on to a lightly floured surface and knead gently until smooth. Cut into eight pieces and pat each one into a 13 cm/5 in round. Heat the oil in a heavy-based frying pan (skillet) and fry (sauté) the corn breads for 2 minutes on each side until browned and lightly puffed.

Swedish Flat Bread

Makes 4

225 g/8 oz/2 cups wholemeal
  (wholewheat) flour
225 g/8 oz/2 cups rye or barley flour
5 ml/1 tsp salt
About 250 ml/8 fl oz/1 cup lukewarm
  water
Oil for greasing

Mix the flours and salt in a bowl, then gradually work in the water until you have a firm dough. You may need a little more or less water, depending on the flour you use. Beat well until the mixture leaves the sides of the bowl, then turn out on to a lightly floured surface and knead for 5 minutes. Divide the dough into four and roll out thinly to 20 cm/8 in rounds. Heat a griddle or large frying pan (skillet) and oil it lightly. Fry (sauté) one or two breads at a time for about 15 minutes on each side until golden.

Steamed Rye and Sweetcorn Bread

Makes one 23 cm/9 in loaf

175 g/6 oz/1½ cups rye flour
175 g/6 oz/1½ cups wholemeal
  (wholewheat) flour
100 g/4 oz/1 cup oatmeal
10 ml/2 tsp bicarbonate of soda
  (baking soda)
5 ml/1 tsp salt
450 ml/¾ pt/2 cups milk
175 g/6 oz/½ cup black treacle
  (molasses)
10 ml/2 tsp lemon juice

Mix together the flours, oatmeal, bicarbonate of soda and salt. Warm the milk, treacle and lemon juice until lukewarm, then stir into the dry ingredients. Spoon into a greased 23 cm/9 in pudding bowl and cover with pleated foil. Place in a large pan and fill with enough hot water to come half-way up the sides of the tin. Cover and boil for 3 hours, topping up with boiling water as necessary. Leave overnight before serving.

Steamed Sweetcorn Bread

Makes two 450 g/1 lb loaves

175 g/6 oz/1½ cups plain
  (all-purpose) flour
225 g/8 oz/2 cups cornmeal
15 ml/1 tbsp baking powder
A pinch of salt
3 eggs
45 ml/3 tbsp oil
150 ml/¼ pt/⅔ cup milk
300 g/11 oz canned sweetcorn (corn),
  drained and mashed

Mix together the flour, cornmeal, baking powder and salt. Beat together the eggs, oil and milk, then stir into the dry ingredients with the sweetcorn. Spoon into two greased 450 g/1 lb loaf tins (pans) and place in a large pan filled with enough boiling water to come half-way up the sides of the tins. Cover and simmer for 2 hours, topping up with boiling water as necessary. Leave to cool in the tins before turning out and slicing.

Wholemeal Chapatis

Makes 12

225 g/8 oz/2 cups wholemeal
  (wholewheat) flour
5 ml/1 tsp salt
150 ml/¼ pt/⅔ cup water

Mix the flour and salt in a bowl, then gradually work in the water until you have a firm dough. Divide into 12 and roll out thinly on a floured surface. Grease a heavy-based frying pan (skillet) or griddle and fry (sauté) a few chapatis at a time over a moderate heat until brown underneath. Turn over and cook the other side until lightly browned. Keep the chapatis warm while you fry the remainder. Serve buttered on one side, if liked.

Wholemeal Puris

Makes 8

*100 g/4 oz/1 cup wholemeal
(wholewheat) flour*
*100 g/4 oz/1 cup plain (all-purpose)
flour*
2.5 ml/½ tsp salt
*25 g/1 oz/2 tbsp butter or margarine,
melted*
150 ml/¼ pt/⅔ cup water
Oil for deep-frying

Mix together the flours and salt and make a well in the centre. Pour in the butter or margarine. Gradually add the water, mixing to a firm dough. Knead for 5–10 minutes, then cover with a damp cloth and leave to stand for 15 minutes.

Divide the dough into eight and roll each one into a thin 13 cm/5 in round. Heat the oil in a large heavy-based frying pan (skillet) and fry (sauté) the puris one or two at a time until they puff up and are crisp and golden. Drain on kitchen paper (paper towels).

Sweet Biscuits and Cookies

*T*here is nothing quite like home-made biscuits (cookies) and there are plenty of recipes here that are quick and easy to prepare so you can offer your family and guests the wonderful taste of home-cooked fare.

Almond Biscuits

Makes 24

100 g/4 oz/½ cup butter or margarine, softened
50 g/2 oz/¼ cup caster (superfine) sugar
100 g/4 oz/1 cup self-raising (self-rising) flour
25 g/1 oz/¼ cup ground almonds
A few drops of almond essence (extract)

*C*ream together the butter or margarine and sugar until light and fluffy. Work in the flour, ground almonds and almond essence to a stiff mixture. Shape into large walnut-sized balls and arrange well apart on a greased baking (cookie) sheet, then press down lightly with a fork to flatten. Bake the biscuits (cookies) in a preheated oven at 180°C/350°F/gas mark 4 for 15 minutes until golden brown.

Almond Curls

Makes 30

100 g/4 oz/1 cup flaked (slivered) almonds
100 g/4 oz/½ cup butter or margarine
100 g/4 oz/½ cup caster (superfine) sugar
30 ml/2 tbsp milk
15–30 ml/1–2 tbsp plain (all-purpose) flour

*P*lace the almonds, butter or margarine, sugar and milk in a pan with 15 ml/1 tbsp of the flour. Heat gently, stirring, until blended, adding the remaining flour if necessary to make the mixture hold together. Place spoonfuls well apart on a greased and floured baking (cookie) sheet and bake in a preheated oven at 180°C/350°F/gas mark 4 for 8 minutes until light brown. Leave to cool on the baking sheet for about 30 seconds, then shape them into curls around the handle of a wooden spoon. If they become too cool to shape, return them to the oven for a few seconds to warm again before shaping the remainder.

Almond Rings

Makes 24

100 g/4 oz/½ cup butter or margarine,
   softened
100 g/4 oz/½ cup caster (superfine)
   sugar
1 egg, separated
225 g/8 oz/2 cups plain
   (all-purpose) flour
5 ml/1 tsp baking powder
5 ml/1 tsp grated lemon rind
50 g/2 oz/½ cup flaked (slivered)
   almonds
Caster (superfine) sugar for
   sprinkling

Cream together the butter or margarine and sugar until light and fluffy. Gradually beat in the egg yolk, then work in the flour, baking powder and lemon rind, finishing with your hands until the mixture binds together. Roll out to 5 mm/¼ in thick and cut into 6 cm/2¼ in rounds with a biscuit (cookie) cutter, then cut out the centres with a 2 cm/¾ in cutter. Place the biscuits well apart on a greased baking (cookie) sheet and prick them with a fork. Bake in a preheated oven at 180°C/350°F/gas mark 4 for 10 minutes. Brush with egg white, sprinkle with the almonds and sugar, then return to the oven for a further 5 minutes until pale golden.

Mediterranean Almond Cracks

Makes 24

2 eggs, separated
175 g/6 oz/1 cup icing (confectioners')
   sugar, sifted
10 ml/2 tsp baking powder
Grated rind of ½ lemon
A few drops of vanilla essence
   (extract)
400 g/14 oz/3½ cups ground almonds

Beat the yolks and one egg white with the sugar until pale and fluffy. Beat in all the remaining ingredients and mix to a stiff dough. Roll into walnut-sized balls and arrange on a greased baking (cookie) sheet, pressing down gently to flatten them. Bake in a preheated oven at 180°C/350°F/gas mark 4 for 15 minutes until golden and cracked on the surface.

Almond and Chocolate Cookies

Makes 24

50 g/2 oz/¼ cup butter or margarine,
   softened
75 g/3 oz/⅓ cup caster (superfine)
   sugar
1 small egg, beaten
100 g/4 oz/1 cup plain (all-purpose)
   flour
2.5 ml/½ tsp baking powder
25 g/1 oz/¼ cup ground almonds
25 g/1 oz/¼ cup plain (semi-sweet)
   chocolate, grated

Cream together the butter or margarine and sugar until light and fluffy. Gradually beat in the egg, then stir in the remaining ingredients to make a fairly stiff dough. If the mixture is too moist, add a little more flour. Wrap in clingfilm (plastic wrap) and chill for 30 minutes.

Roll the dough into a cylinder shape and cut into 1 cm/½ in slices. Arrange, well apart, on a greased baking (cookie) sheet and bake in a preheated oven at 190°C/375°F/gas mark 5 for 10 minutes.

Amish Fruit and Nut Biscuits

Makes 24

100 g/4 oz/½ cup butter or margarine,
*   softened*
175 g/6 oz/¾ cup caster (superfine)
*   sugar*
1 egg
75 ml/5 tbsp milk
75 g/3 oz/¼ cup black treacle
*   (molasses)*
250 g/9 oz/2¼ cups plain
*   (all-purpose) flour*
10 ml/2 tsp baking powder
15 ml/1 tbsp ground cinnamon
10 ml/2 tsp bicarbonate of soda
*   (baking soda)*
2.5 ml/½ tsp grated nutmeg
50 g/2 oz/½ cup medium oatmeal
50 g/2 oz/⅓ cup raisins
25 g/1 oz/¼ cup chopped mixed nuts

Cream together the butter or margarine and sugar until light and fluffy. Gradually beat in the egg, then the milk and treacle. Fold in the remaining ingredients and mix to a stiff dough. Add a little more milk if the mixture is too stiff to work, or a little more flour if it is too sticky; the texture will vary depending on the flour you use. Roll out the dough to about 5 mm/¼ in thick and cut into rounds with a biscuit (cookie) cutter. Place on a greased baking (cookie) sheet and bake in a preheated oven at 180°C/350°F/gas mark 4 for 10 minutes until golden.

Anise Biscuits

Makes 16

175 g/6 oz/¾ cup caster (superfine)
*   sugar*
2 egg whites
1 egg
100 g/4 oz/1 cup plain (all-purpose)
*   flour*
5 ml/1 tsp ground anise

Beat together the sugar, egg whites and egg for 10 minutes. Gradually beat in the flour and stir in the anise. Spoon the mixture into a 450 g/1 lb loaf tin (pan) and bake in a preheated oven at 180°C/350°F/gas mark 4 for 35 minutes until a skewer inserted in the centre comes out clean. Remove from the tin and cut into 1 cm/½ in slices. Place the biscuits (cookies) on their sides on a greased baking (cookie) sheet and return to the oven for a further 10 minutes, turning half-way through cooking.

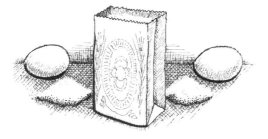

Banana, Oat and Orange Juice Cookies

Makes 24

*100 g/4 oz/½ cup butter or margarine,
  softened*
100 g/4 oz ripe bananas, mashed
120 ml/4 fl oz/½ cup orange juice
4 egg whites, lightly beaten
10 ml/2 tsp vanilla essence (extract)
5 ml/1 tsp finely grated orange rind
225 g/8 oz/2 cups rolled oats
*225 g/8 oz/2 cups plain
  (all-purpose) flour*
*5 ml/1 tsp bicarbonate of soda
  (baking soda)*
5 ml/1 tsp grated nutmeg
A pinch of salt

Beat the butter or margarine until soft, then stir in the bananas and orange juice. Mix together the egg whites, vanilla essence and orange rind, then stir into the banana mixture, followed by the remaining ingredients. Drop spoonfuls on to baking (cookie) sheets and bake in a preheated oven at 180°C/350°F/gas mark 4 for 20 minutes until golden brown.

Basic Biscuits

Makes 40

*100 g/4 oz/½ cup butter or margarine,
  softened*
*100 g/4 oz/½ cup caster (superfine)
  sugar*
1 egg, beaten
5 ml/1 tsp vanilla essence (extract)
*225 g/8 oz/2 cups plain
  (all-purpose) flour*

Cream together the butter or margarine and sugar until light and fluffy. Gradually beat in the egg and vanilla essence, then fold in the flour and knead to a smooth dough. Roll into a ball, wrap in clingfilm (plastic wrap) and chill for 1 hour.

Roll out the dough to 5 mm/¼ in thick and cut into rounds with a biscuit (cookie) cutter. Arrange on a greased baking (cookie) sheet and bake in a preheated oven at 200°C/400°F/gas mark 6 for 10 minutes until golden. Leave to cool on the sheet for 5 minutes before transferring to a wire rack to finish cooling.

Crunchy Bran Biscuits

Makes 16

*100 g/4 oz/1 cup wholemeal
  (wholewheat) flour*
100 g/4 oz/½ cup soft brown sugar
25 g/1 oz/¼ cup rolled oats
25 g/1 oz/½ cup bran
*5 ml/1 tsp bicarbonate of soda
  (baking soda)*
5 ml/1 tsp ground ginger
100 g/4 oz/½ cup butter or margarine
15 ml/1 tbsp golden (light corn) syrup
15 ml/1 tbsp milk

Mix together the dry ingredients. Melt the butter with the syrup and milk, then mix into the dry ingredients to make a stiff dough. Place spoonfuls of the biscuit (cookie) mixture on a greased baking (cookie) sheet and bake in a preheated oven at 160°C/325°F/gas mark 3 for 15 minutes until golden brown.

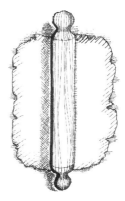

284

Sesame Bran Biscuits

Makes 12

225 g/8 oz/2 cups wholemeal
(wholewheat) flour
5 ml/1 tsp baking powder
25 g/1 oz/½ cup bran
A pinch of salt
50 g/2 oz/¼ cup butter or margarine
45 ml/3 tbsp soft brown sugar
45 ml/3 tbsp sultanas
(golden raisins)
1 egg, lightly beaten
120 ml/4 fl oz/½ cup milk
45 ml/3 tbsp sesame seeds

Mix together the flour, baking powder, bran and salt, then rub in the butter or margarine until the mixture resembles breadcrumbs. Stir in the sugar and sultanas, then mix in the egg and enough of the milk to make a soft but not sticky dough. Roll out to 1 cm/½ in thick and cut into rounds with a biscuit (cookie) cutter. Place on a greased baking (cookie) sheet, brush with milk and sprinkle with sesame seeds. Bake in a preheated oven at 220°C/425°F/gas mark 7 for 10 minutes until golden brown.

Brandy Biscuits with Caraway

Makes 30

25 g/1 oz/2 tbsp butter or margarine,
softened
75 g/3 oz/⅓ cup soft brown sugar
½ egg
10 ml/2 tsp brandy
175 g/6 oz/1½ cups plain
(all-purpose) flour
10 ml/2 tsp caraway seeds
5 ml/1 tsp baking powder
A pinch of salt

Cream together the butter or margarine and sugar until light and fluffy. Gradually beat in the egg and the brandy, then stir in the remaining ingredients and mix to a stiff dough. Wrap in clingfilm (plastic wrap) and chill for 30 minutes.

Roll out the dough on a lightly floured surface to about 3 mm/⅛ in thick and cut into rounds with a biscuit (cookie) cutter. Place the biscuits on a greased baking (cookie) sheet and bake in a preheated oven at 200°C/400°F/gas mark 6 for 10 minutes.

Brandy Snaps

Makes 30

100 g/4 oz/½ cup butter or margarine
100 g/4 oz/⅓ cup golden (light corn)
syrup
100 g/4 oz/½ cup demerara sugar
100 g/4 oz/1 cup plain (all-purpose)
flour
5 ml/1 tsp ground ginger
5 ml/1 tsp lemon juice

Melt the butter or margarine, syrup and sugar in a pan. Leave to cool slightly, then stir in the flour and ginger, then the lemon juice. Drop teaspoonfuls of the mixture 10 cm/4 in apart on to greased baking (cookie) sheets and bake in a preheated oven at 180°C/350°F/gas mark 4 for 8 minutes until golden brown. Leave to cool for a minute, then lift from the baking sheet with a slice and roll around the greased handle of a wooden spoon. Slip off the spoon handle and leave to cool on a wire rack. If the snaps harden too much before you shape them, put them back in the oven for a minute to warm and soften.

285

Butter Biscuits

Makes 24

100 g/4 oz/½ cup butter or margarine,
softened
50 g/2 oz/¼ cup caster (superfine)
sugar
Grated rind of 1 lemon
150 g/5 oz/1¼ cups self-raising
(self-rising) flour

Cream together the butter or margarine and sugar until light and fluffy. Work in the lemon rind, then mix in the flour to a stiff mixture. Shape into large walnut-sized balls and arrange well apart on a greased baking (cookie) sheet, then press down lightly with a fork to flatten. Bake the biscuits (cookies) in a preheated oven at 180°C/350°F/gas mark 4 for 15 minutes until golden brown.

Butterscotch Biscuits

Makes 40

100 g/4 oz/½ cup butter or margarine,
softened
100 g/4 oz/½ cup dark soft brown
sugar
1 egg, beaten
1.5 ml/¼ tsp vanilla essence (extract)
225 g/8 oz/2 cups plain
(all-purpose) flour
7.5 ml/1½ tsp baking powder
A pinch of salt

Cream together the butter or margarine and sugar until light and fluffy. Gradually beat in the egg and vanilla essence. Mix in the flour, baking powder and salt. Shape the dough into three rolls about 5 cm/2 in in diameter, wrap in clingfilm (plastic wrap) and chill for 4 hours or overnight.
Cut into 3 mm/⅛ in thick slices and arrange on ungreased baking (cookie) sheets. Bake the biscuits (cookies) in a preheated oven at 190°C/375°F/gas mark 5 for 10 minutes until lightly browned.

Caramel Biscuits

Makes 30

50 g/2 oz/¼ cup butter or margarine,
softened
50 g/2 oz/¼ cup lard (shortening)
225 g/8 oz/1 cup soft brown sugar
1 egg, lightly beaten
175 g/6 oz/1½ cups plain
(all-purpose) flour
1.5 ml/¼ tsp bicarbonate of soda
(baking soda)
1.5 ml/¼ tsp cream of tartar
A pinch of grated nutmeg
10 ml/2 tsp water
2.5 ml/½ tsp vanilla essence (extract)

Cream together the butter or margarine, lard and sugar until light and fluffy. Gradually beat in the egg. Fold in the flour, bicarbonate of soda, cream of tartar and nutmeg, then add the water and vanilla essence and mix to a soft dough. Roll into a sausage shape, wrap in clingfilm (plastic wrap) and chill for at least 30 minutes, preferably longer.
Cut the dough into 1 cm/½ in slices and arrange on a greased baking (cookie) sheet. Bake the biscuits (cookies) in a preheated oven at 180°C/350°F/gas mark 4 for 10 minutes until golden.

Carrot and Walnut Cookies

Makes 48

175 g/6 oz/¾ cup butter or margarine,
softened
100 g/4 oz/½ cup soft brown sugar
50 g/2 oz/¼ cup caster (superfine)
sugar
1 egg, lightly beaten
225 g/8 oz/2 cups plain
(all-purpose) flour
5 ml/1 tsp baking powder
2.5 ml/½ tsp salt
100 g/4 oz/½ cup mashed cooked
carrots
100 g/4 oz/1 cup walnuts, chopped

Cream together the butter or margarine and sugars until light and fluffy. Gradually beat in the egg, then fold in the flour, baking powder and salt. Fold in the mashed carrots and walnuts. Drop small spoonfuls on to a greased baking (cookie) sheet and bake in a preheated oven at 200°C/400°F/gas mark 6 for 10 minutes.

Orange-iced Carrot and Walnut Biscuits

Makes 48

For the biscuits (cookies):
175 g/6 oz/³⁄₄ cup butter or margarine, softened
100 g/4 oz/¹⁄₂ cup caster (superfine) sugar
50 g/2 oz/¹⁄₄ cup soft brown sugar
1 egg, lightly beaten
225 g/8 oz/2 cups plain (all-purpose) flour
5 ml/1 tsp baking powder
2.5 ml/¹⁄₂ tsp salt
5 ml/1 tsp vanilla essence (extract)
100 g/4 oz /¹⁄₂ cup mashed cooked carrots
100 g/4 oz/1 cup walnuts, chopped
For the icing (frosting):
175 g/6 oz/1 cup icing (confectioners') sugar, sifted
10 ml/2 tsp grated orange rind
30 ml/2 tbsp orange juice

To make the biscuits, cream together the butter or margarine and sugars until light and fluffy. Gradually beat in the egg, then fold in the flour, baking powder and salt. Fold in the vanilla essence, mashed carrots and walnuts. Drop small spoonfuls on to a greased baking (cookie) sheet and bake in a preheated oven at 200°C/400°F/gas mark 6 for 10 minutes.

To make the icing, place the icing sugar in a bowl, stir in the orange rind and make a well in the centre. Gradually work in the orange juice a little at a time until you have a smooth but fairly thick icing. Spread over the biscuits while they are still warm, then leave to cool and set.

Cherry Biscuits

Makes 48

100 g/4 oz/¹⁄₂ cup butter or margarine, softened
100 g/4 oz/¹⁄₂ cup caster (superfine) sugar
1 egg, beaten
5 ml/1 tsp vanilla essence (extract)
225 g/8 oz/2 cups plain (all-purpose) flour
50 g/2 oz/¹⁄₄ cup glacé (candied) cherries, chopped

Cream together the butter or margarine and sugar until light and fluffy. Gradually beat in the egg and vanilla essence, then fold in the flour and cherries and knead to a smooth dough. Roll into a ball, wrap in clingfilm (plastic wrap) and chill for 1 hour.

Roll out the dough to 5 mm/¹⁄₄ in thick and cut into rounds with a biscuit (cookie) cutter. Arrange on a greased baking (cookie) sheet and bake in a preheated oven at 200°C/400°F/gas mark 6 for 10 minutes until golden. Leave to cool on the sheet for 5 minutes before transferring to a wire rack to finish cooling.

Cherry and Almond Rings

Makes 24

*100 g/4 oz/½ cup butter or margarine,
softened*
*100 g/4 oz/½ cup caster (superfine)
sugar, plus extra for sprinkling*
1 egg, separated
*225 g/8 oz/2 cups plain
(all-purpose) flour*
5 ml/1 tsp baking powder
5 ml/1 tsp grated lemon rind
60 ml/4 tbsp glacé (candied) cherries
*50 g/2 oz/½ cup flaked (slivered)
almonds*

Cream together the butter or margarine and sugar until light and fluffy.
Gradually beat in the egg yolk, then work
in the flour, baking powder, lemon rind
and cherries, finishing with your hands
until the mixture binds together. Roll out
to 5 mm/¼ in thick and cut into 6 cm/
2¼ in rounds with a biscuit (cookie)
cutter, then cut out the centres with a
2 cm/¾ in cutter. Place the biscuits well
apart on a greased baking (cookie) sheet
and prick them with a fork. Bake in a
preheated oven at 180°C/350°F/gas mark
4 for 10 minutes. Brush with egg white
and sprinkle with the almonds and sugar,
then return to the oven for a further 5
minutes until pale golden.

Chocolate Butter Biscuits

Makes 24

100 g/4 oz/½ cup butter or margarine
*50 g/2 oz/¼ cup caster (superfine)
sugar*
*100 g/4 oz/1 cup self-raising
(self-rising) flour*
*30 ml/2 tbsp cocoa (unsweetened
chocolate) powder*

Cream together the butter or margarine and sugar until light and fluffy.
Work in the flour and cocoa to a stiff
mixture. Shape into large walnut-sized

balls and arrange well apart on a greased
baking (cookie) sheet, then press down
lightly with a fork to flatten. Bake the
biscuits (cookies) in a preheated oven at
180°C/350°F/gas mark 4 for 15 minutes
until brown.

Chocolate and Cherry Rolls

Makes 24

*100 g/4 oz/½ cup butter or margarine,
softened*
*100 g/4 oz/½ cup caster (superfine)
sugar*
1 egg
2.5 ml/½ tsp vanilla essence (extract)
*225 g/8 oz/2 cups plain
(all-purpose) flour*
5 ml/1 tsp baking powder
A pinch of salt
*25 g/1 oz/¼ cup cocoa (unsweetened
chocolate) powder*
*25 g/1 oz/2 tbsp glacé (candied)
cherries, chopped*

Cream together the butter and sugar
until light and fluffy. Gradually beat
in the egg and vanilla essence, then stir in
the flour, baking powder and salt to make
a stiff dough. Divide the dough in half
and mix the cocoa into one half and the
cherries into the other half. Wrap in
clingfilm (plastic wrap) and chill for 30
minutes.
   Roll out each piece of dough to a
rectangle about 3 mm/⅛ in thick, then
place one on top of the other and press
together gently with the rolling pin. Roll
up from the longest side and press
together gently. Cut into 1 cm/½ in thick
slices and arrange, well apart, on a greased
baking (cookie) sheet. Bake in a preheated
oven at 200°C/400°F/gas mark 6 for 10
minutes.

Photograph opposite: **Honey Scone
Ring (page 266) and Welsh Cakes
(page 278)**

288

Chocolate Chip Biscuits

Makes 24

75 g/3 oz/⅓ cup butter or margarine
175 g/6 oz/1½ cups plain
(all-purpose) flour
5 ml/1 tsp baking powder
A pinch of bicarbonate of soda
(baking soda)
50 g/2 oz/¼ cup soft brown sugar
45 ml/3 tbsp golden (light corn) syrup
100 g/4 oz/1 cup chocolate chips

Rub the butter or margarine into the flour, baking powder and bicarbonate of soda until the mixture resembles breadcrumbs. Stir in the sugar, syrup and chocolate chips and mix to smooth dough. Shape into small balls and arrange on a greased baking (cookie) sheet, pressing down lightly to flatten. Bake the biscuits (cookies) in a preheated oven at 190°C/375°F/gas mark 5 for 15 minutes until golden.

Chocolate and Banana Chip Cookies

Makes 24

75 g/3 oz/⅓ cup butter or margarine
175 g/6 oz/1½ cups plain
(all-purpose) flour
5 ml/1 tsp baking powder
2.5 ml/½ tsp bicarbonate of soda
(baking soda)
50 g/2 oz/¼ cup soft brown sugar
45 ml/3 tbsp golden (light corn) syrup
50 g/2 oz/½ cup chocolate chips
50 g/2 oz/½ cup dried banana chips,
coarsely chopped

Rub the butter or margarine into the flour, baking powder and bicarbonate of soda until the mixture resembles breadcrumbs. Stir in the sugar, syrup and chocolate and banana chips and mix to smooth dough. Shape into small balls and arrange on a greased baking (cookie)

sheet, pressing down lightly to flatten. Bake the biscuits (cookies) in a preheated oven at 190°C/375°F/gas mark 5 for 15 minutes until golden.

Chocolate and Nut Bites

Makes 24

50 g/2 oz/¼ cup butter or margarine,
softened
175 g/6 oz/¾ cup caster (superfine)
sugar
1 egg
5 ml/1 tsp vanilla essence (extract)
25 g/1 oz/¼ cup plain (semi-sweet)
chocolate, melted
100 g/4 oz/1 cup plain (all-purpose)
flour
5 ml/1 tsp baking powder
A pinch of salt
30 ml/2 tbsp milk
25 g/1 oz/¼ cup chopped mixed nuts
Icing (confectioners') sugar, sifted,
for dusting

Cream together the butter or margarine and caster sugar until light and fluffy. Gradually beat in the egg and vanilla essence, then stir in the chocolate. Mix together the flour, baking powder and salt and blend into the mixture alternately with the milk. Stir in the nuts, cover and chill for 3 hours.

Roll the mixture into 3 cm/1½ in balls and roll in the icing sugar. Arrange on a lightly greased baking (cookie) sheet and bake in a preheated oven at 180°C/350°F/gas mark 4 for 15 minutes until lightly browned. Serve dusted with icing sugar.

Photograph opposite: **Chocolate and Banana Chip Cookies (page 289) and Rich Man's Shortbread (page 313)**

American Chocolate Chip Cookies

Makes 20

225 g/8 oz/1 cup lard (shortening)
225 g/8 oz/1 cup soft brown sugar
100 g/4 oz/½ cup granulated sugar
5 ml/1 tsp vanilla essence (extract)
2 eggs, lightly beaten
175 g/6 oz/1½ cups plain
  (all-purpose) flour
5 ml/1 tsp salt
5 ml/1 tsp bicarbonate of soda
  (baking soda)
225 g/8 oz/2 cups rolled oats
350 g/12 oz/3 cups chocolate chips

Cream together the lard, sugars and vanilla essence until light and fluffy. Gradually beat in the eggs. Stir in the flour, salt, bicarbonate of soda and oats, then stir in the chocolate chips. Place spoonfuls of the mixture on to greased baking (cookie) sheets and bake in a preheated oven at 180°C/350°F/gas mark 4 for about 10 minutes until golden.

Chocolate Creams

Makes 24

175 g/6 oz/¾ cup butter or margarine,
  softened
175 g/6 oz/¾ cup caster (superfine)
  sugar
225 g/8 oz/2 cups self-raising
  (self-rising) flour
75 g/3 oz/¾ cup desiccated (shredded)
  coconut
100 g/4 oz/4 cups cornflakes, crushed
25 g/1 oz/¼ cup cocoa (unsweetened
  chocolate) powder
60 ml/4 tbsp boiling water
100 g/4 oz/1 cup plain (semi-sweet)
  chocolate

Cream together the butter or margarine and sugar, then stir in the flour, coconut and cornflakes. Blend the cocoa with the boiling water, then stir into the mixture. Roll into 2.5 cm/1 in balls, arrange on a greased baking (cookie) sheet and press lightly with a fork to flatten. Bake in a preheated oven at 180°C/350°F/gas mark 4 for 15 minutes until golden.

Melt the chocolate in a heatproof bowl over a pan of gently simmering water. Spread over the top of half the biscuits (cookies) and press the other half on top. Leave to cool.

Chocolate Chip and Hazelnut Cookies

Makes 16

200 g/7 oz/scant 1 cup butter or
  margarine, softened
50 g/2 oz/¼ cup caster (superfine)
  sugar
100 g/4 oz/½ cup soft brown sugar
10 ml/2 tsp vanilla essence (extract)
1 egg, beaten
275 g/10 oz/2½ cups plain
  (all-purpose) flour
50 g/2 oz/½ cup cocoa (unsweetened
  chocolate) powder
5 ml/1 tsp baking powder
75 g/3 oz/¾ cup hazelnuts
225 g/8 oz/2 cups white chocolate,
  chopped

Beat together the butter or margarine, sugars and vanilla essence until pale and fluffy, then beat in the egg. Stir in the flour, cocoa and baking powder. Stir in the nuts and chocolate until the mixture binds together. Shape into 16 balls and space out evenly on a greased and lined baking (cookie) sheet, then flatten slightly with the back of a spoon. Bake in a preheated oven at 160°C/325°F/gas mark 3 for about 15 minutes until just set but still slightly soft.

Chocolate and Nutmeg Biscuits

Makes 24

50 g/2 oz/¼ cup butter or margarine, softened
100 g/4 oz/½ cup caster (superfine) sugar
15 ml/1 tbsp cocoa (unsweetened chocolate) powder
1 egg yolk
2.5 ml/½ tsp vanilla essence (extract)
150 g/5 oz/1¼ cups plain (all-purpose) flour
5 ml/1 tsp baking powder
A pinch of grated nutmeg
60 ml/4 tbsp soured (dairy sour) cream

Cream together the butter or margarine and sugar until light and fluffy. Blend in the cocoa. Beat in the egg yolk and vanilla essence, then stir in the flour, baking powder and nutmeg. Blend in the cream until smooth. Cover and chill.

Roll out the dough to 5 mm/¼ in thick and cut out with a 5 cm/2 in cutter. Place the biscuits (cookies) on an ungreased baking (cookie) sheet and bake in a preheated oven at 200°C/400°F/gas mark 6 for 10 minutes until golden.

Chocolate-topped Biscuits

Makes 16

175 g/6 oz/¾ cup butter or margarine, softened
75 g/3 oz/⅓ cup caster (superfine) sugar
175 g/6 oz/1½ cups plain (all-purpose) flour
50 g/2 oz/½ cup ground rice
75 g/3 oz/¾ cup chocolate chips
100 g/4 oz/1 cup plain (semi-sweet) chocolate

Cream together the butter or margarine and sugar until light and fluffy. Mix in the flour and ground rice, then knead in the chocolate chips. Press into a greased Swiss roll tin (jelly roll pan) and prick with a fork. Bake in a preheated oven at 160°C/325°F/gas mark 3 for 30 minutes until golden. Mark into fingers while still warm, then leave to cool completely.

Melt the chocolate in a heatproof bowl over a pan of gently simmering water. Spread over the biscuits (cookies) and leave to cool and set before cutting into fingers. Store in an airtight container.

Coffee and Chocolate Sandwich Biscuits

Makes 40

For the biscuits (cookies):
175 g/6 oz/¾ cup butter or margarine
25 g/1 oz/2 tbsp lard (shortening)
450 g/1 lb/4 cups plain (all-purpose)
flour
A pinch of salt
100 g/4 oz/½ cup soft brown sugar
5 ml/1 tsp bicarbonate of soda
(baking soda)
60 ml/4 tbsp strong black coffee
5 ml/1 tsp vanilla essence (extract)
100 g/4 oz/⅓ cup golden (light corn)
syrup
For the filling:
10 ml/2 tsp instant coffee powder
10 ml/2 tsp boiling water
50 g/2 oz/¼ cup caster (superfine)
sugar
25 g/1 oz/2 tbsp butter or margarine
15 ml/1 tbsp milk

To make the biscuits, rub the butter or margarine and lard into the flour and salt until the mixture resembles breadcrumbs, then stir in the brown sugar. Mix the bicarbonate of soda with a little of the coffee, then stir into the mixture with the remaining coffee, the vanilla essence and the syrup and blend until you have a smooth dough. Place in a lightly oiled bowl, cover with clingfilm (plastic wrap) and leave overnight.

Roll out the dough on a lightly floured surface to about 1 cm/½ in thick and cut into 2 × 7.5 cm/¾ × 3 in rectangles. Score each one with a fork to make a ridged pattern. Transfer to a greased baking (cookie) sheet and bake in a preheated oven at 200°C/400°F/gas mark 6 for 10 minutes until golden brown. Cool on a wire rack.

To make the filling, dissolve the coffee powder in the boiling water in a small pan, then stir in the remaining ingredients and bring to the boil. Boil for 2 minutes, then remove from the heat and beat until thick and cool. Sandwich pairs of biscuits together with the filling.

Christmas Biscuits

Makes 24

100 g/4 oz/½ cup butter or margarine,
softened
100 g/4 oz/½ cup caster (superfine)
sugar
225 g/8 oz/2 cups plain
(all-purpose) flour
A pinch of salt
5 ml/1 tsp ground cinnamon
1 egg yolk
10 ml/2 tsp cold water
A few drops of vanilla essence
(extract)
For the icing (frosting):
225 g/8 oz/1⅓ cups icing
(confectioners') sugar, sifted
30 ml/2 tbsp water
Food colouring (optional)

Cream together the butter and sugar until light and fluffy. Fold in the flour, salt and cinnamon, then mix in the egg yolk, water and vanilla essence and mix to a firm dough. Wrap in clingfim (plastic wrap) and chill for 30 minutes.

Roll out the dough to 5 mm/¼ in thick and cut out Christmas shapes with biscuit (cookie) cutters or a sharp knife. Pierce a hole at the top of each biscuit if you want to hang them from a tree. Place the shapes on a greased baking (cookie) sheet and bake in a preheated oven at 200°C/400°F/gas mark 6 for 10 minutes until golden. Leave to cool.

To make the icing, gradually mix the water into the icing sugar until you have a fairly thick icing. Colour small quantities in different colours, if liked. Pipe patterns on to the biscuits, then leave to set. Thread a loop of ribbon or thread through the hole to hang up.

Coconut Biscuits

Makes 32

50 g/2 oz/3 tbsp golden (light corn) syrup
150 g/5 oz/⅔ cup butter or margarine
100 g/4 oz/½ cup caster (superfine) sugar
100 g/4 oz/1 cup plain (all-purpose) flour
75 g/3 oz/¾ cup rolled oats
50 g/2 oz/½ cup desiccated (shredded) coconut
10 ml/2 tsp bicarbonate of soda (baking soda)
15 ml/1 tbsp hot water

Melt together the syrup, butter or margarine and sugar. Stir in the flour, oats and desiccated coconut. Mix the bicarbonate of soda with the hot water, then stir into the other ingredients. Leave the mixture to cool slightly, then divide into 32 pieces and roll each one into a ball. Flatten the biscuits (cookies) and arrange on greased baking (cookie) sheets. Bake in a preheated oven at 160°C/325°F/gas mark 3 for 20 minutes until golden.

Corn Biscuits with Fruit Cream

Makes 12

150 g/5 oz/1¼ cups wholemeal (wholewheat) flour
150 g/5 oz/1¼ cups cornmeal
10 ml/2 tsp baking powder
A pinch of salt
225 g/8 oz/1 cup plain yoghurt
75 g/3 oz/¼ cup clear honey
2 eggs
45 ml/3 tbsp oil
For the fruit cream:
150 g/5 oz/⅔ cup butter or margarine, softened
Juice of 1 lemon
A few drops of vanilla essence (extract)
30 ml/2 tbsp caster (superfine) sugar
225 g/8 oz strawberries

Mix together the flour, cornmeal, baking powder and salt. Stir in the yoghurt, honey, eggs and oil and mix to a smooth dough. Roll out on a lightly floured surface to about 1 cm/½ in thick and cut into large rounds. Place on a greased baking (cookie) sheet and bake in a preheated oven at 200°C/400°F/gas mark 6 for 15 minutes until golden.

To make the fruit cream, blend together the butter or margarine, lemon juice, vanilla essence and sugar. Reserve a few strawberries for decoration, then purée the remainder and rub through a sieve (strainer) if you prefer the cream without seeds (pits). Mix into the butter mixture, then chill. Spoon or pipe a rosette of cream on to each biscuit before serving.

Cornish Biscuits

Makes 20

225 g/8 oz/2 cups self-raising (self-rising) flour
A pinch of salt
100 g/4 oz/½ cup butter or margarine
175 g/6 oz/⅔ cup caster (superfine) sugar
1 egg
Icing (confectioners') sugar, sifted, for dusting

Mix the flour and salt in a bowl, then rub in the butter or margarine until the mixture resembles breadcrumbs. Stir in the sugar. Stir in the egg and knead to a soft dough. Roll out thinly on a lightly floured surface, then cut into rounds.

Place on a greased baking (cookie) sheet and bake in a preheated oven at 200°C/400°F/gas mark 6 for about 10 minutes until golden.

Wholemeal Currant Biscuits

Makes 36

100 g/4 oz/½ cup butter or margarine,
  softened
50 g/2 oz/¼ cup demerara sugar
2 eggs, separated
100 g/4 oz/⅔ cup currants
225 g/8 oz/2 cups wholemeal
  (wholewheat) flour
100 g/4 oz/1 cup plain (all-purpose)
  flour
5 ml/1 tsp ground mixed (apple-pie)
  spice
150 ml/¼ pt/⅔ cup milk, plus extra for
  brushing

Cream together the butter or margarine
and sugar together until light and
fluffy. Beat in the egg yolks, then stir in the
currants. Mix together the flours and
mixed spice and stir into the mixture with
the milk. Whisk the egg whites until they
form soft peaks, then fold them into the
mixture to make a soft dough. Roll out the
dough on a lightly floured surface, then cut
out with a 5 cm/2 in biscuit (cookie) cutter.
Place on a greased baking (cookie) sheet
and brush with milk. Bake in a preheated
oven at 180°C/350°F/gas mark 4 for 20
minutes until golden.

Date Sandwich Biscuits

Makes 30

225 g/8 oz/1 cup butter or margarine,
  softened
450 g/1 lb/2 cups soft brown sugar
225 g/8 oz/2 cups oatmeal
225 g/8 oz/2 cups plain
  (all-purpose) flour
2.5 ml/½ tsp bicarbonate of soda
  (baking soda)
A pinch of salt
120 ml/4 fl oz/½ cup milk
225 g/8 oz/2 cups stoned (pitted)
  dates, very finely chopped
250 ml/8 fl oz/1 cup water

Cream together the butter or margarine and half the sugar until light
and fluffy. Mix together the dry
ingredients and add to the creamed
mixture alternately with the milk until
you have a firm dough. Roll out on a
lightly floured board and cut into rounds
with a biscuit (cookie) cutter. Place on a
greased baking (cookie) sheet and bake in
a preheated oven at 180°C/350°F/gas
mark 4 for 10 minutes until golden.

Place all the remaining ingredients in a
pan and bring to the boil. Reduce the heat
and simmer for 20 minutes until
thickened, stirring occasionally. Leave to
cool. Sandwich the biscuits together with
the filling.

Digestive Biscuits (Graham Crackers)

Makes 24

175 g/6 oz/1½ cups wholemeal
  (wholewheat) flour
50 g/2 oz/½ cup plain (all-purpose)
  flour
50 g/2 oz/½ cup medium oatmeal
2.5 ml/½ tsp salt
5 ml/1 tsp baking powder
100 g/4 oz/½ cup butter or margarine
30 ml/2 tbsp soft brown sugar
60 ml/4 tbsp milk

Mix together the flours, oatmeal, salt
and baking powder, then rub in the
butter or margarine and mix in the sugar.
Gradually add the milk and mix to a soft
dough. Knead well until no longer sticky.
Roll out to 5 mm/¼ in thick and cut
into 5 cm/2 in rounds with a biscuit
(cookie) cutter. Place on a greased baking
(cookie) sheet and bake in a preheated
oven at 180°C/350°F/gas mark 4 for
about 15 minutes.

Easter Biscuits

Makes 20

75 g/3 oz/⅓ cup butter or margarine,
softened
100 g/4 oz/½ cup caster (superfine)
sugar
1 egg yolk
150 g/6 oz/1½ cups self-raising
(self-rising) flour
5 ml/1 tsp ground mixed (apple-pie)
spice
15 ml/1 tbsp chopped mixed
(candied) peel
50 g/2 oz/⅓ cup currants
15 ml/1 tbsp milk
Caster (superfine) sugar for
sprinkling

Cream together the butter or
margarine and sugar. Beat in the egg
yolk, then fold in the flour and mixed
spice. Stir in the peel and currants with
enough of the milk to make a stiff dough.
Roll out to about 5 mm/¼ in thick and cut
into 5 cm/2 in rounds with a biscuit
(cookie) cutter. Place the biscuits on a
greased baking (cookie) sheet and prick
with a fork. Bake in a preheated oven at
180°C/350°F/gas mark 4 for about 20
minutes until golden. Sprinkle with sugar.

Florentines

Makes 40

100 g/4 oz/½ cup butter or margarine
100 g/4 oz/½ cup caster (superfine)
sugar
15 ml/1 tbsp double (heavy) cream
100 g/4 oz/1 cup chopped mixed nuts
75 g/3 oz/½ cup sultanas
(golden raisins)
50 g/2 oz/¼ cup glacé (candied)
cherries

Melt the butter or margarine, sugar
and cream in a pan over a low heat.
Remove from the heat and stir in the nuts,

sultanas and glacé cherries. Drop
teaspoonfuls, well apart, on to greased
baking (cookie) sheets lined with rice
paper. Bake in a preheated oven at 180°C/
350°F/gas mark 4 for 10 minutes. Leave to
cool on the sheets for 5 minutes, then
transfer to a wire rack to finish cooling,
trimming off the excess rice paper.

Chocolate Florentines

Makes 40

100 g/4 oz/½ cup butter or margarine
100 g/4 oz/½ cup caster (superfine)
sugar
15 ml/1 tbsp double (heavy) cream
100 g/4 oz/1 cup chopped mixed nuts
75 g/3 oz/½ cup sultanas
(golden raisins)
50 g/2 oz/¼ cup glacé (candied)
cherries
100 g/4 oz/1 cup plain (semi-sweet)
chocolate

Melt the butter or margarine, sugar
and cream in a pan over a low heat.
Remove from the heat and stir in the
nuts, sultanas and glacé cherries. Drop
teaspoonfuls, well apart, on to greased
baking (cookie) sheets lined with rice
paper. Bake in a preheated oven at 180°C/
350°F/gas mark 4 for 10 minutes. Leave to
cool on the sheets for 5 minutes, then
transfer to a wire rack to finish cooling,
trimming off the excess rice paper.
Melt the chocolate in a heatproof bowl
set over a pan of gently simmering water.
Spread over the top of the biscuits
(cookies) and leave to cool and set.

Luxury Chocolate Florentines

Makes 40

100 g/4 oz/½ cup butter or margarine
100 g/4 oz/½ cup soft brown sugar
15 ml/1 tbsp double (heavy) cream
50 g/2 oz/¼ cup almonds, chopped
50 g/2 oz/¼ cup hazelnuts, chopped
75 g/3 oz/½ cup sultanas
  (golden raisins)
50 g/2 oz/¼ cup glacé (candied)
  cherries
100 g/4 oz/1 cup plain (semi-sweet)
  chocolate
50 g/2 oz/½ cup white chocolate

Melt the butter or margarine, sugar and cream in a pan over a low heat. Remove from the heat and stir in the nuts, sultanas and glacé cherries. Drop teaspoonfuls, well apart, on to greased baking (cookie) sheets lined with rice paper. Bake in a preheated oven at 180°C/350°F/gas mark 4 for 10 minutes. Leave to cool on the sheets for 5 minutes, then transfer to a wire rack to finish cooling, trimming off the excess rice paper.

Melt the plain chocolate in a heatproof bowl set over a pan of gently simmering water. Spread over the top of the biscuits (cookies) and leave to cool and set. Melt the white chocolate in a clean bowl in the same way, then drizzle lines of white chocolate across the biscuits in a random pattern.

Fudge Nut Biscuits

Makes 30

75 g/3 oz/⅓ cup butter or margarine,
  softened
200 g/7 oz/scant 1 cup caster
  (superfine) sugar
1 egg, lightly beaten
100 g/4 oz/½ cup cottage cheese
5 ml/1 tsp vanilla essence (extract)
150 g/5 oz/1¼ cups plain
  (all-purpose) flour

25 g/1 oz/¼ cup cocoa (unsweetened
  chocolate) powder
2.5 ml/½ tsp baking powder
1.5 ml/¼ tsp bicarbonate of soda
  (baking soda)
A pinch of salt
25 g/1 oz/¼ cup chopped mixed nuts
25 g/1 oz/2 tbsp granulated sugar

Cream together the butter or margarine and caster sugar until light and fluffy. Gradually mix in the egg and cottage cheese. Stir in the remaining ingredients except the granulated sugar and mix to a soft dough. Wrap in clingfilm (plastic wrap) and chill for 1 hour.

Roll the dough into walnut-sized balls and roll in the granulated sugar. Place the biscuits (cookies) on a greased baking (cookie) sheet and bake in a preheated oven at 180°C/350°F/gas mark 4 for 10 minutes.

German Iced Biscuits

Makes 12

50 g/2 oz/¼ cup butter or margarine
100 g/4 oz/1 cup plain (all-purpose)
  flour
25 g/1 oz/2 tbsp caster (superfine)
  sugar
60 ml/4 tbsp blackberry jam
  (conserve)
100 g/4 oz/⅔ cup icing (confectioners')
  sugar, sifted
15 ml/1 tbsp lemon juice

Rub the butter into the flour until the mixture resembles breadcrumbs. Stir in the sugar and press to a paste. Roll out to 5 mm/¼ in thick and cut into rounds with a biscuit (cookie) cutter. Place on a greased baking (cookie) sheet and bake in a preheated oven at 180°C/350°F/gas mark 6 for 10 minutes until cold. Leave to cool.

Sandwich pairs of biscuits together with the jam. Place the icing sugar in a bowl and make a well in the centre. Gradually mix in the lemon juice to make a glacé icing (frosting). Drizzle over the biscuits, then leave to set.

Gingersnaps

Makes 24

300 g/10 oz/1¼ cups butter or
   margarine, softened
225 g/8 oz/1 cup soft brown sugar
75 g/3 oz/¼ cup black treacle
   (molasses)
1 egg
250 g/9 oz/2¼ cups plain
   (all-purpose) flour
10 ml/2 tsp bicarbonate of soda
   (baking soda)
2.5 ml/½ tsp salt
5 ml/1 tsp ground ginger
5 ml/1 tsp ground cloves
5 ml/1 tsp ground cinnamon
50 g/2 oz/¼ cup granulated sugar

Cream together the butter or margarine, brown sugar, treacle and egg together until fluffy. Mix together the flour, bicarbonate of soda, salt and spices. Stir into the butter mixture and mix to a firm dough. Cover and chill for 1 hour.
   Shape the dough into small balls and roll in the granulated sugar. Place well apart on a greased baking (cookie) sheet and sprinkle with a little water. Bake in a preheated oven at 190°C/375°F/gas 5 for 12 minutes until golden and crisp.

Ginger Biscuits

Makes 24

100 g/4 oz/½ cup butter or margarine
225 g/8 oz/2 cups self-raising
   (self-rising) flour
5 ml/1 tsp bicarbonate of soda
   (baking soda)
5 ml/1 tsp ground ginger

100 g/4 oz/½ cup caster (superfine)
   sugar
45 ml/3 tbsp golden (light corn)
   syrup, warmed

Rub the butter or margarine into the flour, bicarbonate of soda and ginger. Stir in the sugar, then blend in the syrup and mix to a stiff dough. Roll into walnut-sized balls, place well apart on a greased baking (cookie) sheet and press down lightly with a fork to flatten. Bake the biscuits (cookies) in a preheated oven at 190°C/375°F/gas mark 5 for 10 minutes.

Gingerbread Men

Makes about 16

350 g/12 oz/3 cups self-raising
   (self-rising) flour
A pinch of salt
10 ml/2 tsp ground ginger
100 g/4 oz/⅓ cup golden (light corn)
   syrup
75 g/3 oz/⅓ cup butter or margarine
25 g/1 oz/2 tbsp caster (superfine)
   sugar
1 egg, lightly beaten
A few currants (optional)

Mix together the flour, salt and ginger. Melt the syrup, butter or margarine and sugar in a pan. Leave to cool slightly, then beat into the dry ingredients with the egg and mix to a firm dough. Roll out on a lightly floured surface to 5 mm/¼ in thick and cut out with shaped cutters. The number you can make will depend on the size of your cutters. Place on a lightly greased baking (cookie) sheet and gently press currants into the biscuits (cookies) for eyes and buttons, if liked. Bake in a preheated oven at 180°C/350°F/gas mark 4 for 15 minutes until golden brown and firm to the touch.

Wholemeal Ginger Biscuits

Makes 24

200 g/7 oz/1¾ cups wholemeal
(wholewheat) flour
10 ml/2 tsp baking powder
10 ml/2 tsp ground ginger
100 g/4 oz/½ cup butter or margarine
50 g/2 oz/¼ cup soft brown sugar
60 ml/4 tbsp clear honey

Mix together the flour, baking powder and ginger. Melt the butter or margarine with the sugar and honey, then stir it into the dry ingredients and mix to a firm dough. Roll out on a floured surface and cut into rounds with a biscuit (cookie) cutter. Place on a greased baking (cookie) sheet and bake in a preheated oven at 190°C/375°F/gas mark 5 for 12 minutes until golden and crisp.

Ginger and Rice Biscuits

Makes 12

225 g/8 oz/2 cups plain
(all-purpose) flour
2.5 ml/½ tsp ground mace
10 ml/2 tsp ground ginger
75 g/3 oz/⅓ cup butter or margarine
175 g/6 oz/¾ cup caster (superfine)
sugar
1 egg, beaten
5 ml/1 tsp lemon juice
30 ml/2 tbsp ground rice

Mix together the flour and spices, rub in the butter or margarine until the mixture resembles breadcrumbs, then stir in the sugar. Mix in the egg and lemon juice to a firm dough and knead gently until smooth. Dust a work surface with the ground rice and roll out the dough to 1 cm/½ in thick. Cut into 5 cm/2 in rounds with a biscuit (cookie) cutter. Arrange on a greased baking (cookie) sheet and bake in a preheated oven at 180°C/350°F/gas mark 4 for 20 minutes until firm to the touch.

Golden Biscuits

Makes 36

75 g/3 oz/⅓ cup butter or margarine,
softened
200 g/7 oz/scant 1 cup caster
(superfine) sugar
2 eggs, lightly beaten
225 g/8 oz/2 cups plain
(all-purpose) flour
10 ml/2 tsp baking powder
5 ml/1 tsp grated nutmeg
A pinch of salt
Egg or milk for glazing
Caster (superfine) sugar for
sprinkling

Cream together the butter or margarine and sugar. Gradually mix in the eggs, then stir in the flour, baking powder, nutmeg and salt and mix to a soft dough. Cover and leave to rest for 30 minutes.
Roll out the dough on a lightly floured surface to about 5 mm/¼ in thick and cut into rounds with a biscuit (cookie) cutter. Place on a greased baking (cookie) sheet, brush with beaten egg or milk and sprinkle with sugar. Bake in a preheated oven at 200°C/400°F/gas mark 6 for 8–10 minutes until golden.

Hazelnut Biscuits

Makes 24

100 g/4 oz/½ cup butter or margarine,
softened
50 g/2 oz/¼ cup caster (superfine)
sugar
100 g/4 oz/1 cup plain (all-purpose)
flour
25 g/1 oz/¼ cup ground hazelnuts

Cream together the butter or margarine and sugar until light and fluffy. Gradually work in the flour and nuts until you have a stiff dough. Roll into small balls and place, well apart, on a greased baking (cookie) sheet. Bake the biscuits (cookies) in a preheated oven at 180°C/350°F/gas mark 4 for 20 minutes.

Crunchy Hazelnut Biscuits

Makes 40

100 g/4 oz/½ cup butter or margarine,
  softened
100 g/4 oz/½ cup caster (superfine)
  sugar
1 egg, beaten
5 ml/1 tsp vanilla essence (extract)
175 g/6 oz/1½ cups plain
  (all-purpose) flour
50 g/2 oz/½ cup ground hazelnuts
50 g/2 oz/½ cup hazelnuts, chopped

Cream together the butter or margarine and sugar until light and fluffy. Gradually beat in the egg and vanilla essence, then fold in the flour, ground hazelnuts and hazelnuts and knead to a dough. Roll into a ball, wrap in clingfim (plastic wrap) and chill for 1 hour.

Roll out the dough to 5 mm/¼ in thick and cut into rounds with a biscuit (cookie) cutter. Arrange on a greased baking (cookie) sheet and bake in a preheated oven at 200°C/400°F/gas mark 6 for 10 minutes until golden.

Hazelnut and Almond Biscuits

Makes 24

100 g/4 oz/½ cup butter or margarine,
  softened
75 g/3 oz/½ cup icing (confectioners')
  sugar, sifted
50 g/2 oz/⅓ cup ground hazelnuts
50 g/2 oz/⅓ cup ground almonds
100 g/4 oz/1 cup plain (all-purpose)
  flour
5 ml/1 tsp almond essence (extract)
A pinch of salt

Cream the butter or margarine and sugar until light and fluffy. Mix in the remaining ingredients to make a stiff dough. Roll into a ball, cover with clingfilm (plastic wrap) and chill for 30 minutes.

Roll out the dough to about 1 cm/ ½ in thick and cut into rounds with a biscuit (cookie) cutter. Place on a greased baking (cookie) sheet and bake in a preheated oven at 180°C/350°F/gas mark 4 for 15 minutes until golden brown.

Honey Cookies

Makes 24

75 g/3 oz/⅓ cup butter or margarine
100 g/4 oz/⅓ cup set honey
225 g/8 oz/2 cups wholemeal
  (wholewheat) flour
5 ml/1 tsp baking powder
A pinch of salt
50 g/2 oz/¼ cup muscovado sugar
5 ml/1 tsp ground cinnamon
1 egg, lightly beaten

Melt the butter or margarine and honey until blended. Stir in the remaining ingredients. Place spoonfuls of the mixture well apart on a greased baking (cookie) sheet and bake in a preheated oven at 180°C/350°F/gas mark 4 for 15 minutes until golden. Leave to cool for 5 minutes before transferring to a wire rack to finish cooling.

Honey Ratafias

Makes 24

2 egg whites
100 g/4 oz/1 cup ground almonds
A few drops of almond essence
  (extract)
100 g/4 oz/⅓ cup clear honey
Rice paper

Beat the egg whites until stiff. Carefully fold in the almonds, almond essence and honey. Place spoonfuls of the mixture well apart on baking (cookie) sheets lined with rice paper and bake in a preheated oven at 180°C/350°F/gas mark 4 for 15 minutes until golden. Leave to cool slightly, then tear round the paper to remove.

Honey and Buttermilk Biscuits

Makes 12

50 g/2 oz/¼ cup butter or margarine
225 g/8 oz/2 cups self-raising (self-rising) flour
175 ml/6 fl oz/¾ cup buttermilk
45 ml/3 tbsp clear honey

Rub the butter or margarine into the flour until the mixture resembles breadcrumbs. Stir in the buttermilk and honey and mix to a stiff dough. Place on a lightly floured surface and knead until smooth, then roll out to 2 cm/¾ in thick and cut into 5 cm/2 in round with a biscuit (cookie) cutter. Place on a greased baking (cookie) sheet and bake in a preheated oven at 230°C/450°F/gas mark 8 for 10 minutes until golden brown.

Lemon Butter Biscuits

Makes 20

100 g/4 oz/1 cup ground rice
100 g/4 oz/1 cup plain (all-purpose) flour
75 g/3 oz/⅓ cup caster (superfine) sugar
A pinch of salt
2.5 ml/½ tsp baking powder
100 g/4 oz/½ cup butter or margarine
Grated rind of 1 lemon
1 egg, beaten

Mix together the ground rice, flour, sugar, salt and baking powder. Rub in the butter until the mixture resembles breadcrumbs. Stir in the lemon rind and mix with enough of the egg to form a firm dough. Knead gently, then roll out on a floured surface and cut into shapes with a biscuit (cookie) cutter. Place on a greased baking (cookie) sheet and bake in a preheated oven at 180°C/350°F/gas mark 4 for 30 minutes. Leave to cool slightly on the sheet, then transfer to a wire rack to cool completely.

Lemon Cookies

Makes 24

100 g/4 oz/½ cup butter or margarine
100 g/4 oz/½ cup caster (superfine) sugar
1 egg, lightly beaten
225 g/8 oz/2 cups plain (all-purpose) flour
5 ml/1 tsp baking powder
Grated rind of ½ lemon
5 ml/1 tsp lemon juice
30 ml/2 tbsp demerara sugar

Melt the butter or margarine and caster sugar over a low heat, stirring continuously, until the mixture begins to thicken. Remove from the heat and stir in the egg, flour, baking powder, lemon rind and juice and mix to a dough. Cover and chill for 30 minutes.

Shape the dough into small balls and arrange on a greased baking (cookie) sheet, pressing flat with a fork. Sprinkle with the demerara sugar. Bake in a preheated oven at 180°C/350°F/gas mark 4 for 15 minutes.

Melting Moments

Makes 16

100 g/4 oz/½ cup butter or margarine, softened
75 g/3 oz/⅓ cup caster (superfine) sugar
1 egg, beaten
150 g/5 oz/1¼ cups plain (all-purpose) flour
10 ml/2 tsp baking powder
A pinch of salt
8 glacé (candied) cherries, halved

Cream together the butter or margarine and sugar until light and fluffy. Gradually beat in the egg, then fold in the flour, baking powder and salt. Knead gently to a smooth dough. Shape the dough into 16 equal-sized balls and place, well apart, on a greased baking (cookie) sheet. Flatten slightly, then top each one with a cherry half. Bake in a preheated oven at 180°C/350°F/gas mark 4 for 15 minutes. Leave to cool on the sheet for 5 minutes, then transfer to a wire rack to finish cooling.

Muesli Biscuits

Makes 24

100 g/4 oz/½ cup butter or margarine
100 g/4 oz/⅓ cup clear honey
75 g/3 oz/⅓ cup soft brown sugar
100 g/4 oz/1 cup wholemeal
(wholewheat) flour
100 g/4 oz/1 cup rolled oats
50 g/2 oz/⅓ cup raisins
50 g/2 oz/⅓ cup sultanas
(golden raisins)
50 g/2 oz/⅓ cup stoned (pitted) dates,
chopped
50 g/2 oz/⅓ cup ready-to-eat dried
apricots, chopped
25 g/1 oz/¼ cup walnuts, chopped
25 g/1 oz/¼ cup hazelnuts, chopped

Melt the butter or margarine with the honey and sugar. Stir in the remaining ingredients and mix to a stiff dough. Place teaspoonfuls on a greased baking (cookie) sheet and press flat. Bake the biscuits (cookies) in a preheated oven at 180°C/350°F/gas mark 4 for 20 minutes until golden.

Nut Biscuits

Makes 24

350 g/12 oz/1½ cups butter or
margarine, softened
350 g/12 oz/1½ cups caster (superfine)
sugar
5 ml/1 tsp vanilla essence (extract)
350 g/12 oz/3 cups plain
(all-purpose) flour
5 ml/1 tsp bicarbonate of soda
(baking soda)
100 g/4 oz/1 cup chopped mixed nuts

Cream together the butter or margarine and sugar until light and fluffy. Stir in the remaining ingredients and mix until well blended. Shape into two long rolls, cover and chill for 30 minutes until firm.

Cut the rolls into 5 mm/¼ in slices and arrange on a greased baking (cookie) sheet. Bake the biscuits (cookies) in a preheated oven at 180°C/350°F/gas mark 4 for 10 minutes until lightly browned.

Crisp Nut Biscuits

Makes 30

100 g/4 oz/½ cup soft brown sugar
1 egg, beaten
5 ml/1 tsp vanilla essence (extract)
45 ml/3 tbsp plain (all-purpose) flour
100 g/4 oz/1 cup chopped mixed nuts

Beat the sugar with the egg and vanilla essence, then blend in the flour and nuts. Place small spoonfuls on a greased and floured baking (cookie) sheet and flatten slightly with a fork. Bake the biscuits (cookies) in a preheated oven at 190°C/375°F/gas mark 5 for 10 minutes.

Crunchy Cinnamon Nut Biscuits

Makes 24

100 g/4 oz/½ cup butter or margarine,
softened
100 g/4 oz/½ cup caster (superfine)
sugar
1 egg, lightly beaten
2.5 ml/½ tsp vanilla essence (extract)
175 g/6 oz/1½ cups plain
(all-purpose) flour
2.5 ml/½ tsp ground cinnamon
2.5 ml/½ tsp bicarbonate of soda
(baking soda)
100 g/4 oz/1 cup chopped mixed nuts

Cream together the butter or mar-garine and sugar. Gradually stir in 60 ml/4 tbsp of the egg and the vanilla essence. Stir in the flour, cinnamon, bicarbonate of soda and half the nuts. Press into a greased and lined Swiss roll tin (jelly roll pan). Brush with the remaining egg and sprinkle with the remaining nuts and press down gently. Bake the biscuits (cookies) in a preheated oven at 180°C/350°F/gas mark 4 for 20 minutes until golden brown. Leave to cool in the tin before cutting into bars.

Oaty Fingers

Makes 24

200 g/7 oz/1¾ cups oatmeal
75 g/3 oz/¾ cup plain (all-purpose)
flour
5 ml/1 tsp baking powder
50 g/2 oz/¼ cup butter or margarine,
melted
Boiling water

Mix together the oatmeal, flour and baking powder, then stir in the melted butter or margarine and enough boiling water to make a soft dough. Knead on a lightly floured surface until firm, then roll out and cut into fingers.

Place on a greased baking (cookie) sheet and bake in a preheated oven at 190°C/375°F/gas mark 5 for 10 minutes until golden brown.

Oat and Banana Biscuits

Makes 36

100 g/4 oz/½ cup butter or margarine,
softened
100 g/4 oz/½ cup caster (superfine)
sugar
1 banana, peeled and mashed
1 egg
100 g/4 oz/1 cup plain (all-purpose)
flour
5 ml/1 tsp ground cinnamon
2.5 ml/½ tsp bicarbonate of soda
(baking soda)
A pinch of salt
100 g/4 oz/1 cup rolled oats

Cream together the butter or mar-garine and sugar until light and fluffy. Stir in the banana. Gradually beat in the egg, then fold in the flour, cinnamon, bicarbonate of soda and salt and stir in the oats. Shape the mixture into walnut-sized balls and place, well apart, on a greased baking (cookie) sheet. Press down lightly with a fork to flatten slightly. Bake the biscuits (cookies) in a preheated oven at 190°C/375°F/gas mark 5 for 15 minutes.

Oat and Raisin Cookies

Makes 20

175 g/6 oz/¾ cup plain (all-purpose)
flour
150 g/5 oz/1¼ cups rolled oats
5 ml/1 tsp ground ginger
2.5 ml/½ tsp baking powder
2.5 ml/½ tsp bicarbonate of soda
(baking soda)
100 g/4 oz/½ cup soft brown sugar
50 g/2 oz/⅓ cup raisins

1 egg, lightly beaten
150 ml/¼ pt/⅔ cup oil
60 ml/4 tbsp milk

Mix together the dry ingredients, stir in the raisins and make a well in the centre. Add the egg, oil and milk and mix to a soft dough. Place spoonfuls of the mixture on an ungreased baking (cookie) sheet and flatten slightly with a fork. Bake in a preheated oven at 200°C/400°F/gas mark 6 for 10 minutes until golden.

Spiced Oatmeal Biscuits

Makes 30

100 g/4 oz/½ cup butter or margarine, softened
100 g/4 oz/½ cup soft brown sugar
100 g/4 oz/½ cup caster (superfine) sugar
1 egg
2.5 ml/½ tsp vanilla essence (extract)
100 g/4 oz/1 cup plain (all-purpose) flour
2.5 ml/½ tsp bicarbonate of soda (baking soda)
A pinch of salt
5 ml/1 tsp ground cinnamon
A pinch of grated nutmeg
100 g/4 oz/1 cup rolled oats
50 g/2 oz/½ cup chopped mixed nuts
50 g/2 oz/½ cup chocolate chips

Cream together the butter or margarine and sugars until light and fluffy. Gradually beat in the egg and vanilla essence. Mix together the flour, bicarbonate of soda, salt and spices and add to the mixture. Stir in the oats, nuts and chocolate chips. Drop rounded teaspoonfuls on to a greased baking (cookie) sheet and bake the biscuits (cookies) in a preheated oven at 180°C/350°F/gas mark 4 for 10 minutes until lightly browned.

Wholemeal Oat Biscuits

Makes 24

100 g/4 oz/½ cup butter or margarine
200 g/7 oz/1¾ cups oatmeal
75 g/3 oz/¾ cup wholemeal (wholewheat) flour
50 g/2 oz/½ cup plain (all-purpose) flour
5 ml/1 tsp baking powder
50 g/2 oz/¼ cup demerara sugar
1 egg, lightly beaten
30 ml/2 tbsp milk

Rub the butter or margarine into the oatmeal, flours and baking powder until the mixture resembles breadcrumbs. Stir in the sugar, then mix in the egg and milk to make a stiff dough. Roll out the dough on a lightly floured surface to about 1 cm/½ in thick and cut into rounds with a 5 cm/2 in cutter. Place the biscuits (cookies) on a greased baking (cookie) sheet and bake in a preheated oven at 190°C/375°F/gas mark 5 for about 15 minutes until golden brown.

Orange Biscuits

Makes 24

100 g/4 oz/½ cup butter or margarine, softened
50 g/2 oz/¼ cup caster (superfine) sugar
Grated rind of 1 orange
150 g/5 oz/1¼ cups self-raising (self-rising) flour

Cream together the butter or margarine and sugar until light and fluffy. Work in the orange rind, then mix in the flour to make a stiff mixture. Shape into large walnut-sized balls and arrange well apart on a greased baking (cookie) sheet, then press down lightly with a fork to flatten. Bake the biscuits (cookies) in a preheated oven at 180°C/350°F/gas mark 4 for 15 minutes until golden brown.

Orange and Lemon Biscuits

Makes 30

50 g/2 oz/¼ cup butter or margarine,
softened
75 g/3 oz/⅓ cup caster (superfine)
sugar
1 egg yolk
Grated rind of ½ orange
15 ml/1 tbsp lemon juice
150 g/5 oz/1¼ cups plain
(all-purpose) flour
2.5 ml/½ tsp baking powder
A pinch of salt

Cream together the butter or margarine and sugar until light and fluffy. Gradually mix in the egg yolk, orange rind and lemon juice, then fold in the flour, baking powder and salt to make a stiff dough. Wrap and clingfilm (plastic wrap) and chill for 30 minutes.

Roll out on a lightly floured surface to about 5 mm/¼ in thick and cut into shapes with a biscuit (cookie) cutter. Place the biscuits on a greased baking (cookie) sheet and bake in a preheated oven at 190°C/375°F/gas mark 5 for 10 minutes.

Orange and Walnut Biscuits

Makes 16

100 g/4 oz/½ cup butter or margarine
75 g/3 oz/⅓ cup caster (superfine)
sugar
Grated rind of ½ orange
150 g/5 oz/1¼ cups self-raising
(self-rising) flour
50 g/2 oz/½ cup walnuts, ground

Beat the butter or margarine with 50 g/2 oz/¼ cup of the sugar and the orange rind until smooth and creamy. Add the flour and nuts and beat again until the mixture begins to hold together. Form into balls and flatten on to a greased baking (cookie) sheet. Bake the biscuits (cookies) in a preheated oven at 190°C/

375°F/gas mark 5 for 10 minutes until brown round the edges. Sprinkle with the reserved sugar and leave to cool slightly before transferring to a wire rack to cool.

Orange and Chocolate Chip Biscuits

Makes 30

50 g/2 oz/¼ cup butter or margarine,
softened
75 g/3 oz/⅓ cup lard (shortening)
175 g/6 oz/¾ cup soft brown sugar
100 g/7 oz/1¾ cups wholemeal
(wholewheat) flour
75 g/3 oz/¾ cup ground almonds
10 ml/2 tsp baking powder
75 g/3 oz/¾ cup chocolate drops
Grated rind of 2 oranges
15 ml/1 tbsp orange juice
1 egg
Caster (superfine) sugar for
sprinkling

Cream together the butter or margarine, lard and brown sugar until light and fluffy. Add the remaining ingredients except the caster sugar and mix to a dough. Roll out on a floured surface to 5 mm/¼ in thick and cut into biscuits with a biscuit (cookie) cutter. Arrange on a greased baking (cookie) sheet and bake in a preheated oven at 180°C/350°F/gas mark 4 for 20 minutes until golden.

Spiced Orange Biscuits

Makes 10

*225 g/8 oz/2 cups plain
(all-purpose) flour
2.5 ml/½ tsp ground cinnamon
A pinch of mixed (apple pie) spice
75 g/3 oz/⅓ cup caster (superfine)
sugar
150 g/5 oz/⅔ cup butter or margarine,
softened
2 egg yolks
Grated rind of 1 orange
75 g/3 oz/¾ cup plain (semi-sweet)
chocolate*

Mix together the flour and spices, then stir in the sugar. Beat in the butter or margarine, egg yolks and orange rind and mix to a smooth dough. Wrap in clingfilm (plastic wrap) and chill for 1 hour.

Spoon the dough into a piping bag fitted with a large star nozzle (tip) and pipe lengths on to a greased baking (cookie) sheet. Bake in a preheated oven at 190°C/375°F/gas mark 5 for 10 minutes until golden brown. Leave to cool.

Melt the chocolate in a heatproof bowl set over a pan of gently simmering water. Dip the ends of the biscuits into the melted chocolate and leave on a sheet of baking parchment until set.

Peanut Butter Biscuits

Makes 18

*100 g/4 oz/½ cup butter or margarine,
softened
100 g/4 oz/½ cup caster (superfine)
sugar
100 g/4 oz/½ cup crunchy or smooth
peanut butter
60 ml/4 tbsp golden (light corn) syrup
15 ml/1 tbsp milk
175 g/6 oz/1½ cups plain
(all-purpose) flour
2.5 ml/½ tsp bicarbonate of soda
(baking soda)*

Cream together the butter or margarine and sugar until light and fluffy. Blend in the peanut butter, followed by the syrup and milk. Mix together the flour and bicarbonate of soda and blend into the mixture, then knead until smooth. Shape into a log and chill until firm.

Cut into slices 5 mm/¼ in thick and arrange on a lightly greased baking (cookie) sheet. Bake the biscuits (cookies) in a preheated oven at 180°C/350°F/gas mark 4 for 12 minutes until golden.

Peanut Butter and Chocolate Swirls

Makes 24

*50 g/2 oz/¼ cup butter or margarine,
softened
50 g/2 oz/¼ cup soft brown sugar
50 g/2 oz/¼ cup caster (superfine)
sugar
50 g/2 oz/¼ cup smooth peanut butter
1 egg yolk
75 g/3 oz/¾ cup plain (all-purpose)
flour
2.5 ml/½ tsp bicarbonate of soda
(baking soda)
50 g/2 oz/½ cup plain (semi-sweet)
chocolate*

Cream together the butter or margarine and sugars until light and fluffy. Gradually blend in the peanut butter, then the egg yolk. Mix together the flour and bicarbonate of soda and beat into the mixture to make a firm dough. Meanwhile, melt the chocolate in a heatproof bowl set over a pan of gently simmering water. Roll out the dough to 30 × 46 cm/12 × 18 in and spread with the melted chocolate almost to the edges. Roll up from the long side, wrap in clingfilm (plastic wrap) and chill until firm.

Cut the roll into 5 mm/¼ in slices and arrange on an ungreased baking (cookie) sheet. Bake in a preheated oven at 180°C/350°F/gas mark 4 for 10 minutes until golden.

Oaty Peanut Butter Biscuits

Makes 24

75 g/3 oz/⅓ cup butter or margarine, softened
75 g/3 oz/⅓ cup peanut butter
150 g/5 oz/⅔ cup soft brown sugar
1 egg
50 g/2 oz/½ cup plain (all-purpose) flour
2.5 ml/½ tsp baking powder
A pinch of salt
A few drops of vanilla essence (extract)
75 g/3 oz/¾ cup rolled oats
40 g/1½ oz/⅓ cup chocolate chips

Cream together the butter or margarine, peanut butter and sugar until light and fluffy. Gradually beat in the egg. Fold in the flour, baking powder and salt. Stir in the vanilla essence, oats and chocolate chips. Drop spoonfuls on to a greased baking (cookie) sheet and bake the biscuits (cookies) in a preheated oven at 180°C/350°F/gas mark 4 for 15 minutes.

Honey and Coconut Peanut Butter Biscuits

Makes 24

120 ml/4 fl oz/½ cup oil
175 g/6 oz/½ cup clear honey
175 g/6 oz/¾ cup crunchy peanut butter
1 egg, beaten
100 g/4 oz/1 cup rolled oats
225 g/8 oz/2 cups wholemeal (wholewheat) flour
50 g/2 oz/½ cup desiccated (shredded) coconut

Mix together the oil, honey, peanut butter and egg, then stir in the remaining ingredients. Drop spoonfuls on to a greased baking (cookie) sheet and flatten slightly to about 6 mm/¼ in thick. Bake the biscuits (cookies) in a preheated oven at 180°C/350°F/gas mark 4 for 12 minutes until golden.

Pecan Nut Biscuits

Makes 24

100 g/4 oz/½ cup butter or margarine, softened
45 ml/3 tbsp soft brown sugar
100 g/4 oz/1 cup plain (all-purpose) flour
A pinch of salt
5 ml/1 tsp vanilla essence (extract)
100 g/4 oz/1 cup pecan nuts, finely chopped
Icing (confectioners') sugar, sifted, for dusting

Cream together the butter or margarine and sugar until light and fluffy. Gradually beat in the remaining ingredients except the icing sugar. Shape into 3 cm/1½ in balls and arrange on a greased baking (cookie) sheet. Bake the biscuits (cookies) in a preheated oven at 160°C/325°F/gas mark 3 for 15 minutes until golden. Serve dusted with icing sugar.

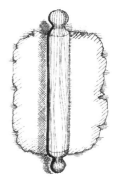

Pinwheel Biscuits

Makes 24

175 g/6 oz/1½ cups plain
  (all-purpose) flour
5 ml/1 tsp baking powder
A pinch of salt
75 g/3 oz/⅓ cup butter or margarine
75 g/3 oz/⅓ cup caster (superfine)
  sugar
A few drops of vanilla essence
  (extract)
20 ml/4 tsp water
10 ml/2 tsp cocoa (unsweetened
  chocolate) powder

Mix together the flour, baking powder and salt, then rub in the butter or margarine until the mixture resembles breadcrumbs. Stir in the sugar. Add the vanilla essence and water and mix to a smooth dough. Shape into a ball, then cut in half. Work the cocoa into one half of the dough. Roll out each piece of dough to a 25 × 18 cm/10 × 7 in rectangle and place one on top of the other. Roll gently so they stick together. Roll up the dough from the long side and press together gently. Wrap in clingfilm (plastic wrap) and chill for about 30 minutes.

Cut into slices 2.5 cm/1 in thick and arrange, well apart, on a greased baking (cookie) sheet. Bake the biscuits (cookies) in a preheated oven at 180°C/350°F/gas mark 4 for 15 minutes until golden.

Quick Buttermilk Biscuits

Makes 12

75 g/3 oz/⅓ cup butter or margarine
225 g/8 oz/2 cups plain
  (all-purpose) flour
15 ml/1 tbsp baking powder
2.5 ml/½ tsp salt
175 ml/6 fl oz/¾ cup buttermilk
Icing (confectioners') sugar, sifted,
  for dusting (optional)

Rub the butter or margarine into the flour, baking powder and salt until the mixture resembles breadcrumbs. Gradually add the buttermilk to make a soft dough. Roll out the mixture on a lightly floured surface to about 2 cm/¾ in thick and cut into rounds with a biscuit (cookie) cutter. Place the biscuits on a greased baking (cookie) sheet and bake in a preheated oven at 230°C/450°F/gas mark 8 for 10 minutes until golden brown. Dust with icing sugar, if liked.

Raisin Biscuits

Makes 24

100 g/4 oz/½ cup butter or margarine,
  softened
50 g/2 oz/¼ cup caster (superfine)
  sugar
Grated rind of 1 lemon
50 g/2 oz/⅓ cup raisins
150 g/5 oz/1¼ cups self-raising
  (self-rising) flour

Cream together the butter or margarine and sugar until light and fluffy. Work in the lemon rind, then mix in the raisins and flour to make a stiff mixture. Shape into large walnut-sized balls and arrange well apart on a greased baking (cookie) sheet, then press down lightly with a fork to flatten. Bake the biscuits (cookies) in a preheated oven at 180°C/350°F/gas mark 4 for 15 minutes until golden brown.

Soft Raisin Biscuits

Makes 36

100 g/4 oz/²⁄₃ cup raisins
90 ml/6 tbsp boiling water
50 g/2 oz/¼ cup butter or margarine,
  softened
175 g/6 oz/¾ cup caster (superfine)
  sugar
1 egg, lightly beaten
2.5 ml/½ tsp vanilla essence (extract)
175 g/6 oz/1½ cups plain
  (all-purpose) flour
2.5 ml/½ tsp baking powder
1.5 ml/¼ tsp bicarbonate of soda
  (baking soda)
2.5 ml/½ tsp salt
2.5 ml/½ tsp ground cinnamon
A pinch of grated nutmeg
50 g/2 oz/½ cup chopped mixed nuts

Place the raisins and boiling water in a pan, bring to the boil, cover and simmer for 3 minutes. Leave to cool. Cream together the butter or margarine and sugar until light and fluffy. Gradually beat in the egg and vanilla essence. Fold in the flour, baking powder, bicarbonate of soda, salt and spices alternately with the raisins and soaking liquid. Stir in the nuts and mix to a soft dough. Wrap in clingfilm (plastic wrap) and chill for at least 1 hour.

Drop spoonfuls of dough on to a greased baking (cookie) sheet and bake the biscuits (cookies) in a preheated oven at 180°C/350°F/gas mark 4 for 10 minutes until golden.

Raisin and Treacle Slices

Makes 24

25 g/1 oz/2 tbsp butter or margarine,
  softened
100 g/4 oz/½ cup caster (superfine)
  sugar
1 egg yolk

30 ml/2 tbsp black treacle (molasses)
75 g/3 oz/½ cup currants
150 g/5 oz/1¼ cups plain
  (all-purpose) flour
5 ml/1 tsp bicarbonate of soda
  (baking soda)
5 ml/1 tsp ground cinnamon
A pinch of salt
30 ml/2 tbsp cold black coffee

Cream together the butter or margarine and sugar until light and fluffy. Gradually beat in the egg yolk and treacle, then stir in the currants. Mix together the flour, bicarbonate of soda, cinnamon and salt and stir into the mixture with the coffee. Cover and chill the mixture.

Roll out to a 30 cm/12 in square, then roll up into a log. Place on a greased baking (cookie) sheet and bake in a preheated oven at 180°C/350°F/gas mark 4 for 15 minutes until firm to the touch. Cut into slices, then leave to cool on a wire rack.

Ratafia Biscuits

makes 16

100 g/4 oz/½ cup granulated sugar
50 g/2 oz/¼ cup ground almonds
15 ml/1 tbsp ground rice
1 egg white
25 g/1 oz/¼ cup flaked (slivered)
  almonds

Blend together the sugar, ground almonds and ground rice. Beat in the egg white and continue to beat for 2 minutes. Pipe walnut-sized biscuits (cookies) on to a baking (cookie) sheet lined with rice paper using a 5 mm/¼ in plain nozzle (tip). Place a flaked almond on top of each biscuit. Bake in a preheated oven at 190°C/375°F/gas mark 5 for 15 minutes until golden.

Rice and Muesli Cookies

Makes 24

75 g/3 oz/¼ cup cooked brown rice
50 g/2 oz/½ cup muesli
75 g/3 oz/¾ cup wholemeal
    (wholewheat) flour
2.5 ml/½ tsp salt
2.5 ml/½ tsp bicarbonate of soda
    (baking soda)
5 ml/1 tsp ground mixed (apple pie)
    spice
30 ml/2 tbsp clear honey
75 g/3 oz/⅓ cup butter or margarine,
    softened

Mix together the rice, muesli, flour, salt, bicarbonate of soda and mixed spice. Cream together the honey and butter or margarine until soft. Beat into the rice mixture. Shape the mixture into walnut-sized balls and place well apart on greased baking (cookie) sheets. Flatten slightly, then bake in a preheated oven at 190°C/375°F/gas mark 5 for 15 minutes or until golden brown. Leave to cool for 10 minutes, then transfer to a wire rack to finish cooling. Store in an airtight container.

Romany Creams

Makes 10

25 g/1 oz/2 tbsp lard (shortening)
25 g/1 oz/2 tbsp butter or margarine,
    softened
50 g/2 oz/¼ cup soft brown sugar
2.5 ml/½ tsp golden (light corn) syrup
50 g/2 oz/½ cup plain (all-purpose)
    flour
A pinch of salt
25 g/1 oz/¼ cup rolled oats
2.5 ml/½ tsp ground mixed
    (apple-pie) spice
2.5 ml/½ tsp bicarbonate of soda
    (baking soda)
10 ml/2 tsp boiling water
Butter Icing (page 229)

Cream together the lard, butter or margarine and sugar until light and fluffy. Beat in the syrup, then add the flour, salt, oats and mixed spice and stir until well blended. Dissolve the bicarbonate of soda in the water and mix in to make a firm dough. Shape into 20 equal-sized small balls and place well apart on greased baking (cookie) sheets. Flatten slightly with the palm of your hand. Bake in a preheated oven at 160°C/325°F/gas mark 3 for 15 minutes. Leave to cool on the baking sheets. When cool, sandwich pairs of biscuits together with the butter icing (frosting).

Sand Biscuits

Makes 48

100 g/4 oz/½ cup butter or hard
    margarine, softened
225 g/8 oz/1 cup soft brown sugar
1 egg, lightly beaten
225 g/8 oz/2 cups plain
    (all-purpose) flour
Egg white to glaze
30 ml/2 tbsp crushed peanuts

Cream together the butter or margarine and sugar until light and fluffy. Beat in the egg, then blend in the flour. Roll out very thinly on a lightly floured surface and cut into shapes with a biscuit (cookie) cutter. Place the biscuits on a greased baking (cookie) sheet, brush the tops with egg white and sprinkle with peanuts. Bake in a preheated oven at 180°C/350°F/gas mark 4 for 10 minutes until golden.

Soured Cream Cookies

Makes 24

50 g/2 oz/¼ cup butter or margarine, softened
175 g/6 oz/¾ cup caster (superfine) sugar
1 egg
60 ml/4 tbsp soured (dairy sour) cream
2.5 ml/½ tsp vanilla essence (extract)
150 g/5 oz/1¼ cups plain (all-purpose) flour
2.5 ml/½ tsp baking powder
75 g/3 oz/½ cup raisins

Cream together the butter or margarine and sugar until light and fluffy. Gradually beat in the egg, cream and vanilla essence. Mix together the flour, baking powder and raisins and stir into the mixture until well blended. Drop rounded teaspoonfuls of the mixture on to lightly greased baking (cookie) sheets and bake in a preheated oven at 180°C/ 350°F/gas mark 4 for about 10 minutes until just golden.

Brown Sugar Biscuits

Makes 24

100 g/4 oz/½ cup butter or margarine, softened
100 g/4 oz/½ cup soft brown sugar
1 egg, lightly beaten
2.5 ml/1 tsp vanilla essence (extract)
150 g/5 oz/1¼ cups plain (all-purpose) flour
2.5 ml/½ tsp bicarbonate of soda (baking soda)
A pinch of salt
75 g/3 oz/½ cup sultanas (golden raisins)

Cream together the butter or margarine and sugar until light and fluffy. Gradually beat in the egg and vanilla essence. Stir in the remaining ingredients until smooth. Drop rounded teaspoonfuls well apart on to a lightly greased baking (cookie) sheet. Bake the biscuits (cookies) in a preheated oven at 180°C/ 350°F/gas mark 4 for 12 minutes until golden brown.

Sugar and Nutmeg Biscuits

Makes 24

50 g/2 oz/¼ cup butter or margarine, softened
100 g/4 oz/½ cup caster (superfine) sugar
1 egg yolk
2.5 ml/½ tsp vanilla essence (extract)
150 g/5 oz/1¼ cups plain (all-purpose) flour
5 ml/1 tsp baking powder
A pinch of grated nutmeg
60 ml/4 tbsp soured (dairy sour) cream

Cream together the butter or margarine and sugar until light and fluffy. Beat in the egg yolk and vanilla essence, then stir in the flour, baking powder and nutmeg. Blend in the cream until smooth. Cover and chill for 30 minutes.

Roll out the dough to 5 mm/¼ in thick and cut into 5 cm/2 in rounds with a biscuit (cookie) cutter. Place the biscuits on an ungreased baking (cookie) sheet and bake in a preheated oven at 200°C/ 400°F/gas mark 6 for 10 minutes until golden.

Shortbread

Makes 8

150 g/5 oz/1¼ cups plain
(all-purpose) flour
A pinch of salt
25 g/1 oz/¼ cup rice flour or ground
rice
50 g/2 oz/¼ cup caster (superfine)
sugar
100 g/4 oz/¼ cup butter or hard
margarine, chilled and grated

Mix together the flour, salt and rice flour or ground rice. Stir in the sugar, then the butter or margarine. Work the mixture with the fingertips until it resembles breadcrumbs. Press into an 18 cm/7 in sandwich tin (pan) and level the top. Prick all over with a fork and mark into eight equal wedges, cutting through to the base. Chill for 1 hour.

Bake in a preheated oven at 150°C/300°F/gas mark 2 for 1 hour until pale straw-coloured. Leave to cool in the tin before turning out.

Christmas Shortbread

Makes 12

175 g/6 oz/¾ cup butter or margarine
250 g/9 oz/2¼ cups plain
(all-purpose) flour
75 g/3 oz/⅓ cup caster (superfine)
sugar
For the topping:
15 ml/1 tbsp almonds, chopped
15 ml/1 tbsp walnuts, chopped
30 ml/2 tbsp raisins
30 ml/2 tbsp glacé (candied) cherries,
chopped
Grated rind of 1 lemon
15 ml/1 tbsp caster (superfine) sugar
for sprinkling

Rub the butter or margarine into the flour until the mixture resembles breadcrumbs. Stir in the sugar. Press the mixture together to a paste and knead until smooth. Press into a greased Swiss roll tin (jelly roll pan) and level the surface. Mix together the topping ingredients and press them into the paste. Mark into 12 fingers, then bake in a preheated oven at 180°C/350°F/gas mark 4 for 30 minutes. Sprinkle with caster sugar, cut into fingers and leave to cool in the tin.

Honeyed Shortbread

Makes 12

100 g/4 oz/½ cup butter or margarine,
softened
75 g/3 oz/¼ cup set honey
200 g/7 oz/1¾ cups wholemeal
(wholewheat) flour
25 g/1 oz/¼ cup brown rice flour
Grated rind of 1 lemon

Cream together the butter or margarine and honey until soft. Stir in the flours and lemon rind and work to a soft dough. Press into a greased and floured 18 cm/7 in cake tin (pan) or shortbread mould and prick all over with a fork. Mark into 12 wedges and crimp the edges. Chill for 1 hour.

Bake in a preheated oven at 150°C/300°F/gas mark 2 for 40 minutes until just golden. Cut into the marked pieces and leave to cool in the tin.

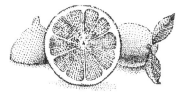

Lemon Shortbread

Makes 12

100 g/4 oz/1 cup plain (all-purpose) flour
50 g/2 oz/½ cup cornflour (cornstarch)
100 g/4 oz/½ cup butter or margarine, softened
50 g/2 oz/¼ cup caster (superfine) sugar
Grated rind of 1 lemon
Caster (superfine) sugar for sprinkling

Sift the flour and cornflour together. Cream the butter or margarine until soft, then beat in the caster sugar until pale and fluffy. Stir in the lemon rind, then beat in the flour mixture until well blended. Roll out the shortbread to a 20 cm/8 in circle and place on a greased baking (cookie) sheet. Prick all over with a fork and flute the edges. Cut into 12 wedges, then sprinkle with caster sugar. Chill in the fridge for 15 minutes. Bake in a preheated oven at 160°C/325°F/gas mark 3 for 35 minutes until pale golden brown. Leave to cool on the baking sheet for 5 minutes before turning out on to a wire rack to finish cooling.

Mincemeat Shortbread

Makes 8

175 g/6 oz/¾ cup butter or margarine, softened
50 g/2 oz/¼ cup caster (superfine) sugar
225 g/8 oz/2 cups plain (all-purpose) flour
60 ml/4 tbsp mincemeat

Cream the butter or margarine and sugar until soft. Work in the flour, then the mincemeat. Press into a 23 cm/7 in sandwich tin and level the top. Prick all over with a fork and mark into eight wedges, cutting through to the base. Chill for 1 hour.

Bake in a preheated oven at 160°C/325°F/gas mark 3 for 1 hour until pale straw-coloured. Leave to cool in the tin before turning out.

Nut Shortbread

Makes 12

100 g/4 oz/½ cup butter or margarine, softened
50 g/2 oz/¼ cup caster (superfine) sugar
100 g/4 oz/1 cup plain (all-purpose) flour
50 g/2 oz/½ cup ground rice
50 g/2 oz/½ cup almonds, finely chopped

Beat together the butter or margarine and sugar until light and fluffy. Mix in the flour and ground rice. Stir in the nuts and mix to a firm dough. Knead lightly until smooth. Press into the base of a greased Swiss roll tin (jelly roll pan) and level the surface. Prick all over with a fork. Bake in a preheated oven at 160°C/325°F/gas mark 3 for 45 minutes until pale golden brown. Leave to cool in the tin for 10 minutes, then cut into fingers. Leave in the tin to finish cooling before turning out.

Orange Shortbread

Makes 12

100 g/4 oz/1 cup plain (all-purpose) flour
50 g/2 oz/½ cup cornflour (cornstarch)
100 g/4 oz/½ cup butter or margarine, softened
50 g/2 oz/¼ cup caster (superfine) sugar
Grated rind of 1 orange
Caster (superfine) sugar for sprinkling

Sift the flour and cornflour together. Cream the butter or margarine until soft, then beat in the caster sugar until

312

pale and fluffy. Stir in the orange rind, then beat in the flour mixture until well blended. Roll out the shortbread to a 20 cm/8 in circle and place on a greased baking (cookie) sheet. Prick all over with a fork and flute the edges. Cut into 12 wedges, then sprinkle with caster sugar. Chill in the fridge for 15 minutes. Bake in a preheated oven at 160°C/325°F/gas mark 3 for 35 minutes until pale golden brown. Leave to cool on the baking sheet for 5 minutes before turning out on to a wire rack to finish cooling.

Rich Man's Shortbread

Makes 36

For the base:
225 g/8 oz/1 cup butter or margarine
275 g/10 oz/2½ cups plain
   (all-purpose) flour
100 g/4 oz/½ cup caster (superfine)
   sugar
For the filling:
225 g/8 oz/1 cup butter or margarine
225 g/8 oz/1 cup soft brown sugar
60 ml/4 tbsp golden (light corn) syrup
400 g/14 oz canned condensed milk
A few drops of vanilla essence
   (extract)
For the topping:
225 g/8 oz/2 cups plain (semi-sweet)
   chocolate

To make the base, rub the butter or margarine into the flour, then stir in the sugar and knead the mixture to a firm dough. Press into the base of a greased Swiss roll tin (jelly roll pan) lined with foil. Bake in a preheated oven at 180°C/ 350°F/gas mark 4 for 35 minutes until golden. Leave in the tin to cool.

To make the filling, melt the butter or margarine, sugar, syrup and condensed milk in a pan over a low heat, stirring continuously. Bring to the boil, then simmer gently, stirring continuously, for 7 minutes. Remove from the heat, add the vanilla essence and beat thoroughly. Pour over the base and leave to cool and set.

Melt the chocolate in a heatproof bowl set over a pan of gently simmering water. Spread over the caramel layer and mark into patterns with a fork. Leave to cool and set, then cut into squares.

Wholemeal Oat Shortbread

Makes 10

100 g/4 oz/½ cup butter or margarine
150 g/5 oz/1¼ cups wholemeal
   (wholewheat) flour
25 g/1 oz/¼ cup oat flour
50 g/2 oz/¼ cup soft brown sugar

Rub the butter or margarine into the flours until the mixture resembles breadcrumbs. Stir in the sugar and lightly work to a soft, crumbly dough. Roll out on a lightly floured surface to about 1 cm/½ in thick and cut into 5 cm/2 in rounds with a biscuit (cookie) cutter. Transfer carefully to a greased baking (cookie) sheet and bake in a preheated oven at 150°C/300°F/gas mark 3 for about 40 minutes until golden and firm.

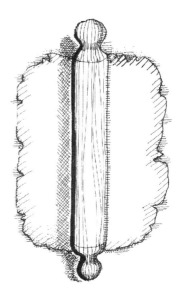

Almond Whirls

Makes 16

175 g/6 oz/³⁄₄ cup butter or margarine,
softened
50 g/2 oz/⅓ cup icing (confectioners')
sugar, sifted
2.5 ml/½ tsp almond essence (extract)
175 g/6 oz/1½ cups plain
(all-purpose) flour
8 glacé (candied) cherries, halved
or quartered
Icing (confectioners') sugar, sifted, for
dusting

Cream together the butter or margarine and sugar. Beat in the almond essence and flour. Transfer the mixture to a piping bag fitted with a large star-shaped nozzle (tip). Pipe 16 flat whirls on to a greased baking (cookie) sheet. Top each one with a piece of cherry. Bake in a preheated oven at 160°C/325°F/gas mark 3 for 20 minutes until pale golden. Leave on the tray to cool for 5 minutes then transfer to a wire rack and dust with icing sugar.

Chocolate Meringue Shortbread

Makes 24

100 g/4 oz/½ cup butter or margarine,
softened
5 ml/1 tsp vanilla essence (extract)
4 egg whites
200 g/7 oz/1¾ cups plain
(all-purpose) flour
50 g/2 oz/¼ cup caster (superfine)
sugar
45 ml/3 tbsp cocoa (unsweetened
chocolate) powder
100 g/4 oz/⅔ cup icing (confectioners')
sugar, sifted

Beat together the butter or margarine, vanilla essence and two of the egg whites. Mix together the flour, sugar and cocoa, then gradually beat into the butter mixture. Press into a greased 30 cm/12 in square tin (pan). Beat together the remaining egg whites with the icing sugar and spread over the top. Bake in a preheated oven at 190°C/375°F/gas mark 5 for 20 minutes until golden brown. Cut into bars.

Biscuit People

Makes about 12

100 g/4 oz/½ cup butter or margarine,
softened
100 g/4 oz/½ cup caster (superfine)
sugar
1 egg, beaten
225 g/8 oz/2 cups plain
(all-purpose) flour
A few currants and glacé (candied)
cherries

Cream together the butter or margarine and sugar. Gradually add the egg and beat thoroughly. Fold in the flour using a metal spoon. Roll out the mixture on a lightly floured surface to about 5 mm/¼ in thick. Cut out people with a biscuit (cookie) cutter or knife, re-rolling the trimmings until you have used all the dough. Place on a greased baking (cookie) sheet and press in currants for eyes and buttons. Cut slices of cherry for the mouths. Bake the biscuits (cookies) in a preheated oven at 190°C/375°F/gas mark 5 for 10 minutes until pale brown. Leave to cool on a wire rack.

314

Iced Ginger Shortcake

Makes two 20 cm/8 in cakes

For the shortcake:
225 g/8 oz/1 cup butter or margarine, softened
100 g/4 oz/½ cup caster (superfine) sugar
275 g/10 oz/2½ cups plain (all-purpose) flour
10 ml/2 tsp baking powder
10 ml/2 tsp ground ginger
For the icing (frosting):
50 g/2 oz/¼ cup butter or margarine
15 ml/1 tbsp golden (light corn) syrup
100 g/4 oz/⅔ cup icing (confectioners') sugar, sifted
5 ml/1 tsp ground ginger

To make the shortcake, cream together the butter or margarine and sugar until light and fluffy. Mix in the remaining shortcake ingredients to make a dough, divide the mixture in half and press into two greased 20 cm/8 in sandwich tins (pans). Bake in a preheated oven at 160°C/325°F/gas mark 3 for 40 minutes.

To make the icing, melt the butter or margarine and syrup in a pan. Add the icing sugar and ginger and blend together well. Pour over both shortcakes and leave until cool, then cut into wedges.

Shrewsbury Biscuits

Makes 24

100 g/4 oz/½ cup butter or margarine, softened
100 g/4 oz/½ cup caster (superfine) sugar
1 egg yolk
225 g/8 oz/2 cups plain (all-purpose) flour
5 ml/1 tsp baking powder
5 ml/1 tsp grated lemon rind

Cream together the butter or margarine and sugar until light and fluffy. Gradually beat in the egg yolk, then work in the flour, baking powder and lemon rind, finishing with your hands until the mixture binds together. Roll out to 5 mm/¼ in thick and cut into 6 cm/2¼ in rounds with a biscuit (cookie) cutter. Place the biscuits well apart on a greased baking (cookie) sheet and prick them with a fork. Bake in a preheated oven at 180°C/350°F/gas mark 4 for 15 minutes until pale golden.

Spanish Spiced Biscuits

Makes 16

90 ml/6 tbsp olive oil
100 g/4 oz/½ cup granulated sugar
100 g/4 oz/1 cup plain (all-purpose) flour
15 ml/1 tbsp baking powder
10 ml/2 tsp ground cinnamon
3 eggs
Grated rind of 1 lemon
30 ml/2 tbsp icing (confectioners') sugar, sifted

Warm the oil in a small pan. Mix together the sugar, flour, baking powder and cinnamon. In a separate bowl, beat the eggs and lemon rind until frothy. Stir in the dry ingredients and oil to make a smooth batter. Pour the batter into a well-greased Swiss roll tin (jelly roll pan) and bake in a preheated oven at 180°C/350°F/gas mark 4 for 30 minutes until golden. Turn out, leave to cool, then cut into triangles and sprinkle the biscuits (cookies) with icing sugar.

Old-fashioned Spice Biscuits

Makes 24

75 g/3 oz/⅓ cup butter or margarine
50 g/2 oz/¼ cup caster (superfine)
sugar
45 ml/3 tbsp black treacle (molasses)
175 g/6 oz/¾ cup plain (all-purpose)
flour
5 ml/1 tsp ground cinnamon
5 ml/1 tsp ground mixed (apple-pie)
spice
2.5 ml/½ tsp ground ginger
2.5 ml/½ tsp bicarbonate of soda
(baking soda)

Melt the butter or margarine, sugar and treacle together over a low heat. Mix together the flour, spices and bicarbonate of soda in a bowl. Pour into the treacle mixture and mix together until well blended. Blend to a soft dough and shape into small balls. Arrange, well apart, on a greased baking (cookie) sheet and press flat with a fork. Bake the biscuits (cookies) in a preheated oven at 180°C/350°F/gas mark 4 for 12 minutes until firm and golden.

Treacle Biscuits

Makes 24

75 g/3 oz/⅓ cup butter or margarine,
softened
100 g/4 oz/½ cup soft brown sugar
1 egg yolk
30 ml/2 tbsp black treacle (molasses)
100 g/4 oz/1 cup plain (all-purpose)
flour
5 ml/1 tsp bicarbonate of soda
(baking soda)
A pinch of salt
5 ml/1 tsp ground cinnamon
2.5 ml/½ tsp ground cloves

Beat together the butter or margarine and sugar until light and fluffy. Gradually beat in the egg yolk and

molasses. Mix together the flour, bicarbonate of soda, salt and spices and blend into the mixture. Cover and chill.

Roll the mixture into 3 cm/1½ in balls and arrange on a greased baking (cookie) sheet. Bake the biscuits (cookies) in a preheated oven at 180°C/350°F/gas mark 4 for 10 minutes until just set.

Treacle, Apricot and Nut Cookies

Makes about 24

50 g/2 oz/¼ cup butter or margarine
50 g/2 oz/¼ cup caster (superfine)
sugar
50 g/2 oz/¼ cup soft brown sugar
1 egg, lightly beaten
2.5 ml/½ tsp bicarbonate of soda
(baking soda)
30 ml/2 tbsp warm water
45 ml/3 tbsp black treacle (molasses)
25 g/1 oz ready-to-eat dried apricots,
chopped
25 g/1 oz/¼ cup chopped mixed nuts
100 g/4 oz/1 cup plain (all-purpose)
flour
A pinch of salt
A pinch of ground cloves

Cream together the butter or margarine and sugars until light and fluffy. Gradually beat in the egg. Mix the bicarbonate of soda with the water, the stir into the mixture with the remaining ingredients. Drop spoonfuls on to a greased baking (cookie) sheet and bake in a preheated oven at 180°C/350°F/gas mark 4 for 10 minutes.

Treacle and Buttermilk Cookies

Makes 24

50 g/2 oz/¼ cup butter or margarine, softened
50 g/2 oz/¼ cup soft brown sugar
150 ml/¼ pt/⅔ cup black treacle (molasses)
150 ml/¼ pt/⅔ cup buttermilk
175 g/6 oz/1½ cups plain (all-purpose) flour
2.5 ml/½ tsp bicarbonate of soda (baking soda)

Cream together the butter or margarine and sugar until light and fluffy, then mix in the treacle and buttermilk alternately with the flour and bicarbonate of soda. Drop large spoonfuls on to a greased baking (cookie) sheet and bake in a preheated oven at 190°C/375°F/gas mark 5 for 10 minutes.

Treacle and Coffee Biscuits

Makes 24

60 g/2½ oz/⅓ cup lard (shortening)
50 g/2 oz/¼ cup soft brown sugar
75 g/3 oz/¼ cup black treacle (molasses)
2.5 ml/½ tsp vanilla essence (extract)
200 g/7 oz/1¾ cups plain (all-purpose) flour
5 ml/1 tsp bicarbonate of soda (baking soda)
A pinch of salt
2.5 ml/½ tsp ground ginger
2.5 ml/½ tsp ground cinnamon
60 ml/4 tbsp cold black coffee

Cream together the lard and sugar until light and fluffy. Stir in the treacle and vanilla essence. Mix together the flour, bicarbonate of soda, salt and spices and beat into the mixture alternately with the coffee. Cover and chill for several hours.

Roll out the dough to 5 mm/¼ in thick and cut into 5 cm/2 in rounds with a biscuit (cookie) cutter. Place the biscuits on an ungreased baking (cookie) sheet and bake in a preheated oven at 190°C/375°F/gas mark 5 for 10 minutes until firm to the touch.

Treacle and Date Cookies

Makes about 24

50 g/2 oz/¼ cup butter or margarine, softened
50 g/2 oz/¼ cup caster (superfine) sugar
50 g/2 oz/¼ cup soft brown sugar
1 egg, lightly beaten
2.5 ml/½ tsp bicarbonate of soda (baking soda)
30 ml/2 tbsp warm water
45 ml/3 tbsp black treacle (molasses)
25 g/1 oz/¼ cup stoned (pitted) dates, chopped
100 g/4 oz/1 cup plain (all-purpose) flour
A pinch of salt
A pinch of ground cloves

Cream together the butter or margarine and sugars until light and fluffy. Gradually beat in the egg. Mix the bicarbonate of soda with the water, then stir into the mixture with the remaining ingredients. Drop spoonfuls on to a greased baking (cookie) sheet and bake in a preheated oven at 180°C/350°F/gas mark 4 for 10 minutes.

Treacle and Ginger Cookies

Makes 24

50 g/2 oz/¼ cup butter or margarine,
softened
50 g/2 oz/¼ cup soft brown sugar
150 ml/¼ pt/⅔ cup black treacle
(molasses)
150 ml/¼ pt/⅔ cup buttermilk
175 g/6 oz/1½ cups plain
(all-purpose) flour
2.5 ml/½ tsp bicarbonate of soda
(baking soda)
2.5 ml/½ tsp ground ginger
1 egg, beaten, to glaze

Cream together the butter or margarine and sugar until light and fluffy, then mix in the treacle and buttermilk alternately with the flour, bicarbonate of soda and ground ginger. Drop large spoonfuls on to a greased baking (cookie) sheet and brush the tops with beaten egg. Bake in a preheated oven at 190°C/375°F/ gas mark 5 for 10 minutes.

Vanilla Biscuits

Makes 24

150 g/5 oz/⅔ cup butter or margarine,
softened
100 g/4 oz/½ cup caster (superfine)
sugar
1 egg, beaten
225 g/8 oz/2 cups self-raising
(self-rising) flour
A pinch of salt
10 ml/2 tsp vanilla essence (extract)
Glacé (candied) cherries to decorate

Cream together the butter or margarine and sugar until light and fluffy. Gradually beat in the egg, then fold in the flour, salt and vanilla essence and mix to a dough. Knead until smooth. Wrap in clingfilm (plastic wrap) and chill for 20 minutes.
Roll out the dough thinly and cut into rounds with a biscuit (cookie) cutter. Arrange on a greased baking (cookie) sheet and place a cherry on top of each one. Bake the biscuits in a preheated oven at 180°C/350°F/gas mark 4 for 10 minutes until golden brown. Leave to cool on the baking sheet for 10 minutes before transferring to a wire rack to finish cooling.

Walnut Biscuits

Makes 36

100 g/4 oz/½ cup butter or margarine,
softened
100 g/4 oz/½ cup soft brown sugar
100 g/4 oz/½ cup caster (superfine)
sugar
1 large egg, lightly beaten
200 g/7 oz/1¾ cups plain
(all-purpose) flour
5 ml/1 tsp baking powder
2.5 ml/½ tsp bicarbonate of soda
(baking soda)
120 ml/4 fl oz/½ cup buttermilk
50 g/2 oz/½ cup walnuts, chopped

Cream together the butter or margarine and sugars. Gradually beat in the egg, then fold in the flour, baking powder and bicarbonate of soda alternately with the buttermilk. Fold in the walnuts. Drop small spoonfuls on to a greased baking (cookie) sheet and bake the biscuits (cookies) in a preheated oven at 190°C/375°F/gas mark 5 for 10 minutes.

318

Savoury Biscuits and Crackers

*T*here are times when a savoury biscuit makes a welcome change, either as part of a buffet, at the tea table, or as a snack.

Crisp Biscottes

Makes 24

25 g/1 oz fresh yeast or 40 ml/
2½ tbsp dried yeast
450 ml/¾ pt/2 cups warm milk
900 g/2 lb/8 cups strong plain (bread)
flour
175 g/6 oz/¾ cup butter or margarine,
softened
30 ml/2 tbsp clear honey
2 eggs, beaten
Beaten egg for glazing

Mix the yeast with a little of the warm milk and leave in a warm place for 20 minutes. Place the flour in a bowl and rub in the butter or margarine. Blend in the yeast mixture, the remaining warm milk, the honey and eggs and mix to a soft dough. Knead on a lightly floured surface until smooth and elastic. Place in an oiled bowl, cover with oiled clingfilm (plastic wrap) and leave in a warm place for 1 hour until doubled in size.

Knead again, then shape into long flat rolls and place on a greased baking (cookie) sheet. Cover with oiled clingfilm and leave in a warm place for 20 minutes.

Brush with beaten egg and bake in a preheated oven at 200°C/400°F/gas mark 6 for 20 minutes. Leave to cool overnight.

Slice thinly, then bake again in a preheated oven at 150°C/300°F/gas mark 2 for 30 minutes until crisp and brown.

Cheddar Biscuits

Makes 12

50 g/2 oz/¼ cup butter or margarine
200 g/7 oz/1¾ cups plain
(all-purpose) flour
15 ml/1 tbsp baking powder
A pinch of salt
50 g/2 oz/½ cup Cheddar cheese,
grated
175 ml/6 fl oz/¾ cup milk

Rub the butter or margarine into the flour, baking powder and salt until the mixture resembles breadcrumbs. Stir in the cheese, then mix in enough of the milk to make a soft dough. Roll out on a lightly floured surface to about 2 cm/ ¾ in thick and cut into rounds with a biscuit (cookie) cutter. Arrange on an ungreased baking (cookie) sheet and bake the biscuits (crackers) in a preheated oven at 200°C/400°F/gas mark 6 for 15 minutes until golden brown.

Blue Cheese Biscuits

Makes 12

50 g/2 oz/¼ cup butter or margarine
200 g/7 oz/1¾ cups plain
(all-purpose) flour
15 ml/1 tbsp baking powder
50 g/2 oz/½ cup Stilton cheese, grated
or crumbled
175 ml/6 fl oz/¾ cup milk

Rub the butter or margarine into the flour and baking powder until the mixture resembles breadcrumbs. Stir in the cheese, then mix in enough of the milk to make a soft dough. Roll out on a lightly floured surface to about 2 cm/ ¾ in thick and cut into rounds with a biscuit (cookie) cutter. Arrange on an ungreased baking (cookie) sheet and bake the biscuits (crackers) in a preheated oven at 200°C/400°F/gas mark 6 for 15 minutes until golden brown.

Cheese and Sesame Biscuits

Makes 24

75 g/3 oz/⅓ cup butter or margarine
75 g/3 oz/¾ cup wholemeal
(wholewheat) flour
75 g/3 oz/¾ cup Cheddar cheese,
grated
30 ml/2 tbsp sesame seeds
Salt and freshly ground black pepper
1 egg, beaten

Rub the butter or margarine into the flour until the mixture resembles breadcrumbs. Stir in the cheese and half the sesame seeds and season with salt and pepper. Press together to form a firm dough. Roll out the dough on a lightly floured surface to about 5 mm/¼ in thick and cut into rounds with a biscuit (cookie) cutter. Place the biscuits (crackers) on a greased baking (cookie) sheet, brush with egg and sprinkle with the remaining sesame seeds. Bake in a preheated oven at 190°C/375°F/gas mark 5 for 10 minutes until golden.

Cheese Straws

Makes 16

225 g/8 oz Puff Pastry (page 136)
1 egg, beaten
100 g/4 oz/1 cup Cheddar or strong
cheese, grated
15 ml/1 tbsp grated Parmesan cheese
Salt and freshly ground black pepper

Roll out the pastry (paste) to about 5 mm/¼ in thick and brush generously with beaten egg. Sprinkle with the cheeses and season to taste with salt and pepper. Cut into strips and twist the strips gently into spirals. Place on a dampened baking (cookie) sheet and bake in a preheated oven at 220°C/425°F/gas mark 7 for about 10 minutes until puffed and golden.

Cheese and Tomato Biscuits

Makes 12

50 g/2 oz/¼ cup butter or margarine
200 g/7 oz/1¾ cups plain
(all-purpose) flour
15 ml/1 tbsp baking powder
A pinch of salt
50 g/2 oz/½ cup Cheddar cheese,
grated
15 ml/1 tbsp tomato purée (paste)
150 ml/¼ pt/⅔ cup milk

Rub the butter or margarine into the flour, baking powder and salt until the mixture resembles breadcrumbs. Stir in the cheese, then mix in the tomato purée and enough of the milk to make a soft dough. Roll out on a lightly floured surface to about 2 cm/¾ in thick and cut into rounds with a biscuit (cookie) cutter. Arrange on an ungreased baking (cookie) sheet and bake the biscuits (crackers) in a preheated oven at 200°C/400°F/gas mark 6 for 15 minutes until golden brown.

Photograph opposite: **Autumn Crown (page 358–9)**

320

Goats' Cheese Bites

Makes 30

2 sheets frozen filo pastry (paste),
  thawed
50 g/2 oz/¼ cup unsalted butter,
  melted
50 g/2 oz/½ cup goats' cheese, diced
5 ml/1 tsp Herbes de Provence

Brush a filo pastry sheet with melted butter, place the second sheet on top and brush with butter. Cut into 30 equal squares, place a piece of cheese on each one and sprinkle with herbs. Bring the corners together and twist to seal, then brush again with melted butter. Place on a greased baking (cookie) sheet and bake in a preheated oven at 180°C/350°F/gas mark 4 for 10 minutes until crisp and golden.

Ham and Mustard Rolls

Makes 16

225 g/8 oz Puff Pastry (page 136)
30 ml/2 tbsp French mustard
100 g/4 oz/1 cup cooked ham,
  chopped
Salt and freshly ground black pepper

Roll out the pastry (paste) to about 5 mm/¼ in thick. Spread with the mustard, then sprinkle with the ham and season with salt and pepper. Roll up the pastry into a long sausage shape, then cut into 1 cm/½ in slices and arrange on a dampened baking (cookie) sheet. Bake in a preheated oven at 220°C/425°F/gas mark 7 for about 10 minutes until puffed and golden.

Ham and Pepper Biscuits

Makes 30

225 g/8 oz/2 cups plain
  (all-purpose) flour
15 ml/1 tbsp baking powder
5 ml/1 tsp dried thyme
5 ml/1 tsp caster (superfine) sugar
2.5 ml/½ tsp ground ginger
A pinch of grated nutmeg
A pinch of bicarbonate of soda
  (baking soda)
Salt and freshly ground black pepper
50 g/2 oz/¼ cup vegetable fat
  (shortening)
50 g/2 oz/½ cup cooked ham, minced
30 ml/2 tbsp finely chopped green
  (bell) pepper
175 ml/6 fl oz/¾ cup buttermilk

Mix together the flour, baking powder, thyme, sugar, ginger, nutmeg, bicarbonate of soda, salt and pepper. Rub in the vegetable fat until the mixture resembles breadcrumbs. Stir in the ham and pepper. Gradually add the buttermilk and mix to a soft dough. Knead for a few seconds on a lightly floured surface until smooth. Roll out to 2 cm/¾ in thick and cut into rounds with a biscuit (cookie) cutter. Place the biscuits, well apart, on a greased baking (cookie) sheet and bake in a preheated oven at 220°C/425°F/gas mark 7 for 12 minutes until puffed and golden.

Photograph opposite: **Onion and Sun-dried Tomato Bread (page 390–1) and Soda Bread (page 343)**

321

Simple Herb Biscuits

Makes 8

225 g/8 oz/2 cups plain
  (all-purpose) flour
15 ml/1 tbsp baking powder
5 ml/1 tsp caster (superfine) sugar
2.5 ml/½ tsp salt
50 g/2 oz/¼ cup butter or margarine
15 ml/1 tbsp snipped fresh chives
A pinch of paprika
Freshly ground black pepper
45 ml/3 tbsp milk
45 ml/3 tbsp water

Mix together the flour, baking powder, sugar and salt. Rub in the butter or margarine until the mixture resembles breadcrumbs. Mix in the chives, paprika and pepper to taste. Stir in the milk and water and mix to a soft dough. Knead on a lightly floured surface until smooth, then roll out to 2 cm/¾ in thick and cut into rounds with a biscuit (cookie) cutter. Place the biscuits (crackers), well apart, on a greased baking (cookie) sheet and bake in a preheated oven at 200°C/400°F/gas mark 6 for 15 minutes until puffed and golden.

Indian Biscuits

Serves 4

100 g/4 oz/1 cup plain (all-purpose)
  flour
100 g/4 oz/1 cup semolina (cream of
  wheat)
175 g/6 oz/¾ cup caster (superfine)
  sugar
75 g/3 oz/¾ cup gram flour
175 g/6 oz/¾ cup ghee

Mix together all the ingredients in a bowl, then rub them with the palms of your hands to form a stiff dough. You may need a little more ghee if the mixture is too dry. Shape into small balls and press into biscuit (cracker) shapes. Place on a greased and lined baking (cookie) sheet

and bake in a preheated oven at 150°C/300°F/gas mark 2 for 30–40 minutes until lightly browned. Fine hairline cracks may appear as the biscuits are cooked.

Hazelnut and Shallot Shortbread

Makes 12

75 g/3 oz/⅓ cup butter or margarine,
  softened
175 g/6 oz/1½ cups wholemeal
  (wholewheat) flour
10 ml/2 tsp baking powder
1 shallot, finely chopped
50 g/2 oz/½ cup hazelnuts, chopped
10 ml/2 tsp paprika
15 ml/1 tbsp cold water

Rub the butter or margarine into the flour and baking powder until the mixture resembles breadcrumbs. Stir in the shallot, hazelnuts and paprika. Add the cold water and press together to make a dough. Roll out and press into a 30 × 20 cm/12 × 8 in Swiss roll tin (jelly roll pan) and prick all over with a fork. Mark into fingers. Bake in a preheated oven at 200°C/400°F/gas mark 6 for 10 minutes until golden.

Salmon and Dill Biscuits

Makes 12

225 g/8 oz/2 cups plain
  (all-purpose) flour
5 ml/1 tsp caster (superfine) sugar
2.5 ml/½ tsp salt
20 ml/4 tsp baking powder
100 g/4 oz/½ cup butter or margarine,
  diced
90 ml/6 tbsp water
90 ml/6 tbsp milk
100 g/4 oz/1 cup smoked salmon
  trimmings, diced
60 ml/4 tbsp chopped fresh dill
  (dill weed)

322

Mix together the flour, sugar, salt and baking powder, then rub in the butter or margarine until the mixture resembles breadcrumbs. Gradually mix in the milk and water and mix to a soft dough. Work in the salmon and dill and mix until smooth. Roll out to 2.5 cm/1 in thick and cut into rounds with a biscuit (cookie) cutter. Place the biscuits (crackers) well apart on a greased baking (cookie) sheet and bake in a preheated oven at 220°C/425°F/gas mark 7 for 15 minutes until puffed and golden.

Soda Biscuits

Makes 12

45 ml/3 tbsp lard (shortening)
225 g/8 oz/2 cups plain
  (all-purpose) flour
5 ml/1 tsp bicarbonate of soda
  (baking soda)
5 ml/1 tsp cream of tartar
A pinch of salt
250 ml/8 fl oz/1 cup buttermilk

Rub the lard into the flour, bicarbonate of soda, cream of tartar and salt until the mixture resembles breadcrumbs. Stir in the milk and mix to a soft dough. Roll out on a lightly floured surface to 1 cm/½ in thick and cut out with a biscuit (cookie) cutter. Place the biscuits (crackers) on a greased baking (cookie) sheet and bake in a preheated oven at 230°C/450°F/gas mark 8 for 10 minutes until golden.

Tomato and Parmesan Pinwheels

Makes 16

225 g/8 oz Puff Pastry (page 136)
30 ml/2 tbsp tomato purée (paste)
100 g/4 oz/1 cup Parmesan cheese,
  grated
Salt and freshly ground black pepper

Roll out the pastry (paste) to about 5 mm/¼ in thick. Spread with the tomato purée, then sprinkle with the cheese and season with salt and pepper. Roll up the pastry into a long sausage shape, then cut into 1 cm/½ in slices and arrange on a dampened baking (cookie) sheet. Bake in a preheated oven at 220°C/425°F/gas mark 7 for about 10 minutes until puffed and golden.

Tomato and Herb Biscuits

Makes 12

225 g/8 oz/2 cups plain
  (all-purpose) flour
5 ml/1 tsp caster (superfine) sugar
2.5 ml/½ tsp salt
40 ml/2½ tbsp baking powder
100 g/4 oz/½ cup butter or margarine
30 ml/2 tbsp milk
30 ml/2 tbsp water
4 ripe tomatoes, skinned, seeded and
  chopped
45 ml/3 tbsp chopped fresh basil

Mix together the flour, sugar, salt and baking powder. Rub in the butter or margarine until the mixture resembles breadcrumbs. Stir in the milk, water, tomatoes and basil and mix to a soft dough. Knead for a few seconds on a lightly floured surface, then roll out to 2.5 cm/1 in thick and cut into rounds with a biscuit (cookie) cutter. Place the biscuits well apart on a greased baking (cookie) sheet and bake in a preheated oven at 230°C/425°F/gas mark 7 for 15 minutes until puffed and golden.

Breads and Rolls

*T*here *is an endless variety of breads you can create and they are not difficult to make. You can use either fresh, dried, or easy-blend yeast for the recipes. Professional bakers always use fresh yeast, which you can buy at the delicatessen or some supermarkets. This does not need as long to activate as dried yeast, so you can simply mix it to a paste and then use it fairly quickly. Ordinary dried yeast needs to be mixed with warm water and sugar and left for about 20 minutes until frothy before being added to the flour. Easy-blend yeast is added to the dried ingredients before the warm liquid is mixed in and the dough is made. This is the easiest way to start if you are not used to making bread, so just adjust the recipe method according to the instructions on the packet.*

The kneading is essential when making bread, so remember to keep going until the dough is smooth and no longer sticky, otherwise the yeast will not work properly. Some people enjoy kneading by hand; others like to make the job quicker and easier by using a food processor – the choice is yours. It will take only a few minutes in a processor, but you should knead for at least 10 minutes if you are working by hand.

Most mixtures are left to rise twice: the second rising is often called proving. Times will vary depending on the recipe and the temperature of the room, but, in a warm room, the dough should take about 1 hour to double in size on the first rising, and about 40 minutes on the second rising. Cover the dough with oiled clingfilm (plastic wrap) or a damp tea towel (dish cloth) to prevent a skin forming on the top.

Between risings, you can shape your dough in almost any way you like – use a loaf tin (pan), form into a traditional bloomer shape, press two pieces into a cottage loaf, make into rolls. Remember that if you make smaller-sized loaves, the cooking time will be reduced. Breads usually need to be baked in a hot oven, and are ready when the loaves sound hollow when tapped on the base.

Basic White Loaf

Makes three 450 g/1 lb loaves

25 g/1 oz fresh yeast or
  40 ml/2½ tbsp dried yeast
10 ml/2 tsp sugar
900 ml/1½ pts/3¾ cups warm water
25 g/1 oz/2 tbsp lard (shortening)
1.5 kg/3 lb/12 cups strong plain
  (bread) flour
15 ml/1 tbsp salt

Blend the yeast with the sugar and a little of the warm water and leave in a warm place for 20 minutes until frothy. Rub the lard into the flour and salt, then stir in the yeast mixture and enough of the remaining water to mix to a firm dough that leaves the sides of the bowl cleanly. Knead on a lightly floured surface or in a processor until elastic and no longer sticky. Place the dough in an oiled bowl, cover with oiled clingfilm (plastic wrap) and leave in a warm place for about 1 hour until doubled in size and springy to the touch.

Knead the dough again until firm, divide into three and place in greased 450 g/1 lb loaf tins (pans) or shape into the loaves of your choice. Cover and leave to rise in a warm place for about 40 minutes until the dough reaches just above the top of the tins.

Bake in a preheated oven at 230°C/450°F/gas mark 8 for 30 minutes until the loaves begin to shrink away from the sides of the tins and are golden and firm, and hollow-sounding when tapped on the base.

Bagels

Makes 12

15 g/½ oz fresh yeast or 20 ml/
  4 tsp dried yeast
5 ml/1 tsp caster (superfine) sugar
300 ml/½ pt/1¼ cups warm milk
50 g/2 oz/¼ cup butter or margarine
450 g/1 lb/4 cups strong plain (bread)
  flour
A pinch of salt
1 egg yolk
30 ml/2 tbsp poppy seeds

Blend the yeast with the sugar and a little of the warm milk and leave in a warm place for 20 minutes until frothy. Rub the butter or margarine into the flour and salt and make a well in the centre. Add the yeast mixture, the remaining warm milk and the egg yolk and mix to a smooth dough. Knead until the dough is elastic and no longer sticky. Place in an oiled bowl, cover with oiled clingfilm (plastic wrap) and leave in a warm place for about 1 hour until doubled in size.

Knead the dough lightly, then cut it into 12 pieces. Roll each one into a long strip about 15 cm/6 in long and twist into a ring. Place on a greased baking (cookie) sheet, cover and leave to rise for 15 minutes.

Bring a large pan of water to the boil, then turn down the heat to a simmer. Drop a ring into the simmering water and cook for 3 minutes, turning once, then remove and place on a baking (cookie) sheet. Continue with the remaining bagels. Sprinkle the bagels with poppy seeds and bake in a preheated oven at 230°C/450°F/gas mark 8 for 20 minutes until golden.

Baps

Makes 12

25 g/1 oz fresh yeast or 40 ml/
2½ tbsp dried yeast
5 ml/1 tsp caster (superfine) sugar
150 ml/¼ pt/⅔ cup warm milk
50 g/2 oz/¼ cup lard (shortening)
450 g/1 lb/4 cups strong plain (bread)
flour
5 ml/1 tsp salt
150 ml/¼ pt/⅔ cup warm water

Blend the yeast with the sugar and a little of the warm milk and leave in a warm place for 20 minutes until frothy. Rub the lard into the flour, then stir in the salt and make a well in the centre. Add the yeast mixture, the remaining milk and the water and mix to a soft dough. Knead until elastic and no longer sticky. Place in an oiled bowl and cover with oiled clingfilm (plastic wrap). Leave in a warm place for about 1 hour until doubled in size.

Shape the dough into 12 flat rolls and arrange on a greased baking (cookie) sheet. Leave to rise for 15 minutes.

Bake in a preheated oven at 230°C/450°F/gas mark 8 for 15–20 minutes until well risen and golden.

Creamy Barley Loaf

Makes one 900 g/2 lb loaf

15 g/½ oz fresh yeast or 20 ml/4 tsp
dried yeast
A pinch of sugar
350 ml/12 fl oz/1½ cups warm water
400 g/14 oz/3½ cups strong plain
(bread) flour
175 g/6 oz/1½ cups barley flour
A pinch of salt
45 ml/3 tbsp single (light) cream

Blend the yeast with the sugar and a little of the warm water and leave in a warm place for 20 minutes until frothy. Mix the flours and salt in a bowl, add the yeast mixture, the cream and remaining water and mix to a firm dough. Knead until smooth and no longer sticky. Place in an oiled bowl, cover with oiled clingfilm (plastic wrap) and leave in a warm place for about 1 hour until doubled in size.

Knead again lightly, then shape into a greased 900 g/2 lb loaf tin (pan), cover and leave in a warm place for 40 minutes until the dough has risen above the top of the tin.

Bake in a preheated oven at 220°C/425°F/gas mark 7 for 10 minutes, then reduce the oven temperature to 190°C/375°F/gas mark 5 and bake for a further 25 minutes until golden brown and hollow-sounding when tapped on the base.

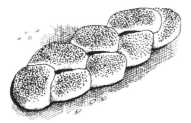

Beer Bread

Makes one 900 g/2 lb loaf

450 g/1 lb/4 cups self-raising
(self-rising) flour
5 ml/1 tsp salt
350 ml/12 fl oz/1½ cups lager

Mix together the ingredients to a smooth dough. Shape into a greased 900 g/2 lb loaf tin (pan), cover and leave to rise in a warm place for 20 minutes. Bake in a preheated oven at 190°C/375°F/gas mark 5 for 45 minutes until golden brown and hollow-sounding when tapped on the base.

Boston Brown Bread

Makes three 450 g/1 lb loaves

100 g/4 oz/1 cup rye flour
100 g/4 oz/1 cup cornmeal
100 g/4 oz/1 cup wholemeal
(wholewheat) flour
5 ml/1 tsp bicarbonate of soda
(baking soda)
5 ml/1 tsp salt
250 g/9 oz/¾ cup black treacle
(molasses)
500 ml/16 fl oz/2 cups buttermilk
175 g/6 oz/1 cup raisins

Mix together the dry ingredients, then stir in the treacle, buttermilk and raisins and mix to a soft dough. Spoon the mixture into three greased 450 g/1 lb pudding basins, cover with greaseproof (waxed) paper and foil and tie with string to seal the tops. Place in a large pan and fill with enough hot water to come halfway up the sides of the bowls. Bring the water to the boil, cover the pan and simmer for 2½ hours, topping up with boiling water as necessary. Remove the bowls from the pan and leave to cool slightly. Serve warm with butter.

Bran Flowerpots

Makes 3

25 g/1 oz fresh yeast or 40 ml/
2½ tbsp dried yeast
5 ml/1 tsp sugar
600 ml/1 pt/2½ cups lukewarm water
675 g/1½ lb/6 cups wholemeal
(wholewheat) flour
25 g/1 oz/¼ cup soya flour
5 ml/1 tsp salt
50 g/2 oz/1 cup bran
Milk to glaze
45 ml/3 tbsp cracked wheat

You will need three clean, new 13 cm/ 5 in clay flowerpots. Grease them well and bake in a hot oven for 30 minutes to prevent them from cracking.

Blend the yeast with the sugar and a little of the warm water and leave to stand until frothy. Mix the flours, salt and bran and make a well in the centre. Mix in the warm water and yeast mixture and knead to a firm dough. Turn out on to a floured surface and knead for about 10 minutes until smooth and elastic. Alternatively, you can do this in a food processor. Place the dough in a clean bowl, cover with oiled clingfilm (plastic wrap) and leave in a warm place to rise for about 1 hour until doubled in size.

Turn out on to a floured surface and knead again for 10 minutes. Shape into the three greased flowerpots, cover and leave to prove for 45 minutes until the dough has risen above the top of the pots.

Brush the dough with milk and sprinkle with the cracked wheat. Bake in a preheated oven at 230°C/450°F/gas mark 8 for 15 minutes. Reduce the oven temperature to 200°C/400°F/gas mark 6 and bake for a further 30 minutes until well risen and firm. Turn out and leave to cool.

Buttered Rolls

Makes 12

450 g/1 lb Basic White Loaf dough
(page 325)
100 g/4 oz/½ cup butter or margarine,
diced

Make the bread dough and leave it to rise until doubled in size and springy to the touch.

Knead the dough again and work in the butter or margarine. Shape into 12 rolls and place them well apart on a greased baking (cookie) sheet. Cover with oiled clingfilm (plastic wrap) and leave to rise in a warm place for about 1 hour until doubled in size.

Bake in a preheated oven at 230°C/450°F/gas mark 8 for 20 minutes until golden brown and hollow-sounding when tapped on the base.

Buttermilk Loaf

Makes one 675 g/1½ lb loaf

450 g/1 lb/4 cups plain (all-purpose)
flour
5 ml/1 tsp cream of tartar
5 ml/1 tsp bicarbonate of soda
(baking soda)
250 ml/8 fl oz/1 cup buttermilk

Mix together the flour, cream of tartar and bicarbonate of soda in a bowl and make a well in the centre. Stir in enough of the buttermilk to mix to a soft dough. Shape into a round and place on a greased baking (cookie) sheet. Bake in a preheated oven at 220°C/425°F/gas mark 7 for 20 minutes until well risen and golden brown.

Canadian Corn Bread

Makes one 23 cm/9 in loaf

150 g/5 oz/1¼ cups plain
(all-purpose) flour
75 g/3 oz/¾ cup cornmeal
15 ml/1 tbsp baking powder
2.5 ml/½ tsp salt
100 g/4 oz/⅓ cup maple syrup
100 g/4 oz/½ cup lard (shortening),
melted
2 eggs, beaten

Mix together the dry ingredients, then blend in the syrup, lard and eggs and stir until well mixed. Spoon into a greased 23 cm/9 in baking tin (pan) and bake in a preheated oven at 220°C/425°F/gas mark 7 for 25 minutes until well risen and golden brown, and beginning to shrink away from the sides of the tin.

Cornish Rolls

Makes 12

25 g/1 oz fresh yeast or 40 ml/2½ tbsp
dried yeast
15 ml/1 tbsp caster (superfine) sugar
300 ml/½ pt/1¼ cups warm milk
50 g/2 oz/¼ cup butter or margarine
450 g/1 lb/4 cups strong plain (bread)
flour
A pinch of salt

Blend the yeast with the sugar and a little of the warm milk and leave in a warm place for 20 minutes until frothy. Rub the butter or margarine into the flour and salt and make a well in the centre. Add the yeast mixture and the remaining milk and mix to a soft dough. Knead until elastic and no longer sticky. Place in an oiled bowl and cover with oiled clingfilm (plastic wrap). Leave in a warm place for about 1 hour until doubled in size.

Shape the dough into 12 flat rolls and arrange on a greased baking (cookie) sheet. Cover with oiled clingfilm and leave to rise for 15 minutes.

Bake in a preheated oven at 230°C/450°F/gas mark 8 for 15–20 minutes until well risen and golden.

Country Flat Bread

Makes six small breads

10 ml/2 tsp dried yeast
15 ml/1 tbsp clear honey
120 ml/4 fl oz/½ cup warm water
350 g/12 oz/3 cups strong plain
 (bread) flour
5 ml/1 tsp salt
50 g/2 oz/¼ cup butter or margarine
5 ml/1 tsp caraway seeds
5 ml/1 tsp ground coriander
5 ml/1 tsp ground cardamom
120 ml/4 fl oz/½ cup warm milk
60 ml/4 tbsp sesame seeds

Blend the yeast and honey with 45 ml/3 tbsp of the warm water and 15 ml/1 tbsp of the flour and leave for about 20 minutes in a warm place until frothy. Mix the remaining flour with the salt, then rub in the butter or margarine and stir in the caraway seeds, coriander and cardamom and make a well in the centre. Mix in the yeast mixture, remaining water and enough of the milk to make a smooth dough. Knead well until firm and no longer sticky. Place in an oiled bowl, cover with oiled clingfilm (plastic wrap) and leave in a warm place for about 30 minutes until doubled in size.

Knead the dough again, then shape into flat cakes. Place on a greased baking (cookie) sheet and brush with milk. Sprinkle with sesame seeds. Cover with oiled clingfilm and leave to rise for 15 minutes.

Bake in a preheated oven at 200°C/400°F/gas mark 6 for 30 minutes until golden.

Country Poppyseed Plait

Makes one 450 g/1 lb loaf

275 g/10 oz/2½ cups plain
 (all-purpose) flour
25 g/1 oz/2 tbsp caster (superfine)
 sugar
5 ml/1 tsp salt
10 ml/2 tsp easy-blend dried yeast
175 ml/6 fl oz/¾ cup milk
25 g/1 oz/2 tbsp butter or margarine
1 egg
A little milk or egg white for glazing
30 ml/2 tbsp poppy seeds

Mix together the flour, sugar, salt and yeast. Warm the milk with the butter or margarine, then mix into the flour with the egg and knead to a stiff dough. Knead until elastic and no longer sticky. Place in an oiled bowl, cover with oiled clingfilm (plastic wrap) and leave in a warm place for about 1 hour until doubled in size.

Knead again and shape into three sausage shapes about 20 cm/8 in long. Moisten one end of each strip and press them together, then plait the strips together, moisten and seal the ends. Place on a greased baking (cookie) sheet, cover with oiled clingfilm and leave to rise for about 40 minutes until doubled in size.

Brush with milk or egg white and sprinkle with poppy seeds. Bake in a preheated oven at 190°C/375°F/gas mark 5 for about 45 minutes until golden brown.

Country Wholemeal Bread

Makes two 450 g/1 lb loaves

20 ml/4 tsp dried yeast
5 ml/1 tsp caster (superfine) sugar
600 ml/1 pt/2½ cups warm water
25 g/1 oz/2 tbsp vegetable fat
  (shortening)
800 g/1¾ lb/7 cups wholemeal
  (wholewheat) flour
10 ml/2 tsp salt
10 ml/2 tsp malt extract
1 egg, beaten
25 g/1 oz/¼ cup cracked wheat

Blend the yeast with the sugar and a little of the warm water and leave for about 20 minutes until frothy. Rub the fat into the flour, salt and malt extract and make a well in the centre. Stir in the yeast mixture and the remaining warm water and mix to a soft dough. Knead well until elastic and no longer sticky. Place in an oiled bowl, cover with oiled clingfilm (plastic wrap) and leave in a warm place for about 1 hour until doubled in size.

Knead the dough again and shape into two greased 450 g/1 lb loaf tins (pans). Leave to rise in a warm place for about 40 minutes until the dough rises just above the tops of the tins.

Brush the tops of the loaves generously with egg and sprinkle with cracked wheat. Bake in a preheated oven at 230°C/450°F/gas mark 8 for about 30 minutes until golden brown and hollow-sounding when tapped on the base.

Curry Plaits

Makes two 450 g/1 lb loaves

120 ml/4 fl oz/½ cup warm water
30 ml/2 tbsp dried yeast
225 g/8 oz/⅔ cup clear honey
25 g/1 oz/2 tbsp butter or margarine
30 ml/2 tbsp curry powder
675 g/1½ lb/6 cups plain
  (all-purpose) flour
10 ml/2 tsp salt
450 ml/¾ pt/2 cups buttermilk
1 egg
10 ml/2 tsp water
45 ml/3 tbsp flaked (slivered)
  almonds

Mix the water with the yeast and 5 ml/1 tsp of the honey and leave to stand for 20 minutes until frothy. Melt the butter or margarine, then stir in the curry powder and cook over a low heat for 1 minute. Stir in the remaining honey and remove from the heat. Place half the flour and the salt in a bowl and make a well in the centre. Add the yeast mixture, the honey mixture and the buttermilk and gradually add the remaining flour as you mix to a soft dough. Knead until smooth and elastic. Place in an oiled bowl, cover with oiled clingfilm and leave in a warm place for about 1 hour until doubled in size.

Knead again and divide the dough in half. Cut each piece into three and roll into 20 cm/8 in sausage shapes. Moisten one end of each strip and press together in two lots of three to seal. Plait the two sets of strips and seal the ends. Place on a greased baking (cookie) sheet, cover with oiled clingfilm (plastic wrap) and leave to rise for about 40 minutes until doubled in size.

Beat the egg with the water and brush over the loaves, then sprinkle with almonds. Bake in a preheated oven at 190°C/375°F/gas mark 5 for 40 minutes until golden brown and hollow-sounding when tapped on the base.

Devon Splits

Makes 12

25 g/1 oz fresh yeast or 40 ml/
2½ tbsp dried yeast
5 ml/1 tsp caster (superfine) sugar
150 ml/¼ pt/⅔ cup warm milk
50 g/2 oz/¼ cup butter or margarine
450 g/1 lb/4 cups strong plain (bread)
flour
150 ml/¼ pt/⅔ cup warm water

Blend the yeast with the sugar and a little warm milk and leave in a warm place for 20 minutes until frothy. Rub the butter or margarine into the flour and make a well in the centre. Add the yeast mixture, the remaining milk and the water and mix to a soft dough. Knead until elastic and no longer sticky. Place in an oiled bowl and cover with oiled clingfilm (plastic wrap). Leave in a warm place for about 1 hour until doubled in size.

Shape the dough into 12 flat rolls and arrange on a greased baking (cookie) sheet. Leave to rise for 15 minutes.

Bake in a preheated oven at 230°C/450°F/gas mark 8 for 15–20 minutes until well risen and golden brown.

Fruited Wheatgerm Bread

Makes one 900 g/2 lb loaf

225 g/8 oz/2 cups plain
(all-purpose) flour
5 ml/1 tsp salt
5 ml/1 tsp bicarbonate of soda
(baking soda)
5 ml/1 tsp baking powder
175 g/6 oz/1½ cups wheatgerm
100 g/4 oz/1 cup cornmeal
100 g/4 oz/1 cup rolled oats
350 g/12 oz/2 cups sultanas
(golden raisins)
1 egg, lightly beaten
250 ml/8 fl oz/1 cup plain yoghurt
150 ml/¼ pt/⅔ cup black treacle
(molasses)
60 ml/4 tbsp golden (light corn) syrup
30 ml/2 tbsp oil

Mix together the dry ingredients and the sultanas and make a well in the centre. Blend together the egg, yoghurt, treacle, syrup and oil, then stir into the dry ingredients and mix to a softish dough. Shape into a greased 900 g/2 lb loaf tin (pan) and bake in a preheated oven at 180°C/350°F/gas mark 4 for 1 hour until firm to the touch. Leave to cool in the tin for 10 minutes before turning out on to a wire rack to finish cooling.

Fruity Milk Plaits

Makes two 450 g/1 lb loaves

15 g/½ oz fresh yeast or 20 ml/
    4 tsp dried yeast
5 ml/1 tsp caster (superfine) sugar
450 ml/¾ pt/2 cups warm milk
50 g/2 oz/¼ cup butter or margarine
675 g/1½ lb/6 cups plain
    (all-purpose) flour
A pinch of salt
100 g/4 oz/⅔ cup raisins
25 g/1 oz/3 tbsp currants
25 g/1 oz/3 tbsp chopped mixed
    (candied) peel
Milk for glazing

Blend together the yeast with the sugar and a little of the warm milk. Leave to stand in a warm place for about 20 minutes until frothy. Rub the butter or margarine into the flour and salt, stir in the raisins, currants and mixed peel and make a well in the centre. Mix in the remaining warm milk and the yeast mixture and knead to a soft but not sticky dough. Place in an oiled bowl and cover with oiled clingfilm (plastic wrap). Leave in a warm place for about 1 hour until doubled in size.

Knead again lightly, then divide in half. Divide each half into three and roll into sausage shapes. Moisten one end of each roll and press three gently together, then plait the dough, moisten and seal the ends. Repeat with the other dough plait. Place on a greased baking (cookie) sheet, cover with oiled clingfilm (plastic wrap) and leave to rise for about 15 minutes.

Brush with a little milk, then bake in a preheated oven at 200°C/400°F/gas mark 6 for 30 minutes until golden brown and hollow-sounding when tapped on the base.

Granary Bread

Makes two 900 g/2 lb loaves

25 g/1 oz fresh yeast or 40 ml/
    2½ tbsp dried yeast
5 ml/1 tsp honey
450 ml/¾ pt/2 cups warm water
350 g/12 oz/3 cups granary flour
350 g/12 oz/3 cups wholemeal
    (wholewheat) flour
15 ml/1 tbsp salt
15 g/½ oz/1 tbsp butter or margarine

Blend the yeast with the honey and a little of the warm water and leave in a warm place for about 20 minutes until frothy. Mix the flours and salt and rub in the butter or margarine. Blend in the yeast mixture and enough of the warm water to make a smooth dough. Knead on a lightly floured surface until smooth and no longer sticky. Place in an oiled bowl, cover with oiled clingfilm (plastic wrap) and leave in a warm place for about 1 hour until doubled in size.

Knead again and shape into two greased 900 g/2 lb loaf tins (pans). Cover with oiled clingfilm and leave to rise until the dough reaches to the top of the tins.

Bake in a preheated oven at 220°C/425°F/gas mark 7 for 25 minutes until golden brown and hollow-sounding when tapped on the base.

Granary Rolls

Makes 12

15 g/½ oz fresh yeast or 20 ml/
2½ tbsp dried yeast
5 ml/1 tsp caster (superfine) sugar
300 ml/½ pt/1¼ cups warm water
450 g/1 lb/4 cups granary flour
5 ml/1 tsp salt
5 ml/1 tbsp malt extract
30 ml/2 tbsp cracked wheat

Blend the yeast with the sugar and a little of the warm water and leave in a warm place until frothy. Mix together the flour and salt, then blend in the yeast mixture, the remaining warm water and the malt extract. Knead on a lightly floured surface until smooth and elastic. Place in an oiled bowl, cover with oiled clingfilm (plastic wrap) and leave in a warm place for about 1 hour until doubled in size.

Knead lightly, then shape into rolls and place on a greased baking (cookie) sheet. Brush with water and sprinkle with cracked wheat. Cover with oiled clingfilm and leave in a warm place for about 40 minutes until doubled in size.

Bake in a preheated oven at 220°C/425°F/gas mark 7 for 10–15 minutes until hollow-sounding when tapped on the base.

Granary Bread with Hazelnuts

Makes one 900 g/2 lb loaf

15 g/½ oz fresh yeast or 20 ml/
4 tsp dried yeast
5 ml/1 tsp soft brown sugar
450 ml/¾ pt/2 cups warm water
450 g/1 lb/4 cups granary flour
175 g/6 oz/1½ cups strong plain
(bread) flour
5 ml/1 tsp salt
15 ml/1 tbsp olive oil
100 g/4 oz/1 cup hazelnuts, coarsely
chopped

Blend the yeast with the sugar and a little of the warm water and leave in a warm place for 20 minutes until frothy. Mix together the flours and salt in a bowl, add the yeast mixture, the oil and the remaining warm water and mix to a firm dough. Knead until smooth and no longer sticky. Place in an oiled bowl, cover with oiled clingfilm (plastic wrap) and leave in a warm place for about 1 hour until doubled in size.

Knead again lightly and work in the nuts, then shape into a greased 900 g/2 lb loaf tin (pan), cover with oiled clingfilm and leave in a warm place for 30 minutes until the dough has risen above the top of the tin.

Bake in a preheated oven at 220°C/425°F/gas mark 7 for 30 minutes until golden brown and hollow-sounding when tapped on the base.

333

Grissini

Makes 12

25 g/1 oz fresh yeast or 40 ml/
2½ tbsp dried yeast
15 ml/1 tbsp caster (superfine) sugar
120 ml/4 fl oz/½ cup warm milk
25 g/1 oz/2 tbsp butter or margarine
450 g/1 lb/4 cups strong plain (bread)
    flour
10 ml/2 tsp salt

Blend the yeast with 5 ml/1 tsp of the sugar and a little of the warm milk and leave in a warm place for 20 minutes until frothy. Melt the butter and remaining sugar in the remaining warm milk. Place the flour and salt in a bowl and make a well in the centre. Pour in the yeast and milk mixture and combine to make a moist dough. Knead until smooth. Place in an oiled bowl, cover with oiled clingfilm (plastic wrap) and leave in a warm place for about 1 hour until doubled in size.

Knead lightly, then divide into 12 and roll out into long, thin sticks and place, well apart, on a greased baking (cookie) sheet. Cover with oiled clingfilm and leave to rise in a warm place for 20 minutes.

Brush the bread sticks with water, then bake in a preheated oven at 220°C/425°F/ gas mark 7 for 10 minutes, then reduce the oven temperature to 180°C/350°F/ gas mark 4 and bake for a further 20 minutes until crisp.

Harvest Plait

Makes one 550 g/1¼ lb loaf

25 g/1 oz fresh yeast or 40 ml/
2½ tbsp dried yeast
25 g/1 oz/2 tbsp caster (superfine)
    sugar
150 ml/¼ pt/⅔ cup warm milk
50 g/2 oz/¼ cup butter or margarine,
    melted
1 egg, beaten
450 g/1 lb/4 cups plain (all-purpose)
    flour
A pinch of salt
30 ml/2 tbsp currants
2.5 ml/½ tsp of ground cinnamon
5 ml/1 tsp grated lemon rind
Milk for glazing

Blend the yeast with 2.5 ml/½ tsp of the sugar and a little of the warm milk and leave in a warm place for about 20 minutes until frothy. Mix the remaining milk with the butter or margarine and leave to cool slightly. Mix in the egg. Place the remaining ingredients in a bowl and make a well in the centre. Stir in the milk and yeast mixtures and mix to a soft dough. Knead until elastic and no longer sticky. Place in an oiled bowl and cover with oiled clingfilm (plastic wrap). Leave in a warm place for about 1 hour until doubled in size.

Divide the dough into three and roll into strips. Moisten one end of each strip and seal the ends together, then plait them together and moisten and secure the other ends. Place on a greased baking (cookie) sheet, cover with oiled clingfilm and leave in a warm place for 15 minutes.

Brush with a little milk and bake in a preheated oven at 220°C/425°F/gas mark 7 for 15–20 minutes until golden brown and hollow-sounding when tapped on the base.

Milk Bread

Makes two 450 g/1 lb loaves

15 g/½ oz fresh yeast or 20 ml/
4 tsp dried yeast
5 ml/1 tsp caster (superfine) sugar
450 ml/¾ pt/2 cups warm milk
50 g/2 oz/¼ cup butter or margarine
675 g/1½ lb/6 cups plain
(all-purpose) flour
A pinch of salt
Milk for glazing

Blend the yeast with the sugar and a little of the warm milk. Leave to stand in a warm place for about 20 minutes until frothy. Rub the butter or margarine into the flour and salt and make a well in the centre. Mix in the remaining warm milk and the yeast mixture and knead to a soft but not sticky dough. Place in an oiled bowl and cover with oiled clingfilm (plastic wrap). Leave in a warm place for about 1 hour until doubled in size.

Knead again lightly, then divide the mixture between two greased 450 g/1 lb loaf tins (pans), cover with oiled clingfilm and leave to rise for about 15 minutes until the dough is just above the tops of the tins.

Brush with a little milk, then bake in a preheated oven at 200°C/400°F/gas mark 6 for 30 minutes until golden brown and hollow-sounding when tapped on the base.

Milk Fruit Loaf

Makes two 450 g/1 lb loaves

15 g/½ oz fresh yeast or 20 ml/
4 tsp dried yeast
5 ml/1 tsp caster (superfine) sugar
450 ml/¾ pt/2 cups warm milk
50 g/2 oz/¼ cup butter or margarine
675 g/1½ lb/6 cups plain
(all-purpose) flour
A pinch of salt
100 g/4 oz/⅔ cup raisins
Milk for glazing

Blend the yeast with the sugar and a little of the warm milk. Leave to stand in a warm place for about 20 minutes until frothy. Rub the butter or margarine into the flour and salt, stir in the raisins and make a well in the centre. Mix in the remaining warm milk and the yeast mixture and knead to a soft but not sticky dough. Place in an oiled bowl and cover with oiled clingfilm (plastic wrap). Leave in a warm place for about 1 hour until doubled in size.

Knead again lightly, then divide the mixture between two greased 450 g/1 lb loaf tins (pans), cover with oiled clingfilm and leave to rise for about 15 minutes until the dough is just above the tops of the tins.

Brush with a little milk, then bake in a preheated oven at 200°C/400°F/gas mark 6 for 30 minutes until golden brown and hollow-sounding when tapped on the base.

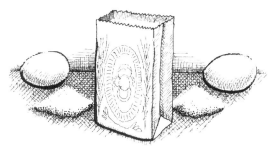

Morning Glory Bread

Makes two 450 g/1 lb loaves

100 g/4 oz/1 cup whole wheat grains
15 ml/1 tbsp malt extract
450 ml/¾ pt/2 cups warm water
25 g/1 oz fresh yeast or 40 ml/
2½ tbsp dried yeast
30 ml/2 tbsp clear honey
25 g/1 oz/2 tbsp vegetable fat
(shortening)
675 g/1½ lb/6 cups wholemeal
(wholewheat) flour
25 g/1 oz/¼ cup milk powder
(non-fat dry milk)
5 ml/1 tsp salt

Soak the whole wheat grains and malt extract in the warm water overnight.

Blend the yeast with a little more warm water and 5 ml/1 tsp of the honey. Leave in a warm place for about 20 minutes until frothy. Rub the fat into the flour, milk powder and salt and make a well in the centre. Stir in the yeast mixture, the remaining honey and the wheat mixture and mix to a dough. Knead well until smooth and no longer sticky. Place in an oiled bowl, cover with oiled clingfilm (plastic wrap) and leave in a warm place for about 1 hour until doubled in size.

Knead the dough again, then shape into two greased 450 g/1 lb loaf tins (pans). Cover with oiled clingfilm and leave in a warm place for 40 minutes until the dough reaches just above the tops of the tins.

Bake in a preheated oven at 200°C/ 425°F/gas mark 7 for about 25 minutes until well risen and hollow-sounding when tapped on the base.

Muffin Bread

Makes two 900 g/2 lb loaves

300 g/10 oz/2½ cups wholemeal
(wholewheat) flour
300 g/10 oz/2½ cups plain
(all-purpose) flour
40 ml/2½ tbsp dried yeast
15 ml/1 tbsp caster (superfine) sugar
10 ml/2 tsp salt
500 ml/17 fl oz/2¼ cups lukewarm
milk
2.5 ml/½ tsp bicarbonate of soda
(baking soda)
15 ml/1 tbsp warm water

Mix the flours together. Measure 350 g/12 oz/3 cups of the mixed flours into a bowl and mix in the yeast, sugar and salt. Stir in the milk and beat to a stiff mixture. Mix together the bicarbonate of soda and water and stir into the dough with the remaining flour. Divide the mixture between two greased 900 g/2 lb loaf tins (pans), cover and leave to rise for about 1 hour until doubled in size.

Bake in a preheated oven at 190°C/ 375°F/gas mark 5 for 1¼ hours until well risen and golden brown.

No-rise Bread

Makes one 900 g/2 lb loaf

450 g/1 lb/4 cups wholemeal
(wholewheat) flour
175 g/6 oz/1½ cups self-raising
(self-rising) flour
5 ml/1 tsp salt
30 ml/2 tbsp caster (superfine) sugar
450 ml/¾ pt/2 cups milk
20 ml/4 tsp vinegar
30 ml/2 tbsp oil
5 ml/1 tsp bicarbonate of soda
(baking soda)

Mix together the flours, salt and sugar and make a well in the centre. Beat together the milk, vinegar, oil and bicarbonate of soda, pour into the dry ingredients and blend to a smooth dough. Shape into a greased 900 g/2 lb loaf tin (pan) and bake in a preheated oven at 180°C/350°F/gas mark 4 for 1 hour until golden brown and hollow-sounding when tapped on the base.

Pizza Dough

Makes enough for two
23 cm/9 in pizzas

15 g/½ oz fresh yeast or 20 ml/
4 tsp dried yeast
A pinch of sugar
250 ml/8 fl oz/1 cup warm water
350 g/12 oz/3 cups plain
(all-purpose) flour
A pinch of salt
30 ml/2 tbsp olive oil

Blend the yeast with the sugar and a little of the warm water and leave in a warm place for 20 minutes until frothy. Blend into the flour with the salt and olive oil and knead until smooth and no longer sticky. Place in an oiled bowl, cover with oiled clingfilm (plastic wrap) and leave in a warm place for 1 hour until doubled in size. Knead again and shape as required.

Oatmeal Cob

Makes one 450 g/1 lb loaf

25 g/1 oz fresh yeast or 40 ml/
2½ tbsp dried yeast
5 ml/1 tsp caster (superfine) sugar
150 ml/¼ pt/⅔ cup lukewarm milk
150 ml/¼ pt/⅔ cup lukewarm water
400 g/14 oz/3½ cups strong plain
(bread) flour
5 ml/1 tsp salt
25 g/1 oz/2 tbsp butter or margarine
100 g/4 oz/1 cup medium oatmeal

Blend the yeast and sugar with the milk and water and leave in a warm place until frothy. Mix together the flour and salt, then rub in the butter or margarine and stir in the oatmeal. Make a well in the centre, pour in the yeast mixture and mix to a soft dough. Turn out on a floured surface and knead for 10 minutes until smooth and elastic. Place in an oiled bowl, cover with oiled clingfilm (plastic wrap) and leave in a warm place to rise for about 1 hour until doubled in size.

Knead the dough again, then shape into a loaf shape of your choice. Place on a greased baking (cookie) sheet, brush with a little water, cover with oiled clingfilm and leave in a warm place for about 40 minutes until doubled in size.

Bake in a preheated oven at 230°C/450°F/gas mark 8 for 25 minutes until well risen and golden brown and hollow-sounding when tapped on the base.

Oatmeal Jarl

Makes 4

25 g/1 oz fresh yeast or 40 ml/
2½ tbsp dried yeast
5 ml/1 tsp honey
300 ml/½ pt/1¼ cups warm water
450 g/1 lb/4 cups strong plain (bread)
flour
50 g/2 oz/½ cup medium oatmeal
2.5 ml/½ tsp baking powder
A pinch of salt
25 g/1 oz/2 tbsp butter or margarine

Blend the yeast with the honey and a little of the warm water and leave in a warm place for 20 minutes until frothy.

Mix together the flour, oatmeal, baking powder and salt and rub in the butter or margarine. Stir in the yeast mixture and the remaining warm water and mix to a medium-soft dough. Knead until elastic and no longer sticky. Place in an oiled bowl, cover with oiled clingfilm (plastic wrap) and leave in a warm place for about 1 hour until doubled in size.

Knead again lightly and shape into a round about 3 cm/1¼ in thick. Cut across into quarters and place, slightly apart but still in the original round shape, on a greased baking (cookie) sheet. Cover with oiled clingfilm and leave to rise for about 30 minutes until doubled in size.

Bake in a preheated oven at 200°C/400°F/gas mark 6 for 30 minutes until golden brown and hollow-sounding when tapped on the base.

Pitta Bread

Makes 6

15 g/½ oz fresh yeast or 20 ml/
4 tsp dried yeast
5 ml/1 tsp caster (superfine) sugar
300 ml/½ pt/1¼ cups warm water
450 g/1 lb/4 cups strong plain (bread)
flour
5 ml/1 tsp salt

Blend together the yeast, sugar and a little of the warm water and leave in a warm place for 20 minutes until frothy. Blend the yeast mixture and remaining warm water into the flour and salt and mix to a firm dough. Knead until smooth and elastic. Place in an oiled bowl, cover with oiled clingfilm (plastic wrap) and leave in a warm place for about 1 hour until doubled in size.

Knead again and divide into six pieces. Roll into ovals about 5 mm/¼ in thick and place on a greased baking (cookie) sheet. Cover with oiled clingfilm and leave to rise for 40 minutes until doubled in size.

Bake in a preheated oven at 230°C/450°F/gas mark 8 for 10 minutes until lightly golden.

Quick Brown Bread

Makes two 450 g/1 lb loaves

15 g/½ oz fresh yeast or 20 ml/
4 tsp dried yeast
300 ml/½ pt/1¼ cups warm milk and
water mixed
15 ml/1 tbsp black treacle (molasses)
225 g/8 oz/2 cups wholemeal
(wholewheat) flour
225 g/8 oz/2 cups plain
(all-purpose) flour
10 ml/2 tsp salt
25 g/1 oz/2 tbsp butter or margarine
15 ml/1 tbsp cracked wheat

Blend the yeast with a little warm milk and water and the treacle and leave in a warm place until frothy. Mix the flours and salt and rub in the butter or margarine. Make a well in the centre and pour in the yeast mixture, blending to a firm dough. Turn out on to a floured surface and knead for 10 minutes until smooth and elastic, or process in a food processor. Shape into two loaves and place in greased and lined 450 g/1 lb loaf tins (pans). Brush the tops with water and sprinkle with the cracked wheat. Cover with oiled clingfilm (plastic wrap) and leave in a warm place for about 1 hour until doubled in size.

Bake in a preheated oven at 240°C/475°F/gas mark 8 for 40 minutes until the loaves sound hollow when tapped on the base.

Moist Rice Bread

Makes one 900 g/2 lb loaf

75 g/3 oz/⅓ cup long-grain rice
15 g/½ oz fresh yeast or 20 ml/
*   4 tsp dried yeast*
A pinch of sugar
250 ml/8 fl oz/1 cup warm water
550 g/1¼ lb/5 cups strong plain
*   (bread) flour*
2.5 ml/½ tsp salt

Measure the rice into a cup, then pour into a pan. Add three times the volume of cold water, bring to the boil, cover and simmer for about 20 minutes until the water has been absorbed. Meanwhile blend the yeast with the sugar and a little of the warm water and leave in a warm place for 20 minutes until frothy.

Place the flour and salt in a bowl and make a well in the centre. Blend in the yeast mixture and the warm rice and mix to a soft dough. Place in an oiled bowl, cover with oiled clingfilm (plastic wrap) and leave in a warm place for about 1 hour until doubled in size.

Knead lightly, adding a little more flour if the dough is too soft to work, and shape into a greased 900 g/2 lb loaf tin (pan). Cover with oiled clingfilm and leave in a warm place for 30 minutes until the dough has risen above the top of the tin.

Bake in a preheated oven at 230°C/450°F/gas mark 8 for 10 minutes, then reduce the oven temperature to 200°C/400°F/gas mark 6 and bake for a further 25 minutes until golden brown and hollow-sounding when tapped on the base.

Rice and Almond Loaf

Makes one 900 g/2 lb loaf

175 g/6 oz/¾ cup butter or margarine,
*   softened*
175 g/6 oz/¾ cup caster (superfine)
*   sugar*
3 eggs, lightly beaten
100 g/4 oz/1 cup strong plain (bread)
*   flour*
5 ml/1 tsp baking powder
A pinch of salt
100 g/4 oz/1 cup ground rice
50 g/2 oz/½ cup ground almonds
15 ml/1 tbsp warm water

Cream together the butter or margarine and sugar until light and fluffy. Gradually beat in the eggs, then fold in the dry ingredients and the water to make a smooth dough. Shape into a greased 900 g/2 lb loaf tin (pan) and bake in a preheated oven at 180°C/350°F/gas mark 4 for 1 hour until golden brown and hollow-sounding when tapped on the base.

Crunchy Rusks

Makes 24

675 g/1½ lb/6 cups plain
(all-purpose) flour
15 ml/1 tbsp cream of tartar
10 ml/2 tsp salt
400 g/14 oz/1¾ cups caster (superfine)
sugar
250 g/9 oz/generous 1 cup butter or
margarine
10 ml/2 tsp bicarbonate of soda
(baking soda)
250 ml/8 fl oz/1 cup buttermilk
1 egg

Mix together the flour, cream of tartar and salt. Stir in the sugar. Rub in the butter or margarine until the mixture resembles breadcrumbs and make a well in the centre. Mix the bicarbonate of soda with a little of the buttermilk, and mix the egg into the remaining buttermilk. Reserve 30 ml/2 tbsp of the egg mixture to glaze the rusks. Mix the remainder into the dry ingredients with the bicarbonate of soda mixture and blend to a stiff dough. Divide the dough into six equal portions and shape into sausages. Flatten slightly and cut each one into six pieces. Arrange on a greased baking (cookie) sheet and brush with the reserved egg mixture. Bake in a preheated oven at 200°C/400°F/gas mark 6 for 30 minute until golden brown.

Rye Bread

Makes two 450 g/1 lb loaves

25 g/1 oz fresh yeast or 40 ml/
2½ tbsp dried yeast
15 ml/1 tbsp soft brown sugar
300 ml/½ pt/1¼ cups warm water
450 g/1 lb/4 cups rye flour
225 g/8 oz/2 cups strong (bread) flour
5 ml/1 tsp salt
5 ml/1 tsp caraway seeds
150 ml/¼ pt/⅔ cup warm milk

Blend the yeast with the sugar and a little of the warm water and leave in a warm place until frothy. Mix together the flours, salt and caraway seeds and make a well in the centre. Mix in the yeast mixture, the milk and remaining water and mix to a firm dough. Turn out on a floured surface and knead for 8 minutes until smooth and elastic, or process in a food processor. Place in an oiled bowl, cover with oiled clingfilm (plastic wrap) and leave in a warm place for about 1 hour until doubled in size. Knead again, then shape into two loaves and place on a greased baking (cookie) sheet. Cover with oiled clingfilm and leave to rise for 30 minutes.

Bake in a preheated oven at 220°C/425°F/gas mark 7 for 15 minutes, then reduce the oven temperature to 190°C/375°F/gas mark 5 for a further 25 minutes until the loaves sound hollow when tapped on the base.

Bavarian Rye Bread

Makes two 450 g/1 lb loaves

For the sourdough:
150 g/5 oz/1¼ cups rye flour
5 ml/1 tsp dried yeast
150 ml/¼ pt/⅔ cup warm water
For the loaf:
550 g/1¼ lb/5 cups wholemeal
(wholewheat) flour
50 g/2 oz/½ cup rye flour
5 ml/1 tsp salt
25 g/1 oz fresh yeast or 40 ml/
2½ tbsp dried yeast
350 ml/12 fl oz/1½ cups warm water
30 ml/2 tbsp caraway seeds
A little flour mixed to a paste with
water

To make the sourdough, mix the rye flour, yeast and water until clear. Cover and leave overnight.

To make the loaf, mix together the flours and salt. Mix the yeast with the warm water and add to the flours with the sourdough. Stir in half the caraway seeds and mix to a dough. Knead well until elastic and no longer sticky. Place in an oiled bowl, cover with oiled clingfilm (plastic wrap) and leave in a warm place for about 30 minutes until doubled in size.

Knead again, shape into two 450 g/ 1 lb loaves and place on a greased baking (cookie) sheet. Brush with the flour and water paste and sprinkle with the remaining caraway seeds. Cover with oiled clingfilm and leave to rise for 30 minutes.

Bake in a preheated oven at 230°C/ 450°F/gas mark 8 for 30 minutes until dark golden and hollow-sounding when tapped on the base.

Light Rye Bread

Makes one 675 g/1½ lb loaf

15 g/½ oz fresh yeast or 20 ml/
 4 tsp dried yeast
5 ml/1 tsp caster (superfine) sugar
150 ml/¼ pt/⅔ cup warm water
225 g/8 oz/2 cups rye flour
400 g/14 oz/3½ cups strong plain
 (bread) flour
10 ml/2 tsp salt
300 ml/½ pt/1¼ cups warm milk
1 egg yolk, beaten
5 ml/1 tsp poppy seeds

Blend the yeast with the sugar and water and leave in a warm place until frothy. Mix together the flours and salt and make a well in the centre. Stir in the milk and yeast mixture and mix to a firm dough. Knead on a lightly floured surface until smooth and elastic. Place in an oiled bowl, cover with oiled clingfilm (plastic wrap) and leave in a warm place for about 1 hour until doubled in size.

Knead again lightly, then shape into a long loaf and place on a greased baking (cookie) sheet. Cover with oiled clingfilm and leave to rise for 30 minutes.

Brush with egg yolk and sprinkle with poppy seeds. Bake in a preheated oven at 200°C/400°F/gas mark 6 for 20 minutes. Reduce the oven temperature to 190°C/ 375°F/gas mark 5 and bake for a further 15 minutes until the bread is hollow-sounding when tapped on the base.

Rye Bread with Wheatgerm

Makes one 450 g/1 lb loaf

15 g/½ oz fresh yeast or 20 ml/
 4 tsp dried yeast
5 ml/1 tsp sugar
450 ml/¾ pt/2 cups warm water
350 g/12 oz/3 cups rye flour
225 g/8 oz/2 cups plain
 (all-purpose) flour
50 g/2 oz/½ cup wheatgerm
10 ml/2 tsp salt
45 ml/3 tbsp black treacle (molasses)
15 ml/1 tbsp oil

Blend the yeast with the sugar and a little of the warm water, then leave in a warm place until frothy. Mix together the flours, wheatgerm and salt and make a well in the centre. Blend in the yeast mixture with the treacle and oil and mix to a soft dough. Turn out on to a floured surface and knead for 10 minutes until smooth and elastic, or process in a food processor. Place in a oiled bowl, cover with oiled clingfilm (plastic wrap) and leave in a warm place for about 1 hour until doubled in size.

Knead again, then shape into a loaf and place on a greased baking (cookie) sheet. Cover with oiled clingfilm and leave to rise until doubled in size.

Bake in a preheated oven at 220°C/ 425°F/gas mark 7 for 15 minutes. Reduce the oven temperature to 190°C/375°F/gas mark 5 and bake for a further 40 minutes until the loaf sounds hollow when tapped on the base.

Sally Lunn

Makes two 450 g/1 lb loaves

500 ml/16 fl oz/2 cups milk
25 g/1 oz/2 tbsp butter or margarine
30 ml/2 tbsp caster (superfine) sugar
10 ml/2 tsp salt
20 ml/4 tsp dried yeast
60 ml/4 tbsp warm water
900 g/2 lb/8 cups strong plain (bread)
flour
3 eggs, beaten

Bring the milk almost to a simmer, then add the butter or margarine, sugar and salt and stir well. Leave to cool until lukewarm. Dissolve the yeast in the warm water. Place the flour in a large bowl and mix in the milk, yeast and eggs. Mix to a soft dough and knead until elastic and no longer sticky. Cover with oiled clingfilm (plastic wrap) and leave to rise for 30 minutes.

Knead the dough again, then cover and leave to rise. Knead it a third time, then cover and leave to rise.

Shape the dough and place in two greased 450 g/1 lb loaf tins (pans). Cover and leave to rise until doubled in bulk. Bake in a preheated oven at 190°C/ 375°F/gas mark 5 for 45 minutes until golden on top and the loaves sound hollow when tapped on the base.

Samos Bread

Makes three 450 g/1 lb loaves

15 g/½ oz fresh yeast or 20 ml/
4 tsp dried yeast
15 ml/1 tbsp malt extract
600 ml/1 pt/2½ cups warm water
25 g/1 oz/2 tbsp vegetable fat
(shortening)
900 g/2 lb/8 cups wholemeal
(wholewheat) flour
30 ml/2 tbsp milk powder
(non-fat dry milk)
10 ml/2 tsp salt
15 ml/1 tbsp clear honey
50 g/2 oz/½ cup sesame seeds, roasted
25 g/1 oz/¼ cup sunflower seeds,
roasted

Blend the yeast with the malt extract and a little of the warm water and leave in a warm place for 10 minutes until frothy. Rub the fat into the flour and milk powder, then stir in the salt and make a well in the centre. Pour in the yeast mixture, the remaining warm water and the honey and mix to a dough. Knead well until smooth and elastic. Add the seeds and knead for a further 5 minutes until well blended. Shape into three 450 g/1 lb loaves and place on a greased baking (cookie) sheet. Cover with oiled clingfilm (plastic wrap) and leave in a warm place for 40 minutes until doubled in size.

Bake in a preheated oven at 230°F/ 450°F/gas mark 8 for 30 minutes until golden brown and hollow-sounding when tapped on the base.

Sesame Baps

Makes 12

25 g/1 oz fresh yeast or 40 ml/
2½ tbsp dried yeast
5 ml/1 tsp caster (superfine) sugar
150 ml/¼ pt/⅔ cup warm milk
450 g/1 lb/4 cups strong plain (bread)
flour
5 ml/1 tsp salt
25 g/1 oz/2 tbsp lard (shortening)
150 ml/¼ pt/⅔ cup warm water
30 ml/2 tbsp sesame seeds

Blend the yeast with the sugar and a little of the warm milk and leave in a warm place until frothy. Mix the flour and salt in a bowl, rub in the lard and make a well in the centre. Pour in the yeast mixture, the remaining milk and the water and mix to a soft dough. Turn out on to a floured surface and knead for 10 minutes until smooth and elastic, or process in a food processor. Place in an oiled bowl, cover with oiled clingfilm (plastic wrap) and leave in a warm place for about 1 hour until doubled in size.

Knead again and shape into 12 rolls, flatten them slightly and arrange on a greased baking (cookie) sheet. Cover with oiled clingfilm (plastic wrap) and leave to rise in a warm place for 20 minutes.

Brush with water, sprinkle with seeds and bake in a preheated oven at 220°C/425°F/gas mark 7 for 15 minutes until golden.

Sourdough Starter

Makes about 450 g/1 lb

450 ml/¾ pt/2 cups lukewarm water
25 g/1 oz fresh yeast or 40 ml/
2½ tbsp dried yeast
225 g/8 oz/2 cups plain
(all-purpose) flour
2.5 ml/½ tsp salt

To feed:
225 g/8 oz/2 cups plain (all-purpose)
flour
450 ml/¾ pt/2 cups lukewarm water

Mix together the main ingredients in a bowl, cover with muslin (cheesecloth) and leave in a warm place for 24 hours. Add 50 g/2 oz/½ cup plain flour and 120 ml/4 fl oz/½ cup lukewarm water, cover and leave for a further 24 hours. Repeat three times, by which time the mixture should smell sour, then transfer to the fridge. Replace any starter you use with an equal mixture of lukewarm water and flour.

Soda Bread

Makes one 20 cm/8 in loaf

450 g/1 lb/4 cups plain (all-purpose)
flour
10 ml/2 tsp bicarbonate of soda
(baking soda)
10 ml/2 tsp cream of tartar
5 ml/1 tsp salt
25 g/1 oz/2 tbsp lard (shortening)
5 ml/1 tsp caster (superfine) sugar
15 ml/1 tbsp lemon juice
300 ml/½ pt/1¼ cups milk

Mix together the flour, bicarbonate of soda, cream of tartar and salt. Rub in the lard until the mixture resembles breadcrumbs. Stir in the sugar. Mix the lemon juice into the milk, then stir it into the dry ingredients until you have a soft dough. Knead lightly, then shape the dough into a 20 cm/8 in round and flatten it slightly. Place it on a floured baking tray and mark into quarters with the blade of a knife. Bake in a preheated oven at 200°C/400°F/gas mark 6 for about 30 minutes until crusty on top. Leave to cool before serving.

Sourdough Bread

Makes two 350 g/12 oz loaves

250 ml/8 fl oz/1 cup lukewarm water
15 ml/1 tbsp caster (superfine) sugar
30 ml/2 tbsp melted butter or
margarine
15 ml/1 tbsp salt
250 ml/8 fl oz/1 cup Sourdough
Starter (page 343)
2.5 ml/½ tsp bicarbonate of soda
(baking soda)
450 g/1 lb/4 cups plain (all-purpose)
flour

Mix together the water, sugar, butter or margarine and salt. Mix the sourdough starter with the bicarbonate of soda and stir into the mixture, then beat in the flour to make a stiff dough. Knead the dough until smooth and satiny, adding a little more flour if necessary. Place in an oiled bowl, cover with oiled clingfilm (plastic wrap) and leave in a warm place for about 1 hour until doubled in size.

Knead again lightly and shape into two loaves. Place on a greased baking (cookie) sheet, cover with oiled clingfilm and leave to rise for about 40 minutes until doubled in size.

Bake in a preheated oven at 190°C/375°F/gas mark 5 for about 40 minutes until golden brown and hollow-sounding when tapped on the base.

Sourdough Buns

Makes 12

50 g/2 oz/¼ cup butter or margarine
175 g/6 oz/1½ cups plain
(all-purpose) flour
5 ml/1 tsp salt
2.5 ml/½ tsp bicarbonate of soda
(baking soda)
250 ml/8 fl oz/1 cup Sourdough
Starter (page 343)
A little melted butter or margarine
for glazing

Rub the butter or margarine into the flour and salt until the mixture resembles breadcrumbs. Mix the bicarbonate of soda into the starter, then stir it into the flour to make a stiff dough. Knead until smooth and no longer sticky. Shape into small rolls and arrange well apart on a greased baking (cookie) sheet. Brush the tops with butter or margarine, cover with oiled clingfilm (plastic wrap) and leave to rise for about 1 hour until doubled in size. Bake in a preheated oven at 220°C/425°F/gas mark 8 for 15 minutes until golden brown.

Vienna Loaf

Makes one 675 g/1½ lb loaf

15 g/½ oz fresh yeast or 20 ml/
4 tsp dried yeast
5 ml/1 tsp caster (superfine) sugar
300 ml/½ pt/1¼ cups warm milk
40 g/1½ oz/3 tbsp butter or margarine
450 g/1 lb/4 cups strong plain (bread)
flour
5 ml/1 tsp salt
1 egg, well beaten

Blend the yeast with the sugar and a little of the warm milk and leave in a warm place until frothy. Melt the butter or margarine and add the remaining milk. Blend together the yeast mixture, butter mixture, flour, salt and egg to make a soft dough. Knead until smooth and no longer sticky. Place in an oiled bowl, cover with oiled clingfilm (plastic wrap) and leave in a warm place for about 1 hour until doubled in size.

Knead the dough again, then shape into a loaf and place on a greased baking (cookie) sheet. Cover with oiled clingfilm and leave to rise in a warm place for 20 minutes.

Bake in a preheated oven at 230°C/450°F/gas mark 8 for 25 minutes until golden and hollow-sounding when tapped on the base.

Wholemeal Bread

Makes two 450 g/1 lb loaves

15 g/½ oz fresh yeast or 20 ml/
4 tsp dried yeast
5 ml/1 tsp sugar
300 ml/½ pt/1¼ cups warm water
550 g/1¼ lb/5 cups wholemeal
(wholewheat) flour
5 ml/1 tsp salt
45 ml/3 tbsp buttermilk
Sesame or caraway seeds for
sprinkling (optional)

Blend the yeast with the sugar and a little of the warm water and leave in a warm place for 20 minutes until frothy. Place the flour and salt in a bowl and make a well in the centre. Stir in the yeast, the remaining water and the buttermilk. Work to a firm dough which leaves the sides of the bowl cleanly, adding a little extra flour or water if necessary. Knead on a lightly floured surface or in a processor until elastic and no longer sticky. Shape the dough into two greased 450 g/1 lb loaf tins (pans), cover with oiled clingfilm (plastic wrap) and leave to rise for about 45 minutes until the dough has risen just above the top of the tins.

Sprinkle with sesame or caraway seeds, if using. Bake in a preheated oven at 230°C/450°F/gas mark 8 for 15 minutes, then reduce the oven temperature to 190°C/375°F/gas mark 5 and bake for a further 25 minutes until golden brown and hollow-sounding when tapped on the base.

Wholemeal Honey Bread

Makes one 900 g/2 lb loaf

15 g/½ oz fresh yeast or 20 ml/
4 tsp dried yeast
450 ml/¾ pt/2 cups warm water
45 ml/3 tbsp set honey
50 g/2 oz/¼ cup butter or margarine
750 g/1½ lb/6 cups wholemeal
(wholewheat) flour
2.5 ml/½ tsp salt
15 ml/1 tbsp sesame seeds

Blend the yeast with a little of the water and a little of the honey and leave in a warm place for 20 minutes until frothy. Rub the butter or margarine into the flour and salt, then mix in the yeast mixture and the remaining water and honey until you have a soft dough. Knead until elastic and no longer sticky. Place in an oiled bowl, cover with oiled clingfilm (plastic wrap) and leave in a warm place for about 1 hour until doubled in size.

Knead again and shape into a greased 900 g/2 lb loaf tin (pan). Cover with oiled clingfilm and leave to rise for 20 minutes until the dough comes above the top of the tin.

Bake in a preheated oven at 220°C/425°F/gas mark 7 for 15 minutes. Reduce the oven temperature to 190°C/375°F/gas mark 5 and bake for a further 20 minutes until the loaf is golden brown and hollow-sounding when tapped on the base.

Quick Wholemeal Rolls

Makes 12

20 ml/4 tsp dried yeast
375 ml/13 fl oz/1½ cups warm water
50 g/2 oz/¼ cup soft brown sugar
100 g/4 oz/1 cup wholemeal
(wholewheat) flour
100 g/4 oz/1 cup plain (all-purpose)
flour
5 ml/1 tsp salt

Blend the yeast with the water and a little sugar and leave in a warm place until frothy. Stir into the flours and salt with the remaining sugar and mix to a soft dough. Spoon the dough into muffin tins (pans) and leave to rise for 20 minutes until the dough has risen to the top of the tins.

Bake in a preheated oven at 180°C/ 350°F/gas mark 4 for 30 minutes until well risen and golden brown.

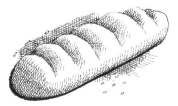

Wholemeal Bread with Walnuts

Makes one 900 g/2 lb loaf

15 g/½ oz fresh yeast or 20 ml/
4 tsp dried yeast
5 ml/1 tsp soft brown sugar
450 ml/¾ pt/2 cups warm water
450 g/1 lb/4 cups wholemeal
(wholewheat) flour
175 g/6 oz/1½ cups strong plain
(bread) flour
5 ml/1 tsp salt
15 ml/1 tbsp walnut oil
100 g/4 oz/1 cup walnuts, coarsely
chopped

Blend the yeast with the sugar and a little of the warm water and leave in a warm place for 20 minutes until frothy. Mix the flours and salt in a bowl, add the yeast mixture, the oil and the remaining warm water and mix to a firm dough. Knead until smooth and no longer sticky. Place in an oiled bowl, cover with oiled clingfilm (plastic wrap) and leave in a warm place for about 1 hour until doubled in size.

Knead again lightly and work in the nuts, then shape into a greased 900 g/2 lb loaf tin (pan), cover with oiled clingfilm and leave in a warm place for 30 minutes until the dough has risen above the top of the tin.

Bake in a preheated oven at 220°C/ 425°F/gas mark 7 for 30 minutes until golden brown and hollow-sounding when tapped on the base.

Sweet Breads and Rolls

*S*ome breads made with eggs, milk or sugar are very much on the borderline between breads and cakes! Here are some interesting ones for you to try.

Almond Plait

Makes one 450 g/1 lb loaf

15 g/½ oz fresh yeast or 20 ml/
  4 tsp dried yeast
40 g/1½ oz/3 tbsp caster (superfine)
  sugar
100 ml/3½ fl oz/6½ tbsp warm milk
350 g/12 oz/3 cups strong plain
  (bread) flour
2.5 ml/½ tsp salt
50 g/2 oz/¼ cup butter or margarine,
  melted
1 egg
  For the filling and glaze:
50 g/2 oz Almond Paste (page 228)
45 ml/3 tbsp apricot jam (conserve)
50g/2 oz/⅓ cup raisins
50 g/2 oz/½ cup chopped almonds
1 egg yolk

*B*lend the yeast with 5 ml/1 tsp of the sugar and a little of the milk and leave in a warm place for 20 minutes until frothy. Mix the flour and salt in a bowl and make a well in the centre. Mix in the yeast mixture, the remaining sugar and milk, the melted butter or margarine and the egg and mix to a smooth dough. Knead until elastic and no longer sticky. Place in an oiled bowl, cover with oiled clingfilm (plastic wrap) and leave in a warm place for about 1 hour until doubled in size.

Roll out the dough on a lightly floured surface to a 30 × 40 cm/12 × 16 in rectangle. Mix together the filling ingredients except the egg yolk and work until smooth, then spread down the centre one-third of the dough. Cut slashes in the outside two-thirds of the dough from the edges at an angle towards the filling at about 2 cm/¾ in intervals. Fold alternate left and right strips over the filling and seal the ends together firmly. Place on a greased baking (cookie) sheet, cover and leave in a warm place for 30 minutes until doubled in size. Brush with egg yolk and bake in a preheated oven at 190°C/375°F/gas mark 5 for 30 minutes until golden brown.

Brioches

Makes 12

15 g/½ oz fresh yeast or 20 ml/
  4 tsp dried yeast
30 ml/2 tbsp warm water
2 eggs, lightly beaten
225 g/8 oz/2 cups strong plain (bread)
  flour
15 ml/1 tbsp caster (superfine) sugar
2.5 ml/½ tsp salt
50 g/2 oz/¼ cup butter or margarine,
  melted

*M*ix together the yeast, water and eggs, then stir into the flour, sugar, salt and butter or margarine and mix to a soft dough. Knead until elastic and no longer sticky. Place in an oiled bowl, cover and leave in a warm place for about 1 hour until doubled in size.

Knead again, divide into 12 pieces, then break a small ball off each piece. Shape the larger pieces into balls and place in 7.5 cm/3 in fluted brioche or muffin tins (pans). Press a finger right through the dough, then press the remaining balls of dough on the top. Cover and leave in a warm place for about 30 minutes until the dough has reached just above the tops of the tins.

Bake in a preheated oven at 230°C/450°F/gas mark 8 for 10 minutes until golden.

Plaited Brioche

Makes one 675 g/1½ lb loaf

25 g/1 oz fresh yeast or 40 ml/
  2½ tbsp dried yeast
5 ml/1 tsp caster (superfine) sugar
250 ml/8 fl oz/1 cup warm milk
675 g/1½ lb/6 cups strong plain
  (bread) flour
5 ml/1 tsp salt
1 egg, beaten
150 ml/¼ pt/⅔ cup warm water
1 egg yolk

Blend the yeast with the sugar with a little of the warm milk and leave in a warm place for 20 minutes until frothy. Mix the flour and salt and make a well in the centre. Add the egg, the yeast mixture, the remaining warm milk and enough of the warm water to mix to a soft dough. Knead until soft and no longer sticky. Place in an oiled bowl, cover with oiled clingfilm (plastic wrap) and leave in a warm place for about 1 hour until doubled in size.

Knead the dough lightly, then divide into quarters. Roll three pieces into thin strips about 38 cm/15 in long. Moisten one end of each strip and press them together, then plait the strips together, moisten and fasten the ends. Place on a greased baking (cookie) sheet. Divide the remaining piece of dough into three, roll out into 38 cm/15 in strips and plait together in the same way to make a thinner plait. Beat the egg yolk with 15 ml/1 tbsp of water and brush over the large plait. Gently press the smaller plait on top and brush with the egg glaze. Cover and leave in a warm place to rise for 40 minutes.

Bake in a preheated oven at 200°C/400°F/gas mark 6 for 45 minutes until golden brown and hollow-sounding when tapped on the base.

Apple Brioches

Makes 12

For the dough:
15 g/½ oz fresh yeast or 10 ml/
  2 tsp dried yeast
75 ml/5 tbsp warm milk
100 g/4 oz/1 cup wholemeal
  (wholewheat) flour
350 g/12 oz/3 cups strong plain
  (bread) flour
30 ml/2 tbsp clear honey
4 eggs
A pinch of salt
200 g/7 oz/scant 1 cup butter or
  margarine, melted
For the filling:
75 g/3 oz apple purée (sauce)
25 g/1 oz/¼ cup wholemeal
  (wholewheat) breadcrumbs
25 g/3 oz/½ cup sultanas (golden
  raisins)
2.5 ml/½ tsp ground cinnamon
1 egg, beaten

To make the dough, blend the yeast with the warm milk and wholemeal flour and leave in a warm place for 20 minutes to ferment. Add the plain flour, honey, eggs and salt and knead well. Pour on the melted butter or margarine and continue to knead until the dough is elastic and smooth. Place in an oiled bowl, cover with oiled clingfilm (plastic wrap) and leave in a warm place for about 1 hour until doubled in size.

Mix together all the filling ingredients except the egg. Shape the dough into 12 pieces, then take one-third off each piece. Shape the larger pieces to fit greased fluted brioche or muffin tins (pans). Press a large hole almost through to the base with a finger or fork handle and fill with the filling. Shape each of the smaller dough pieces into a ball, moisten the top of the dough and press over the filling to seal it into the brioche. Cover and leave in a warm place for 40 minutes until almost doubled in size.

348

Brush with beaten egg and bake in a preheated oven at 220°C/425°F/gas mark 7 for 15 minutes until golden.

Tofu and Nut Brioches

Makes 12

For the dough:
*15 g/½ oz fresh yeast or 20 ml/
  4 tsp dried yeast*
75 ml/5 tbsp warm milk
*100 g/4 oz/1 cup wholemeal
  (wholewheat) flour*
*350 g/12 oz/3 cups strong plain
  (bread) flour*
30 ml/2 tsp clear honey
4 eggs
A pinch of salt
*200 g/7 oz/scant 1 cup butter or
  margarine, melted*
For the filling:
50 g/2 oz/¼ cup tofu, diced
*25 g/1 oz/¼ cup cashew nuts, toasted
  and chopped*
25 g/1 oz chopped mixed vegetables
½ onion, chopped
1 garlic clove, chopped
2.5 ml/½ tsp dried mixed herbs
2.5 ml/½ tsp French mustard
1 egg, beaten

To make the dough, blend the yeast with the warm milk and wholemeal flour and leave in a warm place for 20 minutes to ferment. Add the plain flour, honey, eggs and salt and knead well. Pour on the melted butter or margarine and continue to knead until the dough is elastic and smooth. Place in an oiled bowl, cover with oiled clingfilm (plastic wrap) and leave in a warm place for about 1 hour until doubled in size.

Mix together all the filling ingredients except the egg. Shape the dough into 12 pieces, then take one-third off each piece. Shape the larger pieces to fit greased fluted brioche or muffin tins (pans). Press a large hole almost through to the base with a finger or fork handle and fill with the filling. Shape each of the smaller dough pieces into a ball, moisten the top of the dough and press over the filling to seal it into the brioche. Cover and leave in a warm place for 40 minutes until almost doubled in size.

Brush with beaten egg and bake in a preheated oven at 220°C/425°F/gas mark 7 for 15 minutes until golden.

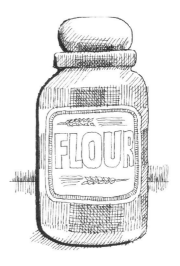

Chelsea Buns

Makes 9

225 g/8 oz/2 cups strong plain (bread)
*   flour*
5 ml/1 tsp caster (superfine) sugar
15 g/½ oz fresh yeast or 20 ml/
*   4 tsp dried yeast*
120 ml/4 fl oz/½ cup warm milk
A pinch of salt
15 g/½ oz/1 tbsp butter or margarine
1 egg, beaten
For the filling:
75 g/3 oz/½ cup mixed dried fruit
*   (fruit cake mix)*
25 g/1 oz/3 tbsp chopped mixed
*   (candied) peel*
50 g/2 oz/¼ cup soft brown sugar
A little clear honey for glazing

Mix together 50 g/2 oz/¼ cup of the flour, the caster sugar, yeast and a little of the milk and leave in a warm place for 20 minutes until frothy. Mix together the remaining flour and salt and rub in the butter or margarine. Blend in the egg, the yeast mixture and the remaining warm milk and mix to a dough. Knead until elastic and no longer sticky. Place in an oiled bowl, cover with oiled clingfilm (plastic wrap) and leave in a warm place for about 1 hour until doubled in size.

Knead again and roll out to a 33 × 23 cm/13 × 9 in rectangle. Mix together all the filling ingredients except the honey and spread over the dough. Roll up from one long side and seal the edge with a little water. Cut the roll into nine equal-sized pieces and place in a lightly greased baking tin (pan). Cover and leave in a warm place for 30 minutes until doubled in size.

Bake in a preheated oven at 190°C/375°F/gas mark 5 for 25 minutes until golden brown. Remove from the oven and brush with honey, then leave to cool.

Coffee Buns

Makes 16

225 g/8 oz/1 cup butter or margarine
450 g/1 lb/4 cups wholemeal
*   (wholewheat) flour*
20 ml/4 tsp baking powder
5 ml/1 tsp salt
225 g/8 oz/1 cup soft brown sugar
2 eggs, lightly beaten
100 g/4 oz/⅔ cup currants
5 ml/1 tsp instant coffee powder
15 ml/1 tbsp hot water
75 ml/5 tbsp clear honey

Rub the butter or margarine into the flour, baking powder and salt until the mixture resembles breadcrumbs. Stir in the sugar. Beat in the eggs to make a soft but not sticky dough, then mix in the currants. Dissolve the coffee powder in the hot water and add to the dough. Shape into 16 flattened balls and place, well apart, on a greased baking (cookie) sheet. Press a finger into the centre of each bun and add a teaspoonful of honey. Bake in a preheated oven at 220°C/425°F/gas mark 7 for 10 minutes until light and golden brown.

350

Crème Fraîche Bread

Makes two 450 g/1 lb loaves

25 g/1 oz fresh yeast or 40 ml/
2½ tbsp dried yeast
75 g/3 oz/⅓ cup soft brown sugar
60 ml/4 tbsp warm water
60 ml/4 tbsp crème fraîche, at room
temperature
350 g/12 oz/3 cups plain
(all-purpose) flour
5 ml/1 tsp salt
A pinch of grated nutmeg
3 eggs
50 g/2 oz/¼ cup butter or margarine
A little milk and sugar for glazing

Blend the yeast with 5 ml/1 tsp of the sugar and the warm water and leave in a warm place for 20 minutes until frothy. Stir the crème fraîche into the yeast. Place the flour, salt and nutmeg in a bowl and make a well in the centre. Mix in the yeast mixture, eggs and butter and work to a soft dough. Knead until smooth and elastic. Place in an oiled bowl, cover with oiled clingfilm (plastic wrap) and leave in a warm place for about 1 hour until doubled in size.

Knead the dough again, then shape into two 450 g/1 lb loaf tins (pans). Cover and leave in a warm place for 35 minutes until doubled in size.

Brush the top of the loaves with a little milk, then sprinkle with sugar. Bake in a preheated oven at 180°C/350°F/gas mark 4 for 30 minutes. Leave to cool in the tin for 10 minutes, then turn out on to a wire rack to finish cooling.

Croissants

Makes 12

25 g/1 oz/2 tbsp lard (shortening)
450 g/1 lb/4 cups strong plain (bread)
flour
2.5 ml/½ tsp caster (superfine) sugar
10 ml/2 tsp salt

25 g/1 oz fresh yeast or 40 ml/
2½ tbsp dried yeast
250 ml/8 fl oz/1 cup warm water
2 eggs, lightly beaten
100 g/4 oz/½ cup butter or margarine,
diced

Rub the lard into the flour, sugar and salt until the mixture resembles breadcrumbs, then make a well in the centre. Mix the yeast with the water, and add to the flour with one of the eggs. Work the mixture together until you have a soft dough that leaves the sides of the bowl cleanly. Turn out on to a lightly floured surface and knead until smooth and no longer sticky. Roll out the dough to a 20 × 50 cm/8 × 20 in strip. Dot the top two-thirds of the dough with one-third of the butter or margarine, leaving a thin gap round the edge. Fold the unbuttered part of the dough up over the next one-third, then fold the top one-third down over that. Press the edges together to seal, and give the dough a quarter turn so the folded edge is on your left. Repeat the process with the next one-third of the butter or margarine, fold and repeat once more so that you have used all the fat. Put the folded dough in an oiled polythene bag and chill for 30 minutes.

Roll, fold and turn the dough again three more times without adding any more fat. Return to the bag and chill for 30 minutes.

Roll out the dough to a 40 × 38 cm/ 16 × 15 in rectangle, trim the edges and cut into 12 15 cm/6 in triangles. Brush the triangles with a little beaten egg and roll up from the base, then curve into crescent shapes and place, well apart, on a greased baking (cookie) sheet. Brush the tops with egg, cover and leave in a warm place for about 30 minutes.

Brush the tops with egg again, then bake in a preheated oven at 230°C/425°F/ gas mark 7 for 15–20 minutes until golden and puffy.

Wholemeal Sultana Croissants

Makes 12

25 g/1 oz/2 tbsp lard (shortening)
225 g/8 oz/2 cups strong plain (bread)
flour
225 g/8 oz/2 cups wholemeal
(wholewheat) flour
10 ml/2 tsp salt
25 g/1 oz fresh yeast or 40 ml/
2½ tbsp dried yeast
300 ml/½ pt/1¼ cups warm water
2 eggs, lightly beaten
100 g/4 oz/½ cup butter or margarine,
diced
45 ml/3 tbsp sultanas
(golden raisins)
2.5 ml/½ tsp caster (superfine) sugar

Rub the lard into the flour and salt until the mixture resembles breadcrumbs, then make a well in the centre. Mix the yeast with the water, and add to the flour with one of the eggs. Work the mixture together until you have a soft dough that leaves the sides of the bowl cleanly. Turn out on to a lightly floured surface and knead until smooth and no longer sticky. Roll out the dough to a 20 × 50 cm/8 × 20 in strip. Dot the top two-thirds of the dough with one-third of the butter or margarine, leaving a thin gap round the edge. Fold the unbuttered part of the dough up over the next one-third, then fold the top one-third down over that. Press the edges together to seal, and give the dough a quarter turn so the folded edge is on your left. Repeat the process with the next one-third of the butter or margarine, fold and repeat once more so that you have used all the fat. Put the folded dough in an oiled polythene bag and chill for 30 minutes.

Roll, fold and turn the dough again three more times without adding any more fat. Return to the bag and chill for 30 minutes.

Roll out the dough to a 40 × 38 cm/16 × 15 in rectangle, trim the edges and cut into twelve 15 cm/6 in triangles. Brush the triangles with a little beaten egg, sprinkle with sultanas and sugar and roll up from the base, then curve into crescent shapes and place well apart on a greased baking (cookie) sheet. Brush the tops with egg, cover and leave in a warm place for 30 minutes.

Brush the tops with egg again, then bake in a preheated oven at 230°C/425°F/gas mark 7 for 15–20 minutes until golden and puffy.

Forest Rounds

Makes three 350 g/12 oz loaves

450 g/1 lb/4 cups wholemeal
(wholewheat) flour
20 ml/4 tsp baking powder
45 ml/3 tbsp carob powder
5 ml/1 tsp salt
50 g/2 oz/½ cup ground hazelnuts
50 g/2 oz/½ cup chopped mixed nuts
75 g/3 oz/⅓ cup vegetable fat
(shortening)
75 g/3 oz/¼ cup clear honey
300 ml/½ pt/1¼ cups milk
2.5 ml/½ tsp vanilla essence (extract)
1 egg, beaten

Mix together the dry ingredients, then rub in the vegetable fat. Dissolve the honey in the milk and vanilla essence and mix into the dry ingredients until you have a soft dough. Shape into three rounds and press to flatten slightly. Cut each loaf partly through into six portions and brush with beaten egg. Place on a greased baking (cookie) sheet and bake in a preheated oven at 230°C/450°F/gas mark 8 for 20 minutes until well risen and golden brown.

Nutty Twist

Makes one 450 g/1 lb loaf

For the dough:
15 g/½ oz fresh yeast or 20 ml/
    4 tsp dried yeast
40 g/1½ oz/3 tbsp caster (superfine)
    sugar
100 ml/3½ fl oz/6 ½ tbsp warm milk
350 g/12 oz/3 cups strong plain
    (bread) flour
2.5 ml/½ tsp salt
50 g/2 oz/¼ cup butter or margarine,
    melted
1 egg
For the filling and glaze:
100 g/4 oz/1 cup ground almonds
2 egg whites
50 g/2 oz/¼ cup caster (superfine)
    sugar
2.5 ml/½ tsp ground cinnamon
100 g/4 oz/1 cup ground hazelnuts
1 egg yolk

To make the dough, blend the yeast with 5 ml/1 tsp of the sugar and a little of the milk and leave in a warm place for 20 minutes until frothy. Mix the flour and salt in a bowl and make a well in the centre. Mix in the yeast mixture, the remaining sugar and milk, the melted butter or margarine and the egg and mix to a smooth dough. Knead until elastic and no longer sticky. Place in an oiled bowl, cover with oiled clingfilm (plastic wrap) and leave in a warm place for about 1 hour until doubled in size.

Roll out the dough on a lightly floured surface to a 30 × 40 cm/12 × 16 in rectangle. Mix together the filling ingredients, except the egg yolk, until you have a smooth paste, then spread over the dough, just short of the edges. Brush the edges with a little of the egg yolk, then roll up the dough from the long side. Cut the dough exactly in half lengthways, then twist the two pieces together, sealing the ends. Place on a greased baking (cookie) sheet, cover and leave in a warm place for 30 minutes until doubled in size. Brush with egg yolk and bake in a preheated oven at 190°C/375°F/gas mark 5 for 30 minutes until golden brown.

Orange Buns

Makes 24

For the dough:
25 g/1 oz fresh yeast or 40 ml/
    2½ tbsp dried yeast
120 ml/4 fl oz/½ cup warm water
75 g/3 oz/⅓ cup caster (superfine)
    sugar
100 g/4 oz/½ cup lard (shortening),
    diced
5 ml/1 tsp salt
250 ml/8 fl oz/1 cup warm milk
60 ml/4 tbsp orange juice
30 ml/2 tbsp grated orange rind
2 eggs, beaten
675 g/1½ lb/6 cups strong plain
    (bread) flour
For the icing (frosting):
250 g/9 oz/1½ cups icing
    (confectioners') sugar
5 ml/1 tsp grated orange rind
30 ml/2 tbsp orange juice

To make the dough, dissolve the yeast in the warm water with 5 ml/1 tsp of the sugar and leave until frothy. Mix the lard into the remaining sugar and the salt. Stir in the milk, orange juice, rind and eggs, then blend in the yeast mixture. Gradually add the flour and mix to a firm dough. Knead well. Place in a greased bowl, cover with oiled clingfilm (plastic wrap) and leave in a warm place for about 1 hour until doubled in size.

Roll out to about 2 cm/¾ in thick and cut into rounds with a biscuit (cookie) cutter. Place a little way apart on a greased baking (cookie) sheet and leave in a warm place 25 minutes. Leave to cool.

To make the icing, place the sugar in a bowl and mix in the orange rind. Gradually mix in the orange juice until you have a firm icing. Spoon over the buns when cool and leave to set.

Pain Chocolat

Makes 12

25 g/1 oz/2 tbsp lard (shortening)
450 g/1 lb/4 cups strong plain (bread) flour
2.5 ml/½ tsp caster (superfine) sugar
10 ml/2 tsp salt
25 g/1 oz fresh yeast or 40 ml/ 2½ tbsp dried yeast
250 ml/8 fl oz/1 cup warm water
2 eggs, lightly beaten
100 g/4 oz/½ cup butter or margarine, diced
100 g/4 oz/1 cup plain (semi-sweet) chocolate, broken into 12 pieces

Rub the lard into the flour, sugar and salt until the mixture resembles breadcrumbs, then make a well in the centre. Mix the yeast with the water, and add to the flour with one of the eggs. Work the mixture together until you have a soft dough which leaves the sides of the bowl cleanly. Turn out on to a lightly floured surface and knead until smooth and no longer sticky. Roll out the dough to a 20 × 50 cm/8 × 20 in strip. Dot the top two-thirds of the dough with one-third of the butter or margarine, leaving a thin gap round the edge. Fold the unbuttered part of the dough up over the next one-third, then fold the top one-third down over that, Press the edges together to seal, and give the dough a quarter turn so the folded edge is on your left. Repeat the process with the next one-third of the butter or margarine, fold and repeat once more so that you have used all the fat. Put the folded dough in an oiled polythene bag and chill for 30 minutes.

Roll, fold and turn the dough again three more times without adding any more fat. Return to the bag and chill for 30 minutes.

Divide the dough into 12 pieces and roll out into rectangles about 5 cm/2 in wide and 5 mm/¼ in thick. Place a piece of chocolate in the centre of each and roll up, enclosing the chocolate. Place well apart on a greased baking (cookie) sheet. Brush the tops with egg, cover and leave in a warm place for 30 minutes.

Brush the tops with egg again, then bake in a preheated oven at 230°C/425°F/ gas mark 7 for 15–20 minutes until golden and puffy.

Pandolce

Makes two 675 g/1½ lb loaves

175 g/6 oz/1 cup raisins
45 ml/3 tbsp Marsala or sweet sherry
25 g/1 oz fresh yeast or 40 ml/2½ tbsp dried yeast
175 g/6 oz/¾ cup caster (superfine) sugar
400 ml/14 fl oz/1¾ cups warm milk
900 g/2 lb/8 cups plain (all-purpose) flour
A pinch of salt
45 ml/3 tbsp orange flower water
75 g/3 oz/⅓ cup butter or margarine, melted
50 g/2 oz/½ cup pine nuts
50 g/2 oz/½ cup pistachio nuts
10 ml/2 tsp crushed fennel seeds
50 g/2 oz/⅓ cup crystallised (candied) lemon rind, chopped
Grated rind of 1 orange

Mix the raisins and Marsala and leave to soak. Blend the yeast with 5 ml/ 1 tsp of the sugar and a little of the warm milk and leave in a warm place for 20 minutes until frothy. Mix the flour, salt and remaining sugar in a bowl and make a well in the centre. Mix in the yeast mixture, the remaining warm milk and the orange flower water. Add the melted butter or margarine and mix to a soft dough. Knead on a lightly floured surface until elastic and no longer sticky. Place in an oiled bowl, cover with oiled clingfilm (plastic wrap) and leave in a warm place for about 1 hour until doubled in size.

Press or roll out the dough on a lightly

floured surface to about 1 cm/½ in thick. Sprinkle with the raisins, nuts, fennel seeds, lemon and orange rinds. Roll up the dough, then press or roll out and roll up again. Shape into a round and place on a greased baking (cookie) sheet. Cover with oiled clingfilm and leave in a warm place for about 1 hour until doubled in size.

Make a triangular cut on the top of the loaf, then bake in a preheated oven at 190°C/375°F/gas mark 5 for 20 minutes. Reduce the oven temperature to 160°C/325°F/gas mark 3 and bake for a further 1 hour until golden and hollow-sounding when tapped on the base.

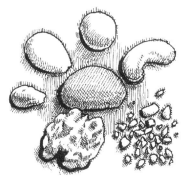

Panettone

Makes one 23 cm/9 in cake

40 g/1½ oz fresh yeast or 60 ml/
4 tbsp dried yeast
150 g/5 oz/⅔ cup caster (superfine)
sugar
300 ml/½ pt/1¼ cups warm milk
225 g/8 oz/1 cup butter or margarine,
melted
5 ml/1 tsp salt
Grated rind of 1 lemon
A pinch of grated nutmeg
6 egg yolks
675 g/1½ lb/6 cups strong plain
(bread) flour
175 g/6 oz/1 cup raisins
175 g/6 oz/1 cup chopped mixed
(candied) peel
75 g/3 oz/¼ cup almonds, chopped

Blend the yeast with 5 ml/1 tsp of the sugar with a little of the warm milk and leave in a warm place for 20 minutes until frothy. Mix the melted butter with the remaining sugar, the salt, lemon rind, nutmeg and egg yolks. Stir the mixture into the flour with the yeast mixture and blend to a smooth dough. Knead until no longer sticky. Place in an oiled bowl, cover with oiled clingfilm (plastic wrap) and leave in a warm place for 20 minutes. Mix together the raisins, mixed peel and almonds and work into the dough. Cover again and leave in a warm place for a further 30 minutes.

Knead the dough lightly, then shape into a greased and lined 23 cm/9 in deep cake tin (pan). Cover and leave in a warm place for 30 minutes until the dough rises well above the top of the tin. Bake in a preheated oven at 190°C/375°F/gas mark 5 for 1½ hours until a skewer inserted in the centre comes out clean.

Tea Breads and Buns

*T*raditional tea breads are actually made with cold tea, but these fruited and tasty breads demonstrate a range of different ingredients.

Apple and Date Loaf

Makes one 900 g/2 lb loaf

350 g/12 oz/3 cups self-raising (self-rising) flour
50 g/2 oz/¼ cup soft brown sugar
5 ml/1 tsp mixed (apple-pie) spice
5 ml/1 tsp ground cinnamon
2.5 ml/½ tsp grated nutmeg
A pinch of salt
1 large cooking (tart) apple, peeled, cored and chopped
175 g/6 oz/1 cup stoned (pitted) dates, chopped
Grated rind of ½ lemon
2 eggs, lightly beaten
150 ml/¼ pt/⅔ cup plain yoghurt

Mix together the dry ingredients, then stir in the apple, dates and lemon rind. Make a well in the centre, add the eggs and yoghurt and gradually mix to a dough. Turn out on to a lightly floured surface and shape into a greased and floured 900 g/2 lb loaf tin (pan). Bake in a preheated oven at 160°C/325°F/gas mark 3 for 1½ hours until well risen and golden brown. Leave to cool in the tin for 5 minutes, then turn out on to a wire rack to finish cooling.

Apple and Sultana Bread

Makes three 350 g/12 oz loaves

25 g/1 oz fresh yeast or 40 ml/2½ tbsp dried yeast
10 ml/2 tsp malt extract
375 ml/13 fl oz/1½ cups warm water
450 g/1 lb/4 cups wholemeal (wholewheat) flour
5 ml/1 tsp soya flour
50 g/2 oz/½ cup rolled oats
2.5 ml/½ tsp salt
25 g/1 oz/2 tbsp soft brown sugar
15 ml/1 tbsp lard (shortening)
225 g/8 oz cooking (tart) apples, peeled, cored and chopped
400 g/14 oz/2⅓ cups sultanas (golden raisins)
2.5 ml/½ tsp ground cinnamon
1 egg, beaten

Blend the yeast with the malt extract and a little of the warm water and leave in a warm place until frothy. Mix together the flour, oats, salt and sugar, rub in the lard and make a well in the centre. Mix in the yeast mixture and the remaining warm water and knead to a smooth dough. Mix in the apples, sultanas and cinnamon. Knead until elastic and no longer sticky. Place the dough in an oiled bowl and cover with oiled clingfilm (plastic wrap). Leave in a warm place for 1 hour until doubled in size.

Knead the dough lightly, then shape into three rounds and flatten slightly, then place on a greased baking (cookie) sheet. Brush the tops with beaten egg and bake in a preheated oven at 230°C/450°F/gas mark 8 for 35 minutes until well risen and hollow-sounding when tapped on the base.

356

Apple and Cinnamon Surprises

Makes 10

For the dough:
25 g/1 oz fresh yeast or 40 ml/
  2½ tbsp dried yeast
75 g/3 oz/⅓ cup soft brown sugar
300 ml/½ pt/1¼ cups warm water
450 g/1 lb/4 cups wholemeal
  (wholewheat) flour
2.5 ml/½ tsp salt
25 g/1 oz/¼ cup milk powder
  (non-fat dry milk)
5 ml/1 tsp ground mixed
  (apple-pie) spice
5 ml/1 tsp ground cinnamon
75 g/3 oz/⅓ cup butter or margarine
15 ml/1 tbsp grated orange rind
1 egg
For the filling:
450 g/1 lb cooking (tart) apples,
  peeled, cored and coarsely chopped
75 g/3 oz/½ cup sultanas
  (golden raisins)
5 ml/1 tsp ground cinnamon
For the glaze:
15 ml/1 tbsp clear honey
30 ml/2 tbsp caster (superfine) sugar

To make the dough, blend the yeast with a little of the sugar and a little of the warm water and leave in a warm place for 20 minutes until frothy. Mix together the flour, salt, milk powder and spices. Rub in the butter or margarine, then stir in the orange rind and make a well in the centre. Add the yeast mixture, the remaining warm water and the egg and mix to a smooth dough. Place in an oiled bowl, cover with oiled clingfilm (plastic wrap) and leave in a warm place for 1 hour until doubled in size.

To make the filling, cook the apples and sultanas in a pan with the cinnamon and a little water until soft and puréed.

Shape the dough into 10 rolls, press your finger into the centre and spoon in some of the filling, then close the dough around the filling. Arrange on a greased baking (cookie) sheet, Cover with oiled clingfilm and leave in a warm place for 40 minutes. Bake in a preheated oven at 230°C/450°F/gas mark 8 for 15 minutes until well risen. Brush with the honey, sprinkle with the sugar and leave to cool.

Apricot Tea Bread

Makes one 900 g/2 lb loaf

225 g/8 oz/2 cups self-raising
  (self-rising) flour
100 g/4 oz/⅔ cup dried apricots
50 g/2 oz/½ cup almonds, chopped
50 g/2 oz/¼ cup soft brown sugar
50 g/2 oz/¼ cup butter or margarine
100 g/4 oz/⅓ cup golden (light corn)
  syrup
1 egg
75 ml/5 tbsp milk

Soak the apricots in hot water for 1 hour, then drain and chop.

Mix together the flour, apricots, almonds and sugar. Melt the butter or margarine and syrup. Add to the dry ingredients with the egg and milk. Spoon into a greased and lined 900 g/2 lb loaf tin (pan) and bake in a preheated oven at 180°C/350°F/gas mark 4 for 1 hour until golden brown and firm to the touch.

Apricot and Orange Loaf

Makes one 900 g/2 lb loaf

175 g/6 oz/1 cup no-need-to-soak
dried apricots, chopped
150 ml/¼ pt/⅔ cup orange juice
400 g/14 oz/3½ cups plain
(all-purpose) flour
175 g/6 oz/¾ cup caster (superfine)
sugar
100 g/4 oz/⅔ cup raisins
7.5 ml/1½ tsp baking powder
2.5 ml/½ tsp bicarbonate of soda
(baking soda)
2.5 ml/½ tsp salt
Grated rind of 1 orange
1 egg, lightly beaten
25 g/1 oz/2 tbsp butter or margarine,
melted

Soak the apricots in the orange juice. Place the dry ingredients and orange rind in a bowl and make a well in the centre. Mix in the apricots and orange juice, egg and melted butter or margarine and work to a stiff mixture. Spoon into a greased and lined 900 g/2 lb loaf tin (pan) and bake in a preheated oven at 180°C/ 350°F/gas mark 4 for 1 hour until golden and firm to the touch.

Apricot and Walnut Loaf

Makes one 900 g/2 lb loaf

15 g/½ oz fresh yeast or 20 ml/
4 tsp dried yeast
30 ml/2 tbsp clear honey
300 ml/½ pt/1¼ cups warm water
25 g/1 oz/2 tbsp butter or margarine
225 g/8 oz/2 cups wholemeal
(wholewheat) flour
225 g/8 oz/2 cups plain
(all-purpose) flour
5 ml/1 tsp salt
75 g/3 oz/¾ cup walnuts, chopped
175 g/6 oz/1 cup ready-to-eat dried
apricots, chopped

Blend the yeast with a little of the honey and a little of the water and leave in a warm place for 20 minutes until frothy. Rub the butter or margarine into the flours and salt and make a well in the centre. Mix in the yeast mixture and the remaining honey and water and mix to a dough. Mix in the walnuts and apricots and knead until smooth and no longer sticky. Place in an oiled bowl, cover and leave in a warm place for 1 hour until doubled in size.

Knead the dough again and shape into a greased 900 g/2 lb loaf tin (pan). Cover with oiled clingfilm (plastic wrap) and leave in a warm place for about 20 minutes until the dough has risen just above the top of the tin. Bake in a preheated oven at 220°C/425°F/gas mark 7 for 30 minutes until golden brown and hollow-sounding when tapped on the base.

Autumn Crown

Makes one large ring loaf

For the dough:
450 g/1 lb/4 cups wholemeal
(wholewheat) flour
20 ml/4 tsp baking powder
75 g/3 oz/⅓ cup soft brown sugar
5 ml/1 tsp salt
2.5 ml/½ tsp ground mace
75 g/3 oz/⅓ cup vegetable fat
(shortening)
3 egg whites
300 ml/½ pt/1¼ cups milk
For the filling:
175 g/6 oz/1½ cups wholemeal
(wholewheat) cake crumbs
50 g/2 oz/½ cup ground hazelnuts
or almonds
50 g/2 oz/¼ cup soft brown sugar
75 g/3 oz/½ cup crystallised (candied)
ginger, chopped
30 ml/2 tbsp rum or brandy
1 egg, lightly beaten

To glaze:
15 ml/1 tbsp honey

To make the dough, mix together the dry ingredients and rub in the fat. Blend together the egg whites and milk and combine with the mixture until you have a soft, pliable dough.

Mix together the filling ingredients, using just enough of the egg to make a spreading consistency. Roll out the dough on a lightly floured surface to a 20 × 30 cm/8 × 10 in rectangle. Spread the filling over all but the top 2.5 cm/1 in along the long edge. Roll up from the opposite edge, like a Swiss (jelly) roll, and moisten the plain strip of dough to seal. Moisten each end and shape the roll into a circle, sealing the ends together. With sharp scissors, make little cuts around the top for decoration. Place on a greased baking (cookie) sheet and brush with the remaining egg. Leave to rest for 15 minutes.

Bake in a preheated oven at 230°C/450°F/gas mark 8 for 25 minutes until golden brown. Brush with honey and leave to cool.

Banana Loaf

Makes one 900 g/2 lb loaf

75 g/3 oz/⅓ cup butter or margarine,
*   softened*
175 g/6 oz/⅔ cup caster (superfine)
*   sugar*
2 eggs, lightly beaten
450 g/1 lb ripe bananas, mashed
200 g/7 oz/1¾ cup self-raising
*   (self-rising) flour*
75 g/3 oz/¾ cup walnuts, chopped
100 g/4 oz/⅔ cup sultanas (golden
*   raisins)*
50 g/2 oz/½ cup glacé (candied)
*   cherries*
2.5 ml/½ tsp bicarbonate of soda
*   (baking soda)*
A pinch of salt

Cream together the butter or margarine and sugar until pale and fluffy. Gradually beat in the eggs, then stir in the bananas. Mix in the remaining ingredients until well blended. Spoon into a greased and lined 900 g/2 lb loaf tin (pan) and bake in a preheated oven at 180°C/350°C/gas mark 4 for 1¼ hours until well risen and firm to the touch.

Wholemeal Banana Bread

Makes one 900 g/2 lb loaf

100 g/4 oz/½ cup butter or margarine,
*   softened*
50 g/2 oz/¼ cup soft brown sugar
2 eggs, lightly beaten
3 bananas, mashed
175 g/6 oz/1½ cups wholemeal
*   (wholewheat) flour*
100 g/4 oz/1 cup oat flour
5 ml/1 tsp baking powder
5 ml/1 tsp ground mixed
*   (apple-pie) spice*
30 ml/2 tbsp milk

Cream together the butter or margarine and sugar until light and fluffy. Gradually beat in the eggs, stir in the bananas, then fold in the flours, baking powder and mixed spice. Add enough of the milk to make a soft mixture. Spoon into a greased and lined 900 g/2 lb loaf tin (pan) and level the surface. Bake in a preheated oven at 190°C/375°F/gas mark 5 until risen and golden brown.

Banana and Nut Bread

Makes one 900 g/2 lb loaf

50 g/2 oz/¼ cup butter or margarine
225 g/8 oz/2 cups self-raising
    (self-rising) flour
50 g/2 oz/¼ cup caster (superfine)
    sugar
50 g/2 oz/½ cup chopped mixed nuts
1 egg, lightly beaten
75 g/3 oz/⅓ cup golden (light corn)
    syrup
2 bananas, mashed
15 ml/1 tbsp milk

Rub the butter or margarine into the flour, then stir in the sugar and nuts. Mix in the egg, syrup and bananas and enough of the milk to give a soft mixture. Spoon into a greased and lined 900 g/2 lb loaf tin (pan) and bake in a preheated oven at 180°C/350°F/gas mark 4 for about 1 hour until firm and golden brown. Store for 24 hours before serving sliced and buttered.

Bara Brith

Makes three 450 g/1 lb loaves

450 g/1 lb/2¾ cups dried mixed fruit
    (fruit cake mix)
250 ml/8 fl oz/1 cup strong cold tea
30 ml/2 tbsp dried yeast
175 g/6 oz/¾ cup soft brown sugar
250 g/12 oz/3 cups wholemeal
    (wholewheat) flour
350 g/12 oz/3 cups strong plain
    (bread) flour
10 ml/2 tsp ground mixed
    (apple-pie) spice
100 g/4 oz/½ cup butter or margarine,
    melted
2 eggs, beaten
2.5 ml/½ tsp salt
15 ml/1 tbsp clear honey

Soak the fruit in the tea for 2 hours. Warm 30 ml/2 tbsp of the tea and mix with the yeast and 5 ml/1 tsp of the sugar. Leave in a warm place until frothy. Mix together the dry ingredients, then blend in the yeast mixture and all remaining ingredients except the honey and mix to a dough. Turn out on to a lightly floured surface and knead gently until smooth and elastic. Divide between three greased and lined 450 g/1 lb loaf tins (pans). Cover with oiled clingfilm (plastic wrap) and leave in a warm place for 1 hour until the dough has risen above the top of the tins.

Bake in a preheated oven at 200°C/400°F/gas mark 6 for 15 minutes, then reduce the oven temperature to 180°C/350°F/gas mark 4 for a further 45 minutes until golden and hollow-sounding when tapped on the base. Warm the honey and brush over the tops of the warm loaves.

Bath Buns

Makes 12 buns

500 g/1 lb/4 cups strong plain (bread)
    flour
25 g/1 oz fresh yeast or 40 ml/2½ tbsp
    dried yeast
150 ml/¼ pt/⅔ cup warm milk
75 g/3 oz/⅓ cup caster (superfine)
    sugar
150 ml/¼ pt/⅔ cup warm water
5 ml/1 tsp salt
50 g/2 oz/¼ cup butter or margarine
2 eggs, beaten
175 g/6 oz/1 cup sultanas
    (golden raisins)
50 g/2 oz/⅓ cup chopped mixed peel
Beaten egg for glazing
Preserving sugar, crushed,
    for sprinkling

Place a quarter of the flour in a bowl and make a well in the centre. Mix the yeast with half the milk and 5 ml/1 tsp of the sugar and pour into the well. Add the remaining liquid. Stir together and leave in a warm place for 35 minutes until frothy. Place the remaining flour in a bowl with the salt. Stir in the remaining sugar, then rub in the butter or margarine until the mixture resembles breadcrumbs. Pour in the yeast mixture and eggs and beat well. Stir in the sultanas and mixed peel. Cover with oiled clingfilm (plastic wrap) and leave in a warm place until doubled in size.

Knead the dough well and divide into 12 pieces. Shape into a round and place on a greased baking (cookie) sheet. Cover with oiled clingfilm and leave in a warm place for 15 minutes. Brush with beaten egg and sprinkle with crushed sugar. Bake in a preheated oven at 200°C/400°F/gas mark 6 for 15–20 minutes until golden.

Cherry and Honey Loaf

Makes one 900 g/2 lb loaf

175 g/6 oz/³⁄₄ cup butter or margarine, softened
75 g/3 oz/¹⁄₃ cup soft brown sugar
60 ml/4 tbsp clear honey
2 eggs, beaten
100 g/4 oz/2 cups wholemeal (wholewheat) flour
10 ml/2 tsp baking powder
100 g/4 oz/¹⁄₂ cup glacé (candied) cherries, chopped
45 ml/3 tbsp milk

Cream together the butter or margarine, sugar and honey until light and fluffy. Gradually stir in the eggs, beating well after each addition. Mix in the remaining ingredients to make a soft mixture. Spoon into a greased and lined 900 g/2 lb loaf tin (pan) and bake in a preheated oven at 180°C/350°F/gas mark 4 for 1 hour until a skewer inserted in the centre comes out clean. Serve sliced and buttered.

Cinnamon and Nutmeg Rolls

Makes 24

15 ml/1 tbsp dried yeast
120 ml/4 fl oz/¹⁄₂ cup milk, boiled
50 g/2 oz/¹⁄₄ cup caster (superfine) sugar
50 g/2 oz/¹⁄₄ cup lard (shortening)
5 ml/1 tsp salt
120 ml/4 fl oz/¹⁄₂ cup warm water
2.5 ml/¹⁄₂ tsp grated nutmeg
1 egg, beaten
400 g/14 oz/3¹⁄₂ cups strong plain (bread) flour
45 ml/3 tbsp butter or margarine, melted
175 g/6 oz/³⁄₄ cup soft brown sugar
10 ml/2 tsp ground cinnamon
75 g/3 oz/¹⁄₂ cup raisins

Dissolve the yeast in the warm milk with a teaspoon of the caster sugar and leave until frothy. Mix together the remaining caster sugar, the lard and salt. Pour in the water and stir until blended. Stir in the yeast mixture, then gradually add the nutmeg, egg and flour. Knead to a smooth dough. Place in a greased bowl, cover with oiled clingfilm (plastic wrap) and leave in a warm place for about 1 hour until doubled in size.

Divide the dough in half and roll out on a lightly floured surface into rectangles about 5 mm/¹⁄₄ in thick. Brush with melted butter and sprinkle with the brown sugar, cinnamon and raisins. Roll up from the longer size and cut each roll into 12 slices 1 cm/¹⁄₂ in thick. Place the slices a little way apart on a greased baking (cookie) sheet and leave in a warm place for 1 hour. Bake in a preheated oven at 190°C/375°F/gas mark 5 for 20 minutes until well risen.

Cranberry Bread

Makes one 450 g/1 lb loaf

225 g/8 oz/2 cups plain
(all-purpose) flour
2.5 ml/½ tsp salt
2.5 ml/½ tsp bicarbonate of soda
(baking soda)
225 g/8 oz/1 cup caster (superfine)
sugar
7.5 ml/1½ tsp baking powder
Juice and grated rind of 1 orange
1 egg, beaten
25 g/1 oz/2 tbsp lard (shortening),
melted
100 g/4 oz fresh or frozen cranberries,
crushed
50 g/2 oz/½ cup walnuts, coarsely
chopped

Mix together the dry ingredients in a
large bowl. Put the orange juice and
rind in a measuring jug and make up to
175 ml/6 fl oz/¾ cup with water. Stir into
the dry ingredients with the egg and lard.
Stir in the cranberries and nuts. Spoon
into a greased 450 g/1 lb loaf tin (pan)
and bake in a preheated oven at
160°C/325°F/gas mark 3 for about 1 hour
until a skewer inserted in the centre
comes out clean. Leave to cool, then keep
for 24 hours before cutting.

Date and Butter Loaf

Makes one 900 g/2 lb loaf

For the loaf:
175 g/6 oz/1 cup stoned (pitted) dates,
finely chopped
5 ml/1 tsp bicarbonate of soda
(baking soda)
250 ml/8 fl oz/1 cup boiling water
75 g/3 oz/⅓ cup butter or margarine,
softened
225 g/8 oz/1 cup soft brown sugar
1 egg, lightly beaten
5 ml/1 tsp vanilla essence (extract)
225 g/8 oz/2 cups plain
(all-purpose) flour

5 ml/1 tsp baking powder
A pinch of salt
For the topping:
100 g/4 oz/½ cup soft brown sugar
50 g/2 oz/¼ cup butter or margarine
120 ml/4 fl oz/½ cup single (light)
cream

To make the loaf, mix together the
dates, bicarbonate of soda and boiling
water and stir well, then leave to cool.
Cream together the butter or margarine
and sugar until light and fluffy, then
gradually beat in the egg and vanilla
essence. Stir in the flour, baking powder
and salt. Spoon the mixture into a greased
and lined 900 g/2 lb loaf tin (pan) and
bake in a preheated oven at 180°C/350°F/
gas mark 4 for 1 hour until a skewer
inserted in the centre comes out clean.

To make the topping, melt together the
sugar, butter or margarine and cream
over a low heat until blended, then
simmer very gently for 15 minutes,
stirring occasionally. Remove the loaf
from the tin and pour over the hot
topping. Leave to cool.

Date and Banana Bread

Makes one 900 g/2 lb loaf

225 g/8 oz/1⅓ cups stoned (pitted)
dates, chopped
300 ml/½ pt/1¼ cups milk
5 ml/1 tsp bicarbonate of soda
(baking soda)
100 g/4 oz/½ cup butter or margarine
275 g/10 oz/2½ cups self-raising
(self-rising) flour
2 ripe bananas, mashed
1 egg, beaten
75 g/3 oz/¾ cup hazelnuts, chopped
30 ml/2 tbsp clear honey

Place the dates, milk and bicarbonate of
soda in a pan and bring to the boil,
stirring. Leave to cool. Rub the butter or
margarine into the flour until the mixture
resembles breadcrumbs. Stir in the
bananas, egg and most of the hazelnuts,

reserving a few for decoration. Spoon into a greased and lined 900 g/2 lb loaf tin (pan) and bake in a preheated oven at 180°C/350°F/gas mark 4 for 1 hour until a skewer inserted in the centre comes out clean. Leave to cool in the tin for 5 minutes, then turn out and remove the lining paper. Warm the honey and brush over the top of the cake. Sprinkle with the reserved nuts and leave to cool completely.

Date and Orange Loaf

Makes one 900 g/2 lb loaf

225 g/8 oz/1⅓ cups stoned (pitted) dates, chopped
120 ml/4 fl oz/½ cup water
200 g/7 oz/scant 1 cup soft brown sugar
75 g/3 oz/⅓ cup butter or margarine
Grated rind and juice of 1 orange
1 egg, lightly beaten
225 g/8 oz/2 cups plain (all-purpose) flour
10 ml/2 tsp baking powder
5 ml/1 tsp ground cinnamon

Simmer the dates in the water for 15 minutes until pulpy. Stir in the sugar until dissolved. Remove from the heat and leave to cool slightly. Beat in the butter or margarine, orange rind and juice, then the egg. Beat in the flour, baking powder and cinnamon. Spoon into a greased and lined 900 g/2 lb loaf tin (pan) and bake in a preheated oven at 180°C/350°F/gas mark 4 for 1 hour until a skewer inserted in the centre comes out clean.

Date and Nut Bread

Makes one 900 g/2 lb loaf

250 ml/8 fl oz/1 cup boiling water
225 g/8 oz/1⅓ cups stoned (pitted) dates, chopped
10 ml/2 tsp bicarbonate of soda (baking soda)
25 g/1 oz/2 tbsp vegetable fat (shortening)
225 g/8 oz/1 cup soft brown sugar
2 eggs, beaten
225 g/8 oz/2 cups plain (all-purpose) flour
5 ml/1 tsp salt
50 g/2 oz/½ cup pecan nuts, chopped

Pour the boiling water over the dates and bicarbonate of soda and leave until lukewarm. Cream together the vegetable fat and sugar until creamy. Gradually beat in the eggs. Mix the flour with the salt and nuts, then fold into the creamed mixture alternately with the dates and liquid. Spoon into a greased 900 g/2 lb loaf tin (pan) and bake in a preheated oven at 180°C/350°F/gas mark 4 for 1 hour until firm to the touch.

Date Tea Bread

Makes one 900 g/2 lb loaf

225 g/8 oz/2 cups plain
(all-purpose) flour
100 g/4 oz/½ cup soft brown sugar
A pinch of salt
5 ml/1 tsp ground mixed
(apple-pie) spice
5 ml/1 tsp bicarbonate of soda
(baking soda)
50 g/2 oz/¼ cup butter or margarine,
melted
15 ml/1 tbsp black treacle (molasses)
150 ml/¼ pt/⅔ cup black tea
1 egg, beaten
75 g/3 oz/½ cup stoned (pitted) dates,
chopped

Mix together the flour, sugar, salt, spice and bicarbonate of soda. Stir in the butter, treacle, tea and egg and mix well until smooth. Stir in the dates. Spoon the mixture into a greased and lined 900 g/2 lb loaf tin (pan) and bake in a preheated oven at 180°C/350°F/gas mark 4 for 45 minutes.

Date and Walnut Loaf

Makes one 900 g/2 lb loaf

100 g/4 oz/½ cup butter or margarine
175 g/6 oz/1½ cups wholemeal
(wholewheat) flour
50 g/2 oz/½ cup oat flour
10 ml/2 tsp baking powder
5 ml/1 tsp ground mixed
(apple-pie) spice
2.5 ml/½ tsp ground cinnamon
50 g/2 oz/¼ cup soft brown sugar
75 g/3 oz/½ cup stoned (pitted) dates,
chopped
75 g/3 oz/¾ cup walnuts, chopped
2 eggs, lightly beaten
30 ml/2 tbsp milk

Rub the butter or margarine into the flours, baking powder and spices until the mixture resembles breadcrumbs. Stir in the sugar, dates and walnuts. Mix in the eggs and milk to make a soft dough. Shape the dough into a greased 900 g/2 lb loaf tin (pan) and level the top. Bake in a preheated oven at 160°C/325°F/gas mark 3 for 45 minutes until risen and golden .

Fig Loaf

Makes one 450 g/1 lb loaf

100 g/4 oz/1½ cups bran cereal
100 g/4 oz/½ cup soft brown sugar
100 g/4 oz/⅔ cup dried figs, chopped
30 ml/2 tbsp black treacle (molasses)
250 ml/8 fl oz/1 cup milk
100 g/4 oz/1 cup wholemeal
(wholewheat) flour
10 ml/2 tsp baking powder

Mix the cereal, sugar, figs, treacle and milk and leave to stand for 30 minutes. Stir in the flour and baking powder. Spoon into a greased 450 g/1 lb loaf tin (pan) and bake in a preheated oven at 180°C/350°F/gas mark 4 for 45 minutes until firm and a skewer inserted in the centre comes out clean.

Fig and Marsala Bread

Makes one 900 g/2 lb loaf

225 g/8 oz/1 cup unsalted (sweet)
  butter or margarine, softened
225 g/8 oz/1 cup soft brown sugar
4 eggs, lightly beaten
45 ml/3 tbsp Marsala
5 ml/1 tsp vanilla essence (extract)
200 g/7 oz/1¾ cups plain
  (all-purpose) flour
A pinch of salt
50 g/2 oz/⅓ cup ready-to-eat dried
  apricots, chopped
50 g/2 oz/⅓ cup stoned (pitted) dates,
  chopped
50 g/2 oz/⅓ cup dried figs, chopped
50 g/2 oz/½ cup chopped mixed nuts

Cream together the butter or margarine and sugar until light and fluffy. Gradually add the eggs, then the Marsala and vanilla essence. Mix the flour and salt with the fruit and nuts, then fold into the mixture and mix well. Spoon into a greased and floured 900 g/2 lb loaf tin (pan) and bake in a preheated oven at 180°C/350°F/gas mark 4 for 1 hour. Leave to cool in the tin for 10 minutes, then turn out on to a wire rack to finish cooling.

Honey and Fig Rolls

Makes 12

25 g/1 oz fresh yeast or 40 ml/
  2½ tbsp dried yeast
75 g/3 oz/¼ cup clear honey
300 ml/½ pt/1¼ cups warm water
100 g/4 oz/⅔ cup dried figs, chopped
15 ml/1 tbsp malt extract
450 g/1 lb/4 cups wholemeal
  (wholewheat) flour
15 ml/1 tbsp milk powder
  (non-fat dry milk)
5 ml/1 tsp salt
2.5 ml/½ tsp grated nutmeg
40 g/1½ oz/2½ tbsp butter or
  margarine
Grated zest of 1 orange
1 egg, beaten
15 ml/1 tbsp sesame seeds

Blend the yeast with 5 ml/1 tsp of the honey and a little of the warm water and leave in a warm place until frothy. Mix the remaining warm water with the figs, malt extract and remaining honey and leave to soak. Mix together the flour, milk powder, salt and nutmeg, then rub in the butter or margarine and stir in the orange rind. Make a well in the centre and pour in the yeast mixture and the fig mixture. Mix to a soft dough and knead until no longer sticky. Place in an oiled bowl, cover with oiled clingfilm (plastic wrap) and leave in a warm place for 1 hour until doubled in size.

Knead lightly, then shape into 12 rolls and arrange on a greased baking (cookie) sheet. Cover with oiled clingfilm and leave in a warm place for 20 minutes. Brush with beaten egg and sprinkle with sesame seeds. Bake in a preheated oven at 230°C/450°F/gas mark 8 for 15 minutes until golden brown and hollow-sounding when tapped on the base.

Hot Cross Buns

Makes 12

For the buns:
450 g/1 lb/4 cups strong (bread) flour
15 ml/1 tbsp dried yeast
A pinch of salt
5 ml/1 tsp ground mixed
(apple-pie) spice
50 g/2 oz/¼ cup caster (superfine)
sugar
100 g/4 oz/⅔ cup currants
25 g/1 oz/3 tbsp chopped mixed
(candied) peel
1 egg, beaten
250 ml/8 fl oz/1 cup milk
50 g/2 oz/¼ cup butter or margarine,
melted
For the crosses:
25 g/1 oz/¼ cup plain (all-purpose)
flour
15 ml/1 tbsp water
A little beaten egg
For the glaze:
50 g/2 oz/¼ cup caster (superfine)
sugar
150 ml/¼ pt/⅔ cup water

To make the buns, mix together the dry ingredients, currants and mixed peel. Stir in the egg, milk and melted butter and mix to a firm dough that comes away from the sides of the bowl. Turn out on to a lightly floured surface and knead for 5 minutes until smooth and elastic. Divide into 12 and roll into balls. Place well apart on a greased baking (cookie) sheet, cover with oiled clingfilm (plastic wrap) and leave in a warm place for about 45 minutes until doubled in size.

Put the flour for the cross in a small bowl and gradually mix in enough of the water to make a dough. Roll out to a long strand. Brush the tops of the buns with beaten egg, then gently press a cross of dough cut from the long strand into each one. Bake in a preheated oven at 220°C/425°F/gas mark 7 for 20 minutes until golden brown.

To make the glaze, dissolve the sugar in the water, then boil until syrupy. Brush over the hot buns, then transfer them to a wire rack to cool.

Lincolnshire Plum Bread

Makes three 450 g/1 lb loaves

15 g/½ oz fresh yeast or 20 ml/
4 tsp dried yeast
45 ml/3 tbsp soft brown sugar
200 ml/7 fl oz/scant 1 cup warm milk
100 g/4 oz/½ cup butter or margarine
450 g/1 lb/4 cups plain (all-purpose)
flour
10 ml/2 tsp baking powder
A pinch of salt
1 egg, beaten
450 g/1 lb/2⅔ cups dried mixed fruit
(fruit cake mix)

Blend the yeast with 5 ml/1 tsp of the sugar and a little of the warm milk and leave in a warm place for 20 minutes until frothy. Rub the butter or margarine into the flour, baking powder and salt until the mixture resembles breadcrumbs. Stir in the remaining sugar and make a well in the centre. Mix in the yeast mixture, remaining warm milk and the egg, then work in the fruit to make a fairly stiff dough. Shape into three greased 450 g/1 lb loaf tins (pans) and bake in a preheated oven at 150°C/300°F/gas mark 2 for 2 hours until golden brown.

London Buns

Makes 10

50 g/2 oz fresh yeast or 30 ml/
  2 tbsp dried yeast
75 g/3 oz/⅓ cup soft brown sugar
300 ml/½ pt/1¼ cups warm water
175 g/6 oz/1 cup currants
25 g/1 oz/3 tbsp chopped stoned
  (pitted) dates
25 g/1 oz/3 tbsp chopped mixed
  (candied) peel
25 g/1 oz/2 tbsp chopped glacé
  (candied) cherries
45 ml/3 tbsp orange juice
450 g/1 lb/4 cups wholemeal
  (wholewheat) flour
2.5 ml/½ tsp salt
25 g/1 oz/¼ cup milk powder
  (non-fat dry milk)
15 ml/1 tbsp ground mixed
  (apple-pie) spice
5 ml/1 tsp ground cinnamon
75 g/3 oz/⅓ cup butter or margarine
15 ml/1 tbsp grated orange rind
1 egg
15 ml/1 tbsp clear honey
30 ml/2 tbsp flaked (slivered)
  almonds

Blend the yeast with a little of the sugar and a little of the warm water and leave in a warm place for 20 minutes until frothy. Soak the currants, dates, mixed peel and cherries in the orange juice. Mix together the flour, salt, milk powder and spices. Rub in the butter or margarine, then stir in the orange rind and make a well in the centre. Add the yeast mixture, the remaining warm water and the egg and mix to a smooth dough. Place in an oiled bowl, cover with clingfilm (plastic wrap) and leave in a warm place for 1 hour until doubled in size.

Shape the dough into 10 rolls and arrange on a greased baking (cookie) sheet. Cover with oiled clingfilm and leave in a warm place for 45 minutes. Bake in a preheated oven at 230°C/450°F/gas mark 8 for 15 minutes until well risen. Brush with the honey, sprinkle with the almonds and leave to cool.

Irish Country Loaf

Makes one 900 g/2 lb loaf

350 g/12 oz/3 cups wholemeal
  (wholewheat) flour
100 g/4 oz/1 cup oatmeal
100 g/4 oz/⅔ cup sultanas
  (golden raisins)
15 ml/1 tbsp baking powder
15 ml/1 tbsp caster (superfine) sugar
5 ml/1 tsp bicarbonate of soda
  (baking soda)
5 ml/1 tsp salt
10 ml/2 tsp ground mixed
  (apple-pie) spice
Grated rind of ½ lemon
1 egg, beaten
300 ml/½ pt/1¼ cups buttermilk or
  plain yoghurt
150 ml/¼ pt/⅔ cup water

Mix together all the dry ingredients and lemon rind and make a well in the centre. Beat together the egg, buttermilk or yoghurt and water. Mix into the dry ingredients and work to a soft dough. Knead on a lightly floured surface, then shape into a greased 900 g/2 lb loaf tin (pan). Bake in a preheated oven at 200°C/400°F/gas mark 6 for 1 hour until well risen and firm to the touch.

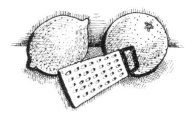

Malt Loaf

Makes one 450 g/1 lb loaf

25 g/1 oz/2 tbsp butter or margarine
225 g/8 oz/2 cups self-raising
(self-rising) flour
25 g/1 oz/2 tbsp soft brown sugar
30 ml/2 tbsp black treacle (molasses)
20 ml/4 tsp malt extract
150 ml/¼ pt/⅔ cup milk
75 g/3 oz/½ cup sultanas
(golden raisins)
15 ml/1 tbsp caster (superfine) sugar
30 ml/2 tbsp water

Rub the butter or margarine into the flour, then stir in the brown sugar. Warm the treacle, malt extract and milk, then blend into the dry ingredients with the sultanas and mix to a dough. Turn into a greased 450 g/1 lb loaf tin (pan) and bake in a preheated oven at 160°C/325°F/gas mark 3 for 1 hour until golden. Bring the sugar and water to the boil and boil until syrupy. Brush over the top of the loaf and leave to cool.

Bran Malt Loaf

Makes one 450 g/1 lb loaf

100 g/4 oz/½ cup soft brown sugar
225 g/8 oz/1⅓ cups dried mixed fruit
(fruit cake mix)
75 g/3 oz All Bran cereal
250 ml/8 fl oz/1 cup milk
5 ml/1 tsp ground mixed
(apple-pie) spice
100 g/4 oz/1 cup self-raising
(self-rising) flour

Mix together the sugar, fruit, All Bran, milk and spice and leave to soak for 1 hour. Stir in the flour and mix well. Spoon into a greased and lined 450 g/1 lb loaf tin (pan) and bake in a preheated oven at 180°C/350°F/gas mark 4 for 1½ hours until firm to the touch.

Wholemeal Malt Loaf

Makes one 900 g/2 lb loaf

25 g/1 oz/2 tbsp butter or margarine
30 ml/2 tbsp black treacle (molasses)
45 ml/3 tbsp malt extract
150 ml/¼ pt/⅔ cup milk
175 g/6 oz/1½ cups wholemeal
(wholewheat) flour
75 g/3 oz/¾ cup oat flour
10 ml/2 tsp baking powder
100 g/4 oz/⅔ cup raisins

Melt the butter or margarine, treacle, malt extract and milk. Pour into the flours, baking powder and raisins and mix to a soft dough. Spoon into a greased 900 g/2 lb loaf tin (pan) and level the surface. Bake in a preheated oven at 200°C/400°F/gas mark 6 for 45 minutes until a skewer inserted in the centre comes out clean.

Freda's Nut Loaf

Makes three 350 g/12 oz loaves

25 g/1 oz fresh yeast or 40 ml/
2½ tbsp dried yeast
10 ml/2 tsp malt extract
375 ml/13 fl oz/1½ cups warm water
450 g/1 lb/4 cups wholemeal
(wholewheat) flour
5 ml/1 tsp soya flour
50 g/2 oz/½ cup rolled oats
2.5 ml/½ tsp salt
25 g/1 oz/2 tbsp soft brown sugar
15 ml/1 tbsp lard (shortening)
100 g/4 oz/1 cup chopped mixed nuts
175 g/6 oz/1 cup currants
50 g/2 oz/⅓ cup stoned (pitted) dates,
chopped
50 g/2 oz/⅓ cup raisins
2.5 ml/½ tsp ground cinnamon
1 egg, beaten
45 ml/3 tbsp flaked (slivered)
almonds

Blend the yeast with the malt extract and a little of the warm water and leave in a warm place until frothy. Mix together the flours, oats, salt and sugar, rub in the lard and make a well in the centre. Mix in the yeast mixture and the remaining warm water and knead to a smooth dough. Mix in the nuts, currants, dates, raisins and cinnamon. Knead until elastic and no longer sticky. Place the dough in an oiled bowl and cover with oiled clingfilm (plastic wrap). Leave in a warm place for 1 hour until doubled in size.

Knead the dough lightly, then shape into three rounds and flatten slightly, then place on a greased baking (cookie) sheet. Brush the tops with beaten egg and sprinkle with the almonds. Bake in a preheated oven at 230°C/450°F/gas mark 8 for 35 minutes until well risen and hollow-sounding when tapped on the base.

Brazil Nut and Date Loaf

Makes three 350 g/12 oz loaves

25 g/1 oz fresh yeast or 40 ml/
2½ tbsp dried yeast
10 ml/2 tsp malt extract
375 ml/13 fl oz/1½ cups warm water
450 g/1 lb/4 cups wholemeal
(wholewheat) flour
5 ml/1 tsp soya flour
50 g/2 oz/½ cup rolled oats
2.5 ml/½ tsp salt
25 g/1 oz/2 tbsp soft brown sugar
15 ml/1 tbsp lard (shortening)
100 g/4 oz/1 cup brazil nuts, chopped
250 g/9 oz/1½ cup stoned (pitted)
dates, chopped
2.5 ml/½ tsp ground cinnamon
1 egg, beaten
45 ml/3 tbsp sliced brazil nuts

Blend the yeast with the malt extract and a little of the warm water and leave in a warm place until frothy. Mix together the flours, oats, salt and sugar, rub in the lard and make a well in the centre. Mix in the yeast mixture and the remaining warm water and knead to a smooth dough. Mix in the nuts, dates and cinnamon. Knead until elastic and no longer sticky. Place the dough in an oiled bowl and cover with oiled clingfilm (plastic wrap). Leave in a warm place for 1 hour until doubled in size.

Knead the dough lightly, shape into three rounds and flatten slightly, then place on a greased baking (cookie) sheet. Brush the tops with beaten egg and sprinkle with the sliced brazil nuts. Bake in a preheated oven at 230°C/450°F/gas mark 8 for 35 minutes until well risen and hollow-sounding when tapped on the base.

Panastan Fruit Bread

Makes three 175 g/12 oz loaves

25 g/1 oz fresh yeast or 40 ml/
2½ tbsp dried yeast
150 ml/¼ pt/⅔ cup warm water
60 ml/4 tbsp clear honey
5 ml/1 tsp malt extract
15 ml/1 tbsp sunflower seeds
15 ml/1 tbsp sesame seeds
25 g/1 oz/¼ cup wheatgerm
450 g/1 lb/4 cups wholemeal
(wholewheat) flour
5 ml/1 tsp salt
50 g/2 oz/¼ cup butter or margarine
175 g/6 oz/1 cup sultanas
(golden raisins)
25 g/1 oz/3 tbsp chopped mixed
(candied) peel
1 egg, beaten

Blend the yeast with a little of the warm water and 5 ml/1 tsp of the honey and leave in a warm place for 20 minutes until frothy. Mix the remaining honey and the malt extract into the remaining warm water. Toast the sunflower and sesame seeds and the wheatgerm in a dry pan, shaking until golden brown. Place in a bowl with the flour and salt and rub in the butter or margarine. Stir in the sultanas and mixed peel and make a well in the centre. Add the yeast mixture, the water mixture and the egg and knead to a smooth dough. Place in an oiled bowl, cover with oiled clingfilm (plastic wrap) and leave in a warm place for 1 hour until doubled in size.

Knead lightly, then shape into three loaves and place on a greased baking (cookie) sheet or in greased baking tins (pans). Cover with oiled clingfilm and leave in a warm place for 20 minutes. Bake in a preheated oven at 230°C/450°F/gas mark 8 for 40 minutes until golden brown and hollow-sounding when tapped on the base.

Pumpkin Loaf

Makes two 450 g/1 lb loaves

350 g/12 oz/1½ cups caster (superfine)
sugar
120 ml/4 fl oz/½ cup oil
2.5 ml/½ tsp grated nutmeg
5 ml/1 tsp ground cinnamon
5 ml/1 tsp salt
2 eggs, beaten
225 g/8 oz/1 cup cooked, mashed
pumpkin
60 ml/4 tbsp water
2.5 ml/½ tsp bicarbonate of soda
(baking soda)
1.5 ml/¼ tsp baking powder
175 g/6 oz/1½ cups plain
(all-purpose) flour

Mix together the sugar, oil, nutmeg, cinnamon, salt and eggs and beat well. Stir in the remaining ingredients and mix to a smooth batter. Pour into two greased 450 g/1 lb loaf tins (pans) and bake in a preheated oven at 180°C/350°F/ gas mark 4 for 1 hour until a skewer inserted in the centre comes out clean.

Raisin Bread

Makes two 450 g/1 lb loaves

15 ml/1 tbsp dried yeast
120 ml/4 fl oz/½ cup warm water
250 ml/8 fl oz/1 cup warm milk
60 ml/4 tbsp oil
50 g/2 oz/¼ cup sugar
1 egg, beaten
10 ml/2 tsp ground cinnamon
5 ml/1 tsp salt
225 g/8 oz/1⅓ cups raisins, soaked in
cold water overnight
550 g/1¼ lb/5 cups strong plain
(bread) flour

Dissolve the yeast in the warm water and leave until frothy. Mix together the milk, oil, sugar, egg, cinnamon and salt. Drain the raisins and stir them into the mixture. Stir in the yeast mixture. Gradually work in the flour and mix to a stiff dough. Place in a greased bowl and cover with oiled clingfilm (plastic wrap). Leave in a warm place for about 1 hour to rise until doubled in size.

Knead again and shape into two greased 450 g/1 lb loaf tins (pans). Cover with oiled clingfilm and leave in a warm place again until the dough rises above the top of the tins. Bake in a preheated oven at 150°C/300°F/gas mark 2 for 1 hour until golden.

Raisin Soak

Makes two 450 g/l lb loaves

450 g/1 lb/4 cups plain (all-purpose) flour
2.5 ml/½ tsp salt
5 ml/1 tsp ground mixed (apple-pie) spice
225 g/8 oz/1⅓ cups raisins, chopped
10 ml/2 tsp bicarbonate of soda (baking soda)
100 g/4 oz/½ cup butter or margarine, melted
225 g/8 oz/1 cup caster (superfine) sugar
450 ml/¾ pt/2 cups milk
15 ml/1 tbsp lemon juice
30 ml/2 tbsp apricot jam (conserve), sieved (strained)

Mix together the flour, salt, mixed spice and raisins. Stir the bicarbonate of soda into the melted butter until blended, then stir all the ingredients together until well mixed. Cover and leave to stand overnight.

Spoon the mixture into two greased and lined 450 g/1 lb loaf tins (pans) and bake in a preheated oven at 180°C/350°F/gas mark 4 for 1 hour until a skewer inserted in the centre comes out clean.

Rhubarb and Date Bread

Makes one 900 g/2 lb loaf

225 g/8 oz rhubarb, chopped
50 g/2 oz/¼ cup butter or margarine
225 g/8 oz/2 cups plain (all-purpose) flour
15 ml/1 tbsp baking powder
175 g/6 oz/1 cup dates, stoned (pitted) and finely chopped
1 egg, beaten
60 ml/4 tbsp milk

Wash the rhubarb and cook gently in just the water clinging to the pieces until you have a purée. Rub the butter or margarine into the flour and baking powder until the mixture resembles breadcrumbs. Stir in the rhubarb, dates, egg and milk and blend together well. Spoon into a greased and lined 900 g/2 lb loaf tin (pan) and bake in a preheated oven at 190°C/375°F/gas mark 5 for 1 hour until firm to the touch.

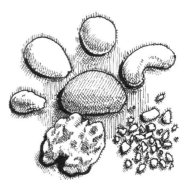

371

Rice Bread

Makes one 900 g/2 lb loaf

75 g/3 oz/⅓ cup arborio or other
medium-grain rice
500 ml/17 fl oz/2½ cups lukewarm
water
15 g/½ oz fresh yeast or 20 ml/
4 tsp dried yeast
30 ml/2 tbsp warm water
550 g/1¼ lb/6 cups strong plain
(bread) flour
15 ml/1 tbsp salt

Put the rice and half the lukewarm
water in a pan, bring to the boil, cover,
and simmer very gently for about 25
minutes until the rice has absorbed all the
liquid and bubble holes appear on the
surface.

Meanwhile, mix the yeast with the
warm water. When the rice is cooked, stir
in the flour, salt, yeast mixture and the
remaining lukewarm water and mix to a
wet dough. Cover with oiled clingfilm
(plastic wrap) and leave in a warm place
for about 1 hour until doubled in size.

Knead the dough on a floured surface,
then shape into a greased 900 g/2 lb loaf
tin (pan). Cover with oiled clingfilm and
leave in a warm place until the dough rises
above the top of the tin. Bake in a
preheated oven at 230°C/450°F/gas mark
8 for 15 minutes, then reduce the oven
temperature to 200°C/400°F/gas mark 6
and bake for a further 15 minutes. Turn
out of the tin and return to the oven for a
further 15 minutes until crisp and brown.

Rice and Nut Tea Bread

Makes two 900 g/2 lb loaves

100 g/4 oz/½ cup long-grain rice
300 ml/½ pt/1¼ cups orange juice
400 g/14 oz/1¾ cups caster (superfine)
sugar
2 eggs, beaten
50 g/2 oz/¼ cup butter or margarine,
melted
Grated rind and juice of 1 orange
225 g/8 oz/2 cups plain
(all-purpose) flour
175 g/6 oz/1½ cups wholemeal
(wholewheat) flour
10 ml/2 tsp baking powder
5 ml/1 tsp bicarbonate of soda
(baking soda)
5 ml/1 tsp salt
50 g/2 oz/½ cup walnuts, chopped
50 g/2 oz/⅓ cup sultanas
(golden raisins)
50 g/2 oz/⅓ cup icing (confectioners')
sugar, sifted

Cook the rice in plenty of boiling salted
water for about 15 minutes until
tender, then drain, rinse in cold water and
drain again. Mix together the orange
juice, sugar, eggs, melted butter or
margarine and all but 2.5 ml/½ tsp of the
orange rind – reserve the rest and the
juice for the icing (frosting). Mix together
the flours, baking powder, bicarbonate of
soda and salt and fold in to the sugar
mixture. Fold in the rice, nuts and
sultanas. Spoon the mixture into two
greased 900 g/2 lb loaf tins (pans) and
bake in a preheated oven at 180°C/350°F/
gas mark 4 for 1 hour until a skewer
inserted in the centre comes out clean.
Leave to cool in the tins for 10 minutes,
then turn out on to a wire rack to finish
cooling.

Blend the icing sugar with the reserved
orange rind and enough of the juice to
make a smooth, thick paste. Drizzle over
the loaves and leave to set. Serve sliced
and buttered.

Curly Sugar Rolls

Makes about 10

50 g/2 oz fresh yeast or 75 ml/
5 tbsp dried yeast
75 g/3 oz/⅓ cup soft brown sugar
300 ml/½ pt/1¼ cups warm water
175 g/6 oz/1 cup currants
25 g/1 oz/3 tbsp stoned (pitted) dates,
chopped
45 ml/3 tbsp orange juice
450 g/1 lb/4 cups wholemeal
(wholewheat) flour
2.5 ml/½ tsp salt
25 g/1 oz/¼ cup milk powder
(non-fat dry milk)
15 ml/1 tbsp ground mixed
(apple-pie) spice
75 g/3 oz/⅓ cup butter or margarine
15 ml/1 tbsp grated orange rind
1 egg
For the filling:
30 ml/2 tbsp oil
75 g/3 oz/⅓ cup demerara sugar
For the glaze:
15 ml/1 tbsp clear honey
30 ml/2 tbsp chopped walnuts

Blend the yeast with a little of the soft brown sugar and a little of the warm water and leave in a warm place for 20 minutes until frothy. Soak the currants and dates in the orange juice. Mix together the flour, salt, milk powder and mixed spice. Rub in the butter or margarine, then stir in the orange rind and make a well in the centre. Add the yeast mixture, the remaining warm water and the egg and mix to a smooth dough. Place in an oiled bowl, cover with oiled clingfilm (plastic wrap) and leave in a warm place for 1 hour until doubled in size.

Roll out the dough on a lightly floured surface to a large rectangle. Brush with oil and sprinkle with demerara sugar. Roll up like a Swiss (jelly) roll and cut into about ten 2.5 cm/1 in slices. Arrange on a greased baking (cookie) sheet about 1 cm/½ in apart, Cover with oiled clingfilm and leave in a warm place for 40 minutes. Bake in a preheated oven at 230°C/450°F/gas mark 8 for 15 minutes until well risen. Brush with the honey, sprinkle with walnuts and leave to cool.

Selkirk Bannock

Makes one 450 g/1 lb loaf

For the dough:
225 g/8 oz/2 cups plain
(all-purpose) flour
A pinch of salt
50 g/2 oz/¼ cup lard (shortening)
150 ml/¼ pt/⅔ cup milk
15 g/½ oz fresh yeast or 20 ml/
4 tsp dried yeast
50 g/2 oz/¼ cup caster (superfine)
sugar
100 g/4 oz/⅔ cup sultanas
(golden raisins)
For the glaze:
25 g/1 oz/2 tbsp caster (superfine)
sugar
30 ml/2 tbsp water

To make the dough, mix the flour and salt. Melt the lard, add the milk and bring to blood heat. Pour on to the yeast and stir in 5 ml/1 tsp of the sugar. Leave for about 20 minutes until frothy. Make a well in the centre of the flour and pour in the yeast mixture. Gradually work in the flour and knead for 5 minutes. Cover and place in a warm place for 1 hour to rise. Turn out on to a floured work surface and work in the sultanas and the remaining sugar. Shape into a large round and place on a greased baking (cookie) sheet. Cover with oiled clingfilm (plastic wrap) and leave in a warm place until doubled in size. Bake in a preheated oven at 220°C/425°F/gas mark 7 for 15 minutes. Reduce the oven temperature to 190°C/375°F/gas mark 5 and bake for a further 25 minutes. Remove from the oven. Dissolve the sugar for the glaze in the water and brush over the hot bannock.

Sultana and Carob Bread

Makes one 900 g/2 lb loaf

150 g/5 oz/1¼ cups wholemeal
  (wholewheat) flour
15 ml/1 tbsp baking powder
25 g/1 oz/¼ cup carob powder
50 g/2 oz/½ cup oatmeal
50 g/2 oz/¼ cup butter or margarine,
  softened
175 g/6 oz/1 cup sultanas
  (golden raisins)
2 eggs, beaten
150 ml/¼ pt/⅔ cup milk
60 ml/4 tbsp oil

Mix together the dry ingredients. Rub in the butter or margarine, then stir in the sultanas. Beat together the eggs, milk and oil, then blend into the flour mixture to make a soft dough. Shape into a greased 900 g/2 lb loaf tin (pan) and bake in a preheated oven at 180°C/350°F/gas mark 4 for 1 hour until firm to the touch.

Sultana and Orange Loaf

Makes two 450 g/1 lb loaves

For the dough:
450 g/1 lb/4 cups wholemeal
  (wholewheat) flour
20 ml/4 tsp baking powder
75 g/3 oz/⅓ cup soft brown sugar
5 ml/1 tsp salt
2.5 ml/½ tsp ground mace
75 g/3 oz/⅓ cup vegetable fat
  (shortening)
3 egg whites
300 ml/½ pt/1¼ cups milk
For the filling:
175 g/6 oz/1½ cups wholemeal
  (wholewheat) cake crumbs
50 g/2 oz/½ cup ground almonds
50 g/2 oz/¼ cup soft brown sugar
100 g/4 oz/⅔ cup sultanas
  (golden raisins)

30 ml/2 tbsp orange juice
1 egg, lightly beaten
For the glaze:
15 ml/1 tbsp honey

To make the dough, mix together the dry ingredients and rub in the fat. Mix together the egg whites and milk and blend into the mixture until you have a soft, pliable dough. Combine the filling ingredients, using just enough of the egg to make a spreading consistency. Roll out the dough on a lightly floured surface to a 20 × 30 cm/8 × 10 in rectangle. Spread the filling over all but the top 2.5 cm/1 in along the long edge. Roll up from the opposite edge, like a Swiss (jelly) roll, and moisten the plain strip of dough to seal. Moisten each end and shape the roll into a circle, sealing the ends together. With sharp scissors, make little cuts around the top for decoration. Place on a greased baking (cookie) sheet and brush with the remaining egg. Leave to rest for 15 minutes.

Bake in a preheated oven at 230°C/450°F/gas mark 8 for 25 minutes until golden brown. Brush with the honey and leave to cool.

Sultana and Sherry Bread

Makes one 900 g/2 lb loaf

225 g/8 oz/1 cup unsalted (sweet)
  butter or margarine, softened
225 g/8 oz/1 cup soft brown sugar
4 eggs
45 ml/3 tbsp sweet sherry
5 ml/1 tsp vanilla essence (extract)
200 g/7 oz/1¾ cups plain
  (all-purpose) flour
A pinch of salt
75 g/3 oz/½ cup sultanas (golden
  raisins)
50 g/2 oz/⅓ cup stoned (pitted) dates,
  chopped
50 g/2 oz/⅓ cup dried figs, diced
50 g/2 oz/½ cup chopped mixed
  (candied) peel

374

Cream together the butter or margarine and sugar until light and fluffy. Gradually add the eggs, then the sherry and vanilla essence. Mix the flour and salt with the fruit, then fold into the mixture and mix well. Spoon into a greased and floured 900 g/2 lb loaf tin (pan) and bake in a preheated oven at 180°C/350°F/gas mark 4 for 1 hour. Leave to cool in the tin for 10 minutes, then turn out on to a wire rack to finish cooling.

Cottage Tea Bread

Makes two 450 g/1 lb loaves

For the dough:
25 g/1 oz fresh yeast or 40 ml/
2½ tbsp dried yeast
15 ml/1 tbsp soft brown sugar
300 ml/½ pt/1¼ cups warm water
15 ml/1 tbsp butter or margarine
450 g/1 lb/4 cups wholemeal
(wholewheat) flour
15 ml/1 tbsp milk powder
(non-fat dry milk)
5 ml/1 tsp ground mixed
(apple-pie) spice
2.5 ml/½ tsp salt
1 egg
175 g/6 oz/1 cup currants
100 g/4 oz/⅔ cup sultanas
(golden raisins)
50 g/2 oz/⅓ cup raisins
50 g/2 oz/⅓ cup chopped mixed
(candied) peel
For the glaze:
15 ml/1 tbsp lemon juice
15 ml/1 tbsp water
A pinch of ground mixed (apple-pie)
spice

To make the dough, blend the yeast with the sugar with a little of the warm water and leave in a warm place for 10 minutes until frothy. Rub the butter or margarine into the flour, then stir in the milk powder, mixed spice and salt and make a well in the centre. Stir in the egg,

the yeast mixture and the remaining warm water and mix to a dough. Knead until smooth and elastic. Work in the currants, sultanas, raisins and mixed peel. Place in an oiled bowl, cover with oiled clingfilm (plastic wrap) and leave in warm place for 45 minutes. Shape into two greased 450 g/1 lb loaf tins (pans). Cover with oiled clingfilm and leave in a warm place for 15 minutes. Bake in a preheated oven at 220°C/425°F/gas mark 7 for 30 minutes until golden. Remove from the tin. Mix together the glaze ingredients and brush over the hot loaves, then leave to cool.

Tea Cakes

Makes 6

15 g/½ oz fresh yeast or 20 ml/
4 tsp dried yeast
300 ml/½ pt/1¼ cups warm milk
25 g/1 oz/2 tbsp caster (superfine)
sugar
25 g/1 oz/2 tbsp butter or margarine
450 g/1 lb/4 cups plain (all-purpose)
flour
5 ml/1 tsp salt
50 g/2 oz/⅓ cup sultanas
(golden raisins)

Blend the yeast with the warm milk and a little of the sugar and leave in a warm place until frothy. Rub the butter or margarine into the flour and salt, then stir in the remaining sugar and the raisins. Stir in the yeast mixture and mix to a soft dough. Turn out on to a lightly floured surface and knead until smooth. Place in an oiled bowl, cover with oiled clingfilm (plastic wrap) and leave in a warm place until doubled in size. Knead the dough again, then divide into six pieces and roll each one into a ball. Flatten slightly on a greased baking (cookie) sheet, Cover with oiled clingfilm and leave in a warm place again until doubled in size. Bake in a preheated oven at 200°C/400°F/gas mark 6 for 20 minutes.

Walnut Loaf

Makes one 900 g/2 lb loaf

*350 g/12 oz/3 cups plain
(all-purpose) flour*
15 ml/1 tbsp baking powder
225 g/8 oz/1 cup soft brown sugar
5 ml/1 tsp salt
1 egg, lightly beaten
*50 g/2 oz/¼ cup lard (shortening),
melted*
375 ml/13 fl oz/1½ cups milk
5 ml/1 tsp vanilla essence (extract)
175 g/6 oz/1½ cups walnuts, chopped

Mix together the flour, baking powder, sugar and salt and make a well in the centre. Stir in the egg, lard, milk and vanilla essence, then stir in the walnuts. Spoon into a greased 900 g/2 lb loaf tin (pan) and bake in a preheated oven at 180°C/350°F/gas mark 4 for about 1¼ hours until well risen and golden brown.

Walnut and Sugar Layer Loaf

Makes one 900 g/2 lb loaf

For the batter:
*350 g/12 oz/3 cups plain
(all-purpose) flour*
15 ml/1 tbsp baking powder
225 g/8 oz/1 cup soft brown sugar
5 ml/1 tsp salt
1 egg, lightly beaten
*50 g/2 oz/¼ cup lard (shortening),
melted*
375 ml/13 fl oz/1½ cups milk
5 ml/1 tsp vanilla essence (extract)
175 g/6 oz/1½ cups walnuts, chopped
For the filling:
15 ml/1 tbsp plain (all-purpose) flour
50 g/2 oz/¼ cup soft brown sugar
5 ml/1 tsp ground cinnamon
15 ml/1 tbsp butter, melted

To make the batter, mix together the flour, baking powder, sugar and salt and make a well in the centre. Stir in the egg, lard, milk and vanilla essence, then stir in the walnuts. Spoon half the mixture into a greased 900 g/2 lb loaf tin (pan). Mix together the filling ingredients and spoon over the batter. Spoon over the remaining batter and bake in a preheated oven at 180°C/350°F/gas mark 4 for about 1¼ hours until well risen and golden brown.

Walnut and Orange Loaf

Makes one 900 g/2 lb loaf

*350 g/12 oz/3 cups plain
(all-purpose) flour*
15 ml/1 tbsp baking powder
225 g/8 oz/1 cup soft brown sugar
5 ml/1 tsp salt
1 egg, lightly beaten
5 ml/1 tsp grated orange rind
*50 g/2 oz/¼ cup lard (shortening),
melted*
375 ml/13 fl oz/1½ cups milk
5 ml/1 tsp vanilla essence (extract)
175 g/6 oz/1½ cups walnuts, chopped
*50 g/2 oz/⅓ cup chopped mixed
(candied) peel*

Mix together the flour, baking powder, sugar and salt and make a well in the centre. Stir in the egg, orange rind, lard, milk and vanilla essence, then stir in the walnuts and mixed peel. Spoon into a greased 900 g/2 lb loaf tin (pan) and bake in a preheated oven at 180°C/350°F/gas mark 4 for about 1¼ hours until well risen and golden brown.

Savoury Fancy Breads and Rolls

*T*his chapter includes a range of interesting breads – some made with yeast and others with baking powder as the raising agent – which use all sorts of interesting grains and ingredients from corn to nuts and mushrooms.

Asparagus Loaf

Makes one 900 g/2 lb loaf

50 g/2 oz/¼ cup butter or margarine
2 shallots, finely grated
100 g/4 oz wholemeal bread, diced
10 ml/2 tsp chopped fresh parsley
1.5 ml/¼ tsp salt
450 g/1 lb asparagus
2 eggs, lightly beaten
450 ml/¾ pt/2 cups hot milk

Melt the butter or margarine and fry (sauté) the shallots, bread, parsley and salt until lightly browned. Remove from the heat and place in a bowl. Trim the tough ends off the asparagus and cut the stems into 2.5 cm/1 in lengths and add to the bowl. Blend together the eggs and milk, then mix into the remaining ingredients. Spoon into a greased 900 g/2 lb loaf tin (pan) and press down lightly. Bake in a preheated oven at 190°C/375°F/gas mark 5 for 30 minutes until firm to the touch.

Savoury Beef Loaf

Makes one 900 g/2 lb loaf

450 g/1 lb/4 cups self-raising
(self-rising) flour
1 packet oxtail soup powder
450 ml/¾ pt/2 cups buttermilk
50 g/2 oz/½ cup Cheddar cheese,
grated
A pinch of cayenne

Mix together the flour and soup powder and make a well in the centre. Stir in the buttermilk and mix to a dough. Shape into a greased 900 g/2 lb loaf tin (pan) and sprinkle with cheese and cayenne. Bake in a preheated oven at 180°C/350°F/gas mark 4 for 1 hour until golden and hollow-sounding when tapped on the base.

Beer and Nut Bread

Makes two 450 g/1 lb loaves

15 g/½ oz dried yeast
30 ml/2 tbsp caster (superfine) sugar
375 ml/13 fl oz/1½ cups warm lager
450 g/1 lb/4 cups plain (all-purpose)
  flour
50 g/2 oz/½ cup rye flour
5 ml/1 tsp salt
120 ml/4 fl oz/½ cup walnut oil
1 onion, finely chopped
100 g/4 oz/1 cup chopped mixed nuts
1 egg, lightly beaten
30 ml/2 tbsp water

Blend the yeast with 5 ml/1 tsp of the sugar and a little of the warm beer and leave in a warm lager for 20 minutes until frothy. Mix the remaining sugar with the flours and salt and make a well in the centre. Stir in the yeast mixture, the remaining warm lager and the oil and mix to a fairly firm dough. Knead until smooth and no longer sticky. Place in an oiled bowl, cover with clingfilm (plastic wrap) and leave in a warm place for 1 hour until doubled in size.

Knead again, then mix in the onion and nuts. Shape into two greased 450 g/1 lb loaf tins (pans), cover and leave in a warm place to rise for 40 minutes until the dough rises above the top of the tins. Beat together the egg and water and brush generously over the top of the loaves. Bake in a preheated oven at 190°C/375°F/gas mark 5 for 45 minutes until golden brown and hollow-sounding when tapped on the base.

Carrot Bread

Makes two 450 g/1 lb loaves

25 g/1 oz dried yeast
5 ml/1 tsp caster (superfine) sugar
45 ml/3 tbsp warm water
500 ml/17 fl oz/2¼ cups hot water
60 ml/4 tbsp black treacle (molasses)
60 ml/4 tbsp oil
5 ml/1 tsp salt
450 g/1 lb carrots, finely grated
675 g/1½ lb/6 cups strong plain
  (bread) flour

Blend the yeast with the sugar and warm water and leave to stand for about 20 minutes until frothy. Mix the hot water with the treacle, oil, salt and carrots, then stir in the yeast mixture and flour and mix to a firm dough. Knead until elastic and no longer sticky. Place in an oiled bowl, cover with clingfilm (plastic wrap) and leave in a warm place for about 1 hour until doubled in size.

Knead the dough again and shape into two greased 450 g/1 lb loaf tins (pans). Cover and leave to rise again for about 30 minutes until the dough rises just above the tops of the tins. Bake in a preheated oven at 220°C/425°F/gas mark 7 for 10 minutes. Reduce the oven temperature to 180°C/350°F/gas mark 4 and bake for a further 30 minutes until golden brown and hollow-sounding when tapped on the base.

Carrot and Coconut Bread

Makes one 900 g/2 lb loaf

3 eggs
175 ml/6 fl oz/³⁄₄ cup oil
5 ml/1 tsp vanilla essence (extract)
350 g/12 oz carrots, coarsely grated
150 g/5 oz/1¼ cups desiccated
  (shredded) coconut
100 g/4 oz/1 cup walnuts, chopped
120 ml/4 fl oz/½ cup clear honey
175 g/6 oz/1 cup raisins
175 g/6 oz/1½ cups wholemeal
  (wholewheat) flour
75 g/3 oz/³⁄₄ cup fine oatmeal
5 ml/1 tsp baking powder
2.5 ml/½ tsp bicarbonate of soda
  (baking soda)
5 ml/1 tsp ground cinnamon
1.5 ml/¼ tsp salt

Beat the eggs, then stir in the oil, vanilla essence, carrots, coconut, walnuts, honey and raisins. Mix the remaining ingredients together and stir them into the carrot mixture until just blended. Spoon into a greased 900 g/2 lb loaf tin (pan) and bake in a preheated oven at 180°C/350°F/gas mark 4 for 1 hour until a skewer inserted in the centre comes out clean. Leave to cool in the tin for 10 minutes before turning out on to a wire rack to finish cooling.

Celeriac Bread

Makes one 900 g/2 lb loaf

350 g/12 oz celeriac (celery root),
  chopped
30 ml/2 tbsp chopped fresh parsley
75 g/3 oz/³⁄₄ cup hazelnuts, chopped
1 onion, sliced
½ green (bell) pepper, sliced
2 eggs, beaten
30 ml/2 tbsp oil
5 ml/1 tsp salt
350 ml/12 fl oz/1½ cups milk
75 g/3 oz/1½ cups fresh breadcrumbs

Process the celeriac, parsley, nuts, onion and pepper until finely chopped and well blended. Stir in the remaining ingredients and press lightly into a greased and lined 900 g/2 lb loaf tin (pan). Bake in a preheated oven at 180°C/350°F/gas mark 4 for 1½ hours until firm to the touch.

Cheese and Almond Ring

Makes one 23 cm/9 in ring

For the dough:
15 g/½ oz fresh yeast
or 20 ml/4 tsp dried yeast
10 ml/2 tsp sugar
90 ml/6 tbsp warm milk
225 g/8 oz/2 cups strong plain (bread)
flour
A pinch of salt
1 egg, beaten
10 ml/2 tsp oil
50 g/2 oz/¼ cup butter or margarine,
diced
For the filling:
15 ml/1 tbsp oil
2 onions, finely chopped
1 egg, beaten
100 g/4 oz/1 cup ground almonds
75 g/3 oz/¾ cup Cheddar cheese,
grated
Salt and freshly ground black pepper

To make the dough, blend the yeast with the sugar and milk and leave in a warm place for about 20 minutes until frothy. Place the flour and salt in a bowl and make a well in the centre. Add the yeast mixture, the egg and oil and work together to a firm dough. Knead well until elastic and no longer sticky. Place in an oiled bowl, cover with clingfilm (plastic wrap) and leave to rise for about 1 hour until doubled in size.

To make the filling, heat the oil and fry (sauté) the onions until soft, then remove from the heat and leave to cool slightly. Reserve a little egg for glazing, then mix in the remainder with all the remaining filling ingredients and leave to finish cooling.

Roll out the dough on a lightly floured surface to a 30 × 10 cm/12 × 4 in rectangle. Dot half the butter over two-thirds of the dough. Fold the plain third of the dough to the centre, covering the butter, then fold the remaining third over the top. Press the side edges together to seal. Turn the dough a quarter turn, roll out and repeat once more with the remaining butter. Wrap in oiled clingfilm and chill for 15 minutes. Roll out and fold once more.

Roll out the dough to a 30 × 23 cm/12 × 9 in rectangle and spread with the filling, almost to the edges. Roll up from the long side like a Swiss (jelly) roll. Shape into a ring, moisten the ends and press together. Make cuts around the dough on the outside edge. Place on a greased baking (cookie) sheet and leave to rise for 20 minutes. Brush with the reserved egg. Bake in a preheated oven at 200°C/400°F/gas mark 6 for 35 minutes until golden.

Cheese and Chive Loaf

Makes one 900 g/2 lb loaf

25 g/1 oz dried yeast
15 ml/1 tbsp caster (superfine) sugar
120 ml/4 fl oz/½ cup warm milk
450 g/1 lb/2 cups Ricotta or cottage
cheese
75 g/3 oz/⅓ cup butter or margarine,
softened
2 eggs
450 g/1 lb/4 cups plain (all-purpose)
flour
30 ml/2 tbsp snipped fresh chives
Salt and freshly ground black pepper

Blend the yeast with the sugar and a little of the warm milk and leave in a warm place for 20 minutes until frothy. Beat the cheese with the butter or margarine and eggs until slightly softened, then beat in the yeast mixture and the remaining warm milk. Mix in the flour and chives, season generously with salt and pepper and mix to a soft dough. Place in an oiled bowl, cover with clingfilm (plastic wrap) and leave in a warm place for 1 hour until doubled in size.

Knead again and shape into a 900 g/2 lb loaf tin (pan). Cover and leave in a warm place for 40 minutes until doubled in size.

Bake in a preheated oven at 180°C/ 350°F/gas mark 4 for 50 minutes until golden brown. Leave to cool in the tin for 10 minutes before turning out on to a wire rack to finish cooling.

Cheese, Chive and Garlic Bread

Makes three 450 g/1 lb loaves

25 g/1 oz fresh yeast or 40 ml/ 2½ tbsp dried yeast
5 ml/1 tsp caster (superfine) sugar
600 ml/1 pt/2½ cups water
450 g/1 lb/4 cups wholemeal (wholewheat) flour
350 g/12 oz/3 cups strong plain (bread) flour
30 ml/2 tbsp milk powder (non-fat dry milk)
10 ml/2 tsp salt
225 g/8 oz/2 cups Cheddar cheese, grated
2 garlic cloves, crushed
30 ml/2 tbsp snipped fresh chives
5 ml/1 tsp made mustard
2.5 ml/½ tsp cayenne
15 ml/1 tbsp rolled oats

Blend the yeast with the sugar and a little of the warm water and leave in a warm place for about 15 minutes until frothy. Mix together the flours, milk powder and salt and make a well in the centre. Stir in the yeast mixture and the remaining warm water and mix to a dough. Knead well until smooth and elastic. Place in an oiled bowl and cover with clingfilm (plastic wrap). Leave in a warm place for 45 minutes until doubled in size.

Add the cheese, garlic, chives, mustard and cayenne and knead into the dough. Shape into three loaves and place on a greased baking (cookie) sheet. Cover and leave to rise for 15 minutes. Sprinkle with the oats and bake in a preheated oven at

230°C/450°F/gas mark 8 for 25 minutes until golden on top and hollow-sounding when tapped on the base.

Cheese and Curried Fruit Bread

Makes three 450 g/1 lb loaves

25 g/1 oz fresh yeast or 40 ml/ 2½ tbsp dried yeast
600 ml/1 pt/2½ cups water
450 g/1 lb/4 cups wholemeal (wholewheat) flour
350 g/12 oz/3 cups strong plain (bread) flour
30 ml/2 tbsp milk powder (non-fat dry milk)
10 ml/2 tsp salt
225 g/8 oz/2 cups Cheddar cheese, grated
100 g/4 oz/⅔ cup dried mixed fruit (fruit cake mix)
5 ml/1 tsp curry powder
2.5 ml/½ tsp ground ginger
15 ml/1 tbsp rolled oats

Blend the yeast with a little of the warm water and leave in a warm place for about 15 minutes until frothy. Mix together the flours, milk powder and salt and make a well in the centre. Stir in the yeast mixture and the remaining warm water and mix to a dough. Knead well until smooth and elastic. Place in an oiled bowl and cover with clingfilm (plastic wrap). Leave in a warm place for 45 minutes until doubled in size.

Add the cheese, mixed fruit, curry powder and ginger to the dough and knead into the mixture. Shape into loaves and place on a greased baking (cookie) sheet. Cover and leave to rise for 15 minutes. Sprinkle with the oats and bake in a preheated oven at 230°C/450°F/ gas mark 8 for 25 minutes until golden on top and hollow-sounding when tapped on the base.

Cheese and Dill Bread

Makes one 900 g/2 lb loaf

For the loaf:
15 g/½ oz dried yeast
60 ml/4 tbsp warm water
225 g/8 oz/1 cup cottage cheese
30 ml/2 tbsp caster (superfine) sugar
15 g/½ oz/1 tbsp butter or margarine
15 ml/1 tbsp chopped onion
10 ml/2 tsp dill seed
5 ml/1 tsp salt
1.5 ml/¼ tsp bicarbonate of soda
   (baking soda)
1 egg
250 g/9 oz/2¼ cups plain
   (all-purpose) flour
For the glaze:
15 g/½ oz/1 tbsp butter or margarine,
   melted
Large pinch of salt

To make the loaf, dissolve the yeast in the water and leave until frothy. Mix into the cheese with the sugar, margarine, onion, dill, salt, bicarbonate of soda and egg. Gradually add the flour and mix to a stiff dough. Cover with clingfilm (plastic wrap) and leave to rise for about 1 hour until doubled in size.

Knead the dough and shape into a greased 900 g/2 lb loaf tin (pan). Cover and leave to rise for about 30 minutes until it comes just above the top of the tin. Bake in a preheated oven at 180°C/350°F/ gas 4 for 45 minutes until golden brown. Leave to cool slightly, then brush with the melted butter and sprinkle with salt.

Georgian Cheese Bread

Makes one 20 cm/8 in round loaf

For the dough:
15 g/½ oz fresh yeast or 20 ml/
   4 tsp dried yeast
5 ml/1 tsp caster (superfine) sugar
150 ml/¼ pt/⅔ cup warm milk
450 g/1 lb/4 cups plain (all-purpose)
   flour
5 ml/1 tsp salt
75 g/3 oz/⅓ cup butter or margarine,
   melted
For the filling:
675 g/1½ lb/6 cups crumbly white
   cheese, broken up
50 g/2 oz/¼ cup butter or margarine
1 egg
1 egg yolk
15 ml/1 tbsp chopped fresh parsley

To make the dough, blend the yeast with the sugar and a little of the warm milk and leave in a warm place for 20 minutes until frothy. Mix the flour and salt in a bowl and make a well in the centre. Blend in the yeast mixture, the remaining warm milk and the butter or margarine and mix to a smooth dough that comes away cleanly from the sides of the bowl. Knead on a lightly floured surface until smooth and elastic. Place in an oiled bowl, cover with oiled clingfilm (plastic wrap) and leave in a warm place for 1 hour until doubled in size.

Knead again, then return the dough to the bowl for a further 1 hour.

To make the filling, beat all the ingredients together until well blended. Chill until the dough is ready.

Roll out the dough to a 50 cm/20 in round and gently place over a greased 20 cm/8 in spring-form cake tin (pan) so that the edge hangs evenly over the sides. Spoon the filling into the centre. Carefully gather the dough into the centre and twist it together. Cover and leave in a warm place for 20 minutes until doubled in size.

Bake in a preheated oven at 200°C/ 400°F/gas mark 6 for 30 minutes, then reduce the oven temperature to 180°C/ 350°F/gas mark 5 and bake for a further 20 minutes until well risen and golden brown. Leave to cool in the tin for 30 minutes, then turn out on to a wire rack to finish cooling.

Harvest Cheese Bread

Makes three 450 g/1 lb loaves

25 g/1 oz fresh yeast or 40 ml/
2½ tbsp dried yeast
600 ml/1 pt/2½ cups warm water
450 g/1 lb/4 cups wholemeal
  (wholewheat) flour
350 g/12 oz/3 cups strong plain
  (bread) flour
30 ml/2 tbsp milk powder
  (non-fat dry milk)
10 ml/2 tsp salt
225 g/8 oz/2 cups Cheddar cheese,
  grated
5 ml/1 tsp made mustard
2.5 ml/½ tsp cayenne
15 ml/1 tbsp rolled oats

Blend the yeast with a little of the warm water and leave in a warm place for about 15 minutes until frothy. Mix together the flours, milk powder and salt and make a well in the centre. Stir in the yeast mixture and the remaining warm water and mix to a dough. Knead well until smooth and elastic. Place in an oiled bowl and cover with clingfilm (plastic wrap). Leave in a warm place for 45 minutes until doubled in size.

Add the cheese, mustard and cayenne to the dough and knead into the mixture. Shape into three loaves and place on a greased baking (cookie) sheet. Cover and leave to rise for 15 minutes. Sprinkle with the oats and bake in a preheated oven at 230°C/450°F/gas mark 8 for 25 minutes until golden on top and hollow-sounding when tapped on the base.

Cheese and Onion Bread

Makes three 450 g/1 lb loaves

25 g/1 oz fresh yeast or 40 ml/
2½ tbsp dried yeast
600 ml/1 pt/2½ cups warm water
450 g/1 lb/4 cups wholemeal
  (wholewheat) flour
350 g/12 oz/3 cups strong plain
  (bread) flour
30 ml/2 tbsp milk powder
  (non-fat dry milk)
10 ml/2 tsp salt
225 g/8 oz/2 cups Cheddar cheese,
  grated
100 g/4 oz onions, chopped
5 ml/1 tsp made mustard
2.5 ml/½ tsp cayenne
15 ml/1 tbsp rolled oats

Blend the yeast with a little of the warm water and leave in a warm place for about 15 minutes until frothy. Mix together the flours, milk powder and salt and make a well in the centre. Stir in the yeast mixture and the remaining warm water and mix to a dough. Knead well until smooth and elastic. Place in an oiled bowl and cover with clingfilm (plastic wrap). Leave in a warm place for 45 minutes until doubled in size.

Add the cheese, onions, mustard and cayenne to the dough and knead into the mixture. Shape into three loaves and place on a greased baking (cookie) sheet. Cover and leave to rise for 15 minutes. Sprinkle with the oats and bake in a preheated oven at 230°C/450°F/gas mark 8 for 25 minutes until golden on top and hollow-sounding when tapped on the base.

Cheese and Tofu Bread

Makes three 450 g/1 lb loaves

25 g/1 oz fresh yeast or 40 ml/
2½ tbsp dried yeast
600 ml/1 pt/2½ cups warm water
450 g/1 lb/4 cups wholemeal
(wholewheat) flour
350 g/12 oz/3 cups strong plain
(bread) flour
30 ml/2 tbsp milk powder
(non-fat dry milk)
10 ml/2 tsp salt
225 g/8 oz/2 cups Cheddar cheese,
grated
100 g/4 oz/½ cup firm tofu, shredded
5 ml/1 tsp made mustard
2.5 ml/½ tsp cayenne
15 ml/1 tbsp rolled oats

Blend the yeast with a little of the warm water and leave in a warm place for about 15 minutes until frothy. Mix together the flours, milk powder and salt and make a well in the centre. Stir in the yeast mixture and the remaining warm water and mix to a dough. Knead well until smooth and elastic. Place in an oiled bowl and cover with clingfilm (plastic wrap). Leave in a warm place for 45 minutes until doubled in size.

Add the cheese, tofu, mustard and cayenne to the dough and knead into the mixture. Shape into three loaves and place on a greased baking (cookie) sheet. Cover and leave to rise for 15 minutes. Sprinkle with the oats and bake in a preheated oven at 230°C/450°F/gas mark 8 for 25 minutes until golden on top and hollow-sounding when tapped on the base.

Corn Bread

Makes one 23 cm/9 in loaf

75 g/3 oz/¾ cup plain (all-purpose)
flour
175 g/6 oz/1½ cups cornmeal
20 ml/4 tsp baking powder
5 ml/1 tsp salt
2 eggs, beaten
350 ml/12 fl oz/1½ cups milk
60 ml/4 tbsp oil

Blend together the dry ingredients, then stir in the eggs, milk and oil and mix until smooth. Spoon into a greased 23 cm/9 in cake tin (pan) and bake in a preheated oven at 200°C/400°F/gas mark 6 for about 30 minutes until well risen and golden brown.

Buttermilk Corn Bread

Makes one 20 cm/8 in square loaf

225 g/8 oz/2 cups cornmeal
75 g/3 oz/¾ cup plain (all-purpose)
flour
5 ml/1 tsp bicarbonate of soda
(baking soda)
10 ml/2 tsp baking powder
A pinch of salt
30 ml/2 tbsp caster (superfine) sugar
450 ml/15 fl oz/2 cups buttermilk
60 ml/4 tbsp milk
1 egg, lightly beaten
60 ml/4 tbsp oil
225 g/8 oz/1 small can sweetcorn
(corn), drained

Mix together the dry ingredients. Mix together the buttermilk, milk, egg and oil and pour into the dry ingredients, mixing to a soft batter. Stir in the sweetcorn. Pour into a greased 20 cm/8 in square baking tin (pan) and bake in a preheated oven at 230°C/450°F/gas 8 for 25 minutes until golden brown.

Quick Soured Cream Corn Bread

Makes one 450 g/1 lb loaf

100 g/4 oz/1 cup plain (all-purpose)
  flour
100 g/4 oz/1 cup cornmeal
15 ml/1 tbsp baking powder
2.5 ml/½ tsp salt
2 eggs
375 ml/13 fl oz/1½ cups soured (dairy
  sour) cream

Mix together the flour, cornmeal, baking powder and salt. Lightly beat the eggs with the soured cream, then stir into the dry ingredients and mix to a soft dough. Spoon into a greased 450 g/1 lb loaf tin (pan) and bake in a preheated oven at 200°C/400°F/gas mark 6 for 20 minutes until well risen and golden brown.

Chilli-corn Bread

Makes one 900 g/2 lb loaf

175 g/6 oz/1½ cups cornmeal
50 g/2 oz/½ cup plain (all-purpose)
  flour
15 ml/1 tbsp caster (superfine) sugar
5 ml/1 tsp baking powder
5 ml/1 tsp bicarbonate of soda
  (baking soda)
1 egg, lightly beaten
250 ml/8 fl oz/1 cup milk
100 g/4 oz/1 small can canned
  chopped green chillies
100 g/4 oz/1 cup Cheddar cheese,
  grated

Mix together the cornmeal, flour, sugar, baking powder and bicarbonate of soda. Beat together the egg and milk, then stir into the dry ingredients with the chillies and cheese. Spoon into a greased 900 g/2 lb loaf tin (pan) and bake in a preheated oven at 180°C/350°F/gas mark 4 for 30 minutes until golden brown.

Corn Muffins

Makes 12

15 ml/1 tbsp oil
1 onion, finely chopped
75 g/3 oz/¾ cup wholemeal
  (wholewheat) flour
75 g/3 oz/¾ cup cornmeal
5 ml/1 tsp baking powder
A pinch of salt
1 egg, beaten
15 ml/1 tbsp clear honey
150 ml/¼ pt/⅔ cup milk
50 g/2 oz/½ cup Cheddar cheese,
  grated

Heat the oil and fry (sauté) the onion until soft. Place the flour, cornmeal, baking powder and salt in a bowl and make a well in the centre. Stir in the onions and oil, then the egg, honey and milk and beat well to form a soft mixture. Stir in the cheese. Spoon into greased bun tins (muffin pans) and bake in a preheated oven at 200°C/400°F/gas mark 6 for 10 minutes until golden brown and firm to the touch.

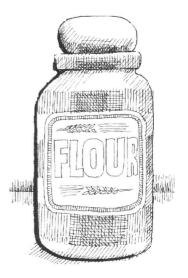

Quick Cheese Croissants

Makes 16

50 g/2 oz/¼ cup butter or margarine
450 g/1 lb/4 cups plain (all-purpose)
    flour
15 ml/1 tbsp baking powder
A pinch of salt
100 g/4 oz/1 cup Cheddar cheese,
    grated
150 ml/¼ pt/⅔ cup milk
1 egg yolk

Rub the butter or margarine into the flour, baking powder and salt until the mixture resembles breadcrumbs. Stir in the cheese. Gradually add enough of the milk to make a firm dough. Divide the dough in half and roll out each half on a lightly floured surface to a 20 cm/8 in round, then cut through the centre into eight portions. Roll up each portion from the outside to the centre, shape into a crescent and place on a greased baking (cookie) sheet. Brush with egg yolk and bake in a preheated oven at 200°C/400°F/gas mark 4 for 15 minutes until golden brown.

Dill Bread

Makes one 900 g/2 lb loaf

15 g/½ oz dried yeast
120 ml/4 fl oz/½ cup warm water
225 g/8 oz/1 cup cottage cheese,
    warmed
15 ml/1 tbsp finely chopped onion
10 ml/2 tsp finely chopped fresh dill
    (dill weed)
5 ml/1 tsp salt
2.5 ml/½ tsp bicarbonate of soda
    (baking soda)
1 egg, lightly beaten
15 ml/1 tbsp oil
350 g/12 oz/3 cups strong plain
    (bread) flour

Dissolve the yeast in the warm water and leave until frothy. Mix together all the remaining ingredients except the flour, then gradually stir in the flour and yeast mixture and knead to a soft dough. Place in a greased bowl, cover with clingfilm (plastic wrap) and leave in a warm place for about 1 hour until doubled in size.

Knead again on a lightly floured surface, then shape into a greased 900 g/2 lb loaf tin (pan). Cover and leave to rise until the dough rises above the top of the tin. Bake in a preheated oven at 180°C/350°F/gas mark 4 for 30 minutes. Cover the top with foil and bake for a further 15 minutes until well risen and golden.

Country Herb Bread

Makes two 900 g/2 lb loaves

40 g/1½ oz fresh yeast or 60 ml/
    4 tbsp dried yeast
50 g/2 oz/¼ cup soft brown sugar
600 ml/1 pt/2½ cups warm water
50 g/2 oz/¼ cup vegetable fat
    (shortening)
900 g/2 lb/8 cups wholemeal
    (wholewheat) flour
5 ml/1 tsp salt
10 ml/2 tsp chopped fresh basil
5 ml/1 tsp chopped fresh thyme
5 ml/1 tsp chopped fresh parsley
5 ml/1 tsp chopped fresh marjoram
2.5 ml/½ tsp dried oregano
15 ml/1 tbsp milk
5 ml/1 tsp poppy seeds

Blend the yeast with half the sugar and a little of the warm water and leave in a warm place for about 15 minutes until frothy. Rub the fat into the flour and salt, then stir in the herbs and make a well in the centre. Add the remaining sugar, the yeast mixture and the remaining warm water and mix to a dough. Knead well until smooth and no longer sticky. Place in an oiled bowl, cover with clingfilm (plastic wrap) and leave in a warm place for about 1 hour until doubled in size.

Knead again and shape into loaves. Place on a greased baking (cookie) sheet, cover and leave to rise for about 15 minutes. Brush with the milk and sprinkle with the poppy seeds. Bake in a preheated oven at 230°C/450°F/gas mark 8 for 30 minutes until well risen and hollow-sounding when tapped on the base.

Herb Rolls

Makes 12

10 ml/2 tsp dried yeast
15 ml/1 tbsp sugar
250 ml/8 fl oz/1 cup warm milk
450 g/1 lb/4 cups wholemeal
　(wholewheat) flour
A pinch of salt
50 g/2 oz/¼ cup butter or margarine
15 ml/1 tbsp chopped fresh marjoram
5 ml/1 tsp chopped fresh thyme
15 ml/1 tbsp chopped fresh parsley
15 ml/1 tbsp snipped fresh chives
2 egg yolks
15 ml/1 tbsp cold milk
15 ml/1 tbsp caraway seeds

Blend the yeast with the sugar and 45 ml/3 tbsp of the warm milk and leave for about 20 minutes until frothy. Mix the flour with the salt and rub in the butter or margarine. Stir in the herbs. Make a well in the centre and add the yeast mixture and egg yolks and mix to make a firm dough. Place in an oiled bowl, cover with clingfilm (plastic wrap) and leave in a warm place for about 1 hour until doubled in size.

Knead again, then roll out on a lightly floured surface to about 4 cm/1½ in thick and cut into rounds. Place on a greased baking (cookie) sheet, cover and leave to rise for a further 15 minutes. Brush with the milk and sprinkle with the caraway seeds. Bake in a preheated oven at

200°C/400°F/gas mark 6 for about 15 minutes until golden and hollow-sounding when tapped on the base.

Herb Baps

Makes 16

40 g/1½ oz fresh yeast or 60 ml/
　4 tbsp dried yeast
50 g/2 oz/¼ cup soft brown sugar
600 ml/1 pt/2½ cups warm water
50 g/2 oz/¼ cup vegetable fat
　(shortening)
900 g/2 lb/8 cups wholemeal
　(wholewheat) flour
5 ml/1 tsp salt
10 ml/2 tsp chopped fresh basil
5 ml/1 tsp chopped fresh thyme
5 ml/1 tsp chopped fresh parsley
5 ml/1 tsp chopped fresh marjoram
2.5 ml/½ tsp dried oregano
15 ml/1 tbsp milk
15 ml/1 tbsp sesame seeds

Blend the yeast with half the sugar and a little of the warm water and leave in a warm place for about 15 minutes until frothy. Rub the fat into the flour and salt, then stir in the herbs and make a well in the centre. Add the remaining sugar, the yeast mixture and the remaining warm water and mix to a dough. Knead well until smooth and no longer sticky. Place in an oiled bowl, cover with clingfilm (plastic wrap) and leave in a warm place for about 1 hour until doubled in size.

Knead again and shape into rolls. Place on a greased baking (cookie) sheet, cover and leave to rise for about 15 minutes. Brush with the milk and sprinkle with the sesame seeds. Bake in a preheated oven at 230°C/450°F/gas mark 8 for about 15 minutes until well risen and hollow-sounding when tapped on the base.

Herb and Cheese Rolls

Makes 16

40 g/1½ oz fresh yeast or 60 ml/
    4 tbsp dried yeast
50 g/2 oz/¼ cup soft brown sugar
600 ml/1 pt/2½ cups warm water
50 g/2 oz/¼ cup vegetable fat
    (shortening)
900 g/2 lb/8 cups wholemeal
    (wholewheat) flour
5 ml/1 tsp salt
10 ml/2 tsp chopped fresh thyme
10 ml/2 tsp chopped fresh parsley
5 ml/1 tsp chopped fresh marjoram
75 g/3 oz/¾ cup Cheddar cheese,
    grated

Blend the yeast with half the sugar and a little of the warm water and leave in a warm place for about 15 minutes until frothy. Rub the fat into the flour and salt, then stir in the herbs and make a well in the centre. Add the remaining sugar, the yeast mixture and the remaining warm water and mix to a dough. Knead well until smooth and no longer elastic. Place in an oiled bowl, cover with clingfilm (plastic wrap) and leave in a warm place for about 1 hour until doubled in size.

Knead again and shape into loaves. Place on a greased baking (cookie) sheet, cover and leave to rise for about 15 minutes. Bake in a preheated oven at 230°C/450°F/gas mark 8 for 10 minutes. Remove from the oven and sprinkle with the cheese. Return to the oven for a further 5 minutes until golden on top and hollow-sounding when tapped on the base.

Quick Herb Bread

Makes one 900 g/2 lb loaf

450 g/1 lb/4 cups plain (all-purpose)
    flour
5 ml/1 tsp salt
2.5 ml/½ tsp ground black pepper

5 ml/1 tsp bicarbonate of soda
    (baking soda)
60 ml/4 tbsp chopped fresh herbs
25 g/1 oz/2 tbsp butter or margarine
300 ml/½ pt/1¼ cups buttermilk

Mix together the dry ingredients and stir in the herbs. Rub in the butter or margarine and make a well in the centre. Stir in the buttermilk to form a stiff dough and knead lightly. Shape into a greased 900 g/2 lb loaf tin (pan) and bake in a preheated oven at 150°C/300°F/gas mark 2 for 1 hour until golden brown and hollow-sounding when tapped on the base.

Mushroom Bread

Makes one 900 g/2 lb loaf

15 g/½ oz fresh yeast or 20 ml/
    4 tsp dried yeast
5 ml/1 tsp sugar
60 ml/4 tbsp warm water
350 g/12 oz/3 cups wholemeal
    (wholewheat) flour
175 g/6 oz/1½ cups plain
    (all-purpose) flour
5 ml/1 tsp salt
30 ml/2 tbsp bran
25 g/1 oz/2 tbsp butter or margarine
60 ml/4 tbsp milk
15 ml/1 tbsp finely chopped onion
100 g/4 oz mushrooms, chopped

Blend the yeast with the sugar and warm water and leave in a warm place until frothy. Mix together the flours, salt and bran, then rub in the butter or margarine and make a well in the centre. Pour in the yeast mixture and milk and knead to a smooth dough. Turn out on to a floured surface and knead for 10 minutes until smooth and elastic, or process in a food processor. Place in a greased bowl, cover with oiled clingfilm (plastic wrap) and leave in a warm place for 1 hour until doubled in size.

Knead again, working in the onion

and mushrooms, then shape into a greased 900 g/2 lb loaf tin (pan), cover with oiled clingfilm (plastic wrap) and leave to rise until the dough has risen to the top of the tins. Bake in a preheated oven at 220°C/425°F/gas mark 7 for 20 minutes. Reduce the oven temperature to 190°C/375°F/gas mark 5 and cook for a further 30 minutes until the bread sounds hollow when tapped underneath.

Nevada Bread

Makes three 450 g/1 lb loaves

25 g/1 oz fresh yeast or 40 ml/
 2½ tbsp dried yeast
50 g/2 oz/¼ cup soft brown sugar
350 ml/12 fl oz/1½ cups warm water
550 g/1¼ lb/5 cups wholemeal
 (wholewheat) flour
2.5 ml/½ tsp salt
15 ml/1 tbsp milk powder
 (non-fat dry milk)
50 g/2 oz/¼ cup vegetable fat
 (shortening)
Grated rind and juice of 1 orange
Grated rind and juice of 1 lemon
Grated rind and juice of 1 lime
75 g/3 oz/½ cup ready-to-eat dried
 apricots, chopped
100 g/4 oz cooking (tart) apples,
 peeled, cored and chopped
100 g/4 oz/⅔ cup stoned (pitted) dates,
 chopped
15 ml/1 tbsp clear honey, warmed

Blend the yeast with 5 ml/1 tsp of the sugar and a little of the warm water and leave in a warm place for 20 minutes until frothy. Mix the flour with the remaining sugar, the salt and milk powder, then rub in the vegetable fat and make a well in the centre. Add the yeast mixture and the remaining warm water and mix to a soft dough. Knead until pliable and no longer sticky. Place in an oiled bowl, cover with oiled clingfilm (plastic wrap) and leave in a warm place

for 1 hour until doubled in size. Mix the fruit juices and rinds with the apricots, apples and dates and leave to soak.

Knead the dough again and work in the fruit mixture. Divide the dough into three equal pieces, and divide each piece into three. Roll into long sausage shapes and plait each set of three together, moistening and pressing the ends together to seal. Cover and leave to rise for 40 minutes until almost doubled in size. Bake in a preheated oven at 220°C/425°F/gas mark 7 for 30 minutes until golden and hollow-sounding when tapped on the base. Brush with the honey while still warm.

Nut Bread

Makes two 450 g/1 lb loaves

75 g/3 oz/¾ cup self-raising
 (self-rising) flour
75 g/3 oz/¾ cup wholemeal
 (wholewheat) flour
25 g/1 oz/½ cup bran
5 ml/1 tsp ground cinnamon
2.5 ml/½ tsp salt
5 ml/1 tsp bicarbonate of soda
 (baking soda)
100 g/4 oz/1 cup chopped mixed nuts
1 egg
100 g/4 oz/½ cup soft brown sugar
60 ml/4 tbsp oil
150 ml/¼ pt/⅔ cup plain yoghurt

Mix together the flours, bran, cinnamon, salt, bicarbonate of soda and nuts. Beat the egg with the sugar and oil, then stir in the yoghurt. Pour into the flour mixture and mix to a firm dough. Spoon into two greased and lined 450 g/1 lb loaf tins (pans) and bake in a preheated oven at 190°C/375°F/gas mark 5 for 1 hour until a skewer inserted in the centre comes out clean.

Oaty Carrot Muffins

Makes 12

75 g/3 oz/³⁄₄ cup rolled oats
250 ml/8 fl oz/1 cup plain yoghurt
1 egg
45 ml/3 tbsp clear honey
175 g/6 oz/1½ cups plain
(all-purpose) flour
15 ml/1 tbsp baking powder
A pinch of salt
100 g/4 oz carrots, finely grated
5 ml/1 tsp grated orange rind

Mix together the oats and yoghurt and leave to stand for 10 minutes. Beat the egg with the honey, then stir into the oat mixture with the remaining ingredients until just blended; do not overmix. Spoon into muffin cases (papers) or greased muffin tins (pans) and bake in a preheated oven at 200°C/400°F/gas mark 6 for 15 minutes until well risen, golden brown and firm to the touch.

Onion and Olive Bread

Makes one 900 g/2 lb loaf

15 g/½ oz fresh yeast or 20 ml/
4 tsp dried yeast
A pinch of sugar
450 ml/³⁄₄ pt/2 cups warm water
675 g/1½ lb/6 cups strong plain
(bread) flour
10 ml/2 tsp salt
45 ml/3 tbsp olive oil
1 onion, finely chopped
175 g/6 oz/1 cup stoned (pitted) black
olives, chopped
15 ml/1 tbsp chopped fresh basil

Blend the yeast with the sugar and a little of the warm water and leave in a warm place for 20 minutes until frothy. Blend the yeast mixture and the remaining water into the flour, salt and olive oil and knead to a firm dough. Place

in an oiled bowl, cover with clingfilm (plastic wrap) and leave in a warm place for 1 hour until doubled in size.

Knead the dough again and roll or press out into a large rectangle. Sprinkle with the onion, olives and basil, then roll up and gently press the dough together. Shape into a greased 900 g/2 lb loaf tin (pan), cover and leave in a warm place for 30 minutes until the dough rises above the top of the tin.

Bake in a preheated oven at 230°C/450°F/gas mark 8 for 25 minutes until golden brown and hollow-sounding when tapped on the base.

Onion and Sun-dried Tomato Bread

Makes one 900 g/2 lb loaf

15 g/½ oz fresh yeast or 20 ml/
4 tsp dried yeast
A pinch of sugar
450 ml/³⁄₄ pt/2 cups warm water
675 g/1½ lb/6 cups strong plain
(bread) flour
10 ml/2 tsp salt
45 ml/3 tbsp olive oil
1 onion, finely chopped
175 g/6 oz/³⁄₄ cup sun-dried tomatoes
in oil, drained and chopped
10 ml/2 tsp dried oregano

Blend the yeast with the sugar and a little of the warm water and leave in a warm place for 20 minutes until frothy. Stir the yeast mixture and the remaining water into the flour, salt and olive oil and knead to a firm dough. Place in an oiled bowl, cover with clingfilm (plastic wrap) and leave in a warm place for 1 hour until doubled in size.

Knead the dough again and roll or press out into a large rectangle. Sprinkle with the onion, sun-dried tomatoes and oregano, then roll up and gently press the dough together. Shape into a greased 900 g/2 lb loaf tin (pan), cover and leave in a warm place for 30 minutes until the dough rises above the top of the tin.

Bake in a preheated oven at 230°C/450°F/gas mark 8 for 25 minutes until golden brown and hollow-sounding when tapped on the base.

Pepper and Onion Bread

Makes one 900 g/2 lb loaf

15 g/½ oz fresh yeast or 20 ml/
  4 tsp dried yeast
A pinch of sugar
250 ml/8 fl oz/1 cup warm water
350 g/12 oz/3 cups plain
  (all-purpose) flour
Salt and freshly ground black pepper
30 ml/2 tbsp olive oil
100 g/4 oz bottled red (bell) peppers,
  drained and finely chopped
1 onion, finely chopped
5 ml/1 tsp dried oregano

Blend the yeast with the sugar and a little of the warm water and leave in a warm place for 20 minutes until frothy. Blend into the flour with a pinch of salt and the olive oil and knead until smooth and no longer sticky. Place in an oiled bowl, cover with clingfilm (plastic wrap) and leave in a warm place for 1 hour until doubled in size.

Knead again and press or roll out into a rectangle. Cover with the peppers, onion and oregano and season with salt and pepper. Roll up, then shape into a cylinder and place on a greased baking (cookie) sheet with the join underneath. Cover and leave to rise in a warm place for 40 minutes until doubled in size.

Bake in a preheated oven at 200°C/400°F/gas mark 6 for 30 minutes until golden brown and hollow-sounding when tapped on the base.

Potato Bread

Makes three 450 g/1 lb loaves

900 ml/1½ pts/3½ cups milk
75 g/3 oz/⅓ cup caster (superfine)
  sugar
75 g/3 oz/⅓ cup butter or margarine
10 ml/2 tsp salt
100 g/4 oz/½ cup mashed potatoes
25 g/1 oz dried yeast
120 ml/4 fl oz/½ cup lukewarm water
350 g/12 oz/3 cups wholemeal
  (wholewheat) flour
800 g/1¾ lb/7 cups strong plain
  (bread) flour

Bring the milk almost to boiling point, then add the sugar, butter or margarine, salt and mashed potatoes and stir until melted. Leave until lukewarm. Meanwhile, dissolve the yeast in the water and leave in a warm place until frothy. Add to the milk mixture with the wholemeal flour and a few spoonfuls of the plain flour and stir to mix. Gradually mix in the remaining flour until you have a stiff dough. Knead until smooth. Place in a greased bowl and cover with clingfilm (plastic wrap). Leave in a warm place to rise for about 1 hour until doubled in size.

Turn on to a floured surface and divide into three. Knead again and shape into loaves. Place on a greased baking (cookie) sheet or into greased 450 g/1 lb loaf tins (pans) and leave to rise until the dough reaches the top of the tins. Bake in a preheated oven at 180°C/350°F/gas mark 4 for 40–45 minutes until well risen and golden brown.

Pumpkin Bread

Makes three 450 g/1 lb loaves

275 g/10 oz/2½ cups wholemeal
  (wholewheat) flour
225 g/8 oz/2 cups plain
  (all-purpose) flour
225 g/8 oz/1 cup muscovado sugar
100 g/4 oz/1 cup chopped mixed nuts
15 ml/1 tbsp bicarbonate of soda
  (baking soda)
5 ml/1 tsp salt
5 ml/1 tsp ground cinnamon
2.5 ml/½ tsp grated nutmeg
225 g/8 oz/1⅓ cups stoned (pitted)
  dates, chopped
675 g/1½ lb cooked pumpkin purée
250 ml/8 fl oz/1 cup clear honey
250 ml/8 fl oz/1 cup oil

Mix together the flours, sugar, nuts, bicarbonate of soda, salt, cinnamon and nutmeg. Stir in the dates. Blend together the pumpkin, honey and oil, then stir into the dry ingredients and mix well. Shape the mixture into three greased 450 g/1 lb loaf tins (pans) and bake in a preheated oven at 180°C/350°F/gas mark 4 for about 1 hour until a skewer inserted in the centre comes out clean.

Sauerkraut Bread

Makes four 450 g/1 lb loaves

15 g/½ oz fresh yeast or 20 ml/
  4 tsp dried yeast
10 ml/2 tsp clear honey
750 ml/1¼ pts/3 cups warm water
15 ml/1 tbsp butter or margarine
675 g/1½ lb/6 cups wholemeal
  (wholewheat) flour
450 g/1 lb/4 cups rye flour
5 ml/1 tsp salt
175 g/6 oz sauerkraut
1 onion, finely chopped
10 ml/2 tsp caraway seeds
5 ml/1 tsp mustard powder

Blend the yeast with the honey and a little of the warm water and leave in a warm place for 20 minutes until frothy. Rub the butter or margarine into the flours and salt, then blend in the yeast mixture and the remaining warm water and mix to a soft dough. Knead until smooth, then place in an oiled bowl, cover with oiled clingfilm (plastic wrap) and leave to rest for 10 minutes. Mix together the sauerkraut, onion, caraway seeds and mustard, then work into the dough. Cover and leave to rest for 10 minutes.

Shape into four 450 g/1 lb loaves and place on a greased baking (cookie) sheet. Cover with oiled clingfilm and leave in a warm place for 45 minutes until doubled in size. Bake in a preheated oven at 220°C/425°F/gas mark 7 for 35 minutes until golden brown.

Seville Bread

Makes three 450 g/1 lb loaves

25 g/1 oz fresh yeast or 40 ml/
 2½ tbsp dried yeast
50 g/2 oz/¼ cup soft brown sugar
350 ml/12 fl oz/1½ cups warm water
550 g/1¼ lb/5 cups wholemeal
 (wholewheat) flour
2.5 ml/½ tsp salt
15 ml/1 tbsp milk powder
 (non-fat dry milk)
50 g/2 oz/¼ cup vegetable fat
 (shortening)
Grated rind and juice of 1 orange
Grated rind and juice of 1 lemon
Grated rind and juice of 1 lime
450 g/1 lb/2⅔ cups sultanas
 (golden raisins)
15 ml/1 tbsp clear honey, warmed

Blend the yeast with 5 ml/1 tsp of the sugar and a little of the warm water and leave in a warm place for 20 minutes until frothy. Mix the flour with the remaining sugar, the salt and milk powder, then rub in the vegetable fat and make a well in the centre. Add the yeast mixture and the remaining warm water and mix to a soft dough. Knead until pliable and no longer sticky. Place in an oiled bowl, cover with oiled clingfilm (plastic wrap) and leave in a warm place for 1 hour until doubled in size. Mix the fruit juices and rinds with the sultanas and leave to soak.

Knead the dough again and work in the sultana mixture. Divide the dough into three equal pieces, and divide each piece into three. Roll into long sausage shapes and plait each set of three together, moistening and pressing the ends together to seal. Cover and leave to rise for 40 minutes until almost doubled in size. Bake in a preheated oven at 220°C/425°F/ gas mark 7 for 30 minutes until golden and hollow-sounding when tapped on the base. Brush with the honey while still warm.

Toledo Bread

Makes two 450 g/1 lb loaves

50 g/2 oz/⅓ cup dried aduki beans
25 g/1 oz fresh yeast or 40 ml/
 2½ tbsp dried yeast
300 ml/½ pt/1¼ cups warm water
450 g/1 lb/4 cups wholemeal
 (wholewheat) flour
5 ml/1 tsp salt
25 g/1 oz/2 tbsp butter or margarine
60 ml/4 tbsp canned chopped
 tomatoes
30 ml/2 tbsp tomato purée (paste)
5 ml/1 tsp chilli powder
2.5 ml/½ tsp dried oregano
1 onion, chopped
1 garlic clove, chopped

Soak the beans overnight in cold water. Drain and rinse, then place in a pan and cover with fresh water. Bring to the boil, boil for 15 minutes, then simmer for 40 minutes until tender. Drain well.

Blend the yeast with a little of the warm water and leave in a warm place for 20 minutes until frothy. Mix together the flour and salt, then rub in the butter or margarine. Add the yeast mixture and the remaining warm water, the tomatoes, tomato purée, chilli powder and oregano and mix to a pliable dough. Place in an oiled bowl, cover with oiled clingfilm (plastic wrap) and leave in a warm place for 10 minutes. Knead in the beans, onion and garlic, cover again and leave to rest for 10 minutes.

Shape the dough into two greased 450 g/1 lb loaf tins (pans), cover with oiled clingfilm and leave in a warm place for 40 minutes until the dough has risen above the tops of the tins.

Bake in a preheated oven at 230°C/ 450°F/gas mark 8 for 15 minutes.

Green Tomato
and Nut Loaf

Makes two 900 g/2 lb loaves

350 g/12 oz/1½ cups caster (superfine)
  sugar
250 ml/8 fl oz/1 cup oil
5 ml/1 tsp salt
5 ml/1 tsp vanilla essence (extract)
3 eggs, beaten
350 g/12 oz/2 cups grated green
  tomatoes, drained
350 g/12 oz/3 cups plain
  (all-purpose) flour
5 ml/1 tsp bicarbonate of soda
  (baking soda)
5 ml/1 tsp baking powder
100 g/4 oz/1 cup chopped mixed nuts
100 g/4 oz/⅔ cup raisins

Mix together the sugar, oil, salt, vanilla essence, eggs and tomatoes. Stir in the flour, bicarbonate of soda and baking powder and mix well. Stir in the nuts and raisins. Spoon into two greased 900 g/2 lb loaf tins (pans) and bake in a preheated oven at 180°C/350°F/gas mark 4 for 40 minutes until well risen and golden brown.

Tomato Loaf

Makes one 900 g/2 lb loaf

15 g/½ oz fresh yeast or 20 ml/
  4 tsp dried yeast
5 ml/1 tsp caster (superfine) sugar
300 ml/½ pt/1¼ cups warm water
550 g/1¼ lb/5 cups strong plain
  (bread) flour
5 ml/1 tsp salt
50 g/2 oz/¼ cup tomato purée (paste)

Blend the yeast with the sugar with a little of the warm water and leave in a warm place for 20 minutes until frothy. Place the flour and salt in a bowl and make a well in the centre. Mix together the tomato purée and the remaining water and stir into the flour with the yeast mixture and mix to a firm dough. Knead until elastic and no longer sticky. Place in an oiled bowl and cover with clingfilm (plastic wrap). Leave in a warm place for 1 hour until doubled in size.

Knead again lightly and shape into a 900 g/2 lb loaf tin (pan), cover and leave in a warm place for 35 minutes until the dough has risen above the top of the tin.

Bake in a preheated oven at 400°C/ 200°F/gas mark 6 for 30 minutes until golden and hollow-sounding when tapped on the base.

Sun-dried Tomato Loaf

Makes one 900 g/2 lb loaf

15 g/½ oz fresh yeast or 20 ml/
4 tsp dried yeast
5 ml/1 tsp caster (superfine) sugar
300 ml/½ pt/1¼ cups warm water
550 g/1¼ lb/5 cups strong plain
(bread) flour
A pinch of salt
50 g/2 oz/¼ cup tomato purée (paste)
50 g/2 oz/¼ cup sun-dried tomatoes in
oil, drained and chopped

Blend the yeast with the sugar and a little of the warm water and leave in a warm place for 20 minutes until frothy. Place the flour and salt in a bowl and make a well in the centre. Mix the tomato purée and the remaining water and stir into the flour with the yeast mixture and mix to a firm dough. Knead until elastic and no longer sticky. Place in an oiled bowl and cover with clingfilm (plastic wrap). Leave in a warm place for 1 hour until doubled in size.

Knead again lightly and work in the sun-dried tomatoes. Shape into a 900 g/ 2 lb loaf tin (pan), cover and leave in a warm place for 35 minutes until the dough has risen above the top of the tin.

Bake in a preheated oven at 400°C/ 200°F/gas mark 6 for 30 minutes until golden and hollow-sounding when tapped on the base.

Sun-dried Tomato and Olive Bread

Makes one 900 g/2 lb loaf

15 g/½ oz fresh yeast or 20 ml/
4 tsp dried yeast
5 ml/1 tsp caster (superfine) sugar
300 ml/½ pt/1¼ cups warm water
550 g/1¼ lb/5 cups strong plain
(bread) flour
A pinch of salt
50 g/2 oz/¼ cup tomato purée (paste)
50 g/2 oz/¼ cup sun-dried tomatoes in
oil, drained and chopped
50 g/2 oz/⅓ cup stoned (pitted) black
olives, chopped

Blend the yeast with the sugar and a little of the warm water and leave in a warm place for 20 minutes until frothy. Place the flour and salt in a bowl and make a well in the centre. Mix the tomato purée and the remaining water and stir into the flour with the yeast mixture and mix to a firm dough. Knead until elastic and no longer sticky. Place in an oiled bowl and cover with clingfilm (plastic wrap). Leave in a warm place for 1 hour until doubled in size.

Knead again lightly and work in the sun-dried tomatoes and olives. Shape into a 900 g/2 lb loaf tin (pan), cover and leave in a warm place for 35 minutes until the dough has risen above the top of the tin.

Bake in a preheated oven at 400°C/ 200°F/gas mark 6 for 30 minutes until golden and hollow-sounding when tapped on the base.

Turnip Bread

Makes one 450 g/1 lb loaf

100 g/4 oz/1 cup strong plain (bread)
  flour
100 g/4 oz/½ cup caster (superfine)
  sugar
2.5 ml/½ tsp bicarbonate of soda
  (baking soda)
2.5 ml/½ tsp baking powder
5 ml/1 tsp ground allspice
A pinch of salt
1 egg, lightly beaten
100 g/4 oz cooked turnip purée
60 ml/4 tbsp oil

Mix together the dry ingredients and make a well in the centre. Blend together the egg, turnip and oil, then mix into the dry ingredients and stir until just blended. Spoon into a greased and lined 450 g/1 lb loaf tin (pan) and bake in a preheated oven at 180°C/350°F/gas mark 4 for 1 hour until a skewer inserted in the centre comes out clean.

Wholemeal Bread with Onion and Nuts

Makes one 900 g/2 lb loaf

15 g/½ oz fresh yeast or 20 ml/
  4 tsp dried yeast
5 ml/1 tsp soft brown sugar
450 ml/¾ pt/2 cups warm water
450 g/1 lb/4 cups wholemeal
  (wholewheat) flour
175 g/6 oz/1½ cups strong plain
  (bread) flour
5 ml/1 tsp salt
15 ml/1 tbsp walnut oil
1 onion, finely chopped
100 g/4 oz/1 cup chopped mixed nuts

Blend the yeast with the sugar and a little of the warm water and leave in a warm place for 20 minutes until frothy. Mix together the flours and salt in a bowl, add the yeast mixture, the oil and the remaining warm water and mix to a firm dough. Knead until smooth and no longer sticky. Place in an oiled bowl, cover with clingfilm (plastic wrap) and leave in a warm place for 1 hour until doubled in size.

Knead again lightly and work in the onions and nuts, then shape into a greased 900 g/2 lb loaf tin (pan), cover and leave in a warm place for 30 minutes until the dough has risen above the top of the tin.

Bake in a preheated oven at 220°C/ 425°F/gas mark 7 for 30 minutes until golden brown and hollow-sounding when tapped on the base.

Index

411